THE HEAVENS.

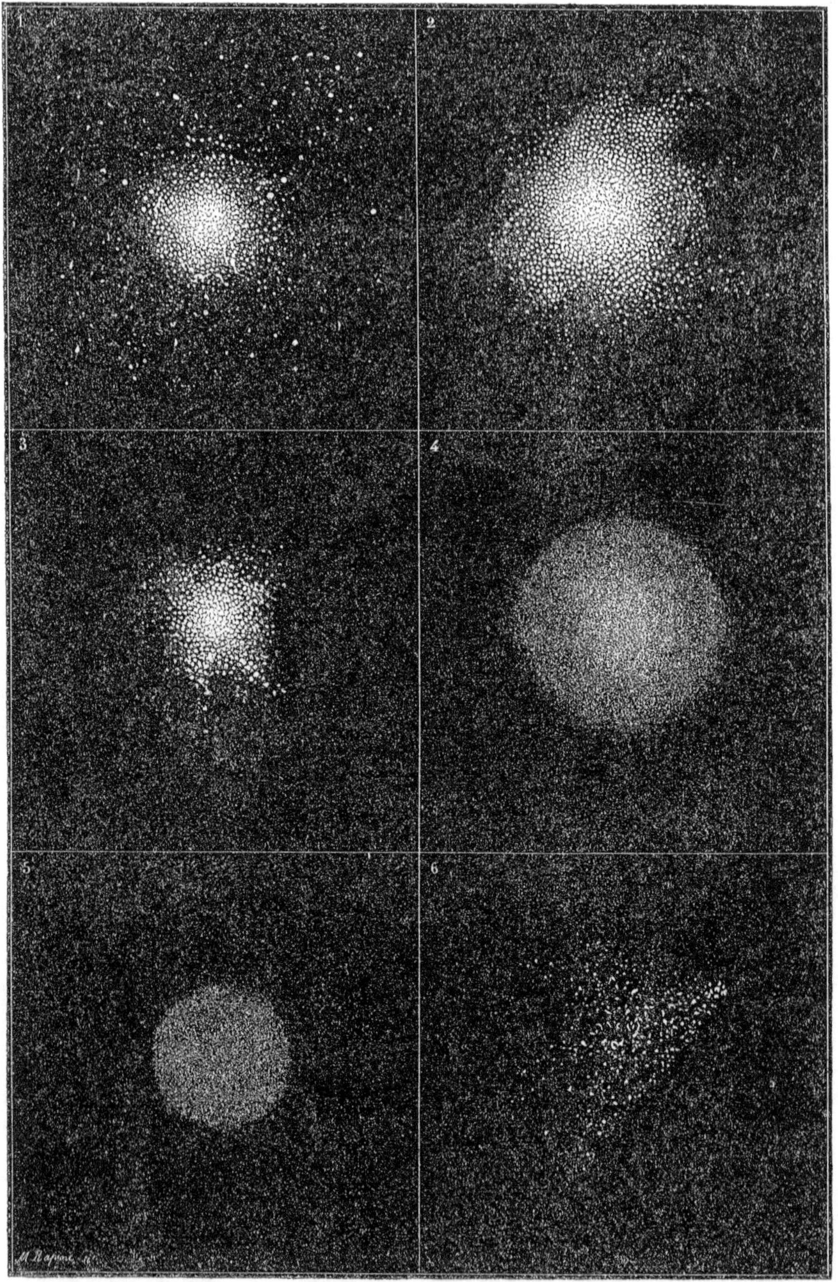

STAR-CLUSTERS.

1. In the Balance. 2. In Hercules. 3. In Capricorn. 4. In Aquarius. 5. In the Serpent
6. In Gemini. (Sir J. Herschel.)

THE HEAVENS.

An Illustrated Handbook

OF

POPULAR ASTRONOMY

BY

AMÉDÉE GUILLEMIN.

EDITED BY J. NORMAN LOCKYER, F.R.A.S., F.R.S.

FOURTH EDITION.

REVISED BY RICHARD A. PROCTOR, B.A., F.R.A.S.

NEW YORK:
G. P. PUTNAM & SONS.

M.DCCC.LXXI.

PREFACE TO THE SECOND EDITION.

The Author, in writing this popular essay, was ambitious of obtaining the support of those for whom it was specially written; that is to say, of the general reader and the young. He has been so generously seconded by the entire press, that in this respect he has succeeded beyond his expectations. He would, therefore, be wanting in gratitude, if he failed to offer in this place his best thanks to those whose praises have been for him so many encouragements in the modest path he has chosen.

But what he did not dare to hope was, to be honoured by the approbation of those who cultivate the highest branches of Astronomy; to see his book presented to the Academy of Sciences by the illustrious Director of the Imperial Observatory, M. Leverrier, and to the Royal Astronomical Society of London by its President, Mr. Warren De La Rue; to receive in flattering letters the congratulations of illustrious Astronomers, among whom he may be permitted to cite the names of Sir John Herschel, the Rev. W. R. Dawes, Professor Piazzi Smyth, Mr. Warren De La Rue, Mr. Lassell, and Professor G. P. Bond; and, lastly, to see an English translation undertaken under the editorship of Mr. Lockyer.

This Second Edition of 'The Heavens' differs much from the first one. The Author has availed himself of the reprint to revise the work with care, and to give, both to the descriptions and explanations of the various phenomena, all the clearness of which they appear to him susceptible.

Newly-published memoirs, and recent observations, have enabled him to add to the different Chapters treating on the Physical Constitution of Stars, all details of a nature likely to interest his readers. The observations of Solar Spots, made by Mr. R. C. Carrington with such admirable perseverance during more than seven years; the work of a like nature by M. Chacornac and Father Secchi, and M. Faye's *résumé* of it; Mr. Lockyer's Memoir on the planet Mars; Lord Rosse's new Catalogue of Nebulæ, &c., have furnished materials for new drawings faithfully copied from the originals.

L'ENVOI.

En présentant au public d'Angleterre un livre dont le succès en France est dû, sans doute, à la rareté des ouvrages vraiment populaires d'Astronomie, j'éprouve le besoin de la mettre sous le patronage du savant distingué qui a bien voulu consentir à en diriger la traduction et la publication.

C'est donc, pour moi, un devoir, bien doux à remplir du reste, que de témoigner, ici même, ma profonde gratitude à Mr. Norman Lockyer pour les soins qu'il a donnés à ce travail de révision, et surtout pour les importantes et savantes additions dont il a enrichi le texte Français. Grace à son zèle, aussi bienveillant qu'éclairé, je me sens plus à l'aise pour solliciter les suffrages des amis des sciences, en faveur d'un livre qui a été composé et inspiré pour le desir d'accroître le nombre des intelligences aptes à comprendre et à admirer les sublimes connaissances de l'Astronomie, et assez courageuses pour se vouer à leurs progrès.

AMÉDÉE GUILLEMIN.

PREFACE TO THE FIRST EDITION.

I AM among those who believe, that the natural and physical sciences possess in themselves attraction sufficient to render any ornaments superfluous. This conviction has been my only guide in the conception and writing of this book, which is not, indeed, a scientific one, but a faithful picture of the phenomena offered by the Heavens to man's intelligent admiration.

My plan was, therefore, ready to my hand, and I had but to follow Nature, as now revealed to us by Astronomy, in all her majestic simplicity. All my efforts have had for their object to represent her in all her details as a whole.

I write for those who, though interested in science, have neither the time nor the wish to become professional astronomers: in a word, for youth and unscientific 'children of larger growth.' It has been my wish, that THE HEAVENS should be read with something of the charm of a romance, or, at least, with that so powerful interest which belongs to travellers' tales of unknown lands. For, after all, is not the mind of a traveller, when it follows Science through the far-off regions of the ethereal sky, journeying on from stage to stage, that is, from Sun to Sun, to the very confines of the visible Universe? In our narrative of this journey through the infinite, the reader, it is true, will find no sudden turns of fortune, no unexpected accident to make the heart beat quicker at the thought of the sufferings of one of our fellow-men: but, on the other hand, it will be given him to contemplate the most sublime of all pictures—the majesty of tremendous phenomena, the unalterable and eternal harmony of the laws of Nature.

What a vast field, moreover, what a magnificent horizon is presented by the Heavens to the most active of human faculties, to the imagination! When our sight, aided by the most powerful instruments, dives into the depths of space, and finds, instead of feebly strung points of light, worlds like our own, some smaller, some larger than it, a thousand questions rise to our lips. We find ourselves involuntarily making in thought a hundred travels, more interesting, more strange, more marvellous than those the scene of which lies on our own planet.

Basing our work on the facts already acquired, we set ourselves to build up our neighbouring worlds; the configuration of their continents and seas, the rivers which water them, their mountains, which are the very skeletons of worlds, the living inhabitants, animal and vegetable, which people them, all present themselves before us in the most various forms. Forced by an irresistible instinct to people these worlds with free and intelligent beings, we help them at their work, in their wars; we ask if they, like us, have a history and traditions; then, the thought that our humanity is but one individual state of being among those, which on all the worlds throughout boundless space work out their destiny, comes to console us; we are no longer alone to seek after truth, and the realization of justice and goodness.

These, doubtless, are questions concerning which Astronomy brings no message to us, and which will long, possibly always, continue in the domain of conjecture. Therefore, we have not dwelt upon them in this book, leaving the reader to solve them as his imagination may lead him. But the coldest mind, the mind least accessible to the suggestions of fancy, cannot entirely banish them. In spite of itself, there comes a moment, an hour of reverie, when it too propounds the same problems; and truly we cannot wish it otherwise. Does it not afford one proof the more of the truth of what day by day becomes more evident, that science borders on poetry?

In order to make Astronomy accessible to all, it was necessary to banish from the work the mathematical portion of the science, which forms the essential element in the special treatises on the subject. But, on the other hand, the most interesting details relative to the constitution of the worlds which people space, the most recent observations made by the magnificent instruments now erected in the Observatories of Europe and America occupy a large place in this physical description of the Universe.

One word on the sources whence I have selected materials for the book.

I wished to place this attempt to popularize science on a level with the most recent and most authentic discoveries. I therefore addressed myself directly to the most illustrious astronomers, both in the Old and New Worlds. All of them have liberally lent me the aid of their knowledge; original memoirs, photographs have been forwarded to me from the various scientific centres, with a generosity for which I must here publicly express my extreme gratitude. Nor have I lacked encouragement and advice. The venerable patriarch of contemporary astronomers, Sir John Herschel, Admiral Smyth, Mr. Warren De La Rue, and Mr. Lassell in England; the illustrious Director of the Observatory of Poulkowa, M. Otto Struve, in Russia; M. Littrow, in Germany; and Professor G. P. Bond, in America, are, among foreign astronomers, those to whom my best thanks are due for their generous aid.

In France, M. Leverrier at once placed the library of the Imperial Observatory at my disposal, and gave me permission to make from nature the drawings of the most important instruments in this magnificent establishment. MM. Laussedat, Chacornac, and Goldschmidt, have aided me by their advice, and have communicated to me their observations.

Nor is this all. I have largely placed under contribution all the ancient and modern publications on Astronomy, the interesting works of Schröter, Laplace, Beer and Mädler, the two Struves: Harding's Celestial Atlas, and that constructed by the illustrious astronomer of Bonn, Argelander; the special periodical so full of facts, the *Astronomische Nachrichten* of Altona, the *Memoirs* and *Monthly Notices* of the Royal Astronomical Society of London; the works of Airy, Hind, Lord Rosse, and Sir Thomas Maclear; the publications of the Academy of Sciences of St. Petersburg, Humboldt's *Cosmos*, Arago's admirable *Astronomy;* and, finally, all the precious communications to be found in the *Comptes Rendus* of the French Academy of Sciences, in which the names of such Frenchmen as Arago, Biot, Babinet, Faye, and Delaunay, are found associated with those of all the *savans*, members of this great republic of science, who belong to other countries.

Such have been my fellow-labourers in the preparation of this book. It will be easily understood that it was not a question of gathering at hazard from the immense collection of ancient and modern works, which form the archives of Astronomy: it was necessary that I should choose the most incontested facts, the most recent and most authentic observations; that I should discuss and compare the numbers, which in Astronomy have such interesting meanings; that I should often go over calculations which lead to them myself: in one word, that I should show to the public, for whom the book has been written, and who have not always the means of verifying an Author's statements, with what respect for the truth, and with what conscientious care, I have acquitted myself of a work so attractive to me.

It rests with the reader now, to say, whether I have known how to profit by these materials, and whether, like a painter before a beautiful landscape, I have been able to portray beauties of the grandest of all scenes, that of the infinite variety of the stars moving in concert through boundless space.

The Editor's Additions and Notes are enclosed in brackets [ ].

The Notes followed by initials have been contributed respectively by

B. S.	Mr. Balfour Stewart.
W. R. D.	Rev. W. R. Dawes.
T. W. W.	Rev. T. W. Webb.
W. R. B.	Mr. W. R. Birt.
R. A. P.	Mr. R. A. Proctor.

CONTENTS.

THE HEAVENS.

PART THE FIRST.—THE SOLAR SYSTEM.

PART THE SECOND.—THE SIDEREAL SYSTEM.

PART THE THIRD.—THE LAWS OF ASTRONOMY.

LIST OF PLATES.

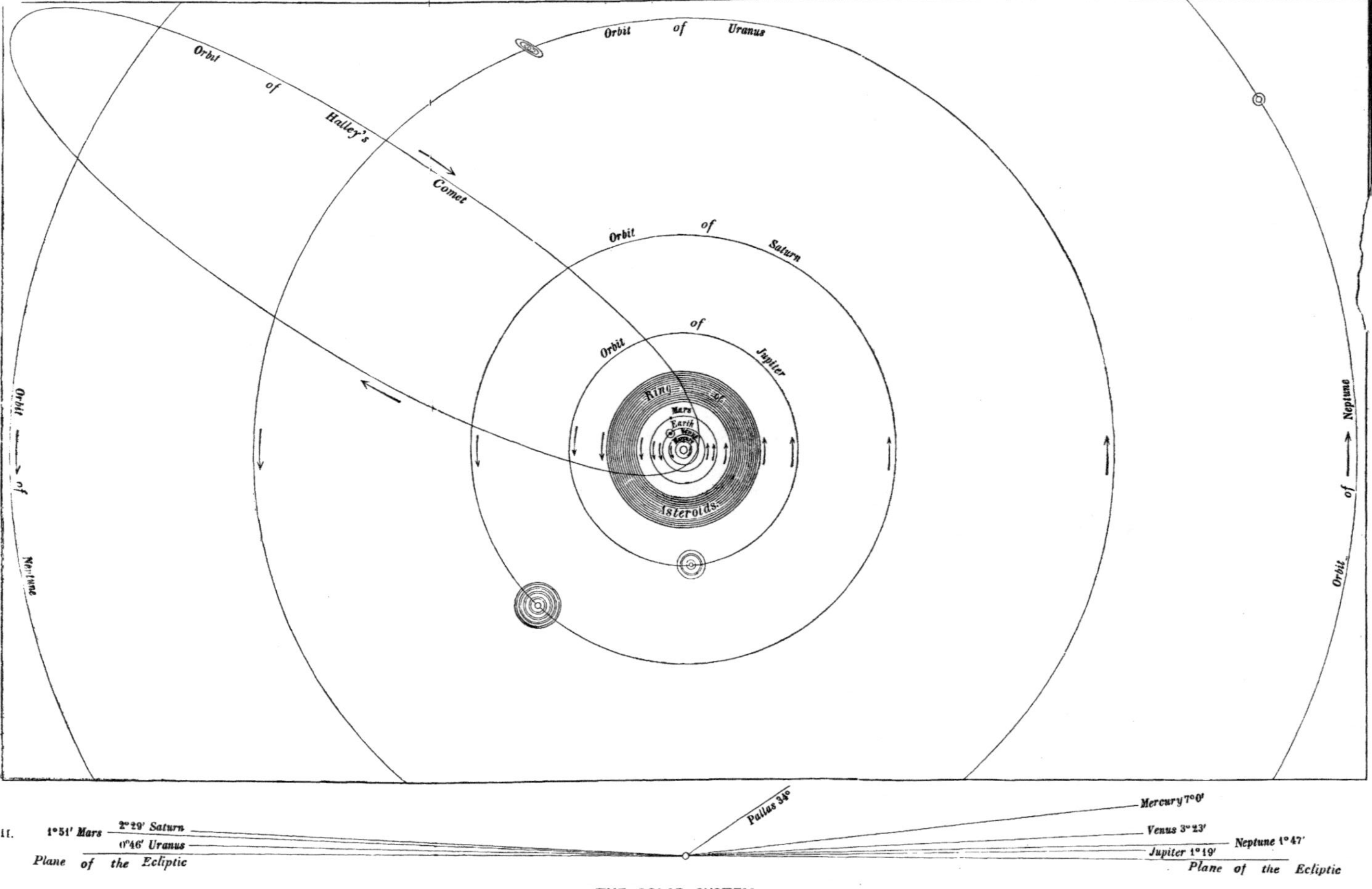

THE SOLAR SYSTEM.

I. Bird's-eye View of the Orbits. II. Inclinations of the Orbits.

THE HEAVENS.

What are the Heavens? Where the shores of that limitless ocean; where the bottom of that unfathomable abyss?

What are those brilliant points—those innumerable stars, which, never dim, shine out unceasingly from the dark profound? Are they sown broadcast—orderless, with no other bond save that which perspective lends to them? Or, if not immovable, as we have so long imagined, if not golden nails fixed to a crystal vault, whither are they bound? And, finally, what are the parts assigned to the Sun, our Earth, and all the Earths attendant on the glorious orb of day, in this tremendous concert of celestial spheres,—this sublime harmony of the Universe?

These are magnificent problems, of which the most fertile imagination would have in vain attempted the solution, if, for the greater glory of the human mind, Astronomy—first-born of the Sciences,—had not at length come to our aid.

How wonderful is the power of man! Chained down to the surface of the Earth, an intelligent atom on a grain of sand lost in the immensity of space, he invents instruments which multiply a thousandfold his vision, he sounds the depths of the ether, guages the visible universe, and counts the myriads of stars which people it; next, studying their most complicated movements, he measures exactly their dimensions and the distances of the nearest of them from the Earth, and next deduces their masses, then, discovering in the seeming disorder of the stellar groupings real bonds of union, he at last evolves order from apparent confusion.

Nor is this all. Rising by a supreme flight of thought to the most abstract speculations, he discovers the laws which regulate all celestial movements, and defines the nature of the universal force which sustains the worlds.

Such are the fruits of the unceasing labours of twenty generations of Astronomers. Such the result of the genius and of the patient perseverance of men who have devoted themselves for two thousand years to the study of the phenomena of the Heavens. The Chaldean shepherds were, they say, the first astronomers. We can well believe it. Dwelling in the midst of vast plains, where the mildness of the seasons permitted them to pass the night in the open air, where the clear sky unfolded before them perpetually the most glorious scenes, they ought to have been, and they were, contemplative astronomers. And all of us would be what they were, did not the rigour of our climate and our variable atmosphere so often prevent us observing the Heavens; and did not, moreover, the turmoil and cares of civilised life deprive us of the necessary leisure.

Nothing is more fitted to elevate the mind towards the infinite than the pensive contemplation of the starry vault in the silent calm of night. A thousand fires sparkle in all parts of the sombre azure of the sky. Varied in colour and brilliancy, some shine with a vivid light, perpetually changing and twinkling; others, again, with a more constant one—more tranquil and soft; while very many only send us their rays intermittently, as if they could scarce pierce the profundity of space.

To enjoy this spectacle in all its magnificence, a night must be chosen when the atmosphere is perfectly pure and transparent—one neither illuminated by the Moon, nor by the glimmer of twilight or of dawn. The Heavens then resemble an immense sea, the broad expanse of which glitters with gold dust or diamonds.

In presence of such splendour, the senses, mind, and imagination, are alike enthralled. (The impression gathered is an emotion at once profound and religious, an undefinable mixture of admiration, and of calm and tender melancholy.) It seems as if these distant worlds, in shining earthwards, put themselves in close communication with our thoughts.

But Sentiment has but one part in this emotion, and soon Intelligence asserts her sway. It asks how these myriads of stars, scattered here and there, can reveal to those who have studied them the structure of the universe; by what method they have succeeded in distinguishing them, in calculating their distances, and determining their movements. Further on, we shall attempt to give an idea of the manner in which these interesting problems have been solved: at present, and before entering into a more detailed description, we shall endeavour to sketch with a free hand the panorama of the Universe.

At a first glance at the starry firmament the stars seem pretty regularly distributed; nevertheless, look at that whitish, undecided, vapoury glimmer which girdles the heavens as with a belt. It is the Milky Way.* As we approach the borders of this star-cloud in our inspection, the stars appear more and more crowded together, and most of them so small that the eye can scarcely distinguish them. The accumulation of stars in the direction of the Milky Way is more especially visible when we examine the heavens with the aid of a powerful telescope.

The Milky Way itself is nothing more than an immensely extended

* *Via Lactea.* It is also called the Galaxy, from γαλαξια, the Greek word for the same thing.

zone of stars, that is, of suns; since, as we know, and as we shall explain in the sequel, each star, from the most brilliant to the faintest, is a sun.

Here, then, is an immense group, a gigantic assemblage of worlds, which seems to embrace all the Universe, if it be true that the greater number of scattered stars situated out of the Milky Way, nevertheless form part of it. In reality, this multitude of millions of suns is divided into numerous and distinct groups, and those into others still more restricted in number, each composed of two or three suns.

What breadth of space does each of these groups occupy? What is the measure of the space which holds them all? The most powerful imagination in vain attempts to answer these questions intelligibly; here numbers fail us.

Let us add—without comment in this place, as we shall return to it,—a fact well proved, and one which will seem strange to many;—our Sun himself is a star of the Milky Way.

The foregoing, however, is but a first sketch of the structure of the visible Universe.

In examining attentively every part of the starry vault, a keen eye perceives here and there whitish spots resembling little clouds. One would say they were so many patches detached from the Milky Way, from which, however, they are often very distinct and very distant. The telescope discovers by thousands these cloud-patches, these—to give them their astronomical name—*Nebulæ.*

[It was formerly imagined, that each of these star-clouds was nothing less than an aggregation of stars very close together, and very numerous—so many Milky Ways lying outside our own, and for the most part so distant that the most powerful instruments were able only to distinguish a confused glimmering. One of the most important observations of modern times, however, has shown that many of these nebulæ, including the most glorious one in our northern hemisphere,—that in the sword-handle of Orion,—are but masses of glowing gases.

Others, again, of these cloud-like masses—cloud-like by reason of their distance—show us, faintly shining on a background apparently nebulous, brilliant stars, larger no doubt, or more brilliant, than their fellows; and some of these objects, called 'Star-clusters,' which are nearest us, are among the most glorious objects revealed to us by our telescopes.]

Let us attempt now to conceive what fearful distances separate these archipelagos of worlds from our own!

Unfathomable abysses whose unspeakable depths the most powerful telescopes increase indefinitely! Profounds, endless, bottomless, but lit up by millions of suns!

Such appears to us the Universe from the natural observatory where we are placed. But to obtain a more complete idea of its constitution, of the infinite variety of its members, we must descend from these regions, where the sight and mind are lost, to a group, nearer to us, and therefore more accessible to the investigations of man,—to that group, or system, of which the Earth forms part. Of this the Sun is the centre.

Round this focus of light and heat, but at various distances, revolve more than a hundred secondary bodies,—Planets, some of which are accompanied by smaller ones—Satellites. Not self-luminous, they would be invisible to us, if the light, which they receive from the Sun, were not reflected towards the Earth, making them also appear as luminous points spread over the celestial vault like so many stars. Such would be the appearance of the Earth seen in space, at a distance sufficiently great.

A common character distinguishes all the celestial bodies that form part of this group—the SOLAR SYSTEM—from the multitude of other stars. For while the Suns, composing what is called the SIDEREAL UNIVERSE, are situated at distances seemingly infinite, the bodies composing the group of which we speak are relatively much nearer the Earth, —are, in fact, our neighbours.

What results from this double fact? Two very simple consequences, easily understood.

The first is, that the stars do not undergo any sensible change of position in the starry vault. Their distance is such, that they appear actually at rest in the depths of space; hence the term *Fixed Stars*,—now abandoned, because a minute and elaborate study of their relative positions has established the fact that the stars really do move in the remote regions of the heavens. The apparent immobility of which we have spoken, and which is one of their characteristics, is evidenced by the uniformity of appearance preserved for centuries by the artificial groups of stars, to which the name of Constellations has been given.

Now, it is otherwise with the bodies that revolve round our Sun; they are near enough to the Earth to allow of their displacements in space being perceived in short intervals of time. Travelling, by virtue of their proper motions along the starry vault, distances which appear greater as their own distance from us is less, these bodies received at the outset the name they have since retained—*Planets*, or Wandering Stars.

It is thus, that, when we stand in the middle of an extensive plain, we judge distant objects—those that border the horizon—to be immovable; whilst we instantly perceive the slightest change of place in the near ones. It is true that when we ourselves move, the real movements become complicated with the apparent movements, but the former must be distinguished, if we wish to have an exact idea of the actual course travelled. This complication of the apparent movements of the planets,—a necessary consequence of the movement of the Earth,—is one of the most striking testimonies to the reality of the latter; but it must be also added, that this was precisely the stone of stumbling of ancient astronomy until the time—and that not long ago—when the real movements were made known.

It will soon be seen, in the detailed description of each of the planets of the solar system, what wonderful variety reigns within its limits. Movements of rotation, movements of revolution around the common centre, the duration of these movements, distances, forms and dimensions, distribution of light and heat, all change in passing from one planet to another. And yet, marvellous thing, the same laws govern all, in such a way, that the unity of plan is not less marked than the astonishing variety of the phenomena.

One circumstance common to all the bodies of the solar system forcibly strikes the imagination. It is, that these enormous masses,—these globes, many of which are much heavier than the Earth, and lastly, the Earth itself, not only are suspended in space, but move through the ether with velocities truly stupendous.

Imagine yourself a spectator, standing immovable in space. A luminous body appears in the distance, little by little you see it approach and increase in size; its immense circumference, which exceeds a hundred thousand leagues, is in rapid rotation, which makes each point on its periphery travel through nine miles a second. The globe itself at last passes before you, carried through space with a velocity twenty-four times greater than that of a cannon-ball. In such a way Jupiter would appear to you travelling in its orbit. This headlong course would banish it for ever, to the most remote regions of the visible universe, if it were not subdued and held by the powerful attraction of a globe a thousand times larger than its own—by the Sun himself. Not only does Astronomy show, by undeniable proofs, the reality of these marvellous movements,—not only has she arrived at the knowledge of their invariable constancy, at least during thousands of centuries; but she has found in their very rapidity the cause of the stability of all the celestial bodies.

If there is difficulty in imagining such masses freely circulating in the ether, how much more are we impressed, when we consider that these rapid movements are not confined to the planets; and when we look upon the Sun with all its retinue, as moving in an orbit yet unknown, himself attracted no doubt by a more powerful Sun, or by a group of Suns! All the stars which by reason of their infinite distances appear immovable, move in different directions; and we shall see later, that if these movements are performed with extreme slowness, the slowness is apparent only. In reality, these are the most rapid celestial movements that we know of.

Thousands of centuries will be necessary before these immense sidereal voyages are accomplished. Their vast periods are to the length of our year what the dimensions of the Earth are to the distances of the stars; and, according to the happy expression of Humboldt, they make of the Universe an eternal timekeeper. Thus, in the contemplation of celestial phenomena, the idea of infinite duration impresses itself on the mind with the same irresistible power as the idea of the infinity of space.

Such is briefly the magnificent field explored by Astronomy.

Other natural and physical sciences teach us to study nature in its more intimate mysteries; they unveil to us the molecular constitution of bodies; the play of their combinations and metamorphoses; their thousand useful and curious properties; the development of organized living beings, both vegetable and animal, and even of man himself, one of whose noblest attributes seems to be the gift of knowing, and who appears by the light of science as the most perfect creation of the organizing forces.

But it is Astronomy that reveals to us the Universe in its majestic whole; it is she who has made us comprehend its structure, and after having gathered its thousand various elements into a gorgeous picture, has initiated us into the eternal laws that govern the Heavens.

PART THE FIRST.

THE SOLAR SYSTEM.

The Bodies which form the Solar System—Direction of movements of Rotation and Revolution—Inclinations of the Planes of the Orbits of the different Planets.

THE group or system of celestial bodies, of which the Earth forms part,—a system known in Astronomy under the name of the Solar or Planetary System, is composed, according to our present knowledge, of a hundred and fifty-nine bodies, which may be classed in the following manner; taking into account at the same time, both the part which they play in the system, and the order of their distances from the Sun:

1. *A central body*, relatively immovable in the group; much larger than all the others, and self-luminous, THE SUN;

2. *One hundred and twenty-three secondary bodies*, or *Planets*, situated at increasing distances from the Sun; revolving round him in orbits nearly circular; and receiving from him the light which renders them visible to us. The planets may again be divided into three principal groups:

The smaller planets, those nearest to the central body, are, in the order of their increasing distances from the Sun: MERCURY, VENUS, THE EARTH, MARS;

The larger planets, those most remote from the central body; JUPITER, SATURN, URANUS, NEPTUNE;

Lastly, the minor planets, or Asteroids, forming between Mars and Jupiter a ring, which separates the two first groups;

One hundred and twelve small planets are now known, but there are, no doubt, many more;

3. *Twenty-two tertiary bodies*, or *Satellites*, revolving round some of the principal planets; such as the Moon, which accompanies the Earth. Jupiter has four such satellites; Saturn, eight; Uranus, eight; Neptune, one;

5. *Thirteen Comets*, the periodical returns of which have been proved by observation, revolving round the Sun in very elongated orbits.

Independently of the hundred and fifty-nine bodies which we have just enumerated, two hundred other comets are known, some of which travel round the Sun in orbits so elongated, and in times so vast, that their return has not yet been proved by observation, although it has been approximately calculated. Others describe curves which may be called infinite, and after having once approached our group, have abandoned it perhaps for ever. A year never passes without new comets being discovered.

We must here also mention a nebulous ring of a lenticular form, the *Zodiacal Light*, which surrounds the Sun at a certain distance, and the position of which in the system is not yet clearly determined: and, besides this, one or two or even more rings composed of a multitude of small bodies, revealed to us by the appearance and fall of *Meteorites, Meteors*, and *Falling* or *Shooting Stars*.

The Sun, the planets and their satellites, all assume a spherical form, sometimes flattened at the extremities of one diameter. In the more important of these bodies, movements of rotation have been detected; these movements all take place in the same direction as that of the Earth. Astronomers, by an analogy based on the laws of mechanics, extend this movement of rotation to all the bodies, which have hitherto baffled our scrutiny in this particular. A second movement, which we call one of revolution or of translation, impels all the planets round the Sun, and all the satellites round their respective planets, in times which vary with the dimensions of the orbits described, by virtue of a remarkable law, the discovery of which we owe to the genius of Kepler.*

The direction of the movement of revolution is the same for all the bodies of the solar system,† and this direction is precisely that of all the movements of rotation. In order that the reader may grasp this important point, let him turn to Plate I., which represents the orbits of all the known planets.‡ The arrow in each case indicates the direction of the planet's revolution round the Sun. Now let us suppose an observer, placed in the centre of the diagram in such a way, that his feet resting on the plane of the paper, his head will be in the northern hemisphere of the heavens. In this position it is easy to see that the movement indicated by the arrow will take place from the right to the left of the observer. Such is the direction of the movements of revolution of planetary bodies.

Let us now compare this movement to the movement of rotation of the Earth on its axis. The centre of our planet is situated on the plane;

* The law which defines the movement of all celestial bodies is referred to in Part III. Book i.

† We must except, however, the satellites of Uranus, one of the seven comets of short period, and a great number of other comets.

‡ In this Plate the orbits of the planets have been represented by the circumferences of circles, although in reality they are of an elliptical or oval form. Nor is the Sun, as represented in the figure, exactly in the centre of each orbit; but it would have been difficult, not to say impossible, to render these differences appreciable on so small a scale.

That which it is absolutely necessary to show correctly in this representation of the Solar System are the relative distances of the different planets from the common focus. The illustration represents the dimensions of the orbits in their true proportion, with the exception of the orbits of the satellites, the dimensions of which have been necessarily enlarged. The positions of the planets are those which these bodies actually occupied in space on the 1st of January, 1865.

the north pole is above it, and the south below it, in such a manner, that the terrestrial rotation which takes place—as proved by the daily movement of the heavens—from west to east, is also to the observer a movement from the right towards the left. If the name of north pole is given to that pole of each of the other planets, which is situated above the plane of which we speak, observation shows that it is always from right to left, or from west to east, that these planets describe both their movements of rotation, and their movements of translation, round the Sun.

It is very evident, that if we had supposed the observer standing on the other side of the paper, with his head towards the south pole of the heavens, all the movements would have seemed inverted; that is to say, would take place from left to right, although they would still remain the same, from the point of view which we occupy. So let us remember, once for all, this fundamental fact of solar astronomy, that the movements, both of rotation and of revolution, of the planets and their satellites, are effected all in the same direction, that is, from right to left or from west to east.

The ideal curves described by the various planets around the Sun, considered at rest, are plain curves, or at least nearly so. This is nearly the same as saying, that the centre of each planetary globe in its movement around the central body, remains always in the same plane. This plane, if prolonged, passes through the centre of the Sun. But the planes of those orbits do not coincide with one another, they are differently inclined to that of the Earth taken as a standard of comparison; from this it results, that each planet describes half its orbit above the plane of the terrestrial orbit, or, as it is called, the *plane of the ecliptic*, and the other half below it.

The inclinations, represented in their true proportions in fig. 2 of the Plate we have mentioned, are, moreover, very small; and it follows that, as seen from the Earth, the principal planets revolve in a narrow zone of the celestial vault; this has received the name of the *Zodiac*.

The Solar System seen in section, or in profile so to speak, would appear therefore, to an observer situated at a great distance beyond its limits (but near its mean plane) as a group of elongated form, having in its centre a luminous point, the Sun, and on both sides of it a multitude of small stars of unequal brightness—the planets and their satellites, oscillating backwards and forwards in paths nearly rectilinear.

After having sketched that entire group of celestial bodies, which interests us the most, seeing that our globe is one of its constituent molecules, we will now describe the members of the group one by one, study their movements, and, by the aid of facts furnished by the persevering observations of modern astronomers, examine them, when possible, in their most minute detail.

We will begin with the Sun.

BOOK THE FIRST.

THE SUN.

Of all the stars which people the immensity of space, the Sun is the most interesting to us the inhabitants of the Earth.

It is at once the largest, at least in appearance, the most brilliant, and that which exercises over our globe the most dominant influence.

The centre of the movements of all the celestial bodies of the system, of all those which are in fact our neighbours, he is to them and to us the inexhaustible source of light, heat, and life. It is from him that all the energies, developed on the surface of the Earth or on the other planets,—energies manifested under so many various forms—incessantly flow without ever draining their source.

[And yet all the action on this our Earth is carried on by the two thousand three hundred millionth part of the force radiated by the Sun; for that is all the Earth can grasp, as it were, of his rays given out in all directions, and it is by this fraction of his mighty power that all the Earth's work is done.]

Lastly, the Sun would seem to be the common father of the whole family of bodies that gravitate round him, and which he holds in hand by his powerful attraction. It is from him that at epochs immensely distant from ours, have been thrown out successively, at first under the form of nebulous rings, those agglomerations of matter which have become in the end, by a natural concentration, nearly spherical globes; Jupiter, Saturn, Mars, the Earth, Venus, are so many children of the Sun. The part played by the Sun in the group, of which he is the centre, we have already stated. Farther on, we shall see how he figures in the Sidereal Universe; and we shall find him midst the millions of stars which form the Milky Way.

Our present object is to study his individuality, to measure his apparent and real dimensions, to study the physics of his surface, and his movement of rotation, and to deduce from all the facts gathered by the most able and distinguished observers, the structure of this tremendous star, and the most probable conjectures as to its physical constitution.

I.

Form and apparent Size of the Sun—Its Distance from the Earth, and real Size—Its Surface, Volume, Mass, and Weight.

As every one knows, the naked eye cannot bear the brightness of the Sun. Nor can this be wondered at, if we remember that the intensity of its light as seen from the Earth is eight hundred thousand times greater than that of the full Moon, or twenty-two thousand million times that of the most brilliant star.* To obtain therefore, a clear idea of its form, we must take advantage of opportunities when clouds, or, better still, dense fogs, interpose themselves between the eye and its radiant body. The use of telescopes would be still more dangerous than that of the unaided sight, if observers did not take the precaution to use dark or coloured glasses to shield the eye, inasmuch as lenses and reflectors concentrate to their *foci* a considerable quantity of light- and heat-rays. The eye would be dazzled, or even utterly destroyed, without this indispensable precaution. †

A first rough glance shows us that the disk of the Sun is circular. But the use of accurate instruments leaves not the least doubt in this respect, and numerous micrometric ‡ measurements have proved that all the diameters of the disk are exactly equal. The Sun has then the appearance of a perfect luminous circle, and as it is not less certain that it turns on an axis, and therefore successively presents different faces to us, we can only conclude that its form is in reality that of a perfect sphere without any trace of irregularity or flattening.

In the morning when the Sun rises, or in the evening a little time before its setting, if the atmosphere be rather misty, the solar disk may often be observed by the naked eye: it then appears to be larger than

* [There is, however, to judge from the different results obtained by different physicists, some uncertainty attaching to these numbers. The comparative brightness of the Sun to Vega in Lyra, as given by different observers, is as follows:—

Wollaston .	180,000,000,000	to 1.
Bond . . .	24,000,000,000	to 1.
Clark . . .	10,400,000,000	to 1.

The absolute amount of light emitted by the Sun is another matter; he would really appear less bright than α Centauri, if we could see both at the same distance. The intrinsic light of the Sun, or the amount emitted by a unit of area of his surface, is yet another matter. It has been supposed that α Centauri is intrinsically brighter than the Sun; but as we do not know the real dimensions of this star, we can form no certain opinion on the point.

† In our Chapter on Astronomical Instruments in Part III, we shall describe the various methods of solar observation by which these objections are avoided.

‡ That is to say, made with micrometers—instruments which serve to measure very small objects and small angles, of which more anon in Part III.

usual, and its contour differs sensibly from that of a circle. But these are illusions, the cause of which we shall try to explain farther on.

The apparent dimensions of the Sun do not remain the same throughout the course of a year. The average size is such, that three hundred and thirty-seven disks equal to its own, placed side by side, would cover a half-circle of the celestial vault: its average diameter being somewhat more then half a degree.* But in winter it appears larger than in summer, at least to the inhabitants of the northern hemisphere of the Earth. In the southern hemisphere it seems larger in summer than in winter, because, of course, our winter is their summer. This change of size must not be attributed to a real change in the dimensions of the Sun. It is easily explained when we know that the annual revolution of the Earth round the central body is effected in a curved path, of which the Sun does not occupy exactly the centre. The distance of the two bodies varies therefore from one day to another, and it is towards the first days of winter in our northern hemisphere that the Earth is at its least distance from the Sun. The different sizes of the solar disk, as seen from the Earth when at its least, mean, and greatest distances from it, are shown in the following diagram:—

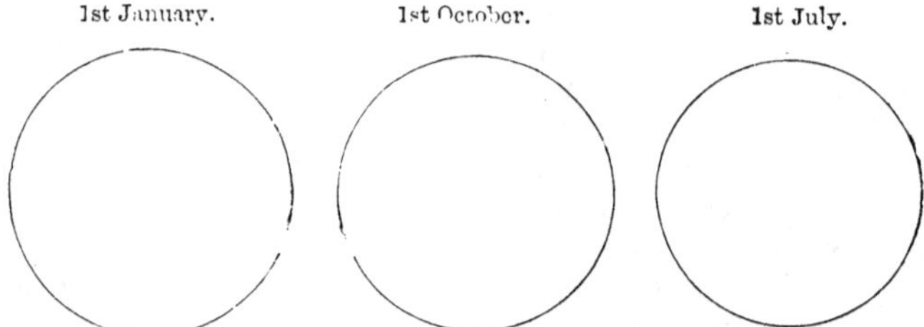

Fig. 1.—Apparent dimensions of the solar disk at the Earth's extreme and mean distances.†

We see, then, that the apparent size of an object varies with the distance: similarly the size of the solar disk ought to vary, seen from each of the planets of the system. The more distant the planet from the Sun, the smaller will the Sun appear. To avoid giving numbers, which would convey no definite idea to the reader, we have included in the same

* It is usual in geometry to divide the circumference of the circle into 360 equal parts, each of which is called a degree, and is represented thus: 1°. Each degree is subdivided into 60 minutes, and each minute into 60 seconds: a minute is written 1′; and a second, 1″. [Properly speaking, however, degrees, minutes, and seconds are the angles subtended by these arcs respectively.—R.A.P.]

† If we represent the luminous surface of the Sun by 1000 at its mean distance from the Earth, the numbers 967 and 1034 will represent the same surface as it appears to us at the Sun's greatest distance in July, and at its least distance about the 1st of January. The same numbers give us also the relative quantities of heat and of light received by the Earth at these different epochs, so that in summer the Sun warms and lights our globe less than during winter. This apparent anomaly will be explained when we describe the terrestrial seasons.

diagram (fig. 2) the comparative sizes of the Sun as seen from each of the principal planets at their mean distance. But it must not be forgotten,

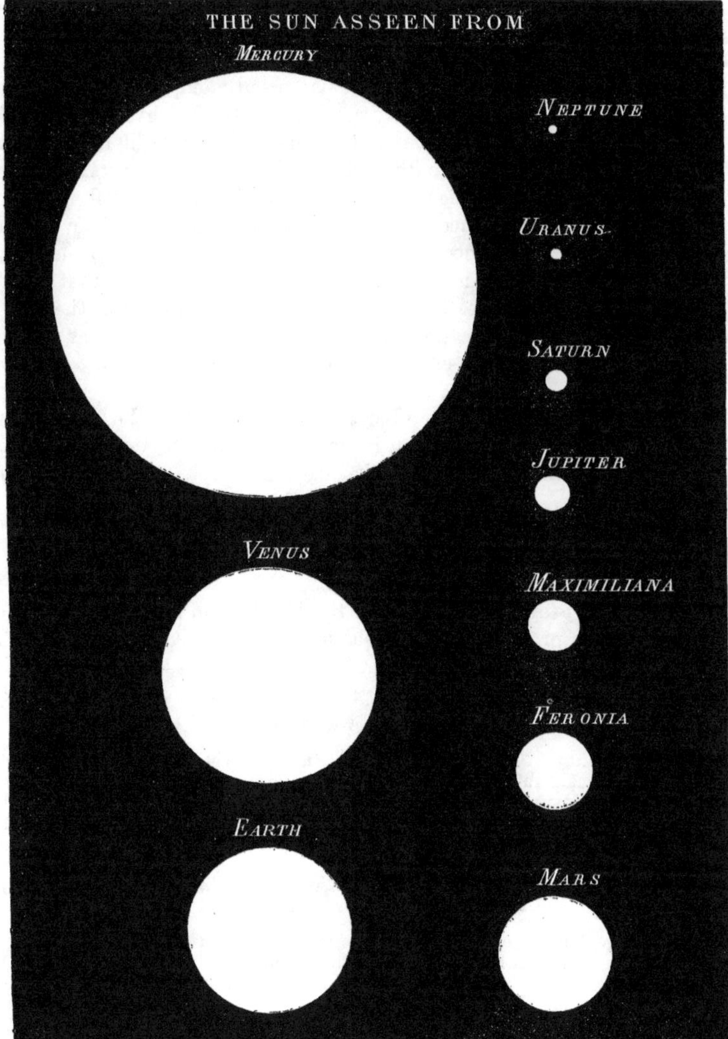

Fig. 2.—The apparent size of the Sun as seen from the principal planets.

that if the apparent size varies, the intrinsic intensity of the light remains the same, of course leaving out of consideration absorption by the planetary atmospheres, of the power of which nothing precise is yet known. The quantity of light or of heat received by a planet depends upon the extent of the apparent surface of the solar disk.

From Mercury, the planet nearest the Sun, this body is seen with its greatest apparent dimensions; from Neptune, on the contrary, with its smallest. The luminous surface appears 6670 times larger from the former of these planets than from the latter, situated, as we know, on the confines of our system. When we come to study the physical constitution of these bodies, we shall return to the quantities of light and heat with which the solar effulgence bathes the surface of the planets. We need only say here, that, if to the inhabitants of the Earth, the disk of the Sun presents an apparent surface seven times less than that seen from Mercury, if, in Neptune this surface is further reduced a thousand times, it still preserves, as seen from this last globe a brilliancy superior to that of all the bodies, whether planets or stars, that we on the Earth see in the heavens, although at this distance the immense luminary would appear but as a point, lost amid the innumerable fires of the starry vault.

The *apparent* size of an object—in other words, the angle formed by the visual rays coming from its two extremities to our eye—teaches us, however, nothing of its *real* size, so long as we are ignorant of its distance from us.

What is, then, the distance of the Sun from the Earth and from the other bodies of our planetary system?

Let us take, first, the distance of the Earth from the Sun, without considering for the present the particular methods employed to determine it.

This distance is 95,298,260 miles,* equal to 24,000 (more precisely to 23,984) semi-diameters of our planet. It was about the middle of the last century that this determination was arrived at.

* It is certain that the distance of the Sun from the Earth as stated above requires to be considerably diminished. The labours of Le Verrier and Hansen, the observations of Mars made by Stone and Winnecke, the new determination of the velocity of light by Léon Foucault, all point to the necessity for this correction, which will entail a series of modifications in the numbers at present adopted for the various elements of the solar system.

[The old value of the Sun's parallax (a word which we shall subsequently explain), and the values recently obtained, are as follows:—

	Seconds.
The old value obtained by Bessel from the transit of Venus	8·578
The new value obtained by Hansen from the Moon's parallactic equation .	8·916
" " " Winnecke from the observations of Mars . .	8·964
" " " Stone	8·930
" " " Foucault, from the velocity of light . . .	8·860
" " " Leverrier, from the motions of Mars and Venus, and the apparent motion of the Sun . .	8·950

This small correction, amounting to only two-fifths of a second of arc, brought to light in the first instance by small disturbances in the motion of the Moon and planets, should, it has been well remarked, inspire astronomers with additional

Very different from the distance just given was that adopted hypothetically by Pythagoras. This philosopher, who held ideas of the system of the world so similar to those which a long series of labours has definitely established, assigned 44,000 miles as our distance from the body, which warms and lights us, a distance which would give as its diameter 75 miles. Bearing these figures in mind, we can understand the ancient assertion which, perhaps, would still astonish many of us, that the Sun is larger than the Peloponnesus.*

The very large numbers, which are so often met with in Astronomy, leave for the most part only a very vague impression on the mind. It is difficult for the imagination to figure the objects that they represent; and where it is a question even of moderate distances, it is only by the aid of comparisons that we can arrive at any precise idea. If these distances are greater than those which we can actually see on a terrestrial horizon, say than 25 or 50 miles, the image properly so called vanishes, and we are compelled to have recourse to other means of representation; for example, we ask how much time a locomotive, going at a known rate, will require to traverse the given distance. The idea of duration comes then in aid of that of space to complete and perfect it.

Let us see with what exactness we can by this means form a conception of the distance which separates the Earth from the Sun.

Light—the propagation of which is the most rapid movement known, and which travels at the rate of 192,000 miles in a second of time—requires 8 minutes 17 seconds to flash from the Sun to the Earth. If we suppose the intervening space to contain atmospheric air, a sound, with an intensity sufficiently great to put in motion a sphere of such enormous dimensions, would take fourteen years and two months to reach our ears, sound travelling, as we know, about 1115 feet a second.

confidence (if that were needed) in the exactness of their science and in the fixedness of the laws which bind the Kosmos together. And if, on the other hand, a contrary misgiving is created in other minds from the fact, that this abrupt alteration of so important an element as the solar parallax implies an alteration of some four millions of miles in the Sun's reputed distance from our Earth, this misgiving may, perhaps, be removed, as Sir John Herschel has suggested, by the consideration that after all this improvement of our knowledge amounts to no more than a correction to an observed angle represented by the apparent breadth of a human hair viewed at the distance of about 125 feet.]

* Before 1769, astronomers had endeavoured to determine the distance of the Sun in various ways. Aristarchus of Samos, and afterwards Ptolemy, Copernicus, and Tycho, supposed it equal to 1200 radii of the Earth, nearly 4,800,000 miles, that is to say, twenty times less than the actual distance. Kepler tripled this number. Cassini and Lacaille approached the nearest to the truth. According to D'Alembert, the latter of these *savants* valued the distance in question at 21,000 terrestrial radii: Cassini at 28,000. The same author again quotes a distance of 12,000 diameters of the Earth, which is precisely that now adopted; but he does not give the name of the astronomer who arrived at this estimate. Arago, in his "Popular Astronomy," alludes to the measures of Riccioli and Hevelius, giving 7000 and 5200 terrestrial radii respectively; lastly, those of Richer and Maraldi, deduced from oppositions of Mars, fixed the mean distance of the Sun at 21,712, and at 20,626 terrestrial radii.

Finally, an express train going at the rate of about 30 miles an hour, leaving the Earth the first of January, 1866, would not arrive at the Sun until the year 2213, nearly 347 years after the day of its departure.

We can thus form an idea of the immensity of the chasm which lies between the Sun and our globe,— an immensity, the measure of which is expressed by the round number, so simple in appearance, of 95,000,000 miles. It is this number—this 95,000,000 miles—which will henceforth form the unit, the 'standard measure,' by means of which the other celestial distances will be expressed.

The distance of the Sun once known, we have only to solve an easy problem in geometry, to deduce its real dimensions from the apparent size of its disk.* We thus know that its diameter is about 112 times (112·06) the diameter of the Earth, or, as it may be expressed in miles, 887,076. The circumference of our great light-giver, therefore, exceeds 2,785,400 miles.

The Moon, as we shall see in the sequel, revolves round the Earth at a mean distance of 30 diameters of our Earth. If, then, we imagine the centre of the solar orb to coincide with the centre of the Earth, not only would the orbit of the Moon lie entirely within the Sun, but to reach its surface, a distance equal to 26 Earth-diameters would still remain to be traversed. Fig. 4, drawn to scale, will show this clearly.

So much, then, for the linear dimensions of our Sun.

If we ask what is the extent of the Sun's surface, and what its volume, we find that the first comprises the enormous number of 2,471,665,000,000 square miles, that is, 12,611 times the entire surface of the terrestrial

* This problem is so simple, in fact, that we cannot resist the temptation of proving our assertion. Take a disk of white pasteboard, say of about four inches (the French equivalents are given in the figure) in diameter, place it vertically, and

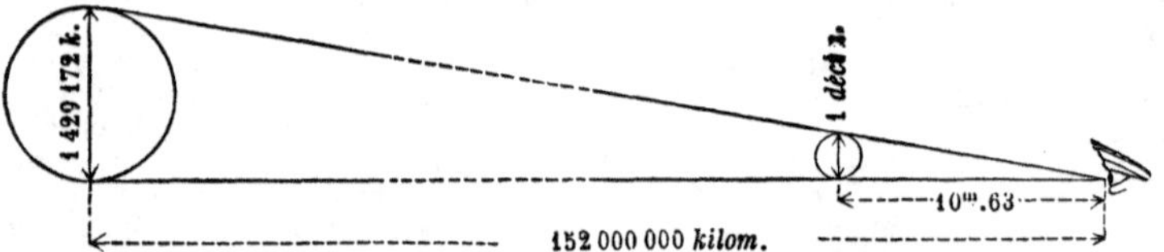

Fig. 3.—Dimensions of the Sun reduced from its distance and its apparent diameter.

move away from it little by little until its apparent dimensions are precisely the same as those of the Sun, that is, until the pasteboard disk will exactly cover the solar disk. Observation shows us that the distance between the eye and the disk is very nearly 12 yards.

Now it is easy to see from the preceding figure, that there is between the real dimensions of the pasteboard disk and those of the Sun precisely the same relation as between the distances which separate the observer from each of the two objects in question. The diameter of the Sun is therefore to the diameter of the disk as 95,000,000 miles are to the distance of the disk from the eye. The method employed by astronomers is less elementary; but in the main it is based on the same principle.

sphere. If we pass to its volume, it is impossible not to be startled at the colossal number of 364,345,641,000,000,000 cubic miles, a number which represents more than 1,400,000 times the cubic contents of the Earth.

Arago, in his 'Popular Astronomy,' quotes the following comparison, well adapted to give an idea of the immensity of this volume: 'A certain Professor at Angers, wishing to give his pupils a tangible notion of the size of the Earth compared with that of the Sun, counted the number of grains of wheat of ordinary size contained in a measure called a litre; he found this to be 10,000; consequently a decalitre would hold 100,000; a hectolitre 1,000,000, and 14 decalitres, 1,400,000. After having

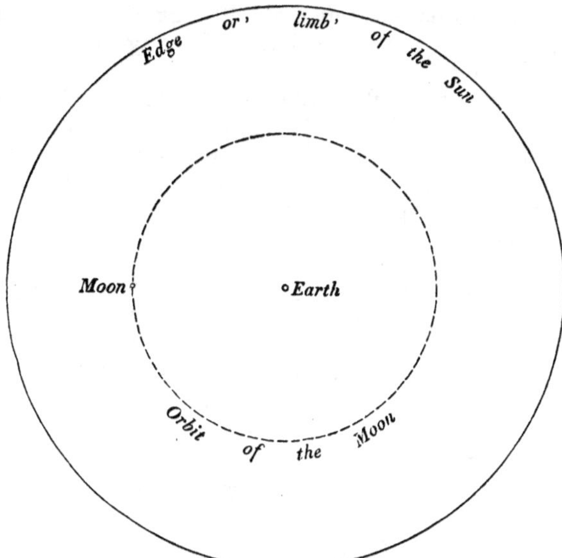

Fig. 4.—Comparative dimensions of the Sun and of the orbit of the Moon.

gathered into one heap the 14 decalitres, he held up one grain, and said to his listeners, "Here is the volume of the Earth, and here is the Sun." This statement of the case struck the pupils infinitely more than if he had announced it in abstract numbers, 1 to 1,400,000.'

When we shall have seen what are the actual dimensions of this grain of corn which represents the Earth, we shall be more surprised still, and our imagination will be crushed under the prodigious size of our world's light-giver, which, nevertheless, is but itself a grain of luminous dust lost in infinite space.

Our Earth being only one of the members of the planetary family, it would be only natural to extend the comparisons that we have made between its volume and that of the Sun to the principal celestial bodies which revolve with it round the central focus. But, in the detailed description that we shall subsequently give of each of these bodies, we shall take occasion to enlarge more on their proper dimensions. To deal with them here as a whole, we may remark that the volume of the Sun is itself equal to 600 times the united volumes of all the planets and their satellites put together.

That we have been able, by means of the data supplied by observation, and the laws of geometry and optics, to measure the true distances of the celestial bodies — at least of those nearest to us; that from their distances we have determined their dimensions in diameter, in surface, and in volume, is not difficult to understand, and our readers will doubtless readily admit what we have already said, although we have not finished with the subject, as the question of distance will be again discussed in the third part of this book.

But that astronomers should pretend even to know the weight of the different celestial bodies, and to say how many Earths may be placed in one scale of a balance to hold the Sun in equilibrium in the other, will seem paradoxical, at all events, to many. We shall, farther on, show the possibility of conclusions apparently so audacious, the inquiry into which may seem to border on presumption. We must, however, in the interim invoke a sentiment which is but rarely required in science — faith in our assertions, not a faith which shelters itself under the impenetrability of the mysterious, but one which will become by future study clear and demonstrated truth.

Compared with the mass of the Earth, the mass of the Sun is only about 355,000 times as great, although its volume, as we have seen, is 1,400,000 times larger. This indicates a less density; and it is found that the matter of which the Sun is composed weighs but little more, volume for volume, than a quarter of that of which our own globe is formed. The weight of the Sun may thus be expressed in tons:

2,154,106,580,000,000,000,000,000,000

It ranks, as we see, among those numbers which present nothing to the mind, and leave the imagination itself powerless.

We shall find that among the bodies of the solar system, there are many planets whose dimensions and masses are considerable when compared to our Earth. The mass of the Sun alone, however, is equal to 750 times the united masses of all the bodies which it maintains in its sphere of attraction, and to which it dispenses light and heat.

II.

Solar Observations—Sun-spots—The Sun's movement of Rotation—The Kew Photographs of the Sun—The Telescopic appearance of the General Surface—Mr. Nasmyth's 'Willow-leaves'—Opinions of other Astronomers—The appearance of the Penumbra—Umbra and Penumbra of Spots—Enormous Spots—Their rapid Change of form—Mr. Carrington's Researches on their Proper Motion.

When clouds or mists are thick enough to mitigate the dazzling splendour of the Sun's rays, but yet sufficiently transparent to enable us to see its disk, with its distinctly circular form, the surface of the luminary appears to us uniformly luminous, with no spot dimming its brightness. The same appearance, as every one knows, is presented when we observe it through a plate of black or smoked glass.

But if, instead of confining ourselves to observations with the naked eye, we examine the body with a telescope of moderate magnifying power, our eye being properly protected, the enlarged image of the disk will usually appear to us, as if sprinkled with irregularly grouped dark points. These are the 'Sun-spots,' real movable appurtenances of the surface of the Sun, the observation of which, as we shall soon see, is surrounded with the greatest interest, as it helps us in the study of the physical constitution of our luminary.

The following representation of the Sun (fig. 5) will give an idea of the manner in which the spots are distributed, and of their grouping at a given time.

Let us remark at once, that the number of the spots, their relative positions, and their forms even, vary constantly according to the period of observation. Sometimes, but rarely, the solar disk is perfectly clear, no spot varying the uniformity of its splendour. During a period of ten years, from 1840 to 1850, out of a total number of 1982 days, when the Sun was observed, there were only 372 days on which spots were not observed on its disk.

As many as 80 spots have been visible at one time. On the other hand, whole years, it is stated, have passed without any being observed.

But we must be allowed to consider the latter fact a negative one, resulting from the want of assiduity of observers; for since such astronomers as Schwabe of Dessau, Wolf of Zurich, Carrington of Redhill, Dawes of Haddenham, [De La Rue of Cranford, and Stewart of Kew], have devoted themselves to the continuous observation of these phenomena, the number of days in the year when the disk of the Sun has not presented any spot has always been less than those on which groups have been recognised.

We shall see, subsequently, that the number of spots follows a certain periodicity, which seems to establish a most interesting correlation between Sun-spots and the phenomena of terrestrial magnetism.

When observed with care during several consecutive days, the spots are seen to vary in form and position. But midst all these variations, a common movement, a progression of the whole, by virtue of which they all move in the same direction, can be distinguished. From this movement has been deduced the rotation of the solar globe round an axis that passes through its centre.

Let us look again through our telescope. The reversed image of the Sun presents itself in such a manner, that the eastern edge—or *limb* as

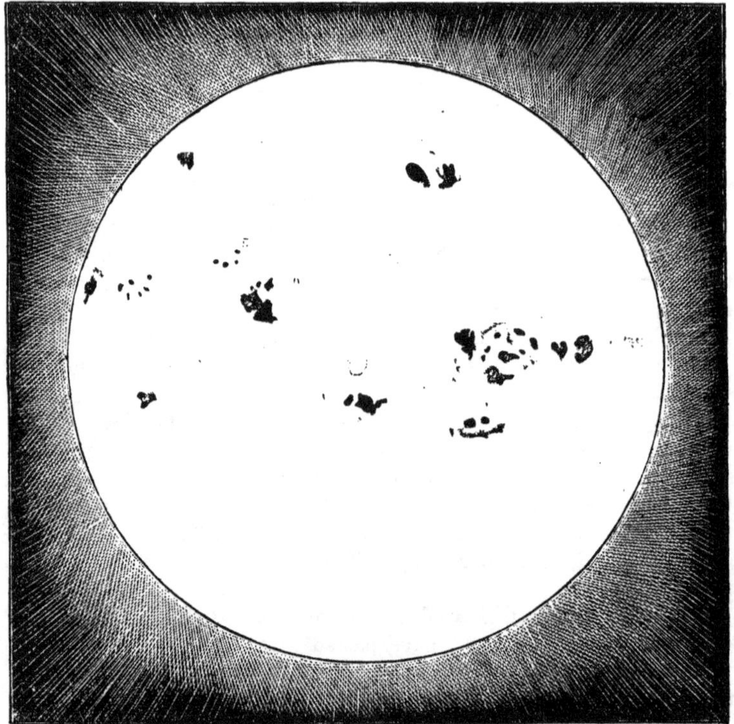

Fig. 5.—Sun-spots observed on the 2nd September, 1839. (Captain Davis.)

it is called by astronomers—occupies the right, the western one the left, whilst the south and north regions of the Sun are, the former at the top, the latter at the bottom of the image, as seen in the telescope.

Observe a spot on the eastern edge. From one day to another we shall see it progress, and that with gradually increasing rapidity, until it occupies a central position on the disk. Then it will continue to advance towards the left, but, in this second half of its journey, its rapidity will decrease, and the spot will finally disappear on the western border. The same phenomena will take place with all the spots which, at the commencement of observation, are scattered over the solar disk; all will describe in the same direction with a nearly equal velocity either straight lines or slightly curved ones (according to the period of observation), the convexity of the latter lying in the same direction for all the spots observed at the same time.

Let us suppose that the particular spot that we have noticed is of an oval form, its greatest length being at right angles to its motion across the Sun at the moment when it appeared at the eastern border. In proportion as it approaches the centre the spot widens, so that it becomes nearly circular, then, having passed the centre, its form becomes more and more oval again, until its disappearance, its apparent size meanwhile in one direction not having sensibly varied.

Fig. 6 shows the changes of form of which we speak during the first or last half of the period of the visibility of the spot. The effects are

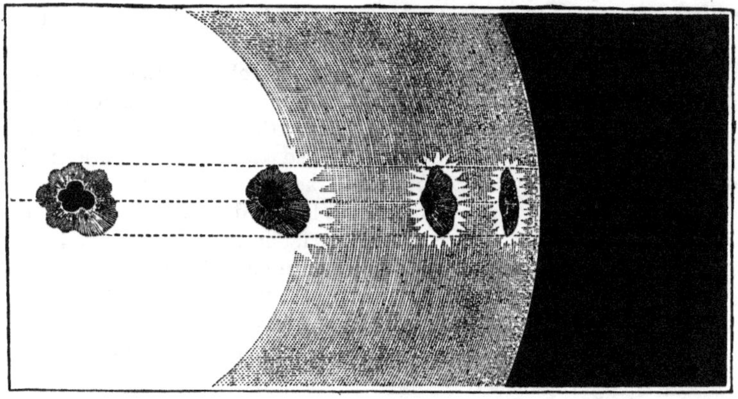

Fig. 6.—Apparent change in the form of spots approaching or receding from the centre.

produced precisely as the laws of perspective demand, if we admit that the Sun is of a spherical form, and that the dark spot observed passes over its surface with an uniform movement.

About fourteen days is the time during which a spot remains visible, and this time is the same for all, although they do not all traverse arcs of precisely the same length on the Sun's surface.

It is also fourteen days after the disappearance of a spot on the western border before it appears again on the eastern, often changed in form, it is true, but, nevertheless, generally recognisable.

Precise measurements have proved both the general uniformity and the parallelism of all these movements, although, independently of the rotation of the whole, the spots undergo slight displacements among themselves.

It was asked at first if the black points which form the spots really belonged to the body of the Sun, whether they were not small bodies revolving like planets around the great light-giver and presenting to us their unilluminated faces. But the variation in their apparent rapidity which we have noticed, combined with the change of form which some of them undergo in passing from one border to the other, does not allow us to adopt this hypothesis.

It was also thought possible to explain the movement of the spots from the eastern to the western border, by an actual translation of them across the surface of the Sun, itself immovable. But if so, how shall we account for this absolute uniformity in their movements?

Thus there are two facts of great importance placed beyond all question by the attentive and continued observation of these black points which are scattered over the surface of the Sun; on the one hand, the spherical form of the body, on the other the existence of a movement of general rotation. Moreover, this movement takes place from right to left, or from west to east; that is, as we have already seen, precisely in the same direction as the movements, both of rotation or revolution, of the other bodies of the solar system.

When, three centuries ago, the discoveries of Copernicus at last brought to light the true system of the world, the Sun was promoted from the secondary rank of satellite to the Earth to that of sovereign of the planetary kingdom, and it was imagined that he was enthroned, immovable, in the centre of his court. It was not suspected either that he was whirling through space accompanied by his dependants, or that he turned on an axis. Why, it was said, this latter movement, in a body which itself is light and heat, and knows only an eternal day?

These two movements are, nevertheless, real movements. The recent progress of Sidereal Astronomy has demonstrated the movement of translation of the solar system in space, as the observation of the Sun-spots has proved the rotation of the Sun.

It was in 1611 that this last and important discovery was made. Before that time, Jordano Bruno and Kepler had suspected the movement of rotation; anticipating, as remarked by Arago, actual observation by their genius, while the astronomer, Jean Fabricius, discovered both the spots and their general displacement on the surface of the disk.

We have said before, that about 28 days elapse between the appearance and disappearance of a spot on the same edge of the Sun; the time of the actual rotation is actually less by two days.*

* Let us endeavour to understand this important distinction.

If we take a spot, *a*, on the accompanying diagram at the moment when, as seen from the Earth, it coincides with the centre of the Sun, and disregard the irregular displacements to which it will be subjected on the surface of that body, an entire rotation will seem to us to be effected when the same spot returns to occupy the same central portion after 27 days 12 hours. But, during this time, the Earth, our movable observatory, will be displaced in its orbit, and will have described an arc, from T, its primitive position, to T′, its new position. At this moment,

We are here content to state the time of the Sun's rotation thus broadly, as we shall have to return to it by-and-bye.

The plane of the Sun's equator is but slightly inclined (7° 15′ according to Carrington's latest researches) to the ideal plane in which our Earth moves round the Sun. If this inclination were *nil*, we should always see the spots moving in right lines over the disk, parallel to the solar equator. But this inclination causes us to be sometimes above and sometimes below the plane of the Sun's equator. Hence the curved paths of the spots at some seasons, the convexity sometimes being towards the north, at others towards the south. But at the two intermediate seasons, that is, on the 6th of June and the 8th December, the Earth is exactly in the plane of the equator,* and at these times we see the spots moving in straight lines. Fig. 8 will render our statements clear, [but it must be understood that the feature illustrated is greatly exaggerated.]

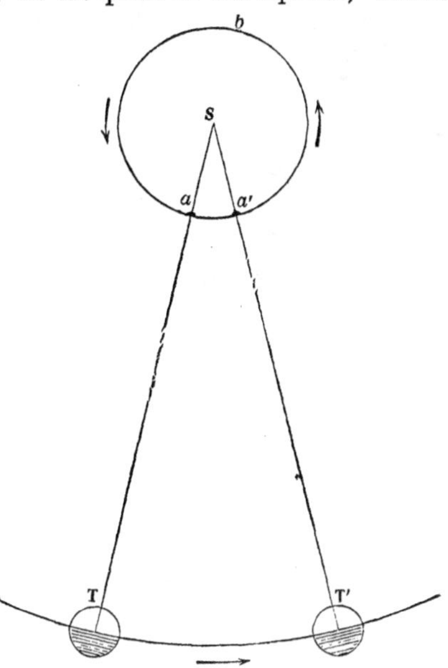

Fig. 7.—Difference of time in the apparent rotation of the Sun, and its real rotation.

Sun-spots are confined in the main to two zones, situated on each side of the equator, and they are seldom observed on other parts of the disk, whence it seems to follow, that the phenomena which give rise to them have a certain relation to the movement of rotation of the solar globe. If the luminous surface of the Sun be an incandescent fluid [or be composed of masses of gas or cloud], it is conceivable that the rapidity of rotation gives rise to a centrifugal force which, though absent at the poles, constantly increases towards the equator, where it attains its maximum. Hence arise currents, whirlwinds, and, no doubt, breaks or rents in the luminous surface.

The rapidity of rotation increases of course from the poles towards the equator, and is much greater than would be imaginable at first sight

the spot has revolved not only back to *a* again, but also through an additional part of the arc *a a′*, so that it has actually effected more than an entire rotation. In other words, the point of the surface of the Sun, which corresponded first to the centre of the disk, is now to the east of the new central point *a′*, by the fact of the movement of the Earth. The apparent period of the rotation exceeds thus the real period by the time necessary to traverse the path *a a′*. A simple calculation shows that this period is about two days.

* [The ascending node of the Sun's equatorial plane is situated in heliocentric longitude 73° 40′ for 1850·0 (Carrington).]

to judge from the slowness of its angular movement. A point situated on the solar equator, however, travels with a velocity of 4560 miles an hour, or about $1\frac{1}{4}$ miles a second; that is, nearly four times and a half faster than a point situated on the terrestrial equator.

Now that the spots of the Sun have revealed to us its movement of rotation, and the direction, manner, and duration of that movement, let us study in detail these interesting phenomena, and see what knowledge we can gather of the physical constitution of this giant of our planetary system.

Turn to Plate II, which represents a series of Sun-spots. It will be seen that the spots consist almost invariably of one or several dark portions called *umbræ*, which seem black when compared with the luminous parts of the disk.

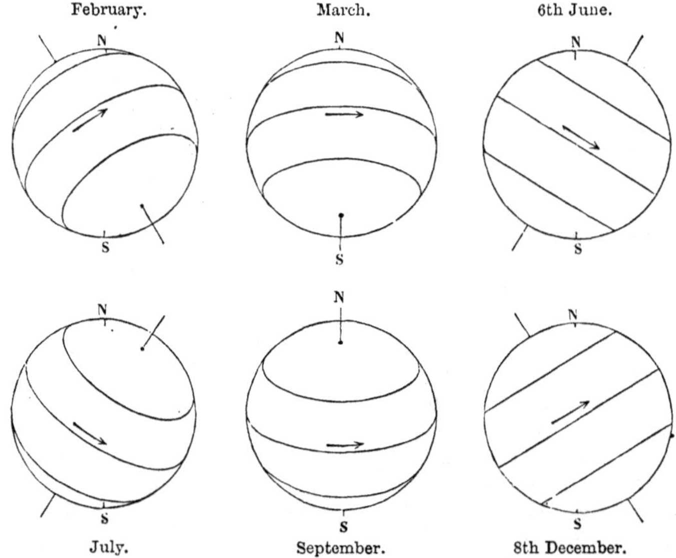

Fig. 8.—Different paths of Sun-spots at different periods of the year.

Around these, a grey tint furrowed with dark striæ forms what is named, improperly, the *penumbra*. The majority of spots are composed of one or several *umbræ*, enclosed in one penumbra. But sometimes spots appear without the greyish envelope, as also occasionally penumbræ unprovided with *umbræ*.

The forms of the spots, as shown by the drawings placed before the reader, are most varied. The penumbra most frequently reproduces the principal contours of the umbra, and often presents a great variety of shades, when examined with considerable magnifying powers. On the exterior edges of the penumbra, the grey tint seems generally the deepest, either by the effect of contrast with the brilliant portions that surround it, or because in reality it possesses at these points a more decided tint.

Fig. 9 affords a striking example of this aspect of the penumbra.

This spot presents the peculiarity, not at all unfrequent, that the dark umbra is divided into several fragments by luminous bridges, spanning it, as it were, from one side of the penumbra to the other.

The umbra itself is far from offering an uniform black tint. In reality it always presents the appearance of varied shades, as if the penumbra and umbra were mingled, and mixed up their tints in varied proportions.

[We owe to the Rev. W. R. Dawes the discovery that the *umbra* is but a darker kind of penumbra; for under the best conditions of air and

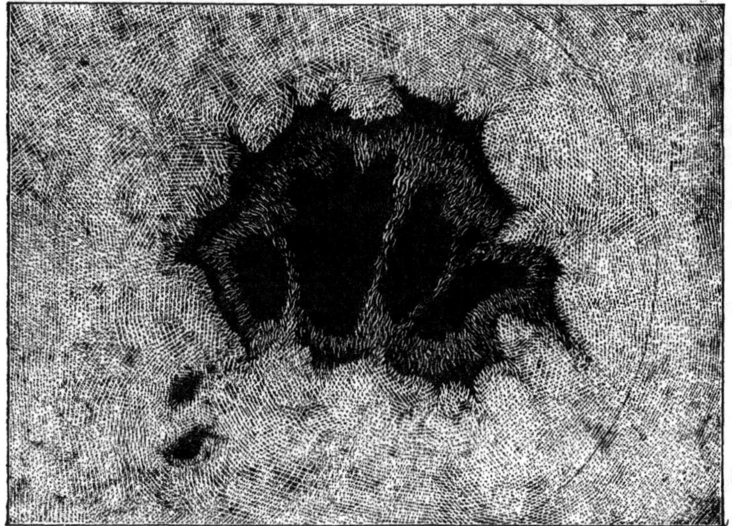

Fig. 9 —Sun-spots, showing umbra, penumbra, and luminous bridges. (Nasmyth.)

nstrument, he has found within some umbræ a much darker portion—which he calls the *nucleus.* This he finds to be of the most intense blackness; but in saying this we must warn our readers that such a word as applied to the Sun is comparative only. Sir J. Herschel has shown, that a ball of ignited quicklime, in a Drummond's oxyhydrogen lamp, which itself gives out an apparently near approach to sunlight, when projected on the Sun *appears as a black spot.* So that the Sun-spots, properly so called, may not be so black after all!]

The transits of Mercury, moreover, over the Sun's disk have taught us that the umbra is less dark than the unilluminated face of a planet.

We shall now speak of the real dimensions of the spots, the successive changes which they undergo, and what astronomers call their 'proper motion,' that is, their actual movement on the Sun's surface in any direction.

The dimensions of the spots are extremely variable, and they sometimes cover enormous areas. It is not uncommon to see one with a surface larger than that of the Earth. Schröter measured one, the extent of which was equivalent to sixteen times the surface embraced by a great circle of our Earth, or four times the entire superficies of our globe; its

Fig. 10.—Enormous Sun-spots. (Davis.)

diameter, therefore was nearly four times the diameter of the Earth, that is to say, more than 29,000 miles. Sir W. Herschel, in 1799, measured a spot consisting of two parts, the diameter of which was not less than 50,000 miles. Some spots observed by Captain Davis on the 30th of August, 1839, show what enormous proportions they sometimes attain. The most extensive was not less than 186,000 miles in its greatest length, its surface embracing about 25,000,000,000 square miles.

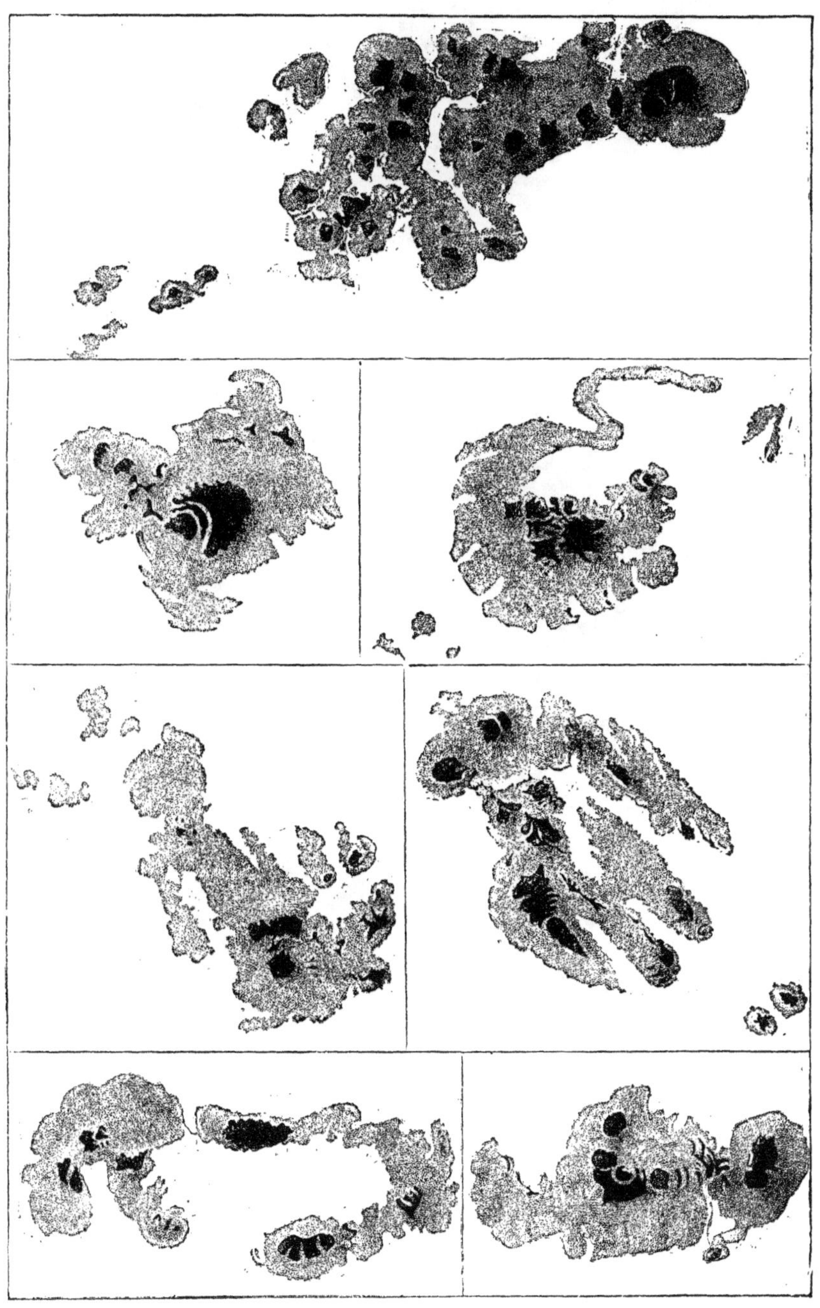

SUN-SPOTS. (Sir J. Herschel.)

If the spots are deep rents in the envelope, of what enormous capacity must be those gulfs, those gigantic abysses, at the bottom of which the Earth would only be as a boulder in the crater of a volcano!

Not only are Sun-spots not permanent—it is rare that one lasts for many successive rotations—but their forms and dimensions differ from one rotation to the other; sometimes even in the interval of a day.

The modification undergone by groups of spots, in about the interval of one rotation, can be seen in figs. 11 and 12.

These different groups, though easily recognised again, form, nevertheless, a new *ensemble*, and the details of the spots are still more modified.

These changes indicate two phenomena going on simultaneously, which observers have separately studied. On the one hand, we have here indicated a proper motion of the spots, more or less rapid and distinct from the apparent movement produced by rotation. According

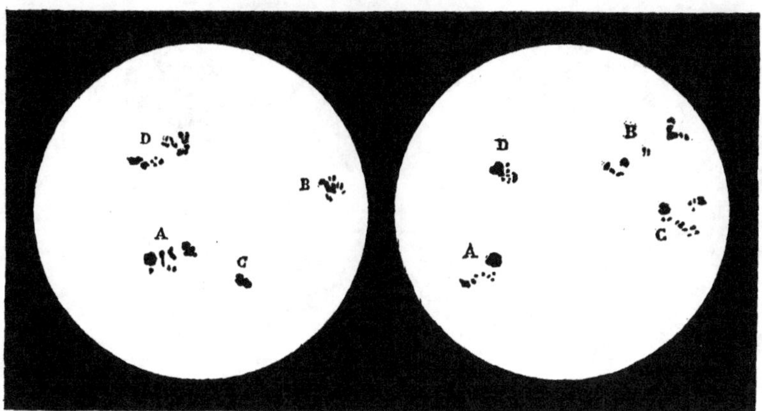

Fig. 11.—Transformation of groups of Solar spots in the interval of a rotation. Observed by M. Pastorff on 24th May and 21st June, 1828.

to Laugier, the proper motion of a spot observed by him was not less than 363 feet a second; that is to say, three times greater than that of clouds carried along by the most violent hurricane.

[The proper motion of the spots has recently been inquired into in the most complete manner by Mr. Carrington, who has been willing to observe the Sun every fine day for eight and a half years, in order to supply his share of information for the solution of that great question, 'What is a Sun?' What he has discovered shows us that there need be no wonder that various observers have differed so greatly in the time they have assigned to the Sun's rotation. As our readers already know, that rotation has been deduced from the time taken by the spots to cross the disk. Mr. Carrington now shows that all Sun-spots have a movement of their own, and that the rapidity of this movement varies regularly with their distance from the solar equator. In fact, the spots near the equator travel faster than those away from it, so that if we take the estimated motion for the Sun's equator we shall say that the Sun rotates in about 25 days; and if we take a spot situated half-way between the equator and the poles (in either hemisphere), we shall say that it rotates in about 28 days. This, truly, is an important stand-point gained, but while it aids our knowledge of the photosphere—that silver sea over which the spots, like gondolas, so slowly glide—it tells us that of the rotation of the Sun itself lying underneath this fiery envelope we are yet entirely ignorant, for if it be a solid mass it can only have one period of rotation. Which is it?]

We now come to the other phenomenon indicated. The *change of form* is not less rapid than the proper movement. Sometimes a spot divides into several separate nuclei; sometimes many distinct nuclei

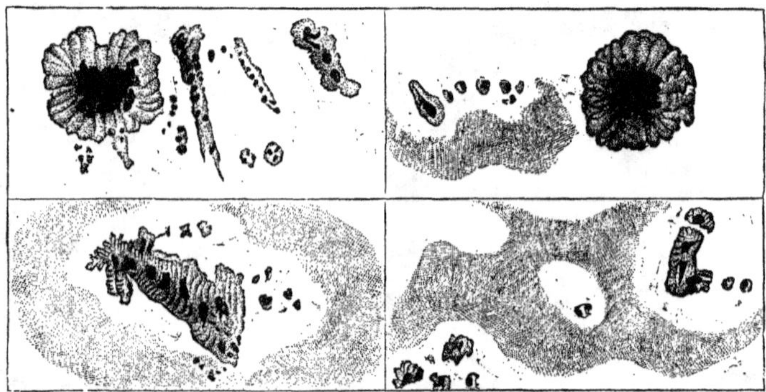

Fig. 12.—Changes of Solar spots in the interval of one rotation. Details of groups A. and B. (See last figure.) (Pastorff.)

reunite into one. Arago quotes from Wollaston a curious instance of a spot which seemed to break upon the surface of the solar globe, in the same manner as a fragment of ice thrown on the frozen surface of a sheet of water divides into several pieces, and slides in all directions.

[Diligent observation, moreover, of the umbra and penumbra with a powerful instrument, reveals to us the fact that *change* is going on incessantly in the region of the spots. Sometimes, after the lapse of an hour, many changes in detail are noticed: here a portion of the penumbra setting sail across the umbra; here a portion on the umbra melting from sight; here, again, an evident change of position and direction in masses which retain their form.]

Are, then, these spots the only exceptions to the uniform brightness of the Sun's surface? They are not.

[Near the edge of the solar disk, and especially about spots approaching the edge, it is quite easy, even with a small telescope, to discern certain very bright streaks of diversified form, quite distinct in outline, and either entirely separate or coalescing in various ways into ridges and network. These appearances, which have been termed 'faculæ,' are the most brilliant parts of the Sun. Where, near the limb, the spots become invisible, undulated shining ridges still indicate their place—being more remarkable thereabout than elsewhere on the limb, though everywhere traceable in good observing weather. Faculæ appear of all magnitudes; and Professor Phillips, whose description we are quoting, has observed them from barely discernible, softly-gleaming, narrow tracts, 1000 miles long, to continuous, complicated, and heapy ridges, 40,000 miles and more in length, 1000 to 4000 miles broad. By the frequent meeting of the bright ridges, spaces of the Sun's surface are included of various magnitudes and forms, somewhat corresponding to the areas and forms of the irregular spots with penumbræ. They are never regularly arched, and

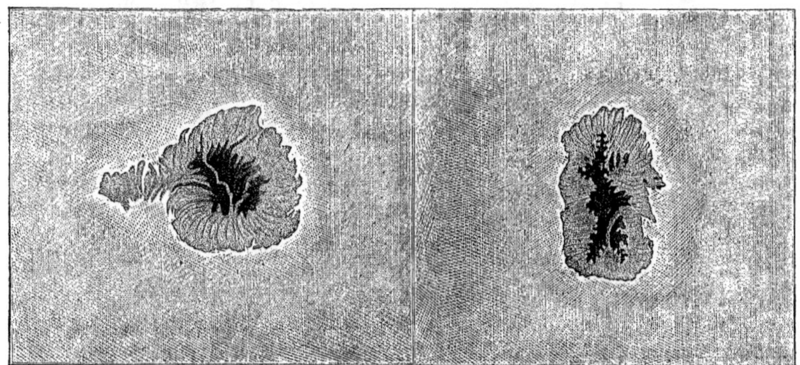

Fig 13.—Sun-spots surrounded by a platform of faculæ. (Capocci.)

never formed in straight bands, but always devious and minutely undulated, like clouds in the evening sky, or irregular ranges of snowy mountains.

Ridges of this kind often surround a spot as shown in fig. 13, and hence appear the more conspicuous; but sometimes there appears a very broad white platform round the spot, and from this the white crumpled ridges pass in various directions. Towards the limb the ridges appear parallel to it; away from it, this character is exchanged for indeterminate direction and lessened distinctness; over the remainder of the surface they are much less conspicuous, but can certainly be traced.]

There would seem to be a close connexion between spots and faculæ, for M. Chacornac, an eminent French observer, holds that spots are distributed for the most part in groups, with their greatest length parallel to the Sun's equator, and that the first spot of the group is the blackest, the most regular, and lasts the longest. As the spots on the wake of the first disappear, they give place to faculæ, which invade and cover over the regions where the spots showed themselves: then the original spot appears followed by a train of faculæ.*

[The Sun himself has bestowed a great boon upon observational Astronomy. Thanks principally to the labours of Mr. De La Rue, who has now brought the art and science of Astronomical Photography almost to perfection, the Sun, whether brightly shining or hid in dim eclipse, now tells his own story, and prints his image on a retina which never forgets, and withal so docilely, that each day he shines on the Kew Observatory a young lady† takes observations which surpass immeasurably in value those made by the hardest-headed astronomers of by-gone times. We have mentioned in a note one fact which these new pictures have taught us; there are others of equal, possibly greater value, which we shall discuss by-and-bye.

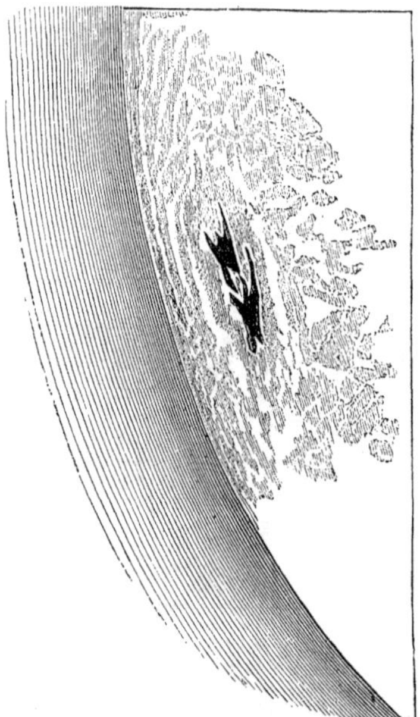

Fig. 14.—Spot with faculæ, May 24, 1863. (Capt. Noble.)

So much for the more salient phenomena of the Sun's surface, which we can study with our telescopes. There is much more, however, to be inquired into; and astronomers—so far from being dismayed at the enormous distance of our central luminary, and at the fact, that with our most powerful instruments we can only watch the changes perpetually going on its surface as we could do with the naked eye at a distance of 180,000 miles,—are at the present moment engaged in a discussion on the more minute appearances revealed to us under the best conditions of air and instrument.

We may begin by saying, that the whole surface of the Sun, except those portions occupied by the spots, is *coarsely mottled;* and, indeed, the mottled appearance requires no very large amount of optical power to render it visible. It has been often observed with a good refractor of only $2\frac{1}{2}$ inches aperture. Examined, however, with a large instrument, it is seen that the surface is principally made up of luminous masses—described by Sir W. Herschel as 'corrugations' and small points of unequal light—imperfectly separated from each other by rows of minute dark dots, called

* A fact agreeing with the deductions made by Mr. Balfour Stewart from an elaborate study of the Sun-pictures taken at Kew.

† [Shall we be divulging too much if we recognise here the 'qualified assistant' of the Kew Reports?]

pores, the intervals between them being extremely small, and occupied by a substance decidedly less luminous than the general surface. Mr. Nasmyth has recently announced his discovery that these pores are the 'polygonal interstices between certain luminous objects of an exceedingly definite shape and general uniformity of size (at least as seen in projection, in the central portions of the disk), which is that of the oblong leaves of a willow-tree.'* According to other observers, however, these luminous masses present almost every variety of irregular form: they are 'rice-grains,' 'granules or granulations,' 'untidy circular masses,' 'things twice as long as broad,' 'three times as long as broad,' and so on. Mr. Dawes asserts, indeed, that he has seen some nearly in contact differ so greatly in size that one was four or five times as large as the other; and while, in a

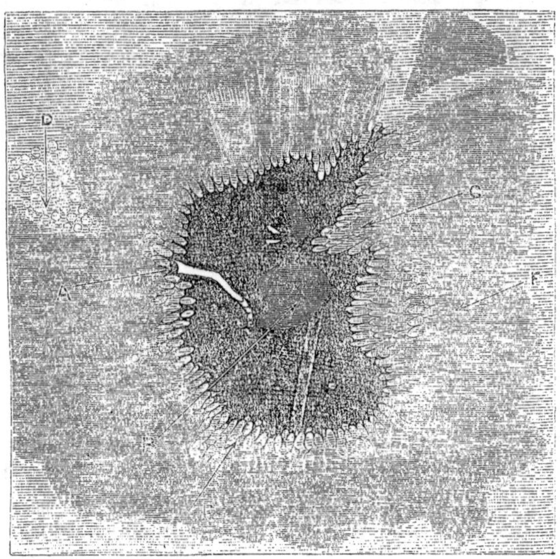

Fig. 15.—Sun-spot, April 2, 1865. (Lockyer.)

The interior outline of the penumbra and other appearances projected on the umbra are alone intended to be shown.

A. Tongue of facula (?) stretching out into the umbra. B. Clouds (?)

C. A Promontory in which the 'things' are changing the direction of their larger axes with respect to the centre of the spot.

D. The 'things' on the general surface of the Sun; these are shown by the engraver too regularly and too near together, as opposed to the 'things' on the penumbra.

F. Here the penumbra seems composed of layers, and the 'things' are arranged like feathers on a duck's wing.

remarkably bright mass, one somewhat resembled a blunt and ill-shaped arrow-head, another, very much smaller, and within 5″ of it, was an irregular trapezium, with rounded corners.

With regard to the general surface of the Sun, therefore, it is not so easy to reconcile the conflicting opinions to which we have alluded. The

* Herschel's 'Outlines of Astronomy,' p. 695.

appearances which, according to Mr. Nasmyth, arise from the interlacing and irregular arrangement of his 'willow-leaves,' Mr. Dawes, who is one of the most assiduous observers of the present day and who has closely studied the solar surface, explains very differently. He looks upon them not as individual and separate bodies of a peculiar nature, but as merely rendering visible to us different conditions as to brightness or elevation of the larger masses forming the mottled surface, 'just as the brightest portions of that surface, and the faculæ also, are different conditions of the general photosphere.' 'Their forms and sizes,' he says, 'are so various as to defy every attempt to describe them by any one appellation or comparison. But the rarest of all forms is the long and narrow.'

The word 'willow-leaf,' however, very well paints the appearance of the minute details *sometimes* observed in the penumbræ of spots, which occasionally, as seen in fig. 9, appear to be made up of elongated masses of unequal brightnesses, so arranged that for the most part they point like so many arrows to the centre of the nucleus, giving to the penumbra a radiated appearance. At other times, and sometimes in the same spot, the jagged edge of the penumbra, projecting over the nucleus, has caused Mr. Dawes to liken the interior edge of the penumbra to coarse thatching with straw, the edge of which has been left untrimmed. But other appearances are assumed, depending upon the amount and kind of action going on in the spot at the time. This has recently been abundantly demonstrated by Father Secchi. The occasional 'willow-leaf' appearance of the penumbra is represented in fig. 15.

Mr. Dawes has come to the conclusion, that the 'granules' or 'granulations' are generally larger and brighter, on the brightest parts than on the darkest ones; the difference in brightness of the individual 'granules' in each part being much the same as in the different masses themselves: on each of the larger masses, the individual granules are all very nearly of equal brilliancy, throughout the mass to which they belong. They are not in general, if ever, mixed together—some much brighter, and others far less bright, on the same mass. There are also darker or shaded portions between the granules, often pretty thickly covered with dark dots, like stippling with a soft lead-pencil; these are what have been called 'pores' by Sir John Herschel, and 'punctulations' by his father. Some of these are almost black, and are like excessively small eruptive spots.]

III.

Theories of the Physical Constitution of the Sun—Wilson's Theory—Kirchhoff's Theory—Their Antagonism—Opinions of M. Faye and Mr. Herbert Spencer—Solar Cyclones—Probable downrush of Clouds into a spot, and Consequent Disappearance—Spectroscopic Observations by Mr. Lockyer—Recent Discoveries respecting the Prominences and Chromosphere—Intensity of the Sun's Light and Heat.

Great interest, doubtless, attaches to a knowledge of the relative movements of the celestial bodies, and to the possession of the secret of the successive changes of position of the luminous points in the starry vault, which we are enabled to contemplate. These phenomena, studied with admirable perseverance during twenty centuries, have at length unveiled to us the structure of the universe, by enabling us to comprehend in all its details that of the system to which the Earth belongs.

But the domain of Astronomy is not restricted to the study of these general laws, so great in their simplicity. It embraces also all the phenomena appertaining to each celestial body considered singly; phenomena which, when taken as a whole, allow us to form the most reasonable conjectures as to its particular constitution. The Earth, naturally enough, was the first body of which the physical constitution was studied and known, and this, of course, apart from all astronomical considerations, and by direct methods very different from those employed by astronomers.

The bodies nearest to us and most easy to observe, thanks to their apparent dimensions—the Moon and the Sun—came next in turn. Then followed the several planets of our system; and at length the investigators of science, overcoming the abysses which separate us from the other systems of the sidereal universe, have attacked with success the problems which deal with the physical constitution of the Stars and Nebulæ.

The nature of the light by which a celestial body reveals its existence to us; its intensity; the heat which it receives or gives out; the nature of the matter of which it is composed; the various phenomena which it reveals to us; the changes of form and of colour which these phenomena undergo; the succession of day and night and of seasons deduced from its various movements; the mass; density; and force of gravity at its surface—these are some of the principal points, the study of which belongs to that part of our subject called Physical Astronomy; a part of the science which has from the earliest times been privileged to excite human curiosity to its highest degree.

We propose, in the course of this work, to collect together all the facts of this kind with which observers have, up to the present time, enriched our science, in such a manner as to amply satisfy this legitimate curiosity; and we will begin with the Sun.

We have been made acquainted with its dimensions, mass, and movement of rotation; and we have dwelt upon the curious phenomena of which the surface of its immense globe is eternally the theatre. We have now to try to explain these phenomena, and to see in what manner they can be connected with the Sun's constitution.

The first attempt to do this was made as long ago as 1774, by Alexander Wilson; and his theory, developed and modified by Bode,

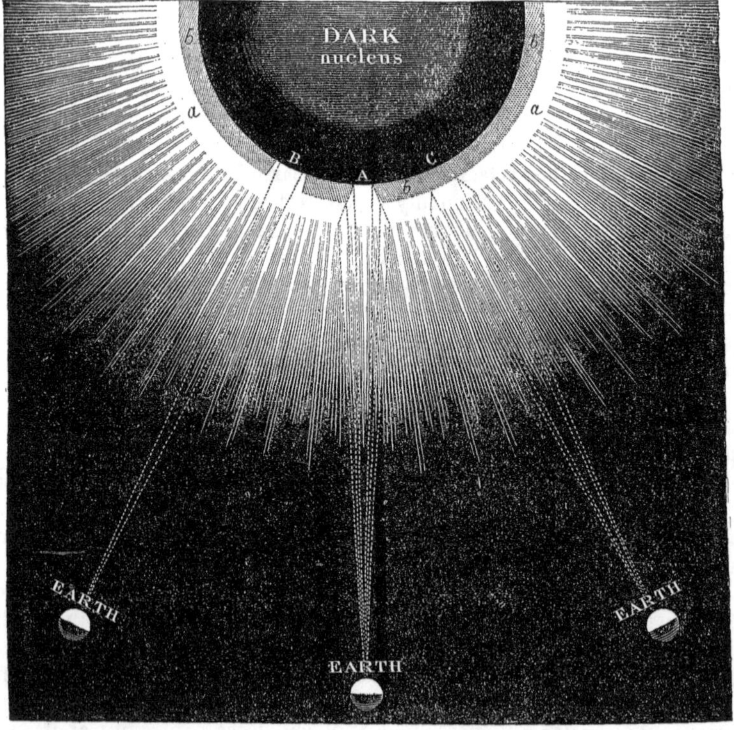

Fig. 16 —Explanation of Sun-spots on Wilson's hypothesis: *a a*, photosphere; *b b*, cloudy stratum. A, spot with nucleus (umbra) and penumbra; B, nucleus (umbra without penumbra); C, penumbra without nucleus (umbra).

Mitchell, and Schröter, and completed by Sir W. Herschel and Dawes, has been confirmed, and partly verified, by the important experiments of Arago.

According to Wilson's theory, the Sun is composed of a dark spherical globe, or at least a globe not self-luminous, surrounded, at different distances, by three atmospheres, or gaseous envelopes, entirely distinct.

The first atmosphere, the one nearest the central nucleus, is formed of an opaque, cloudy stratum, reflecting light, but giving out none, except that light which it receives itself.

To this envelope succeeds another, either close to the first, or separated from it by a certain interval. This second atmosphere is self-luminous, being formed of a gas in a permanently incandescent state. The outer surface of this stratum, called the *photosphere*, gives rise to the visible limits—the well-defined edge, or *limb*, of the sun's disk.

We have, lastly, a third atmosphere, which is illuminated by the photosphere, is transparent, and surrounds all the others, and is composed of strata the density of which decreases as they increase in distance from the central body.

Let us see now how this hypothesis accounts for the appearances presented by Sun-spots, and the shaded or luminous portions of the remainder of the disk.

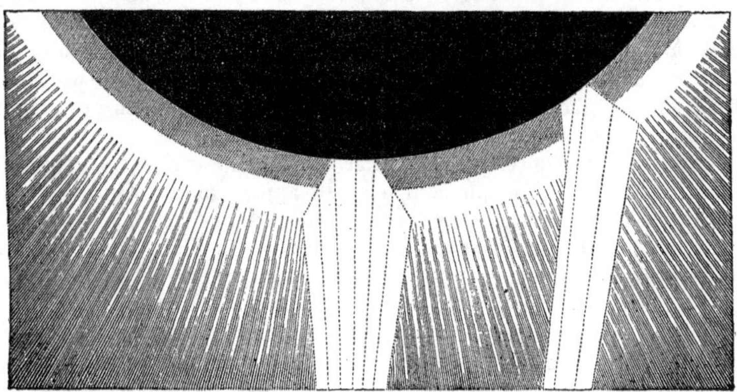

Fig. 17.—Explanation of Sun-spots on Wilson s hypothesis. Appearances pre ented by the same spot as seen at the centre and near the limb.

If we imagine that on the surface of the dark nucleus there are formed from time to time gaseous masses, incandescent by reason of their high temperature; or again, if there exist on the same surface centres of volcanic disturbance, the eruptions proceeding from these craters, piercing and tearing away successively the two interior atmospheres of the Sun, would produce holes of the greater or less extent, openings through which the central nucleus or the overlying umbra could be seen. These openings, therefore, should present generally the form of an irregular cone, widened at the upper part, exposing at its centre the solid and obscure part of the Sun, and all around this the cloudy atmosphere of a greyish tint. Hence, black spots surrounded with penumbræ.

But it may happen that the opening thus made in the photosphere will be smaller than that in the cloudy stratum. In this case the black nucleus will be alone visible, and it is thus that a spot without penumbra is explained. If, on the contrary, the rupture in the first envelope closes up before the photosphere, then the obscure body will be invisible, a circumstance which easily explains penumbræ without a nucleus. These different cases are all represented in fig. 17, where the conditions necessary to present these appearances to an observer on the Earth are indicated.

When a fissure is violently and suddenly produced in a gaseous mass like the photosphere, we must expect to see round the opening a heaping up of the matter of which it is formed, and consequently much greater luminous intensity.

Such would seem to be the origin of faculæ, which generally, as we have seen, surround the spots.

The theory of the physical constitution of the Sun accounts in a very satisfactory manner for the details of the phenomena observed. The various forms of the spots, their disappearance, their motions even, are easily and naturally explained. The fact often observed, that the nucleus diminishes little by little, and is reduced to a mere point, leaving the penumbra visible sometimes after its disappearance, is admirably explained: it is precisely in this manner that the edges of the two atmospheres should gradually come together when the cause which gave rise to their disturbance diminishes in energy and disappears.

It may also be conceived, that after the disappearance of a spot, the faculæ ought still to remain and even to appear more brilliant, since a certain time must be necessary to re-establish the perfect homogeneity of the gaseous strata; and that the gaseous matter, in filling up the cavity formerly occupied (apparently) by the umbra or nucleus and the penumbræ, would naturally condense, and thus become more luminous.

Besides the ascending currents, the rapidity of which is powerful enough to pierce the atmospheric envelopes of the Sun, it is thought that there exists a continual agitation in the gaseous strata and on the surface of the photosphere. This surface is not smooth, but furrowed with elevations and depressions in every direction, analogous to the waves of the ocean. Hence the luminous ridges, and darker intervals, and multitude of pores, giving the Sun the mottled aspect before mentioned.

The apparent changes of form, which result from the rotation of the Sun, now remain to be explained. In fig. 6 are represented the appearances presented by a spot as it travels from the edge to the centre of the disk, or *vice versâ*. The elongated form of a spot at the edges, compared to its rounded form at the centre, is an effect of perspective, and results from the spherical form of the Sun. But this is not all. If the spot and its penumbra are formed by a conical opening, the sloping sides of which reveal to us the thickness of the envelopes,* the portion of the penumbra

* M. Petit, of Toulouse, has succeeded recently in measuring the height of the cloudy stratum which gives rise to the appearance of the penumbra. He has found

turned towards the centre will disappear first, while the penumbra on the side nearest the limb will apparently increase. The same appearance will be produced at the moment of the appearance of a spot on the eastern limb. This is due to a simple effect of perspective, which fig. 17 will show at once.

The preceding theory is entirely founded upon the hypothesis that the light of the Sun does not belong to the nucleus, but that it is radiated by a gas in a state of incandescence.*

The physical constitution of the Sun is much more simple, if we accept the reasoning of those who adopt a second theory which is less at variance with the ideas held by those unfamiliar with Astronomy on the subject of our great luminary. But, perhaps (at least such is our way of viewing it), it scarcely renders a more satisfactory explanation than the other of all the observed phenomena, and it leaves without explanation many circumstances of these phenomena. According to it, the Sun is formed of an incandescent nucleus, the direct source of the light and heat which it emits; whether it be a solid or liquid nucleus matters not. The nucleus is surrounded with a very dense atmosphere, formed of the constituent elements of the body,—elements which the intensity of the temperature maintains in a gaseous state.

If partial coolings take place at different points of the atmosphere by the action of unknown causes, what happens? There will be formed at these points precipitations analogous to the clouds of aqueous vapour in the terrestrial atmosphere. Very dense agglomerations of vapours in the vesicular state, dark clouds intercepting the luminous rays of the body of the Sun, will appear to us as spots on its disk.

A cloud, once formed, becomes a screen to the upper regions, hence a cooling down of these regions, and the formation of a lighter cloud-screen, less opaque, and which as seen from the Earth will present the appearance of the penumbræ which surround the spots.

it to be upwards of 4000 miles. [Professor Phillips has found a much smaller height—300 miles—to be a probable limit. Faye, however, adopts a value not differing greatly from Petit's.]

* That the Sun is not a solid body, at least that its visible surface is not solid, we must admit, in consequence of the extreme mobility displayed by the phenomena of that surface. But it is not so evident that it is not an incandescent liquid or body in a state of fusion. This fact has been held to be established by an experiment of Arago's. The optical properties of the luminous rays radiated by an ignited gas are very different from those of rays the source of which is a liquid or solid mass, at least if these rays leave the surface of the incandescent body at a very small angle from the limb of a sphere. Whilst the latter rays, examined by means of a very ingenious instrument, called a 'polariscope,' by its able inventor, are decomposed into two coloured pencils, the others, in passing through the same artificial medium, remain in their natural state. Now it is precisely the latter phenomenon which is presented by the light emanating from the borders of the Sun. Hence Arago concluded that the luminous surface of the solar globe consists of gas in a state of ignition. But this does not preclude that the interior nucleus may be liquid, that is to say, composed of mineral substances in a state of fusion.

According to this hypothesis, the apparent changes which the spots undergo in moving from the border to the centre, or *vice versâ*, are explained also by an effect of perspective, which fig. 17 will convey to our readers.

Seen in ground-plan on the centre of the Sun, the spot will seem to occupy the middle of the penumbra; but in travelling towards the border part of the upper cloud situated towards the centre will be projected on the dark nucleus, and will be confounded with it, whilst the portion of the same cloud towards the limb will apparently increase by exposing to view the thickness of the light cloudy mass which overlies the darker one.*

This theory has been put forward in support of some recent discoveries of great importance to which we must now call attention.

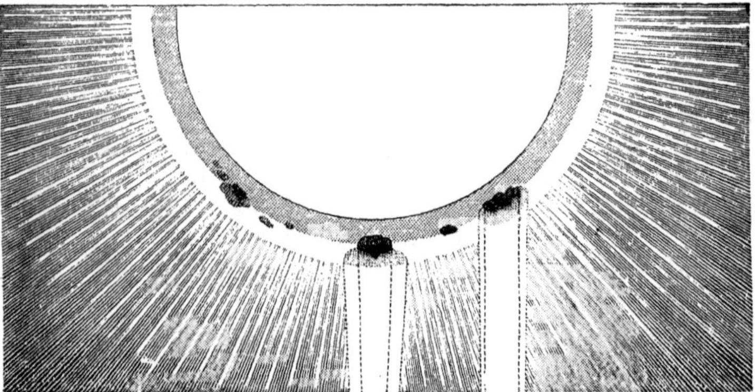

Fig. 18.—Explanation of Sun-spots on Kirchhoff's hypothesis.

Every one is acquainted with the glorious coloured band called 'the spectrum,' which is produced by the decomposition of white light by means of a prism. Every one knows, too, that, besides the seven primary colours, there is in the spectrum of sunlight a multitude of dark lines, which completely divide the coloured bands in the direction of its breadth. By comparing these dark lines with the brilliant lines of the different spectra of the light given out by the flames of different metallic substances, philosophers have arrived at the knowledge, that the light

* It has been said that the second theory leaves some important facts without explanation. It accounts neither for the existence of faculæ, nor from the granulations. One does not see also why spots should not be found near the poles, or why, when a spot disappears, the penumbra still subsists after the disappearance of the nucleus. It does not explain the difference which exists between the spots without penumbræ and the penumbræ deprived of umbræ. Besides, a general fact of observation, which seems inexplicable if the spots are clouds in suspension in the solar atmosphere, is, that the spots *always* disappear a little before they reach the limb, when, according to this hypothesis, they should invariably notch it.

emitted by the luminous nucleus of the Sun must traverse, before it reaches us, an atmosphere charged with certain metallic vapours. The nature of these vapours even has been determined with precision; and 'spectrum analysis,'—the name devoted to this new and already fertile branch of science,—teaches us that the solar atmosphere contains, in the metallic state, vapours of sodium, iron, nickel, copper, zinc, and barium. The presence of cobalt is doubtful. The presence of gold, silver, mercury, lead, tin, or silicium, so abundant in the terrestrial crust, or of arsenic, antimony, strontium, cadmium, or lithium, has not yet been proved. As the six metals of the first series exist in the Sun's atmosphere, they must also exist in the very body of the Sun.

Here we have, then, a wonderful instance of a celestial body, separated from us by an enormous distance, the constituents of which are studied in their most minute detail,—analysed, if one may so say, with the same certainty as if they were put into one of the crucibles of our chemical laboratories. We shall have more to say about spectrum analysis when we try to answer the question, 'What is a star?'*

[But, in the meantime, we recall the fact, that these theories are antagonistic in the main. One declares for a cool nucleus, the other for an incandescent one; one for a gaseous photosphere, the other for a liquid one; and the experiments made by the polariscope are apparently negatived by those made by the spectroscope. Again, although Wilson's theory accounts for the telescopic appearance of spots, it does so on an altogether improbable assumption; and although Kirchhoff's theory is more in harmony with our present knowledge, he supports it by a statement as to the spots which is justly rejected by all who have ever observed the Sun through a telescope. But are they entirely antagonistic? Here M. Faye and Mr. Herbert Spencer come to our rescue; and, in spite of some differences of detail, propound an explanation of the observed phenomena, which is certainly worthy of careful consideration, while, very opportunely, the Sun-pictures taken at Kew have put in a mass of new evidence to help us in our inquiries.

The first important point in this new evidence is, that the Sun himself tells us that his spots are cavities; this supports the notion always held by astronomers and strengthened by the beautiful stereoscopic combinations suggested by De La Rue; it also equally upsets an important statement made by Kirchhoff. Astronomers, doubtless, would have sooner asserted the small mean density of the Sun and its enormous heat in support of the evidence of their telescopes, if they had not so long held to the theory of the cool and habitable globe underneath. So that

* According to the recent experiments of Mitscherlich it is the pure metals, not their chemical combinations, which exist in the solar atmosphere. The bodies which support combustion, such as oxygen and chlorine, do not exist in it, or if they do, they are mixed with combustible bodies in a state of dissociation, of which we have examples when these bodies are raised to a very high temperature.

Arago's deduction from his experiments on the polarisation of the Sun's light—a deduction which supported the theory of the gaseous nature of the photosphere from a new point of view—was doubly welcome.

M. Faye has removed the grounds for Sir John Herschel's objection to this experiment, and has shown, moreover, that it can be reconciled with Kirchhoff's spectroscopic one. He considers the formation of a photosphere to be a simple consequence of cooling, and looks upon it, in fact, as the limit which separates the intense heat of the interior portions of the Sun from the vacuum and cold of space.

From this point of view, the beautiful experiments of Arago and Kirchhoff are seen to be no longer contradictory. The term *incandescent*

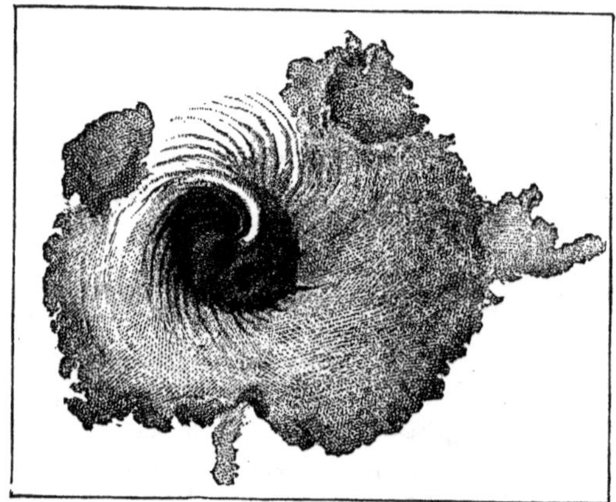

Fig. 19.—Solar cyclone, May 5th, 1857. (Secchi.)

gas was not used by Arago in the sense attributed to it now. The flame he used was that of an ordinary gas-jet, and not the *obscure* one of a Bunsen's burner, or of a simple gas. Incandescent molecules diffused in a gaseous medium, itself heated to a high temperature, give a continuous spectrum, with the exception of the dark lines due to the absorption of the medium.*

The formation of the photosphere enables us to account for the spots and their movements. The successive layers are constantly traversed by vertical currents, both ascending and descending. In this perpetual agitation we can readily imagine that where the ascending current becomes

[* The researches of Frankland, however, throw doubt on this conclusion. He has been able to show that increase of atmospheric pressure alone suffices to cause an increase in the brilliancy of a flame. A candle burning at the summit of a lofty mountain, for instance, is much less luminous than one burning near the sea-level; yet the difference is not due to any difference in the rate of combustion. This is proved by the fact that a candle loses in a given time the same amount of weight whatever the level at which it burns.—R.A.P.]

more intense, the luminous matter of the photosphere is momentarily dissipated. Through this kind of unveiling it is not the solid cold and black nucleus of the Sun that we perceive, but the internal ambient, gaseous mass, of which the radiating power at the temperature of the most vivid incandescence is so feeble, in comparison to that of the luminous clouds of the non-gaseous particles, that the difference of these powers suffices to explain the striking contrast between the two tones observed in our telescopes.]

[Kirchhoff may be said, however, to have overthrown M. Faye's theory, by showing that it is not in accordance with the well-known law called 'the theory of exchanges,' according to which the radiating and absorbing powers of the same body are strictly complementary. 'M. Faye imagines,' he reasons, 'that' the nucleus of the Sun is even hotter than the photosphere, and yet dark. He conceives this nucleus to be gaseous, and because gases have but slight radiating power, he imagines that these two properties can both appertain to the solar nucleus. But from the proportion which holds between the radiating and absorbing powers of bodies, it follows inevitably that, even if the light emitted by the nucleus were altogether imperceptible by the eye, the nucleus, whatever its nature, would be transparent; so that we should see through the opening in that half of the photosphere turned towards us the inner side of the other half (viewing it through the whole of the solar nucleus), and we should recognise no sign whatever of the existence of an opening.'

Even more decisive is the evidence supplied by the spectroscope. For the spectrum of the umbra of a spot should, according to M. Faye's theory, exhibit bright lines, superposed, perhaps, on a faint continuous spectrum; but, instead of this, the spectrum of the umbra has been shown, both by Mr. Lockyer and by Dr. Huggins, to differ chiefly from the spectrum of the photosphere in the increased strength of certain dark lines. From this observation (which has been confirmed by Father Secchi and others) it follows conclusively that the spots are regions of increased absorption. This accords with Herbert Spencer's theory, with which, also (as already remarked) the observations of Mr. De La Rue and Dr. Balfour Stewart are in satisfactory agreement.—R.A.P.]

[Let us now pass to the theory of Mr. Herbert Spencer.

M. Faye, as we have seen, considers the Sun to be at present a gaseous spheroid, having an envelope of metallic matters precipitated in the shape of luminous cloud, the local dispersions of which, caused by currents from within, appear to us as spots. Mr. Spencer, on the contrary, holds that a liquid film exists beneath the visible photosphere.

Mr. Spencer's remarks as to possible causes of solar spots are very valuable; for, whatever theory of their formation be the true one, it is certain that the rapid formation of the spots, their movements, and their disappearances, indicate meteorological phenomena on the most gigantic scale of which the imagination can scarcely form an idea. Immense cyclones pass over the surface of the Sun with fearful rapidity, as is rendered evident by the form and changes of certain spots, as observed by Secchi and others. In one instance, recorded by Mr. Dawes, the rotation of a spot amounted to 110° in six days.

Here also (fig. 20), in a series of sketches representing a spot as observed by Mr. Dawes, is abundant proof of the rapidity of these move-

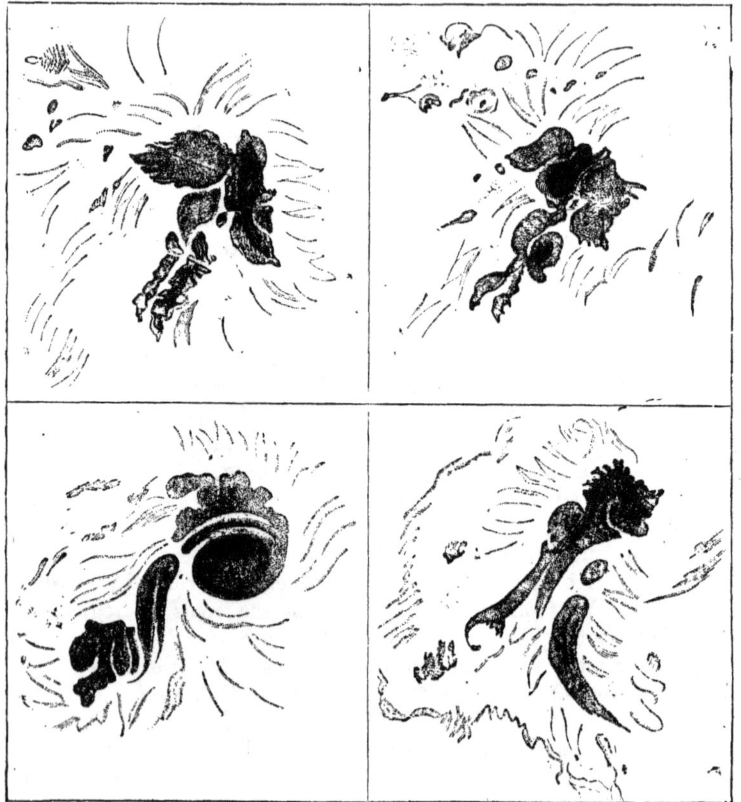

Fig. 20.—Change in the shape of a Sun-spot, October 27, 29, 31, and November 2. (Dawes)

ments. The form here indicates clearly the cyclones of which we are about to speak: although in a manner less precise than in fig. 19. It should, however, be added, that these cyclonic spots are somewhat rare.

The spot figured at page 42, also afforded remarkable evidences of rapid change, which seems to put the cloudy nature of the Sun's photosphere beyond all doubt.* It was a spot of the normal character, by no means cyclonic, but with a tongue of what appeared to be a portion of facula, stretching half way into the spot. When the observation commenced, about half-past eleven on the date given, the tongue of facula was extremely brilliant; by one o'clock, it had become apparently less brilliant than any portion of the penumbra. At the same time it seemed to be 'giving out,' at its end, and a portion of the umbra between it and the penumbra appeared to be veiled with a stratus cloud evolved out of it. After a time, condensation seemed going on on the following portion of the cloudy mass. So that a very brilliant mass of what appeared to be faculæ gradually melted away into umbra, and then the umbra condensed again; three or four cloud-masses on the inner edge of the penumbra were observed to detach themselves from it at different points, and to traverse the umbra towards the centre of the spot.

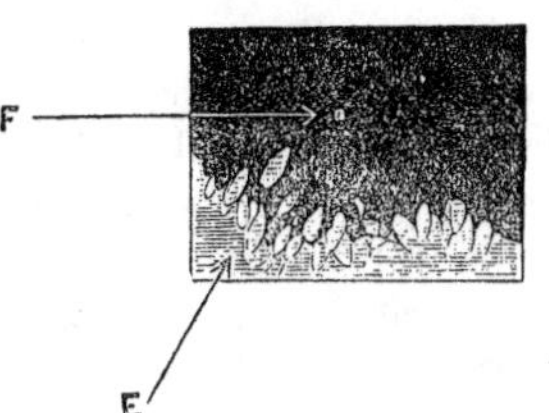

Fig. 21.—Cloud-masses detaching themselves from the penumbra. A very faint one at F. 1865, April 2, 12h 30m. (Lockyer.)

It has long been taken for granted that there are upward and downward currents on the Sun. And this down-rush into a spot seems proved, for the first time, so far as we know, by the observations to which we are alluding. The fact, also, that this down-rush was accompanied by first a dimming and then a melting of the cloud-masses carried down, was also thought to be established.†

The cloud-masses, in one region of the penumbra, were also seen to change the direction of their longer axes in about three-quarters of an hour with regard to the centre of the spot, in fact they turned round bodily through a considerable angle. Others, projected on the umbra, gradually melted away out of sight. One cloud-mass was distinctly observed to set sail, as it were, over the umbra, and it had travelled a considerable distance when the observations were terminated.

It would seem from these observations, that there is a running down of the shape, as if the cloud-mass seen on the general surface of the Sun were gradually drawn out in its journeying towards the umbra.

Mr. Spencer, basing his reasoning on terrestrial analogies, thus accounts for the spots. The central region of a cyclone must be a region of rarefaction, and consequently a region of refrigeration. In an atmosphere of metallic gases rising from a molten surface, and reaching a limit at which condensation takes place, the molecular state, especially towards its upper

* 'Monthly Notices, Royal Astronomical Society,' 1865, p. 236.

† [While this book is passing through the press, Messrs. De La Rue, Stewart, and Loewy, are publishing a paper in which a new theory of Sun-spots is discussed, which is confirmed by the above observation made by Mr. Lockyer. It seems at the same time in accordance with other facts. In this paper all differences of luminosity on the surface of the Sun are referred to the same cause, namely, the presence to a greater or less extent of a comparatively cold absorbing atmosphere.—B. S.]

part, must be such that a moderate diminution of density and fall of temperature will cause precipitation; that is to say, the rarefied interior of a solar cyclone will be filled with cloud; condensation, instead of taking place only at the level of the photosphere, *will here extend to a great depth below it.* It will be seen that Mr. Spencer, as opposed to Kirchhoff, not only accounts for the formation of a cloud, but places it where the objections made to Kirchhoff's clouds do not hold good. He next shows that a cloud thus occupying the interior of a cyclone will have a rotatory motion; and this accords with observation. Being funnel-shaped, as analogy warrants us in assuming, its central parts will be much deeper than its peripheral parts, and therefore more opaque. This, too, corresponds with observation. Nor are we, on this hypothesis, without some interpretation of the penumbræ. If we may suppose the so-called 'willow-leaves'—the 'things' on the Sun,—to be the tops of the currents ascending from the Sun's body, what changes of appearance are they likely to undergo in the neighbourhood of a cyclone? For some distance round a cyclone there will be a drawing-in of the superficial gases towards the vortex. All the luminous spaces of more transparent clouds, forming the adjacent photosphere, will be changed in shape by these centripetal currents; they will be greatly elongated; and those peculiar aspects which the penumbra presents will so be produced.

We must now, however, pass from this part of our subject—interesting as it is,—and we can do so full of hope, for never before was it engaging the attention of so many minds.]

In examining with care the contour of the solar disk when the Mocn interposes between it and the Earth, as in the case of a total eclipse, there have been observed in the luminous aureola which envelopes the lunar disk several very curious prominences—some in form of mountains, others of boomerangs, others resembling columns, the upper part of which appeared out of the perpendicular; others, again, entirely detached from the disk, seem to float like immense clouds in the atmosphere of the Sun.

The total eclipse of the 18th of July, 1860, furnished most valuable information relating to these strange phenomena, and the magnificent photographs taken by Mr. Warren De La Rue on that occasion showed clearly the aspect of the reddish prominences we have just described. Astronomers hesitated long between opposite explanations, some only seeing in these appearances effects produced by the interposition of the Moon, others believing in the objective reality of these phenomena, and looking upon them as agglomerations of matter resting on the Sun, or suspended in the external atmosphere which surrounds it at a certain distance. In 1860, all doubts as to their belonging to the Sun were removed, but astronomers were not much nearer to an explanation of them. Some looked upon them as clouds, others as solar auroræ. The fact that they had been seen all round the limb of the Moon, that they were found to exist in all regions near the poles in the same manner as at the equator, seemed to negative all idea of their being in any way connected with the spots or with the causes which give rise to them, although at first the opinion was entertained by some that they were in some manner correlated.

[But, during and since the great eclipse of August 1868, much light has been thrown upon the subject of these strange objects.

Until the epoch of this eclipse the light of the prominences had not been submitted to spectroscopic analysis; and much was anticipated from the use of that powerful mode of research in 1868. Few, however, could have anticipated how important a series of discoveries would be initiated by the observations made in this way.

Major Tennant, Lieutenant Herschel, M. Janssen, and M. Rayet, observing the eclipses at different stations, all succeeded in determining the nature of the spectrum belonging to the prominences. This spectrum consists of bright lines, indicating that the prominences are formed of glowing gas. Major Tennant counted five lines, which his measurements led him to associate with the bright lines belonging to hydrogen and sodium. Lieutenant Herschel saw three lines,—red, orange, and blue. Janssen saw five or six lines, two of which (red and blue) he associated with the bright lines of hydrogen. M. Rayet saw nine lines, five of which appeared much more conspicuous than the others.

But the most important result of the eclipse-observations remains to be noticed.

M. Janssen, even while his observations were in progress, felt convinced that he should be able to see the bright lines when the Sun is not eclipsed; and on the following day he succeeded in doing this. He could thus determine where there were prominences, and even the shape of such prominences, as satisfactorily as though the Sun were eclipsed. 'I have enjoyed to-day,' he said, 'a continuous eclipse.'

But before the news of his success reached Europe, the same method had been applied by Mr. Lockyer. After the discovery by Mr. Huggins that the temporary (or rather variable) star which shone out in the constellation Corona in May 1868, had a spectrum in which bright lines were conspicuous, the idea occurred to spectroscopists that, if bright lines could be discerned in the spectrum of a star, they might be visible also in the solar spectrum. More particularly it was thought that, if the prominences consist of glowing gas, the bright lines corresponding to the gaseous constituents of the prominences might be visible, even though the prominences themselves cannot be seen. Mr. Lockyer, who had expressed this opinion two years before the eclipse of 1868, had failed to recognise the bright lines of the prominences, owing to the inadequate dispersive power of his spectroscope. For a like reason Mr. Huggins had not succeeded; while Father Secchi was deterred, he tells us, from pursuing similar researches by the announcement of Mr. Lockyer's want of success. It will be readily understood why great dispersive power is required. The light of the prominences is far feebler than that of the illuminated terrestrial atmosphere near the solar limb; so that any plan for merely reducing the light of that atmosphere obliterates the prominences altogether. But the spectroscope acts differently. It spreads the light of the atmosphere into a rainbow-tinted streak, while it resolves the light of the prominences into a few coloured lines. When we increase its dispersive power, the rainbow tinted streak is lengthened and made proportionately fainter, whereas the coloured lines are thrown further apart without being diminished in brightness. It is only necessary to increase the dispersion up to a certain point in order that the coloured lines belonging to the prominences may be visible on the background formed by the rainbow-tinted streak.

Mr. Lockyer therefore applied for, and obtained a grant of money from the Royal Society for the construction of a spectroscope of suitable dispersive power. The death of Mr. Cooke, to whom the construction of this instrument was in the first place intrusted, caused some delay; and when eventually Mr. Browning had designed and completed a spectroscope of the requisite power, the news had already reached Europe that the spectrum of the prominences consists of certain bright lines. We need not doubt, however, that in the long-run, even without this information, Mr. Lockyer would have succeeded in recognising the lines, since the optical difficulties had been so perfectly mastered by Mr. Browning that the prominence lines can be seen (so Mr. Lockyer assures us) even by the least practised observer. Be this as it may, Mr. Lockyer had seen the lines and announced their exact position, before the news had reached Europe that M. Janssen had solved two months earlier the same problem.

Mr. Lockyer was also able to confirm by the new method the discovery which Leverrier and Secchi had made in 1860,* that the solar photosphere is covered by a layer of gaseous matter, of which the prominences are but the most elevated portions. For all round the Sun's limb he could recognise the existence of bright lines similar to those belonging to the prominences. He assigned to this layer the title—in some respects not altogether satisfactory—of the *chromosphere.* He has found (as have other observers) that at times the spectrum of the chromosphere shows many more bright lines than that of the prominences, or, at least, of their more elevated portions.

The new method has also enabled observers to decide the question of the position of the bright lines; for as these are brought into juxtaposition with the dark lines of the solar spectrum, it is easy to see whether they coincide or not. In this way the lines which had been assumed to indicate the presence of glowing hydrogen in the prominences, have been found nearly to correspond to the hydrogen lines in the solar spectrum. But the bright line supposed to indicate the presence of sodium has been found not to accord with the sodium line in the solar spectrum.

Even these results, however, were surpassed in interest and importance

* Before this Grant and Swann had suspected the existence of such a layer.

by one which yet remains to be described. By the new method, the place and shape of the prominences could be determined, indeed, but the prominences could not be actually seen. It was much as though one were to determine the position and shape of a distant mountain by looking in different directions through a long slit in an opaque screen, which permitted only a long strip of the mountain to be visible at each instant. It occurred to Mr. Huggins that if the slit of the spectroscope were opened, so that instead of the bright-coloured lines, bright-coloured images of the prominences were formed, these might be visible notwithstanding the resulting increase in the brightness of the rainbow-tinted background. He found that with the dispersive power at his command this did not happen, but by using a deep-coloured ruby glass, which absorbed nearly all the light but that coming from the part of the spectrum near the red hydrogen line, he was able to see the red image of a prominence.

Afterwards, Mr. Lockyer, availing himself of the greater dispersive power at his command, succeeded in seeing the prominences without using any absorbing medium. Dr. Zöllner, of Germany, has also observed the prominences in this way. But the Italian astronomer. Respighi, has been, perhaps, the most successful of all who have applied Mr. Huggins' method. For he has been able to make drawings showing the varying aspect of the whole of the Sun's limb from day to day. We quote some of the most important results of his researches:—

In the circumpolar solar regions, great prominences are not formed, but only small and short-lived jets. In the spot-zone the great prominences are seen, the equatorial, like the polar zones, being regions of relatively small activity. Where faculæ are present, prominences are usually seen, but they are not identical with faculæ. Over spots the jets are seen, but they are not high. There is a great difference in the duration of prominences. Some develope and disappear in a few minutes; others remain visible for several days. They originate, generally, in rectilinear jets, either vertical or oblique, very bright and well defined. These rise to a great height,—often to a height of at least 80,000 miles, and, in one instance observed by Respighi, to twice that height,—then, bending back, fall again upon the Sun like the jets of our fountains. Then they spread into figures resembling gigantic trees, more or less rich in branches. In general, the highest parts are the regions of the most remarkable transformations.

Respighi and Zöllner agree in thinking that the well-defined bases of these jets prove them to be due to eruptions taking place, not through gas, but through a compact substance forming a sort of crust (Zöllner's 'Trennungschicht'). Respighi considers that the expelling force may be due to electric action, but Zöllner is disposed to regard it as due rather to the compression of the imprisoned gas; and he applies this theory to form an estimate of the temperature and pressure of the Sun's surface-layers.

Mr. Lockyer has been able to show that the substance of prominences is often agitated by cyclonic motions of a surprising nature, the velocity of these solar wind-storms, amounting sometimes to as much as 120 miles per second.

The researches of Plucker, Wüllner, Frankland, and others, into the nature of the hydrogen spectrum under various conditions of pressure and temperature, serve, when combined with the observations of Lockyer, Wüllner, and others, on the nature of the lines in the spectrum of the prominences, to show that the pressure near the base of solar atmosphere is not nearly so great as the pressure of our own atmosphere near the sea-level. This would seem to dispose of the theory that the corona seen during total eclipses is an atmosphere of the Sun; for in that case the pressure at the Sun's surface could scarcely fail to be enormously greater than it is observed to be. Mr. Lockyer therefore considers that the corona is not a solar appendage at all, but due to the passage 'of the Sun's rays through our own atmosphere near the Moon's place,' some action on the rays as they pass near the Moon causing them to be deflected into the region of the terrestrial atmosphere which is illuminated (according to this hypothesis) during total solar eclipses. The present writer has pointed out objections to this view, founded on optical and mathematical considerations; and while admitting the evidence against the theory, that the corona is a solar atmosphere, he expresses his belief that it is beyond all question a solar appendage. Further observations are required, however, to show what sort of solar appendage the corona may be, the spectroscopic observations hitherto made having been somewhat contradictory. If the American observations of August 7, 1869, are to be accepted, the coronal spectrum resembles that of the terrestrial aurora and the zodiacal light. But whether this, if confirmed, would imply that the three phenomena are closely related, and (still more) whether, as the present writer believes, meteoric astronomy is to be looked to for the solution of the problem, remains yet to be demonstrated.—R. A. P.]

Let us return, in order to finish what we have to say of the constitution of the Sun, to the purely physical facts which Astronomy has set forth.

One word now on the intensity of Sun-light. This intensity is not the same in all parts of the disk. The edges are less luminous than the centre, and Arago valued at one-fortieth the difference of their intensity, which is much more considerable according to other astronomers, Faye among the number.

[This fact, fully established for the luminous rays given out by the Sun, applies also to the chemical ones; but with this difference, that whereas the light, broadly speaking, diminishes regularly and very gradually, from centre to border, the chemical brightness is much more 'patchy,' so to speak. Professor Roscoe, by receiving the image of the Sun on a properly prepared photographic plate, has observed remarkable differences of this kind; and, with Mr. De La Rue, is inclined to attribute to them some connexion with the phenomena of the red prominences to which we have before drawn attention. The latter distinguished physicist is not without hope of obtaining photographic pictures of them without the intervention of a total eclipse. He imagines that an extension of his beautiful experiment—in which he combines Sun-pictures stereoscopically, and shows the faculæ to be above, and the spots below, the general surface,—will enable him to show the red flames as very delicate dark markings on the more brilliant mottled background of the photosphere. These delineations, except with the aid of the stereoscope, would be confounded with the other markings of the Sun's surface; but they would assume their true aspect and stand out from the rest as soon as two suitable photographic pictures were viewed by the aid of that instrument.]

The gradual diminution of both the Sun's luminous and chemical brightness towards the limb indicates without doubt the existence of an atmosphere enveloping the body to a great distance.* And it is in this envelope, as we have said, that the red clouds observed in total eclipses float.

According to Sir W. Herschel, the general brightness of the disk being represented by 1000, that of the penumbra is not more than 469, and that of the darkest portion of the nucleus as low as 7.

Considered in each of these points of view, the solar light as it arrives on the surface of the Earth, is, according to Arago, at least 15,000 times more intense than the flame of a wax-candle. 'According to the energy of the battery employed,' he adds ('Astronomie Populaire,' ii. p. 172), 'it is found that the electric light varies in intensity from a fiftieth part to a quarter of that of the Sun.' So much for the comparative intensity of Sun-light.

Compared with the brightness of the full Moon, the light of the Sun, according to Wollaston, is 800,000 times brighter than that of the lunar disk; in other words, 800,000 full Moons would be required in the heavens to produce a day as brilliant as that illuminated by a cloudless Sun.

As to the origin of this light, some, as we have seen, attribute it to the incandescence of a gaseous mass, others to that of a solid or liquid nucleus. Other *savants* again, among whom we must class Sir J. Herschel, regard the solar light as having an electro-magnetic origin, rather than arising from the combustion of solid, liquid, or gaseous matter; it is, according to them, a perpetual aurora.

From the intensity of the light, let us pass to the intensity of solar heat. Without any doubt, this heat must be enormous on the surface of the Sun; and, if we base our estimation on the law of decrease of radiant heat, the conclusion is arrived at that its intensity is about 300,000 times greater than that of the heat received on a given point on the surface of the Earth. The quantity of heat, incessantly radiated into space by the

* [Not necessarily to a great distance. Indeed it is easily seen that the greater the observed diminution, the shallower the atmospheric envelope must be, and the greater its absorbing power.—R. A. P.]

immense focus of our system, has also been calculated. The following comparison made by Sir J. Herschel will give an idea of its calorific activity. Let us imagine a cylindrical pillar of ice, 45 miles in diameter, to be continually darted into the Sun, and that the water produced by its fusion is continually carried off. In order that the heat given off constantly by radiation should be wholly expended on its liquefaction, it would be necessary to plunge the cylinder of ice into the Sun with the velocity of light, or, in other words, the heat of the Sun can, without diminishing its intensity, melt in a second of time a pillar of ice 1590 square miles at its base, and 194,626 miles in height.

As with the luminous and chemical rays, so with the heat-rays there is a difference in the calorific intensity of the centre and limb, the radiation being greatest from the centre. The polar regions, also, are colder than the equatorial ones; and Secchi has shown that less heat is radiated from the spots than by other portions. Sir John Herschel thinks that one of the hemispheres of the Sun is hotter than the opposite one.

It has been held that there exists a close correlation between the periods of maximum and minimum of the solar spots and the Earth's temperature. There is no doubt an intimate relation existing between them and the Earth's magnetism. This has been proved by delicate researches extending over a long period of years, carried on by such physicists as Major-General Sabine, the President of the Royal Society of London, Schwabe of Dessau, and Wolf of Zurich.

[Thus we come upon another bond of union between the different members of our system besides gravitation, and there is good reason for believing that our luminary was once caught in the act of creating a magnetic disturbance on our Earth. On the 1st of September, 1859, two astronomers, Messrs. Carrington and Hodgson, were independently observing a large spot, when they noticed a very bright star of light suddenly break out over it, moving with great velocity over the Sun's surface. At the same moment the magnetograph at Kew, where all the changes in the Earth's magnetism unceasingly register themselves, was violently affected.]

A question of great interest, of which a solution has lately been attempted, is that of the permanence or the decrease of the solar heat in the course of ages.

A philosopher of great eminence—Professor William Thomson—has enunciated the idea that the solar temperature is constantly sustained by a fall of meteorites, the motion of which is transferred into heat at the moment of impact. Whether this theory be true [and we believe Professor Thomson has abandoned it*], or whether the solar globe

* [The strongest evidence in its favour has, however, been discovered since Sir W. Thomson expressed doubts respecting its validity. We refer to the discovery that the meteor-systems encountered by the Earth travel for the most part in orbits of remarkable eccentricity, instead of nearly circular orbits, as has been surmised.

loses its heat year by year, it is perfectly certain that there will be still sufficient heat left to support life on the Earth and the other planets for millions of years to come — a perspective view which in truth is very consoling.

The question of the habitability of the Sun has also been agitated: on the hypothesis which makes of this body an incandescent globe, the answer can only be in the negative. We have no idea of an organised being capable of living in a temperature so enormous. But the case is altered if we suppose that the solar globe itself is neither very luminous nor incandescent; if we admit that it can be protected against the radiation of the photosphere, by an envelope of great density, which absorbs the light, and is at the same time a non-conductor of heat. Arago remarks, 'If any one were to ask me simply the question, Is the Sun inhabited? I should answer that I did not know. But, if he asked me if the Sun *could* be inhabited by beings organised in a manner analogous to those who people our globe, I should not hesitate to make an affirmative reply.'

Questions of this kind will never be resolved categorically; their solution, whatever it may be, will remain eternally to humanity in the domain of the probable. But what we must acknowledge, what ought to strike our minds, now so much evidence has been placed before us, is the varied and continual influence of the Sun on the conditions of existence on the surface of our globe.

He acts on the Earth by his mass, whether he maintains it in its orbit at distances the variation of which is regulated by inflexible laws, or combines his action with that of the Moon, to produce the semi-diurnal oscillatory movement of the waters of the ocean,—the tides. The heat of the solar rays is the principal cause of the perturbations of equilibrium of the atmospheric strata. It is that which gives rise to the wind, to the aërial and marine currents, to the evaporation of the water of the rivers, of the lakes, of the sea, and which produces a continual circulation of fluids on the surface of the planet. This action is thus found to be the cause of the secular modifications of the geological strata, by the slow but increasing denudation of the rocks, and by the transport of material due to currents. It is the heat and the light of the Sun which everywhere distribute life to the beings of the vegetable and animal world. 'At one time,' says Humboldt in his Cosmos, 'its action manifests itself tranquilly and in silence, by chemical affinities, and determines the divers phenomena of life, in vegetables by the endosmosis of the cellular wall, in animals in the tissue of the muscular and nervous fibres; at another it fills the atmosphere with thunder, waterspouts, and hurricanes. The light-waves do not act only on the world of matter; they do not confine themselves

It is probable, however, that only a portion of the Sun's heat-supply can be accounted for in this way, and possibly not the most important portion. Another portion may be accounted for, as Helmholtz has suggested, by the distribution of heat corresponding to the gradual contraction of the Sun's volume.—R. A. P.]

to decomposing and recomposing substances; they do not merely draw from the bosom of the Earth the delicate germs of plants, and develope the green matter or chlorophyl in the leaves; they do not simply tinge the odorous flowers, or repeat thousands and thousands of times the image of the Sun, in the midst of the graceful break of the waves, and on the light stems of the prairie, bent with the breath of the winds. The light of heaven, according to its varying degrees of duration and brilliancy, is also in mysterious relation with the inner man, with the development more or less decided of his faculties, with the gay or melancholic disposition of his mind. This is what Pliny the elder referred to in these words: '*Cœli tristitiam discutit sol, et humani nubila animi serenat.*'*

* 'The Sun chases sadness from the sky, and dissipates the clouds which darken the human heart.'

BOOK THE SECOND.

THE PLANETS.

We have seen that round the Sun—that immense focus of light and heat—revolve at different distances, and in widely varying periods, a multitude of secondary bodies, and among them our Earth. Sometimes solitary, sometimes arranged in groups which reproduce in miniature the Solar System itself, these bodies form so many distinct worlds of which the dimensions, distances, movements, form, structure, and physical constitution, deserve a separate examination and study.

This study will now occupy us. The numerous phenomena of which these worlds are the theatre—phenomena observed by our astronomers as each planet has glided past us—not only make us acquainted with the mechanism of the system as a whole, but permit us also to examine somewhat closely into the details of the physical organisation of each of these bodies.

If we look through the most powerful telescopes, we shall see the form of the planets and their characteristic features; and the markings visible on their disks will tell us if they rotate, and what is the duration of their day and night. The forms and dimensions of the orbits, and the periods of revolution, will give us precise information respecting the succession of seasons and climates, and the lengths of their years. Even the climatic variations will be partly revealed to us by the degree of inclination of the axis of rotation to the plane in which the body moves round the Sun.

The presence of satellites will not offer less interest, whether we consider the partial illumination of the planet's night, caused by the reflection from the illuminated faces of these—in their turn—secondary planets, or the eclipses, necessary consequences, occurring more or less frequently, of the interposition of an opaque body between the illuminated disk of the planet and the source of light.

We shall encounter the Earth in our wanderings through the planetary spaces. The study of the astronomical phenomena which relate to it will afford assistance by no means to be despised in enabling us to comprehend the analogies and differences which these phenomena present in the various planetary worlds.

Starting, then, our journey from the Sun, we shall visit in succession all the bodies which revolve round him, following the most natural order, that of their distances.

I.

MERCURY.

Apparent Movement and phases—Distances from the Sun and Earth—Form and Dimensions; its Transit across the Sun's disk—Length of Day and Night, Seasons and Climates—Equatorial Belts, Atmosphere and Mountains of Mercury—Mass, Density, and Force of Gravity on its surface.

When the sky is clear, and the atmosphere at the horizon is not too much charged with vapour, there may be perceived sometimes in the evening, after the setting of the Sun, a star, whose brilliant twinkling light renders it conspicuous in the ruddy and faint glimmer of twilight. Its apparent elevation above the horizon, at first small, increases little by little each evening, but it never recedes from the Sun more than 28°.*

This star is the planet Mercury.

If we continue to observe it on favourable evenings, it will be seen finally to approach the Sun, and, lost in the dazzling brightness of his rays, set with him.

Some days after, in the morning before sunrise, the same star, again emerging from the Sun's rays, will rise earlier and earlier, mounting day by day to a higher elevation above the horizon; the maximum of this to the east will be precisely equal to that it formerly attained to the west. At last it begins to retrograde, approaching the Sun, until the moment when it again disappears in his rays. Mercury accomplishes then, in this manner, a complete revolution round the Sun; to us it appears like an oscillation, and one which it repeats continually; its duration varies between 106 and 130 days.

The ancients, who did not know the true system of the world, deceived by the double appearance of Mercury, sometimes after the setting and sometimes before the rising of the Sun, believed at first that two distinct bodies were in question; they named one Apollo, god of day and light, and the other Mercury, god of thieves. The Indians and the Egyptians also gave it two different names. But observers remarked, at last, that one only of the two bodies was visible at the same time, and that the appearance of the one coincided very nearly with the disappearance of the other. To conclude their identity from this fact was not a difficult matter.

If, instead of confining ourselves to naked-eye observations,—which, by the way, are by no means easy—we employ a telescope of pretty high

* Nor does it always attain this distance from the Sun before commencing its return towards that luminary; its greatest elongation sometimes not exceeding 18°.

magnifying power, it will be found that the form of the planet varies according to the time of observation. This remark also holds good with its apparent size.

Let us speak first of its form. Mercury, in the course of one of its oscillations, presents phases entirely analogous to those of our Moon. It

Fig. 22.—Phases of Mercury when seen after sunset.

is at first a luminous disk, nearly circular, which by degrees is reduced on the side towards the east, until not more than a half-circle is visible at the period of its greatest apparent distance from the Sun; the crescent form henceforward characterises it more and more, until it is only visible as a fine luminous thread. We give some of these phases. The progressive increase of its apparent dimensions is also shown in exact proportion.

Fig. 23.—Phases of Mercury, when seen before sunrise.

The same appearances are observed, but in inverse order, when Mercury is observed during the period in which he is a morning star.

It is easy to account for these facts which observations have placed before us. The phases prove that Mercury has the form of a spherical globe, which is not self-luminous. Its movement round the Sun places it, relatively to the Earth, in a series of very different positions, and shows us portions, sometimes smaller, sometimes larger, of its illuminated half. The same movement varies its distance from the Earth,—this explains the variations in the apparent dimensions of its disk.

On the preceding page is a diagram of the positions of Mercury in different parts of its orbit, during the period of an entire oscillation compared to the successive positions occupied by the Earth.

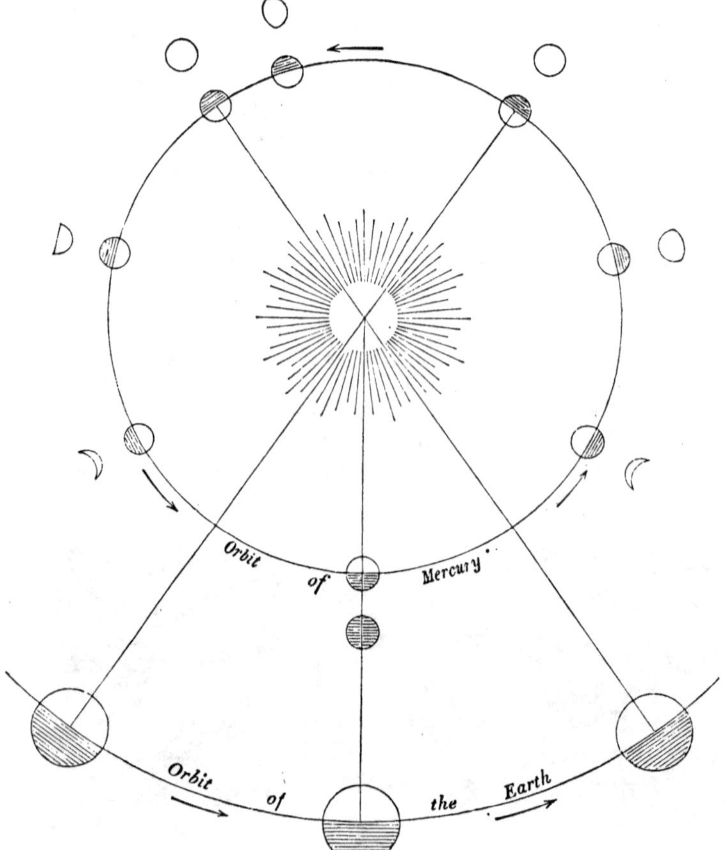

Fig. 24.—Explanation of the Phases of Mercury.

When Mercury is in the same direction as the Sun, we say that the planet is in *conjunction*. It is in *superior* conjunction when beyond the Sun; and in *inferior* conjunction when on our side of it. In the first case, it turns towards us its bright hemisphere; in the second, its dark one.

If the Earth itself were immovable, the interval of 106 to 130 days, which we have seen to be the period of an entire oscillation, would be also the period of a revolution of Mercury round the Sun. But it is easy to see from the preceding diagram, that, by the time the planet has returned to the same conjunction again, the Earth has travelled onwards in its orbit, and Mercury has, therefore, accomplished more than a complete revolution.

In reality, the time of a revolution of Mercury is less than that of a complete oscillation; it is about 88 of our days.*

If the orbit of Mercury were a perfect circle, its distance from the Sun would not vary. But it is known that the orbits described by the planets are ellipses—oval curves more or less elongated, of which the Sun does not occupy the centre, but one of the foci.

Amongst the eight principal planets, Mercury's orbit differs most from the circular form. Hence, its distances from the Sun are very variable. While at its greatest distance from the central body its distance is 44,475,000 miles, it approaches at its least distance to within 29,305,000 miles, the difference being over 15 millions of miles. In each of its revolutions Mercury traverses little less than 210 millions of miles.

Fig. 25.—Apparent dimensions of the disk of Mercury at its extreme and mean distances from the Earth.

This gives a velocity of 2,400,000 miles a-day, 100,000 miles an hour, and finally close upon 28 miles a second.

As we are speaking of distances, let us say a word with regard to those which separate Mercury from the Earth. These vary still more than those we have before mentioned; and this can easily be conceived, because, firstly, the distance of the planet from the Sun varies; and secondly, because Mercury, as we have seen, is sometimes between our Earth and the common focus; and sometimes beyond that focus,—the Sun.

In the first of these positions, Mercury approaches within 49,223,000 miles, while in the second it is distant 132,000,000 miles; these distances vary in the ratio of one to three; and its apparent diameter changes in inverse proportion to these numbers.

* More exactly, 87 days 23 hours 15 minutes and 46 seconds. Such is the precision with which astronomers have succeeded in measuring celestial phenomena. This revolution is called a *sidereal revolution* in contradistinction to the 'synodic revolution,' because, relatively to the Sun, the planet again occupies the same portion of the heavens. By the *synodic revolution* of a planet is expressed the interval of time taken to return to the same position relatively to the Sun as seen from the Earth.

As to its real dimensions, they have been easily determined from the two elements which precede: we allude, on the one hand, to the measure of its apparent diameter; on the other, to the distance of the planet from the Earth. We hence derive the first physical datum relating to Mercury, that it has the form of a globe, of 3089 miles in diameter: this is about two-fifths of the mean diameter of the Earth. Fig. 26 gives an exact idea of the relative sizes of the two planets.

Hence it follows that the surface of Mercury is nearly six times and a half less than that of our dwelling-place; seventeen globes, of the same volume as Mercury, would be required to equal the volume of the Earth.

Is Mercury of a perfectly spherical form? It is difficult to be assured of this in observing the planet in its phases. The brightness of its light is such that precise measures are extremely difficult.*

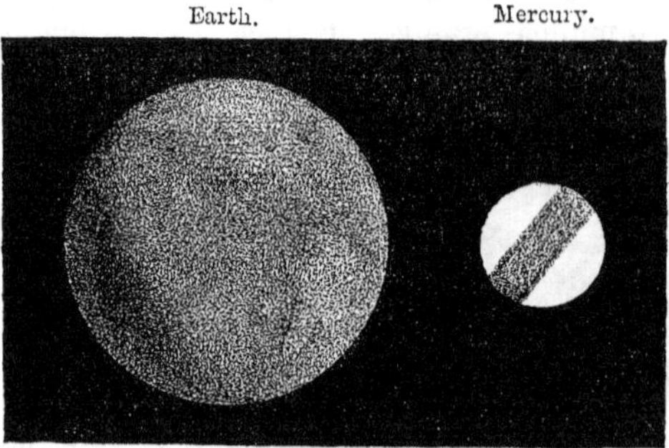

Fig. 26.—The size of Mercury compared with the Earth.

Astronomers have therefore preferred to take advantage of a phenomenon which occurs pretty frequently, and sufficiently so to control the observations. We allude to the passages, or transits, of Mercury across the Sun's disk (fig. 27).

It must be borne in mind that once in each of its revolutions round the Sun, Mercury passes between the Earth and that radiant body.

If the plane in which the planet moves were identical with that of the terrestrial orbit, that is to say, coincided with it, at each inferior conjunction Mercury would be projected on the Sun. But this is not the case; owing to the inclination of the plane of the orbit of Mercury to that of our Earth, sometimes the planet is thrown above the solar disk, sometimes it passes below. It happens, however, occasionally, that it is precisely

* In 1832, Saturn and Mercury occupied the same region of the heavens, in appearance, that is to say. According to Beer and Mädler, who observed them at that time, 'Saturn compared to Mercury appeared pale and without brilliancy, Mercury presented a variable brightness, and remained perfectly visible after the rising of the Sun, whilst Saturn disappeared from the sight. Mercury was illuminated a little more than half.'

of the same apparent height as the Sun. Mercury is then seen as a black round spot, traversing in the course of several hours* the Sun's disk, which is then partially eclipsed.†

The sharpness of the planet's circular form, the uniformity of the movement of the black spot over the Sun, and, lastly, the time of the transit, are circumstances which sufficiently prevent the phenomena being confounded with those of solar spots.

Astronomers have chosen the favourable occasions offered by these transits, to measure, by the aid of micrometrical instruments, the apparent diameter of Mercury, from which, by an easy calculation, they have been able to determine its real dimensions. They have, at the same time,

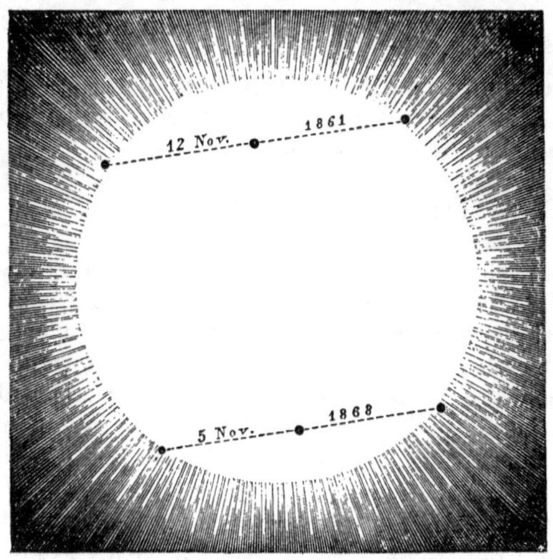

Fig. 27.—Transits of Mercury over the Sun, 1° the 12th November, 1861, 2° the 5th November, 1868.

observed that the black spot was always perfectly round, that is to say, that the globe shows no trace of flattening.‡

We now know the movement of Mercury round the Sun, the time of

* The duration of the transit is very variable. It may last about eight hours. The last passage took place on the 12th of November, 1861. We may add that up to the end of the present century there will be six others, the first of which will take place on the 5th of November, 1868. The transits of Mercury always occur in May or November.

† 'The first of these observations was made at Paris, by Gassendi, on the 7th of November, 1631, and, as mentioned by him, in accordance with the wish and suggestion of Kepler, for Kepler had predicted this transit, and had printed or written on it the preceding year, which was that of his death.'—*D'Alembert's Encyclopædia.*

‡ A single observation of this kind would not always be conclusive, since Mercury might be in such a position as to present to us one of its poles of rotation. Besides, the flattening might be so slight as not to be measurable at this distance.

its revolution, its distances from the Sun and from the Earth, and, lastly, its dimensions in diameter, in surface, and in volume. It only remains now to speak of what is known of its physical constitution. The facts that science has succeeded in gathering on this curious and important point of the monography of the planets ought to present a lively interest to us all, by reason of the likeness or contrast which each of these worlds possesses to our own. The manner in which light and heat are distributed on the surfaces of the planetary bodies, the succession of their days, nights, and seasons, the existence or the want of an atmosphere like ours; lastly, the markings that the telescope has permitted us to observe on their surfaces, are so many valuable particulars which enable us to make the most probable conjectures on the organisation of the living beings which doubtless people them. Supported by such positive data, imagination can then launch boldly in the field of conjecture.

The intensity of the light which Mercury receives from the Sun, at its mean distance, is nearly seven times* as great as that with which our globe is illuminated under the same conditions of distance.

It is not then surprising that the ancients gave Mercury the epithet of 'Twinkler' (στίλβων). This is not all. The laws governing the propagation of radiant heat are the same as those of light. Mercury then receives seven times more heat than the Earth, or, more properly, a heat the intensity of which is in the mean seven times as great.

To judge by the impression which the light-rays make on our eyes, seeing that we cannot bear their dazzling brightness without pain, and, again, by that which they make on our body when it is subjected to their influence, the inhabitants of Mercury should be extremely uncomfortable. But are they formed like us? and have their senses the same degree of impressionability? We know not. Variations of temperature are also disagreeable to us. In this respect, again, we must own that the inhabitants of Mercury have more to suffer than we. Owing to the planet's elongated orbit, we have seen that sometimes it recedes from, and sometimes approaches, the Sun, and that the difference between the extreme distances amounts to fifteen millions of miles. So that whilst at aphelion,† the intensity of the luminous and heat-rays is no more than four times and a half that of rays received by the Earth; at perihelion, on the contrary, it rises to more than ten times the same quantity.

Lastly, and this adds still more to the contrasts of temperature, the variations occur in a period of time less than a quarter of one of our terrestrial years. Presently, we shall see that the seasons present still greater anomalies.

* Exactly, 6·67.

† *Aphelion*—the greatest distance of a body from the Sun; from ἀπὸ *from*, and ἥλιος *the Sun*. *Perihelion*—least distance; from περὶ *near to*, and ἥλιος. If the orbit of a body were rigidly circular, there would be neither aphelion nor perihelion points.

We must not forget, however, that one circumstance may modify all this to an extent sufficient to render the conditions of vegetable and animal life in Mercury either similar to our own or more different still. This circumstance is the existence or absence of a gaseous or vaporous envelope,—in a word, of an atmosphere? Has Mercury, then, an atmosphere? According to many astronomers, Mercury presented the following aspect (fig. 28) in its transit (1799) across the solar disk. Instead of a black round spot, perfectly clear and well defined, there was seen all round the disk of the planet a circular band less luminous than the rest of the surface of the Sun, forming a sort of nebulous ring. It was thence inferred that there existed a very high and dense atmosphere. Recent observers have not seen anything like it. But, on the other hand, they have remarked in the phases of the planet, that the line of separation of the light and shade, which astronomers call the *terminator*, is never very decided, so that the breadth of the luminous part seemed diminished. 'Hence,' say Beer and Mädler, 'we may conclude that Mercury has a pretty sensible atmosphere.'

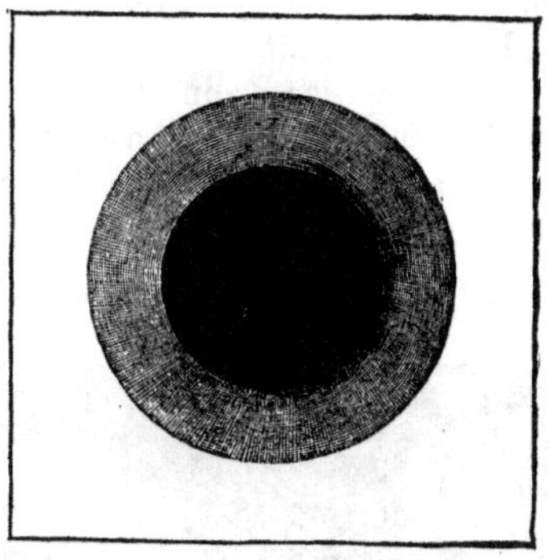

Fig. 28.—Aspect of the disk of Mercury during its transit over the Sun. 7th May, 1799, Vaporous aureola, and bright point on the disk. (Schröter.)

If this be so, we can form an idea of the modifications which a somewhat dense atmosphere would induce in the intensity of the light and heat, by comparing the days when on our Earth the sky is clear and without clouds—when the Sun darts its rays on the surface without obstacle, with the dark and dull days when the clouds completely hide him from us. The density of the atmospheric envelope we see then can strikingly change the effects of solar radiation. Let us compare, for instance, the temperature of one of our valleys with that of the mountainous summits which surround it. It is like passing from summer to the cold of winter, from the burning heat of July to the frost of November, and yet the Sun shines alike on the mountains and on the valley.

Finally, the chemical composition of the atmosphere of Mercury, the nature of the gases of which it is formed, and which are perhaps very different from the nitrogen and oxygen of our air, are also features which may influence the climate of the planet; concerning these matters we have no data. Let us confine ourselves, then, to describe the astronomical phenomena of which the influence is incontestable.

In the first place, let us consider the length of the day. Mercury turns on its axis in 24 hours and $5\frac{1}{2}$ minutes, and his year comprises $87\frac{2}{3}$ of these sidereal rotations.* The number of his solar days in this period is

[* Great doubt rests, however, both on this estimate and on the estimate of the planet's inclination.—R. A. P.]

therefore 86$\frac{2}{3}$, whence results as the length of one of them 24 hours and 54 seconds. This is nearly the length of one of our own solar days, so that the organised beings of the two planets have the same periods of light and darkness, of activity and repose. But the relative length of the days and nights in the course of the entire year is much more variable than on the Earth, owing to the great inclination of the axis of Mercury to the plane of its orbit.

Fig. 29 shows, according to the old observers, at what angle Mercury presents itself to the Sun at the commencement of each of its seasons.

Very extensive zones around the two poles enjoy at one season, during their summer, continuous day; at another, during their winter, they are

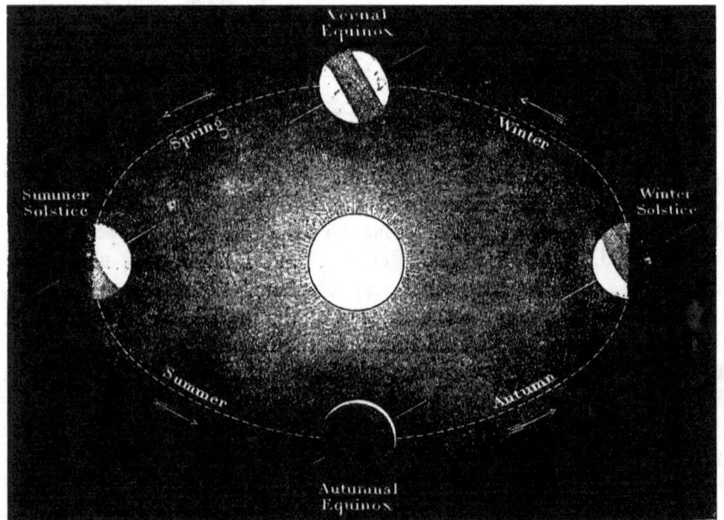

Fig. 29.—Orbit of Mercury.

plunged in profound darkness. It is only during a short period and near the planet's equinoxes, that these zones see light and darkness succeed in the interval of the same day.

The glacial and torrid zones are not distinct on Mercury, and temperate climates do not exist, or rather their zones change their character twice during each revolution. The equatorial regions alone have the advantage of possessing all the year, day and night, light and darkness, and of experiencing heat during the day, cold and calm during the night. It is true, however, that if the Sun towards the equinoxes rises so far as the zenith, it descends nearly to the horizon in the extreme seasons.

We have said above, that the orbit of Mercury is very elongated, or, in astronomical language, that its excentricity * is considerable. It results that the seasons in Mercury are of very unequal duration, and, seeing that, according as we consider the northern or the southern hemisphere, the spring and the summer of the one are the autumn and the winter of the other, a like inequality should exist between the extreme temperatures of the two hemispheres.

The great proximity of Mercury to the solar rays renders the observation of the planet somewhat difficult; very little, therefore, is known of its surface. One diligent observer, Schröter, at the end of the last century, was able, however, to observe some dark bands on its disk (fig. 30), which he considered as an equatorial zone; it was from the direction of these bands that he deduced the inclination of the axis of rotation. Besides this, during the crescent phases many observers (Schröter, Beer and Mädler) have seen indentations which make the line of separation of light and shade appear jagged; they also observed that the southern horn of the crescent was truncated (fig. 31). These markings were not always visible, but disappeared, to show themselves anew at intervals, the periodicity of which

Fig. 30—Equatorial band of Mercury. (Schröter.)

Fig. 31.—Crescent of Mercury, showing irregularities on the terminator and the truncation of the Southern Horn. (Schröter.)

* We have already remarked that it is not in the centre of the oval curve traversed by each planet that the Sun is situated, but in a point by so much more distant from this centre as the curve is more elongated. The name of *excentricity* is given to the distance between these two points, compared to the half of the greatest diameter of the orbit. Let us add that the place where the Sun is, is called the *focus* of the curve, and that the focus is always one of those points in the greater diameter to which we have alluded.

has enabled us to determine the period of rotation of Mercury. They evidently indicate the existence of high mountains, which intercept the light of the Sun, and of valleys plunged in shade, which lie near the parts of the surface of the planet then illuminated.

Mercury, therefore, has mountains. The measurement of the amount of truncation of the crescent, has also shown the height of one of them, and if this measure is not exaggerated it is not less than the $\frac{1}{253}$rd part of the diameter of the planet; that is more than eleven miles! Now the highest mountain known on the Earth, Gaurisankar of the Himalaya, is not more than 29,000 feet in vertical height; this giant of terrestrial mountains, therefore, does not rise above the sea-level more than the $\frac{1}{1400}$th part of the Earth's diameter.

Schröter, when examining Mercury during its transit over the Sun on the 7th of May, 1799, saw, or believed that he saw, on the black disk of the planet a luminous point. It has been concluded from this observation, which has not however been confirmed, that there exist on the surface of Mercury active volcanoes. This would be another analogy between the physical constitution of this planet and that of the Earth.

We have already said, in speaking of the Sun, that astronomical science has succeeded in ascertaining the masses, or the relative weights, of the celestial bodies of the solar system. The mass of Mercury is such that 4,866,000 globes of the same weight as its own would be required to balance the mass of the Sun. As the latter is itself 354,936 times as heavy as the mass of the Earth, it follows that the weight of Mercury is the $\frac{81}{100}$ths, or more simply four-fifths, of the weight of our globe. In comparing these numbers with those which measure the volumes of the two planets, it is found that the matter of which Mercury is formed is much denser than that of which the Earth is composed. Its density is half as much again. It lies between the specific gravity of iron and copper. . . .

Lastly, there is another physical fact which we must take into account if we would form an idea of the beings which people the planets of the solar system. We refer to the force of gravity on the surface. The influence of this force is all-important; according as its intensity is greater or less, the muscular movements, for example, are more or less difficult, requiring an expenditure of force more or less considerable. According to the most recent determinations, the force of gravity on Mercury is but three-fifths of what it is on the Earth. To sum up. By the aid of all the astronomical, physical, and meteorological, data which we have reviewed in this study of Mercury, and compared with the corresponding elements of the terrestrial globe, it has been possible for us to point out both the resemblances and differences of these two worlds, revolving in regions of the heavens, which are, after all, near each other, when we consider the extent of the whole planetary system.

II.

VENUS.

Distance from the Sun — Apparent and real Movements; Form of the Orbit — Distance of Venus from the Earth — Real Dimensions, Form, and Surface-markings; Rotation — Day and Night on Venus; Atmosphere, Seasons, and Climates — Physical Constitution.

THE two planets nearest to the Earth — Mars and Venus — are precisely those which present the most striking analogies to it; Mars especially, which we have more particularly studied. This fact is a very natural one, and it will appear to us still more so when we try to form an idea of the origin of the system, according to the views of Laplace. For the present let us study in detail the various phenomena which each planet in turn presents to us.

Mercury is the first planet which we encountered on leaving the Sun. Venus comes after Mercury in the order of distance, whilst of all the principal planets Mercury is that which describes an orbit of the most elongated form, and that by very much. Venus, on the contrary, moves in an orbit the form of which approaches nearest to a perfect circle. There is not between its greatest and least distances from the Sun — between its aphelion and its perihelion, to use the language of astronomers — a difference equal to the $\frac{1}{145}$th part of the maximum distance.

The mean distance of Venus from the Sun is 68,932,000 miles; its maximum distance is 69,405,000 miles; and when nearest to the Sun, it is still removed from him 68,459,000 miles.

What is the result of this quasi equality in the movement of Venus? It is, that the quantity of light and heat which it receives from the Sun varies little in the different points of its orbit; or, what comes to the same thing, in the different seasons of its year. Yet, this quantity is still nearly double in intensity that which our globe receives, — a fact we must take into account when we treat on the physical constitution of the planets.

Venus, like Mercury, is sometimes an evening, sometimes a morning star. It appears to us to oscillate in the same manner round the Sun. But the amplitude and the duration of its periodical oscillations are much greater. Thus, in that part of its apparent orbit in which it recedes each evening from the setting Sun, it advances at its maximum eastern elongation to a distance of 48°, while that of Mercury is 29°. When in the morning before sunrising, it gradually leaves that body, its maximum western elongation attains the same value.

Who does not know the Shepherd's Star? Who has not contemplated its soft and brilliant light, rarely twinkling, and intense enough at times to cast shadows? Where a light cloud veils that portion of the sky occupied by the planet, a pretty strong glimmer will still indicate its position in the centre of the luminous ring formed by the illuminated molecules of the interposing cloud. The brilliancy of this planet is, indeed, sometimes so intense that in a very clear sky it is visible by day.

The evening star received from the ancients the name of Vesper, whilst they gave to the morning star the name of Lucifer. The same error which led them to double Mercury—if we may be allowed the expression,—made them see in Venus also two distinct bodies. But they at length recognised the identity of the two stars, and Venus eventually replaced Vesper and Lucifer.

Venus takes 584 days to accomplish an entire oscillation. At the end of this time, it is again found in an identical position with regard to the Sun and the Earth, and recommences this apparent movement round the central body.

This similarity in the apparent movements of the two planets nearest to the Sun would lead us to infer that their real movements are similar. This is the case. Venus describes round the Sun a curve entirely enclosed by the orbit of the Earth.

Accordingly, when, instead of observing it with the naked eye we use a telescope of considerable magnifying power, we perceive that it presents phases * like Mercury, and that, like this latter planet, its apparent dimensions vary as in its movement it recedes from or approaches our Earth. We need not here repeat the explanations that we gave in the case of Mercury, inasmuch as they would be quite identical for Venus.

We must not confound the period of a complete oscillation of Venus with the period of its real revolution. As the Earth moves at the same time and in the same direction, the planet requires in reality much more time to return to the same position relatively to the Sun and the Earth than to accomplish an entire revolution, or, as it may be expressed, to return to the same part of its orbit. So, while the synodic revolution of Venus is accomplished in about 584 days, its sidereal revolution requires only 225 days ($224^{d}\ 16^{h}\ 49^{m}\ 7^{s}$), or less than $\frac{5}{8}$ths of one of our years. In this interval, the distance which it travels is upwards of 430 millions of miles, so that its mean velocity is 80,000 miles an hour, or nearly 22 miles a second. We have seen already that Mercury travels at the rate of 28 miles a second; the generalisation of these facts will show us that the velocity of the planets decreases as we advance from the common centre of their movements.

Viewed from the mean distance of Venus, the disk of the Sun seems nearly double (in surface) its apparent size as seen from the Earth. (See fig. 2, p. 24.)

A word now on the different distances which separate the two planets when in various positions in their orbits.

* Galileo recognised them first.

When Venus is between the Sun and the Earth, it is obviously nearest to us; and when it is beyond the Sun, it is farthest from us.

In the first case, to know the distance between the two planets, we must find the difference of their distances from the Sun; in the second, we must add them together. But let us say, once for all, in respect of Venus as in respect of the other bodies of the system, that as the orbits are not circles, but ellipses or ovals, there is for each of the two cases a maximum and a minimum. We will dwell upon these details when their importance renders it necessary.

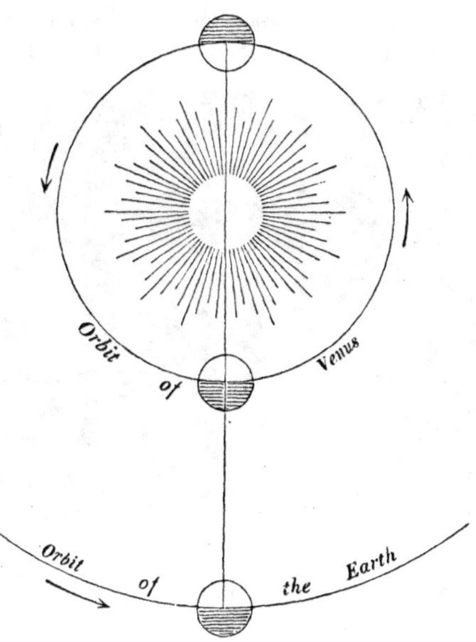

Fig. 32.—Superior and inferior conjunction of Venus. Greatest and least distance from the Earth.

The greatest distance of Venus from the Earth varies between 166,304,000 and 162,157,000 miles,—its least distance between 24,839,000 and 24,293,000 miles. The divergence of these numbers would leave us to believe at first, that the observations of Venus ought to be much more favourable in the case of short distances. This, however, is not the case. In this part of its orbit, in fact, Venus presents to us more and more of its dark hemisphere, and, besides, its light is extinguished by the brightness of the solar rays. This last circumstance is repeated at the period of its maximum distance, so that it is in the intermediate phases that it is most distinctly visible and its light most brilliant.

From figure 33 we can understand both the change in the apparent size, and in the degree of illumination of its disk at its extreme and mean distances from the Earth. The diameter varies nearly in the proportion of the numbers 10, 18, and 65.

When both the distance of an object and its apparent size are known, nothing is easier, as already remarked, than to determine its real dimensions. It has been calculated* that the diameter of the globe of Venus measures 8108 miles which is within the $\frac{15}{1000}$th part of that of the Earth. The dimensions in volume and surface also differ very little

* By Sir W. Herschel, Arago, Beer and Mädler, &c. [Leverrier, however, assigns to the planet a smaller diameter.]

from those of the terrestrial spheroid. But up to the present time no perceptible polar compression has been observed.

This last result is not at all astonishing, for if such a flattening really existed, if it did not exceed that of the terrestrial poles, even the most delicate measures would not be able to detect it. Although Venus is one

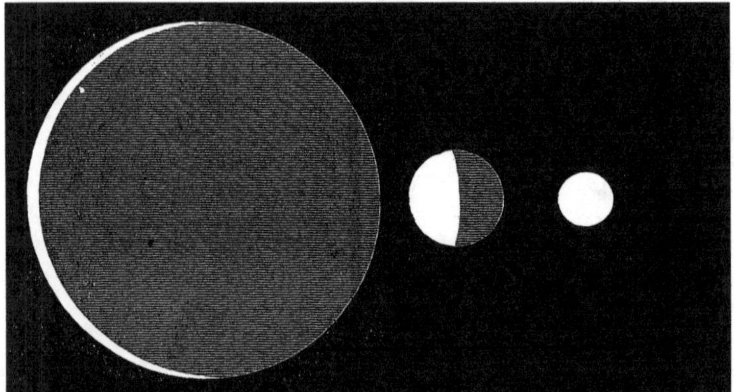

Fig. 33.—Apparent dimensions of Venus at its extreme and mean distances from the Earth.

of the nearest planets to the Earth, astronomers have experienced great difficulty in measuring its apparent diameter in a precise manner. This is

Fig. 34.—Comparative dimensions of Venus and the Earth.

owing to the astonishing brilliancy of the light of Venus, and to the irradiation* which is produced in its image in our instruments—a cause of

* The effect of irradiation may be observed in fig. 35. If two circles, one of which is black, the other white on a black ground, are examined, it will be seen that the last seems perceptibly larger; and nevertheless their diameters are rigorously the same. This effect is by so much the more perceptible as the light of the object is more intense.

error which it is very difficult to estimate. How can we then be astonished if we are not sure of its diameter within the $\frac{3}{100}$th part?

If the flattening of the globe of the planet is unknown, this is not the case with the period of its rotation, although its determination has also necessitated very delicate observations.

Venus turns on itself in 23 hours 21 minutes 23 seconds. That is a period less than that of the rotation of the Earth by 35 minutes only. As in the case of Mercury, it is by the careful watching of the irregularities which the illuminated part of the planet presents at the limit of light and shade, and their successive and periodical reappearances, that various astronomers* have been able to measure this period.

Bianchini, an Italian astronomer of the last century, endeavoured to deduce the rotation of Venus from the observations of the spots which he

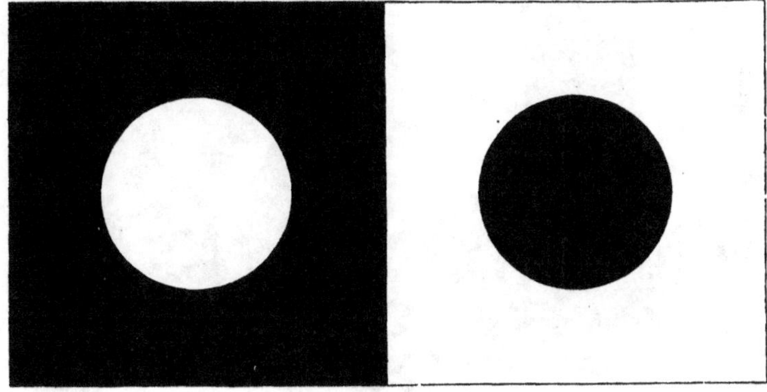

Fig. 35.—Effect of irradiation.

observed on its disk. Although the number he found is completely at variance with the recognised and adopted period, his observations, nevertheless, have their value, as they give an idea of the features which distinguish the surface of the planet.†

Venus, in its various phases, is far from showing perfectly regular forms. The horns of the crescent, especially the southern one, have nearly always been observed blunted—truncated, so to speak. Schröter also saw a bright point completely separated from the luminous crescent. Fig. 33 shows some of these forms observed by this able astronomer.

These inequalities, besides serving by their periodical return to enable

* D. and J. Cassini, Schröter, Vico, Beer and Mädler.

† They were, however, permanent spots. if it be true, as stated by Arago ('Astronomie Populaire,' ii. 523), that Bianchini's spots were again seen by Vico, from 1840 to 1842, with all their old forms. We give these spots from Schröter's drawings in *Aphroditographische Fragmente*. [Doubts still rest on the subject of the permanence of these markings; and accordingly the rotation-period and axial inclination of Venus are still held as doubtful by many astronomers.—R. A. P.]

us to measure the rotation of the planet, are evidences of the irregularities of its surface. Thus the solid ground of Venus is uneven, like that of Mercury and of the Earth; it is covered with high mountains. But is it certain that these asperities attain such a considerable height as is stated? Do mountains exist on Venus to the vertical elevation of 27 miles; that is to say, five times higher than the most elevated peak in Thibet, ten times the colossal Mont Blanc? This is a delicate question which subsequent

Fig. 36.—Irregularities in the terminator of Venus. (Schröter.) Spots on its two hemispheres. (Bianchini.)

measurement may perhaps settle. But if the first results were confirmed, we could scarcely help thinking of the strange aspect the mountainous regions of Venus would offer; the sublime peaks of our Alpine regions would be but mere mole-hills in comparison. If we refer to the drawings of Schröter (fig. 36), which represent Venus in three of its phases, we shall notice that the luminous part of the disk is far from terminating abruptly along the line of shade. Its light, on the contrary, diminishes gradually; and this diminution may be entirely explained by the twilight on the planet. The existence of an atmosphere of a considerable heighth as hence been inferred, which, by refracting the rays of the Sun, enables them to penetrate into regions where that body is already set. Thus the evenings in Venus would be like ours, lighted by twilight, and the mornings by the dawn.

Venus, during each of its periodical oscillations, should, one would think, when it passes between the Earth and the Sun, be projected on the disk of the latter body. But the occurrence is, on the contrary, rare, because the plane which Venus describes is not coincident with the plane of the Earth's orbit. Sometimes the globe of the planet, always, be it remembered, with its unilluminated half towards us, passes higher than the solar disk, sometimes it passes below. Two transits occur in an interval of eight years, after which they do not again occur until the end of another interval of more than a century. When two transits have taken place both in December, the two following invariably occur in June. The last observed were those on the 5th of June, 1761, and the 3rd of June, 1769. The two next transits will take place on the 8th of December, 1874, and the 6th December, 1882. We shall see further on, that it was by observations of these transits, made very carefully at different stations on the surface of the globe, that the Sun's distance was for the first time calculated. Venus, in traversing the solar disk, appears as a perfectly round black spot.

Now, in what manner do the days and nights vary according to the latitudes and the seasons? This depends both on the way in which Venus in the course of its year presents its polar and equatorial regions to the Sun, and on the relative durations of its two movements of rotation and revolution. Let us return to some of our former statements.

Venus turns on itself in 23 hours and 21 minutes and 23 seconds; this is the duration of its sidereal day.* Its year contains 225 terrestrial days (224·7). It comprises, therefore, 231 entire rotations, or sidereal days of Venus, which are equivalent to 230 solar days of Venus. Each ordinary day then on Venus consists of 23 hours 26 minutes.

On the other hand, the nearly circular form of its orbit gives a nearly equal length to the four seasons, and the light and the heat of the Sun are distributed with a like constancy. But that which establishes a marked difference between the terrestrial seasons and climates and those of the planet which we are exploring, is the great inclination of its axis of rotation to the plane of its orbit. In this respect Venus resembles Mercury. Fig. 37 shows the position of the planet at one of its solstices, at the

* On each planet, as on the Earth, we can distinguish the sidereal day, the length of which is identical with that of a rotation, and the solar day, a little longer than the sidereal day. We shall explain, in the chapter relating to the Rotation of the Earth, the reason for this essential distinction.

commencement of the summer of the hemisphere which presents its pole to the Sun. At the winter solstice, Venus occupies a diametrically opposed position. It follows that the polar regions undergo alternately the torrid temperature of summer and the prolonged cold of winter. At the equator, the Sun then attains but a small elevation above the horizon.

Towards the equinoxes, on the contrary, the regions nearest the equator are exposed to the heat of the Sun, the intensity of which is nearly double the intensity of the solar heat on our globe. Perhaps a very dense, cloudy atmosphere, constantly charged with vapours arising from the heat, envelopes the globe of Venus, and thus moderates the rigour of its opposite seasons. A fact which gives to this hypothesis a certain degree of truth is the observation of the transit of Venus over the Sun in 1761. A nebulous ring seemed to surround the black disk of the body; and, moreover, at

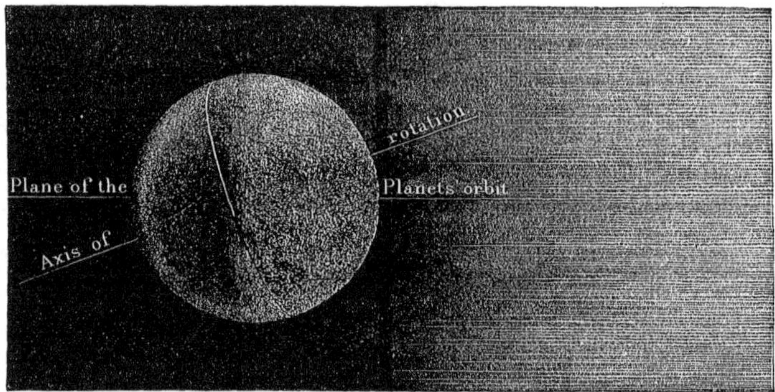

Fig. 37.—Venus at one of its solstices. Inclination of the axis of rotation.

the moment when it was but partly projected on the Sun, the contour of the exterior limb of the planet was seen edged with a luminous ring.

These two phenomena are easily explained if we suppose the globe of Venus to be enveloped with a very dense atmosphere.

There still remain some other interesting physical data bearing on the constitution of Venus. Thus, for instance, calculation has shown that its mass is such, that more than 400,000 globes of the same weight would be required to balance the mass of the Sun; it is nearly $\frac{88}{100}$ths of the mass of the Earth. Taking into consideration the difference of the volumes of the two planets, we find that the density of the matter of which Venus is composed is more than nine-tenths (0·987) of the density of our globe.

Finally, the force of gravity on its surface is also a little more than nine-tenths of the mean intensity of this force on the surface of the Earth.

To sum up. The world we have explored resembles in many points, in its dimensions and astronomical and physical constitution, that which we inhabit. And, if we were to accept the observations of several astronomers of the 17th and 18th centuries,* it would present an additional resemblance; as the Moon accompanies the Earth, so also would Venus, according to them, be provided with a satellite. But this singular body has not been since seen, and high scientific† authorities are now convinced that the observers in question were the victims of an optical illusion. It must be confessed that the doubt which still exists on this point is, at least, very curious, and testifies the progress which still remains to be accomplished in the domain of planetary astronomy.

[Before we quit Mercury and Venus, we must fairly state that the decision and positiveness with which the physical data are given by the old astronomers, are by no means borne out by modern observation, although we might imagine, to say the least, that if the observations of Schröter and others, faithfully recorded by M. Guillemin, were correct, the vastly superior telescopes of the present day would have verified them. This, however, they have failed to do. The different features, although stated to have been seen by De Vico during the present century, have not once been observed either by Admiral Smyth or the Rev. W. R. Dawes; indeed, the only physical fact which modern observation has placed before us, and this we owe to Professor Phillips and the Rev. T. W. Webb, is the possible existence of snow-zones on Venus as on Mars. This, however, is not certain. We must, therefore, caution our readers against receiving absolutely the inferences drawn from the old observations.]

III.

THE ZODIACAL LIGHT.

Aspect of the Zodiacal Light in the various regions of the Earth — Probable existence of a large Luminous Ring situated between the Earth and the Sun.

In the evenings, about the time of the vernal equinox — in March and April, when in our climate the twilight is of short duration, if we examine the horizon towards the west, a little after sunset, we may perceive a faint light that rises in the form of a cone among the starry constellations.

This is what astronomers call the *Zodiacal Light*. Those unfamiliar with it, or little accustomed to the ordinary aspect of the sky, might confuse this glimmering either with the Milky Way, or with the ordinary twilight, or even with an aurora. But, with a little attention, it is impossible to mistake it.

* D. Cassini, Short, Montaigne, Rœdkier, Horrebow, Montbaron, Lambert.

† De Lalande (*Encyclopédie Méthodique*.)

The triangular form of this luminous cone, its elevation, and its inclined position to the horizon, make it a thing apart and one eminently deserving particular mention.

As the days lengthen, and with them the duration of twilight, the Zodiacal Light disappears, it becomes invisible, at least in our climate. But it may again be seen in the morning, in the east, about the time of the autumnal equinox, in September and October, when the dawn has an equally short duration—again, however, to disappear during the period of long nights and long twilights.*

It is needless to add that the sky must be clear, and the night moonless, for observations of the Zodiacal Light to be possible.

The brightness of this light is comparable with that of the Milky Way, or with the tails of comets, its transparence is such, that all but the smallest stars are visible through it. Nevertheless, according to Mairan, who occupied himself with this phenomenon in the days most favourable for observation, its light is more intense than that of the Milky Way, and more uniform, generally less white, and inclining somewhat towards yellow or red in the parts nearest the horizon. It was only towards the apex that he could discern the small stars in the region on which the light was projected.

This yellowish-red colour was observed also, in 1843, by Arago and other astronomers of the Observatory of Paris, who compared it to the tail of the comet of that same year. Moreover, the same red tint was, in 1707, noticed by Derham.

Now, if from temperate regions of the two hemispheres we travel towards the tropical zones, the Zodiacal Light increases in intensity and height, and it can be observed throughout the year. The illustrious Humboldt thus relates in his 'Cosmos,' the impressions made on him in his travels by the sight of this curious phenomenon: 'The much greater luminous intensity which the Zodiacal Light presented in Spain, on the coast of Valentia and in the plains of New Castile, had already determined me, before I quitted Europe, to observe it assiduously. The brightness of this light—I should say of this illumination—still increased in a surprising manner, as I gradually approached the equator on the American continent, or on the South Seas. Through the dry and transparent atmosphere of Cumana, on the grassy plains or Llanos of Caracas, on the

* In large towns, the thousands of gas-lamps or other lights render the observation of the Zodiacal Light very difficult, not to say impossible, at all times. On the other hand in stations conveniently situated, it can be seen at various epochs of the year, even in the temperate zones.

Mr. Heis (of Munster) cites some observations made by him in the month of December, in Germany, and Mr. Jones had observed it at the same time in Japan.

M. Chacornac observed the Zodiacal Light in January and February in Paris, and in December in Lyons, in 1864. A fact little known, established by him, is, that the light is intense enough to efface stars of the twelfth and thirteenth magnitude. 'It is beyond doubt,' he writes, 'that this phenomenon covers with a yellowish red veil the region of the sky on which it is projected.'

THE ZODIACAL LIGHT.

Its aspect in Europe, as observed by M. Heis, at Munster.

table-lands of Quito, and on the Mexican lakes, particularly at a height of eight or twelve thousand feet, where I could stay a longer time. I saw the Zodiacal Light sometimes surpass in brilliancy the most striking parts of the Milky Way, comprised between the prow of the Ship and Sagittarius, or, to cite the regions of the sky visible in our hemisphere, between the Eagle and the Swan.'*

Let us see now if it is possible to account for the nature of the Zodiacal Light, which evidently is not a purely meteorological phenomenon, since its participation in the diurnal movement, its visibility in regions of the Earth very distant one from the other, and, lastly, its nearly invariable inclination along the ecliptic, indicate sufficiently that the cause which produces such appearances lies outside our atmosphere, in the celestial spaces.

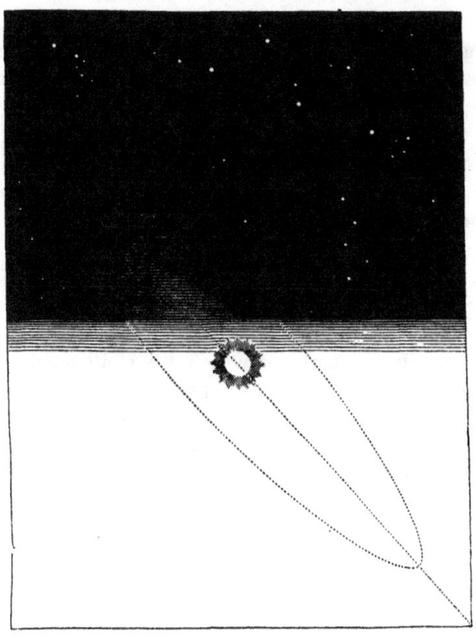

Fig. 38.—Direction of the axis of the Zodiacal Light.

Among the explanations that have been given, the most probable one is that which likens the Zodiacal Light to a flattened nebulous ring surrounding the Sun at some distance. It is to be remarked, that the direction of the axis of the cone, or of the pyramid, prolonged below the horizon, always passes through the Sun. (Fig. 38.)

It was believed at first that this direction precisely coincided with the solar equator; but it seems more certain that it coincides with the plane of the Earth's orbit, or the ecliptic.†

The length of the longer axis of the ring is variable, or, as it may be expressed, the distance from the summit of the cone to the middle of its base,—to the horizon,—is more or less considerable, according to the

* 'Cosmos,' vol. ii. p. 594.

† The recent observations of Mr. Heis at Munster, and of Mr. Jones at Japan, made simultaneously, show, however, the axis of the luminous cone as forming an angle with the latter plane.

time of observation. Very simple geometric considerations point to the conclusion that the luminous ring sometimes extends as far as the orbit of the Earth, and even surpasses it, sometimes it is enclosed within this same orbit. This may be explained in two ways: either by admitting that the form of the ring is elliptical or oval, or, if it be circular, that the Sun does not lie exactly in the centre.

Now, what is the nature of this luminous mass? Must it be considered as a zone of vapours thrown off by the Sun when in the process of consolidation, when our central star passed from a nebulous state to that of a condensed fluid sphere? This was the opinion of Laplace.

Another hypothesis, also connected with the first, is, that the Zodiacal Light is formed of myriads of solid particles, analogous to the aërolites, possessing a general movement, but travelling separately around the focus of our solar world. The light of the ring would be thus produced by the accumulation of this multitude of brilliant points, reflecting towards us the light borrowed by each of them from the Sun.

This explanation accounts for the variation of the intensity of the Zodiacal Light at different epochs; it would suffice to admit that the condensation of the particles or the density of the ring is not the same throughout its extent, and that its movement of circulation round the Sun presents successively different parts to the Earth. In this case, it becomes a question whether this lenticular ring of matter is distinct from the systems of meteors, of which we shall soon speak, and the existence of which seems at length established.

Lastly, some astronomers regard the Zodiacal Light as a vaporous ring which belongs to the Earth, surrounding it at some distance. But this is an opinion which appears somewhat wild (it can be upset by the most simple geometric consideration), and is utterly at variance with observation.*

We omit to mention various other theories now completely abandoned. But it must be owned, in concluding what we have to say on this interesting phenomenon, that while the observations remain so vague and so few in number, we are not yet permitted to pronounce, in a definite way, on its nature.

Cassini and Mairan have observed in the luminous cone momentary sparklings, which they explain by the rapid movements of its particles, alternatively presenting faces of unequal size; nearly in the same way as one sees the grains of dust sparkling in the rays of the Sun when they penetrate into the interior of a dark room.

This is an explanation which must be presented with the more

* Whatever may be the true nature of the Zodiacal Light, observation proves that the substance of which it is composed lies in a region which sometimes extends beyond the Earth's orbit, sometimes lies within it. Our readers will therefore understand why the description of it is found in this part of the Solar System.

reserve, as the observations of Mairan and Cassini have not been, as far as we know, confirmed.

The intermittent brightness described by Humboldt—the sudden undulations which he observed to traverse the luminous pyramid, also await explanation. Arago did not think this fact could be explained merely by variations in the strata of our atmosphere.

IV.

THE EARTH.

The Earth suspended in Space—Proof of its Spheroidal Form—Its Dimensions, Mass, and Mean Density—Atmospheric Refraction; its effects on the appearance of the Disks of the Sun and Moon.

THE Earth considered as a celestial body—as a planet—will now be the object of our study. It is the globe we meet with next in our journey from the focus of the Solar System.

The Earth does not voyage alone, as do Venus and Mercury; but, drawing the Moon after it, in its annual course, it is continually escorted by this faithful satellite. It is the first planet that rejoices in such a privilege.

If the Earth be a body travelling through space, as do the multitudes of those which people the heavens, it may be asked, under what aspect it appears to the nearest celestial bodies. This will evidently depend on the distance of the observer.

The form of the Earth is that of a nearly spherical globe, of which one-half receives the light of the Sun, whilst the other half is plunged in gloom; to a spectator who moves from it gradually, it would appear under the form of a disk, gradually becoming more and more diminutive, but more and more luminous at the same time; presenting phases like Mercury and Venus, according to the relative position of the Earth with regard to the spectator and the Sun.

At the distance of the Moon, the Earth will be seen under the form of a luminous disk, sprinkled with spots, the bright ones marking the continents and islands, and the snow and ice of the poles; the darker ones indicating the place of the seas; but besides these permanent spots, variable and movable ones would be distinguished, produced by the cloudy strata of the atmosphere.

Its apparent diameter would be nearly four times that of the Moon, so that, seen at the full, the Earth would shine like thirteen united full moons. At about four times the distance of our satellite, the terrestrial globe would still seem as large as the latter. But as the spectator moved away by degrees, the diameter of the disk would diminish, and would end by

Fig. 39.—The Earth suspended in Space.

becoming insensible. The Earth would then shine in the heavens like a star.

These statements of Science regarding the form of our globe, and its real dimensions,—statements now familiar to every one,—are not based on simple analogies. Exact facts, which it is easy to verify, place the rotundity of the Earth beyond doubt, and trigonometrical surveys of extreme precision have determined its true dimensions. Let us dwell an instant on these different points.

It is well known that the horizon of a plain presents the form of a circle, surrounding the observer. If the latter moves, the circle moves also, but its form remains the same, and is modified only when mountains, or other obstacles of some elevation, limit the view. Out at sea, the circular form of the horizon is still more decided, and changes only near the coasts, the outline of which breaks the regularity.

Here, then, we obtain a first notion of the rotundity of the Earth, since a sphere is the only body which is presented always to us under the form of a circle, from whatever exterior point of view it is examined. Moreover, it cannot be said that the horizon is formed by the limit of distinct

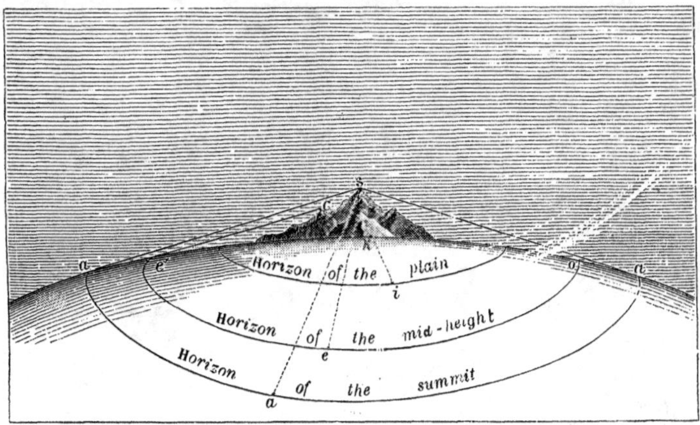

Fig. 40.—Curvature of the Continents. Horizons of the same place at different altitudes.

vision, and that it is this which causes the appearance of a circular boundary, because the horizon is enlarged when we mount vertically above the surface of the plain.

The preceding drawing, in which a mountain is figured in the middle of a plain, whose uniform curvature is that of a sphere, will prove our assertion. From the foot of the mountain the spectator will have but a very limited horizon. Let him ascend half-way, his visual radius extends, is inclined below the first horizon, and reveals a more extended circular area. At the summit of the mountain, the horizon still increases, and if the atmosphere be pure, the spectator will see numerous objects appear, where from the lower stations the sky alone was visible.

This extension of the horizon would be inexplicable if the Earth had the form of an extended plane.

The curvature of the surface of the sea manifests itself in a still more striking manner. Suppose yourself on the coast, at the summit of a high tower, hill, or steep, rocky shore; a vessel appears on the horizon, you see only the tops of the masts, the highest sails; the lower sails and the hull are invisible. As the vessel approaches, its lower part comes into view above the horizon, and soon it appears entire (fig. 41).

Fig. 41.—Curvature of the surface of the sea.

This fact, of the successive appearances on the surface of the sea, of the different parts of an object, beginning by the highest parts of it, is manifested in the same manner to the sailors who from the ship observe

Fig. 42.—Curvature of the sea.

the land. The explanation is rendered clear in the second sketch, where the course of a vessel, seen in profile, is figured on the convex surface of the sea.

As the curvature of the ocean is the same in every direction, it follows that the Earth has really the form of a sphere, or at least differs from it but little.

We may also mention two proofs of another kind, which, like the preceding ones, are more interesting as facts than as elements of conviction. Who could doubt at the present time of the rotundity of the Earth, and of its suspension in space, after so many voyages of circumnavigation, after the daily testimony of the movement of the stars, setting on one side of the horizon, to reappear after twenty-four hours on the opposite side? These are the proofs.

One of the stars of the northern heavens,—the Pole-star—we shall speak of it again subsequently—remains nearly immovable, and at the same height in the heavens above the horizon of any given place. Now, when we move towards the south, this star by degrees approaches the horizon; whilst, on the other hand, it rises if we advance to the north.

This is a fact which can be explained very naturally by the convexity of the surface of the Earth, for if this change of height were held to be the result of a real approach of the traveller to, and removal from, the observed star, the known distance of the stars from the Earth shows that the displacement of the observer is, so to speak, indefinitely small, compared to the distance of the star, and cannot in any way account for its apparent movement. Besides, if instead of walking from north to south, the observer travels from east to west, the Pole-star will always appear at the same point of the heavens as referred to the movable horizon, and at the same height above this horizon. But, in this case, it will be the hour of the rising and setting of the stars that will vary; as should happen if the curvature of the terrestrial surface is in every direction; and if, as indeed is known, our globe every day performs an entire rotation round one of its diameters.

We may announce, then, as a fact, demonstrated by experience and observation, that the Earth, in spite of the irregularities of its surface, which seem to us so considerable, is a spheroid, which, seen in space, appears as well defined, regular and smooth, as the disks of the other planets.

Some numbers relative to the real dimensions of the Earth will support these results, so astonishing to those, who, learning them for the first time, seek to figure them as so many real facts. But before we give them, we will state a little more exactly the form of the Earth, as determined by the most exact measures. Its form is not rigorously spherical; the diameter or axis, round which the movement of diurnal rotation is performed, is the smaller diameter. Our globe, then, is flattened at the poles, that is to say, at the extremities of the axis. The existence of this flattening has been determined in the following manner.

Let us consider a meridian, one of the ideal curved lines, indefinite in number, which encircle the Earth, each one passing through the two poles. If the earth were exactly spherical, each meridian would be a circle, that is, if we leave out of consideration the irregularities of the Earth's surface

On this hypothesis, the successive verticals which, from the Equator to the Pole, would form between themselves equal angles—an angle of one degree, for instance,—would be equally distant the one from the other. The distances between the feet of the verticals on the surface of the earth, would be expressed by equal numbers.

Observation contradicts this supposition, and it has been found that the length of the successive degrees of the meridian increases, in a continuous manner, from the Equator to the Pole.*

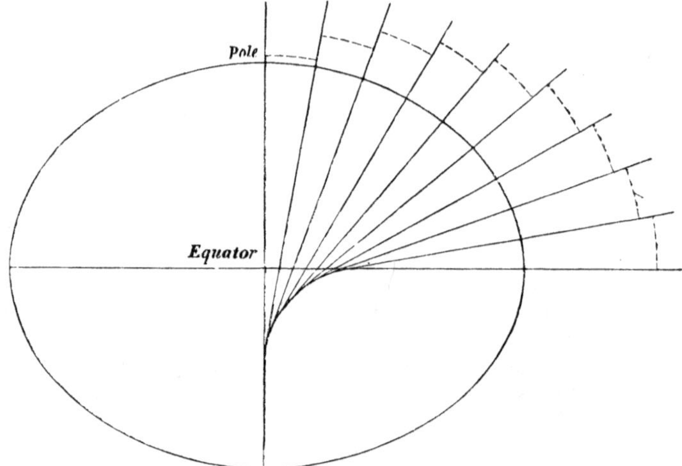

Fig. 43.—Elliptical form of the terrestrial meridians. Diminution in the length of a degree from the Pole to the Equator.

The following table shows the differences of length of the arcs of a degree, measured in the northern hemisphere of the Earth, at increasing latitudes, that is to say, at gradually increasing distances from the Equator :

	Mean Latitude of Arc.			Length of one Degree in English Feet.
India	12°	32′	20″	362,956
"	16	8	21	363,044
America	39	12	0	363,786
Italy	42	59	0	364,262
France	44	51	2	364,572
England	52	2	19	364,951
Denmark	54	8	14	365,087
Russia	56	3	55	365,291
Sweden	66	20	10	365,744

* It is easy to see from fig. 43, that the meridian ought, in fact, to present really the form of an ellipse or oval, the greater diameter of which terminates in the equator, and the smaller in the two poles. In such a curve, the curvature is the more strongly marked, as we consider the arcs nearest the major axis. We shall then require to traverse a shorter distance nearer the Equator to find the same angle between successive verticals than we shall near the poles. But it is well to remark that the flattening is much exaggerated in the drawing.

The differences are unmistakable, and their constancy puts the fact of the polar flattening quite beyond doubt. But their relative smallness,—there is only a difference of 2788 feet between the extreme latitudes—proves that the compression is in truth very small, as may be proved by comparing the length of the equatorial diameter, and the polar one, deduced from the preceding data:

	Feet.
Equatorial diameter	= 41,848,380
Polar ,,	= 41,708,710

Thus, if we represent the Earth by a sphere, a yard in diameter, the polar diameter will be about the $\frac{1}{10}$th part of an inch too long.

[But this is not all. The most recent results arrived at by geodesists have taught us that the Earth is not quite truly represented by an orange, at all events, unless the orange be slightly squeezed, *for the equatorial circumference is not a perfect circle, but an ellipse,* the larger and shorter equatorial diameters being respectively 41,852,864 and 41.843,896 feet. That is to say, the equatorial diameter which pierces the Earth from longitude 14° 23′ east, to 194° 23′ east of Greenwich, is two miles longer than that at right angles to it.*]

What then, on this scale, are the irregularities produced by the mountains and valleys; what the depth of the seas? The calculation is easy: Kunchinjinga and Gaurisankar, the giants of the Himalayan range, the highest known mountains of our globe, would only be elevated above the surface of a sphere of this size the $\frac{1}{2000}$th part of its diameter; Mont Blanc, about half as much. In chains of mountains of ordinary elevations, the hills and valleys would be unnoticeable. The greatest depth of the ocean would but indent the surface about $\frac{15}{10000}$th of an inch. Fig. 44 shows on a larger scale the relative dimensions of the height of the mountains, of the depth of the ocean, and the presumed thickness of the terrestrial crust. To obtain these dimensions, we have given the terrestrial globe a diameter of fourteen yards.

The inequalities of the surface of the Earth have often been compared to the roughness of the skin of an orange. It will be seen by the preceding statements how exaggerated this comparison is. Our globe, reduced to the dimensions of an orange, would not present to the naked eye any trace of projection or of depression, nor would the flattening be perceptible unless to a practised eye.

The study of the structure of the Earth—the configurations of its surface, its watercourses and seas, the geological constitution of its crust, and of the interior nucleus which composes it—presents the highest possible degree of interest, but its consideration would be out of place in the present volume.

We will only refer to the opinion, now generally entertained of its

* Mem. Roy. Ast. Soc. vol. xxix 1860.

primitive fluidity; because this hypothesis has its astronomical confirmation in the ellipticity which has been detected. It can be demonstrated by the laws of mechanics, that a fluid mass, animated by a movement of rotation, tends to take the form of a spheroid, flattened at the extremities of the axis around which the movement is effected.

Among the planets which we have still to explore, we shall find many which assume, like the Earth, a spheroidal form, but with a much more considerable flattening at their poles. Now, their movement of rotation is much more rapid.

One word more on the form and dimensions of the Earth.

We shall be able to form an idea of the curvature of the surface of the globe over a limited extent of country, from the following facts: A traveller who starts on a journey from a given place, descends more and more below the horizon of that place. When he shall have traversed a

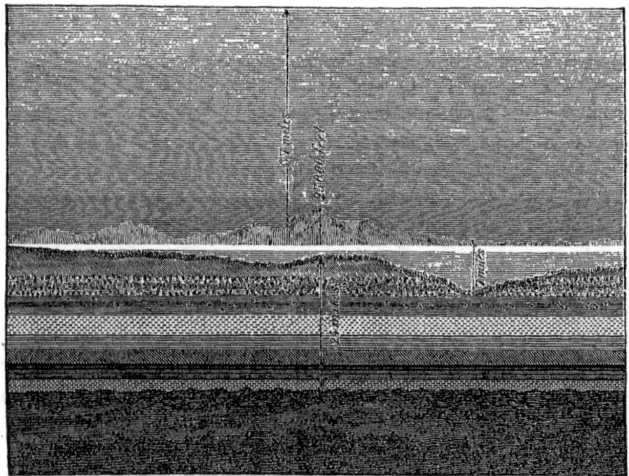

Fig. 44.—Comparative heights of Mountains; depth of the Seas, and thickness of the solid crust of the Earth.

degree (69½ miles), he will actually be more than a thousand yards below the horizon-plane of the point of departure, disregarding differences of level proceeding from irregularities of surface. The horizon of Paris, prolonged as far as Marseilles, would pass above that town at a height of over 18 miles.

By reason of the flattening of the poles, the circumference of a meridian is shorter than that of the Equator by nearly 42 miles.

It follows from the preceding numbers, that the surface of the Earth contains about 196,626,000 square miles. Of this immense surface the oceans embrace more than three-quarters; the remainder comprises the continents and islands. It is not a little curious that one hemisphere of the terrestrial globe comprises the land, whilst the other hemisphere is nearly entirely occupied by water. If we adjust a globe in such a way that London would occupy the centre of the visible hemisphere, and place it at some distance from the eye, we shall see on the hemisphere turned towards us the whole of Europe, Asia, Africa, North America, and part of South America. If we place ourselves on the opposite side, with our antipodes in the centre, we shall see a hemisphere, with the exception of New Holland and the lower point of Southern America, nearly entirely covered by the ocean, only here and there scattered with islands.

The figures in Plate V give an idea of the distribution of the solid and liquid portions of the terrestrial surface.

If, from the measures of the surface of the globe, we pass to those of its volume and weight, we arrive at numbers of which it is extremely difficult to form a definite idea, so much are they beyond our ordinary notions.

But we can conceive a cubic volume of which the length, breadth, and height, are each one mile—this we call a cubic mile; of such cubes our globe contains 259,800,000,000! Experiments and calculations, into the details of which we cannot enter in this place, have taught us the mean density of the materials of which our Earth is composed; we say *mean* density, because the density varies in different strata. [And, moreover, the solid crust may not extend to the centre.] This *mean* density then is such that the Earth weighs $5\frac{1}{2}$ times more than an equal volume of water would do.

Hence we have been able, as it were, to weigh the Earth, and we have found that it weighs 6,069,000,000,000,000,000,000 tons! This is exclusive of the weight of the air. Does then the air weigh anything? Yes; if we suppose it to extend only 37 miles [and we have positive proof that it extends much higher], it will weigh 5,178,000,000,000,000 tons; this however, is, after all, less than the millionth part of the weight of the Earth.

Such are the dimensions, such is the mass of the planet which serves us as a dwelling-place. What in comparison, and considered merely from a material point of view, are the works of man both individually and collectively?

Nevertheless, this sphere which appears to us so colossal, must, after all, be classed only among the smaller planets of our system, and is but a grain of sand compared with our central Sun, and a mere point lost in the immensity of the space comprised within the limits of our system. What idea then shall we have of the infinity of space, when, leaving our own system behind, as we shall shortly do, we shall see that even that entire system is but an atom of the Visible Universe?

We have just spoken of the total weight of the atmosphere: this is a point of mere curiosity. But the pressure which this fluid mass exercises on every inch of surface, on organised beings which are enveloped and move in it, on liquids and vapours, is of extreme importance to organised life and to the physical conditions under which life is possible. The density of the atmosphere, the law of decrease of this density, both in the lower and upper strata, are so many facts which have an intimate relationship with the temperature of the surface at different altitudes, with climate, and consequently with the distribution of animal and vegetable life on the surface of our globe.

Moreover, there is a relationship no less decided between the constitution of the gaseous envelope in which we live, and the way in which the solar rays traverse it.

Every one knows that a luminous ray proceeds in a straight line when it traverses a homogeneous medium, that is to say, one of unvarying density. The object which this luminous ray brings to our view under these circumstances is exactly where it appears to be.

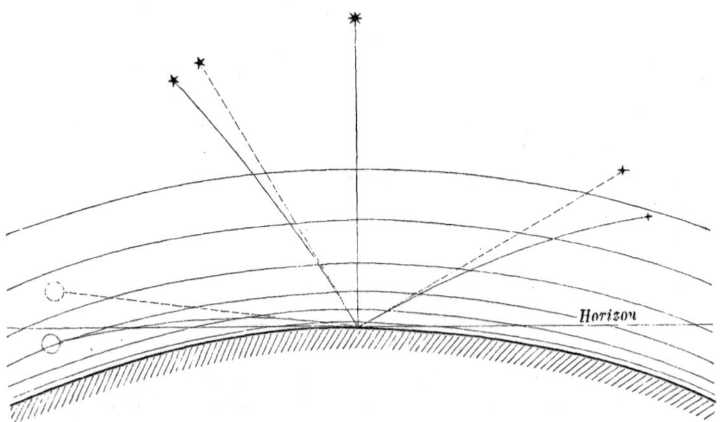

Fig. 45.—Atmospheric refraction, showing its effect on the apparent places of bodies in the celestial vault.

If, on the other hand, before it reaches us, the luminous ray has to traverse media of different densities, obliquely, each change of density makes it deviate from its direct route; and when it reaches the eye, the total deviation causes the object not to appear in the true direction which it occupies. Its apparent position does not then indicate its real position. This phenomenon of deviation takes place in the atmosphere, and is called *atmospheric refraction*. The importance of a proper knowledge of refraction in astronomical observations will be understood when we state that all celestial bodies are thus more or less displaced: the error resulting from this displacement is not the same in every part of the celestial vault: it is much more considerable when the strata traversed are thicker, or are

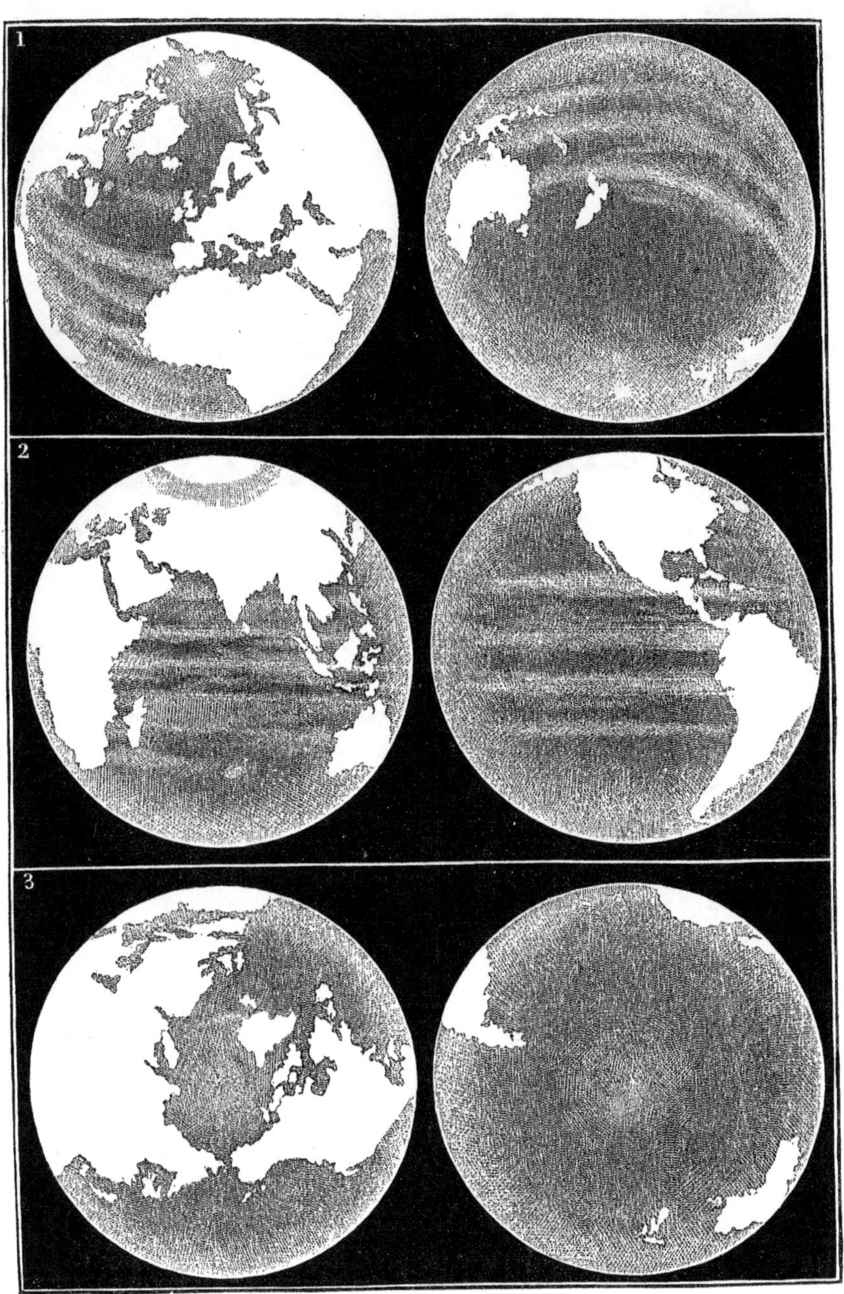

THE EARTH VIEWED FROM SPACE.

presented obliquely to the luminous rays; in other words, when the object observed is near the horizon.

The light proceeding from all celestial bodies in all their positions, therefore, is refracted unequally, and the effect of refraction is to make them appear higher than they really are; to place them nearer the zenith.

Hence follows a rather curious fact, namely, that the entire disks of the Sun or Moon remain still visible when they are mathematically set, that is to say, when they are really below the plane of the horizon. The duration of the day is then increased by refraction. The same phenomenon, of course, occurs both morning and evening.

Refraction still prolongs the day, even when the Sun has actually disappeared; the upper strata of the atmosphere are still illuminated, when the surface of the Earth is already in shade. They reflect earthwards a portion of this light, and by this means it is that the night passes into day, and day into night, by imperceptible gradations. Such is the cause of the morning and evening twilight. In fine, the duration of dawn and twilight varies according to the seasons and latitudes.

Not only is the apparent position of bodies altered by the refraction of the atmosphere,* but for the same reason, the form of those with large disks, as the Sun and Moon, is modified. Refraction, the intensity of which, as we have seen, increases as it approaches nearer the horizon, affects the lower limbs of these luminaries more strongly than it does the upper ones, so that the body, already flattened in its upper half, is still more so in the lower one. The sea-view represented in fig. 46 represents this curious phenomenon, which can be seen inland as well as at sea, at both the rising and setting of the Sun and Moon. Sometimes this deformation of the solar and lunar disks is far from presenting the regularity and symmetry which are seen in our drawing. The irregularities in the density of the lower strata of the air make the body appear under the most curious aspects.

[Recent researches into the action of the light-rays of the Sunbeam have made us acquainted with another class of facts of the utmost value to physical astronomers, as bearing upon the atmospheres of our sister Planets. Indeed, the more we study the marvellous mechanism of our own atmosphere, its manipulation, so to speak, of sunshine, the reinforcing, tempering and economising power it possesses by reason of the aqueous vapours which it contains, the more we see that, in spite of many ideas which it will be our duty to lay before our readers, it is not impossible that the actual heat experienced on the surfaces of all our Planets may be vastly different from

* Tables of corrections have been calculated for different heights. These tables enable us to find the true position of a celestial body, when the apparent position is known by observation. Nevertheless astronomers avoid observing too near the horizon, and wait until the body, by virtue of its diurnal motion, has attained its maximum height, at the moment of culmination, or of the upper transit of the meridian as it is called.

that to which they would be apparently entitled taking only their distance from the Sun into account. It has been proved that the heat which the Earth receives from the Sun is prevented from passing away again into space so rapidly as it otherwise would, by the aqueous vapour present in the atmosphere. Hence, though the proportion of heat received at Mercury, Venus, Jupiter, and Saturn, must correspond to their distance from the Sun, yet their atmospheres may be so constituted that the amount of heat actually retained may not greatly exceed or fall short of that which we enjoy. How far the excess or deficiency of direct heat may thus be compensated has not yet been demonstrated.]

Fig. 46.—Deformation of the Sun's limb at Sunset.

Let us add, in concluding our notice of the atmosphere with which our planet is surrounded, that, by diffusing on all sides the light of the Sun, it interposes a bright curtain between the celestial bodies and the Earth, which during the day veils, as it were, the starry vault, as the stars are not sufficiently bright in comparison to remain visible. Without this diffused light the sky, instead of presenting that azure tint which we all know so well, would assume the appearance of a black ground, on which the stars would appear and shine in broad daylight, as they do when a solar eclipse cuts off the source of its diffused light.

V.

THE EARTH.

MOVEMENT OF ROTATION.

Apparent Diurnal Movement of the Stars and Sun—Real Rotation of the Earth—The difference between Sidereal and Solar Days—The Rapidity of the Earth's Rotation varies with the Latitude.

MERCURY, Venus, and the Sun, the three celestial bodies the movement of which we have studied, each turns round one of their diameters; this is a phenomenon which seems general; and it has, in fact, been observed in all the bodies near enough and large enough to permit of their surface-markings being observed from the Earth.

The rotatory movement of the Earth was established before that of any of the other celestial bodies, and no one at the present time is ignorant of the manner in which it daily manifests itself to us.

At an hour of the morning, which varies according to the seasons, the Sun is seen to appear on the eastern horizon. By degrees it rises, its disk becomes entirely visible, and mounts gradually in the sky. At noon it reaches the highest point of its course; it then commences its downward course, describing in the second half of the day an arc symmetrical to the first; it then sets, and finally disappears in the evening in the west. The rotation of the Earth is thus shown during the day.

During the night the stars accomplish the same apparent movement. The entire heavens seem then to possess a movement of rotation, which always takes place from east to west round a line of constant direction, to which astronomers give the name of Axis of the World. This is no other than the axis of the Earth.

It was for some time imagined that the heavens themselves actually revolved in this direction; but in fact, it is our Earth which rotates in a contrary one, that is to say, from west to east, with an uniform movement, the duration of which for each rotation is a little less than four-and-twenty hours. Since the time of Copernicus and Galileo, the fact of the rotation of the Earth, demonstrated beyond all contradiction, has been universally admitted, as well as its annual translation round the Sun; but it is none the less true now, that there is still in some minds a singular confusion, arising from the fact that they cannot distinguish clearly between these two movements.

The rotation of the Earth, let us repeat, is a daily or diurnal movement, which is accomplished in about twenty-four hours, and which produces, besides an apparent revolution of the entire celestial vault, the phenomena of day and night.

Independently of this diurnal rotation, the Earth has a movement in space, describing round the Sun, like all the other planets, a nearly circular curve or orbit. This movement of translation gives rise to the year and the seasons, but it does not cause the apparent diurnal revolution of the starry sphere, nor the succession of days and nights ; it only modifies their relative length, as will be seen in the sequel.

Let us return to the Earth's movement of rotation.

We have before seen, that this movement is uniform ; that is to say, its angular velocity is constant. The proof of this uniformity is easy, and astronomers have satisfied themselves about it by measuring the length of

Fig. 47.—Comparative length of the sidereal and solar day.

the arcs described in the same time by different stars. These arcs always measure an equal number of degrees. If we note with precision the interval of time which elapses between two consecutive passages (or *transits*, as they are called) of the same star over the meridian of a place from night to night—between two successive culminations*—we shall know the exact length of an entire rotation.

It has thus been found to be about twenty-three hours fifty-six minutes.

This interval of time has received the name of a *sidereal day*,† whilst

* Astronomers call the vertical plane which passes through the north and south points of the horizon of a place, indefinitely prolonged into space, the meridian of that place. When a star passes the meridian it is at the highest point of its apparent diurnal course. Hence the name of *culmination* is given to this passage (or transit).

† The sidereal day is divided, like the solar day, into twenty-four hours. Sidereal and solar hours are divided into sidereal and solar minutes respectively, and so on: of this more presently.

the term *solar day* is reserved for the interval of time which elapses between two successive passages of the Sun over the meridian; this second interval is about four minutes longer than the first.

Between the solar day and the sidereal day there is a fundamental difference,—that of length. There is another not less important; whilst the length of the sidereal day is invariable, that of the solar day varies throughout the year.*

We must linger somewhat on the fundamental fact that the sidereal day is shorter than the solar one, as it is a fact which follows from the annual revolution of the Sun, and in truth is one of the best proofs of its existence. This proof is rendered evident by fig. 47.

We there see the Earth in two positions in its orbit, positions which we will suppose separated one from the other, by an interval of a sidereal day; that is to say, by an entire rotation.

In the first of these positions—that on the left, the meridian S O passes on one side through the Sun; it is noon for the parts of the Earth situated along this meridian in the illuminated hemisphere; on the opposite side it passes, let us say, through some particular star; it is midnight on that part of the Earth, situated along this meridian in the dark hemisphere.

Let us imagine an entire rotation accomplished, while our planet is travelling along its orbit. What will happen? This, namely, that the meridian considered in its first position, after having rotated round the Earth's axis, is again parallel to that position, so that if the Earth had remained fixed in space, the Sun and stars would reappear at the same time in the meridian; the sidereal day would have been of the same length as the solar day.

But the Earth is not so fixed, she has travelled onward to another point. The star, because it is situated at an infinite distance, is again found, after a complete rotation, in the meridian, which, on the illuminated side, no longer passes through the Sun. It is clear from the figure, that the Earth must still describe a fraction of its movement of rotation, in order to bring the meridian we have lettered S O, again to the Sun.

Thus, the difference in the length of the diurnal rotation of the Earth, and of the solar day, is explained by the annual revolution of our globe round the Sun, which is thus proved geometrically.

* Hence it is that astronomers, with a view of obtaining a convenient and uniform measure of time, have recourse to a *mean solar day*, the length of which is equal to the mean or average of all the apparent solar days in a year. An imaginary Sun, called the 'Mean Sun,' is conceived to move uniformly with the real Sun's mean (or average) motion, and the interval between the departure of the mean Sun from a meridian, and its succeeding return to it, is the duration of the mean solar day. Clocks and chronometers are adjusted to mean solar time, so that a complete revolution (through twenty-four hours) of the hour-hand shall be performed in exactly the same interval as the revolution of the Earth on its axis with respect to the mean Sun.

As the time deduced from observation of the *true* Sun is called 'true' or 'apparent' time, so the time deduced from the *mean* Sun, or indicated by the machines which represent its motion, is denominated '*mean* time.'

Since the Earth has the form of a sphere, and turns with an uniform angular velocity round an ideal line of invariable direction, there ought to result from this movement different rates of movement for the various points of its surface.

At the two poles this velocity is *nil:* but from the poles to the Equator it increases constantly, as the radii of the circles described by the different points along a meridian,—or, in other words, the distance from the axis of rotation,—increase as these points are nearer the Equator.

In twenty-four hours, the circle described by a part of the globe, situated in the latitude of Paris, is entirely traversed, as is that parallel to it, in the latitude of Reikiawitz in Iceland, or, finally, in the latitude of Quito on the Equator itself. These circles are of very different lengths. Hence very unequal real velocities. These velocities are, at Reikiawitz, 221 yards; at Paris, 333 yards; and at Quito (on the Equator), 507 yards a second; or 450,682 and 1038 miles an hour respectively.

How is it then, that, carried with such rapidity, we do not ourselves perceive our movement? It is because the entire bulk of the Earth, atmosphere, and clouds, participate in the movement.*

This constant velocity, with which all bodies situated on the surface of the Earth are animated, would be the cause of the most terrible and general catastrophe that could be imagined, if, by any possibility, the rotation of the Earth were abruptly to cease. Such an event would be the precursor of a most sweeping destruction of all organised beings.

But the constancy of the laws of nature permits us to contemplate such a catastrophe without fear. It is demonstrated that the position of the poles of rotation on the surface of the Earth is invariable. It has also been asked whether the velocity of the Earth's rotation has changed, or, which comes to the same thing, if the length of the sidereal day and that of the solar day deduced from it have varied within the historical period? Laplace has replied to this question, and his demonstration shows that it has not varied the one hundredth of a second during the last two thousand years.

* Who was that ingenious inventor who, seriously or otherwise, suggested that we should utilise the Earth's rotation as the most rapid mode of locomotion at once the most simple and economical that could be conceived? This was to be accomplished by rising, in a balloon for instance, to a height inaccessible to aërial currents. Then the balloon, remaining immovable in this calm region, would simply await the moment when the Earth, rotating underneath, would present the place of destination to the eyes of the travellers, who would then descend. A well-regulated watch, and an exact knowledge of longitudes, would thus render possible travelling from east to west, all voyages from north to south, or from south to north, naturally being interdicted. This suggestion has only one fault; it supposes that the atmospheric strata do not participate in the movement of rotation of the solid part of the globe.

The inventor did not remark that on the hypothesis of an immovable atmosphere, while we rotate at London with a velocity of 333 yards a second, there would result a wind in the contrary direction ten times more violent than the most terrible hurricane. Is not the absence of such a state of things a convincing experimental proof of the participation of the atmospheric envelope in the general movement?

VI.

THE EARTH.

REVOLUTION ROUND THE SUN.

The Year—Dimensions of the Earth's Orbit—The Seasons—Difference in the Length of Days and Nights, according to the Seasons and Latitudes—Zones and Climates.

THE movement of the Earth on its axis manifests itself to us, as we have seen, by an apparent revolution of the whole heavens in the space of a day.

By a similar illusion, the Sun seems to describe in a year, round our planet, an orbit, which, in reality, is traversed by the Earth round the Sun.

The exact time of this revolution, in mean solar days, is 365 days 6 hours 9 minutes 10 seconds and 75 hundredths of a second. In this interval of time, the Earth sets out from one part of its orbit, travelling in a direction from right to left, or from west to east, and regains the point of departure; accomplishing thus, without end, and always in the same manner, its movement of translation.

This orbit is not a circle, but an ellipse, of which the Sun occupies one focus. The mean radius of the orbit, that is to say, the mean distance of the Sun from the Earth, measures 95,298,000 miles.

The velocity of the Earth's passage along this immense curve is variable, but its average rate is 33,290 yards a second, or 68,000 miles an hour. So that, we not only rotate every instant, describing arcs round the terrestrial axis, the length of which, varying with the latitude, may reach as high as 500 yards a second; but we are again carried through space with a velocity which exceeds 19 miles a second.

If we contemplate the dimensions of the globe and the enormous mass of the Earth, the imagination will be confounded in the presence of the gigantic ball, which glides through space with such rapidity.

A calculation of two contemporary philosophers, Helmholtz and Mayer, will perhaps give an idea of the prodigious movement which impels our globe. These physicists have endeavoured to ascertain what amount of heat would be developed by the abrupt stoppage of the Earth in its orbit. They have found that this heat would suffice to melt the entire globe, and to reduce a great portion of it to a state of vapour.

If it be true that the Earth moves thus around the Sun relatively fixed, in proportion as she travels in one direction along a certain portion of her orbit, the Sun itself will seem to describe an equal arc in a contrary direction when we consider the arcs described separately; but if we compare, in fig. 48, the real curve described by the Earth with the apparent one described by the Sun, we shall see that the directions are the same. So that, as the proper movement of the Sun, which causes the delay of its passage across the meridian, or, what is the same thing, the inequality of the solar and sidereal days, takes place from west to east, the real movement of the Earth is also effected in the same direction. It is for want of comprehending this, that some authors with rather imaginative minds have cried out against the fallacies of astronomers.

The Sun, then, must move each instant across the starry vault of the heavens, and its centre will coincide from day to day with different stars. During the day this displacement is not perceptible when no exact measure of the position of the Sun is taken. But we need only recognise that, corresponding with the displacement of the Sun during the day, there must be an analogous movement of the heavens during the night, to

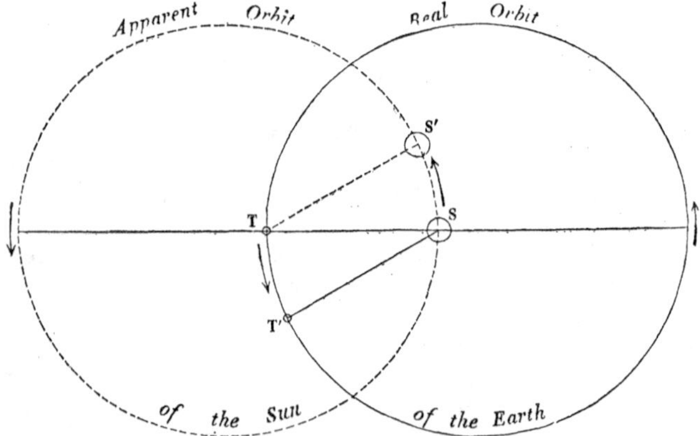

Fig. 48.—Real Orbit of the Earth, and apparent Orbit of the Sun.

comprehend that the aspect of the constellations must vary throughout the whole year. It is in consequence of the translation of the Earth, that the heavens defile progressively over the horizon of any given place, or if not the whole heavens, at least that portion of them which are brought by the diurnal movement above that horizon.

The length of the year, that is to say, of the interval of time which elapses between two successive passages of the Earth through the same point of its orbit, is about $365\frac{1}{4}$ mean solar days. How many entire rotations on its axis does our globe execute during that time?—$366\frac{1}{4}$; in other words, if the number of the solar days of the year is $365\frac{1}{4}$, the number of the sidereal days is exactly greater by unity.

This is a direct consequence of the yearly revolution of the Earth, combined with its diurnal movement of rotation. The same phenomenon, which at first seems paradoxical, is produced in all the other planets, whatever the number of rotations accomplished during a complete revolution round the Sun, and whatever the durations of their sidereal and solar days.

Let us recall the fact that after an entire rotation, the Sun, which at the point of departure passed the meridian at the same time as a given star, lags behind about four minutes. At the following rotation there is further delay, which is added to the preceding one; and so on, until the annual revolution being terminated, matters are found in the same state as at the beginning. Now, if in order to return to a coincidence of the Sun with the star which serves as a means of comparison, the Earth has effected 366 rotations on its axis, the star will have passed 366 times over the meridian, whilst the Sun, exactly behind one transit, will have returned to the meridian once less, that is to say, only 365 times.

Let us now pass to other phenomena of great interest to the inhabitants of the Earth,—phenomena which have their source in the double movement of our planet.

From one day to another, the inhabitants of the same place—let us rather say the inhabitants of the same latitude—see the Sun ascend above the horizon to variable heights. The points in the east and west, where the radiant body rises and sets, change their places; the Sun at noon attains a greater or less altitude, and, the length of its daily sojourn above the horizon gives to the days and nights their variable and unequal lengths: hence different temperatures and diversified climatic conditions; hence, *the Seasons.* On the other hand, these conditions themselves change, not only in both hemispheres of the Earth, but even in the same hemisphere, according to the latitude of the place considered. Hence, *climate,* frigid zones with long days and nights, temperate zones, torrid zones, and the regions nearest to the equator, which have each year two summers and two winters, and where the length of the day is always equal to that of the night.

The astronomical reason of all these phenomena rests in the simultaneous movements of the Earth. But there is a circumstance which influences their succession in a dominant manner, and on which we must now fix our attention.

Let us glance at Plate V, which represents the orbit of the Earth and the position of our planet in various points of it. We shall see that the axis of rotation is neither perpendicular to the plane in which the orbit lies, nor in this plane, but that it forms with it a certain angle (66° 32′ 42″) nearly equal to two-thirds of a right angle. This inclination is constant during the whole year, or at least varies only between very small limits: besides this, the axis always remains parallel to itself. It is the parallelism of the axis which accounts for the nearly invariable position of the celestial pole above the horizon in each locality, provided we bear in mind the nearly infinite distance of the stars from the Earth.

Among all the positions which the Earth occupies in its orbit, there are four principal ones, diametrically opposed, in pairs, which influence in a most important manner the relative lengths of day and night, and the seasons; these are the two equinoxes and the two solstices.

Here are the order and dates of their succession:

Towards the 21st of March, the Earth is at the first of these points, called the Spring Equinox; then comes the Summer Solstice, about the 21st of June; the Autumnal Equinox, near the 22nd of September; and, lastly, the Winter Solstice, which generally falls on the 21st of December. Each of these points marks the commencement of the season after which it is named. The precise epochs of these four fundamental positions vary each year, but within a somewhat restricted limit, as may be seen from the following table:—

COMMENCEMENT OF THE FOUR SEASONS.

	1865.				1864.			
SPRING . . .	March 20,	8^h	19^m	a.m. . .	March 20,	2^h	15^m	p.m.
SUMMER . . .	June 21,	5	25	a.m. . .	June 21,	10	55	a.m.
AUTUMN . . .	Sept. 22,	7	1	p.m. . .	Sept. 23,	1	8	a.m.
WINTER . . .	Dec. 21,	1	13	p.m. . .	Dec. 21,	6	59	p.m.

When the Earth is at one or the other of the equinoxes, the plane of the Equator prolonged passes precisely through the centre of the Sun. The two poles of the planet are then symmetrically placed with regard to the radiant body, and the circle of separation of the illuminated hemisphere and the dark hemisphere lies in a meridian.

It results from this particular position, that each part of the Earth, whatever its latitude, describes half its daily journey imposed on it by the Earth's rotation in shade, and half in sunshine. Fig. 49 will explain this.

Thus, at the time of the equinoxes, the length of the day is equal to that of the night all over the world. The Sun remains twelve hours above the horizon of each place, and twelve hours below it.

From the spring equinox to the summer solstice, the Earth traverses the portion of its orbit which corresponds to the months of April, May, and June. Its axis remaining always parallel to itself, one of its poles,—the North Pole,—is turned more and more towards the Sun; during the same period, the South Pole, on the contrary, is turned more and more away from it. The day and night become more and more unequal in length, and this inequality attains its maximum towards the 21st of June (fig. 50).

The circle of separation of sunshine and shade having travelled farther from the Pole, it follows that the lengths of the nights of the northern hemisphere has continuously decreased; the day, on the contrary, increasing, and in much greater proportion as the places are more distant from the equator.

The southern hemisphere has, during this period, experienced inverse phenomena; at the equator only has the day continued to be equal with the night.

From the 21st of June to the 22nd of September, the Earth passes

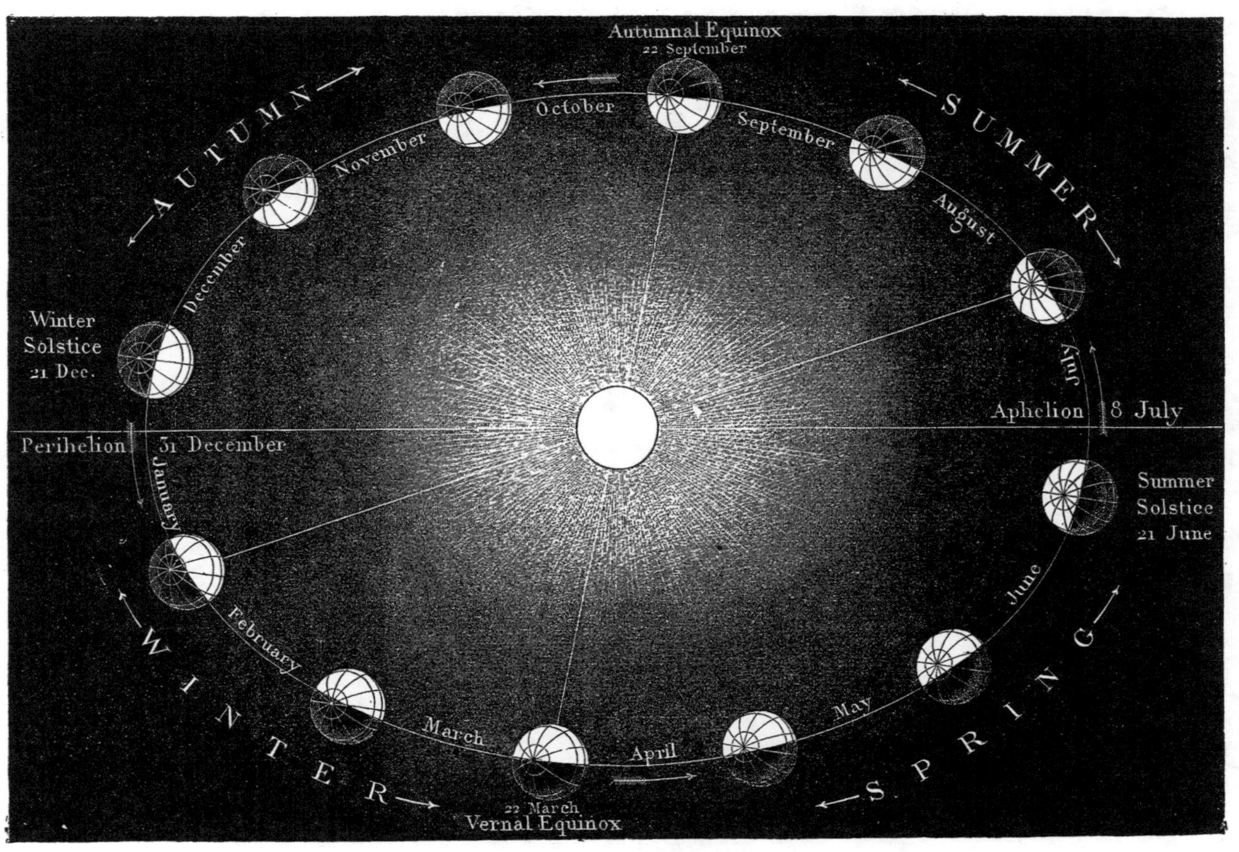

ORBIT OF THE EARTH.

from the summer solstice to the autumnal equinox. During the second period, the North Pole is turned towards the Sun, while the South Pole remains plunged in darkness; the alternations of day and night present, in inverse order, during the summer the same phenomena as during the spring.

Thus, for six months, the regions near the North Pole have continually seen the Sun above the horizon, those of the South Pole have always had it below. Hence, in their icy deserts, here a day of six months, there a night of six months, tempered, it is true, by a continual twilight. During each twenty-four hours, in consequence of the diurnal rotation, the Sun thus describes a curve, which grazes the horizon, though

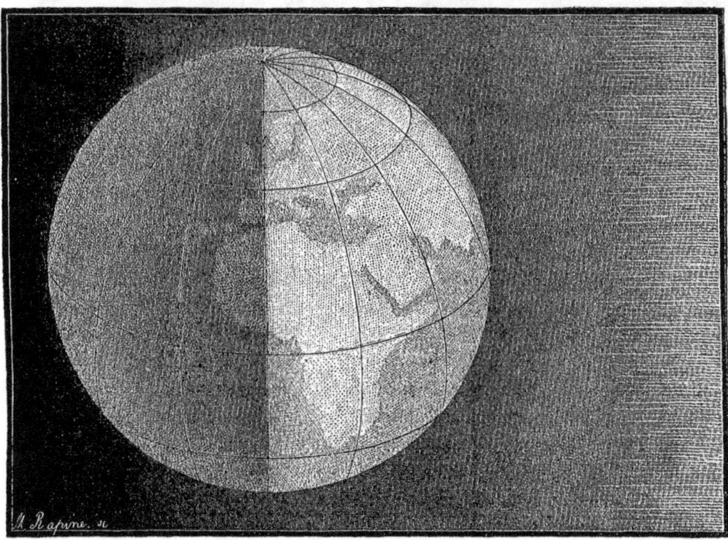

Fig. 49.—The Earth at an equinox. Equal day and night all over the world.

not quite parallel to it, describing a double spiral, which rises constantly until the 20th of June, and afterwards descends to the beginning of autumn.

If the course of the Earth during one half of the year has been well understood, it will be easily seen how, during the other half, similar phenomena will occur in symmetrically inverse order. At the autumnal equinox we shall have equal days and nights throughout the Earth. The autumn and winter of the northern hemisphere will be the spring and summer of the southern one. The same differences in the relative lengths of night and day will also be presented: the only difference arising from the different length of the corresponding seasons in the two hemispheres.

A word now on the inequality of seasons.

Let us once more insist upon the fact, that the orbit of the Earth is not a circle, but an ellipse, and that the Sun is not in its centre, as would appear from Plate VI, but in one of its foci. More than this, the major axis of the ecliptic—which is the astronomical term for the orbit of the Earth—does not exactly pass through the solstices. In fig. 51 their non-coincidence has been purposely exaggerated.

We shall immediately comprehend from an inspection of the diagram that winter ought to be the shortest, and summer the longest, of the four seasons: the two other seasons are of intermediate lengths, spring being the longer of the two.

This would be true, owing to the fact of the inequality of the arcs

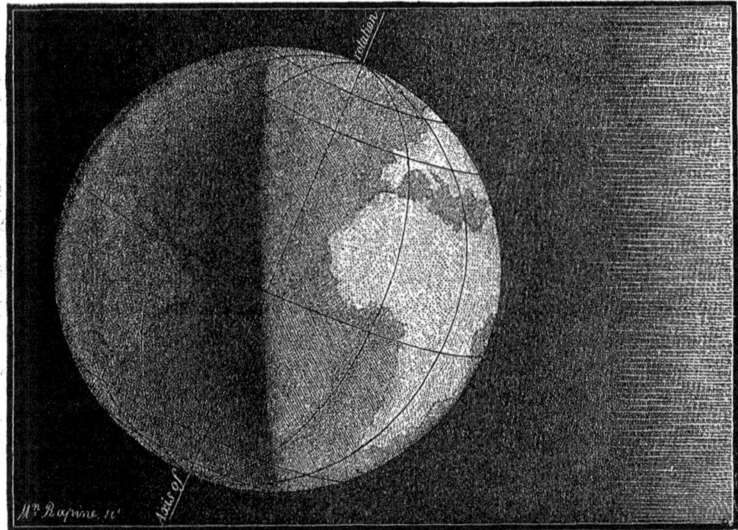

Fig. 50.—The Earth at a Solstice. Unequal day and night.

traversed alone even if the Earth travelled with a constant velocity over every portion of its orbit. But the inequality is largely increased from another cause.

We shall see in the sequel, that every planet moves round the Sun with variable velocities, and more rapidly as it approaches the common focus. The Earth, therefore, moves less quickly during the summer season of the northern hemisphere than during the winter season, and this again contributes to increase the difference in their lengths.

The mean durations of the seasons in the order in which we have spoken of them, are as follow:—

	Days.		Days.
Spring	92·9	Autumn	89·7
Summer	93·6	Winter	89·0

The first two seasons, as do the two others, differ only but seven-tenths of a day, that is to say, 16 hours 48 minutes. But the spring exceeds the autumn by 3 days 4 hours 48 minutes, and the summer is longer than the winter by 4 days 14 hours and 24 minutes.

At the extremities of the larger diameter (or 'major axis,' as it is called) of its orbit, the Earth is nearest to and most distant from the Sun. It is at its maximum distance, or *aphelion,* in the first days of July, and at its maximum distance, or *perihelion,* a few days after the winter solstice—about the 31st of December.

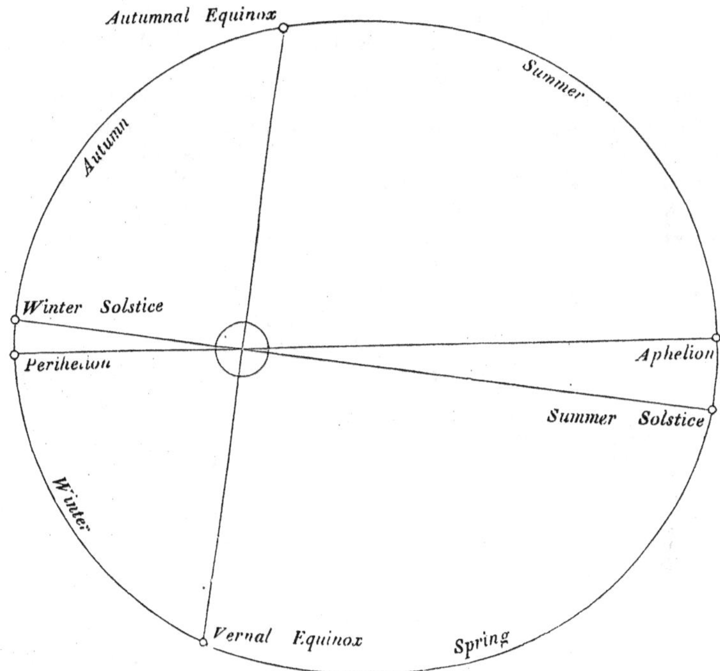

Fig. 51.—Orbit of the Earth. Varying length of the different Seasons.

Thus the Sun is farther from us during the spring and summer than during the autumn and winter of the northern hemisphere, a circumstance which proves that it is not to the decrease of the Sun's distance that we must attribute the increase of heat, or rather of temperature, of any given place on our hemisphere.

During the northern spring and summer the Sun remains above the horizon of a place longer than in autumn and winter; the length of the day exceeds more and more that of the night as the solstice is approached. That is the most important cause of the increase of temperature during the summer months. Another cause, not to be passed over, is the height of the Sun above the horizon. The diurnal arc described by the great light-giver rises higher and higher from the time of the spring equinox to the summer solstice, returning in inverse order from the summer solstice to the autumnal equinox. The rays that he sheds on the divers points of the northern hemisphere traverse the atmosphere less obliquely than in winter and autumn; and the intensity of the heat received is much greater when this obliquity is less, a circumstance easily explained by the smaller thickness of the atmospheric strata traversed. Besides, if we leave the thickness of the atmosphere out of the question, the obliquity of which we speak is in itself a cause why the heat received should be less considerable.

The preceding explanation applies to the southern hemisphere during the seasons of autumn and winter, which are to it what spring and summer are to us. And as the Sun is, besides, at a less distance from the Earth, the intensity of the heat is greater: as also in the winter seasons of the same hemisphere, the cold is more intense. In the long run, however, these inequalities are compensated, and the mean temperatures of the year are nearly the same, both north and south of the Equator.

We speak here merely of the purely astronomical influences, leaving out of the question the thousand local disturbing causes which may exist or arise; the climate of a place being a resultant of them all. From this point of view, it is also easy to comprehend why the maxima of heat and cold do not fall exactly at the solstices, but some little time after, in July and January. From the 20th of June, the Earth, already warmed by the days of spring, continues to receive from the Sun during the day more heat than it radiates during the night: its temperature, therefore, still increases. On the other hand, towards the 21st of December, the Earth, already chilled by the long nights of the autumnal period, still continues to get colder, because it loses more heat during the night than it receives during the day.

More than this, the seasons are very different for every point of the same hemisphere. From the equator to one or the other pole, we pass by imperceptible degrees from an intense heat to an extreme cold. On the surface of the globe, five zones or climates are distinguished, which succeed in the following order:

The Torrid Zone, which comprises all the regions north and south of the equator, where the Sun is vertical twice a-year; it is bounded by the tropics in lat. 23° north and south.

Two *Temperate Zones*, which extend on either side the tropics to a latitude of 66°. To all the countries comprised in these zones, the Sun never rises to the zenith, and the limit of its least meridional altitudes is comprised between 66° and the horizon.

Lastly, two *Frigid* or *Circumpolar Zones.* Within the limits of these zones the Sun descends to the horizon and disappears even beneath it, here for one day, there for six months. It never rises to an altitude greater than 46°, and at the pole itself the maximum altitude is but half that quantity.

The superficial areas of these zones are very unequal: the torrid zone embraces $\frac{40}{100}$ths of the total surface of the terrestrial spheroid; the two temperate zones, $\frac{52}{100}$ths; and, lastly, the two frigid zones, $\frac{8}{100}$ths. Thus the two temperate zones, the most favourable to human habitation and to the development of civilised life, comprise more than half the extent of the Earth; the frigid zones, which may almost be termed uninhabitable, from a very small fraction. In these quantities both land and sea are included.

The various phenomena which we have just considered depend directly upon the rotation of the Earth and its annual movement of translation in space. The length of this rotation, or of the sidereal day, the inclination and the parallelism of the axis, the duration of the year, the form of the orbit and its real dimensions, are so many elements which combine to produce them. If all, or some of them, were to change, the days and nights, the seasons and climates, would change also, and the consequences which would result to the conditions of life on our planet would produce, either in the long run, or suddenly, the most profound modifications and most considerable changes.

We have already seen that the length of day has remained invariable during the historic period. The same may be said of the year. But if the form of the terrestrial orbit and the inclination of the axis of rotation vary imperceptibly, the periodical variability of these elements is confined within narrow limits, so that, except for unforeseen and improbable catastrophes, the astronomical conditions of our planet can be considered as invariable. The source of the light and heat, and even of life, on our own globe, and on the other planets, no doubt, is being gradually dried up, but calculation has shown that millions of years must elapse before the gradual weakening of its rays can modify perceptibly our terrestrial climates.

When we come to study the other members of our system, we shall soon find the most curious variety in the astronomical—and therefore climatic—conditions of each of them. Governed by identical laws, they, nevertheless, will present to us the most wonderful diversities, in the same manner as the organic kingdom constructed with a small number of simple elements on a plan, the unity of which is, day by day, becoming more evident, furnishes, nevertheless, to the intelligent admiration of man a considerable number of various substances, and a still more prodigious number of genera, species, and varieties.

VII.

THE MOON.

Phases of the Moon—Its Movement round the Earth—Dimensions and Distances; recent measures, Effect of Irradiation in the Case of the Moon—Rotation—Rotation and Revolution performed in the same time—The Moon's Orbit always Concave to the Sun—The Moon's Rotation on its Axis.

Owing to its successive and periodical appearances and disappearances, —the variety of form of its luminous portion, and the varying illumination due to its light, the Moon is certainly the body which above all others gives the greatest diversity to the aspect of our nights. The white and soft light with which it inundates the landscape is the delight of all those who are sensible to the beauties of nature; poets have not failed to introduce it in their descriptions, and painters in their pictures. But the absence or the presence of the Moon in the starry vault is not less interesting to astronomers than to artists—to science than to poetry. It is only from the astronomical point of view that we shall here speak of it.

When the Moon shines in the heavens, when even she shows us a small part only of her illuminated side, the brightness of her light effaces the smallest stars visible to the naked eye. The number of stars thus rendered invisible—put out as it were, is much more considerable as the Moon approaches the full; then the glimmer of the Milky Way is lost in the diffused light of the atmosphere, and only the most brilliant stars remain perceptible to the unaided vision. Moreover, as the time during which the Moon is visible, increases with its brightness, it soon becomes impossible for astronomers to make delicate observations, at least if they do not propose to study the Moon itself, or the more brilliant stars.

Happily for observers, the Moon disappears periodically from the heavens, and thus restores to the celestial vault, when the air is clear and calm, all its splendour and magnificence. The great proximity of the Moon to the Earth, which it incessantly accompanies in its revolution round the Sun, makes it one of the most interesting among the celestial bodies. What can be, in fact, more curious than this little system in the vast system of the solar world; this Earth in miniature, perpetually executing round our globe a series of movements entirely similar to those that our Earth in turn performs round the Sun. Further on, when we shall see other planets, accompanied also by satellites, and forming with some so many little systems, we shall more easily be able to appreciate the phenomena which these satellites present to observers situated in the primary body, if we in this place study those presented by our own Moon and Earth in detail.

Let us begin with our satellite as it appears to the naked eye.

Two facts are known to every one; first, that in an interval of twenty-nine or thirty days, the Moon is seen under a series of appearances which are called *phases*, which are reproduced periodically in the same order. Second, that it always presents the same face to the Earth, in such a manner that we only see one of its hemispheres; the other half of the lunar globe remaining for ever invisible to us.

Now, these two facts are proofs positive, that the Moon has two motions, one of revolution round the Earth, another of rotation on itself. These two movements, by a curious coincidence, are made in the same interval of time. If we follow the Moon through the course of one of its revolutions, we shall be convinced of the reality of these movements, and of the fact, that they are both performed in the same time.

We know that there is a *New Moon*, when our satellite is invisible, both during the day and night. It then occupies in the heavens a place very near the Sun, presenting to us its dark hemisphere; for this reason, and because also it is lost in the splendour of the solar rays, it is invisible to us.

About four days elapse between the disappearance of the Moon in the morning in the east, and its reappearance in the evening in the west, a little after the setting of the Sun; the instant of new moon occurs precisely in the mid interval; after this epoch it gradually emerges from the Sun's rays.

We see it first (Plate VI) in the form of a very slender crescent, the convexity of which is turned towards the point below the horizon occupied by the Sun; at this time the obscure portion of the Moon's disk is seen very distinctly. The delicate transparent tint which renders it visible is known under the name of Earth-shine, or *lumière cendrée*, and is due to the reflected light of the Earth.

Drawn along, apparently, by the diurnal movement, the body soon sets below the horizon. The next day, the same appearance again occurs, but already the crescent is less delicate, the luminous portion larger, and the Moon somewhat farther from the Sun, setting also a little later.

The fourth day after the new Moon, the form and appearance of our Satellite, which sets only three hours after the Sun, is that which is represented in the second figure of Plate VI. The Earth-shine is still very perceptible, although it diminishes more and more, to disappear altogether at the following phase, which is called the *First Quarter*.

Between the seventh and eighth days of the Moon, it is presented to us under the form of a semicircle, partly visible during the day, as this time the diurnal movement only causes it to approach the horizon some six hours after sunset. In the preceding phase, the various features spread over the Moon's surface were visible. But at this time these markings are distinguished with great clearness on the luminous half circle, more especially at the division between the illuminated and the dark portion called 'the terminator.'

Between the first quarter and the *Full Moon*, seven days again elapse, during which the form of the illuminated part approaches nearer and nearer to that of a complete circle; the Moon rises and sets later and later, always turning towards the west the circular portion of its disk.

Lastly, it presents to us the whole of its illuminated portion, about fifteen days after the new Moon; then the hour of its rising is nearly that of the setting of the Sun, which in turn rises when the Moon sets. It is midnight when it attains the highest part of its course, or, in astronomical language, when it passes the meridian; then the Sun itself passes the lower meridian under the horizon; that is to say, relatively to the Earth, the Moon is precisely opposite the Sun.

Fig. 52.—Last phase of the Moon.

From the time of full Moon to the next new Moon, the circular form of the visible portion of the disk diminishes by degrees, and at last puts on the appearance first noticed,—that of a slender crescent. But this time the convexity is turned towards the east; in fact, the half circle bounding the illuminated portion naturally always faces the Sun.

In the mid interval which separates the full Moon from the following period, at the *Last Quarter* we get a phase like that presented at the first quarter, but inversely situated. In this second part of the lunar period, or *Lunation*, the apparent position of the Moon in the Heavens approaches nearer and nearer that of the Sun. Towards the last days, it precedes its rise by very little, until it is again lost in its rays, finally to disappear, and then to again appear as a *new moon*, at the commencement of the next lunation. The Earth-shine again becomes visible, after the last as before the first quarter, and becomes more apparent as the visible portion of the disk diminishes.

This succession of the phases of the Moon, which is constantly reproduced, and always in the same manner, results evidently from the movement of the Moon round the Earth. This will be easily understood from fig. 53, and it will be there seen why the phases of successive lunations are precisely the same, when the Sun, the Earth, and the Moon occupy the same relative positions; while if we referred the place occupied by the Moon to the stars, in two or more similar and consecutive phases, it would be seen that it does not occupy the same point of the sky—that it does not even traverse the same constellations; a fact which results not only from the movement of the Earth in its orbit, but from the variations of the movement of the Moon in hers. In a little more than 29½ days,*

* 29 days, 12 hours, 44 minutes, 3 seconds.

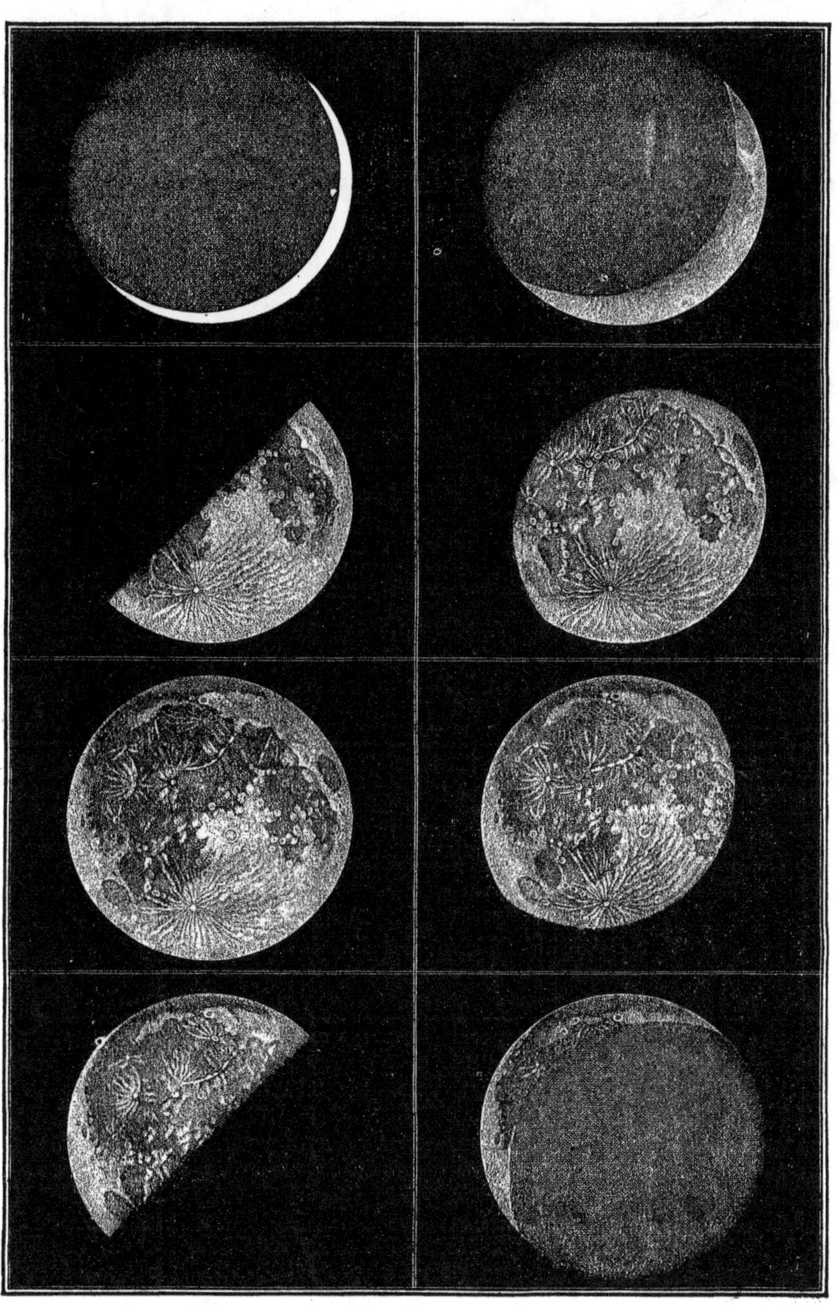

THE PHASES OF THE MOON.

the Moon returns to occupy the same position with respect to the Sun and Earth; this marks the length of the lunar month or lunation.

It must be added, that this length exceeds by more than two days the time of a complete revolution of the Moon in its orbit, that is, of its

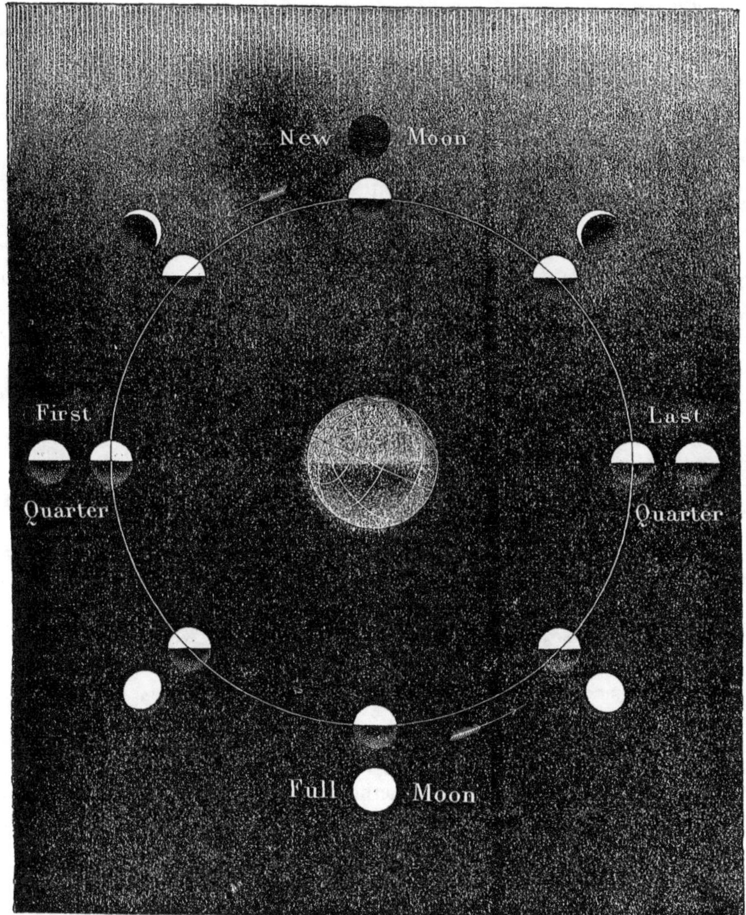

Fig. 53.—Orbit of the Moon. Explanation of the Phases.

sidereal revolution.* This difference is due to the movement of the Earth round the Sun.

Considering the Earth as fixed, the orbit which its satellite describes round it is an ellipse of which the Earth occupies one of the foci. The

* The Moon's sidereal day is 27 days, 7 hours, 43 minutes, 11½ seconds long.

distance, therefore, which separates the two bodies, varies incessantly, and as a consequence, the apparent diameter of the Moon varies also, but inversely; a fact proved by observation, and especially by micrometrical measures of its disk.

The figures here given will enable us to form a precise idea of these variations.

The greatest distance of the Moon from the Earth is about $64\frac{3}{4}$ times the equatorial radius of our globe. When the Moon is at this distance, it is said to be in *apogee*. At the time of *perigee*,* that is to say, its least distance, it is not further from us than $57\frac{3}{4}$ of these radii, whence it results that its mean distance is $60\frac{1}{4}$ radii, that is, nearly equal to the 400th part of the distance of the Earth from the Sun, which is, as we have seen, in round numbers 24,000 terrestrial radii. We must then make a chain of thirty globes, equal in size to the Earth, touching each other, and in a straight line, to reach the Moon. [According to the latest researches of Professor Adams, the mean distance of the centres of the Earth and Moon is 238,793 miles, and this we know to be correct within a very few miles.]

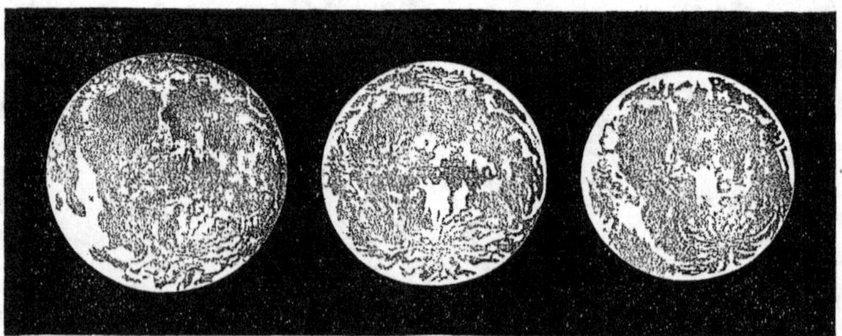

Fig. 54.—Apparent dimensions of the Moon at its extreme and mean distances from the Earth.

After we have passed the heavens under review, we shall return to the interesting question of the distances of the different bodies, and we shall attempt to give an idea of the methods which enable us to determine them. We shall then see how, relying on very simple geometrical principles, and aided by instruments of great perfection, astronomers can measure the distances of some bodies near the Earth, infer from these measures the distances of the other members of the system, and, finally, gauge the profundities of the ethereal vault without quitting the movable stand-point where Nature has placed us.

The mean distance which separates us from the Moon is but little more than nine times the circumference of the Earth at the Equator. There are many sailors who have, in their voyages, traversed as long a

* *Apogee*, from ἀπὸ, *from*, and γῆ, *the Earth*. *Perigee*, from περὶ, *near*, and γῆ.

distance — one that an express train would easily accomplish in less than 300 days.

The apparent magnitude of the lunar disk varies, as we have seen, with the distance of the Earth from the Moon: but even on the surface of our globe, and at the same instant, the diameter of the disk does not appear of equal magnitude to all observers. It appears smaller to an observer who sees the Moon rising or setting at the horizon than to him who sees it at the zenith.

To the former, the distance A L of the Moon is nearly equal to the actual distance of the centres of the two bodies. To the latter, on the contrary, the distance A′L, is equal to the first diminished by the terrestrial radius, or by the sixteenth part of the total distance.

Hence it follows, that as the Moon is carried by the Earth's rotation from the horizon of any place to its zenith, that place is actually brought nearer to it some 4000 miles. The lunar disk should, therefore, appear

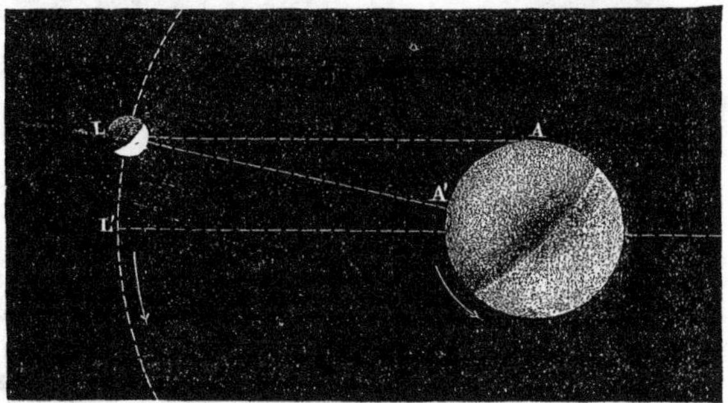

Fig. 55.—Difference of the distances of the Moon, at the horizon and at the zenith.

to us larger at the zenith than at the horizon; but, singularly enough, by a pure illusion, the opposite effect obtains; at the rising and setting of the Moon its disk appears to us enormous; it seems, on the contrary, to diminish insensibly when it is removed from the objects situated on the horizon and mounts the starry sky.

We have remarked, that this is a pure illusion. To be convinced of it, it is sufficient to take exact measures when the Moon is in the two positions; if this be done with rigorous exactness by means of an instrument, to make the result independent of our ordinary way of judging, it is entirely opposite to the appearance. How is this singular phenomenon explained?

By an error of our judgment. When the luminous disk of the body is near the horizon, it seems placed beyond all the objects on the surface of the Earth interposed between us and it, and therefore more distant than at the zenith where nothing separates it from us. Now an object which keeps the same apparent dimensions is to us, by virtue of the instinctive habits of our eye, by so much greater as it appears to be more distant.*

We next come to the real dimensions of the Moon. These are readily determined, since we know, with the most wonderful exactness, both the apparent magnitude of the Moon's diameter and our distance from it.†

[A recent discovery of very great interest shows us that in the case of the Moon, the word 'apparent' means much more than it does with regard to other celestial bodies. Indeed, the brightness of the Moon causes our eyes to play us false. As is well known, the crescent of the new moon, by an effect of irradiation, seems part of a much larger sphere than that which it has been said, time out of mind, to 'hold in its arms.' We now learn that the bright portion of the Moon, as seen in our measuring instruments as well as with the naked eye, covers a larger area in the

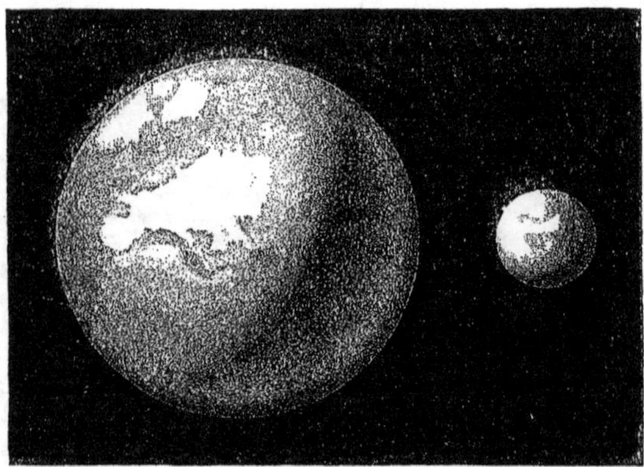

Fig. 56.—Comparative dimensions of the Earth and Moon.

field of view of the telescope, than it would do if it were not bright. This has recently been proved by measuring the *dark moon.* Our readers may possibly ask how this has been done? Well, we get an approach to a dark moon when we observe the occultation of a star at the dark limb; and under these circumstances, it has been recently found by the Astronomer Royal, that in the main, all such occultations go to show that the limb of the Moon is not so far away from its centre, in other words, that its radius is not so great, as we thought. Again, in total or annular eclipses, we deal entirely with the dark Moon, and Mr. De La Rue's exquisite photographs of the total eclipse of 1860 entirely endorse the results of the twenty-five years' labours at Greenwich.

* If, when the disk of the Moon appears at the horizon with these illusory dimensions, it is looked at with the naked eye through a tube, or the hands placed tubewise, the illusion disappears; it does not seem then to exceed in size the lunar disk seen at the zenith.

† The diameter of the Earth being 1, that of the Moon is 0·2729.

The Astronomer Royal's result is, that the Moon's angular diameter hitherto received, is too large by 2″. Mr. De La Rue's, that it is too large by 2″·15. And this quantity must be looked upon as a 'telescope-fault.'

Hansen gives the mean angular semi-diameter of the Moon as 15′ 33″·36. We must now call it 15′ 31″·36; and its diameter, which was formerly supposed to be 2160 miles, or a little more than a quarter of the diameter of the Earth, must be reduced by something like seven miles. We shall have something else to say on this discovery when we refer to the question of the lunar atmosphere.]

Supposing the Moon spherical, the total surface of its two hemispheres, visible and invisible, is equal to a little less than the thirteenth part of the surface of the terrestrial globe; that is to say, that it measures 14,568,000 square miles. Lastly, if from its superficial extent we pass to its volume, we find that the Moon is scarcely more than the forty-ninth part of that of our Earth, or 5,200,000,000 cubic miles.

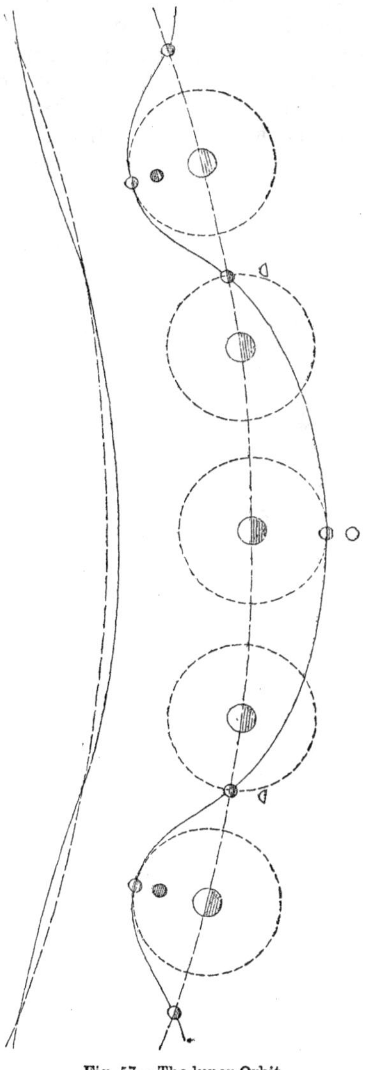

Fig. 57.—The lunar Orbit.
1. Amplified. 2. In its relative dimensions.

The Moon's motion, we have before remarked, is effected along an elliptical curve or oval, at one of the foci of which is the Earth. Such would be, indeed, the lunar orbit if the Earth remained fixed in space. But it is well known, that, far from remaining at the same spot, our globe itself travels round the Sun in an orbit the mean radius of which is four hundred times greater than that of the Moon. As the Moon accompanies the Earth in its stupendous journey, keeping the relative positions necessitated by its circum-terrestrial movement, it follows that the form of its real orbit is much more complicated than a simple elliptic one would be.

[Its real path consists of a series of curves, or rather of an epitrochoidal curve, *concave throughout to the Sun,* and intersecting the orbit of the Earth twice during a lunar month.]

But the total departure of the Moon from the Earth's orbit, does not exceed the $\frac{1}{400}$th part of the radius; so that, if drawn to scale on a large sheet of paper, it would be almost impossible to detect the departure of the Moon's orbit from that of the Earth.

If the Earth and the Moon, instead of moving simultaneously along their orbits in such a way as to occupy the five positions indicated in

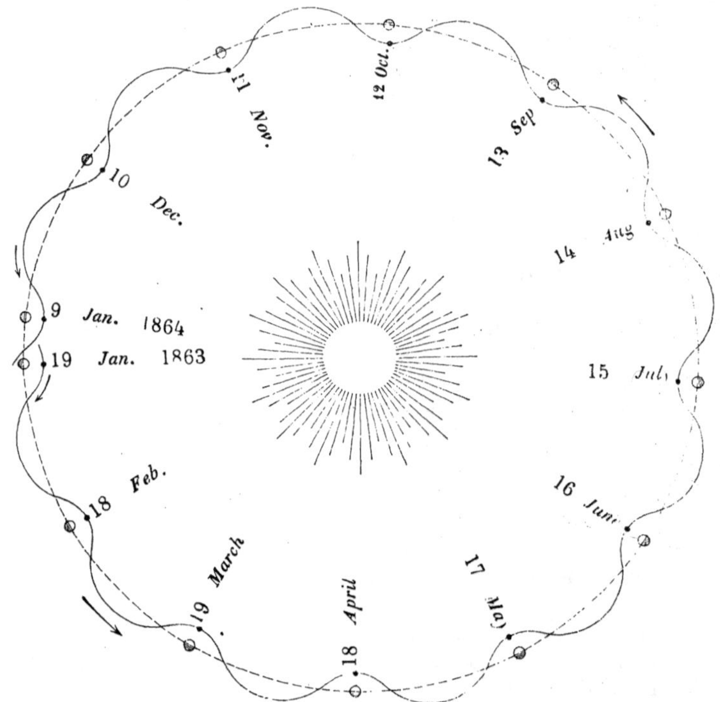

Fig. 58.—The curve described in a year, by the Moon round the Earth.

fig. 57 [which will be understood to be grossly exaggerated, nor is the real orbit precisely represented], were simply, the first to remain at rest, and the second to circulate in its orbit round our globe; it is easily seen that the appearances presented would be precisely the same, at least if we compare the positions of the two bodies with regard to the Sun.

It is in this manner that a person, on the deck of a vessel in motion, believes that in walking round the mast, he is moving in a circle, whilst the curve which he describes on the surface of the sea, is a sinuous curve, the form of which is analogous to that of the real orbit of the Moon. In reality, the path which this person traverses is more complicated still; and to obtain its real form, we must take into account his proper movement, the movement of the vessel on the sea, the double movement of rotation and of revolution of the Earth itself. It will be seen later on, that the Sun moves also through space, drawing with it the Earth, the other planets, and their satellites, whence follow, for the orbits of all those bodies,

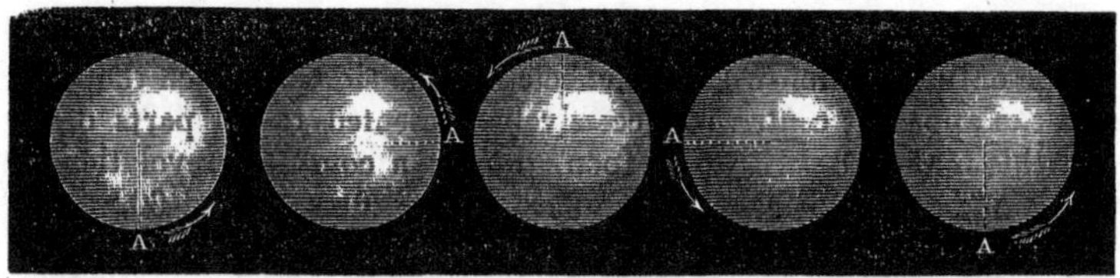

Fig. 59.—Rotation of a sphere, supposed to be at rest.

sinuous curves, the degree of complexity of which varies with the number of the various motions with which they are animated.

We must recollect that it is the phases of the Moon which have demonstrated to us its revolution round the Earth. This movement, added to the fact, that the Moon constantly presents the same hemisphere to the Earth, proves that it turns also on itself, in a period of time exactly equal

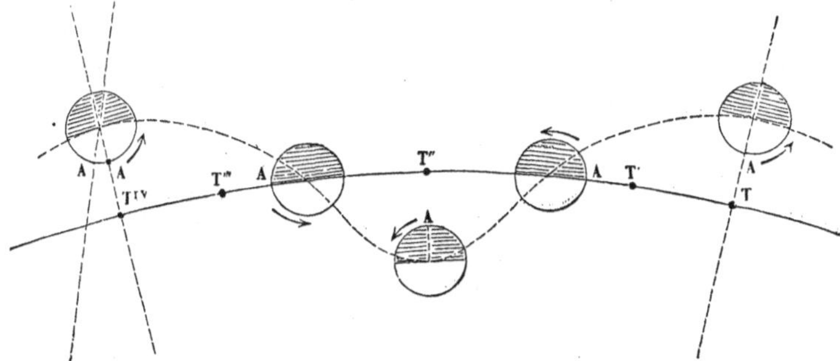

Fig. 60.—Actual movement of rotation of the Moon in the interval of a lunation.

to the length of its sidereal revolution, that is to say, in about twenty-seven days and a third.

In speaking of the movement of rotation of the Moon on its axis, it is right to anticipate an objection often made, proceeding from a false idea sometimes conceived of the rotatory movement of a movable body. 'Since the Moon,' it is said, 'always presents the same face to us, it cannot turn on itself. If it turned on an axis or pivot, it ought to present us all its sides successively.' Such is the objection simply put.

To solve this difficulty, let us examine into the phenomena. What is a movement of rotation? How is it known that a body, a sphere for example, does rotate? and how is it known when an entire rotation has been completed? Evidently, when the sphere has presented successively one of its sides towards every point of the space which surrounds it. If we divide the entire rotation into four periods, the accompanying diagram will show how the sphere would be seen at the comencement of each of those periods, to an observer at rest.

Now, if the sphere, during the exact time that it takes to effect this rotation round its axis, executes a movement of revolution round the observer, whether the observer be at rest or not, it is none the less evident, that the entire rotation would be effected, if the side, of which the point A forms the apparent centre, is successively presented to all parts of space. Now, this is the case with the Moon, during a complete revolution in its orbit, as may be seen from the comparison of figures 59 and 60.*

We shall see further on, that it is not rigorously true to affirm that the Moon always presents the same face to the Earth; our satellite, in fact, undergoes what astronomers call a *libration*, or apparent swinging from east to west, and another from north to south.

These librations result from causes of which more anon; it is sufficient here to know that they do not modify the fundamental fact of the equal duration which characterises the two simultaneous movements of rotation and revolution of the Moon. More than this, the central point of the disk is not precisely the same to observers situated in different parts of the Earth.

We shall now proceed to describe the Moon as it is seen in the telescope, and to inquire into what is known of its physical constitution, a question of absorbing interest from so many points of view.

VIII.

THE MOON.

PHYSICAL CONSTITUTION.

The Aspect of the Moon to the naked eye—The Seas or *Maria;* Mountains—Principal Mountain Chains—Volcanic character of the Lunar Mountains—The Craters Tycho and Copernicus—Walled Plains—Annular Mountain-ramparts—Craters, Peaks, and Cones—Terrestrial Analogies—Heights and Dimensions of the Mountains—Bright Rays; Centres from which they emanate; Mr. Nasmyth's Explanation of them—Rilles or Furrows—Suggested Explanations; Recent Labours of Schmidt.

THE world which we are about to explore,—somewhat in detail, thanks to its small distance and to the great power of our modern optical instruments,—though like the Earth in some general characters, totally differs from it in others. If an inhabitant of the Earth were transported to the

* The sphere in fig. 59 occupies five positions in inverse order to those of the Moon in fig. 60. But this does not affect the demonstration.

surface of the Moon, he would be at once struck with the strangeness of the scene. The configuration of the surface, every corner broken up and rugged, here circular cavities, there elevated peaks; the aspect of the heavens; the bright stars shining in the broad day; the sharpness of the lights and shades; the eternal silence which reigns in these desolate regions; the extreme temperatures, now glacial, now torrid; the singular life-conditions of organised beings—if it be that life is possible there; all would unite to upset the most familiar notions.

Nevertheless, whatever may be the contrasts between the lunar world and our own globe, it will be seen that the variety which is manifested with a marvellous richness, here, as in all the works of Nature, is the effect of but a small number of causes, or rather the result of simple modifications of elements which are really the same for all celestial bodies. The simplicity of the laws which govern astronomical phenomena causes the unity of plan of the whole solar system to shine forth with incomparable clearness.

The full moon in a very pure sky allows the naked eye to distinguish the principal dark and bright features—features, the permanence of which, as we have before remarked, shows that the same face—the same hemisphere, is always turned towards us. From east to west, going northward, several large greyish spaces are distinguished, the uniform aspect of which contrasts with the southern half of the disk, which is almost entirely covered with a multitude of bright points. The north-east and north-west borders of the disk are terminated by whitish and bright marks, whilst the central regions participate in the general tone of the southern part.

Of old the name of 'seas' was given to the large dark spots which mottle the Moon's northern hemisphere and part of the southern one, towards the west and east. The name is still retained, although its literal meaning must not be attached to it. The lunar seas are now regarded as plains, whilst the most brilliant portions are principally mountainous regions. We will now briefly describe both, asking the reader to follow the description on Plate VII, which represents the full Moon as seen with the aid of a telescope of small magnifying power.

[As the image of a celestial object seen in a telescope is inverted, the top of the plate represents the South Pole, and the bottom the North Pole, the right hand is east and the left hand west.]*

To begin with the Seas, or *Maria*.

Close to the western border or limb, is seen a greyish spot, of an oval form, plainly visible by contrast and isolated in the brighter portions: this is the *Mare Crisium*—the Sea of Crisis. Between this spot and the centre of the disk, a large dark space divided by a kind of sharp promontory has

* [A slight change has been made here in the translation, at the suggestion of the Rev. T. W. Webb, to accommodate the expressions 'east' and 'west' to the general usage of selenographers, according to which the terms employed in describing the relative position of objects upon the disk, imply a reversion of E. and W., compared with their situation on terrestrial maps, but not an inversion of N. and S.]

been named the Sea of Tranquillity,—*Mare Tranquillitatis.* It throws out towards the south two portions the largest and most western of which is the Sea of Fecundity—*Mare Fecunditatis,* whilst the other, smaller and nearer the centre, is the Sea of Nectar—*Mare Nectaris.*

If now, leaving the Sea of Tranquillity, we travel northward, we find the Sea of Serenity—*Mare Serenitatis,* which is traversed throughout its length by a very bright and nearly rectilinear ray, which gives to the whole spot the form of the Greek capital *phi,* Φ. The Sea of Vapours—*Mare Vaporum,* is a prolongation towards the centre of the disk of the Sea of Serenity.

Lastly, the Sea of Rains—*Mare Imbrium,* of round form, the largest of all those which have been named, forms the northern termination of the series of greyish spots to which the incorrect appellation of seas is still applied.

We must now re-descend towards the east to find the Ocean of Tempests—*Oceanus Procellarum,* of which the outlines, not very well defined, are lost toward the south in the Sea of Moistures—*Mare Humorum,* and the Sea of Clouds—*Mare Nubium,* at a short distance from a luminous point, whence diverge in all directions whitish rays of great length.

This last point, which may be considered as the centre of the mountainous regions which surround the southern pole, is no other than Tycho, one of the most important elevations of the visible hemisphere of the Moon.

If now, in order to observe the details of the lunar disk, we employ a telescope of considerable magnifying power, we shall be astonished at the prodigious multitude of small spots of annular form, round or oval, which cover the entire surface. At the time of full Moon, these features are not well defined, which arises from the position of the visible hemisphere with regard to the Sun.

If, on the contrary, we choose for the time of observation the epoch of the first or last quarter, the portions near the edge of the illuminated portion of the Moon will appear eaten into cavities, surrounded by circular ramparts, throwing their shadows away from the Sun, here towards the interior, there towards the exterior of the cavity. More than this, along the whole line of separation of the light and shadow called the *Terminator* the interior of the annular cavities seems quite black, whilst here and there luminous points show themselves detached from the illuminated portions of the Moon. These spots indicate mountain-tops or ranges, which accordingly as we observe at the first or last quarter, receive the rays of the Moon's morning sun, or the sunset rays which linger after the lowlands are in shade.

Such are the mountains of the Moon. Figs. 61 and 62 give an idea of the appearance of the mountainous regions with which our satellite is overspread.

The chains of mountains, as distinguished from the annular mountain-ramparts, are not relatively numerous in the visible hemisphere of the Moon.

THE FULL MOON.

The greatest number is found in the northern part of the disk. The Alps, the Caucasian range, and the Apennines, are the most remarkable. This last chain separates the Seas of Serenity and of Vapours from the Sea of Rains, which is surrounded as with a belt of semicircular form by the three ranges we have named. It is well seen in the drawing of the full Moon which we have before given. We may also notice the Carpathian and the Oural mountains, which separate the Ocean of Tempests from the Sea of Rains, and the Sea of Clouds; the Taurus mountains, west of the Sea of Serenity; the mountains Dörfel and Leibnitz, at the southern pole; the Pyrenees, which separate the Seas of Fecundity and of Nectar; towards the west, the Altai mountains, near this last sea, which extends 276 miles from north to south. [The Altai mountains approach closely to the arc of an ellipse, the major axis of which is terminated on the south by the crater Piccolomini, and on the north by the twin craters Isidorus and Capella, which are in a very disturbed region. The monster craters, Catherina, Cyrillus, and Theophilus, are just within the north-east portion. There are two concentric crater ranges separated by plains between the Altai mountains and the *Mare Nectaris.*] Lastly, we have the Cordilleras and the mountains D'Alembert, near the western limb. The range of the Apennines, the most considerable* of these mountain-chains, is, however, but 373 miles in length.

SOUTH.

WEST. EAST.

NORTH.

Fig.		
1. Clavius.	8. Orontius.
2. Maginus.	9. Sasserides.
3. Longomontanus.	10. Lexell.
4. Pictet.	11. Gauricus.
5. Saussure.	12. Wurzelbauer.
6. Tycho.	13. Hell.
7. Nasireddin.	

It is impossible not to recognise the eminently volcanic character of the lunar mountains. All the crust of our satellite is pierced by craters which indicate an innumerable series of volcanic eruptions, some limited to a small space, others embracing an immense area on the surface. We give in the margin a rough sketch of Tycho, and the region lying to the west and south, deduced from the large photograph (38 inches in diameter) of Warren De La Rue. We also give (fig. 61) an additional

* [Or rather 'the most familiarly known.' It is surpassed in height, and possibly in extent, by the ranges (if they are not annular ramparts in profile) of the S. and E. limbs.—T. W. W.]

representation of crateriform abysses lying to the south-east of the same crater, as observed and drawn by Mr. Nasmyth, who is second to none

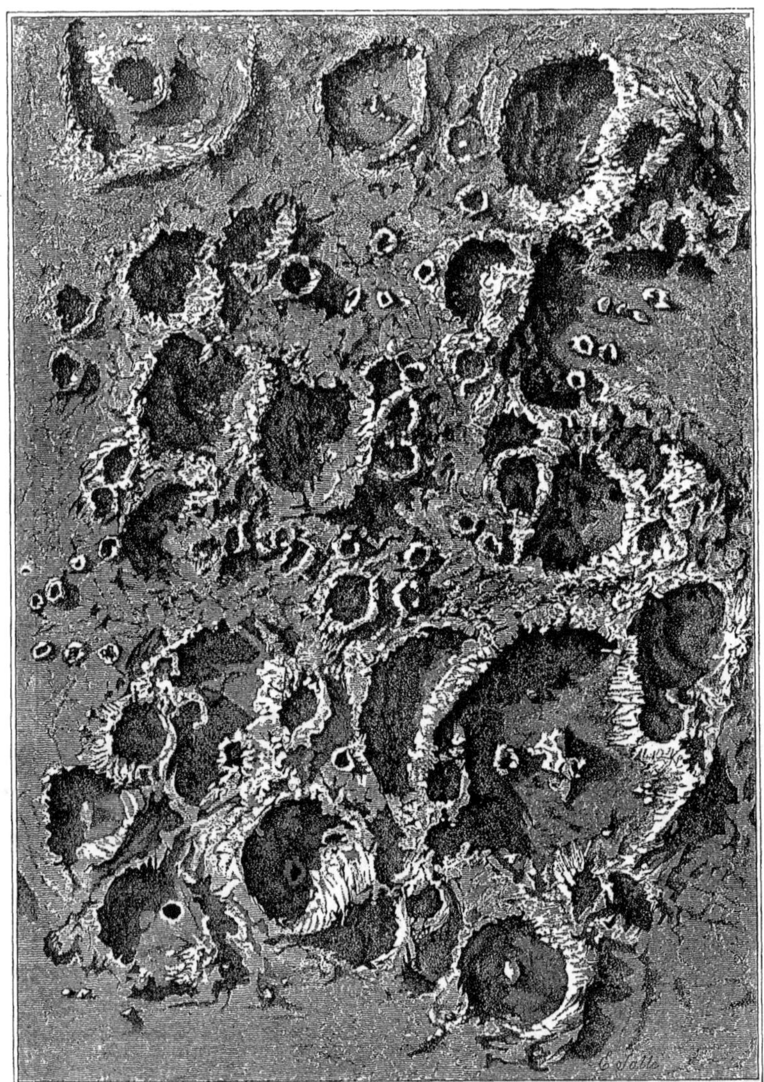

Fig. 61.—Mountains of the Moon. View of the region to the south-east of Tycho. (Nasmyth.)

in his hand-drawings of the lunar surface. The circular rampart of

Copernicus, one of the largest annular mountains of the Moon, near the Carpathians, is represented in detail, in fig. 62, as observed by Mr. Nasmyth. We are indebted to the kindness of the late Admiral Smyth for permission to present it to our readers, it forms one of the illustrations of his magnificent work, the 'Speculum Hartwellianum.'

The regions near Tycho are formed, as may be seen, of a number of craters of various dimensions, some of which are hollowed out in the form

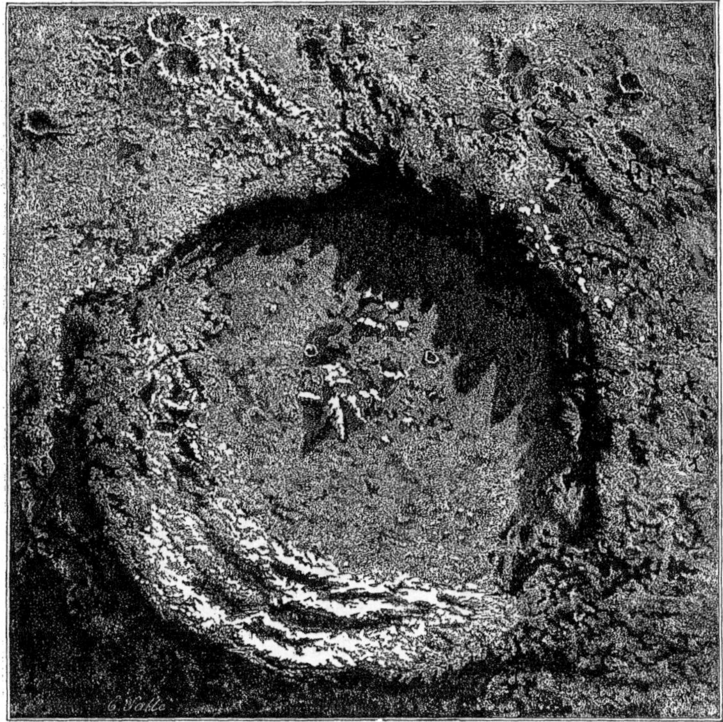

Fig. 62.—The Mountains of the Moon. View of Copernicus. (Nasmyth.)

of cups or funnels, whilst the largest present the appearance of circles with flat bottoms, at the centre of which rise peaks of pyramidal form. One crater is situated at the centre of a circle which it surpasses in altitude; whilst at the bottom of a crater with very elevated ramparts, and here and there in the winding valleys which the circular walls leave between them, other small volcanic vents scarcely rise above the neighbouring surface. The irregular edges of all these openings bear testimony to the convulsions, rents, and dislocations, which the surface of our satellite underwent at the period when these eruptions took place.

The crater-wall of Copernicus shows numerous traces of *débris* ejected from the crater. Many other lunar mountains present, like Copernicus, evident traces of stratification [or terraces, if the common geological meaning of 'stratification' should be thought to imply aqueous action], doubtless owing to the deposits of successive eruptions.

If the volcanic mountains of the Moon present great analogies to the volcanoes of our Earth, they are also distinguished by very marked characters. If the preceding drawings be compared with the topographic

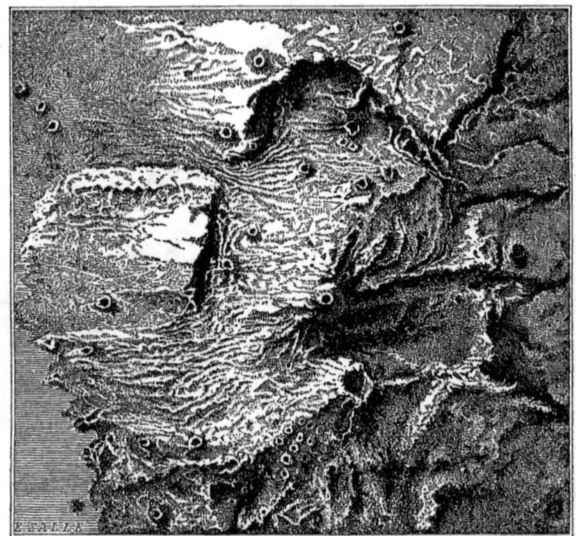

Fig 63.—The Peak of Teneriffe and its Environs. (Piazzi Smyth.)

view (fig. 63) of the Peak of Teneriffe and its environs, the differences, as well as the analogies, will be seen. Whilst the craters on the Moon have enormous dimensions,—the diameter of Ptolemy being 114½ miles, of Copernicus 56, and of Tycho 54,—the dimensions of the terrestrial volcanoes are relatively extremely small. The relief of the Isle of Bourbon (fig. 64), which we reproduce as constructed by a French engineer, M. L. Maillard, shows large depressions of nearly circular form, at the points where cones of eruption originally existed. It is, perhaps, to sinkings of this nature that the circles of the Moon are due.* But it must be

* [The elevation, however, of the surrounding ramparts seems to render this improbable, as they would on such a supposition indicate the former existence of cones of most disproportionate dimensions. The exterior of the lunar craters seldom exhibits any approach to a vertical position.—T. W. W.]

remarked that the exterior profile of these volcanic cavities has not that sharp vertical direction which on our satellite distinguishes the walled craters, the elevation of the sides of which is less on the exterior than in the interior, as demonstrated by the differences in the lengths of the shadows cast. The bottom of a lunar crater is generally of lower level than that of the plain which surrounds it; the contrary always holds in terrestrial volcanoes. It is true that this observation applies to the walled craters of great extent, rather than to the craters properly so called.

If, as is believed, the generally rounded form of the lunar features, including even the chains of mountains, proceeds from the action of the interior strata against the solidified crust of the spheroid—if the walled

Fig. 64.—Topographical relief of the Isle of Bourbon. (Maillard.)

craters are but craters of upheaval, would it not be allowable to attribute the interior depression of the bottom of the circular cavities to a kind of sinking of the half-liquid matter?*

* [Mr. Mallet, in his fourth report on Earthquake Phenomena (*Reports of the British Association for the Advancement of Science*, 1858, p. 61) shows that the Earth's surface is to a great extent divided into saucer-shaped shallow depressions, bounded by flowing coast lines, generally uniting in closed curves; and on p. 64 he says: 'Enough, however, has probably been stated, to indicate that, viewed on the broadest scale, the surface of our globe consists, as respects its solid surface, of a number of saucer-like depressions, when large having also *convex* central areas, all having plain

One word now on the heights of the lunar mountains.

The highest of all are in the vicinity of the southern pole: there Dörfel is found, the summit of which attains 8897 yards in altitude; the mountains Casatus and Curtius are 7078 and 7409 yards high, and the annular crater Newton is 7951 yards deep. 'The excavation of this last is such,' say Beer and Mädler, 'that neither Earth nor Sun is ever visible from a great part of its bottom.'

In the northern regions, considerable heights are also found: Calippus and Caucasus, Huygens in the Apennines, respectively attain 6193 and 6020 yards in height. The central peaks and cones are nearly always much surpassed in height by the annular mountains. The central cone of Tycho measures 5000 feet, and that of Eratosthenes, at the extremity of the chain of the Apennines, rises to a height of 5250 yards above the floor of the crater.

To sum up; of the 1095 heights measured by Beer and Mädler, 39 are higher than the summit of Mont Blanc, and 6 are more than 6500 yards high.

Thus the vertical heights of the lunar mountains are not less astonishing than their lateral dimensions. We have already mentioned the immense walled plains of Ptolemy, Copernicus, and Tycho; but among the craters, properly so called, it is not rare to find some which have diameters of 100 to 120 miles. The crater of Schickard is one of the most considerable on the visible hemisphere of the Moon: its diameter is not less than 133 miles; and the height of one of the mountains which lies near it is 3500 yards. It is a noteworthy circumstance that an observer placed at the centre of the immense walled plain Schickard, would not be able to see the summit even of the lofty irregular wall which surrounds it on every side. The distance would be so great, that the borders of the crater would lie below the visible horizon. How different to the craters of our own volcanoes, which, as remarked by Humboldt, would at the distance of the Moon, be scarcely visible with the telescope.

To complete this description of the Moon, which is at once geological, geographical, and topographical, we must mention two singular phenomena which have much puzzled astronomers. We refer to the luminous bands and rilles.

In Plate VII there are seen to start from two principal points, Tycho and Copernicus, two series of luminous rays, which, traversing the moun-

outlines approximating to extremely irregular ovals, or other closed curves, and *bounded by mountain chains*, or more rounded or flat-topped ridges, or elevations of the solid sphere, greater or less;' and also on p. 61 he says, 'Each great oceanic saucer, bounded by the existing continents and their fragmentary outliers, presents an almost continuous fringe around, of *mountain chains* and *volcanic* foci.' It is not a little remarkable, that the lunar volcanic vents are arranged similarly to those of the terrestrial, either breaking out on, or even piercing through, the walls of the smaller craters, or arranged in lines across the larger lunar depressions, not unlike the sub-oceanic linear volcanic ranges of which Mr. Mallet speaks.—W. R. B.]

tains and the neighbouring features, extend to a great distance from those brilliant centres. More than a hundred luminous bands thus diverge from Tycho. Aristarchus, Kepler, and the Carpathians, [and many other centres] present analogous systems, which appear to converge, intermingle, and connect themselves together. These singular appearances, of which no entirely satisfactory explanation has yet been given, are only visible about the time of the full moon. They disappear at the other phases; and this seems to show that they are not due to elevations, as then they would cast shadows, and would be, on that account, clearly visible. Do they owe their origin to the eruptions of the volcanoes which occupy their centre? If this be so, would they not seem to be crevices filled subsequently with reflecting and crystalline substances, thus forming on the surface of the Moon so many slightly luminous threads?

[Mr. Birt has informed us, that some of these rays are visible under all illuminations; one, which emanating from Tycho, crosses a crater on the north-east of Fracastorius, is not only distinctly visible when the terminator grazes the west edge of Fracastorius, but is even brighter as the terminator approaches it. Those emanating from Tycho are evidently different in their character from those emanating from Copernicus, while those from Proclus form a third class. The rays from Copernicus and Kepler appear to be very similar. One very bright ray, in the neighbourhood of Geminus, we have found to coincide in direction with a ridge of high land.

Mr. Nasmyth has been able to produce somewhat similar appearances on a glass globe by filling it with cold water, closing it up and plunging it into warm water. This causes the enclosed cold water to expand very slowly, and the globe eventually bursts, its weakest point giving way and forming a centre of radiating cracks similar to the fissures—if they be fissures—in the Moon.]

According to the views of an eminent observer, M. Charconac, the ring-formed mountains, or craters, which form points of divergence for these radiations, are of relatively recent origin. At the time of the eruption which produced these craters, the gaseous masses escaping by the new volcanic vents, or becoming precipitated, swept before them the pulverulent and whitish substances which covered the summits of the neighbouring craters of anterior origin, or in case of concentric divergence, the summit of the craters existing on the same spot; hence the long white bands which radiate from Tycho in the direction of meridians having this volcano for a common pole. This explanation of the singular luminous bands which radiate from Tycho, Proclus, Aristarchus, Copernicus, and Euler, may, perhaps, throw some light on the physical constitution of our satellite.*

The rilles differ from the luminous bands in that they are evidently

* [The enormous length and smoothness of these rays, together with their perfect uniformity of level, seem, however, to militate against any explanation which has yet been attempted.—T. W. W.]

formed of two parallel slopes, more or less steep, leaving a sort of sunken way between them. They appear bright in the full moon, and in the other phases as dark lines, one of the two ridges projecting its shadow on the bottom of the trench.

It was at first believed that these were ancient river-beds; but their form, often wider at the centre than at the extremities, their immense breadth, which sometimes reaches 1½ miles, and still more their depth, which varies between 450 and 700 yards, render this hypothesis untenable. Besides which, their length is relatively slight, being usually comprised between 10 and 125 miles. Lastly, one circumstance which is frequently observed, and which will show that it is not possible to consider them ancient river-beds, is, that many of them traverse mountains, and cut through the sides of high craters in such a way as to present the greatest diversity of level. Some of them are widened in parts, and form oval valleys; others again present a series of small craters, joined together.* We here reproduce (Plate VIII) from the beautiful map of Beer and Mädler two regions of the central mountainous parts of the Moon, which contain some of the most curious of these appearances.

Beer and Mädler, in their remarkable work 'Der Mond,' have added 70 to the list, and point out, as an important fact, the constancy of direction of the majority of them.† All these facts tend to show that these singular markings date from the last period of geologic change on the lunar surface, and are, therefore, posterior to the craters and ring-formations, as is proved by the *rainure* of Hyginus, which penetrates to the interior of this crater, breaking through its boundary wall.

* [They are not unfrequently met with in the interior of great walled plains, a fact, perhaps, of some selenological import.—T. W. W.]

† Schröter, Pastorf, Gruithuisen, and Lohrmann preceded the two German astronomers in these interesting discoveries.

[Dr. Schmidt of Athens has been most indefatigable in this department of lunar astronomy; he has discovered no less than 278 of these curious formations, making with previous discoveries 425, which he has arranged in classes; the order of discovery is as follows:—

From 1787 to 1801	Schröter discovered .	11
„ 1823 „ 1827	Lohrmann . . .	75
„ 1823 „ 1841	Mädler	55
„ 1847 „ 1848	Kenan	6
„ 1842 „ 1865	Schmidt . . .	278
		425

Mr. Birt has recorded an observation in which a rille appears to have been diverted from its course by *two* craters, and the same rille, in a further part of its course, is completely interrupted by another crater, as if the craters were of more recent origin.]

[In connexion with rilles, Mr. Mallet has in his report on Earthquake Phenomena, p. 62, this remarkable passage: 'A vast fissure (noticed by Humboldt), and marked by an almost continuous line of volcanic rents, extends in a direction nearly east and west, right across Mexico, between 18° and 19° lat. It is nearly 500 miles in length. Its main direction if produced, bears upon the volcanic island of Revillegigedo, and, as Humboldt also thinks, probably extends to Monna Roa in the Sandwich Islands. The Mexican extremity of this enormous crevasse, probably marks the continental end of one of the great dividing ridges of the sub-basins of the Pacific.' It would be desirable to know the *breadth* of this crevasse.—W. R. B.]

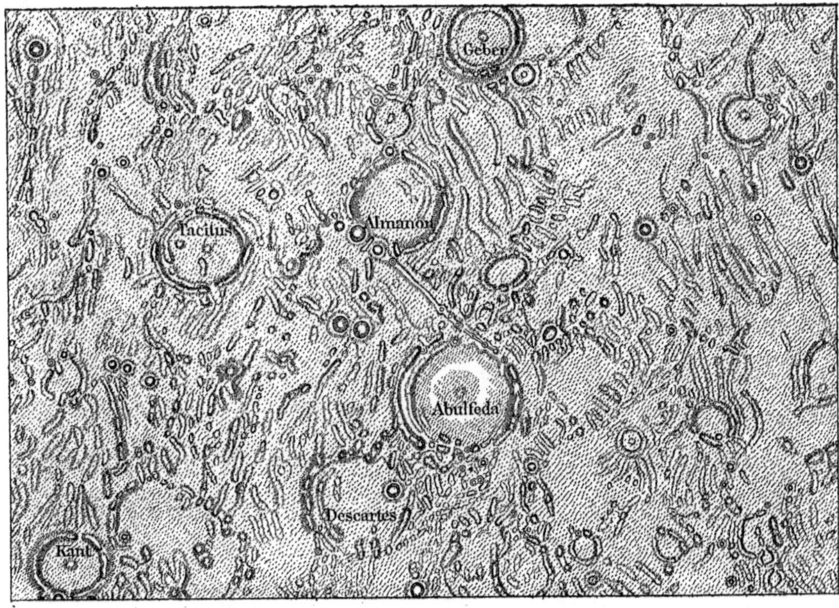

2

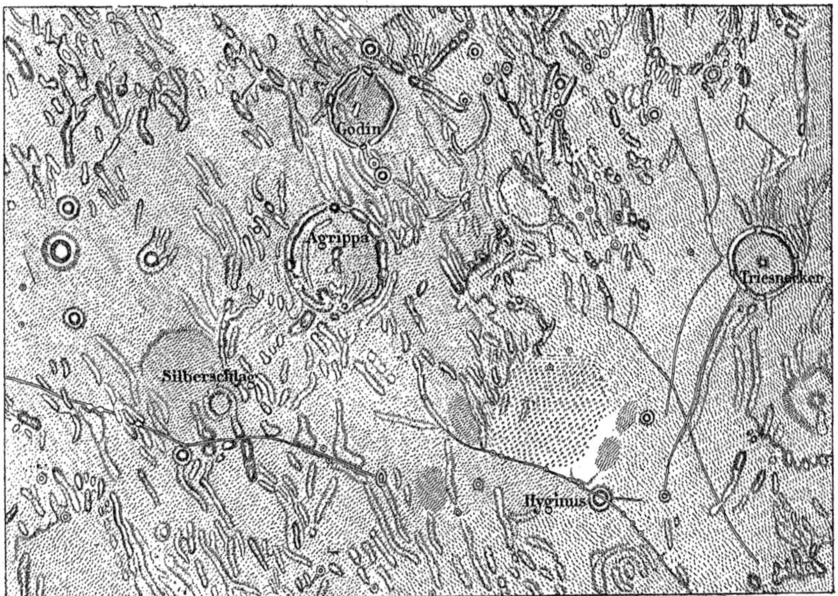

Godin
Agrippa
Triesnecker
Silberschlag
Hyginus

Gravé chez Erhard, R. Bonaparte 42.

LUNAR TOPOGRAPHY.

1. Walled Plains, Craters, and Rilles. Rilles of Abulfeda. 2. Rilles of the central regions near the Sinus Medii.

IX.

THE MOON.

PHYSICAL CONSTITUTION (*continued*).

Absence of Air and Water on the Moon's Surface—Has the Moon an Atmosphere?—Aspect of a Lunar Landscape—The Moon's Past History; Professor Frankland's Hypothesis based on Traces of Glacier-action—The Moon's Climate—Days, Nights, and Seasons—Extent of the Visible and Invisible Portions of the Lunar Globe—Astronomy from a Lunarian's point of view—Lunar Photography; the British Association 'Moon Committee.'

We have already supposed an inhabitant of the Earth landing on the desolate lunar world bristling with mountains and covered with thousands of volcanic vents. We have described him contemplating with wonder this strange globe. But we ought to mention one fact, which would render his sojourn much more than painful—impossible; namely, that he would not find on the surface of the Moon, the most indispensable elements to his existence,—air and water.

The Moon, indeed, it would appear, is entirely devoid of atmosphere.

This fact seems demonstrated by the occultation of stars. When, by reason of the Moon's movement across the constellations, one of the luminous points of the starry vault is covered by the dark part of the lunar disk, it is extinguished suddenly, without any gradual diminution of its light indicating the presence of a gaseous envelope. This fact holds good with the smallest as with the largest stars, even during the eclipses of the Moon, when the terrestrial atmosphere is longer illuminated by our satellite.

If, moreover, an atmosphere, however slight its density, enveloped the lunar spheroid, such atmosphere would refract, that is to say, a star, after its real immersion behind the disk, would still remain visible for an instant. In the same way, it would again become visible on its emersion a little before its actual occultation had terminated, so that the duration of the occultation would be, for two reasons, *less* than the time assigned by calculation, and deduced from precise and mathematical knowledge of the movement of the Moon. Now nothing like this has been observed. Hence, it results that, if the atmosphere of the Moon really exists, its density is less than the 2000th part of the density of the Earth's atmosphere. Such an atmosphere would be more rare than the vacuum which is obtained, under the best conditions, in the most perfect air-pumps.

The only objections that can be made to the consequences drawn from the preceding fact, are, as Arago remarked, that the apparent diameter of the Moon is not perhaps known with sufficient precision; and again, the singular phenomenon observed in the total eclipse of the Sun in 1860, and pointed out by M. Laussedat, that the horns of the solar crescent were truncated and rounded, near the Moon's limb.

There is also another point. It is known that the exterior edge of the lunar disk forms a line unbroken in appearance, whilst near the centre, the terminal ellipse, or terminator, marking the separation of the light and shade, is deeply indented and irregular. The cause of this difference is easily understood; the summits of the craters and peaks, situated at the edge of the disk, form a series of undulations which are averaged and levelled by the effect of perspective, and prevent therefore a regular and uniform outline; at the centre of the disk, on the contrary, the irregularities are presented to us in face, as in a bird's-eye view, so to speak, so that the summits illuminated by the light of the Sun stand out from the dark lower levels of the plains. But after all the uniformity of the limb is not so decided that it can be argued that in an occultation of a star the difference between the observed and the calculated times is, or is not, due to the existence of an atmosphere.

[Now, with regard to the recent discovery to which we have before referred; of the $2''\cdot0$, by which we now know that the Moon's apparent diameter must be reduced, certainly a part, probably the whole, is due to the irradiation of the telescopic semidiameter. But the reader may perhaps attribute a part to refraction by the Moon's atmosphere. If the whole were attributable to that cause, it would imply, according to the Astronomer Royal, a horizontal refraction of $1''\cdot0$, which is only about the $\frac{1}{2000}$ part of the Earth's horizontal refraction; probably implying a tenuity of lunar atmosphere which would make the atmosphere undiscoverable in any other way.]

Is it possible that there may be an atmosphere confined to the bottom of the lowest plains and the deepest craters? Nothing renders probable or contradicts this hypothesis. But at all events no cloud ever disturbs the purity of its sky; for clouds, even of slight dimensions, would be easily perceived from the Earth, and no convincing observations of any are recorded.*

In consequence of this want of atmosphere, the lunar landscapes have a very peculiar aspect—the shadows have everywhere the same blackness. At the most, the crudity of the bright and luminous tints, which stand out on a nearly black sky, and of the nearly black shadows, is tempered by reflexions, which are, however, very numerous as the levels are so broken. Then again, there is no aërial perspective—none of those effects of light, of those cloud-tints, which give our terrestrial landscapes so much charm and softness. There refraction does not decompose sunshine into glorious colouring, and a thousand varied tints; the rainbow and other

* [After all fair deductions on the score of imperfection of observation or precipitancy of inference, there are still residuary phenomena,—such as, for instance, the extraordinary profusion of brilliant points which, on rare occasions, diversify the *Mare Crisium*,—so difficult of interpretation, that we may judge it wisest to avoid too positive an opinion.—T. W. W.]

phenomena of the same kind are unknown on the surface of the Moon. But then the stars and the other celestial bodies shine in full day in the starry vault.

Plate IX may give an idea of the aspect of the landscape in the mountainous parts of the southern hemisphere.

The absence of air on the surface of the Moon implies absence of water. If there existed lakes, seas, or even rivers, the liquids forming these reservoirs or currents, would be reduced to vapour by the fact that they would not be maintained as such by atmospheric pressure. But the solar heat, acting still more energetically, would develope a gaseous envelope, — thick clouds of vapour. A cloud of 200 yards in diameter would be easily visible. Now, as we have before said, no moving object has ever been seen on the disk of the Moon.

No air and no water! This implies, of necessity, absence of winds and currents, — absence of motion everywhere — in the sky as on the surface. At the most, under the influence of the alternations of heat and cold, the disintegration of the rocks and the destruction of equilibrium of the heavy bodies causing the fall of *débris* break the monotony of the stillness and eternal silence. Nor sound, as it cannot be communicated without an aërial medium, can only make itself known by the contact of solid molecules. To an inhabitant of the Earth, our light-giver by night would appear, according to the expression of Humboldt, but a silent and voiceless desert.

It has been said before that the large dark spots, which the first observers took for seas, are now known to be vast plains, lower in level than the valleys of the mountainous regions. One thing, which, doubtless, in the first instance, increased the illusion, was, that many of these spots appear of a light greyish green colour: others are greenish grey, reddish, or, again, of a deep grey, like steel. The absence of seas, waters, and — as a natural consequence — of rains, is so much the more probable, as it well explains the present appearance of the surface of the Moon, or, in other words, the geology of its superficial strata.* 'The Moon,' says Humboldt, 'is nearly such as the Earth must have been in its primitive state, before being everywhere covered, owing to the continuous action of tides and currents, with sedimentary beds rich in shells, gravels, and alluvium.' It is necessary, however, to distinguish between the mountainous regions and the regions of the plains. These latter offer a much more uniform surface, and it appears probable that it is owing to sedimentary beds which are there deposited.

[Instead of seas they are most probably old sea-bottoms.

Such, then, are the results of the telescopic observations of the side of our satellite turned towards us. Do we know anything about the like

* [The long continuance of eruptive action, so distinctly marked by the successive encroachment of more recent craters upon the boundaries of older ones, and the decrease of its energy, equally traceable in the diminished magnitude of the results, are too evident to admit of a question. But many other features are of a more equivocal character.—T. W. W.]

conditions of the side turned away from us? or, again, can we dive into the past history of the Moon?

The illustrious Hansen has held that it is quite possible that the lunarians on the side away from us may possess both water and an atmosphere, and that the side turned towards us may be regarded as one vast mountain. Adams and Le Verrier, however, have shown that such a hypothesis is not very securely based.

Professor Frankland has perhaps provided us with some data towards answering the second question. A study of the glacial epoch on our own globe, he asserts, renders it probable that the other bodies belonging to our solar system have either already passed through a similar epoch or are destined still to encounter it. With the exception of the polar ice of Mars we have hitherto obtained no certain glimpse into the thermal and meteorological condition of the planets; and, indeed, the Moon is the only body whose distance is not too great to prevent the visibility of comparatively minute details upon her surface. Professor Frankland believes, and his belief rests on a special study of the lunar surface, that our satellite has, like its primary, also passed through a glacial epoch, and that several, at least, of the *valleys*, *rilles*, and *streaks* of the lunar surface, are not improbably due to former glacial action. Notwithstanding the excellent definition of modern telescopes, it could not be expected that other than the most gigantic of the characteristic details of an ancient glacier bed would be rendered visible. What then may we expect to see? Under favourable circumstances the terminal moraine of a glacier attains enormous dimensions; and, consequently, of all the marks of a glacial valley this would be the one most likely to be first perceived. Two such terminal moraines, one of them a double one, have appeared to them to be traceable upon the Moon's surface. The first is situated near the termination of that remarkable streak which commences near the base of Tycho, and, passing under the south-eastern wall of Bullialdus, into the ring of which it appears to cut, is gradually lost after passing Lubiniezky. Exactly opposite this last, and extending nearly across the streak in question, are two ridges forming the arcs of circles whose centres are not coincident, and whose external curvature is towards the north. Beyond the second ridge a talus slopes gradually down northwards to the general level of the lunar surface, the whole presenting an appearance reminding the observer of the concentric moraines of the Rhone glacier. These ridges are visible for the whole period during which that portion of the Moon's surface is illuminated; but it is only about the third day after the first quarter, and at the corresponding phase of the waning moon, when the Sun's rays, falling nearly horizontally, throw the details of this part of the surface into strong relief, and these appearances suggest this explanation of them. The other ridge, answering to a terminal moraine, occurs at the northern extremity of that magnificent valley which runs past the eastern edge of Rheita.

With regard to the probability of former glacial, or even aqueous,

LUNAR LANDSCAPE.
Ideal View, taken in the mountainous regions of the south-west.

agency on the surface of the Moon, difficulties of an apparently very formidable character present themselves.* There is not only now no evidence whatever of the presence of water, in any one of its three forms, on the lunar surface, but, on the contrary, all selenographic observations tend to prove its absence. Nevertheless, the idea of former aqueous agency in the Moon has received almost universal acceptation. It was entertained by Gruithuisen and others. But, if water at one time existed on the surface of the Moon, whither has it disappeared? If we assume, in accordance with the nebular hypothesis, that the portions of matter composing respectively the Earth and the Moon once possessed an equally elevated temperature, it almost necessarily follows that the Moon, owing to the comparative smallness of the mass, would cool much more rapidly than the Earth; for whilst the volume of the Moon is only about $\frac{1}{49}$th, its surface is nearly $\frac{1}{13}$th that of the Earth. This cooling of the mass of the Moon must, in accordance with all analogy, have been attended with contraction, which can scarcely be conceived as recurring without the development of a cavernous structure in the interior. Much of this cavernous structure would doubtless communicate, by means of fissures, with the surface; and thus there would be provided an internal receptacle for the ocean, from the depths of which even the burning sun of the long lunar day would be totally unable to dislodge more than traces of its vapour. Assuming the solid mass of the Moon to contract on cooling at the same rate as granite, its refrigeration, through only 180° Fahrenheit, would create cellular space equal to nearly $14\frac{1}{2}$ millions of cubic miles, which would be more than sufficient to engulf the whole of the lunar oceans, supposing them to bear the same proportion to the mass of the Moon as our own oceans bear to that of the Earth.

Now, if such be the present condition of the Moon, we can scarcely avoid the conclusion that a liquid ocean can only exist upon the surface of a planet so long as the latter retains a high internal temperature. The Moon, then, becomes to us a prophetic picture of the ultimate fate which awaits our Earth, when, deprived of an external ocean, and of all but an annual rotation upon its axis,† it will revolve round the Sun an arid and lifeless wilderness, one hemisphere being exposed to the perpetual glare of the solar rays, the other shrouded in eternal night.]‡

The climate of our satellite must be not less extraordinary than its geology. During about fifteen days the Sun pours its rays, without any cloudy curtain or aërial current to temper them. To this temperature,

* [It may be objected to this ingenious theory that the traces of such an action would be far more numerous, there being great probability that there would be a regular gradation in their proportions, and an absolute certainty that they would be visible in modern telescopes, even if of far less magnitude than those referred to.— T. W. W.]

† [Mayer has recently endeavoured to prove that the action of the tides tends to arrest the motion of the Earth upon its axis. And although it has been asserted that, since the time of Hipparchus, the length of the terrestrial day has not increased by the $\frac{1}{100}$th part of a second, yet this fact obviously leaves untouched the conclusion to which Mayer's reasoning points.]

‡ Professor Frankland, 'Proc. Royal Institution,' vol. iv. p. 175.

more intense even than that of our torrid zone, succeeds an intense cold, which a night of fifteen days' length renders more glacial than that of our polar winters. It is true, that during the day the radiation of the solar heat into space again is not prevented. We must conclude, therefore, that the climates of the various regions of the Moon have a certain analogy with those of our Alpine regions; seeing that the depression of the temperature, and the reverberation of the intense light there, become insupportable by the continuity of their action.

There are, properly speaking, no seasons on the Moon. The slight inclination of its axis of rotation maintains the Sun at a nearly constant inclination in each latitude. But whilst in the equatorial regions the radiant body scarcely leaves the zenith; at the middle of the day, in the polar regions, it scarcely rises above the horizon. The polar mountains enjoy perpetual day.*

One can understand, also, that the inclination of the Sun to the lunar surface, variable according to the latitudes, can never have on the Moon the same importance as on the Earth; since the rays, whether luminous or calorific, are transmitted directly to the surface without having to traverse atmospheric strata of unequal thicknesses.

The revolution of our satellite is effected with variable velocity, whilst its movement of rotation is uniform. Hence results a want of correspondence between the two movements; and the Earth is found sometimes to the east, sometimes to the west, of the point of space opposite to a fixed point of the surface of the Moon, considered as the centre of the visible hemisphere. We thus discover regions both at the eastern and western limbs, which, without this circumstance, would remain hidden to us.

Nor is this all; the inclination of the plane of the lunar orbit, added to that of its equator, to the plane of the terrestrial orbit, causes the Moon to present to us sometimes the north, sometimes the south pole, of its globe, and thus to uncover certain portions of its polar regions which otherwise we should not see.

From these two *librations*, which is the name given to these movements, it follows that of 1000 parts of the surface of the Moon, 569, or more than half, are visible to the Earth, whilst only 431 remain constantly hidden from us.

But as the dimensions of the Earth are very appreciable when compared to its distance from the Moon, it follows that an observer, as he moves on the terrestrial spheroid, displaces the apparent centre of the lunar disk,—or, what comes to the same thing, perceives the different portions near the limbs.

* 'The Sun does not descend below the real horizon of a lunar pole, at the most, to an angle greater than the inclination of the equator of the Moon; that is to say, 1° 30′; but the smallness of the globe of our satellite is such, that at an elevation of 650 yards we see 1° 30′ below the true horizon. Now there exist at the North Pole mountains upwards of 4000 yards in height; consequently the summit of these mountains can never be hidden from the light of the Sun.'—*Beer and Mädler*, '*Fragments sur les Corps Célestes.*'

The effect of this displacement again increases the dimensions of the portion of the Moon which is accessible to us, in such a manner, that of 1000 parts 424 only remain definitely and absolutely hidden, 576 are visible to us.

From east to west, the part of the Moon which must for ever remain unknown to us embraces 2780 miles; from north to south, 2815 miles; from the lat. of 40° north, to the same latitude south, 2690 miles. Whilst the same dimensions, calculated for the visible surface, are respectively 3310, 3266, and 3390 miles, according to Beer and Mädler.

A complete zone, therefore, of the half of the Moon which is turned away from the Earth, is accessible to the eyes of man. [So much foreshortened, however, that our knowledge of great part of it must always remain very defective.]

'Now, observations have not indicated,' we quote these two most diligent explorers of the Moon, 'any essential difference between those regions which form the seventh part of the lunar surface generally hidden from our gaze, and those with which we are acquainted; the same mountainous countries and the same *maria* are found there.' Hence, it is most natural to conclude the similarity of the invisible portions to those which we see.

That the part actually invisible will for ever remain unknown to the Earth, follows from the searching analysis of Laplace.

To bring to an end the description of the physical particularities which make the Moon a body so different from the globe which we inhabit, let us see if the astronomical phenomena are the same for her as for the Earth. Without examining into the interesting—almost insoluble question, of the existence of living and organised beings on the surface of the satellite of our little Earth,* we shall suppose an observer successively placed on each of its hemispheres.

The phases of the Moon indicate, that she presents all the points of her sphere to the Sun in an interval of $29\frac{53}{100}$ days, or, as it may be put, in about 709 hours; each of these points, therefore, receives during $354\frac{1}{2}$ hours the solar light and heat, for this is the length of the Moon's

* Others, more daring than ourselves, will doubtless cut the knot of this difficulty. They will assert, with a great chance of being believed, that an organised being cannot live without air and water, and that the climatic conditions of the Moon are evidently opposed to such organisms; we will not contradict them. The cause of our reserve, however, is easy to understand. If, before having observed any of the innumerable organisms which people the waters on our planet, and before having heard of their existence, any one had suddenly learned that it is possible to exist, breathe, and move in water, and if he then referred to simple experiment, which teaches that prolonged immersion in a liquid is fatal to all the organisms known to him, even to man himself: without doubt, the assertion would cause him the greatest surprise. Such would be our surprise were it ever demonstrated by facts beyond dispute, that living beings exist on the surface of the Moon. Nature is so varied in its modes of action, so infinite in the manifestations of its power, that nothing in Nature can be pronounced by man to be absolutely impossible.

day. During 354½ hours the same point is entirely deprived of light and heat, this is the length of its night. From this point of view there is an entire equality between the visible and the invisible hemispheres.

The absence of atmosphere must give to the lunar days a singular aspect. The disk of the Sun, seen sharp and distinct, is deprived of those rays which surround him to a great distance as seen from the Earth. If it be true that the Sun is surrounded by an atmosphere, this envelope should be clearly visible in the lunar sky, which everywhere else, as we have said, remains dark, and even in broad day is overspread with stars.

But the intensity of the light of the Sun and that of his direct heat, are not the same at mid-day in each hemisphere of the Moon. In fact, it is noon for the points of the lunar meridian which is presented to us at the exact moment of full moon; while for the other half of this meridian, our lunar antipodes, noon coincides with the instant of the new moon. Now, in the first position the Moon is further from the Sun than in the second by double its mean distance from the Earth, or by the 200th part of the distance of the Sun from the Earth. So the apparent diameter of the Sun is greater in the second case than in the first by about the two-hundredth part.

During the nights of this latter hemisphere, the lunar observer will constantly see the Earth under the form of a luminous disk, fourteen times larger than the Moon in our own sky, and presenting successively a series of phases analogous to her own. The nights, therefore, will never be quite dark, as in fact is indicated by the Earth-shine. At midnight, that is, at the Moon's midnight, the side of which we speak—the one turned towards us, then invisible because it is lost in the Sun's rays—will have *full Earth.* The light, which she then receives from the luminous disk of our planet, is equal to that which would be received by ourselves, if fourteen full Moons equal to our own were at the same time lighting up our evening sky.

On the other hand, the Earth is unknown to the lunarian observer situated on the invisible hemisphere, and the darkness of the nights there can only be imagined by bearing in mind that they are tempered by no twilight, and that the only illumination received by that hemisphere is star-light. Between these two regions, which form together six-sevenths of the surface of the Moon, is the zone, near the limb, which comprises the parts in which the Earth is sometimes in view, sometimes invisible. In this zone the Earth rises and sets, but its disk rises only a short distance above the horizon.

In the visible hemisphere, the phases of the Earth, the observation of the different features which appear and disappear in turn by the effect of rotation, serve as a clock: it is a dial, all but fixed in the same point of the sky, like an immense lamp, behind which the stars defile slowly along the dark sky.

As to those regions of the Moon which are invisible to the Earth, as soon as the Sun has disappeared below their horizon they are suddenly plunged into the deepest night. During 350 hours, an astronomer, if he were transported to such a favourable sky, would be able to carry on his observation of planet and star unimpeded by cloud, moon, or twilight. Another difference which characterises the invisible hemisphere is, that there the Sun is never eclipsed, whilst in the hemisphere turned towards us solar eclipses last sometimes two hours.

Here, then, we may bring our notice of the details of the lunar world and its singular constitution to a conclusion. The phenomena to which we have just referred—Eclipses of the Sun and Moon—which are invested with such absorbing interest, now demand our attention.

[Before, however, parting company with the Moon, we would refer the reader who would know more about her to the Rev. T. W. Webb's work, 'Celestial Objects for Common Telescopes.' That observer has for many years made the Moon his special study. We may also congratulate ourselves that at last, thanks to the example set by Mr. Webb, Mr. Birt, and other observers, and to the advance of lunar photography, in the hands of Mr. De La Rue, whose latest result is an exquisitie photographic portrait of the Moon, 38 inches in diameter, the investigation of the Moon's surface is being taken up in earnest, and there is now a standing 'Moon Committee' of the British Association, under whose auspices good work is being done; and a map, 8 feet 4 inches in diameter, is being constructed by Mr. Birt, whose perseverance in this field of investigation is worthy of all praise.* In spite of the general excellence of Beer and Mädler's map, some parts so ill represent the actual appearance of the Moon, that in some minds the idea has arisen of changes actually going on. This is improbable, but we must wait for a larger map and for more observations before we can positively assert that this is not the case. As has been pointed out by Mr. Grove, observations of the geologically or selenologically recent observations will from this point of view be the most hopeful and valuable. We may venture to express our belief that this and similar work will be best done by filling in from eye-observations a skeleton map prepared from photographs of the various regions, on the largest scale possible, reduced to a mean libration.†]

* [The labours in lunar astronomy, more especially as regards the Moon's surface, of Julius Schmidt of Athens, have been very extensive. Since the year 1842 he has made and calculated 4000 micrometrical measures (made at the observatory at Olmutz, between 1853 and 1858) of the altitudes of lunar mountains. In addition to these he has nearly 1000 original sketches, which he is now engaged in combining into a map of three feet radius.]

† [Since this was written, the Moon Committee have determined upon constructing such a skeleton map as is here proposed, and zones 1° or 2° broad will be distributed among different observers. We may thus hope for a complete map on an adequate scale in a comparatively short space of time.]

X.

ECLIPSES OF THE SUN AND MOON.

General Theory of Eclipses—Eclipse of the Sun can only take place at the time of New Moon—The Eclipses of the Moon happen at Opposition—Why each Lunation is not accompanied by two Eclipses.

WHEN the movements of the Moon and the Earth bring these two bodies in such a position, that their centres and the centre of the Sun are all in the same straight line, the phenomenon which follows from this particular situation of the three celestial bodies is what is called an Eclipse. If it be the Moon which occupies the intermediate position, it turns its dark hemisphere towards the Earth; and the interposition of its black disk between us and the luminous body of the Sun prevents the rays of the latter reaching us, and an Eclipse of the Sun is produced. If it be the Earth which occupies the mid-interval, our globe acts as a screen; the lunar hemisphere turned towards the Sun no longer receives his rays, its disk is obscured, and we have an Eclipse of the Moon.

But this way of considering the phenomena is only from our own point of view. In reality, in both these cases, there is simultaneously an eclipse to each of the three bodies in question.

What happens, in fact, in the first case?

To an observer placed on the Sun, the Moon seems projected on the Earth, hiding a portion of the surface, although it is true that the two superposed disks, as they are both luminous, would not permit the darkened part of the surface of the terrestrial globe to be seen from the Sun. An observer situated on the dark hemisphere of the Moon will perceive an eclipse of the Earth, that is to say, a successive darkness over all the regions of our globe in which the eclipse of the Sun is visible. Lastly, in the case which produces an eclipse of the Moon as seen from the Earth, there is also an eclipse [occultation] of the Moon to the Sun, whilst there is an eclipse of the Sun to the lunar hemisphere turned towards us.

Eclipses may be regarded and explained in another way.

The Earth and the Moon are two spherical and opaque bodies, and the halves of both are constantly illuminated by the rays of the Sun, whilst the other halves are in the shade. The illuminating body is itself a sphere of much greater dimensions. Not only, therefore, have the Moon and the Earth always one of their hemispheres dark, but each of these two bodies throws behind it, away from the Sun, a shadow of conical form, the length and diameter of which depend on the distance and diameter of the illuminating body, and the diameter of the illuminated body.

This cone of shade encloses all those parts of space where, by reason of the interposition of the opaque body, no ray of light from the Sun can be received. Beyond the summit of this cone of pure shadow—of *umbra*—and in its prolongation, are situate all those points of space which see a part of the Sun, under the form of a luminous ring, bordering the obscure disk of the opaque body.

Lastly, these two regions are themselves surrounded by what is called

Fig. 65.—General theory of Eclipses.

a *penumbra.* Every part of space situated in the penumbra only receives light from one part of the Sun, the luminous disk of which seems partially invaded by the obscure disk of the opaque body. The darkness produced by the penumbra is so much more intense as the point in question is nearer the umbra.

The Moon and the Earth, in their movements, carry with them their cones of umbra and penumbra, and it is by projecting these total and partial shadowings one on the other that they produce the phenomena of eclipses.

Now, if we look at fig. 65, it will be at once seen why an eclipse of the Sun, when it does happen, always takes place at the moment of the new moon, and why, on the contrary, an eclipse of the Moon is only possible at the period when our satellite is in opposition, that is to say, at the moment of full moon. In all the other positions of our satellite, that is to say, in all the other phases of the lunation, the lunar cone of shade is projected into space away from the Earth, and the terrestrial cone of shade does not meet the Moon.

This is confirmed by all the observations of eclipses. It does not, however, follow that there is an eclipse at every full moon, or at each new moon; and the reason for this is not far to seek.

There would be really two eclipses in each lunar month, one of the Sun, the other of the Moon, if the orbit of the Earth round the Sun and the orbit of the Moon round the Earth were described in the same plane. Then, at the epoch either of opposition or of conjunction, the centres of the three bodies would be necessarily in a straight line.

But it has been seen that this is not the case. The orbit of the Moon is inclined to the plane of the ecliptic, so that it often happens that, at the moment of the new moon, our satellite projects its cone of shade above or below the Earth. Similarly, at the period of opposition, the Moon, in consequence of its position out of the plane of the ecliptic, passes sometimes above, sometimes below the terrestrial cone of shade. Every time that this happens of course there is no eclipse.

Let us see, then, what conditions are necessary for an eclipse of the Sun or the Moon.

The orbit of the Moon, we repeat, is situated in a plane which makes with the plane of the terrestrial orbit a certain angle, nearly constant.

It follows that half of the monthly revolution is effected above this latter plane, whilst the other half is accomplished below it. The Moon then passes through the ecliptic twice every lunation.

The two positions which it occupies during these passages are the *Nodes*. One is called the *ascending node*, the other the *descending node;* because they correspond, the first to the movement of the Moon when it rises from the south side to the north side of the ecliptic, the second to the inverse movement.

If the nodes remained invariable in their relative positions with regard to the Sun, one of two things would happen; either there would be no eclipses at all, or there would be two in each lunar month. But the nodes are displaced from one lunation to another; and it is easy to comprehend that an eclipse will take place every time that they coincide with the phases of the full and the new moon — with the *syzygies*, as they are called.* This coincidence need not be absolute; it suffices that the nodes be so near these phases, that the size of the cones of shade makes an immersion either of the Moon or of the Earth possible.

Such is the first general condition of possibility of these phenomena. There are still others which are proper to each kind of eclipse, which we shall discuss in describing the two kinds of eclipses separately.

XI.

ECLIPSES OF THE SUN.

Conditions of the Possibility and Visibility of Eclipses of the Sun — Total, Annular, and Partial Eclipses — Path of the Moon's Shadow along the Earth — Longest possible Duration of Solar Eclipses — The Corona, Red Prominences; they belong to the Sun: their Shape and Height — Influence of the Phenomena of Eclipses on Living Beings.

SOLAR eclipses are of three kinds. Some are total; the dark disk of the Moon then entirely covers the Sun. Others are partial; that is, a portion only, large or small, of the solar disk is eclipsed. Lastly, there are annular eclipses, which take place when the disk of the Moon is not large enough to entirely cover that of the Sun, and leaves a luminous ring visible round its own body.

As the Moon is much smaller than the Sun, it will be understood that it is its small relative distance which causes its disk to appear of equal, and even greater dimensions than that of the Sun. This distance varies by reason of the elliptical form of its orbit, and hence the dimensions of the lunar disk are sometimes larger, sometimes smaller than, and sometimes equal to, those of the Sun.

This is the same as saying that the cone of real shadow or umbra, projected by the new moon towards the Earth, reaches or does not reach

* [The plane of the Moon's orbit may be regarded as shifting parallel to itself as the Earth travels round the Sun. Thus, precisely as there are two epochs in the year — the equinoxes — when the Earth's equator-plane is directed towards the Sun; so also there are two epochs in the year when the plane of the Moon's orbit is directed towards the Sun. At new moon or full, near these epochs, there will be solar or lunar eclipses. Hence there are two eclipse-months (so to speak) in each year. During each, at least one eclipse must take place (if only one the eclipse will be solar), and there may be as many as three. Add to these considerations the fact that the plane of the Moon's orbit shifts its nodes precessionally — much as the Earth's equator-plane does — only in a period of about 18½ years (instead of more than 25,000 years) and the chief general relations of eclipses will be understood. The effect of this precessional motion is somewhat to shorten the mean interval between eclipse-months, which is thus reduced to about 5½ months.— R. A. P.]

the surface of our globe. If it reach this surface, there is a total eclipse to all parts of the Earth which are plunged in it; a partial eclipse to all the regions contained in the penumbra. This will be understood from the following figure.

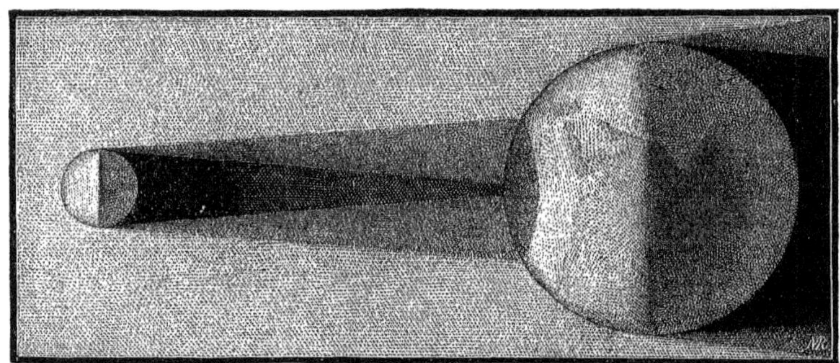

Fig. 66.—Total Eclipse of the Sun; Theory.

If the cone of the Moon's shadow does not reach the Earth, there will be an annular eclipse visible in those parts comprised in the prolongation of the cone: a partial eclipse to those which are only found in the penumbra. This case is represented by the next figure.

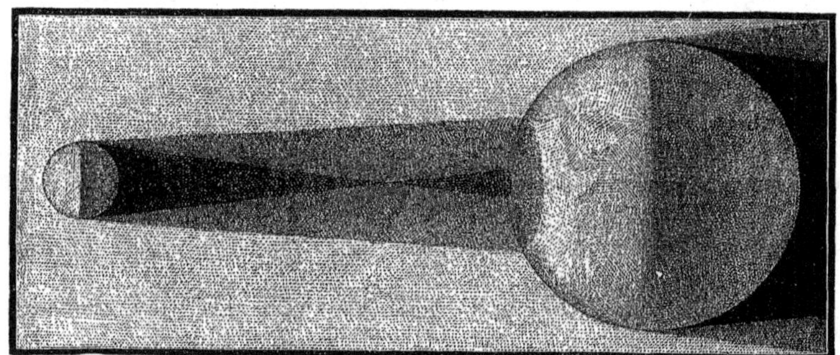

Fig. 67.—Annular Eclipse of the Sun; Theory.

It will be seen, therefore, that the conditions of the possibility of a total eclipse of the Sun are the following:—

The Moon must be in conjunction, that is, she must be new;

She must at the same time be near a node;

Lastly, her distance from the Earth must be less than the length of the cone of shadow projected by her into space.

The same conditions, except the last, are necessary for an annular eclipse.

Those who are accustomed to read in scientific journals or in almanacs the announcements of eclipses, which are calculated long beforehand by astronomers, must often have noticed these words, *invisible at London* (or some other place). An eclipse of the Sun (we shall speak further on of those of the Moon) may then take place without being visible to all parts of the Earth. A little thought will convince us of this, and make it easy to account for the circumstance.

First, it is evident that there will be no eclipse at those places where the Sun remains invisible during its entire duration; secondly, in many

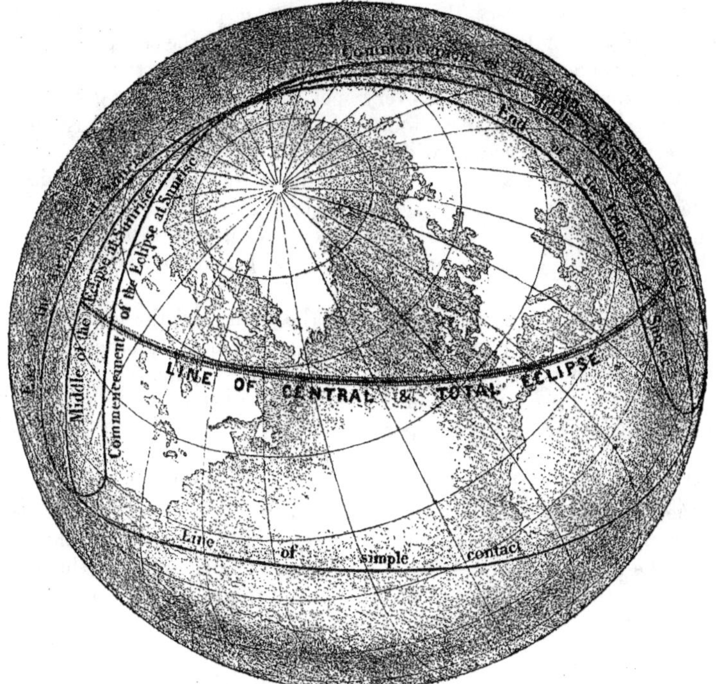

Fig. 68.—Total Eclipse of the Sun of the 18th July, 1860. Path of the shadow and penumbra on the surface of the Earth.

places which have the Sun above their horizon, if the Moon's shadow is not large enough to cover the illuminated surface, there will be no eclipse.

But the Moon has a diameter nearly four times less than that of the Earth. Its cone of shade, therefore, at its greatest, is much too small to enshroud the whole Earth; and near the extremities of this cone its dimensions are small enough to throw on the surface of our globe but a very small circle of shadow, about 50 miles in diameter. An eclipse of the Sun is then only total at the same instant, in a circle of these dimensions. But the rotation of the Earth and the movement of translation of the Moon combined, cause the cone of shadow to travel in reality over a very large surface, tracing a dark curve on the surface of the continents and seas.*

The same observations apply to the penumbra.

Thus, according to the position of places relatively to the Sun and to the Moon, the first of these bodies may be eclipsed totally or partially, or even appear only in simple contact with the obscure disk of our satellite.

The astronomical theories of the movements of the Moon and of the Earth are now so perfect, that astronomers can predict these phenomena with the most wonderful precision. Not only does the calculation indicate the day of the eclipse; but the exact second, the time, the dimensions or phases of the phenomenon for every spot of the Earth are given. Maps are generally added to these numerical details, and show those parts of the Earth where the eclipse will be visible.

We have drawn a map of this kind, for the total eclipse which took place on the 18th of July, 1860, according to the indications of the 'Connaissance des Temps' and the 'Nautical Almanac,'—works published many years in advance for the benefit of astronomers and navigators.

A curve in the form of ∞ marks the points of the globe where the eclipse commenced or ended at sunrise or sunset. Another line, which cuts the first two in parts, passes through those places which only saw half the eclipse, because the middle of it coincided at those places, either with the rising or setting of the Sun.

One line, darker than the rest, marks the line in which the eclipse was total and central. Parallel to this line, other lines which are not marked on the diagram would indicate the regions where the partial eclipse was visible under smaller and smaller phases,† until the line is reached which limits the phenomenon, passing through all the places where the eclipse is reduced to the simple contact of the disks of the Sun and Moon.

The black line of central eclipse is in reality but the path of the shadow thrown by the Moon on the surface of the Earth, as the complete figure represents the path of the penumbra on the same surface.

The duration of an eclipse of the Sun is variable. But we must distinguish carefully between the total duration of the phenomenon on the whole Earth, and on any given place. We here give, according to the

* The length of the cone of shade projected by the Moon into space, varies between 57 and 59 radii of the Earth. On the other hand, we have seen that the distance between the centres of the Earth and the Moon also varies between 57 and 64 terrestrial radii. From the centre of the Moon to the nearest point of our globe there are then from 56 to 63 of these radii.

† Astronomers formerly expressed the size of the phases by the number of digits, a digit being the twelfth part of the diameter of the solar disk. Thus, if the phase was $\frac{6}{12}$ digit, the Moon's limb extended to the centre of the Sun.

calculations of Dionis de Séjour, cited by Arago, a table showing the greatest possible duration of the different phases:

		Greatest possible duration. h.	m.	s.
A total eclipse . .	At the Equator . . .	4	29	44
	At the latitude of Paris	3	26	32
Annular phase . .	At the Equator . . .		12	46
	At the latitude of Paris		9	56
Total obscurity .	At the Equator . . .		7	58
	At the latitude of Paris		6	10

The total eclipse of the Sun, of which the preceding figure gives the path on the surface of the terrestrial globe, commenced at 0 hour 3 minutes P.M. Paris mean time, and ended at 5 hours 6 minutes P.M. after having lasted in the whole of its phases 5 hours 3 minutes. At Paris, where the eclipse was only partial, the duration of the phenomenon was only 2 hours 14 minutes.

Total eclipses of the Sun are very rare, even for the Earth in general; they are much more so for particular places. From the 16th until the beginning of the 19th century, there were altogether nine total eclipses of the Sun, and seven annular ones. Paris, during all the 18th century, only witnessed a single total eclipse, that of 1724. London also, as little favoured as the capital of France, has not seen one since 1715.

Since 1801, seven total eclipses have been observed, those of 1806, 1842, 1850, 1851, 1856, 1860, and 1861. We give here those which will take place before the end of the present century, with the places where they will be total:

1870.	22nd December	Azores, south of Spain, north of Africa, Sicily, and Turkey.
1887.	19th August .	North-east of Germany, south of Russia, Central Asia.
1896.	9th August . .	Greenland, Siberia, and Lapland.
1900.	8th May . . .	Spain, Algeria, Egypt, the United States.

None of them will be total at London.

The eclipses of the Sun and Moon no longer are privileged to excite fear, at least among civilised nations. Instead of a superstitious terror, they inspire an interest of curiosity. Announced a long time beforehand, they testify to the precision of astronomical calculations; and all are getting accustomed by degrees to admire the fixed laws, order and harmony, where formerly ignorance supposed but accidents, precursors of evil, and testimonies of the celestial anger.

As to the astronomer, he finds in them matter for researches of the highest importance. Even the partial eclipses, the least interesting of all, give him occasion to verify the exactitude of his tables, by the agreement, or otherwise, between the hour predicted by calculation, and the hour really observed. But it is the total eclipses, especially the last ones—those of 1842, 1850, 1851, 1858, 1860, and 1861,—which have been so fertile in new and precious facts.

We propose to give a brief description of these facts, besides placing under the eyes of the reader, in Plate X. drawings which represent some of the various phenomena observed.

Let us follow the phenomenon in its progressive march.

It is always the western border of the Sun which first receives the impression of the contact of the Moon; and consequently it is the eastern border of the lunar disk which by degrees encroaches on the radiant body, until it covers it entirely. The eclipse is necessarily partial, therefore, before the moment when the last luminous thread disappears. The total obscuration,—the totality, as astronomers call it,—then commences. At the end of some minutes a fine luminous thread appears at the western edge, and the partial eclipse passes, in inverse order, through the same phases as in the first part of the phenomenon. There are then, in all, four contacts of the two disks—two exterior contacts and two interior ones.

Attempts have been made to prove by the form of the horns of the luminous crescent the existence of a lunar atmosphere. Most observers have seen nothing. Nevertheless, the eclipse of the 18th of July, 1860, furnished a curious fact on this point: one of the horns of the solar crescent appeared rounded and truncated. At the other extremity a contraction was remarked, which was followed by the separation of a luminous point, and of a truncation identical with the first. To M. Laussedat we owe the communication of the photographic negative obtained by him: the drawing (fig. 69) is an exact reproduction.

Fig. 69.—Total Eclipse of the Sun of the 18th July, 1860. Rounded and truncated form of the horns of the Solar Crescent. (Laussedat.)

[The phenomenon observed would appear to be somewhat similar to the peculiar notched appearance sometimes presented, called 'Baily's Beads.' These, however, are considered by Mr. De La Rue to arise from atmospheric disturbance. This and the irregularity of the Moon's limb are, doubtless, sufficient to account for the singular appearance.]

Some minutes before and after, but especially during the totality, a luminous appearance in the form of a halo surrounds the Sun, and throws in every direction rays of light, separated by dark spaces. In many total eclipses, independently of the regular corona, other light portions, the rays of which have directions more or less eccentric, have been remarked irregularly situated on its contour. Plate X shows in detail the coronas of several total eclipses. The colour of the corona which immediately surrounds the dark disk is sometimes of a pearly or silvery white, sometimes yellowish, and even red.

The explanation generally given of this corona is, that it indicates the existence of a solar atmosphere, enveloping the radiant body to an enormous distance.*

We now come to a phenomenon of great interest, which was noticed for the first time in the total eclipse of 1842, and which has since been the object of important and minute observations.

Prominences of various forms and of a reddish colour were visible throughout the contour of the Moon's limb, during the period of totality. Some took the form of mountain-peaks, others rose normally from the disk, and turned at right angles, others, again, appeared completely detached, as floating clouds might do. Their tint was sometimes of a bright red, sometimes rosy, here and there varied by greenish-blue. Arago regarded the latter colour as a simple effect of contrast.

It has now been proved, beyond all question, that these protuberances belong to the Sun. If we examine with care the two drawings made by Mr. Warren De La Rue, on the total eclipse of the Sun of the 18th of July, 1860, representing these remarkable phenomena at the beginning and at the end of the totality, this fact will appear evident.

We have already, however, in the chapter on the Sun, had occasion to discuss yet more convincing and instructive evidence on these points.

As soon as the last luminous thread of light disappeared behind the eastern edge of the Moon, the rose-coloured prominences were seen on the contour of the limb, where the solar crescent had just disappeared. On the opposite side—the western one—they were not yet entirely visible; their tops only extended beyond the obscure disk, at its upper and lower parts. The Moon, advancing, hid by degrees the prominences first observed, exposing to view, at the opposite side, those previously covered.

The facts, then, occur absolutely as the hypothesis, now accepted on all hands, requires; namely, that the prominences do not belong to the lunar disk, and are not optical effects caused by its presence, but are absolutely part and parcel of the Sun.

They were first supposed to be enormous mountains on the surface of the Sun. But the form of many of the prominences, and their occasional complete separation from the solar disk, soon caused this hypothesis to be abandoned. All the observed facts led to the conclusion that these immense appendages, the dimensions of which reach 25,000 and even 50,000 miles, in height and length,† are possibly clouds, here adherent to a continuous stratum, which reposes on the Sun, here floating in an atmosphere limited by the corona.

The intensity of the illumination of the atmosphere naturally diminishes gradually during the entire duration of a total eclipse, from its commencement until the beginning of the totality, to again as gradually recover its primitive intensity. This obscurity, during the phase of

* [This, however, has been since disproved as mentioned in the chapter on the Sun, by the spectroscopic observations made by Lockyer, Wüllner, and others on the solar prominences and chromosphere.—R. A. P.]

† The highest prominence, in the form of a peak, measured by Mr. Warren De La Rue in 1860, was 45,000 miles in vertical height above the solar surface.

totality, is, however, very far from being complete. Thus only the brightest stars, and some of those of the second magnitude, are seen. The planets Venus and Mercury, Jupiter, Mars, and Saturn, however, have been likewise observed.

Terrestrial objects take by degrees a livid hue; they are coloured with various tints, among which olive-green predominates. Orange, yellow, vinous-red, and copper tints, give to the landscape a singular appearance, which, joined to a very perceptible lowering of temperature, contributes to produce a profound impression on all animated beings.

Arago thus describes the attitude of an entire population, awe-impressed by the magnificent and solemn spectacle offered by the total eclipse of the 8th of July, 1842.

'At Perpignan, people dangerously ill alone remained in their rooms. The population from early morning covered the terraces, the ramparts of the town, and the hills outside, whence they hoped to see the rising of the Sun. At the citadel, we had under our eyes, besides the numerous groups of citizens on the *glacis*, the soldiers who were being reviewed in the vast court.

'The hour of the commencement of the eclipse approached. Nearly twenty thousand people, with smoked glasses in hand, examined the radiant globe, projected on an azure sky. Scarcely, armed with our powerful telescopes, had we begun to perceive a little encroachment on the western border of the Sun, when an immense shout, mixed with a thousand different exclamations, told us that we had anticipated only by a few seconds the observations made with the naked eye by twenty thousand improvised astronomers. A lively curiosity, an emulation, a desire not to be beaten, seemed to have given to the unarmed sight an extraordinary penetration.

'Between this moment and that which preceded the totality, we remarked nothing in the behaviour of the spectators which deserves relating. But, when the Sun, reduced to a narrow thread, began to throw on our horizon but very feeble light, a sort of inquietude seized upon every one; each felt the desire to communicate his impressions to those by whom he was surrounded. Hence, a dull roar like that of the distant sea after a tempest. The uproar became stronger in proportion as the solar crescent became thinner. The crescent disappeared; at last, darkness suddenly succeeded to light, and an absolute silence marked this phase of the eclipse, as absolutely as the pendulum of our astronomical clock. The phenomenon, in its magnificence, triumphed over the petulance of youth, the careless air which some men take for a sign of superiority, and over the noisy indifference ordinarily assumed by soldiers. A profound calm also reigned in the air; the birds ceased to sing.

'After a solemn waiting of about two minutes, transports of joy—frenzied plaudits greeted, with the same accord, the same spontaneity, the reappearance of the first solar rays. . . .' *

* 'Annuaire du Bureau des Longitudes,' 1846, pp. 303–5.

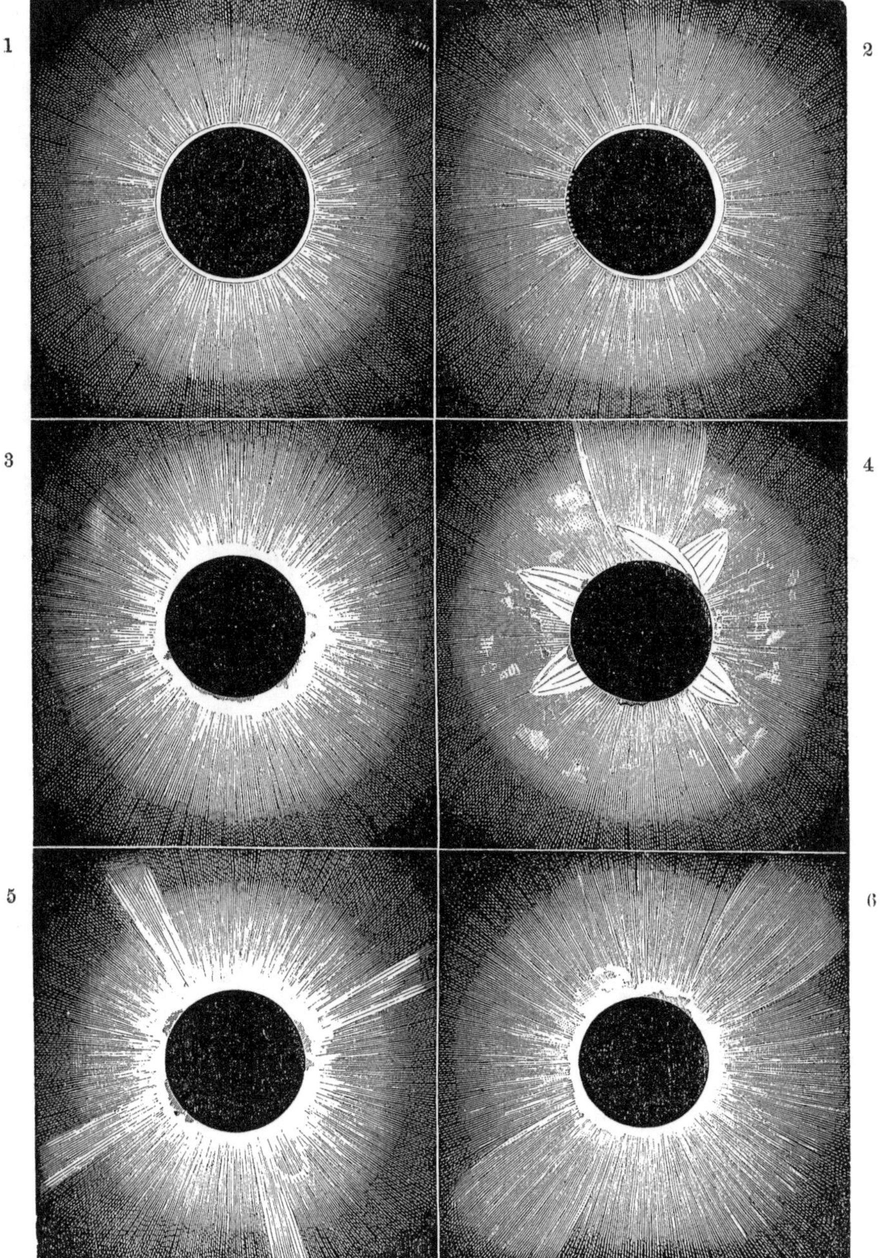

ECLIPSES OF THE SUN.

1. Annular Eclipse. 2. Annular Eclipse of the 15th May, 1836, showing 'Baily's Beads.' 3. Total Eclipse of the 28th July, 1851 (Dawes). 4. Eclipse of 1858 (Liais). 5. Total Eclipse of the 18th July, 1860 (Feilitzsch). 6. Total Eclipse of the 8th July, 1842.

Animals testify, by unmistakable signs and movements, the effect which eclipse-phenomena produce upon them. Vegetation even is not altogether unaffected. In 1842, the leaves of certain plants were shut. During the eclipse of July, 1860, M. Laussedat, who observed it in Algeria, relates this fact:—'The plants showed how rapid is the action of light, which they receive as by a kind of diffused sense in their corollas, for, in spite of the short duration of the totality, daturas, convolvuli, poppies, and night-shades, which had been closely shut, were observed to half open during the total eclipse.'

The observations made during total eclipses of the Sun are very important and interesting from a physical and astronomical point of view, but so numerous that they would fill volumes. We shall confine ourselves, therefore, to saying one word more on the phenomenon of the fringes of the waves, alternately light and dark, which sweep over the Earth, in a direction perpendicular to their length, and the direction of which, when carefully measured, has been found to be parallel to the tangent at the first point of interior contact. These fringes are referred by M. Faye,* to an effect of oblique mirage, produced by a difference of density in the atmospheric strata which compose the cone of the umbra.

[It is to be hoped that the famous 'Himalaya' expedition to Spain in 1860, to watch the eclipse which occurred in that year, will on all future similar occasions be drawn into a precedent. Mr. Warren De La Rue's Memoir, published in the 'Philosophical Transactions,' containing a complete account of the results of all his observations, and especially of his photographic ones, is one of the most valuable contributions to this branch of our subject possessed by astronomers. We would gladly, if space permitted, make large extracts from it.]

XII.

ECLIPSES OF THE MOON.

Conditions of Possibility and Visibility of Eclipses of the Moon—Partial and Total Eclipses—Colour of the Lunar Disk during the Phases of a Total Eclipse—Periodicity and Calculation of Eclipses—Occultations of the Fixed Stars and Planets.

Like the eclipses of the Sun, those of the Moon may be either partial or total; but they are never annular, the Earth's cone of shade being always,

* This interesting phenomenon was observed with minute care by MM. Laussedat and Mannheim, members of the Commission sent by the Polytechnic School to Batna (Algeria), in July, 1860. They furnish us with the first exact measures of the direction and rapidity of these phenomena. The following year (during the eclipse of 1861) a French officer, M. Poulain, repeated the measures, according to the indications of M. Mannheim. The *Monthly Notices of the Royal Astronomical Society of London*, mentioning in 1862 this last observation, have omitted (we know not why) to refer to the original observation published in detail in the *Comptes Rendus de l'Académie des Sciences de Paris*, and in the *Annales de Physique et de Chimie*, in the year 1860.

at the greatest distances of our satellite from us, much more considerable than the lunar disk itself.

A fundamental distinction, however, between the two phenomena is, that while an eclipse of the Sun is visible in a part only of that terrestrial hemisphere which has that body above the horizon, an eclipse of the Moon is visible from every part of the Earth where she has not set. This is not all: it is only successively that an eclipse of the Sun is observed at different stations, in proportion as the umbra and penumbra of the Moon traverse the surface of our globe, but, on the contrary, the obscuration of the lunar disk begins and terminates everywhere, not at the same hour, because the hour varies according to the longitude of the place of observation, but at the same physical instant.

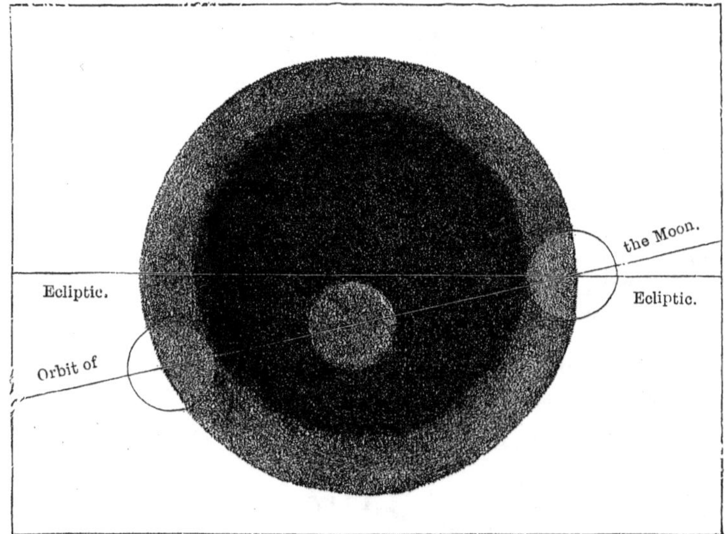

Fig. 70.—Path of the Moon in the Earth's cone of shade. Total Eclipse.

The reader has already understood the reason of this essential difference. In the solar eclipse, the surface of the radiant body is not really darkened, but only hidden by the obscure disk of the Moon, so that the interposition is an effect of perspective, varying according to the respective positions of the observer, of the Moon and of the Sun. The lunar eclipse is, on the contrary, produced by a real fading of the Moon's light, and the darkness consequent upon it is observed at the same instant everywhere where the Moon is in view.

The two diagrams, figs. 70, 71, show under what conditions an eclipse of the Moon is partial or total. When the Moon, in opposition, traverses the cone of shadow thrown by the Earth, at its thickest part, the eclipse is total and central, and its duration the greatest possible.

The eclipse may, however, be still total, without being central, when the orbit of the Moon traverses a sufficient breadth of the cone. But if the Moon's node is too far from the centre of the cone, its disk, penetrating the umbra only in part, will only be incompletely darkened — the eclipse will be partial.*

At the commencement of a total eclipse of the Moon, there is first noticed a marked diminution of the brightness of the disk, this is due to the Moon's entering the penumbra. Then, suddenly, a small patch of darkness is seen, which by degrees invades the luminous parts of the disk, but the outline of the portion thus eaten out is far from being as sharp as that observed in solar eclipses. The form is circular, but the curvature is less decided, a fact easily imagined, and confirmed by calcu-

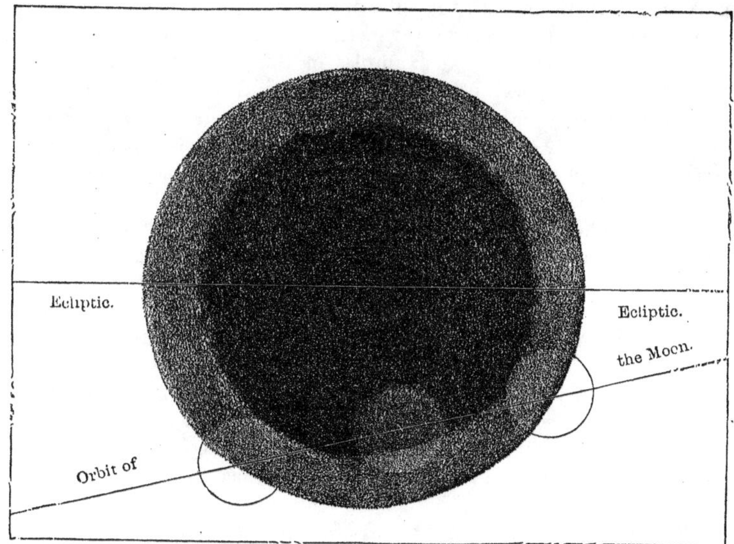

Fig. 71.—Path of the Moon in the Earth's cone of shade. Partial Eclipse.

lation, the diameter of the Earth's shadow being nearly three times as great as that of the Moon itself.†

The colour of the shadow is at first a greyish black, which permits us to see nothing of the part eclipsed; but, as the shadow gains on the lunar disk, a reddish tint makes its appearance, and the details of the principal spots become visible. Between the luminous crescent and the ruddy centre of the shadow is observed a band of greyish blue.

* [There are occasions also when the Moon passes partially within the Earth's penumbra, without reaching the umbra. These eclipses are not noted in the Nautical Almanac, but the theory of eclipses can hardly be regarded as complete without a consideration of them. An eclipse of this sort took place in September, 1868. I have proposed that they should be called penumbral lunar eclipses.—R. A. P.]

† The mean diameter of the Earth's shadow at the distance at which eclipses occur, is about 82′, whilst the lunar diameter is only 31′.

From the time of totality the red becomes more intense, and is soon spread over the whole of the disk. According to Beer and Mädler the bluish tint is of a dark grey when compared with that part of the Moon illuminated by the Sun; it seems blue, and clearer than the red, if compared with the latter.

Some minutes before the reappearance of the light on the opposite side of the disk, the bluish tint slightly colours that side also, and the phases of the eclipse are reproduced in an inverse order, until the entire emersion of the Moon.

The Moon, therefore, does not always completely disappear in total eclipses. The cause of this fact lies in the refraction of the solar rays in traversing the lower strata of the Earth's atmosphere; they are diverted, and purple our Moon with the tints of sunset.

It sometimes happens, however, that the Moon becomes quite invisible during a total eclipse; as examples of this we may quote the eclipses of 1642 and 1816. At other times, the visibility, without being absolutely *nil*, is very indistinct; we find the explanation of these circumstances in the state of our atmosphere at the time on the periphery of our Earth which comprises the places where the Sun is rising and setting at the moment of the eclipse.

Another phenomenon, which happens, however, very rarely, appears contradictory to the geometric and astronomical theory of eclipses. We refer to the simultaneous presence of the Sun and Moon during the phenomenon. The first of these bodies setting at the moment when the other rises, it would seem that the Moon, the Earth, and the Sun, are no longer in a straight line. This appearance again is owing to refraction. The Sun, actually already below the horizon, is raised up by refraction, and remains visible to us. The same thing happens to the Moon, which is not yet really risen, although we see it. The eclipses of 1666, 1668, and the 19th of July, 1750, may be quoted as having presented this singular circumstance.

We must now bring our notices of eclipses to a conclusion, by saying a word on their periodicity.

About every eighteen years, the Earth, Moon, and Sun, again occupy the same relative positions. This is a fact which the ancients proved by observation long before the theory of the celestial movements had demonstrated its near approach to the truth. If, then, we start from the epoch of an eclipse of the Sun or Moon, that is to say, from a lunar opposition or conjunction coinciding with one of the nodes of the Moon, after eighteen years the three bodies will again be found in a situation nearly identical. Hence, the eclipses which succeed one another in the first period follow again and in the same order during the second period.

This is the principal point of departure in the calculation of eclipses; but the approximation is too rough for modern astronomers to content themselves with, and nowadays eclipses are foretold for many years in advance, true to a second of time.

The Moon, in traversing its orbit round the Earth, produces again another kind of eclipse, to which the name of *occultation* has been given.

We say that a planet or a star is *occulted* when it passes behind the lunar disk. We have spoken of these phenomena with reference to the question of the existence of an atmosphere on the surface of the Moon.

Let us add that the occultations of stars are calculated like eclipses, and that, as they are frequent, they have been made of use to our navigators. The Moon being very near the Earth, compared with the distance of the stars and even of the planets, it follows that two observers, placed in two different parts of the globe, do not see it projected at the same instant on the same part of the heavens. The occultation of a star, therefore, does not take place to them at the same instant of time.

The starry heavens resemble, from this point of view, an universal dial, of which the Moon is the minute hand, marking the time at once in all parts of the Earth. Thanks to the tables calculated by astronomers, these various hours can be converted the one into the other; and the traveller in the desert, as well as he who traverses the ocean, is thus enabled to arrive at his position and to determine his route.

XIII.

THE METEORIC RINGS.

Shooting or Falling Stars—'Star-showers'—Their Numbers—Radiant Points—Recent Discoveries respecting the Position, Form, and Inclination of the Meteoric Rings—Heights, Velocities, and Weights of Shooting Stars—Luminous Meteors (Bolides), their Telescopic Appearance—Meteorites; Professor Maskelyne's Classification; Mr. Sorby's Microscopic Examination of them, and its results—Remarkable Meteorites.

Every one is familiar with shooting or falling stars. We have all seen their luminous trains furrowing the heavens during the night, like so many brilliant points suddenly detached from the celestial vault. Are these appearances, now rare and isolated, now numerous and periodical, due to meteors of atmospheric origin, or must they be considered as manifesting the existence of bodies situated in the extra-terrestrial regions? The place which our description of these phenomena of the solar system occupies shows pretty clearly that it is to this last conclusion that science has definitely come.

The number of shooting stars is very variable according to the time of the year; hence the distinction between *sporadic meteors* and the *showers* of shooting stars which appear in the nocturnal sky in large numbers, and generally periodically. During ordinary nights, the mean number of shooting stars observed in an interval of an hour is from four to five, according to some observers; it is as high as eight according to others.*

But at two periods of the year, about the 10th of August and the 11th of November, these phenomena are much more numerous, and the number of shooting stars observed in one hour is often more than tenfold that seen on ordinary nights. Let us quote, for the month of August, the observations of Capocci and Nobile, who, in four hours, counted at Naples 1000 shooting stars (10th of August, 1839), and those of M. Walferdin, who in an hour observed 316 (at Bourbonne-les-Bains, in the night of the 8th–9th of August, 1836). It is to this phenomenon that popular tradition formerly gave the name of 'St. Lawrence's tears.' The luminous trains being nothing else, to the *naïve* populations of Catholic Ireland, than the burning tears of the martyr whose feast falls on the 10th of August.

The month of November has furnished still more extraordinary facts, and the appearances of the 12th of November, 1799, and of the night of the 12th–13th of November, 1833, are well worthy of mention. Humboldt and Bonpland, who were at Cumana on the first of these dates, relate that between the hours of two and five in the morning, the sky was covered with innumerable luminous trains, which incessantly traversed the celestial vault from north to south, presenting the appearance of fireworks let off at an enormous height; large meteors, having sometimes an apparent diameter of one and a half times that of the Moon, blending their trains with the long, luminous, and phosphorescent paths of the shooting stars. In Brazil, Labrador, Greenland, Germany, and French Guyana, the same phenomena were observed.

The showers of the 12th–13th of November, 1833, were not less extraordinary. 'The meteors were observed,' says Arago,† 'along the eastern coast of America, from the Gulf of Mexico as far as Halifax, from nine o'clock in the evening till sunrise, and even, in some places, in full day, at eight o'clock in the morning. They were so numerous, and were visible in so many regions of the sky at once, that in trying to count them one could only hope to arrive at a very rough approximation. An observer (Olmsted) at Boston compared them at the moment of maximum to half the number of flakes which are seen in the air during an ordinary fall of snow. When the brilliancy of the display was considerably reduced, he counted 650 in 15 minutes, though he confined his observations to a zone which was not a tenth of the visible horizon. According to him, this number was but two-thirds of the total; thus he estimates the number at 866, and in all the visible hemisphere, 8660. This last value would give during each hour 34,640 shooting stars. Now, the phenomenon lasted more than seven hours, and therefore the number seen at Boston exceeded

* This hourly mean is from five to six, according to Olbers; from four to five, according to Dr. J. Schmidt; five to seven is given by M. Coulvier-Gravier, and Saigey; and, lastly, eight by M. Quételet.

† 'Astronomie Populaire,' vol. iv. p. 310.

240,000; and yet it must not be forgotten that the bases of this calculation were obtained at a moment when the display was already notably on the decline.'

[Mr. Newton, an American astronomer, who has given much attention to this subject, finds that the average number of meteors which traverse the atmosphere daily, and which are large enough to be visible to the naked eye on a dark clear night, is no less than 7,500,000; and applying the same reasoning to telescopic meteors, their numbers will have to be increased to 400,000,000! If allowance be made for the space occupied by the Earth's atmosphere, we find that, in the mean, in each volume as large as the Earth, of the space which the Earth traverses in its orbit about the Sun, there are as many as 13,000 small bodies, each body such as would furnish a shooting star visible under favourable circumstances to the naked eye. If telescopic meteors be counted, this number should be increased at least forty-fold.]

Several less important periods have been recognised at other times of the year, but they have not the same regularity as those of August and November.

These last-mentioned periods also present a rise and fall in the hourly number of shooting stars observed. From a maximum of 110 stars, in August, 1848, the number was reduced to 40 in 1858, and since then the numbers in the same month have regained their upward march. The November shower, of old so remarkable, is now reduced to the point of being less remarkable than that observed at night towards the end of October. Since 1862, however, this shower is again increasing in numbers, [and in 1866, 1867, and 1868, it has afforded very remarkable displays.]

Most frequently the paths described by shooting stars have the appearance of straight lines. The luminous trains left in the heavens by their rapid movement, enable us easily to verify this fact. But there are exceptions, and stars of this kind have been seen to describe, before disappearing, strangely curved paths.

Their brilliancy is also very variable: some have surpassed in apparent size the most brilliant fixed stars, and even Venus and Jupiter. The colour likewise varies.

On observing a given number of shooting stars, it has been found that about two-thirds are white; while yellow, reddish yellow, and green characterise the remainder.

We now come to a fact of great importance, which has thrown much light on the origin of these meteoric showers, and revealed their cosmical nature. In observing the direction of the trajectories on the celestial vault, it has been noticed that the greatest number of those observed at any one time are emitted from the same part of the heavens, called the *radiant point*, because from it they radiate in all directions.

The star Mu in the constellation of the Lion (μ Leonis) is the point of the November showers, whilst Gamma in Perseus (γ Persei) is the radiant points of the stars observed in the month of August. No less than

56 radiant points have been shown to exist in different seasons of the year.

We must infer from these facts, that shooting stars are luminous bodies, the movement of which is independent of the rotation of the Earth, and that they are external to our atmosphere. This conclusion is singularly corroborated by this other fact, that the radiant points in the Lion and Perseus are precisely those towards which our globe is travelling, in its annual movement round the Sun, at the two epochs of November and August.

Astronomers have therefore concluded, that the appearance of shooting stars is caused by the Earth's passage through rings composed of myriads of these bodies circulating, like the larger planets, round the Sun, and the parallel movements of which seen from the Earth seem to radiate towards

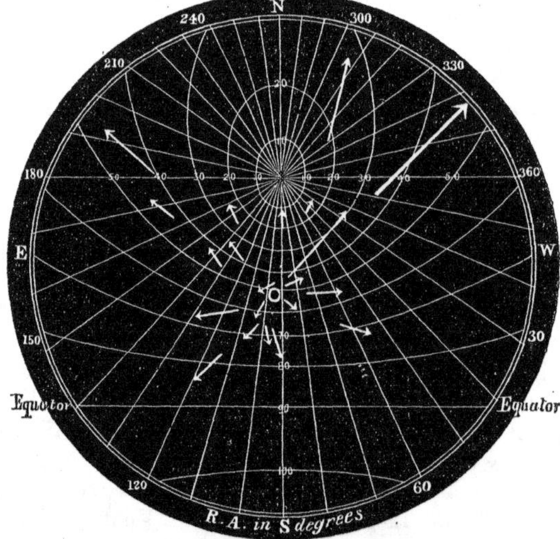

Fig. 72.—Radiant Point of Shooting Stars. R.A. 94°, N. Decl. 37°.
Radiant Point of Meteors observed at Hawkhurst, Nov. 28. (Mr. Alexander Herschel.)

that part of the heavens approached by our Earth. The appearance required by this theory is exactly that which is represented to us.

At first it was a question, whether there existed one ring, the various regions of which, sometimes richer, sometimes poorer in cosmical matter, could give rise to the varying phenomena observed. Or whether we should admit the existence of many separate rings, successively traversed by the Earth.

It will be seen, in fig. 73, how the periodical appearances of August and November can be explained on the hypothesis of a single ring. We may suppose that the plane of the meteoric ring coincides exactly, or nearly so, with that of the ecliptic, and that the orbit of the meteors is a more elongated curve, or one of greater excentricity, than the terrestrial orbit,

[This view, however, is not in accordance with the observed positions of the 'radiant-points' of these systems; and has recently been completely disproved.—R. A. P.] A single inspection of the figure will show that the Earth should encounter a large number of meteors, in travelling from its aphelion in July to its perihelion at the end of December, than in the opposite period of its revolution.

Now, if we suppose two rings inclined at different angles to the plane of the ecliptic, and cutting this plane, one in August and in February, the other in May and November, we can also account both for the two maxima and minima of the year.

[It has now been demonstrated that meteors belong to systems of bodies, travelling in orbits of all degrees of excentricity around the Sun; and further, that the Earth encounters more than a hundred such systems in the course of her annual revolution.

As regards the two systems which produce the November and August showers, our evidence is very complete. The first circumstance which suggested the possibility that shooting stars may travel in very eccentric orbits, was a somewhat singular one. Schiaparelli had noticed that the comet of 1862 passed very close to that part of the Earth's orbit where she encounters the August meteors, and he was led to inquire whether on the supposition that the meteors have an orbit as excentric as that of the comet, the two orbits would agree *in other respects*. He found the agreement singularly close. The evidence thus adduced, though founded on an assumption, was of a very remarkable character, because there are millions of possible orbits fulfilling this assumption and also crossing the Earth's orbit in the same place as the path of the comet of 1862, which yet would show no resemblance whatever to the path of that comet. Schiaparelli accordingly expressed the opinion that the agreement could not possibly result from accident,—that in other words some physical association exists between the August meteors and the comet of 1862 (described and pictured further on.) But, although the evidence rightly understood was demonstrative, it is probable that very little attention would have been paid to it, but for an unexpected confirmation which it presently received.

In 1866, the November meteors attracted an unusual degree of attention on account of the wonderful display they presented on the morning of November 13th, in that year. Since these meteors attain their maximum of splendour at intervals of about 33 years, or more exactly about three times in each century, the idea would naturally have been suggested that they travel in an orbit whose period is about 33⅓ years, had it not been for the circumstance that an orbit of that period would carry them beyond the orbit of Uranus. Astronomers were not prepared to admit so surprising a result, where a simpler explanation was available. Accordingly the theory was suggested that the meteors travel in a period of one year, *plus* or *minus* a thirty-third part. This would account for the observed tri-secular recurrences of maximum displays. But the place where the November meteors cross the Earth's orbit is slowly shifting, owing to planetary perturbations, and this fact enabled Professor Adams to test the various orbits assigned to the meteor system. He found that orbits of short period would not account for the observed displacement of the nodes of the meteor-system. He was led accordingly to try the period of 33⅓ years. After overcoming the great difficulties resulting from the very eccentric character of the the corresponding orbit, he found that this widely extended path, by which the meteors are carried beyond the orbit of Uranus, and subjected to the perturbations of the giant planets outside the zone of asteroids, accounts perfectly for the observed motion of the node.

It was demonstrated, therefore, that the November meteors revolve in

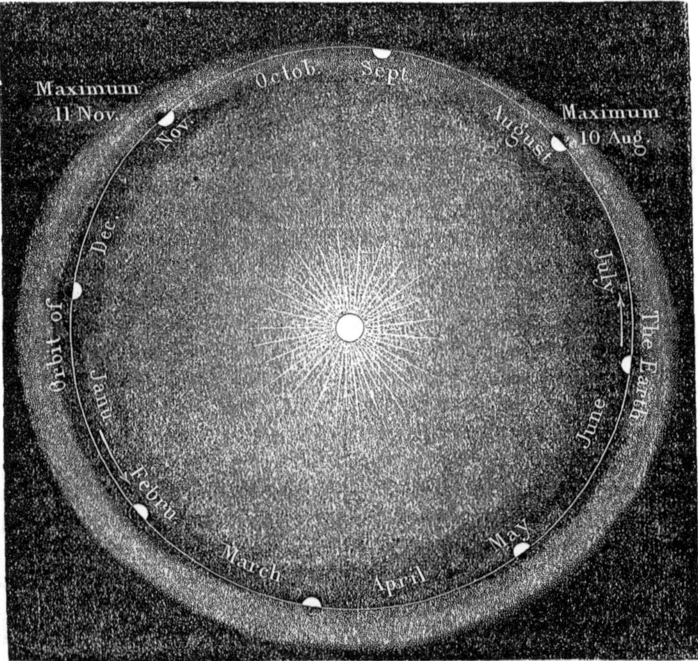

Fig. 73.—Ring of meteorical bodies circulating round the Sun.

a period of about 33⅓ years, and in an orbit resembling the eccentric cometary orbits. Schiaparelli's discovery respecting the August meteors now naturally attracted fresh attention. The question was asked, whether a comet could be found whose orbit should correspond with that of the November meteors. After searching among all the more noted comets, astronomers examined telescopic ones. At length they found a small comet (Tempel's), *only discovered a few months before,* whose path agreed in the most remarkable manner with the orbit of the meteors. Peters, Leverrier, Adams, and other astronomers, helped to demonstrate the identity of the two orbits, respecting which there is now no shadow of doubt.

This comet, too, it fortunately chances, is one of three which have been subjected to spectroscopic analysis by Mr. Huggins, with results which are described further on.

Now that we know that the meteor-systems encountered by the Earth travel in orbits of great extent, excentricity, and inclination, we have every reason for believing (or rather it must be held to be demonstrated) that the total number of meteor-systems within the solar domain is practically infinite; for only on this supposition can it be accounted for that the Earth encounters so many of these systems.—R. A. P.]

The heights of a great number of shooting stars at the moment of their appearance and disappearances have been determined.

'Shooting stars,' says Humboldt,* 'descend nearly to the summits of Chimboraco and of Aconcagua, at 8750 yards above the level of the sea.'.

[Much attention has lately been given in England, America, and Italy, to this subject. Mr. Herschel, who is to England what Mr. Newton is to America, has recently collated the observations undertaken to determine the heights of meteors. It appears that the heights of shooting stars at Rome are sensibly the same as in those latitudes of Northern Europe and America where they have chiefly been observed; and this height, as determined from the most trustworthy observations since 1798, may be stated to be respectively 73 and 53 miles, at first appearance and disappearance above the surface of the Earth, with a probable error of *not more than two or three miles*.]

The height of a shooting star, at the two extremities of its path, and the time of its flight, are elements which enable us to determine the mean velocity of the body. This velocity often exceeds the velocity of the translation of the Earth, which is nearly 18 miles a second. Meteors have been observed which have traversed space with the enormous rapidity of 43 miles, and others 50, and even 100 miles a second; that is, from two to five times the velocity of the Earth.

[The average velocity of shooting stars, however, in 66 instances observed by Mr. Herschel, is 34·4, or in round numbers 35 miles per second.]

The tremendous velocity with which these meteors traverse the celestial spaces enables us readily to understand their incandescence when they enter our atmosphere; composed of easily inflammable matter, like some sulphureous metallic combinations, the intensity of the friction which they undergo in the upper strata of our atmosphere results in a very great rise of temperature sufficient to produce incandescence.

[Mr. Herschel has roughly estimated, according to the dynamical theory of heat, the weight of twenty shooting stars, and found it to be on an average a little more than two ounces. A similar estimate of the largest meteor observed in 1863 gave two hundredweight.]

Differences of chemical composition and of degrees of incandescence also account for the diversity of colours which are observed.

* 'Cosmos,' vol. iii. p. 615.

In the immense number of meteors which invade the regions of the air in a year, there are some perhaps that only pass through its domain and continue their path in space, after having presented us with the spectacle of a transient illumination. A great number, on the other hand, not only do not again leave our atmosphere, being vaporised therein, but, when of large size, attain the very surface of the Earth. Falls of stones, ferruginous masses, and dust, from the upper regions of the air, are proofs of this assertion.

From shooting stars to meteors, or *bolides*, the transition in our narrative is easy: the difference between these two orders of phenomena is not very strongly marked.

Bolides are luminous bodies of circular, or rather of spherical, form, and of sensible apparent diameter. Like shooting stars, they appear suddenly, but generally they move more slowly, and disappear after some seconds. Their light is ordinarily less vivid, but their much more considerable apparent dimensions are sufficient to compensate this difference of intensity. The illumination of the landscape by the presence of a

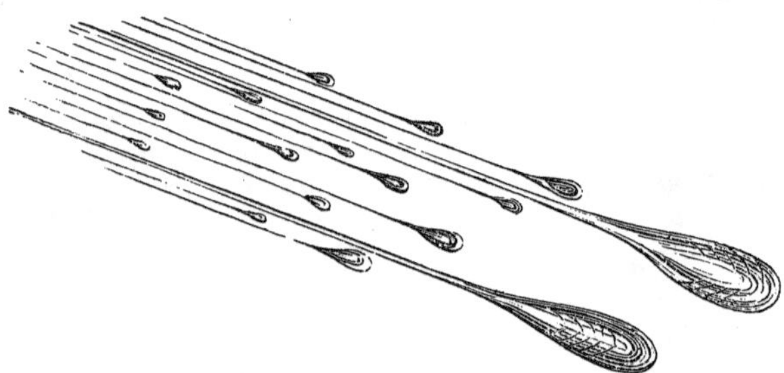

Fig. 74.—Appearance of a Meteor in a Telescope. (Schmidt.)

meteor sometimes approaches that of moonlight. Most of them leave behind a luminous train; others explode with violence, and sometimes the explosion is accompanied with reports like discharges of artillery.

The appearance of meteors is more rare than that of shooting stars, the total number of observations recorded amounting at most to a thousand, reckoning those recorded by the ancients.

A curious circumstance, and one which helps to prove the relationship between the shooting stars and meteors, is the fact that the appearances of meteors are more frequent in August and November than at other epochs of the year; and the total number from July to December exceeds also that observed from December to July.

[One of the most curious observations of a meteor which have been recorded, leaving that of 1783 out of the question, was recently made by Dr. Schmidt, who was fortunate enough to observe a large meteor in a telescope, under a magnifying power of eight times. The fire-ball was twin, and was followed by several smaller ones, following side by side with parallel motions of translation until all were extinguished (fig. 74). This observation lends force to the supposition that meteors exist in space as a crowd of bodies, revolving round each other, before they enter our atmosphere.]

The heights of meteors from the surface of the Earth are often very considerable; they vary between 7 and 310 miles. It must then be held, as remarked by Arago, that the sudden incandescence of meteors is produced in regions where it was formerly supposed that the strata of the terrestrial atmosphere were so rarefied that all action of its elements on the matter of the shooting stars would be regarded as impossible.

It has been suggested, not without some probability, that the attraction of the Earth is susceptible of retaining meteors in the state of permanent satellites; and astronomical treatises quote the calculations of a French astronomer, M. Petit, of Toulouse, who assigns to one of these bodies a revolution round our globe, the period of which would be three hours and twenty minutes. The distance of this singular companion of our Moon is 5000 miles from the surface of our Earth.

We are here brought naturally to say a word of the falls of meteorites —stony and ferruginous masses, which, leaving the interplanetary spaces, have at various times astonished our populations by their unexpected fall.

[Professor Maskelyne has recently made a convenient classification of meteorites into 'Aërolites or Meteoric *Stones*;' 'Aërosiderites or Meteoric *Iron*;' and 'Aërosiderolites,' which includes the intervening varieties.

Thinking that, unlike all terrestrial rocks, meteorites are probably portions of cosmical matter, which has not been acted upon by water or volcanic heat, Mr. Sorby was led to study their microscopical structure. He has thus been able to ascertain that the material was at one time certainly in a state of fusion; and that the most remote condition, of which we have positive evidence, was that of small, detached, melted globules, the formation of which cannot be explained in a satisfactory manner, except by supposing that their constituents were originally in the state of vapour, as they now exist in the atmosphere of the Sun; and, on the temperature becoming lower, condensed into these 'ultimate cosmical particles.' These afterwards collected together into larger masses, which have been variously changed by subsequent metamorphic action, and broken up by repeated mutual impact, and often again collected together and solidified. The meteoric irons are probably those portions of the metallic constituents which were separated from the rest by fusion when the metamorphism was carried to that extreme point. Though at present he looks upon it as a mere hypothesis, he ventures to suggest that there is a similar relation between these ultimate cosmical globules and planets that there is between the minute drops of water in the clouds, and an ocean; and that the study of the microscopical structure of meteorites reveals to us the physical history of the solar system at the most remote period of which we have any evidence.]

It is now universally admitted that there is an intimate relation between the phenomena of shooting stars, meteors, and meteoric falls; as the falls have been in several instances known to occur after the appearance of a meteor.

On the 26th of April, 1803, at Aigle, Department of Orne, a few minutes after the appearance of a large meteor, moving from south-east to north-west, which was also perceived at Alencon, Caen, and Falaise, a frightful explosion, followed by detonations similar to the noise of cannon, or the roll of musketry, proceeded from a single black cloud in a very clear sky. A large quantity of meteorical stones, still fuming, was found

Fig. 75.—Mass of meteoric iron, weighing 15 cwt., found in 1828 by Brard, at Caille (Var).

on the surface of the ground, over an extent of country measuring not less than six miles, in the direction of its greatest length. The largest of these stones weighed rather less than twenty-four pounds.

More recently, in the evening of the 15th of May, 1864, the identity of meteorites and meteors was evidenced by the appearance, explosion, and fall of a splendid meteor, which was observed over a great extent of France. A globe of brilliant light, leaving behind it a whitish train, was shattered rocket-wise into numerous fragments. A noise like the prolonged rumbling of thunder followed the explosion at some minutes' interval, and a fall of stones which took place over about two square leagues enabled the extra-telluric matters of which the meteor was composed to be examined.

Aërolites and aërosiderites of the same origin, but of much more considerable size, have been collected in different museums. M. Daubrée has permitted us to reproduce here, in figs. 75 and 76, two of the most beautiful specimens of meteorites now known. The first is a block of pure iron, found in a plain in the department of Var, which weighs upwards of eleven hundredweight. It is very remarkable for its crystalline structure, visible even on its exterior, but rendered still more evident by a section made artificially at one of its angles.

This is one of the treasures of the mineralogical galleries of the Natural History Museum of Paris; where, thanks to the zeal of M. Daubrée, the number of meteorites gathered from different points of the globe is increasing daily.

Mineralogists and chemists have analysed these meteorites with great

Fig. 76.—Aërolite found at Juvénas (rdèche), the 5th of June, 1821.

care, and it has been found that their composition is nearly always the same, whatever difference their external aspect presents. Oxygen, sulphur, phosphorus and carbon, silicium and aluminium, potassium, sodium, sulphide of iron, metallic and magnetic iron, and other metals, such as nickel, cobalt, manganese, tin, copper, &c., have been recognised among the substances of which meteorites are composed. Latterly, the presence of nitrogen has been detected, besides the eighteen simple bodies, of which the principal have just been cited.

It is worthy of remark that all the simple bodies found in meteoric stones are known in our own planet. The chemical combinations of these bodies do not differ from those with which we are acquainted, excepting two or three, of which one, *schreiberzite,* has been recently artificially reproduced.*

* By MM. Faye and H. Deville.

Thus, thanks to the phenomena which we have described—meteorites, meteors, and shooting stars—the planetary spaces, which seemed for ever shut out from direct investigation, have been correlated with our Earth. These masses, undefiled until the time of their fall by living contact, relate to us the mineralogy and chemistry of a whole region of the sky. By combining the indications which they furnish with the marvellous revelations of spectrum analysis, man is beginning to obtain precise notions on the composition of the most distant celestial bodies; and he will thus expand those ideas which the laws of attraction, of light, and of heat, have already enabled him to hold on their physical constitution.

XIV.

MARS.

Movement of Mars round the Sun — Mars, in Opposition; Conditions necessary for a favourable Opposition — Bright and Dark Spots — Effects of the Transit of Clouds — Colour of the Planet's Disk; Why Mars is sometimes Red — Polar Snows — Melting of the Polar Snows — Rotation — Seasons and Climate.

In pursuing our exploration of the solar world, we meet with Mars after the Earth; it is the next planet in the order of distance from the Sun, and therefore the first, the orbit of which encircles that of the Earth, or of those bodies which are called by astronomers *Exterior* or *Superior Planets.*

At successive [average] intervals of two years, one month, and nineteen days, its movement of revolution brings it in opposition with the Sun; that is to say, in a line passing respectively through the centres of the Sun, Earth, and the planet. Mars is then comparatively very near to us, and in an extremely favourable situation for observations of its disk; indeed, excepting the Moon, there is no planetary body, the physical constitution of which has been better studied.

Mars appears to the naked eye as the reddest star in the heavens,* but its brightness varies considerably, on account of the variability of its distance from the Earth. Occasionally its light scintillates, but most frequently this does not happen: and it is thus, like all other planets, distinguished from the stars of the same apparent magnitude.

If, instead of observing with the naked eye, a telescope of sufficient magnifying power is used, the scintillation entirely disappears, the luminous point takes the form of a clearly defined disk, and the degree of intensity of the red colour diminishes and passes to a general tint of a yellowish red.

As is the case with Venus and Mercury, the light which Mars emits is borrowed from the Sun; but it is more difficult to prove this fact, common to all the bodies which revolve round the central fire, absolutely,

* Beer, Mädler, and Arago.

because the phases of its disk are extremely small. They exist, however. It is easy to account for this difference, which we shall find more decided still in the planets furthest from the Sun.

When Mars and the Earth are brought, by their movements of translation round the Sun, into a straight line with it (see fig. 77), but in such a manner that we are placed between the Sun and the planet, Mars is presented to us under the form of a completely illuminated disk. It

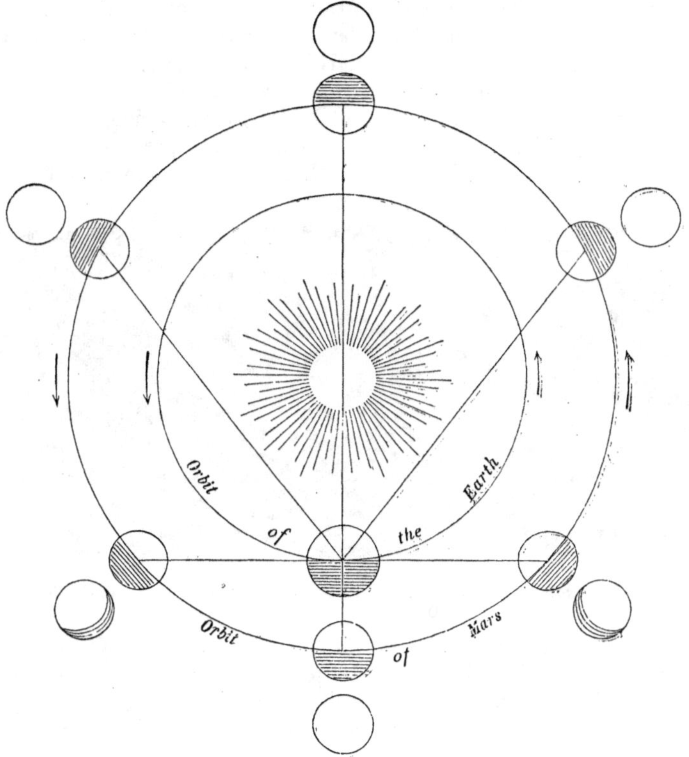

Fig. 77.—Orbit and Phases of Mars.

presents the same appearance when it is on the other side of the Sun. In the intermediate positions, there is but little perceptible change in the appearance to that presented at conjunction or opposition.* At certain distances, however, from these two extreme positions,† Mars presents to

* Let us remind the reader that a planet is in *Conjunction* when it is on the same line as the Sun, between it and the Earth. It is in *Opposition* when on the same line as the Sun, but on the opposite side of the Earth to the Sun.

† At the *quadratures*, or in the position in which lines drawn to the Earth and Sun form the greatest possible angle.

us a slight portion of its dark hemisphere, although the luminous part is always by far the larger.

The aspect of Mars at this time caused Sir J. Herschel to apply the term *gibbous*. The apparent form of the planet then is that of the Moon, two or three days before or after full.

However slight this phase, it suffices to prove, as we have before said, that Mars is not self-luminous, and we shall see that it is thus with all the other planets.

If we consider the orbit which Mars describes round the Sun, we shall readily see how it is that this planet is most favourably situated for observations of the physical particularities of its surface.

The two inferior planets, Mercury and Venus, oscillating at small distances round the Sun, are often hid in its rays; besides, during their periods of visibility, they show us a considerable portion of their dark sides. It is not thus with Mars, which is only lost once in a revolution

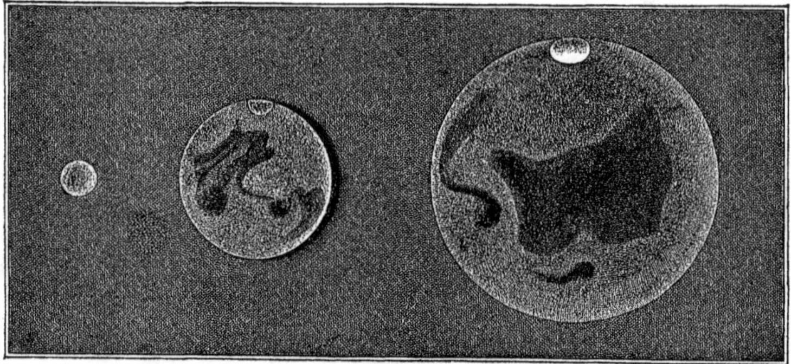

Fig. 78.—Apparent dimensions of Mars at its mean and extreme distances from the Earth.

in the solar rays, and is almost without phases. We have before said that when a superior planet is in opposition with the Sun, its distance from the Earth is least. At this epoch, indeed, this distance is measured by the difference between the distances of the planet and the Earth from the Sun.

Let us look into this statement a little closer with regard to Mars.

Like all planets, Mars describes an orbit which is not circular, so that its distance from the focus of the system varies continually. At its greatest distance from the Sun, Mars is 159,000,000 miles removed; at its minimum distance, 132,000,000: its mean distance being 145,000,000 miles. Thus the difference in the distance from the Sun at perihelion and aphelion amounts to 27,000,000 miles. These numbers indicate an orbit of considerable ellipticity.

From this follow also enormous differences in the distance of Mars from the Earth; in their various relative positions; whilst the planet is sometimes distant from us 256,000,000 miles, in its most favourable opposition t is not more than 35,000,000 miles away from us — a distance seven times less than the first.

It will not be astonishing, then, in glancing at figure 78, to find such great differences between the apparent dimensions of the disk of Mars, seen from the Earth at its extreme and mean distances.

[We may, with advantage, pursue this subject a little further. In the case of an *inferior* planet, if we suppose, bearing the elliptic form of the orbit in mind, the perihelion of the Earth to coincide in direction — or, as astronomers put it, to be in the same heliocentric longitude — as the aphelion of the planet, it will be obvious that the *conjunctions* which happen in this part of the orbits of both will bring the bodies nearer together than will the conjunctions which happen elsewhere. Similarly, if we suppose the aphelion of the Earth to coincide with the perihelion of a *superior* planet — let us say of Mars — it will be obvious that the

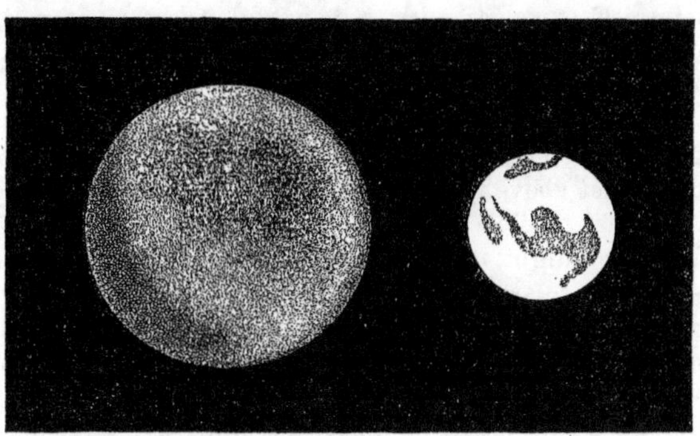

Fig. 79.—Mars and the Earth; comparative dimensions.

oppositions which happen in that part of the orbit will be the most favourable for observation. It happens, however, that these points are in no case coincident.*

The perihelion of the Earth is situated in 99° of heliocentric longitude, its aphelion is therefore situated in long. 279° (=99°+180°). The perihelion of Mars is in long. 332°. The oppositions, therefore, which occur near the part of his orbit are looked forward to with the greatest interest, and utilised to the utmost by astronomers — the oppositions of 1830 and 1862 to wit.†]

Mars traverses its orbit with varying velocities. Its mean rate of motion is upwards of 54,000 miles an hour, or about 16 miles a second.

* [The orbit of the Earth, however, is so nearly circular, that practically nothing is lost. Were it as elliptical as that of Mars, this consideration would be of great importance.]

† [In Mr. Lockyer's 'Elementary Lessons of Astronomy' will be found at p. 185, a figure showing the successive conjunction lines of Mars and the Earth during the years 1856–1871. It is borrowed from a plate illustrating an article by the present writer in the 'Popular Science Review' for January, 1867.—R. A. P.]

The apparent diameter of Mars is less than that of Venus; this is due to two causes; firstly, Venus approaches nearer the Earth, and, secondly, the diameter of that planet is larger in reality than that of Mars; it exceeds it by about three-fourths. The diameter of Mars is 4113 miles, that is, a little less than half that of the Earth, which is nearly 8000 miles.

Lastly, whilst the surface of Mars is scarcely more than a quarter of the Earth's surface, its volume does not exceed the seventh part. Nevertheless, it is more than double that of Mercury, and about seven times that of the Moon.

We now arrive at a subject of extreme interest—the physical constitution of the planet.

To observe Mars, we must choose the most favourable epoch—that of opposition; and, if possible, of an opposition when the planet, as we have before explained, is at its greatest possible proximity to the Earth. We must also furnish ourselves with a powerful telescope, one, if possible, driven by clockwork, so that it exactly keeps pace with the planet in its westward course.

Let us turn our instrument on the reddish luminous point of light, on a clear night, when the air is calm and charged with moisture, and the height of the planet above the horizon is the greatest possible, so that we shall have the least possible thickness of atmosphere to penetrate. It will be then nearly midnight, since it is towards that hour that all planets culminate—that is to say, pass the meridian—at opposition.

The disk of the planet will appear of a nearly circular form, perfectly well defined, and overspread with light and dark spots, which differ considerably in tone and colour—tone especially. The brighter portions, excepting in two points nearly diametrically opposed, are sometimes of a reddish tint, whilst the dark spots, as some hold, by the effect of contrast, as others hold, absolutely, seem of a blue or greenish grey. Throughout its circumference the disk is more luminous than the central part; the dark spots also are effaced and disappear at the limb.

Lastly, at two points, of which mention has been before made, which are not situated at the extremities of a diameter, two spots of unequal extent and of extreme whiteness, which contrasts with the reddish parts, shine with a very particular brightness.* These two spots mark near the poles of Mars. [Both are visible when the planet is observed at the time of its solstices; at others, only the one bowed down towards the Earth can be seen.]

* 'The colour of the polar spots' (we quote Beer and Mädler) 'were, every time the planet was distinctly seen, always of a bright and pure white, in no way similar to the colour of the other parts of the planet. In 1837 it happened once that Mars, during the observations, was completely obscured by a cloud, with the exception of the polar spot, which remained distinctly visible to the view.'—*Fragments sur les Corps Célestes.*

Arago estimated that the brightness of the polar spots is more than double that of the other bright spots, on the edge of the disk.

All the appearances on the surface of the planet may be divided into permanent and variable ones. The permanence of the features, that is to say, the constancy of their principal shapes, and of their relative situations, has been proved by numerous and minute observations—a matter more difficult than might be imagined at a first examination. Indeed, as the observation of the spots shows, the planet has a movement of rotation effected in about 24½ hours. Hence it follows that in a few hours the aspect of the disk changes: of this we may gain an idea by examining figures 80 and 81. Besides, when, in consequence of the movement of rotation, a spot approaches the edge, it disappears before having attained it. This disappearance is owing, doubtless, to the atmosphere of Mars, seen in these points under a great obliquity, and the brightness of which effaces the darker tint of the spot.

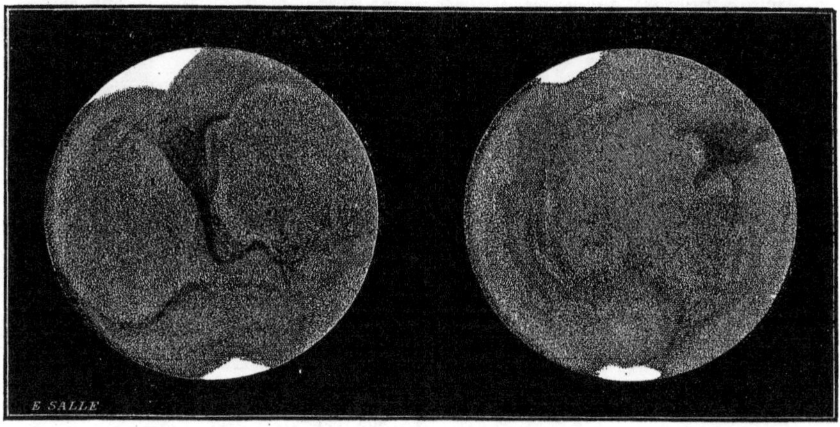

Fig. 80.—Views of Mars at two hours' interval. (Warren De La Rue.)

Lastly, the orbit of Mars does not coincide with the ecliptic: the two planes form a slight angle (1° 51′). But if to this is joined the much greater inclination of the axis of rotation, we shall readily see why, at successive opposition, Mars does not present to the Earth the same portions of its surface. Hence changes produced by perspective, so much more decided as a spherical surface is in question.

The variability, often very rapid, which is observed in the form of the features which overspread the disk, has suggested the opinion that these phenomena are owing to the interposition of cloudy masses in the planet's atmosphere above the general level of land and sea. Mr. Lockyer, who carefully followed the changing features of Mars during the opposition of 1862, thus writes in his Memoir* on the planet: 'Although the complete fixity of the main features of the planet has been placed beyond all doubt, daily—nay, hourly—changes in the detail and in the tones of the

* 'Memoirs of the Royal Astronomical Society,' vol. xxxii. p. 183.

different parts of the planet, both light and dark, occur. These changes are, I doubt not, caused by the transit of clouds over the different features.' The drawings which accompany this Memoir seem to fully justify this opinion.

It is generally held that the reddish and bright spots of Mars are the solid parts of the surface on the continents, whilst the dark bluish spots form the liquid parts on the seas. This distinction is founded on the unequal reflexion of the light by the land and the water. According to Mr. Lockyer, if we admit that the darkest spots indicate water, the darkest among them are those portions which are most land-locked.

Whence comes the reddish colouring, which characterises the bright parts of the disk? If Mars were self-luminous, this tint would doubtless, be attributed to the very nature of its light; but it only reflects to us the white light of the Sun; it is evident, therefore, that the colour is imparted by the planet or its atmosphere. Several hypotheses have been

Fig. 81.—Rotation of Mars. Movement of the spots observed during the opposition of 1830. (Beer and Mädler.)

suggested on this subject. Some have attributed the red tint of the continents to the nature of the soil, composed of red sandstone. Others, among them Lambert, have thought that the colour of the vegetation, instead of being green, as it is on our Earth, is red on Mars. This explanation is not an impossible one; but, if it be true, there should be variations in the intensity of the tint on each of the hemispheres of the planet corresponding to the seasons; the tint should diminish during winter, to reappear in spring, and to attain its maximum in the summer.

It has also been proposed to explain the colour of the spots by the refraction of the rays of the Sun through the atmosphere of Mars. Arago has refuted this hypothesis by the simple remark, that at the borders of the planet the redness should be more decided than in the central portions, since the luminous rays traverse a greater thickness of atmosphere, and traverse it more obliquely, in the regions near the limb, where the contrary effect is observed. Let us add, that this hypothesis does not explain why the red tint is not general. The ruddy light of Mars cannot, therefore, in this manner be assimilated to our twilight hues.

[But the question is altered if we take the existence of clouds into consideration. Observations of the planet in 1862 suggested to Mr. Lockyer that the colour might depend upon the cloudy state of the planet, and the spectroscope substantiates this hypothesis. In 1862 the planet was clearer of clouds, *and more ruddy*, than in 1864. The suggested explanation is that, when Mars is clouded, the light reflected by the clouds undergoes less absorption than that reflected by the planet itself; and on one occasion the spectroscope indicated this increased absorption by revealing the fact that the sunlight was reflected to us *minus* a large portion of the blue rays.]

We must now occupy ourselves with the polar snows. We have seen that they are distinguished from the other features by their brilliant white light; they are equally distinct from the rest by reason of the variation in their dimensions. In proportion as the white spot on one of the poles diminishes, the other increases; the minimum of both always corresponding with the summer, and the maximum with the winter, of the hemisphere in which it is situated. Thus, during the opposition of 1830 the southern snow-zone was seen to diminish by degrees, and its outline to recede till the time which corresponds, for that hemisphere of Mars, to the middle of the month of July on our northern hemisphere; from this moment it increased again. (Beer and Mädler.) In 1837 similar diminutions were observed in the dimensions of the spot of the northern pole. At the same time the snowy regions of the southern pole had a considerable extension. Now these variations corresponded equally to the summer season of the northern hemisphere, and to the winter of the southern hemisphere of Mars.

Thus from the Earth we can watch the formation of the polar ice, and the fall and thaw of the snows on the surface of a neighbouring planet; in a word, all the vicissitudes of heat and cold which distinguish the seasons of winter and spring, autumn and winter. The succession of these changes is now so well established, that astronomers can predict approximately the form, relative size, and position of the northern and southern snow-zones.

We have said that the two white spots are not of the same extent either during their respective winters or summers. The snowy cap of the southern hemisphere varies within much greater limits than that of the opposite pole: it is much more extensive during the winter season, and it diminishes during the summer to such an extent that it does not occupy more than the fifth part of the superficies of the snowy spot of the northern pole. This difference is easily explained by the great inclination of the axis of the planet to the plane of its orbit, and by the fact that the southern pole is turned towards the Sun, when Mars is nearly at its smallest distance from the focus of light and heat. The summer time, on the other hand, of the northern hemisphere, occurs at the epoch of its greatest distance. The quantities of heat received by the globe of Mars, at these two opposite points of its orbit, vary in the ratio of seven to five.*

In truth, these differences of temperature are partly compensated in the course of a revolution; but the extremes of heat and cold are still very decided.

We have seen that Mars presents the most curious analogies with the

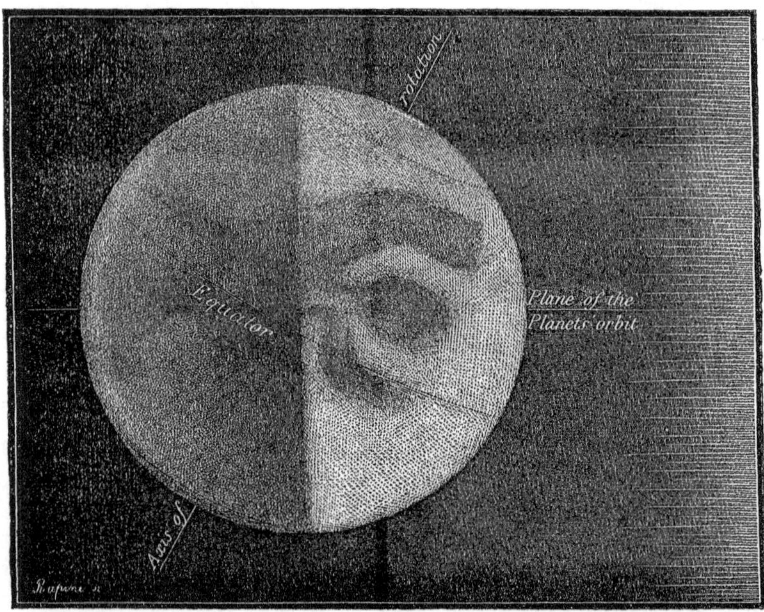

Fig. 82.—Inclination of the axis of rotation. Mars at one of its solstices.

Earth; and it is probable that to the inhabitants of Venus our planet presents the same appearances that Mars does to us. Like the poles of Mars, the poles of the Earth are covered with snow and ice: it is also our Southern pole which is the most frost-bound, and for the same astronomical reasons, by the congelation of the aqueous vapour. Lastly, the points of greatest cold on Mars, as on the Earth, do not coincide exactly with the poles of of rotation. This excentricity is very evident in the views of Mars given in fig. 80.

If snow falls in Mars, it is because water is there evaporated by heat;

* At the mean distance of Mars from the Sun, the disk of this last body is but $\frac{43}{100}$ths of that presented to us, or less than half; but at its shortest distance, the Sun's apparent diameter is about three-fourths; the apparent surface of its disk is then a little more than half that which is presented to us.

hence, the water must spread on the surface under the form of clouds, which condense sometimes in a liquid state in the form of rain, sometimes as snowy crystallisations. Thus Mars certainly possesses an atmosphere of aqueous vapour.

But we see the permanent spots of the disk too distinctly, not to be certain of the existence of an atmosphere analogous to our own, the pressure of which, by counterbalancing the expansion of the aqueous vapour, prevents it from usurping all the surface. We have already said that the more luminous borders of the disk allow us to infer the existence of a cloud-bearing atmosphere, which effaces by its brightness the dark spots when the rotation brings them towards the limb.

The meteorology of Mars is, then, to a great extent known. It presents, we repeat, the greatest analogies with the meteorology of our Earth. But at the same time notable differences distinguish them. As Professor Phillips has remarked, the considerable periodical exchange of moisture which is made between the two hemispheres, especially between the two poles, must give rise to hurricanes and storms, of the violence of which we can form no idea; while the melting of the snows over such large areas must produce terrible periodical inundations.

We have seen that Mars turns on itself in about $24\frac{1}{2}$ hours.* Thus the duration of its movement of rotation exceeds that of our sidereal day by 41 minutes.

Mars accomplishes an entire revolution round the Sun in 687 of our terrestrial days. But, the year of Mars only contains $669\frac{2}{3}$ of its own sidereal days; and as the number of the solar days—we have explained this for the Earth—is always less by one than that of the rotations, the year of Mars is in reality composed of $668\frac{2}{3}$ of its own solar days, which gives, for the duration of one of these days, 24 hours, 39 minutes, 35 seconds.

Thus a whole day of Mars exceeds one of our days by 39 minutes 35 seconds. The difference is not very perceptible.

Besides, the inclination of the axis of rotation to the plane of the ecliptic is nearly the same as that of the axis of the Earth.† It follows that in the course of a year Mars presents its various regions to the Sun, nearly like our globe, so that the length of the days and the nights, in the different latitudes, is distributed in the same manner. The extreme zones, torrid and frigid, are a little more extended, proportionally, which consequently reduces the surface of the temperate zones. But it must not be forgotten that this is a favourable circumstance, at least for the tropical regions, since the solar light and heat arrive at the planet with an intensity much less than on our globe.

Between Mars and the Earth, however, there is an important distinction, and it lies in the difference between the lengths of the Terrestrial and

* $24^h\ 37^m\ 22{\cdot}62^s$ (Kaiser); $24^h\ 37^m\ 22{\cdot}73^s$ (Proctor).

† 61° 9′ for Mars; 66° 33′ for the Earth.

Martial seasons. In the northern hemisphere of the planet, the 668 days of its year are divided as follows:

Spring lasts	191 days	8 hours.
Summer	181 „	0 „
Autumn	149 „	8 „
And Winter	147 „	0 „

But the summer seasons of the northern hemisphere are the winter seasons of the southern hemisphere, whence it follows that the spring and summer, taken together, last 76 days longer in the northern hemisphere than in the southern one.

The globe of Mars is not exactly spherical; it is flattened at the poles, and it bulges, like our Earth, at the equator. But the measurement of this flattening presents considerable difficulties, which most of the observers attribute to errors of measurement induced by the irradiation caused by the polar spots. Arago, who made a series of measures of the two diameters with great care, concluded that the latter is shorter than the former by the thirtieth part of its value. Herschel, in 1784, found the same quantity, $\frac{1}{26}$; whilst more recent measures appear to reduce it to the third of the value measured by Arago. M. Kaiser (of Leyden) gives $\frac{1}{118}$ for the flattening, as measured during the opposition of 1862. Supposing that the planet was fluid in the first instance, the figures which precede are too great to be in accordance with the laws of hydrostatics, which govern the configuration of the celestial bodies. But it is to be regretted that the uncertainty of the measures is here, perhaps, the only cause of this apparent anomaly, and we hope that, at the next most favourable oppositions, astronomers will arrive at more precise data on this point.

It remains for us, before we complete this monograph of Mars, to speak of its density, which is very near that of the Earth;* of its mass, which is rather more than an eighth of the terrestrial mass; and, lastly, of the force of gravity by which the bodies are retained on its surface. This last is half that which is observed on the surface of the Earth, whence we may conclude that the organisation of the living bodies which people Mars differs notably from that with which we are familiar.

It may be seen, also, that the conditions of temperature to which these beings are subjected are very variable, and that the solar illumination varies very largely. But before we can draw from these facts positive conclusions, the constitution and density of the atmosphere, an element so important in the physiology of the celestial bodies, must be known.

Mars has no satellites. Its nights are therefore completely dark, if indeed they are not lit up by auroræ and long lingering twilights.

At all events, this is not a great privation, to judge by the imperfect manner in which our Moon acquits itself of its function of torch-bearer to our Earth.

* 0·948, that of the Earth being 1.

XV.

THE MINOR PLANETS.

Considerable number of Celestial Bodies circulating round the Sun between Mars and Jupiter—Bode's Law—Olbers' Hypothesis—Interlacing of their Orbits—Some Details on the principal Planets of the group, Juno, Pallas, Ceres, and Vesta—How to discover a New Planet.

The number of the known planets in the Solar System, sixty-four years ago, was only seven, among which was counted the large planet Uranus, discovered by Sir W. Herschel. At the present time this number is increased to 92, so that without reckoning the new comets and the recently discovered satellites, the solar system has been increased by 85 bodies. It is true that, with the exception of Neptune, which forms part of the group of large planets, all these bodies are of extreme smallness, and, taken separately, do not even equal in size the satellites of the principal planets.

Hence they have been named *Asteroids*, *Minor Planets*, and *Telescopic Planets.*

In spite of their smallness, they form a very interesting group, which gives a new appearance to the solar system, at the same time that it throws a fresh light on the problem of its formation and development. The 84 telescopic planets now known—the number increases every year—are all situated between Mars and Jupiter; the orbits which they describe round the Sun are so near one another, and so interlaced, that a contemporary astronomer, M. D'Arrest, deduced from this circumstance the evident proof of a common origin.

'One fact,' he says, 'seems above all to confirm the idea of an intimate relation between all the minor planets; it is, that, if their orbits are figured under the form of material rings, these rings will be found so entangled, that it would be possible, by means of one among them taken at hazard, to lift up all the rest.'

At the time when these lines were written, only 14 asteroids were known; since then, 70 more newly discovered planets have been found to occupy the mid-interval. The comparison of D'Arrest, and the inference that he draws from it, are therefore so much the more strengthened.

Before the discovery of the minor planets, astronomers, in comparing the intervals which separated the known planets from the Sun, noticed the relative considerable distance between the two planets, Jupiter and Mars. The imagination of Kepler, which led the illustrious disciple of Tycho into theoretical views of extreme hardiness, placed an undiscovered planet in the vacant space; and this hypothesis seemed corroborated by a discovery made by an astronomer of the eighteenth century—Titius, who detected a singular connexion, since known under the name of Bode's Law, between the successive distances of the planets.

This connexion was as follows. If we write down the following series of numbers—

0	3	6	12	24	48	96

and add 4 to each of them, we shall have another series—

4	7	10	16	28	52	100

Now, the terms of this series, with the exception of the fifth—28,—very nearly represent the relative distances of the planets known in Titius' time:—

Mercury,	Venus,	Earth,	Mars,	—	Jupiter,	Saturn.

After this empirical law was announced, the discovery of Uranus in 1781, extended the series, and it was found that the distance of the new planet was precisely that represented by the eighth term, 196, of the regularly formed series. Hence, to conclude the existence of a planet, which should fill the blank existing between Jupiter and Mars, was natural. 'Baron de Zach,' says M. Lespiault, in his excellent monograph of the asteroids,* 'went so far as to publish beforehand, in the Berlin Almanac, the elements of the supposed planet, and he organised an association of astronomers to search for this body. The Zodiac was divided into twenty-four zones, each of which was confided to the special *surveillance* of one of the members of the Society.' The discovery was made, but certainly not in the manner contemplated.

In fact, on the 1st of January, 1801, at Palermo, Piazzi inaugurated the nineteenth century by the discovery of Ceres, thus filling the gap indicated by Titius and Bode, of which, truth to tell, he thought very little. Singularly enough, however, Ceres precisely occupied the vacant number 28, which expressed the distance of the new planet from the Sun, the distance of the Earth being represented by 10. Fifteen months after, a second planet, Pallas, was added to the list, and this greatly disturbed the views of the prophets of the first discovery.

The able astronomer, Olbers, who had discovered Pallas, then hit upon an ingenious theory. He considered the two new bodies were fragments of a planet which had been destroyed. Now, the laws of mechanics indicated that after such a catastrophe, whatever might be the cause, the fragments, in whatever directions they might be thrown, ought to lie at the same mean distance from the focus of their movements, the Sun; and should pass, moreover, at each of their revolutions, through the point of space in which the catastrophe took place.

Pallas and Ceres very nearly fulfilled those conditions, and it was the same with the third planet discovered, Juno, which was supposed to be a third fragment of the hypothetical planet.

The researches were continued under the influence of these views; and lastly, Olbers himself, in 1807, discovered Vesta. But, curious contradic-

* 'Memoirs of the Physical and Natural Sciences of Bordeaux,' vol. ii. p. 171.

tion, this discovery, which it was expected would definitely consolidate an ingenious and otherwise rational theory, on the contrary, shook it to its foundations. The distance, and other elements of the orbit of Vesta, presented serious differences both with this theory and Bode's law; and both have since received their *coup-de-grâce.**

In fact, since 1845, the epoch of the discovery of the fifth asteroid, the number of these bodies has rapidly increased, and we have every reason for believing that it will continue to do so.

In the actual state of discovery, the 109 small planets form a zone, almost entirely confined to that half of the interval between Mars and Jupiter nearest to Mars. One only, Maximiliana, which is consequently the furthest from the Sun, is found to be nearer to Jupiter than to Mars. The breadth of the zone is upwards of 100,000,000 miles; † but throughout this interval the planets are very irregularly distributed, since 81 are situated in the half of the zone nearest Mars, and 28 only in the other half. It follows, from these numbers, that the 81 minor planets nearest the Sun are only separated from each other, on an average, by 990,000 miles, or less than four times the distance of the Moon from the Earth.

Flora and Maximiliana are the names of the two extreme planets; the first is at a mean distance of 210,000,000 miles, the second at 323,000,000, so that the middle of the zone is 266,000,000 from the central body. The distance of the Earth from the Sun being represented by 10, this last distance would be represented by 28,—the term of Bode's series, which at first pointed out the gap; but the uneven distribution of the minor planets much reduces the value of this coincidence.

We have seen that, if averaged, the orbits of these bodies lie near together. If we compare them one by one from this point of view, we shall find the real distance, in some cases, to be much smaller.

The orbits of Egeria and Astrea are separated by a mean interval of 50,000 miles; those of Eurydice and Clytie, 30,000; lastly, Leto and Bellona are only 26,000 miles apart. But it must be well understood that these numbers do not apply to the planets themselves, first, because, at a given epoch, they are found in very different directions, and also because their orbits are more or less elongated, and the planes in which they move are very diversely inclined.

The forms of the orbits are far from being circular. The least elongated of all, that of Freia, is proportionately much more elliptical than the orbits of the Earth, Neptune, or Venus, which are the nearest to the cir-

* The planet Neptune, the last of the known planets of the solar system in the order of distance, is far from satisfying the empirical formula of Titius. Its distance, which should be represented by the number 388, is in reality only 300. Let us add, as noticed by others, that the first number of the series, that which corresponds to Mercury, is not formed in a regular manner. Instead of 0 it should be 1·5, which, by adding 4, would become 5·5, whilst the true distance of Mercury is 3·87.

It seems, however, well to retain, as an aid to the memory, the series we owe to Titius; it is, moreover, intimately connected with the history of Astronomy.

† This breadth is increased to 248,000,000 miles, if we take the extreme distances into account.

cular form among the orbits described by the bodies of our solar system. The most elongated is the orbit of Polyhymnia, of which the major axis surpasses the minor axis by one-third of its length, which causes between its greatest and least distances from the Sun a difference of 184,800,000 miles. Fig. 83 shows the form and relative size of these two orbits, compared with each other and with that of the Earth.

The planes in which the telescopic planets move are very diversely inclined to each other. In comparing them with the plane of the Earth's orbit, it is found that some among them, those of Massilia and Angelina, for example, nearly coincide with it; whilst the orbit of Pallas, as may be

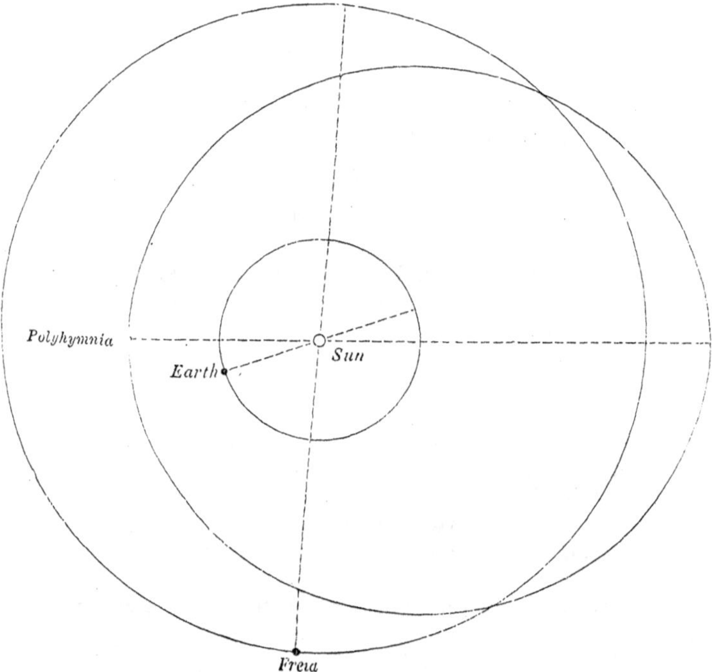

Fig. 83.—Orbits of Freia and Polyhymnia, compared together, and with that of the Earth.

seen in Plate I., rises at an angle of 34°, that is to say, nearly $\frac{2}{5}$ths of a right angle.*

It now remains to us to terminate this general sketch, by saying a word on the times occupied in their revolutions round the Sun. These periods are comprised between 1193 and 2310 mean solar days, that is to say, between 3 years, 3 months, and 7 days, and 6 years, 3 months, and 28 days, which mark the length of the years of Flora and Maximiliana

* These considerable inclinations have caused the name of *ultra zodiacal planets* to be given to the asteroids; as a great number of them, in consequence of their inclination are observed out of the zone in which the principal planets move.

respectively. It happens, as it does also with the mean distances, that some of the asteroids perform their journey round the Sun in times almost equal. In the case of Egeria and Astrea the difference is not more than half a day; for Eurydice and Clytie a quarter of a day; and, lastly, Leto and Bellona accomplish their revolutions, one in 1688·295 days, the other in 1688·546, that is to say, with a difference of about six hours and two minutes only. This is a direct consequence of one of the laws of Kepler, which connects the time of revolution and mean distances of the planets of the system.

We will now pass under review some of the principal bodies of this group, and see whether we have yet discovered any facts relating to their dimensions and physical constitution.

Vesta is the most brilliant of the entire family. It is visible to the naked eye in a very clear sky, and its light, a palish yellow, is whiter than those of the three planets discovered before it. It takes three years and eight months to accomplish its entire revolution round the Sun, at a mean distance of 223,000,000 miles. As its orbit is relatively but little elongated, there is only a difference of 4,000,000 miles between its perihelion and aphelion. Its real diameter, measured by Mädler, is about 300 miles, not the twenty-fifth part of the diameter of the Earth, so that the surface of our globe comprises nearly 700 times that of Vesta. Here, then, is a planet, the entire surface of which contains but the ninth part of the European continent. The volume of the Earth is nearly 18,000 times that of Vesta.

Juno has the aspect of a star of the eighth magnitude, and is, consequently, invisible to the naked eye. Its colour is reddish, and its light is subject to variations, which are not less remarkable than the rapidity with which they are accomplished. This phenomenon is not peculiar to Juno; it is observed in Vesta—which sometimes becomes very bright,—in Ceres, and in many other of the minor planets. Several hypotheses have been suggested to explain this fact. Some suppose that the different faces of these small bodies do not reflect the solar light with the same intensity; that some are formed of crystalline facets, or even have a light of their own. Others believe that the small planets are irregularly formed, presenting to us consequently sometimes very extensive, and at others very limited, surfaces. Whichever hypothesis we admit, both take for granted a *rotation.* Perhaps, in studying with care the periods of these variations, we may learn the durations of these rotatory movements. M. Goldschmidt, who ranks almost highest among living astronomers in this branch of research, has already made some interesting observations with this object in view.

Juno recedes from the Sun, at aphelion, to a distance of nearly 300,000,000 miles; at perihelion, it approaches within 180,000,000 miles; hence its mean distance is about 240,000,000, and there is a difference of

120,000,000 miles between its extreme distances. Its orbit is far from having a circular form.

Mädler estimated the diameter of the planet at 360 miles; which is thus 22 times less than that of the Earth, and its surface is a little more extensive than that of Vesta. It travels over its orbit in $1592\frac{1}{3}$ days, or in 4 terrestrial years and 4 months.

Ceres, the 56th of the group in the order of distance, and, as has been seen, the first in the order of discovery, appears as a reddish star, the brightness of which is intermediate between that of Juno and Vesta.

An illustrious observer, Schröter, thought he detected in the vaporous appearance of its disk the proof of the existence of a very extensive atmosphere. The same seemed to hold good for Pallas, and he concluded that these two planets were surrounded with a gaseous envelope of 500 miles in thickness. Since his time it has been found that these appearances were due to the imperfection of his telescope.

Ceres revolves round the Sun in $1680\frac{3}{4}$ days, at a mean distance of 260,000,000 miles. But, at its minimum distance, it is nearer by 42,000,000 miles than at its greatest distance. The heat and light received from the Sun by these bodies, the distance of which varies in such considerable proportions, vary also between rather wide limits. But as nothing is known of the physical constitution of Ceres or of the condition of its surface, it is impossible to draw certain conclusions from these data relative to the actual variations in the planet's temperature.

The diameter of Ceres has been measured several times. But the results are not concordant: whilst it is 450 miles according to Schröter, it is only 160 according to Sir W. Herschel, and Argelander valued it at 220. If we adopt this last number, we find that the surface of Ceres is only the 1300th part of that of the terrestrial globe, so that 46,000 globes as large as the planet would be required to equal the volume of the Earth.

We now pass to *Pallas*, which revolves round the Sun in $1683\frac{1}{2}$ days, in an orbit nearly as elongated as that of Juno, greatly inclined to the plane of our ecliptic, and at a mean distance of 260,000,000 miles. At its aphelion, Pallas is 320,000,000 miles away from the Sun, whilst at its least distance it is scarcely 200,000,000. At the time of its nearest approach to the Earth, Pallas has the aspect of a star of the seventh magnitude, of a beautiful yellow colour. Its diameter has been estimated at 600 miles.* It is the most important of all the smaller planets, although its diameter is 13 times, its surface 168 times, and its volume 2177 times less than than that of our Earth. All these numbers, it will be understood, are merely approximate, and we give them principally in order that a clear idea may be formed of the relative importance of all the celestial bodies of our system. Fig. 84 should make this point clearer still.

* Lamont.

The four planets of which we have just given some details, are among the most important of the group. The smallness of nearly all the others is such, that it is not possible to measure their diameters; as they appear in a telescope merely as luminous points. It is probable that the least of these microscopic bodies have diameters which do not reach many score miles, so that their surface is less than that of one of our English counties. M. Lespiault, from whom this comparison is borrowed, adds that a good walker could easily in a day make a tour of many of these miniature worlds.

How long shall we go on making discoveries of fresh bodies in this zone between Mars and Jupiter? This is a difficult question to solve, but it is probable that we are now acquainted, if not with the largest of the minor planets, at all events with all those most easily visible from the Earth. The discovery of others will, therefore, become more and more difficult, and the extension of their number is partly subordinate to the use of larger instruments in the research, and more detailed celestial maps. At all events, M. Leverrier, from mathematical considerations, has assigned to the total mass of the bodies which compose the ring such a limit, that, if we suppose them to possess a density equal to that of our own globe, those already discovered form only the $\frac{1}{1800}$th part of it. This would make the number of the minor planets about 150,000. But, admitting that this number may be excessive, and in reducing it to the tenth of its value, this swarm of celestial bodies will still be counted by thousands.

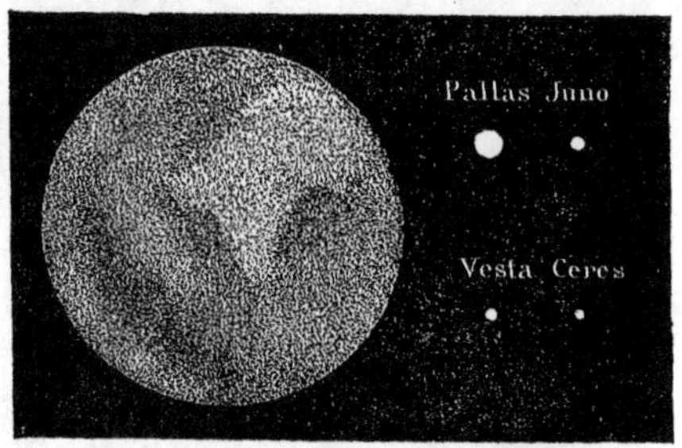

Fig. 84.—Comparative dimensions of the Earth and Juno, Ceres, Pallas, and Vesta.

We have heard so often during the last twenty years of the discoveries of new asteroids, that some of our readers may be interested to know the way in which these discoveries are made. Let us begin by stating that it is not chance that presides over these researches. From the discovery of Piazzi down to our own time, it is only by special and systematic examination that our knowledge of the Solar System has been increased in such an astonishing manner.

It is not, as we have already said, by its aspect, that a planet is distinguished in the midst of the starry vault from the multitude of luminous points which surround it; and this remark applies especially to these small bodies, the diameter of which is insensible. It is by its proper motion,—by its progressive displacement, that it is recognised. How, then, can this be detected? By using very detailed celestial maps, containing all the very small stars, and incessantly watching the regions mapped for the appearance of new ones. Such is the first *sine quâ non* for such a research, and the astronomer who undertakes the construction of celestial maps, executed with the necessary detail and precision, is of necessity the fellow-labourer of him who actually discovers the planets. Let us add, that often these two *collaborateurs* are one and the same person.

It is not necessary to explore the entire sky. It is sufficient to examine the regions nearest the ecliptic, because, as the orbit of a planet must necessarily, twice in each revolution, pass through the plane of the orbit of

Fig. 85.—Ecliptic chart, from M. Chacornac's 'Star Atlas.'

the Earth, it is enough to look out for the body at one or other of these nodal passages.

Fig. 85 reproduces, on a reduced scale, one of the maps constructed by a distinguished observer, M. Chacornac, to whom astronomy owes, besides numerous observations of different kinds, the discovery of eight telescopic planets.

This map includes all stars down to the thirteenth magnitude. Furnished with a map of this kind, and a telescope powerful enough to show all the stars marked on it, the observer who intends to devote himself to the search after small planets will proceed in the following manner:—

He will place in the field of view of his telescope six spider lines at right angles to each other, and all of them the same distance apart, in such a manner that several squares will be formed, embracing just as much of the heavens as do those shown in the map. He will then direct his telescope to the region of the sky he wishes to examine, represented by the map, so as to be able to compare successively each square with the corresponding portion of the sky.

He can then assure himself if the numbers and positions of the stars mapped, and the stars observed, are identical. If he observe in the field of view a luminous point which is not marked in the map, it is evident that this can only arise from two causes, if the map be well made. It may be that the new body is a star of variable brightness, and that it was not

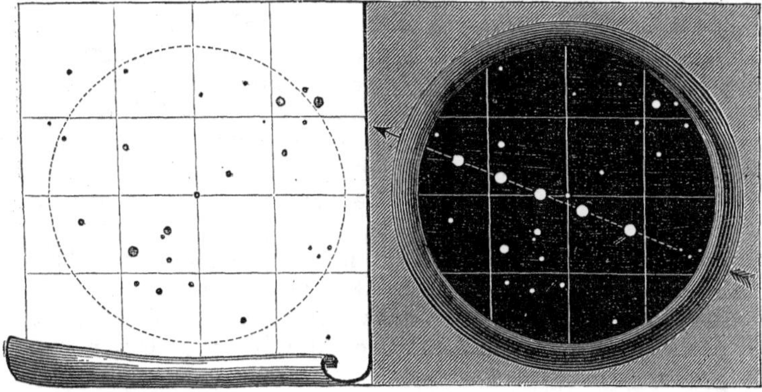

Fig. 86.—Discovery of a small planet by means of Ecliptic Charts.

visible at the time the map was made; or indeed that it is a planet. It then becomes necessary to distinguish between these two possible cases. We must examine whether the new body remains invariably fixed at the same point, or, on the other hand, if it changes its position with regard to the neighbouring stars. The proper motion is generally so sensible, that in the course of one evening the change of position may be detected. In this last case a new planet, or perhaps a comet, has been discovered.

Fig. 86, which represents, on the left the map itself, on the right the field of view of the instrument, will be sufficient to give an idea of the manner in which this result is attained. The stars shown in both are the same, and in the field of view of the telescope is seen the new body, which, absent from the map, by its successive positions indicates the presence of a body belonging to our solar system.

It is scarcely necessary to add after this that these researches are not only laborious, but demand the greatest patience and watchfulness.*

XVI.

JUPITER.

Distance of Jupiter from the Earth and Sun—Real and apparent Dimensions—Movement of Rotation; Days and Nights—Years and Seasons—Dark and Light Belts on the Disk; Atmosphere—Satellites, their Movements and Distances—Eclipses of the Satellites—Their real Dimensions.

FROM that region of space where we have just seen the smallest members of our system circulating in their orbits, we pass without transition to the largest planet—the colossal Jupiter.

To the naked eye, Jupiter appears as a star of the first magnitude, the brightness of which, variable with its distance from the Earth, is sometimes, when the Moon is absent, sufficient to throw a shadow. Its light is constant, and scintillates but rarely. But if, to examine it, a rather powerful telescope is used, the point expands into a well-defined disk, and is generally seen to be accompanied by three or four little points of light, which oscillate in short periods of time round the central planet: these are the satellites of Jupiter.

Venus, Mercury, and Mars, as we have seen, are without satellites; the Earth has only one. Jupiter, with its four moons, which the powerful attraction of its bulk compels to revolve round him, exhibits to us therefore a small system analogous to the solar one of which it forms part and which it reproduces on a smaller scale.

To arrive in our journey from the Sun as far as the Jovian system, we must pass over a distance which exceeds five times the mean distance of the Sun from the Earth, or, in the mean, nearly 500,000,000 miles. But the orbit described by Jupiter round the Sun differs from the circular form more than does the Earth's. Its distance, therefore, is more variable, and while at perihelion it reaches 472,000,000 miles, at its greatest distance it is not less than 520,000,000 miles from the Sun, the difference being therefore 48,000,000 miles.

Jupiter, therefore, as seen from the Sun, presents an apparent diameter sometimes greater, sometimes less, than its mean one; and of course the

* In 1861 nine minor planets were discovered, in 1862 five, and in 1863–4 six only. If we suppose the watch kept constant, there is here exhibited a decrease, resulting apparently from a downward march, which may be explained by the fact that the minor planets actually discovered, being the largest of the group, the others more and more escape observation. The hypothesis of a large number of asteroids is not shaken.

[In 1868, twelve minor planets were discovered, a fact which disposes at once of the difficulty and the explanation in the preceding note.—R. A. P.]

same phenomenon is seen by observers situated on the Earth, but in a much greater proportion. Fig. 87 will give an idea of the variations of size which the disk of Jupiter, at the times of its mean and extreme distances from the Earth, presents to us.

The reason of this difference between the apparent diameters of the disk is easily explained. The orbit of Jupiter, like that of Mars, encircles the terrestrial one, and the motions of the two bodies in their respective orbits bring them, once in every 13 months, in the same straight line with the Sun, and on the same side of it; Jupiter is then in *opposition*, and its distance from the Earth is measured by the difference of the distances of the two bodies from the Sun. In a similar period the two planets are still in a straight line with regard to the Sun, but on opposite sides of it. This is the *conjunction* of Jupiter, and the distance of the two planets is found by adding their respective distances from the Sun. These distances them-

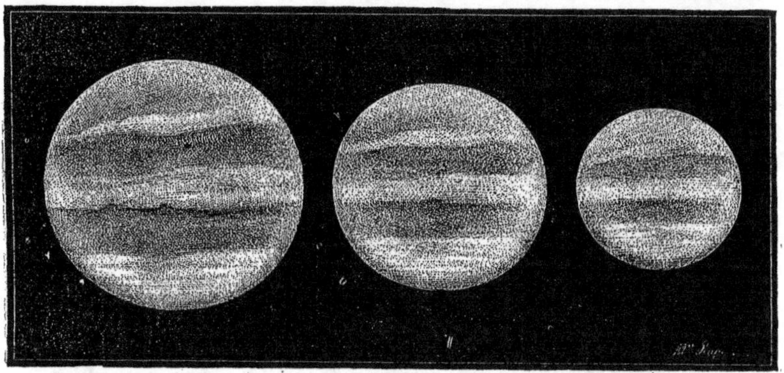

Fig. 87.—Apparent dimensions of Jupiter at its mean and extreme distances from the Earth.

selves are sometimes smaller and sometimes greater than at others, and therefore the same thing happens with regard to those which separate the Earth from Jupiter at the time of *opposition* and *conjunction*.

At its greatest distance from the Earth, Jupiter is 617,000,000 miles from us; at opposition it may be within 375,000,000 miles; but in the mean, the distance of Jupiter at conjunction with the Sun is 591,000,000 miles, and at opposition 400,000,000 miles, the difference being the diameter of the Earth's orbit.

From the preceding numbers we may perceive the immense development of the orbit described by this member of our planetary system. Thus, to traverse this path, it requires 12 years. This gives a mean rate of upwards of 700,000 miles a-day, or nearly 30,000 miles an hour.

The movements with which we are acquainted on the Earth can give us no idea of such a mass travelling eternally through the depths of space with a velocity 80 times greater than that of a cannon-ball.

We look upon the volume of the Earth as immense when we compare it to the objects which we are in the habit of seeing about us; but how much more stupendous is the size of Jupiter, which is 1400 times larger than our globe! This value has been deduced from the real diameter of the planet, which has in turn been deduced from its apparent size and real distance.

Fig. 88 gives an idea of the comparative dimensions of the Earth and the planet which we are about to describe. The diameter of Jupiter is nearly 11 times greater than that of the Earth, being 89,000 miles. Seen at the distance of the Moon, this immense globe would appear to us with a diameter $34\frac{1}{2}$ times larger than that of our satellite, and its disk would embrace, on the celestial vault, 1200 times the space that the full moon occupies.

The form of the globe of Jupiter is not that of a perfect sphere: it is an ellipsoid, flattened, like the Earth, at the poles of rotation. But whilst

Fig. 88.—Comparative dimensions of Jupiter and the Earth.

the polar compression of the terrestrial spheroid is but about $\frac{1}{300}$th, that of the globe of this immense planet is $\frac{1}{18}$th, so that there is between the polar diameter—the smallest, and the equatorial diameter, a difference of 4900 miles, which gives for the flattening of each pole 2450 miles.

This elliptical form is very perceptible in the telescope; it is perceived at once without any measurement. The drawings which accompany our description convey a good idea of this flattened form.

If it be true, as physical experiments and geological facts tend to show, that the planets are bodies the primitive state of which was fluid, the elliptical form of their meridians is but a consequence of their rotation. The flattening of a sphere, therefore, gives rise to the idea of its rotation round an axis which passes through its centre.

Venus, the Earth, Mars, have movements of rotation—is it the same with Jupiter? It is, and the velocity of its movement, taken in connexion with its small density, explains at once the extent of the flattening to which we refer, which has been carefully measured.

Very early * observations of the planet demonstrated the rotatory movement of Jupiter. This was accomplished by observing the movement of the spots on its surface. We give two views of the planet, after Beer and Mädler, at an interval of 37 minutes 15 seconds, which clearly show the apparent displacement of the two dark spots produced by this movement.

This immense globe revolves on itself in about 10 hours (9 hours, 55 minutes, 26 seconds). A point situated on the equator of Jupiter travels, therefore, by virtue of this movement, eight miles a second, or 27 times as rapidly as one situated on our equator.

The rotation of Jupiter of course produces the phenomena of day and

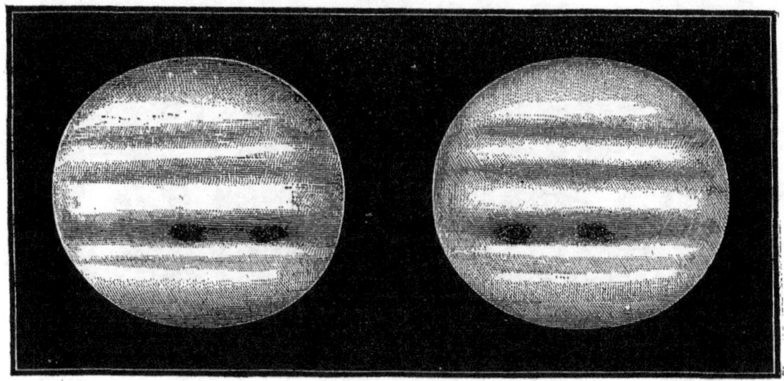

Fig. 89.—Rotation of Jupiter. Apparent displacement of two spots in 37 minutes 15 seconds.

night on the planet. But, as the axis of rotation is nearly at right angles to the plane of the orbit,† there is but little difference in their length, the maximum of which is five hours, for the greater portion of the surface, throughout the length of the planet's long year. Two very narrow zones, situated at the two poles, comprise those regions of the planet where the day and night exceed the time of rotation. At the poles themselves, the Sun is visible for nearly six years, and remains set afterwards for a like period.

The seasons are also very slightly varied on Jupiter; at least at any given place. Summer reigns during the whole year in the zones nearest to the equator, whilst the temperate regions rejoice in a perpetual spring, those which surround the poles being subject to a continual winter. Nothing is known as to the real climatic or meteorological conditions of

* Cassini, in 1665, first measured the time in which this rotation is accomplished. After him we must mention Sir W. Herschel, Airy, Beer and Mädler.

† The angle of inclination is about 87°.

these seasons. At Jupiter's distance from the Sun, the light and heat of that radiant body only possess but a small fraction of their intensity at the distance of the Earth; but this diminution, consequent upon the increasing distance, may be compensated by physical conditions, such as a greater density of the atmosphere, a higher calorific or luminous capacity of the matters composing the soil. Does the globe of Jupiter still possess an internal heat considerable enough to raise the temperature of the crust to an extent sufficient to make up for the relative feebleness of the solar heat? These are questions on which science is still silent.

Jupiter's year is, as we have said, equal to about twelve of ours: to be exact, the length of his year is $4232\frac{6}{10}$ days, or 11 years, 10 months, 14 days, 19 hours. It follows, therefore, that, measured in sidereal days of the planet, the year of Jupiter comprises 10,478 rotations, or 10,477 Jovian sidereal days. From these numbers, it is easily found that between

Fig. 90.—Inclination of the axis of Jupiter to the plane of its orbit.

the sidereal and solar day of Jupiter there is scarcely three seconds difference—that is, three of our seconds.

Seen from the Earth, Jupiter does not present perceptible phases; its great distance, and the fact that its orbit is so far removed from our own and away from the Sun, render a reason for this, which of course does not in any way affect what we have said concerning the planet's days and nights. We possess decisive proofs that the planet does not shine by its own light; and we may remember that Mars, at a less distance from the Earth and Sun, presents only small indications of phases.

We must now look upon the planet from a physical point of view. What we know of the planet's physical constitution has been derived from observations of the belts or patches of different shades which girdle the planet in a direction parallel to its equator. The drawings we have already given indicate these appearances, but to give our readers the best idea possible, we reproduce, in Plate XI, a magnificent drawing by Mr. De La Rue.

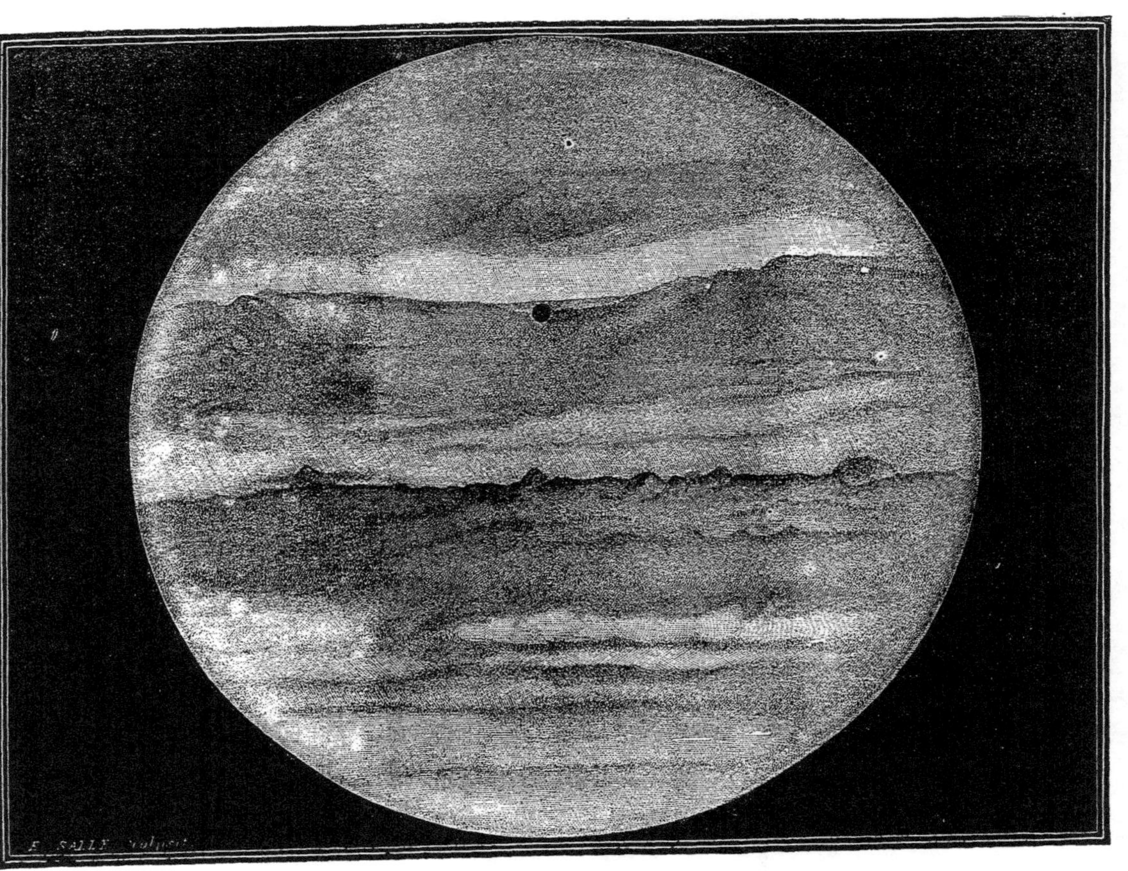

JUPITER.

Bright and dark belts, transit of a Satellite and its shadow across the disk. (Warren De la Rue.)

Broad greyish belts stretch across the disk, north and south of the equator, and between these a brighter [often rose-coloured] space marks the equatorial regions. On either side of the principal belts approaching the polar regions, other narrower bands are seen, sometimes dark, sometimes light. The brightness of the disk is decidedly more feeble at the poles.

With a low magnifying power these belts seem perfectly straight, but under better optical conditions it is easy to see numerous irregularities and transverse markings, vandyking and crossing the more visible features in various directions, in the middle even of the bands. One important circumstance is, that the dark bands do not reach the borders of the disk. [Webb, however, is of another opinion. He tells us that he commonly sees the belts right up to the limb.]

Independently of the bright and dark belts, spots of various forms are seen; and it is by the observation of these points that the time of rotation has been determined. The spots and belts vary besides in form and position. On several occasions one or other of the two large dark belts has entirely disappeared. This happened to the northern belt in 1834 and 1835.

It is, then considered certain that these phenomena are atmospheric, aud the parallelism of the strata of clouds is very naturally explained by the direction and velocity of the rotation. The equatorial regions of Jupiter are doubtless regions of great aerial currents, analogous to the trade-winds of our planet—with this difference, however, as remarked by Arago, that the direction in which the cloud-belts move is opposite to that of our own trade-winds.

The variability of position of the irregular spots indicates a proper motion; according to Beer and Mädler, the rapidity of their displacement is about 100 miles a-day,—the velocity of a light wind on our Earth. We have, therefore, no reason for supposing the existence of violent tempests and hurricanes, which were at first imagined. We may hold, on the contrary, that the Jovian meteorological phenomena are produced very calmly. The long year of the planet, the slight and gradual variations of its seasons, the no doubt considerable density of its atmosphere, the force of gravity at its surface, are so many facts which tend to produce a great atmospheric stability.*

The mass of Jupiter equals 338 times that of our globe, whilst its volume, as we have seen, exceeds the Earth's nearly 1400 times. This gives, for the matter of which it is formed, a mean density less than a quarter of the terrestrial density. It is a third more than that of water; it is easy to conjecture that the strata forming the surface have, at most, the density of water. Is the surface of Jupiter, then, in a liquid state? Here observations fail us.

* [During the autumn and winter of 1869–70, Mr. Browning, F.R.A.S. noticed a very remarkable change in the colour of the equatorial belt, which, in place of being, as usual, nearly a pure white, passed through many tints of yellow and yellowish-red. Other observers subsequently noticed the same peculiarity.—R.A.P.]

Four luminous points—four small stars—unceasingly accompany Jupiter in its twelve-yearly revolution. They are easily observed with small telescopes.

From hour to hour their positions vary, and they seem to oscillate from one side to the other of the disk, in paths nearly parallel to the direction of the belts, that is to say, to the equator of Jupiter. These are its moons or satellites. They are besides frequently seen to disappear, one, two, and even three at a time. It sometimes, indeed, even happens that not one of the four is visible. Jupiter then appears alone, deprived of its companions. This state of things was observed by Mr. Dawes on the 27th of September, 1843. But it only happens very rarely.

Fig. 91.—Jupiter and its Four Satellites.

Taking these satellites in the order of their distances, the times of their revolutions are as follows:

First satellite (Io)	1 day,	18 hours,	28 minutes
Second „ (Europa) . .	3 „	13 „	43 „
Third „ (Ganymede) .	7 „	3 „	43 „
Fourth „ (Callisto) . .	16 „	16 „	32 „

In comparing these times with that of the revolution of the Moon, it is seen that the movements of the satellites of Jupiter are much more rapid than that of our Moon. This rapidity is the more marked, as their distances from the planet, and therefore the lengths of their orbits, are more considerable than in the case of our satellite. Measured from the centre of the planet, the mean distances of these satellites are, of Io, 278,000 miles; of Europa, 443,000; of Ganymede, 707,000; and of Callisto, 1,243,000. These distances are, of course, the radii of their orbits.

The orbits of the two first satellites are nearly circular; those of the other two are more elongated. But on the scale on which figure 92 presents the system of Jupiter to us, these elongations are imperceptible.

The total space occupied by this interesting system measures nearly 2½ millions of miles in diameter.

The study of the other phenomena observable in the Jovian system presents great interest. Among these phenomena, we must especially mention eclipses.

Jupiter, like all celestial bodies not self-luminous, casts into space, in the direction opposite to the Sun, a cone of shade, the axis of which is always situated in the plane of the orbit, and the length of which is proportionate to the dimensions of the planet and its distance from the Sun. Now, the three first satellites revolve round Jupiter in planes but little inclined to the planet's orbit, so that at each revolution they pass through the cone of shade; thereby causing, to themselves an eclipse of the Sun, and to Jupiter an eclipse of its satellites. From the Earth, we can distinctly see the disappearance, or *immersion*, of the satellites in the planet's shadow, as also their reappearances, or *emersions*.

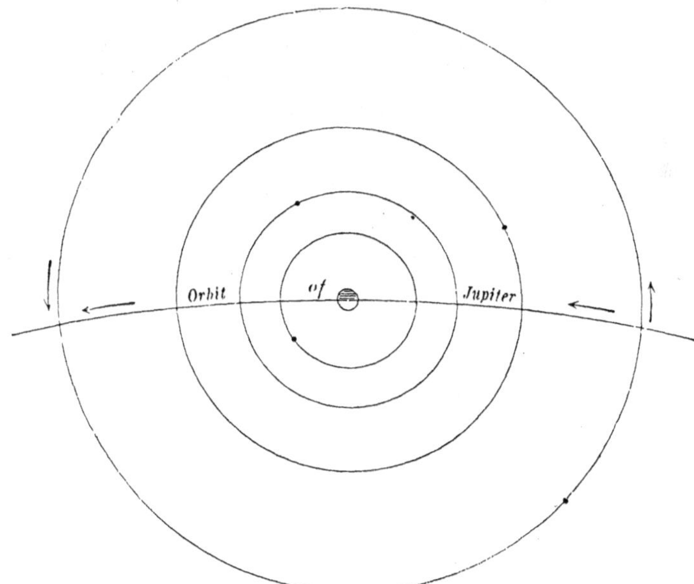

Fig. 92.—The Jovian system. Orbits of the Satellites.

The fourth satellite also undergoes eclipse, but, on account of the much greater inclination of the plane of its orbit, these eclipses are less frequent, sometimes it grazes, as it were, the limit of the cone of shade, and the small loss of light which the satellite undergoes shows us that it is but partially eclipsed.

The nights of Jupiter, then, are illuminated by four moons, which are to be seen, sometimes singly, sometimes together, above the horizon, and which may present at the same time all the varying phases of our single satellite. The nearest appears to the inhabitants of the planet with dimensions nearly equal to those of the Moon seen from the Earth. It is always eclipsed when full, that is, about every 42 hours, or four of Jupiter's days.

The second and third satellites in the order of distance, seen from Jupiter, appear of equal apparent diameter—a little more than half of that of our Moon: their eclipses take place, for the second, every 85 hours, —8½ of Jupiter's days; and, for the third, at successive intervals of 171 hours, or 17⅓ of the planet's days.

Jupiter's moons, at each of their revolutions, pass also between the planet and the Sun. At the time of each new moon, then, as their distances are such that the cone of shade which they throw behind them

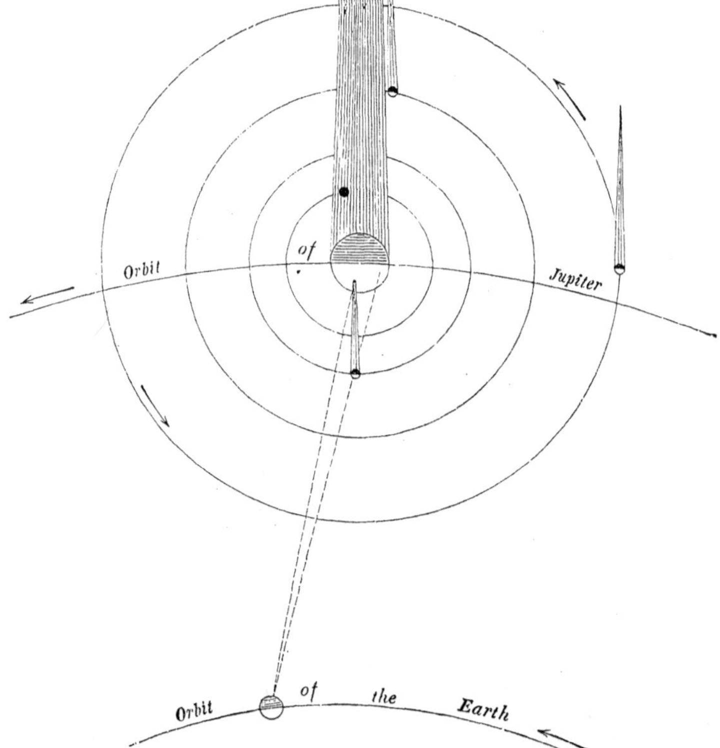

Fig. 93.—Eclipses and passages of the Satellites of Jupiter, seen from the Earth.

reaches the surface of Jupiter, they give rise, on the regions they pass over, to eclipses of the Sun, either partial or total. These phenomena are also visible from the Earth, and Plate XI represents Jupiter at the moment when the shadow of a satellite appears on the disk in the form of a small black dot, whilst the satellite itself is seen, a small bright circle, on the greyish belts of the planet. The three first satellites are never subject to simultaneous eclipses; this follows from a law of their motions and relative distances, discovered by Laplace.

This consequence is only applicable to eclipses properly so called, that is to say, to the passages of the satellites through the cone of the planet's shadow. But to an observer placed on the Earth, a satellite may disappear without undergoing an eclipse; it may pass behind the disk of the planet and be occulted.

Lastly, as mentioned above, it may happen that during the disappearance of the three satellites, the fourth is between the Earth and the planet. Then the planet equally appears solitary and deprived of its companions.

Figure 93 will render clear the various positions which the satellite may occupy with reference to the Earth. One of them in this figure is represented eclipsed, the other is seen projected on the disk, on which also its shadow is thrown; a third is hidden by the planet, and the fourth is entirely visible.

We have seen what are the apparent dimensions of the four satellites,

Fig. 94.—Dimensions of the Satellites of Jupiter compared with those of the Earth and the Moon.

as seen from Jupiter, compared to the apparent size of our Moon. But we must not confound the apparent with the real diameters. It follows, from the measures made by astronomers, that the diameter of the first satellite is 2440 miles; of the second, 2192; of the third, 3579; and of the fourth, 3062 miles. So the third and fourth in the order of distance are the first and second in order of magnitude; one only is less than our Moon; taken together, they would form a body 9½ times larger than it, or about one-fifth of the volume of the Earth.

Lastly, the volume of the largest exceeds by two-thirds the volume of the planet Mercury. Here, then, we have a secondary body larger than a primary one of the first order, and far surpassing in size those which circulate between Mars and Jupiter.

Sir W. Herschel studied with great care the variations of brightness of each satellite, and found that they occurred in each period of revolution. He hence imagined that this variability was owing to the nature of the faces which each of these bodies successively presents to the Earth. It follows from these observations that, as in the case of the Moon, the same face is always turned towards the primary: this of course would render the times of rotation and revolution equal. The disks of the third and fourth satellite present spots which are represented in the preceding drawing (fig. 94).

There is another point. These moons can be distinguished not only by their dimensions and the brightness of their light, but also by their colour. According to Beer and Mädler, the first and second satellites have a bluish tint, especially when compared with the third, the light of which is yellow. Some difference in colour is certain, although contrast may go for something. The light of the fourth satellite is bluish,* like that of the first two.

[Bringing our Mars observations to bear, we might almost be justified in supposing these varying colours to be caused by different distributions of land and water.]

The united masses of Jupiter and its four satellites are the $\frac{1}{1047}$th part of the mass of the Sun; that of Jupiter alone is 6000 times the mass of its satellites, or, as we have said, 338 times the mass of our Earth. Lastly, Jupiter exceeds in mass all the other bodies of the Solar system, the Sun excepted, by 2½ times.

XVII.

SATURN.

Its Exceptional Physical Constitution—Distance of Saturn from the Sun and from the Earth—Apparent and real Dimensions—Movement of Rotation and Polar Compression—Days, Nights, and Seasons—Rings; Movement of Rotation—Satellites—Celestial Phenomena to an Inhabitant of the Planet.

If Jupiter be the largest planet of the Solar System, Saturn is by far the most gorgeously attended among the secondary systems of which that system itself is composed.

Not by four only, but by even eight satellites, is the central planet encircled; and if these eight moons in their revolution do not give rise to eclipses as frequently as do those of Jupiter, the inhabitants of Saturn possess a much stranger spectacle, one, as far as we know, *unique* in the planetary system; we allude to the wondrous ring system which surrounds the planet at some distance from its equator and revolves eternally round it. Thus, then, we see that the further we go in our exploration of the Solar System, the more have we to admire the wonderful variety in the constitution of the bodies which people it. Now we have to deal with isolated planets, such as Mercury, Venus, and Mars; now, with such a

* [The light of the fourth satellite is reddish, decidedly.—W. R. D.]

group of celestial pigmies as the telescopic planets; and, again, with matter more finely divided still, like the Zodiacal light, and the shooting stars. Then we find the Earth accompanied by a single Moon in its annual revolution round the common focus; and, lastly, the group of large planets, which are not only distinguished by their enormous dimensions, but by the number of secondary bodies maintained in their sphere of attraction, which with their primaries form real systems in miniature.

Up to this point, however, whatever may have been the variety of the elements of each planet, there has been a common point of resemblance—the form of each has been a regular spheroid. Nor have the revelations of the telescope taught us that the planets which we have already described are surrounded with anything save the satellites we have described.

[The first peep at Saturn, however, infinitely extends our mental horizon; besides eight satellites, it is surrounded by a system of rings, some shining with a golden light, others transparent; and it may possibly be, that the Zodiacal light, and the meteoric and asteroidal rings, may be to the Sun what Saturn's rings are to Saturn—an innumerable company of satellites, as the sands on all shores for multitude.]

Before, however, describing the rings of Saturn in detail, as they deserve, we must chronicle the principal astronomical data of the planet itself.

The mean distance of Saturn from the Sun exceeds 9½ times that of the Earth, a distance expressed by the enormous number of 909,000,000 miles,—not far from double the distance of Jupiter. Seen from such a distance, the solar disk is reduced to the hundredth of its apparent size to us; and it is in this proportion that the intensity of the light and heat is reduced, unless there be some compensating power in its atmosphere.

The orbit of Saturn is not circular; it has, like that of the other planets, the form of an ellipse, of which the Sun does not occupy the centre, but the focus. The planet is therefore sometimes nearer to, and sometimes more distant from, the radiant body. At its perihelion and aphelion respectively, these distances are 858,000,000 and 960,000,000 miles. There is, therefore, between the extreme distances a difference of some 100,000,000 miles. From these numbers it is easy to deduce the length of the path described by Saturn in his long year of 10,760 of our days, or 29 years 167 days. Saturn travels along this orbit with a mean velocity of 529,000 miles a-day, or 22,000 miles an hour.*

If Saturn, by reason of the elliptical form of its orbit, approaches more or less to the focus of the solar system, it is easy to understand that

* If this velocity be compared with those that we have given for the planets lying between the Sun and Saturn, we shall see that the movement of the planets in their orbits is slower as the distance increases. This is a direct consequence of a law of Kepler's, of which more anon.

its distances from the Earth must vary still more, according to the relative positions of the two planets and the Sun. It is at opposition that they are nearest; at conjunction, on the contrary, their distance is much more considerable. These two periods occur at intervals of 378 days, or a little more than a year. But the maximum or minimum distances themselves vary, from one period to another, because each of the two planets, according to the point of its orbit which it occupies, is itself more or less removed from the Sun. The distance of Saturn from the Earth may vary between 1,057,000,000 and 761,000,000 miles. This difference of 296,000,000 miles produces, as may be imagined, a corresponding variation in the apparent dimensions of the planet: fig. 95 shows between what limits that variation lies.

Nevertheless, as seen from the Earth, Saturn always appears under the aspect of a star of the first magnitude, which our best telescopes present to us under the form of a spheroidal globe, surrounded, as we have seen, with a ring brighter than itself.

Let us continue to consider but the nucleus of this singular system. Its distance being known, it is easy to deduce its real dimensions: these show Saturn to be the second of the principal planets, as far as its size is concerned.

Fig. 95.—Apparent dimensions of Saturn at its extreme and mean distances from the Earth, showing also the different appearances presented by its ring-system.

As it turns rapidly on one of its diameters, it is much flattened at the poles of rotation, so that it is necessary, in giving its dimensions, to distinguish between the axis, or polar diameter, and that of its equator. While the latter measures $9\frac{1}{2}$ times more than that of the Earth's mean diameter, or 75,100 miles, the former is only $8\frac{1}{2}$ times greater, or 68,270 miles. The difference of 6830 miles represents a flattening of $\frac{1}{11}$th, that of the Earth being $\frac{1}{300}$, or 26 miles.

To make a tour of this immense globe, taking the shortest way, its inhabitants would have to travel nearly 214,000 miles passing through the poles, or 236,000 along the equator.

These distances are less than on Jupiter, but they are more than nine times greater than those of our globe. These dimensions give a surface of 16,655,000,000 square miles, and a volume more than 776 times greater than that of our Earth.

But the mass of this enormous spheroid is far from being comparable with its volume—at least, if we compare this with that of the Earth: it is but a little more than 100 times greater* (102·683). This indicates, on the supposition that it is equally dense throughout, that it is composed of matter seven times lighter than the materials of our Earth, and consequently less dense than water; [in fact, about the density of oak or sulphuric ether.]

The rotatory movement of Saturn has been determined by observations of the dark bands which cross the disk in a direction parallel to its equator; the inequalities of these bands, by their periodical return, have enabled astronomers to calculate the time of rotation, which is 10 hours, 29 minutes, 17 seconds.

Here, then, we find one of the largest planets with a period of rotation less than half those of Mercury, Venus, Mars, or the Earth. Day and night succeed each other on the average at intervals of five hours, but the

Fig. 96.—Saturn and the Earth; Comparative dimensions.

length of the year, which comprises 24,631 complete rotations, or 24,630 solar days of Saturn, causes the seasons to modify the lengths of day and night but very slowly.

As to the seasons themselves, they are much more varied than on Jupiter, since, owing to the considerable inclination of the axis [to] the plane of the orbit,† Saturn presents to the Sun sometimes one, and sometimes another, of its poles of rotation. For the same place on its surface,

* That is, the $\frac{1}{3500}$th part of the mass of the Sun.
[† This inclination is 63° 10′ 32″, according to Proctor.]

the altitude of the Sun above the horizon is still more variable than on the Earth; but if we wish to form an idea of the change of temperature due to this cause, it is important to remark that the altitude of which we speak varies thirty times less rapidly than with us. Each of Saturn's seasons lasts more than seven of our years, and there is nearly fifteen years' interval between the autumn and spring equinoxes, and between the summer and winter solstices.

But we should have but an incomplete idea of the phenomena presented by the days, nights, and seasons of Saturn, if we did not take into account the modifications produced in these elements by the existence of the annular appendages by which this magnificent planet is surrounded, and by the presence on the horizon of the eight satellites which escort it in its long revolution of thirty years. The drawings given in Plate XII show Saturn as it was observed, at an interval of nearly three years, in two points of its orbit, distant enough to modify perceptibly its position relatively to the Earth and the Sun; all the details of the disk and of the rings perceived by the most powerful instruments are faithfully reproduced.

At the time of the discovery of this strange system, telescopes had just been invented. The imperfections of these instruments threw Galileo, says Arago, 'into great perplexity.' A letter to the Grand Duke of Tuscany informs us that Saturn seemed to him *tricorps*. 'When I observe Saturn,' he remarks, 'with a glass of a power of more than thirty times, the central body seems the largest; the two others, situated one on the east, the other on the west, and on a line which does not coincide with the direction of the zodiac, seem to touch it. They are like two supporters, who help old Saturn on his way, and always remain at his side. With a glass of smaller magnifying power, the planet appears elongated and of the form of an olive.'

Saturn subsequently appeared to the illustrious astronomer perfectly round. He regarded his preceding observations as optical illusions, and in his disappointment exclaimed, 'Can it be possible some demon has mocked me?' This is the first record we have of the disappearance of the rings, of which more presently. Huyghens subsequently observed these appendages of Saturn, and he first gave the explanation which the theory of the planet's motion and the employment of more powerful instruments have definitely confirmed.

[Most encouraging is the chapter of the history of Modern Astronomy which tells us how eye and mind have bridged over the tremendous gap which separates us from the planet. We have seen by degrees a ring evolved out of the triform planet, and the great division in the ring and the irregularities on it, brought to light. Enceladus, and coy Mimas, faintest of twinklers, are caught by Herschel's giant mirrors, and he, too, first among men, realises the wonderful tenuity of the ring along which he saw those satellites travelling, 'like pearls strung on a silver thread.' Then Bond comes on the field, and furnishes evidence to show that we must multiply the number of separate rings we know not how many fold.

SATURN.

From the observations of Bond, Struve, and Warren De La Rue.
November 1852, and March 1856.

And here we reach the golden age of Saturnian discovery, when Bond, with the giant refractor of Cambridge, U.S., and Dawes, with his eagle gaze and $6\frac{1}{3}$-inches Munich glass, first beheld that wonderful dark semi-transparent ring which still remains one of the wonders of our system. But the end is not yet; ere summer on the southern surface of the ring fades into autumn, Otto Struve in turn comes upon the field, detects, as Dawes had previously done, a division even in the dark ring, and measures it while it is invisible to Lassell's mirror—a proof, if one were needed, of the enormous superiority possessed by refractors in such inquiries. Then we approach 1861, when the ring-plane again passes through the Earth, and Otto Struve and Wray observe those curious nebulous appearances, of which more anon.]

We know indeed, now, that surrounding Saturn, and nearly in the plane of its equator, is extended a system of rings which may be broadly divided into three, of unequal breadths: of these the thickness is relatively very small. The exterior ring, the one farthest from the planet, is separated from the intermediate one by a very distinct break, whilst the interior ring, that nearest to Saturn, seems joined on to the second. Their brightnesses are very different: the intermediate ring, the most brilliant of the three, is more luminous than the globe of Saturn; the exterior ring is of a greyish tint, nearly of the same shade as the dark bands of the disk. Both of these are opaque, and throw on Saturn a very distinct shadow. The interior ring, on the contrary, is dusky, and almost of a purple tinge, and transparent; it stands out on the globe of Saturn as a dark band, through which the luminous disk is readily seen, [and without distortion.]

[Let us dwell for a moment on this transparent ring, the physical features of which are perhaps less remarkable than the fact that it was not discovered till 1850, and had been entirely overlooked, if it existed, till then, not only by all ordinary observers, but by Herschel's great telescopes. When Bond and Dawes discovered it, it was by no means easy of observation, but now it may be seen in a four-inch achromatic. Another remarkable fact is the probable increase in width since the time of its discovery, which we shall see subsequently to have an important bearing on one of the hypotheses suggested to account for the entire appendage.]

In order that a clear idea may be obtained of the positions and breadths of the rings, we give in fig. 97 a view of the system, such as would be obtained by an observer placed above the plane of the rings in the prolongation of the planet's polar axis.

The exterior diameter of the outer ring is 173,500 miles, and its inner diameter 153,500 miles; its breadth therefore is 10,000 miles. These dimensions for the middle ring are respectively 150,000, 113,400, and 18,300 miles. The distance which separates these two rings is 1750 miles. The dark ring joins the middle (or bright) ring. The space between its interior edge and the surface of the planet is 10,150 miles; its breadth therefore is 9000 miles. The entire breadth of the ring-system, therefore, is 39,050 miles. Its thickness is probably not more than 100 miles.

Can then, such a material system, whether solid or liquid, sustain itself, without point of contact or support, in a constant—or nearly constant—position with regard to the planet? And, if so, how do its different parts resist the 'pull' which the attraction of Saturn exercises on each of them? It would seem that this immense bridge ought by degrees to break up, and then—catastrophe far beyond anything the face of heaven has yet presented to man's eye—be precipitated in unutterable and headlong fall upon the surface of the planet.

Laplace first considered this problem. He showed that its equilibrium

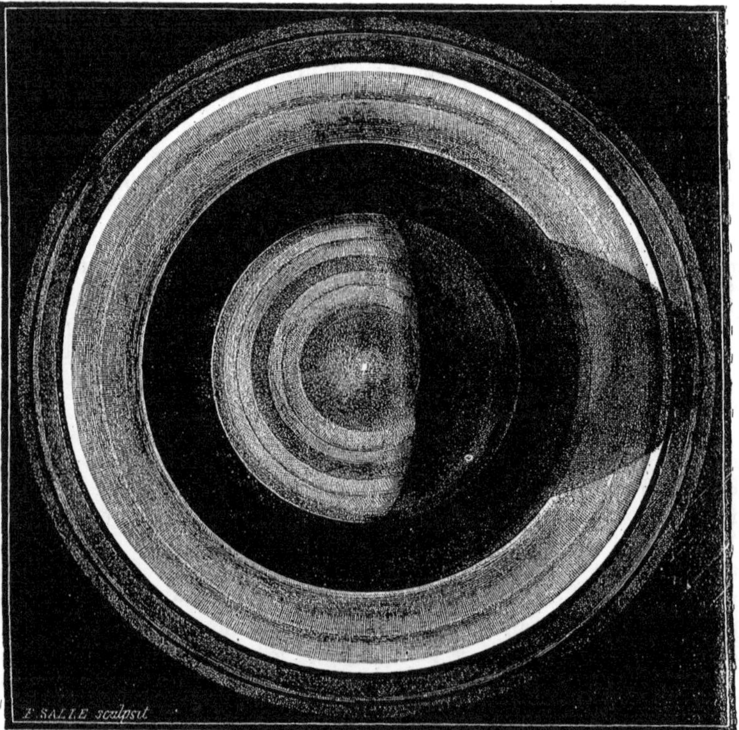

Fig. 97.—Bird's-eye View of Saturn and its ring-system.

could not be possible and stable, unless the section of the ring, of elliptical form, presented in several points inequalities of breadth or curvature. Observation has shown that these conditions exist, as the centre of gravity of the ring does not coincide with that of the planet, and slow oscillations in their relative positions take place. Moreover, he showed that there was another essential condition—the ring ought to rotate in its plane with a velocity of little more than ten hours. Herschel imagined that he had also detected this rotation, which thus agreed with the result of calculation.

His observations, made in 1790, gave a period of rotation of 10 hours, 32 minutes.

[Since this time, however, Laplace's investigation has been shown to be insufficient, and Pierce and Maxwell have in turn demonstrated that the rings are not solid, and are not liquid; and their non-solidity appears to be shown, not only by the variable traces of divisions in the ring and the appearance—may we not almost say the birth?—of the dark ring, but by the possible increase in the breadth of the ring-system. The least favourable measure of the width of the ring in Huyghens' time gives 23,667 miles; Herschel found it 26,297. The most modern recorded measurements give 28,300, so that if we accept these measurements, the present annual increase in the breadth of the ring is 29 miles.

Of what, then, are the rings composed? It is now held by some that they are composed of *Satellites*, and Proctor has pointed out that on this hypothesis,—

'The temporary divisions and mottled stripes are easily explained.

Fig. 98.—Saturn, Dec. 26, 1861, at $18^h\ 30^m$. (Wray.)
Luminous appendages of the ring. The satellites are also seen apparently on the ring.

It is conceivable, for instance, that the streams of satellites forming the rings might be temporarily separated along arcs of greater or less length by narrow strips altogether clear of satellites, or in which satellites might be but sparsely distributed. Divisions of the former kind would appear as dark lines, while those of the latter kind would present precisely that mottled appearance seen in the dusky or ash-coloured stripes. The transparency of the dark inner ring is easily understood if we consider the satellites to be sparsely scattered throughout that formation. The fact that this ring has only become visible of late years no longer presents an insuperable difficulty, for it is readily conceivable that the satellites forming the dark ring have originally belonged to the inner bright ring, whence collisions or disturbing attractions have but lately propelled or drawn them. The gradual spreading out of the rings is explicable when the system is supposed to consist of satellites only connected by their mutual attractions; while the thinness of the system is obviously a necessary consequence of such a formation, for the attraction of Saturn's bulging equatorial regions would compel each satellite to travel near the plane of Saturn's equator.'*

Fig. 99.—Saturn, Jan. 5, 1862, at $14^h\ 0^m$. Luminous appendages of the ring. (Wray.)

The elliptical shading on the inner bright ring at the ends of the apparent longer axis of the dark ring, which is represented in our figures,

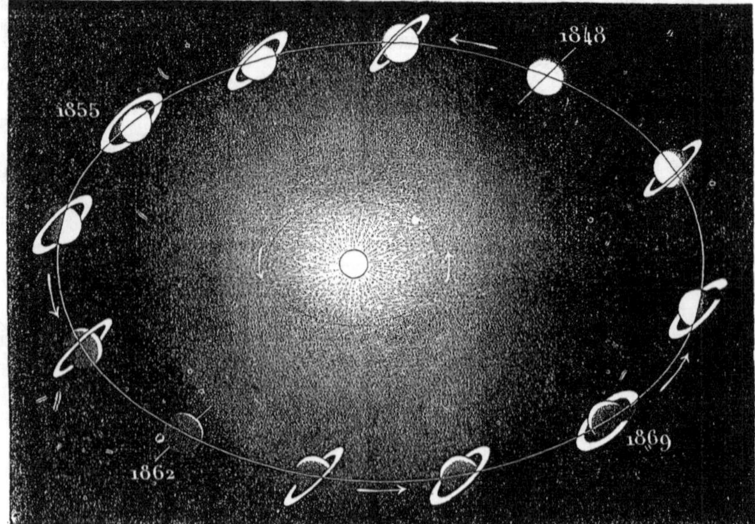

Fig. 100.—Explanation of the Phases of Saturn's rings. Periodical disappearances of the rings.

and has been a sore puzzle to our observers, also finds a possible explanation :—

'We have only to imagine that the satellites are strewn more densely

* Proctor's *Saturn and its System*, p. 118. This volume forms the most complete monograph of the planet yet published.

near the outer edges of the bright rings, and especially of the inner bright ring, and that this density of distribution gradually diminishes inwards. For instance, we may conclude that along the inner edge of the inner bright ring the satellites are so sparsely strewn, that, at the extremities of the apparent longer axis of that edge, *the dark background of the sky becomes visible through the gaps between the satellites.*'

Mr. Dawes attributes this shading to the overlapping of the dark ring, which may be thicker than the inner edge of the bright ring.

Otto Struve and Wray also noticed, in 1861 and 1862, curious appendages, like clouds of a less intense light, lying on the ring, differing much in colour from the ordinary colour of the rings—not yellow, but more of a livid colour, brown and blue. These appearances, on the hypothesis to which we refer, are supposed to be due to the satellites drawn out of the plane of the ring by the attraction of Saturn's outer satellite.]

Fig. 101.—Saturn, Nov. 22, 1848 (Bond). Luminous points visible near the period of the disappearance of the ring.

In its movement round the Sun, the axis of Saturn, like that of the other planets, remains parallel to itself. The axis of motion of the rings is also constant, and, as their inclination to the plane of the planet's orbit is considerable,* it follows that the Sun sometimes illuminates one of the faces of the system, sometimes the other. In two diametrically opposed positions in Saturn's orbit, the plane of the rings is directed to the Sun, and consequently their edge only receives its light. This takes place at the epoch of Saturn's equinoxes.

What, then, are the appearances presented to us Earth-dwellers? Evidently that the rings, by an effect of perspective easily gathered from

* [This inclination of the Planet's orbit to the plane of the ecliptic is . . . . 2° 29′ 26″
The inclination of the plane of the rings to the same plane is . 28 10 22]

fig. 100, appear sometimes more and sometimes less open; and that during one-half of the planet's year, the part of the ring between us and the planet is apparently projected on the northern hemisphere; and during the other half the 'dip' is in an inverse direction, and the ring is seen to cover a part of the south hemisphere. At two particular periods the ring, being only illuminated at the edge, disappears entirely, except in the most powerful instruments, which then show a light luminous line near the prolongation of Saturn's equator.

We give two drawings which represent Saturn in this particular position. The first (fig. 101) shows the planet as it was observed by Professor Bond, in November, 1848. The other (fig. 102), which we also owe to the same astronomer, gives the explanation of the luminous points recorded in fig. 101.

[He supposes them due (as the Earth was not in the plane of the ring) to the light reflected from the edges of the different rings, which near the

Fig. 102.—Explanation of the brilliant points observed near the epoch of the disappearance of the ring.

epoch of the passage of the ring-plane through the Sun, received the Sun's light.]

Besides this cause for the disappearance of the rings, which is independent of the position of the Earth in its orbit, and depends only upon the passage of the plane of the rings through the Sun, there is another, which depends upon our Earth passing through the plane of the ring. An observer, situated on our globe, would then, equally, only see the edge of the ring; he could observe neither the upper nor lower surface, but merely, near the time of passage, the luminous points to which we have referred.

There is still another cause for the disappearance of the ring, and this occurs when the Earth is on one side of the plane of the rings and the

Sun is on the other. At such times obviously, as the dark surface is turned towards us, we cannot see it.

Such appears to us Saturn at its enormous distance from the Earth. We have said that it is the richest of the systems, or worlds in miniature, which surround the Sun. It is distinguished from all the others, not only by its wondrous rings, which bear witness, perhaps, of the method of formation of our planetary worlds, but in addition by eight satellites, the incessant revolution of which round the central globe adds to the variety of its celestial phenomena.

We give below the names of the eight moons of Saturn, with their distances from the centre of the planet, and the time of their revolutions in terrestrial mean solar days :—

	Distance from Saturn's centre in miles.	Time of sidereal revolutions. d.	h.	m.	s.
Mimas	119,725	0	22	37	23
Enceladus	153,630	1	8	53	7
Tethys	190,225	1	21	18	26
Dione	243,670	2	17	41	9
Rhea	340,320	4	12	25	11
Titan	788,915	15	22	41	25
Hyperion	954,160	21	7	7	41
Japetus	2,292,790	79	7	54	40

The first four satellites are all nearer to Saturn than the Moon is to the Earth. Mimas is, moreover, but 82,000 miles from Saturn's surface, and Dione about 206,000; Mimas' distance from the edge of the ring being but about 31,000 miles. On the other hand, Japetus is nearly ten times more distant from Saturn than we are from our satellite, so that the diameter of the Saturnian system measures nearly 4,500,000 miles.

Fig. 103.—Saturn and its satellites. (Sir J. Herschel.)

Figure 104 shows the system of the orbits of the satellites, supposing their planes coincident with the plane of Saturn's orbit. These curves are not circular; but their excentricity is not accurately known, and the elliptical form would not be perceptible, on the small scale we have adopted.

We see, by the times of revolution, that the movements of the satellites are extremely rapid; their phases, therefore, must vary rapidly to the inhabitants of the planet. Mimas passes from new to full moon in less than twelve hours, a little more than Saturn's day. In one or two days, the four following moons present the same succession of appearances. Japetus alone accomplishes its entire revolution in a longer time than our lunar month. The two interior satellites and Hyperion are very difficult to observe, and require experienced observers, provided with the most powerful instruments. The remaining five satellites, however, are well seen with careful watching in a five-foot achromatic. The diameter of Titan, the largest satellite, has been measured. It is about the sixteenth part of that of Saturn. It is, therefore, more than half the diameter of the Earth. Thus, as in the case of Jupiter's satellites, one of the secondary bodies of this marvellous system exceeds in size such planets as Mercury and Mars; its volume is about nine times that of our Moon.

We have before referred to the days, nights, and seasons in this planet. It will be readily understood, by referring to what we have said of these

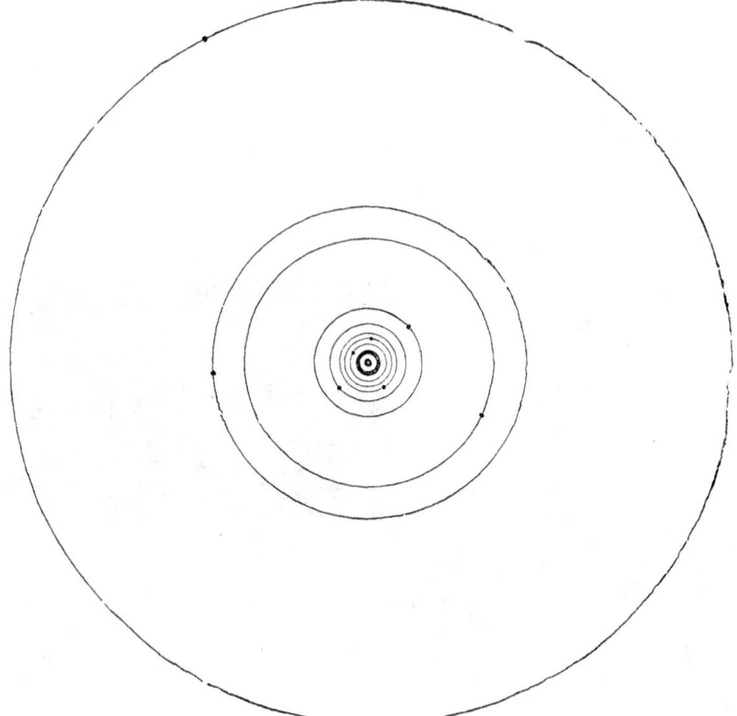

Fig. 104.—Bird's-eye View of the Orbits of Saturn's satellites.

matters in the case of the Earth, that similar variations must also take place in this planet in a given place, in the course of the year, and at the same moment, in different latitudes.

At the two poles, and throughout the polar zones, these variations attain their maximum. During fifteen of our years the Sun does not leave the north pole, and a night of the same length envelopes the south pole of Saturn; the reverse phenomena occur during the fifteen following years. Doubtless, an intense cold is the consequence of this prolonged privation of the rays of light and heat. To this long winter, and the ice and snow with which the polar regions are doubtless covered, may perhaps be attributed the whitish zone which has been remarked round the poles; but at such a distance physical facts elude us, and we must rest content with hypotheses.

The atmosphere of Saturn is doubtless very dense, especially near the equatorial regions; the bright belts with which the disk is girdled are probably produced by the reflexion of light from immense cloud-masses, which the rapidity of the movement of rotation incessantly accumulates. The darker belts possibly, as we remarked in the case of Jupiter, indicate a more serene atmosphere.

Let us imagine ourselves on the globe of the Saturn. Thence let us gaze on the appearances of the celestial vault during the day and night.

If we start from either pole, in advancing as far as 63° of Saturnicentric latitude, we shall traverse those regions of the hemisphere where the ring is never visible; only the satellites appear above the horizon, and present to the spectator the varied aspect of their phases.

Leaving this latitude, the ring-system begins to be visible. But it is only during the two seasons of spring and summer that the surface of the rings, turned towards the hemisphere where we are placed, receives the rays of the Sun, and lights up, by reflexion, the planet's nights. During the day their arcs send forth but feeble light, analogous possibly to that reflected by our Moon when visible in broad day.

The form and extent of the immense luminous arches vary, moreover, according to the latitude; starting from 63°, and advancing towards the equator, they rise higher and higher above the horizon. We first see a part of the exterior ring, then the ring in its entirety. At the mean latitude of 45°, the two first rings are observed. In proportion as we descend towards the equatorial regions, the entire system becomes visible, but at the same time, the visual rays having a more oblique direction, the rings diminish in apparent breadth, continually, however, rising more and more above the horizon. At the equator, they are only visible by their interior edge. This edge is then presented as an immense luminous band, stretched from east to west, passing through the zenith.

To give an idea of the magnificent spectacle which the starry vault presents during the nights of the summer season, we have sketched, according to the laws of perspective, the appearance of the rings from a latitude comprised between 25° and 30°. These two ideal views represent the ring at midnight, the one a little after the equinox, the other at the beginning of summer, towards the period of the solstice.

In the first of these Saturnian landscapes (fig. 105), the ring-system is seen forming an immense arch, interrupted by a large space at the summit. The sky is visible through the division, which separates the two principal rings, and it again appears below the arch. The interruption at the summit is produced by the shadow cast by Saturn, and is only distinguished from the sky by the absence of stars. It is possible, however, that this eclipsed portion of the rings may be sometimes rendered visible by the refraction of the solar rays by the atmosphere of the planet. The eclipsed band may take a coloured tint, analogous to the reddish colour of the Moon during total eclipses.

The second ideal landscape (fig. 106) allows us to see the exterior ring in its entirety. At the solstices, the shadow of the planet is thrown only on the interior rings. We must remark, also, that at the different hours of the night the position of the shadow is not the same. It only occupies the middle of the arc at midnight. It hence follows that after sunset the western part of the ring first appears; by degrees, as the night advances, the western arc diminishes, and the other portions appear at the

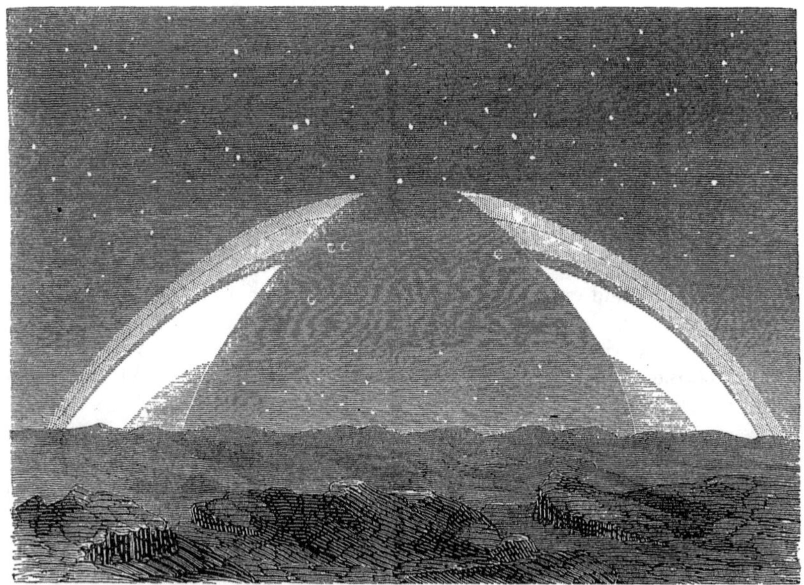

Fig. 105.—The Rings seen from Saturn at a latitude of about 28°. Ideal View, at midnight towards the period of the Saturnian solstices.

east; until, at midnight, the lengths of the two arcs are equal. From midnight, the western portion still diminishes, and at last disappears, whilst the eastern arc increases in length. When we add to the strange beauty of this spectacle the presence of the satellites, presenting different phases, some full, others new, others gibbous, or crescent, an idea will be formed of the variety of aspects of the Saturnian night. [Compared with our Moon, however, the moons of Saturn give very little light. Even if all full together, they would give but one-sixteenth part of the light of our full moon.—R. A. P.]

During the winter seasons, the rings present their dark sides, and are only visible during the night, negatively; that is to say, by the absence of the stars on the celestial vault which they eclipse. Nevertheless, towards the morning and evening they may possibly reflect the light they receive from the illuminated part of the planet; at the east and west they show doubtless a slight glimmer, similar to the Earth-shine of our Moon, or, again, to the Zodiacal light.

But if the winter nights are deprived of the light of the rings, the days of the same seasons present, on the other hand, the most curious phenomena. As, by reason of the diurnal rotation, the Sun moves apparently along circular arcs, sometimes more, sometimes less elevated above the horizon, the god of day, being compelled thus to pass behind the rings, undergoes long and frequent eclipses. The duration of these phenomena is shorter

Fig. 106 —The Rings seen from Saturn at a latitude of about 28°. Ideal View, taken at midnight, between the Saturnian equinoxes and the solstices.

than was at first supposed, because, as the apparent path of the Sun is not paralled to the arcs of the rings, he, though eclipsed at rising, reappears under the ring, to again disappear before sunset.

[Mr. Proctor, in the book from which we have already quoted, remarks that in latitude 40° we have morning and evening eclipses for more than a year, gradually extending until the Sun is eclipsed during the whole day, and these total eclipses continue for nearly 7 years, eclipses of one kind or another, taking place for 8 years 292·8 days. 'If we remember,' he adds, 'that latitude 40° on Saturn corresponds with the latitude of Madrid on our Earth, it will be seen how largely the rings must influence the conditions of habitability of Saturn's globe, considered with reference to the wants of beings constituted like the inhabitants of our Earth.']

Nearer the equator and poles solar eclipses are still very frequent, but the period of time during which they last is gradually reduced. Judging of the loss of light by the intensity of the shade thrown on the planet, the apparent night produced by these eclipses is doubtless very decided, although atmospheric refraction would prevent them from being absolute. If we could watch the various celestial phenomena from the rings, the appearance of the sky would be very different: if we supposed ourselves located over the edge of the ring, we should have a long night of fifteen years succeeding a day of the same length.

During the period of illumination of each side of the rings, the Sun is

Fig. 107.—Ideal view of a phase of Saturn.

eclipsed every 10½ hours. These eclipses, due to the interposition of Saturn's disk, produce partial nights, the duration of which varies between 1½ and 2 hours over a large surface of the ring. These are the phenomena which caused the interruption of the luminous arc seen from Saturn, as represented in two different epochs in our two ideal views.

But for nearly fifteen years each side of the rings is entirely deprived of the light of the Sun. This long night is partly compensated by the light reflected by the illuminated hemisphere of the planet, or at least by the part of that hemisphere visible from the ring. During every period of 10½ hours the immense globe appears under various phases. It is first a luminous point, which rises from the horizon, taking more and more the form of a half crescent (fig. 107), but much less curved than that of the Moon. After $5\frac{1}{4}$ hours it is nearly a half circle, which embraces the eighth part of the whole celestial vault, the surface of this half circle is thus more than 20,000 times that of the lunar disk (fig. 108). On this disk is perceived a dark zone, divided by a bright line: it is the shadow projected by the ring on the planet. Bright and dark belts, and, doubtless, many other physical details that we cannot see at our enormous distance from Saturn, distinguish the various parts of this immense disk.

The more we leave the inner ring, the more does the visible portion of the planet increase; but its apparent dimensions diminish, on the other

Fig. 108.—The globe of Saturn, seen from the ring.

hand, with the distance always however remaining considerable. Figs. 107 and 108 will give an idea of the aspect of Saturn seen from a point on the middle ring at an interval of about 3 hours.*

It remains for us to point out, in terminating our review of Saturn's phenomena, and of the celestial phenomena presented to the Saturnians, the numerous eclipses produced by the eight satellites, both when they pass over the solar disk and when they themselves plunge into the shadow

* [In these two ideal views, as in the two preceding ones, M. Guillemin has been compelled, naturally enough, to appeal in his foregrounds, to our terrestrial prejudices. Of course, the rights of the different hypotheses referred to in the text are 'strictly reserved.']

thrown by the planet. These phenomena can be watched from the Earth in powerful instruments. The last occasion took place in 1862, when Mr. Dawes and Mr. Lockyer were enabled to observe the shadow of Titan traversing the planet's disk, the satellite itself on one occasion grazing the planet's lower limb. [Mr. Dawes also witnessed an eclipse of Titan—'a unique observation,' he remarks.]

XVIII.

URANUS.

Discovery of Uranus in the last Century—Form and Dimensions of its Orbit—Its apparent and real Dimensions—Its Satellites; Inclinations of their Orbits, and Directions of their Movements.

THE Solar System, as known to the ancients, comprised all those celestial bodies the movements and physical constitution of which we have just studied, with the exception of the telescopic planets and the satellites of Saturn and Jupiter. A century ago the number of the planets remained the same as for ages past, and the confines of the system did not extend beyond Saturn. It was reserved for one of the most illustrious observers of modern times, Sir William Herschel, to double the radius of the sphere which embraces the bodies subject to the attraction of the Sun, by the discovery of a new planet—Uranus.

It was on the 13th of March, 1781, between ten and eleven o'clock at night, that Herschel, employed in exploring with his telescope the constellation of the Twins, observed a star the disk of which attracted his attention. Perceiving, after a few nights of observation, that the new body moved, he first took it for a comet. His observations, when submitted to calculation, soon showed that he had discovered a body which was at such a great distance from the Sun, and the orbit of which was so circular, that it was impossible long to hesitate as to its real character: it was a planet.

Uranus, usually—but this depends upon its distance from the Earth—shines as a star of the sixth magnitude. It is therefore sometimes visible to the naked eye. This insignificant size and brightness, however, are merely relative, and are caused by the immense distance of the planet from the Sun, and therefore from the Earth, and also by the feeble intensity of the light received from the first-named body. But if it be examined with a telescope of high magnifying power, the circular form of its disk appears with clearness, and its apparent diameter may be measured.

The orbit described by Uranus round the Sun surrounds the orbit of the Earth at so great a distance, that it is impossible to perceive on its disk any appearance of phases. It has the appearance of always turning its bright side towards us.

The orbit is not a perfect circle, but, like those of the other planets, is elliptical; so that, during the whole course of its revolution, which lasts about 84 years—more exactly, 30,686 $\frac{8}{10}$ days—the distance of Uranus from the Sun constantly varies between 1,743,000,000 and 1,913,000,000 miles: there is thus a difference of 170,000,000 miles.

Its distance from the Earth varies even more, being greatest when the two planets are on opposite sides of the Sun, and of course least when they are on the same side. In the former case, Uranus is in conjunction, and its mean distance from the Earth exceeds 1,923,000,000 miles, whilst at opposition the mean distance is 1,733,000,000. Its apparent diameter, seen from the Earth, then varies in a way which may thus be exhibited:—

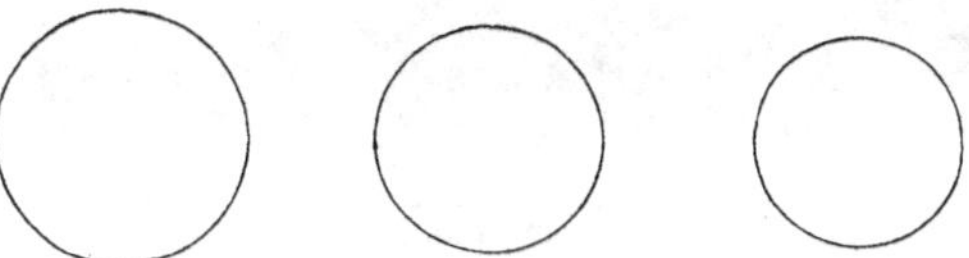

Fig. 109.—Apparent dimensions of Uranus at its mean and extreme distances from the Earth.

From the distance of Uranus and its apparent size, its real dimensions have been deduced: it is a spherical body, 82 times larger than our Earth, the diameter of our planet being $4\frac{1}{3}$ times less than that of Uranus (4·344). The real diameter, therefore, is 34,500 miles. Fig. 110 shows the comparative dimensions of these two bodies.

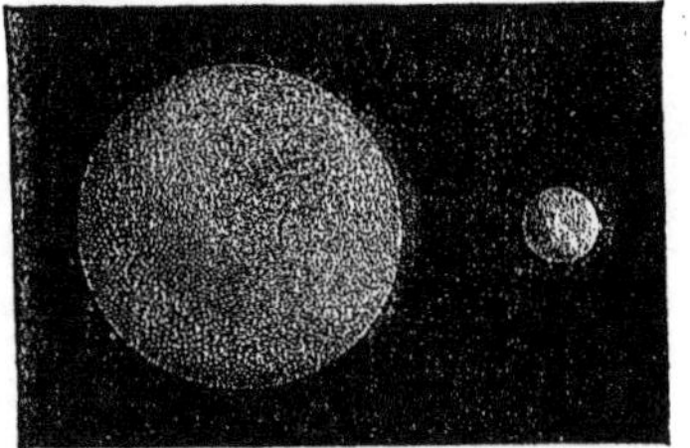

Fig. 110.—Comparative size of Uranus and the Earth.

Astronomers are not agreed as to whether Uranus is perfectly spherical or flattened at the poles of rotation. Sir William Herschel asserted the latter, and Mädler found some years ago a flattening of $\frac{1}{10}$th, which is suggestive of a rapid rotation; but other astronomers, Otto Struve among them, have not been able to detect any perceptible flattening. This, however, does not, perhaps, militate against the observations of Mädler and Herschel; for if, as Arago remarks,* we assume that the equator of Uranus is situate nearly in the plane of the orbits of its satellites, this will explain how, at different epochs, observers have arrived at different results. The axis of rotation of the planet would, on this supposition, nearly coincide with the plane of the orbit of the Earth. If the axis be turned towards our globe, the ellipsoid will seem to us circular; if, on the other hand, it be at right angles with us, the polar compression will become visible.

The following figure explains both the difference of position, and the change of appearance resulting therefrom.

* 'Popular Astronomy,' vol. iv. p. 493.

Uranus, like Saturn, is the centre of a little system, comprising, besides the principal planet, eight* moons or satellites, revolving in planes nearly per-

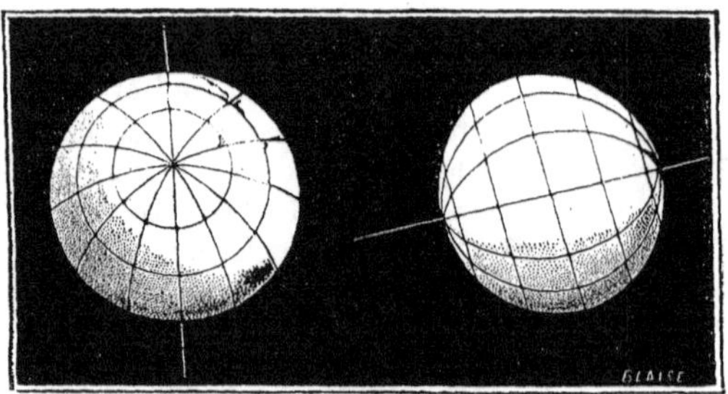

Fig. 111.—Difference between the apparent forms of a flattened globe, seen in two different positions.

pendicular to the plane of the planet's orbit. These bodies, whose revolutions are accomplished, the nearest in two days, and the most distant in about 108

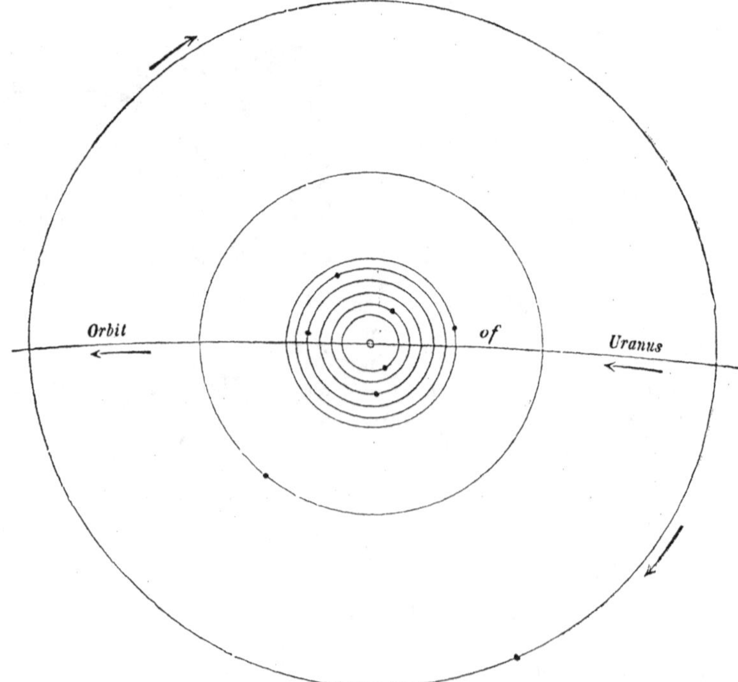

Fig.—112.—System of the Satellites of Uranus; relative dimensions of the Orbits.

* [Mr. Lassell is inclined to believe from his own observations of Uranus, that only four satellites have been discovered, and that those supposed to have been seen by Herschel were in reality fixed stars. As a matter of fact, however, Herschel paid

days, possibly compensate, in some degree, by their reflected light, during the nights of the planet, the feeble intensity of the daylight. The Sun is visible at Uranus as a small disk, whose superficial extent is but one 370th of the extent of the solar disk as seen from our globe. The heat received from it, too, is but one 370th of that we receive from the Sun.

We have shown, in fig. 112, the relative dimensions of the orbits of the satellites, as they would be seen if we could obtain a bird's-eye view of the plane in which they revolve. We have already mentioned the fact, that their movements are performed in a direction nearly perpendicular to the plane in which the planet revolves round the Sun. Another peculiarity, and this is found nowhere else throughout the Solar system, further distinguishes Uranus; the direction of these movements is retrograde, that is to say, it is contrary to that of all the other known movements of satellites and planets. But this anomaly probably results from the very great inclination of their orbits, shown in fig. 113.

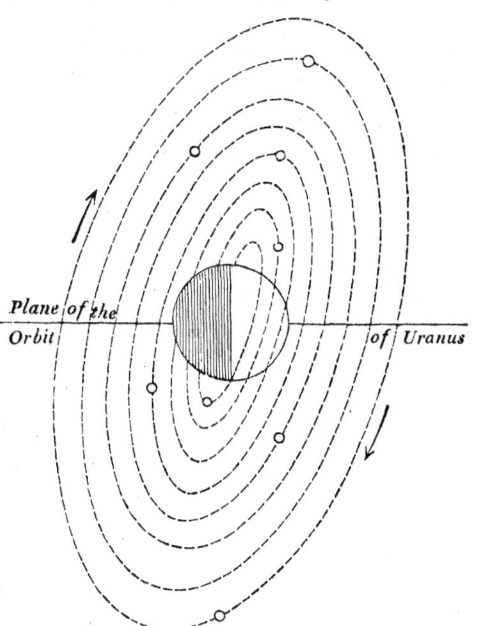

Fig. 113.—Inclination of the planes of the orbits of the satellites to the orbit of Uranus.

The first satellite is but 128,000 miles, or about half the distance of our Moon, from the planet. The most distant of the four of which we have certain knowledge is 392,000 miles. Of these four, the two nearest, *Ariel* and *Umbriel*, were discovered by Lassell and Otto Struve respectively; the six remaining ones (two of which have received the names *Titania* and *Oberon*), by Sir W. Herschel.

Observations of the variations of the quantity of light reflected by these enormously distant bodies—and these observations, we need scarcely say, are extremely difficult—have led to the inference that they possess movements of rotation, an idea strengthened by other planetary analogies: it is, however, as yet by no means certain. Nor have we yet observed their eclipses by the shadow of the planet, or those of the Sun, which doubtless sometimes take place when they pass between the planet and that body.

special attention to the necessity of carefully distinguishing fixed stars from satellites. We have no sufficient grounds as yet for rejecting (for the first time) observations made by Sir W. Herschel, and regarded by him as demonstrative.—R. A. P.]

We may, however, infer these phenomena as well as phases; and the simultaneous presence or absence of these bodies from the Uranian sky doubtless affords a great variety in the appearances presented to the inhabitants—if such exist—of this distant planet.

Observations have at present given us no information on the physical constitution of Uranus. No feature is visible on the disk at such a distance. Astronomical calculations can only tell us of its mass, which is fifteen times that of the Earth; taking this and its volume into account, we find, for the density of the matter of which it is composed, a value equal to one-sixth of that of our Earth: the density of Uranus, therefore, is a little more than that of ice.

On the surface of Uranus, the force of gravity is $\frac{1}{20}$th greater than on the surface of our Earth, so that the phenomena of equilibrium and movement are about the same as with us—with this difference, that the surface of the planet *may* be much less solid.

XIX.

NEPTUNE.

Discovery of Neptune—The Method of Discovery—Distance—Apparent and real Dimensions—Volume and Density—Satellite of Neptune.

At a mean distance from the Sun of 2,862,000,000 miles, that is to say, more than thirty times the radius of the Earth's path, the most distant of the known planets of the system circulates in its orbit. The nearly circular orbit which it describes round the common centre is so great, that it requires nearly 165 years to accomplish its revolution.

This planet is Neptune. Scarcely eighteen years separate us from the time when it was first distinguished as a planet; so that we have merely yet seen it traverse the ninth part of its orbit. The recent date of its discovery, and the immense distance of the planet from the Earth, are sufficient reasons for the few data we possess regarding it. But it is surrounded with another kind of interest to compensate for this insufficiency—we refer to the method, unique in the annals of astronomy, which served as a basis for its discovery.

We have seen that among the known bodies which compose the solar system, eight only were distinguished by the ancients from the multitude of brilliant points which spangle the starry vault: the dimensions of some,—the Sun, Moon, and Earth; the proper motion of others among the constellations,—Mercury, Venus, Mars, Jupiter, and Saturn, were the characters which early led to their being classed by themselves as wanderers.

Later, the telescope enlarged man's field of view, and permitted astronomers to add to these eight bodies a considerable number of new ones. Uranus, the Asteroids, the Satellites of Jupiter, Saturn, and Uranus, were ranked successively among the Solar family. But what was the method employed to discover all these celestial bodies? An attentive and minute survey of every part of the starry sky, the comparison of celestial maps with the field of view of powerful optical instruments, the happy discovery of a change of place of a luminous point. But in all this there was no prevision founded on theory, no preconceived notion on future discovery, which, indeed, in all cases has been due to the persevering zeal of observers and to happy chances.

The method to which the discovery of Neptune is owing was entirely a different one.

We shall speak subsequently on the principles of the movements of celestial bodies round their foci of revolution, as they act and react on each other in such a manner as to disturb the regularity of their movements; on the observed perturbations, and on the manner in which the perturbations observed are connected with the laws which govern them. Now, among these perturbations, there was one which utterly defied explanation on any known theory, and which astronomers had in vain attempted to ascribe to the action of one of the known bodies. The tables constructed for the planet Uranus did not at all agree with the observations, and the motion of this body was evidently disturbed by some unknown body. This body was, nevertheless, for some time suspected by Bouvard, Hansen, and many other astronomers, who held that the perturbations were due to an undiscovered planet beyond the orbit of Uranus. But the complete solution of the problem was accomplished independently by an Englishman,—Professor Adams, and a Frenchman,—M. Leverrier, both of whom now take rank among the foremost living astronomers.

[When we consider the problem in all its grandeur, we need not be surprised that two mathematicians who felt themselves competent to its solution should have independently undertaken it. As far back as July, 1841, Mr. Adams determined to investigate the irregularities of Uranus; early in September, 1846, the new planet had fairly been grappled. We find Sir John Herschel remarking: 'We see it as Columbus saw America from the shores of Spain. Its movements have been felt trembling along the far-reaching line of our analysis with a certainty hardly inferior to ocular demonstration.'

On the 29th of July, 1846, the Equatorial at Cambridge was first employed to search for the planet in the place theoretically assigned to it by Mr. Adams. M. Leverrier's theoretical researches were published on the 31st August, and his letter to the Berlin astronomers pointing out where he expected it would be found, was received on the 23rd September, his theoretical place and Mr. Adams' being not 1° apart. There, thanks to the Berlin star-maps, which the English astronomers had not received, Dr. Galle found the planet the same evening.

We need not now refer to the unfortunate, though perhaps necessary, discussion as to the comparative merits of these two astronomers, which almost clouded the brilliancy of their discovery. Let us rather look upon the work of each as a stupendous triumph of intellect, and the result to which the labours of both have led us as one which for ever establishes the theory of universal gravitation.]

In the words of Arago, 'Such a discovery is one of the most brilliant manifestations of the exactitude of the system of modern astronomers. It will encourage our most eminent geometers to seek with fresh ardour the eternal truths which remain hidden, as Pliny expresses himself, in the majesty of theories.'

Neptune is invisible to the naked eye. In telescopes, it has the aspect of a star of the eighth magnitude. Its apparent movement is extremely slow; but, as the orbit which it describes round the Sun is so immense, its real velocity is nevertheless considerable; it is about 12,400 miles an hour.

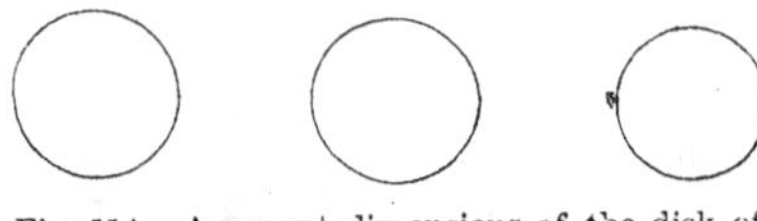

Fig. 114.—Apparent dimensions of the disk of Neptune at its mean and extreme distances from the Earth.

Like all other planets, it is sometimes nearer and sometimes further from the Earth. At the time of conjunction it is distant from us, on the average, 2,958,000,000 miles, whilst its minimum distance at opposition is less by 218,000,000 miles. The apparent dimensions vary in inverse ratio, their limits are shown in fig. 114.*

The real dimensions are somewhat considerable, and in virtue of them Neptune is the third planet of the system. Its diameter is 4·72 times greater than the diameter of the Earth, or 37,000 miles. The surface of the globe of Neptune is more than 22 times that of the Earth, and its volume is nearly 105 times.

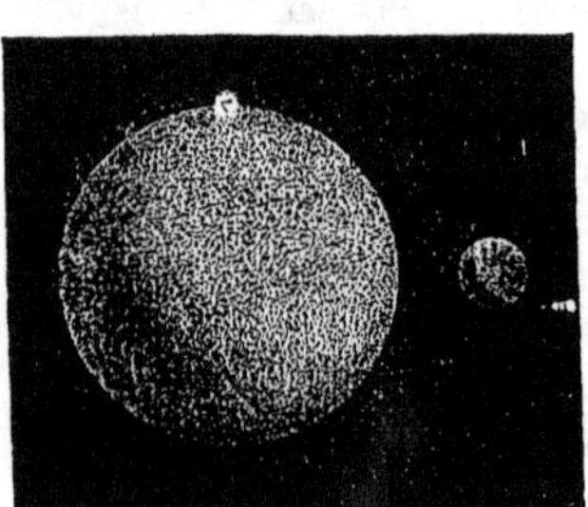

Fig. 115.—Neptune and the Earth; comparative dimensions.

If we turn to fig. 2, page 13, we shall see to what small dimensions the apparent diameter of the Sun is reduced, as seen from Neptune. The intensity of the heat and light received by that planet is but little more, at that enormous distance, than the thousandth part of that received by us. But as nothing is known of its physical and atmospheric conditions or of its rotation, nothing can be determined on the climatic conditions of the planet.

At a distance nearly equal to that of the Moon from the Earth, that is to say, about 225,000 miles, a satellite revolves round Neptune, in a

* This disk has not yet presented any perceptible trace of flattening, neither can any spot be distinguished on it, so that the time of its rotation remains unknown.

very circular orbit, in 5 days, 21 hours, 8 minutes:* this has enabled astronomers to calculate the mass of the primary. It is equal to about the $\frac{1}{17000}$th part of the mass of the Sun, or to 21 times that of the Earth. Hence, the density of the matter of which Neptune consists is less than

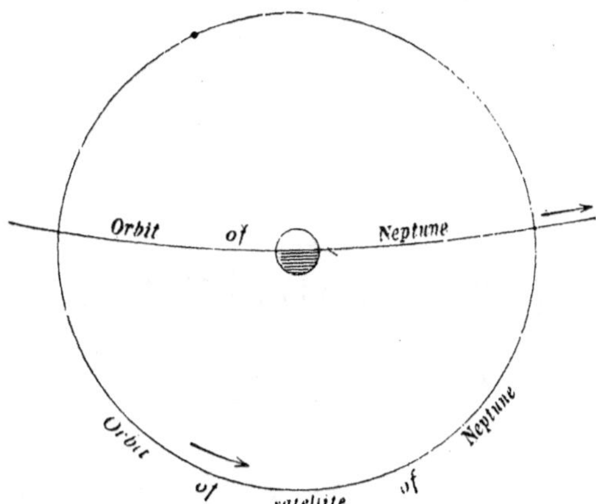

Fig. 116.—Satellite of Neptune.

the fourth of that of the Earth, or nearly equal to the density of nitric acid, and a little less than that of sea-water. From this point of view Jupiter is the planet most analogous with this body, whilst the force of gravity at its surface is about the same as on Saturn and Uranus.

* Observers have also imagined that Neptune is surrounded by a ring; but it is now certain that this appearance, which was also suspected in Uranus, must be considered an optical illusion.

BOOK THE THIRD.

COMETS.

The name of 'Comet' for the most part gives rise to the idea of a body of curious form, accompanied with a luminous train, travelling capriciously through space, appearing suddenly and disappearing in like manner, and at once astonishing by its strange aspect both learned and vulgar. This manner of distinguishing comets from other celestial bodies is no longer strictly accordant with the discoveries of science, which has succeeded in discovering the laws of their movements, and in assigning to them their true place in astronomical classification.

It is now proved that most of the observed comets, if not all, form part of the solar system, and that, if they are distinguished from the principal and secondary planets, it is by characteristics entirely different from those which are ordinarily assigned to them.

Let us see what these are.

I.

Aspect of Comets—Head; Nucleus; Tails, simple and multiple—How Comets are distinguished from the other bodies of the Solar System—Forms and Inclinations of their Orbits; Direction of their Movements.

If we refer to the etymology of the word, 'comet' signifies a hairy body. Most frequently, indeed, a comet appears as a star, the nucleus of which is surrounded with a nebulosity more or less brilliant, to which ancient astronomers gave the name of hair.

Independently of this nebulosity, the body is frequently accompanied by a train, the length of which varies in each comet, or in the same comet at different times: this luminous train is called the *tail.* The form of the head and its apparent and real dimensions, and the form and dimensions of the tail, are extremely variable, and, indeed, comets have been seen with two or even several tails.

But the nebulous aureola and luminous nucleus which generally form the head of the comet, and the single or multiple train with which the

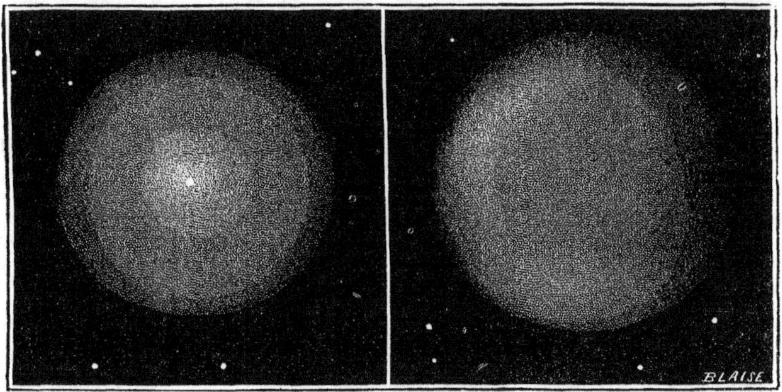

Fig. 117.—1. Tailless Comet. 2. Head without tail or nucleus.

head is accompanied, cannot be considered absolutely as specific characters, seeing that bodies without these characteristics would be required to be ranged in a different category.

There exist, in fact, some comets deprived both of tail and nucleus; such is the one represented in the right hand drawing of fig. 117, which consists, as we see, of a simple rounded nebulosity.* Others, like that represented in the first drawing in the same figure, possess a nucleus surrounded with a nebulosity, but no tail.

* We shall describe further on the nebulous appearances entirely distinct from comets; these are the *nebulæ*, properly so called. The difference between them is, that whereas the nebulæ retain a fixed position, the comet moves more or less rapidly across the sky.

Nor is the nebulous character of the head always constant; comets have been observed which have presented the appearance of stars, with which, indeed, they have been confounded. The astronomical history of the last century offers a striking example. When Sir W. Herschel, by the aid of his powerful instruments, discovered in the distant regions of the solar system the planet which now bears the name of Uranus, he first mistook this body for a comet. Still, there was no trace of nebulosity to mislead the illustrious astronomer of Slough. His opinion was founded upon a rough determination of its orbit.

But it is right to say that, among the numerous comets observed up to the present time, either with the naked eye, or by means of telescopes, the majority are distinguished by a nebulosity surrounding the nucleus, and a great number, especially of the most brilliant ones, possess a luminous train or tail. With others, the tail, displayed fan-like, is divided into many branches, as if the body had in reality several distinct tails. Plate XIII and fig. 118 give an idea of the varied forms of these cometary appendages.

Fig. 118.—Comet of 1744 (Chéseaux's Comet), with multiple tails.

This diversity of aspect will, perhaps, some day, enable astronomers to class comets into genera, species, and varieties, and will doubtless facilitate the perfection of the theory of the phenomena which these bodies present, which is still so obscure.

Comets, as we have said, form part of our Solar System. Like the planets, they revolve round the Sun, traversing with very variable velocities extremely elongated orbits; the form of the cometary orbits furnishes us with the first of their specific characters.

Whilst the planets now known move in nearly circular, closed curves, and thus remain continually visible, if not to the naked eye, at least with the aid of telescopes, most of the comets revolve round the Sun either in extremely elongated ellipses, or in infinite curves, or at least in curves which appear so. Hence it results that comets are observable only in a very limited portion of their paths, that is, when they approach nearest

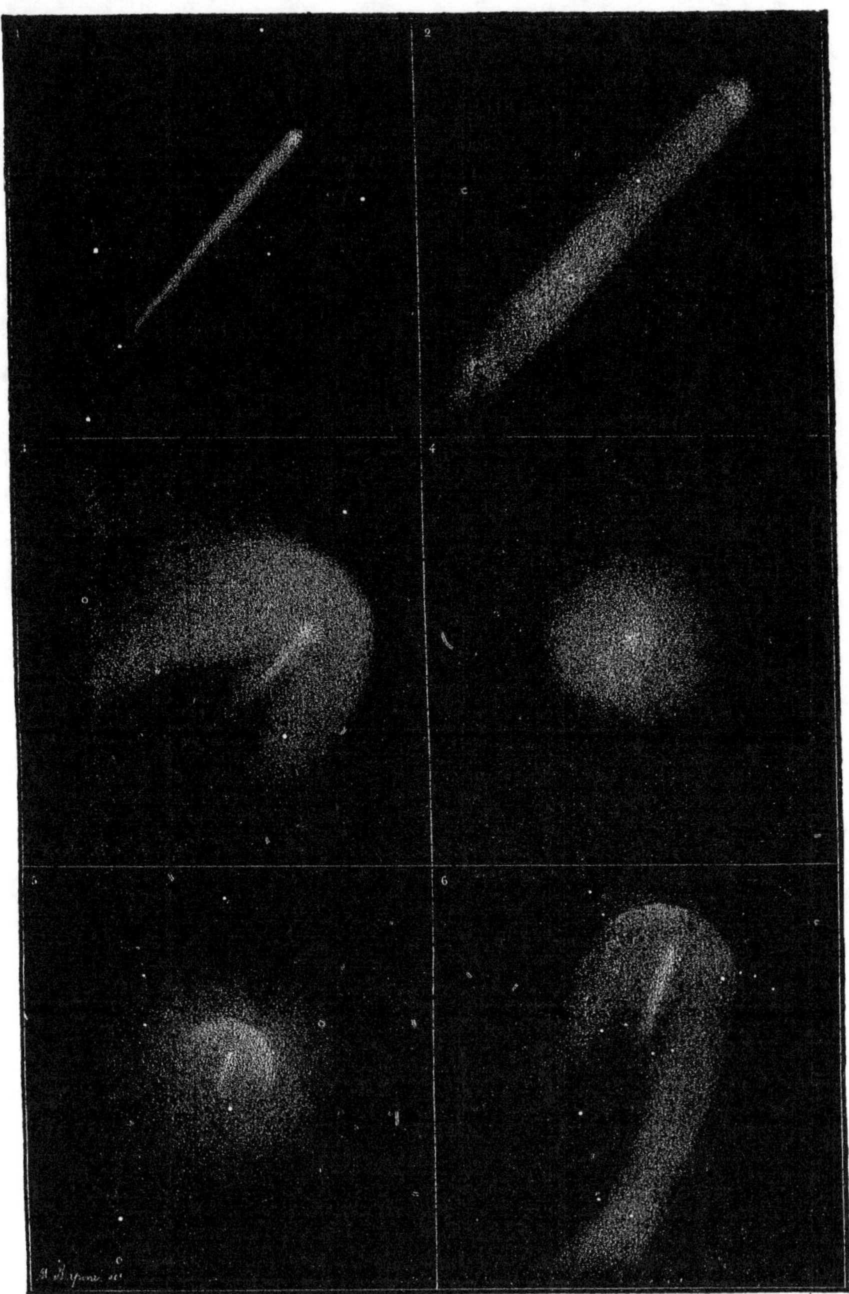

HALLEY'S COMET. (Sir J. Herschel.)

1. View of the comet in Ophiuchus with the naked eye, Oct. 22, 1835.
2. The same viewed with a telescope of 7 feet focal length.

3, 4, 5, 6. Details of the head of the comet, October, 1835—February, 1836.

to the Sun and Earth. Moreover, as the period of their revolutions increases with the departure of their orbits from a closed curve, it has only been possible to determine the return of a very small number of these solar satellites. There are some, which, judging by what we know, will never revisit our system.

In fig. 119 are represented the three kinds of orbits described by comets.

The first, of oval form, having the Sun for its focus, is the *ellipse.* It is a closed or re-entering curve. Although elongated, it is clear that the

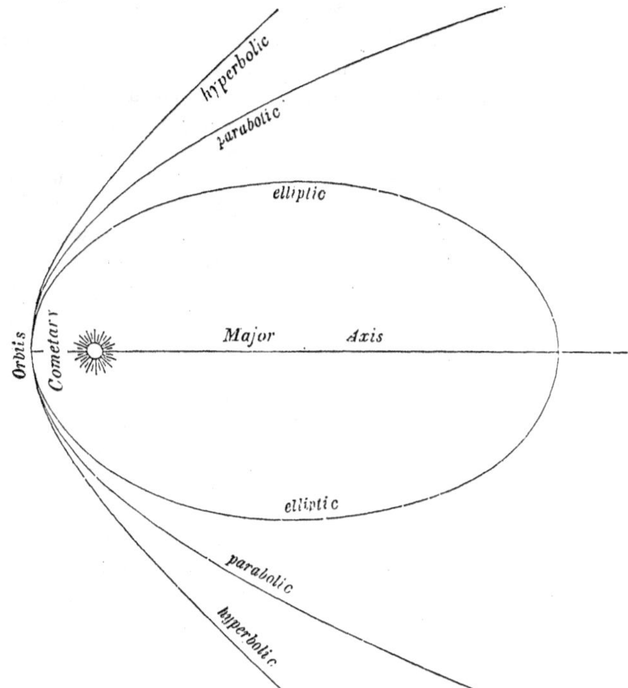

Fig. 119.—Form of cometary orbits.

body that traverses it must return periodically, to the Sun, at epochs more or less distant.

The second is of a form very analogous to the ellipse, but it is distinguished from it by the fact that its two branches constantly get further apart, and therefore never join. This is the *parabola;* but it is quite possible that those comets the orbits of which appear parabolic really describe extremely elongated ellipses, and that this form is taken for the parabolic one during the period of visibility of the body, in consequence of this similarity; but on this hypothesis, the period of revolution necessary to give rise to this confusion, must be so great, that a return can never be proved: still, strictly speaking, a return may take place.

It is another matter, however, when the comet describes the third kind of orbit, to which geometers give the name of *hyperbola.* The two branches of the hyperbola not only are infinite, but they are distinguished essentially from the ellipse, as the branches depart much more from the re-entering form which characterises an ellipse, with which form no portion of the hyperbola can be confounded.*

Several comets move in orbits of this kind, so that, after having once formed part of our solar system, they go away for ever, seeking perhaps in the depths of the heavens another Sun, which they will afterwards abandon as they do our own. Among the elliptic cometary orbits now known, that which the nearest approaches the circle is much more elongated than the planetary orbit which departs from it most. In fig. 120 are given, on the one hand, the most excentric of the planetary orbits, and, on the other, the least excentric cometary one, so that this difference may be appreciated by the eye.

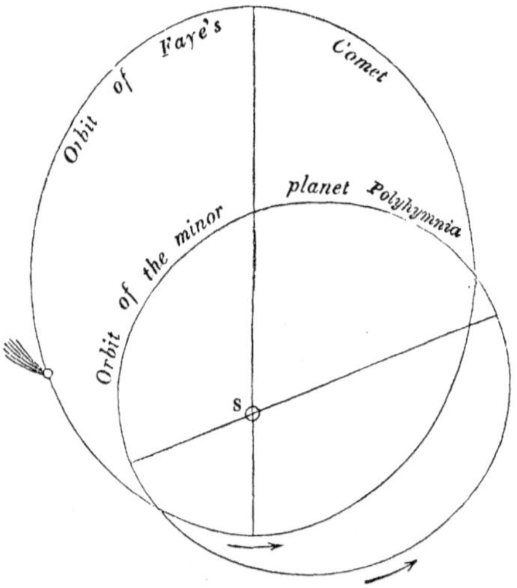

Fig. 120.—Comparison of the excentricity of the planetary and cometary orbits.

Thus comets are distinguished from planets, in the first place, by the extreme elongation of the curves which they describe round the Sun.

There are two other characters which are not less important than this: these are, first, that the inclinations of their orbits, instead of being contained, like those of the planetary orbits, within small limits, take every possible value. Hence comets traverse the starry vault in every direction, different in this from the other bodies of the solar system, the apparent paths of which never vary much from the narrow zone known under the name of the Zodiac.

Lastly, the direction of movement is sometimes from west to east, sometimes in the contrary direction, or, if we recall the signification of these words, sometimes *direct,* sometimes *retrograde.* Now the fundamental fact should be ever present in our memory, that all the planets

* [Or rather, though the form of a hyperbola near the vertex closely resembles that of an ellipse near the extremity of the minor axis, yet the motion of a comet even near the vertex of a hyperbolic orbit cannot (when its velocity is considered) be confounded with the motion in any elliptic orbit.—R. A. P.]

move in the same direction, that is to say, from right to left, or from west to east, to an observer placed on the northern side of the plane of the ecliptic.

Such are the essential differences which render comets a peculiar family of celestial bodies, and a most interesting one in the double point of view of their movements and physical constitution; indeed, they give to the solar group, already so varied, an incomparable richness.

II.

Periodic Comets—Halley's Comet; its return in 1759 and in 1835—Encke's Comet of Short Period; Acceleration of its Movement—Division of Gambart's Comet—Elements of the Principal Periodical Comets.

In spite of the oft-renewed protests of astronomers, a singular reproach is often launched against them. When a comet, visible to the naked eye, appears in the sky attracting notice on all sides by its brightness perchance, or the length of its tail, a number of people are astonished at the carelessness or ignorance of astronomers in having failed to predict it. We shall, therefore, now show how it happens that they are unable to predict, except in a few instances, the approach of a comet, as they do the position of a planet or the phenomena of eclipses.

All comets, as we have seen, have the Sun for the focus of their movements, and all describe a curve round it—an orbit the concavity of which is always turned towards the Sun. But, as we have also stated, most of the cometary orbits are so elongated, that they appear to be parabolic, the branches of which are infinite; others, again, are hyperbolic. What must we expect, then, in the case of comets which describe such orbits? Either they will never return to us, the immense distance to which they travel from the Sun perhaps carrying them into the sphere of attraction of some other system; or if they do return, it will be at an enormous interval of time, perhaps after a lapse of thousands of centuries.

Thus most of the comets observed visit the celestial regions occupied by our world for the first time, or, if they have already been with us, their visit happened at periods so remote from ours that no human observation has been handed down to us, even if man then existed on the Earth. On these hypotheses the impossibility of a scientific preparation is evident: we must observe a comet and ascertain the elements of its motion, before we are able to predict its return.

A certain number of comets, it is true, move in closed orbits—in ellipses. Among these we distinguish the comets of short period from those the revolutions of which occupy centuries—the anterior observations of which are unknown, or so confused, that it is impossible to base any calculations on them. Of these, however, science has also predicted the return, if not on a given day, at all events between certain limits. But in the case of the periodical comets of short period, their movements are known to a precision which permits the return to be easily announced, and we can predict for any given day and hour the various places they will occupy in the starry vault.

Let us enter somewhat into detail.

The first of these comets, the periodicity of which has been well established, both by observation and calculation, bears the name of Halley, an English astronomer of the seventeenth century. It is to him that we owe, in fact, the identification of the comet of 1682 with those of 1531 and 1607, and the prediction of its return at the end of 1758, or the beginning of 1759. The event justified the prediction. This was not all: at this latter period cometary astronomy was elevated at once to a state of perfection comparable with that of the other branches of the science. A French geometer, Clairaut, calculated the effect of perturbations of the two large planets, Jupiter and Saturn, in the vicinity of which the body was expected to pass, on the path of the announced comet. He assigned a delay of 618 days; 100 due to the action of Saturn, 518 to that of Jupiter.

The return of the body to its perihelion was predicted, therefore, to occur in the middle of April, 1759, with an error of a month more or less, the uncertainty arising from the neglect of some terms in the calculation which Clairaut, pressed for time, omitted. It actually returned to perihelion on the 13th of March.

Since then, in 1835, Halley's comet reappeared in our regions of the sky, but this time its passage was predicted with such precision, that there was only three days' difference between calculation and observation.

The form of the orbit of Halley's comet is shown in fig. 121, which also gives those of the other comets of short period at present known in our system. This orbit, too elongated to be represented in its entire development, is shown in Plate I, where it is seen that at its more distant point from the Sun, it reaches beyond the orbit even of Neptune. The comet requires more than 76 years—27,866 days—to traverse this immense curve. We also see that in consequence of one of those characteristics which especially distinguish such a body from the planets of the solar system—the elliptical form of its orbit—Halley's comet is sometimes nearer to the Sun than Venus, within, indeed, a distance which does not exceed 56,000,000 miles, and sometimes it recedes from the focus of heat and light to a distance 60 times more removed—a distance exceeding 3,200.000,000 miles.

These enormous variations in distance would lead us to suppose most astonishing differences in the quantity of light and heat received by the comet from the Sun. And, in fact, the intensity of these physical agents varies in the ratio of 3000 to 1, or, as it may be put, the Sun's light and heat arrive at the comet with a force 3000 times more considerable at perihelion than at aphelion.

FORMS OF COMETS.

1. Comet of 1577. (Cornelius Gemma.) 2. Comet of 1680. (J. C. Sturm.)
3. Comet of 1769.

Halley's comet moves from east to west in a plane inclined to the orbit of the Earth the fifth part of a right angle. In Plate XIV are represented the various appearances assumed by it in 1835, both in its general aspect and in the portion of it surrounding the nucleus.

Following the order of discovery, we must next describe Encke's comet.

Invisible to the naked eye, it appears in the telescope under the form of a nebulous mass, nearly spherical, and without either tail or nucleus. It is a singular fact that the head of this comet varies both in form and dimensions at the same time, and it is at its nearest approach to the Sun that its volume is smallest.

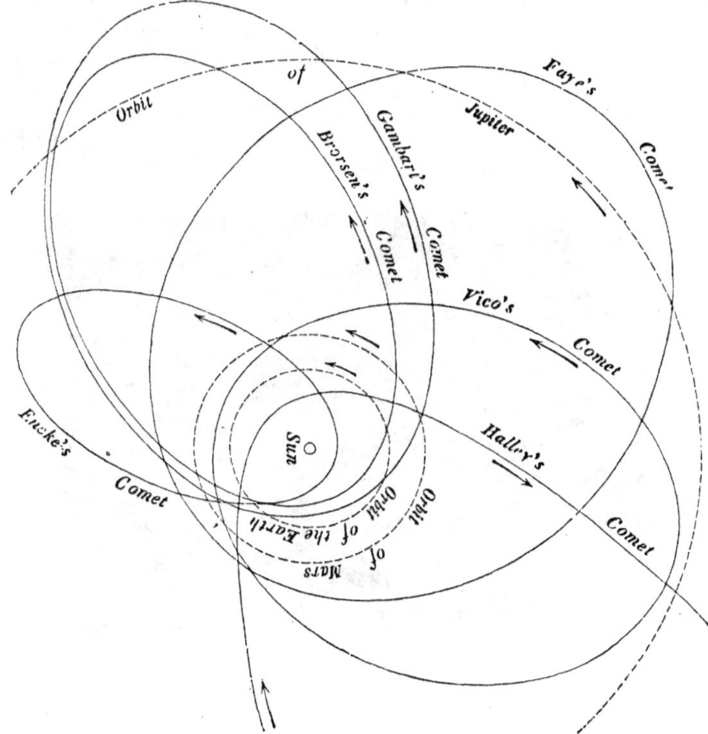

Fig. 121.—Orbits of the periodic Comets.

Of all the comets, the periodical return of which has been demonstrated, this comet accomplishes its revolution round the Sun in the shortest space of time, which in the mean is 1205 days, or a little less than $3\frac{1}{3}$ years. It moves from west to east in an orbit such that its perihelion and aphelion distances are respectively 32,000,000 and 387,000,000 miles.

Here, then, is a body which, at each of its revolutions, penetrates within the orbit of Mercury, and at its greatest distance from the Sun surpasses the orbits of the asteroids, and almost reaches that of Jupiter. Since 1818, the time of its discovery, all its returns to the number of fourteen have been regularly observed; but, singular circumstance, the period of its revolution is constantly diminishing; so that, if this progressive diminution always follows the same rate, the time when the comet, continually describing a spiral, will be plunged into the incandescent mass of the Sun can be calculated. This continued approach has been attributed to the existence of a resisting medium in the regions of space.*

Encke's comet is also specially designated by the appellation of *the comet of short period.*

Among the other comets, of which both calculation and observation have confirmed the periodicity, bearing the names of Gambart or Biela, Faye, De Vico, Brorsen, and others, the first only requires a special

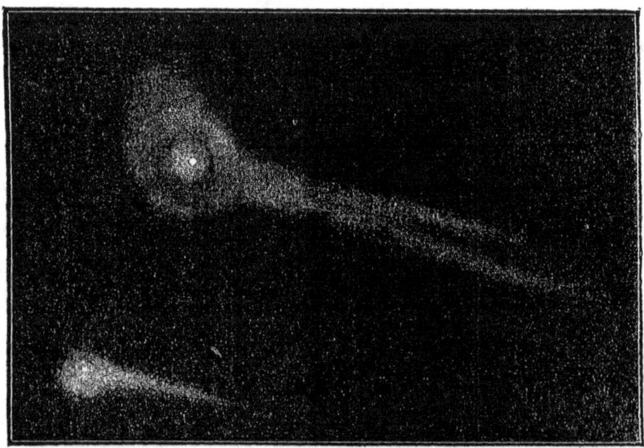

Fig. 122.—Subdivision of Gambart's Comet. (Struve.)

* It appears at first paradoxical to say that a resistance to a movement can produce an acceleration in the time of the successive revolutions: the first tendency of the mind is to see, on the contrary, a cause of slackening; but with a little reflection it is easy to convince oneself of the exactitude of the first explanation, or, at least, of its probability. We have shown, in another work ('Les Mondes,' XIX. Causerie), that acceleration, combined with the third law of Kepler, and the theory of universal gravitation, is a direct consequence of such a resistance. The explanation of this would here be premature; we must refer to the third part of the present work, in which an exposition of astronomical laws is given.

It is possible that the nebulous ring which forms the zodiacal light can be the medium which accelerates the period of Encke's comet? Or, again, may not the same effect be attributed to the perturbations to which the body is subjected at its periodical passage through the regions of shooting stars or the telescopic planets? All these questions are still extremely problematical, and it will be understood that this is not the place to discuss the various degrees of probability of each of them. We may, however, remark that M. Faye, in attributing to the solar heat a repulsive force, has suggested a theory of the physical constitution of comets which accounts at once for the form of the appendices of these bodies, and for the acceleration of the period which observation has demonstrated for Encke's comet.

mention. The latter are all telescopic, and do not offer any particular interest in their physical aspect.

This is not the case, however, with Gambart's comet. Discovered in 1826, its first reappearance occurred in the autumn of 1832, and much excitement was caused by the somewhat premature announcement that it must in its passage meet the Earth. More precise calculations demonstrated, before the event, that the comet would cross our orbit a month before our globe would reach the point of passage, and thus contact was impossible.

But the alarm had been sounded. The imagination was excited, and the idea of the end of the world—of our little world—occupied numerous minds. Even among those who placed confidence in the precision of astronomical calculations, there were some who at least feared a derangement of our orbit. Doubtless, to them, an orbit was something material—a metallic circle, for example. 'As if,' says Arago, in relating this curious notion, 'the form of the parabolic path in which a bomb after leaving a mortar, traverses space, was dependent on the number and positions of the paths which other bombs had formerly described in the same region.'

Further on we will say a few words on this question, which some day or another may largely interest the inhabitants of our globe—we allude to the danger and the probability of a comet's contact with the Earth.

If Gambart's planet did not justify the fears that were conceived, it was itself subjected a little later to a strange transformation—it subdivided itself into two. In 1846 it appeared under the form of two comets, of unequal size, which gradually separated more and more. In 1852 the two comets reappeared travelling together, but the distance between the two nuclei, which had reached 150,000 miles in 1846, then amounted to 1,240,000 miles.

Astronomical annals have before recorded similar transformations; but as they related to comets which have not reappeared, authorities hesitated to believe them. Gambart's comet, however, leaves no doubt on the fact.

We here give some data on the short-period comets to which we have referred:—

Comets.	Time of revolution in years.	Distances from the Sun. Aphelion. Miles.	Perihelion. Miles.	Time of next return.
Encke's	3·29	387,000,000	32,000,000	1868, October.
De Vico's	5·46	475,000,000	110,000,000	1866 (?).
Winnecke's	5·54	—	—	1869, June.
Brorsen's	5·58	537,000,000	64,000,000	1868, May.
Biela's (or Gambart's)	6·61	585,000,000	82,000,000	1866, January.
D'Arrest's	6·64	—	—	1870, October.
Faye's	7·44	603,000,000	192,000,000	1866, Feb.
Méchain's	13·60	—	—	1871, October.
Halley's	76·78	3,200,000,000	56,000,000	1910 (?).

All these have their direction of movement the same as that of the movement of the planets, that is, from west to east. Among the periodical comets, already mentioned, that of Halley is the only exception. [Besides the comets included in the preceding table, others with periods of about seventy years have been discovered,—by Westphal (1852); Pons (1312);

De Vico (1846); Olbers (1815); Brorsen (1847); Tempel's comet (1866) has a period of 33¼ years.]

We shall content ourselves with the preceding details of the astronomical short period of the periodical comets. It remains for us to give some details on those comets the return of which is either very remote or has not been determined.

III.

Comets of Long Period—Large Comets visible to the Naked Eye—Physical Constitution of Comets; Mass, Density—Nature of their Light—Danger which might result from the contact of a Comet—Spectroscopic Observations by Mr. Huggins.

Must we accept literally the comparison of Kepler, who affirmed that comets are scattered throughout the heavens with as much profusion as fishes in the ocean? Arago, adopting the hypothesis of an equal distribution of comets in every region of the Solar System, and basing his calculations on the number of comets between the Sun and Mercury, estimated the number of these bodies which traverse the solar system with its known limits, that is to say, within the orbit of Neptune, at 17,500,000.*

Whatever we may think of these hypotheses, observation proves, from year to year, that the number of comets is really considerable. Leaving mere reappearances out of the question, new ones are constantly found to arrive from the depths of space, describing round the Sun orbits which testify to the attractive power of that radiant body, and, for the most part, going away for centuries, to return again from afar after their immense revolutions.

During the two or three centuries in which comets have been observed with care, more than 200 have been recorded. Adding them to those noted in ancient annals, we must reckon them at five or six hundred, among which there are only about forty of which we have been enabled to determine the period of revolution.

Of this number, five complete their revolutions in periods which vary betweeen sixty-nine and seventy-five years. But what shall we say of those which take thousands of years to accomplish their circuit, of the famous comet of 1680, the perihelion point of which was so near the Sun, that Newton valued its temperature while passing through that part of its orbit at 2000 times the heat of red-hot iron? Its period is about 8814 years. But there are some longer still; and the period of the comet of July 1844 has been estimated at not less than 100,000 years. If the

* As early as 1765 Lambert, basing his calculations on other data, regarded 500,000,000 as a very moderate estimate of those within the orbit of Saturn.

DONATI'S COMET.

1. 24 September, 1858. 2. 26 September, 1858. (G. P. Bond.)

calculation is exact, here is a comet the return of which will be observed by the astronomers of the year 101,844! At a mid date of this immense period, it will be travelling in space at a distance not less than 4000 times that of the Earth from the Sun.

The velocity of comets, diminishing like that of the planets as their distances from the Sun increase, varies between very large limits, and at their greatest distance from the central body it is extremely small; thus the comet of 1680 scarcely traverses, at its aphelion, more than three yards a second!

Among the numerous comets observed, there are very few that are visible to the naked eye, and a still less number which strike ordinary

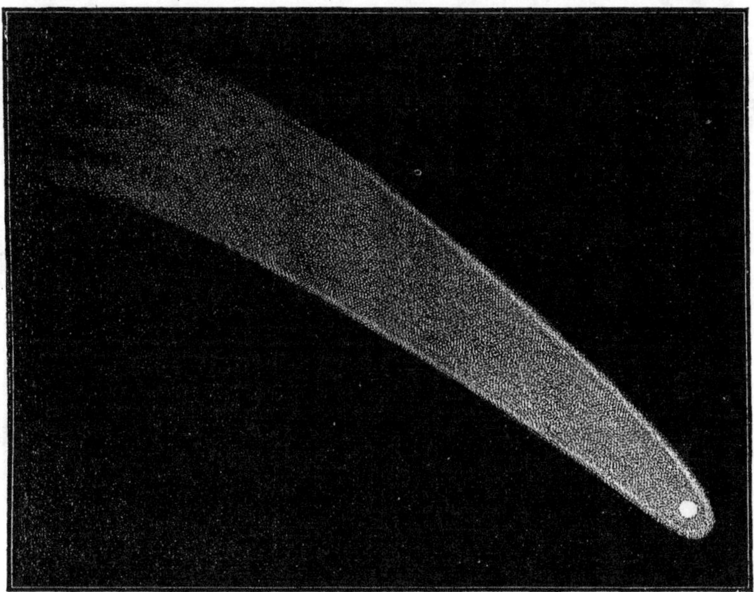

Fig. 123.—Great Comet of 1811, from a drawing by Admiral Smyth, in the 'Speculum Hartwellianum.'

observers by their large dimensions and the brightness of their light. It is these, nevertheless, which possess the greatest interest, by reason of the peculiar phenomena presented by their tails and nuclei—phenomena which throw great light on their physical constitution.

Among the most remarkable comets of by-gone centuries must be mentioned the large comet of 1500, which the Italians surnamed *Il Signor Astone*; the comet of Charles the Fifth, of 1556, which, according to astronomical calculations having already appeared in 1264, ought to have made its reappearance about 1860, and has not been again seen; that of

1686, the bright nucleus of which shone as a star of the first magnitude; the comet of 1744, with several tails; and that of 1769, which is represented, as given in the drawings of the time, in Plate XIII and fig. 118.

The portion of the nineteenth century already elapsed has been rich in brilliant comets, visible to the naked eye. We here reproduce some of the most remarkable; first, the large comet of 1811, the appearance of which made an extraordinary sensation. It will not again return for thirty centuries. The head measured 112,000 miles in diameter, whilst the diameter of the luminous nucleus was little more than 400 miles. The tail, of prodigious dimensions, attained a length of 112,000,000 miles.

The great comet of 1843 was one of the most brilliant ever observed. Not only the nucleus, but a portion of the tail, was visible in full day. The tail was besides very remarkable for its length, and still more for the uniformity of its breadth. This is, of all known comets, that which is the nearest to the Sun. At the time of its shortest distance from the centre of our system, the nucleus was not more than 470,000 miles from the centre of the Sun, and consequently only 30,000 miles from its surface.

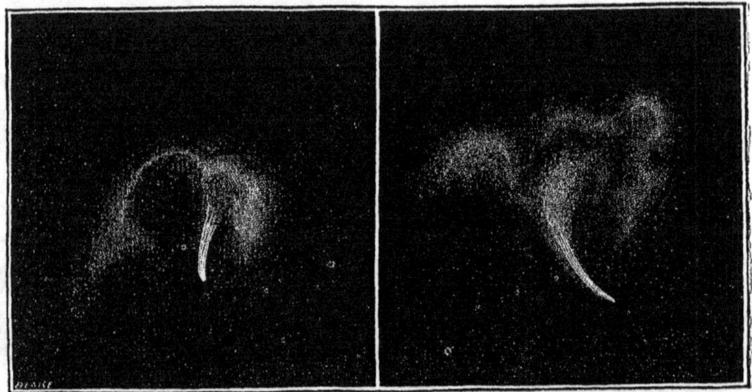

Fig. 124.—Comet of 1862. Forms and positions of the luminous jets on August 23, at one o'clock in the morning, and at nine in the evening.

In these latter years three comets, visible to the naked eye, have been the object of the most interesting observations. The most brilliant of all, Donati's comet, made its appearance in 1858. Perceived at Florence, for the first time on the 2nd of June, by the astronomer whose name it bears, it became visible to the naked eye towards the first days of September, and was soon distinguished among the northern constellations by the brightness of its brilliant nucleus, and the magnificent development of its tail.

Those persons who were witness to the splendid spectacle offered by the nights when this beautiful body was visible, will be able to recognise and follow, in Plates XV and XVI, the aspect of the comet at different epochs, and its path across the starry vault.

In 1861 and in 1862 two other comets were also visible, although

DONATI'S COMET.

1. October 3, 1858. 2. Oct. 5, 1858. (G. P. Bond.)

inferior in brilliancy to that of 1858. There will be found further on (figs. 124 and 125, and Plate XVIII), detailed representations of the head and nebulous envelopes of these bodies—details extremely interesting from a physical point of view.

The problems connected with the study of the physical constitution of comets are numerous, and of extreme difficulty. It may be asked, in the first place, What is the nature of the matter which composes them? or whether this matter be entirely gaseous? or, again, if the nuclei enclose liquid or even solid particles, and if so what is their bulk and their density; if the tail is of the same nature as the head or nucleus; or by virtue of what influence these singular appendages are formed, which, almost unnoticeable when the comet is far from the Sun, are developed as it

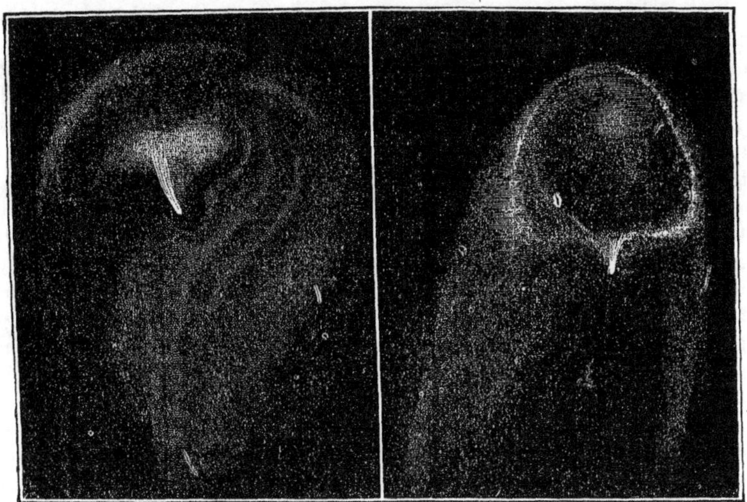

Fig. 125.—Comet of 1862. Aspect of the head of the Comet, at nine in the evening, the 23rd August, and the 24th August at the same hour.

approaches it, to diminish, and finally disappear again in the more distant half of its orbit?

Next comes the question of the light which renders the comets visible in space. Do comets shine with their own light? do they borrow their light from the Sun? or do they send us rays proceeding from both these sources? Again, can anything plausible be conjectured on their temperature, or on the changes induced upon this element by the prodigious variations of distance which are the consequence of the extreme elongations of their orbits?

Lastly, what is the cause of the modifications to which these strange bodies are subjected, not only from one revolution to another, but under our very eyes, during the short interval of a single appearance? Not only is the tail formed, developed, diminished, and again absorbed, but the envelope of the nucleus is subject to the most curious transformations. If we look at the drawings (figs. 124 and 125) of the comet of 1862, drawings which represent the head of the body at intervals of a day at the most, we shall be astonished at the rapidity of the changes of position and form of the luminous jets which successively were emitted from the nucleus, in a direction nearly always opposed to that of the tail. In an interval of seventeen days, the able observer to whom we owe the communication of these drawings, M. Chacornac, was able to distinguish the formation of thirteen of these jets, similar to jets of steam, and alternately directed towards the Sun and to the east of it, that is to say, in a direction opposite to the movement of the comet. After each of these emissions, the nebulous matter, accumulated at the end of the jet, seemed driven back by a repulsive force emanating from the Sun, and then flowed in the direction of the tail. These phenomena would seem to confirm the hypothesis of M. Faye, to which we have before alluded, which attributes to the Sun, independently of an attracting force by virtue of its mass, a repulsive power by virtue of its heat. By means of this hypothesis, M. Roche has been enabled to account for the variation in form of the nucleus and envelopes.

[We may here remark that these last have recently been specially the object of a searching inquiry by the lamented Professor Bond, in his most admirable memoir on the comet of 1858. These envelopes, however, must not be confounded with the *Umhüllung*, or outer faint veil, which may extend for some distance around the head. They were observed to regularly expand outward from the nucleus, and the history of no less than seven of them has been recovered.]

To what forces are these strange phenomena due?

To these questions of great interest, which, it must be admitted, are still very obscure, may be added others which at different times have been privileged to captivate the attention of the public. We have seen that Gambart's periodical comet was expected in 1832, to come in contact with the Earth. What would have resulted from such an event?

A century ago, *savans* still considered comets to be bodies, the impact of which on our globe, or with another planet, would entail the most frightful consequences.

'When the movement of the comets is considered,' says Lambert, in his *Lettres Cosmologiques*, 'and we reflect on the laws of gravity, it will be readily perceived that their approach to the Earth might there cause the most woeful events, bring back the universal deluge, or make it perish in a deluge of fire, shatter it into small dust, or at least turn it from its orbit, drive away its Moon, or, still worse, the Earth itself outside the orbit of Saturn, and inflict upon us a winter several centuries long, which neither men nor animals would be able to bear. The tails even of comets would not be unimportant phenomena, if the comets in taking their departure left them either in whole or in part in our atmosphere.'

Maupertuis, at the same time, had already described in nearly the

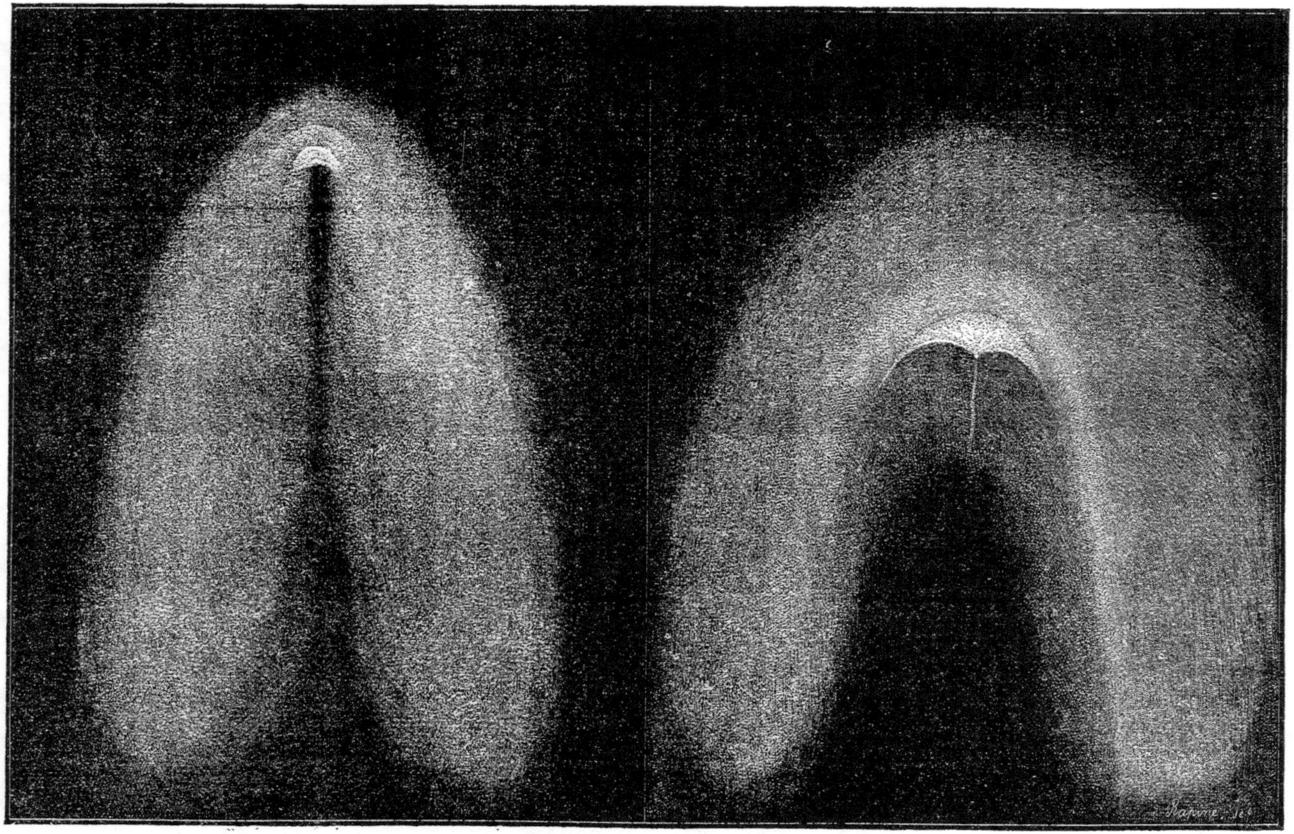

HEADS AND TAILS OF COMETS.

1. Donati's comet, September 29, 1858. (G. P. Bond.) 2. Comet of 1861, July 2nd. (Warren De La Rue.)

same manner the catastrophes which the fear of the Earth's contact with a comet had led astronomers to imagine. Only, by the side of possible inconveniences, he enumerated the advantages that might be derived from the distant influence of these bodies, such as changes of the seasons into a perpetual spring, the acquisition of new moons, or of a ring like that of Saturn. He then adds: 'However dangerous might be the shock of a comet, it might be so slight, that it would only do damage at that part of the Earth where it actually struck; perhaps even we might cry quits if while one kingdom were devastated, the rest of the Earth were to enjoy the rarities which a body which came from so far might bring to it. Perhaps we should be very surprised to find that the *débris* of these masses that we despised were formed of gold and diamonds; but who would be the most astonished, we, or the comet-dwellers, who would be cast on our Earth? What strange beings each would find the other!'*

At the present day astronomers have abandoned these fears. Not only, according to them, is the probability of a shock so slight, that it is not worth while to trouble ourselves about such an event; but, again, the mass of comets appears such a small fraction of the mass of the terrestrial globe, that the shock would be quiet imperceptible.

This way of looking at the matter rests on considerations and on facts which render it very probable. In 1770 a comet was seen to traverse the system of Jupiter, without inducing the smallest perturbation in the movement of the satellites, whilst the nebulous body itself was so much disturbed that its entire orbit was changed.

[Then again, we have good reason to believe that we actually passed through the tail of the comet of 1861, and the only effect observed was a peculiar phosphorescent mist.]

But would it be the same with all comets? In our opinion, it is at least prudent not to generalise too hastily. If comets exist, the nebulosity of which seems entirely gaseous, and so transparent that small stars remain visible through them, there are others, the nucleus of which is doubtless very dense, since their light has been strong enough to be perceptible in full day, even in the vicinity of the Sun. The mass of Donati's comet has been valued by MM. Faye and Roche at about the seven-hundredth part of the bulk of the Earth.

'That is,' says M. Faye, 'the weight of a sea of 40,000 square miles 109 yards deep; and it must be owned that a like mass, animated with a considerable velocity, might well produce by its shock with the Earth very perceptible effects.'

Of the heat peculiar to the comets, and of the nature of the light that they emit, very little is yet known. Doubtless, in the vicinity of the Sun, the action of the high temperature of the radiant body cannot fail to be felt on the exterior strata of the cometary nuclei; and it is thus that the formation of the luminous jets which, becoming detached from the

* 'Lettre sur la Comète. Œuvres de M. de Maupertuis,' p. 203. Dresden, 1752.

central mass and acted upon by some unknown force, give rise to the tail, may be accounted for.

On the other hand, it seems proved that the light of the comets is, in part at least, borrowed from the Sun. But may they not also possess besides a light of their own? and, on this last hypothesis, is this brightness owing to a kind of phosphorescence, or to the state of incandescence of the nucleus? Truly, if the nuclei of comets be incandescent, the smallness of their mass would eliminate from the danger of their contact with the Earth only one element of destruction; the temperature of the terrestrial atmosphere would be raised to an elevation inimical to the existence of organised beings; and we should only escape the danger of a mechanical shock to run into a not less frightful one of being calcined in a many days' passage through an immense furnace.

If we enlarge on these considerations, which are merely hypothetical, it is not with the intention of reviving the fears or superstitious terrors of another age. We but wish to show to what conjectures science is still reduced on the problem, so interesting from so many points of view, of the physical constitution of comets.

[The spectroscopic observations made by Mr. Huggins on the light of three faint comets show that a certain portion at least of the light of these objects is inherent. The outer part of each gave a continuous spectrum, in which dark lines may have existed but could not be recognised owing to the extreme faintness of the light. The nucleus gave in each case three bands of light, indicating that the substance of the nucleus consisted of glowing vapour. In the case of the third comet thus examined by Mr. Huggins—that known as Brorsen's—the spectrum of the nucleus closely resembled, or was in fact practically identical with that of carbon as shown when the electric spark is taken through olefiant gas. But in what condition the carbon of the comet's nucleus may be, in order to account for this result, it is difficult indeed to say. Carbon, as we know, is of a remarkably 'fixed' character, and it seems difficult to conceive that the heat to which Brorsen's comet was actually subjected at the time could be sufficient to volatilize such an element. Mr. Huggins remarks that probably the carbon exists in the nucleus in a state of excessively minute division. 'In such a form,' he says, 'it would be able to take in nearly the whole of the Sun's energy, and thus acquire more speedily a temperature high enough for its conversion into vapour.' But he admits that the whole subject is full of difficulty, and doubtless we must wait until some bright comet shall have presented itself for examination with the powerful spectroscopic appliances recently placed at Mr. Huggins's disposal.—R.A.P.]

GENERAL SURVEY OF THE SOLAR SYSTEM.

We have now terminated our description of the various phenomena presented by the Solar System.

We have reviewed successively all the bodies which compose it, from the immense central body—the fountain-head of heat and light—to the most distant planets which its powerful attraction maintains in their orbits, and to those vagabond bodies, the comets, some of which perhaps visit but once those regions of the sky in which the movements of our system take place.

We are about to quit the system of which our Earth forms part—a system so prodigiously vast, when the dimensions are compared either with the most gigantic construction of man, or even with the terrestrial globe itself, the magnitude of which reduces man to nothingness. We shall now launch out into space, far, very far beyond Neptune, to such distances that the Earth, the planets, the Sun itself even, when looked back upon, would but appear as luminous points, and the whole Solar System would dwindle down to a single speck of light.

There we shall find myriads of other Suns, other worlds, of which the physical constitution, distances, and movements, must also be studied. But before undertaking this immense voyage in the infinite, let us sum up in a few general remarks the more striking features of the Solar System, which will constantly serve us for comparison with the other systems with which we shall have to deal.

We have seen how the different celestial bodies which revolve round the Sun are grouped. In describing each of them we have given their real dimensions, both absolute, and compared with those of our Earth. Plate XVIII contains all these comparative dimensions grouped together, whence we may gather by a *coup d'œil* how much the volume of the Sun preponderates over that of all the planets and their satellites put together. Calculation shows indeed that the solar globe itself contains 600 times the united volumes of all these bodies. Its mass is still more considerable; and if the Sun were placed in one of the scales of a celestial balance, 750 times the weight of all the planetary masses must be placed in the other to equal it.

We have from the commencement divided the planets into three principal groups; that of the planets of average size, that of the asteroids or telescopic planets, and that of the larger planets. A fact which renders this division more striking is, that the celestial bodies, of which each group is formed, not only present a similarity in size, while the distances of all from the Sun seem to obey a law, but other physical analogies seem to indicate that they form so many natural families, the members of which have perhaps a common origin.

Thus Mercury, Venus, the Earth, and Mars, have a movement of rotation the time of which is nearly equal; and, except in the case of Mercury,* their density is very similar, and the polar flattening is either very slight or imperceptible.

With regard to the inclinations of their axes to the planes of their orbits, a condition of things which has an overpowering influence on the seasons in each planet, the four smaller planets of which we speak must [if we accept the old observations] be divided into two sub-groups, Mercury and Venus in one category, Mars and the Earth in the other.

We know very little of the physical constitution of the minor planets; but, besides the fact that they are all accumulated in one narrow zone, and are all of small dimensions, they possess a family likeness in the great excentricity of their orbits, and the generally very great inclinations of the planes in which they revolve round the Sun.

We come now to the four larger planets, Jupiter, Saturn, Uranus, and Neptune; at once we are struck with their much more rapid rotation, which we should have predicted from the considerable polar flattening of the two first bodies. With regard to the two other planets, Uranus and Neptune, we are still in the dark on these points. Their density is at most but a quarter of that of the smaller planets, and this is almost the case for all the members of the group.

But the other elements do not offer such close analogies. The inclination of the axis, small in the case of Jupiter, is larger in the case of Saturn, and probably excessive in Uranus.

But another point of resemblance is, that all these larger planets have a great number of satellites, whilst the Earth alone, of all the planets of the system, is accompanied by a single moon.

The question as to the habitability of the other planets of the system has been much agitated. It has been asked if only the Earth's surface is embellished by the productions of animal and vegetable life, if it alone is inhabited and governed by intelligent and sensible beings.

Astronomy can only indirectly touch on these interesting questions, the solution of which will, doubtless, long remain beyond us, although we have seen with what minute care science collects together all the elements of the problem, all the data which observation can furnish on the meteorological and physical conditions belonging to each member of the solar system.

Doubtless, if we reason by the analogies which are permitted us, there are strong probabilities that most of the planets and their moons are inhabited. But what is the organisation of the vegetable and animal kingdoms which people them? Of this it is difficult to form an idea, in the actual state of our knowledge.

But is it not probable that the ages of the planets are very different, and that, if we suppose that they all must pass through the same geological phases, these phases will be far from being the same at the same epochs?

* According to Encke, the density of Mercury is really much less than that at present adopted; it is not very different from the density of the Earth.

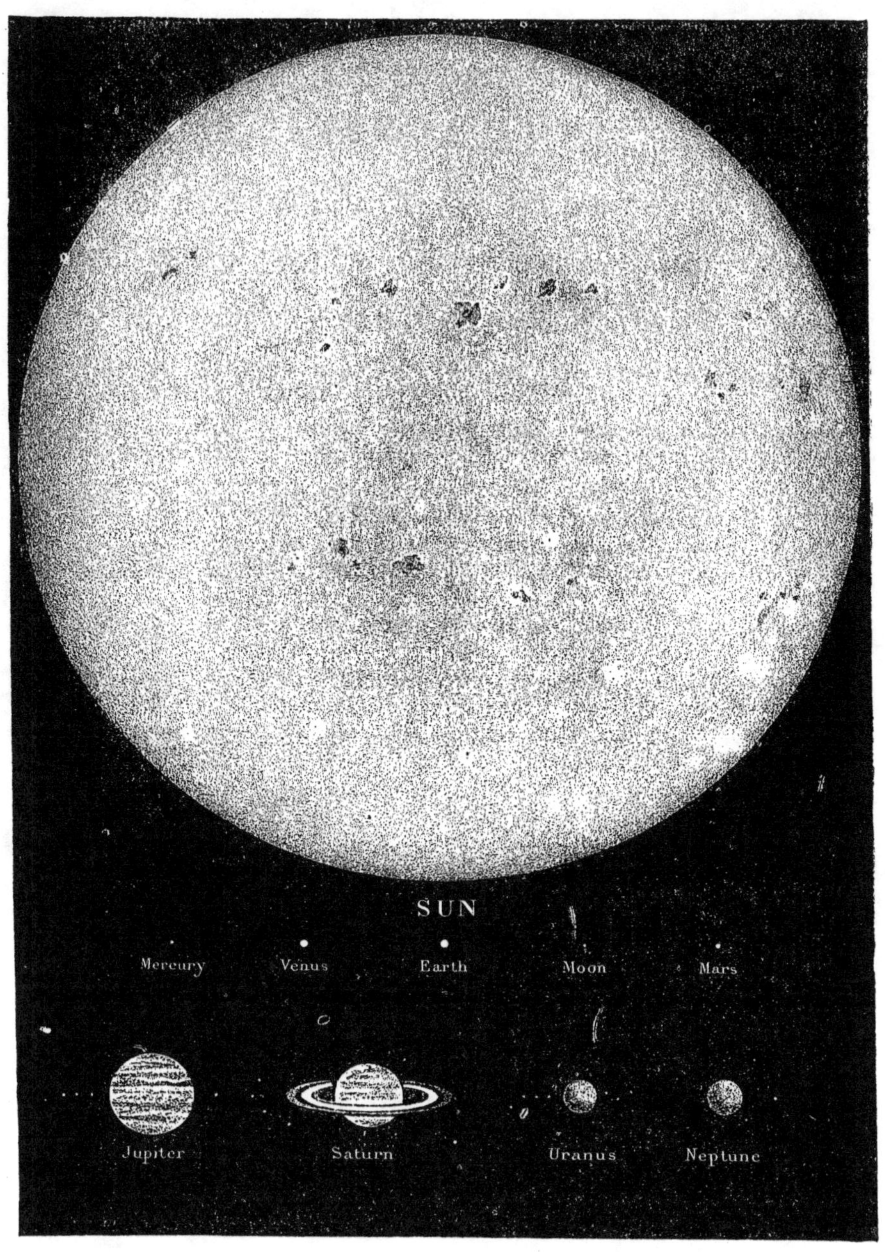

COMPARATIVE DIMENSIONS OF THE SUN, THE PLANETS AND THEIR SATELLITES.

PART THE SECOND.

THE SIDEREAL SYSTEM.

BOOK THE FIRST.—THE STARS.

Let us imagine a sphere, having the Sun for its centre, the ideal surface of which lies at a distance of thirty times the mean radius of the Earth's orbit; this sphere will comprise in its vast extent all the celestial bodies, the comets excepted, which periodically effect their revolutions round the Sun, and of which we have described the movements and physical constitution.

Do other planets exist more distant still than Neptune? and do the comets of long period which, after having shone once in our regions, bury themselves in depths exceeding many thousands of times the distance of the Sun from the Earth, really belong to our system?

These are questions which at present cannot be answered, and for the solution of which we must wait, perhaps for centuries. We may, therefore, be allowed to regard the sphere which we have just imagined, as fixing an approximate limit to the dimensions of the Solar System.

Let us, however, in thought, triple the radius of this sphere; let us give it a radius of a hundred radii of our orbit, that is, a radius of some 9,500,000,000 miles,—an enormous distance, which the imagination can with difficulty grasp, and which a ray of light would require more than eleven days to traverse, in spite of its extraordinary velocity of 192,000 miles a second!

Nevertheless, we shall soon see that this immense line is but a point, when we compare it with the dimensions of that portion of the universe which our sight is able to grasp. The nearest of the innumerable systems which people that universe would be removed from the then confines of the solar system to a distance two thousand times greater than the radius of our imaginary sphere. We could scarcely hope, therefore, that it would ever be possible, even with the aid of the most powerful telescopes, to make out the physical peculiarities of celestial bodies so immensely distant. But thanks to some ingenious appliances and to methods of an extreme delicacy, the latest investigations have furnished observers with a rich series of interesting phenomena.

The constitution even of the visible universe has thus by degrees been revealed: the distribution of the various bodies, their groupings and movements, the intensity and colour of their light, and a thousand other interesting facts, are so many points, the positive knowledge of which now surrounds sidereal astronomy with the highest interest.

We are, therefore, about to consider the Heavens as a whole and in detail. The knowledge we have acquired of the system to which the Earth belongs will be a great help to us in this study, as it will continually afford us points of comparison to reason by analogy on other systems.

I.

THE STARS.

Scintillation of the Stars—Apparent Fixity of their relative Distances—Number of Stars visible to the Naked Eye—Approximate Number of Stars visible in Telescopes.

No sight, as we said at the beginning of this work, is at once so awe-inspiring and so grand as that of the Heavens on a beautiful night. If care be taken to choose as a stand-point for observation an open place, such as a plain or the summit of a hill on land, or, again, the open sea; and if the atmosphere, somewhat charged with dew, possess all its transparency and purity, we shall see thousands of luminous points twinkling in all directions, accomplishing slowly and together their silent march. The contrast of the obscurity which reigns on the surface of the Earth with the brightness of that resplendent vault, gives an indefinite depth to the celestial ocean that deepens over our heads. But let us here leave the magnificence of the spectacle, to study it in its most minute details.

Let us commence with the appearances. A character common to all the stars is an incessant and very rapid change of brightness, which has received the name of *scintillation*. This is accompanied by variations of colour equally rapid, due to the same cause as the successive disappearances and reappearances. All stars scintillate, whatever may be their brilliancy, at least in our temperate regions. But the intensity of this luminous movement is not the same in all, and it varies, moreover, both with the degree of purity of the sky, the elevation of the stars above the horizon, and the temperature of the night.

According to Arago, scintillation is due to the difference of velocity of the various-coloured rays traversing the unequally warm, unequally dense, unequally humid atmospheric strata. Thus, in tropical regions, where the atmospheric strata are more homogeneous, scintillation is rarely observed in stars the elevation of which above the horizon is more than 15°, or the sixth of the distance of the horizon from the zenith. 'This circumstance,' says Humboldt, 'gives to the celestial vault of these countries a particularly calm and soft character.'

As to the planets, they scintillate little or not at all; it is rare that traces of this phenomenon are observed in Saturn or Jupiter, but it is more perceptible in Mars, Venus, and Mercury. This difference suffices, in our climates, to afford to those who are not very familiar with the configuration of the celestial groups the first means of distinguishing a planet from a star.

Another specific character of the stars is, that their diameters are without appreciable dimensions. To the naked eye this distinction would be insufficient, since, the Moon and the Sun excepted, the most considerable planets have not sensible diameters. But, while the magnifying power of optical instruments shows us the principal planets under the form of clearly defined disks, the most powerful glasses only show a star as a luminous point. The distance which separates us from these bodies is so great, that there is nothing to astonish us in such a result.

Wollaston affirms that the apparent diameter of the most brilliant star in the heavens, Sirius, is not more than the fiftieth part of a second of arc. But let us hasten to say that this result still leaves a good margin as to the real dimensions of the star, since, at the distance of Sirius, an apparent diameter of this size would represent a real diameter of 11,000,000 miles; that is, twelve times the diameter of our Sun.

Let us add, lastly, that the absence of appreciable apparent dimensions does not suffice to distinguish absolutely the stars from the planets, since a certain number of the latter, as we have before seen, appear in telescopes only as simple luminous points. Let us come, then, to a permanent specific character, the knowledge of which will always prevent us from confounding a star with one of the known or unknown bodies which form part of our solar group. This characteristic is as follows:—

The stars, properly so called, preserve among themselves—nearly enough for our present purpose—the same relative distances. They form, then, on the celestial vault apparent groups, the configuration of which is nearly invariable. Centuries must elapse to show a change of form, unless we employ extremely delicate measures. A planet, on the contrary, moves rapidly across these groups, to such a degree that, in the interval of a night, or at most of a few nights, this displacement is very perceptible: hence the old denomination of *fixed* stars, in opposition to the *wandering* ones, or planets.

We must be careful, however, to guard against assigning to this word a rigidity which it does not possess, for we shall shortly see that the stars really move with a velocity not inferior to that which animates the members of our system. Their immense distance is the only cause of their apparent immobility, which vanishes when precise observations, embracing a sufficient interval of time—some years, for example—are made.

A fact which strikes every one is the great diversity of brightness in the stars which people the heavens. All degrees of intensity are remarked, from the resplendent light of Sirius to the scarcely perceptible glimmer of those hardly visible to the naked eye.

Whence arises this difference of brightness? This question we cannot answer for any star in particular; but it is easy to imagine that it may result from various circumstances, such as their less or greater distance, the real and various dimensions of the bodies, and, lastly, the intrinsic brightness of the light peculiar to each. However this may be, astronomers, without regard to the unknown causes which may influence the intensity of the stellar light, have divided stars into *classes* or *magnitudes:* and when we speak of a star of the first, second, or fifth magnitude, it is understood that this way of speaking refers only to the apparent brightness, and that nothing is affirmed either as to the real dimensions or distance, or even intrinsic brightness.*

Besides, as the stars, arranged in the order of their brightness, would form a progression decreasing by imperceptible degrees, the classes adopted are themselves conventional and arbitrary. The first six magnitudes comprise all stars visible to the naked eye. But the use of the most powerful telescopes brings to view stars of feebler light, descending to the sixteenth and seventeenth magnitudes. In truth, the progression has no inferior limit; it extends more and more in proportion as the progress of the optician's art increases the penetrating power of our instruments.

To gain an idea of the respective intensities of the light emitted by the stars of the first six magnitudes, following the scale adopted by astronomers, the following drawing should be inspected; in it the stars are figured by disks, the surfaces of which are in proportion to their brilliancy.

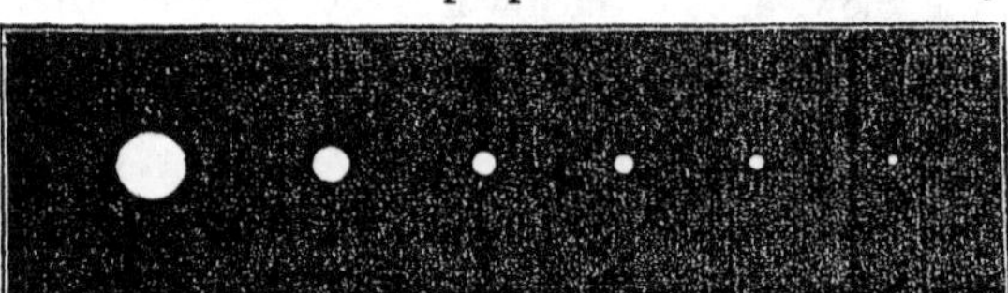

Fig. 126.—Relative brightness of the stars of the first six magnitudes.

But, we repeat, it must not be thought that the stars ranked in the same class are, on that account, of the same brightness.† Thus the light of Sirius is estimated at four times that of the star Alpha (or α) Centauri; but both, nevertheless, are included by astronomers in the number of the stars of the first magnitude.

* What we have said of a particular star is not rigorously true when the whole of the stars are considered. The calculus of probabilities enables us, in this case, to deduce from the brightness of the stars of a certain size some inferences on their mean distances. We shall return to this point.

† [Astronomers not only class the stars in magnitudes, but tabulate them in the order of their brightness in each constellation, the principal stars being denoted by the letters of the Greek alphabet. A star is described by a Greek letter, followed by the name of the constellation in Latin: thus α, or Alpha Centauri, denotes the brightest star in the constellation of the Centaur. β Lyræ is the second brightest star in the Lyre, and so on.] [The order of brightness is, however, not very strictly adhered to.—R. A. P.]

We here give the names of the twenty most brilliant stars of the two hemispheres, which it is usual to consider as forming the first class. They are here arranged in the order of their brightness:—

1. Sirius.
2. Eta (η) Argûs.*
3. Canopus.
4. Alpha (α) Centauri.
5. Arcturus.
6. Rigel.
7. Capella.
8. Vega.
9. Procyon.
10. Betelgeuse.†
11. Achernar.
12. Aldebaran.
13. Beta (β) Centauri.
14. Alpha (α) Crucis.
15. Antares.
16. Atair.
17. Spica.
18. Fomalhaut.
19. Beta (β) Crucis.
20. Pollux.

Lastly, Regulus, a bright star in the constellation of the Lion, is also ranked by some astronomers in the first magnitude, while others only admit in this class the first seventeen stars in the above list. These divergencies are of no importance.

In proportion as the scale of brilliancy or magnitude is descended, the number of the stars contained in each class rapidly increases. The number of second-magnitude stars in the entire heavens is about 65; of the third, about 200; of the fifth, 1100; and of the sixth magnitude, 3200. Adding these numbers together, we obtain a few over 5000 stars of the first six magnitudes, and these comprise very nearly all those that can be seen with the naked eye.

The smallness of this number nearly always astonishes those who have not tried to form an exact estimate of the number of stars which shine in the celestial vault on the most favourable nights.

The aspect of the multitude of sparkling points which are scattered over the sky makes us disposed to believe that they are innumerable, and to be counted, if not by millions, at all events by hundreds of thousands. This is, nevertheless, an illusion. All observers who have taken the trouble to make an exact enumeration of the stars visible to the naked eye, have arrived at a maximum of 3000 as the mean number which can be observed in every part of the heavens, visible at the same time, at the same place: this, of course, is but half of the entire heavens.

Argelander has published an exact catalogue of the stars visible on the horizon of Berlin during the course of the year. This catalogue comprises 3256 stars.‡ According to Humboldt, there are 4146 visible on

* It will be seen, subsequently, that the brightness of this star undergoes astonishing changes.

† The brightness of this star is variable; it has recently descended to the sixth magnitude.

‡ M. Heis (of Munster) affirms that his sight is so penetrating that he can perceive with the naked eye 2000 more stars than those catalogued by Argelander in his *Uranometria Nova*. On the other hand, there are many eyes which distinguish at most stars of the fifth magnitude, and do not see any of those of the sixth.

The degree of visibility of the stars to the naked eye depends also on the state of the atmosphere, on its degree of purity, and on the altitude of the place. Londoners, to be assured of these differences, have only to compare the sparkling sky of the country with that which they see through the haze which almost constantly envelopes their city.

the horizon of Paris in the whole course of the year ; and as this number increases in proportion as we approach the Equator, that is to say, in proportion as the double movement of the Earth unfolds to us during a year a more extensive portion of the heavens, 4638 stars are already visible to the naked eye on the horizon of Alexandria.

We repeat, the maximum number is comprised between 5000 and 6000 stars for the entire heavens,* including those seen by the most

Fig. 127.—A part of the constellation of the Twins, as seen through a telescope.†

piercing and most accustomed eyes in the best nights for observation. When the atmosphere is lit up by the Moon, or by twilight, or, as happens in the great centres of population, by the illumination of the houses and streets, the lowest magnitude stars are effaced altogether, and the number

* [In the British Association Catalogue, which is intended to include all stars visible to the naked eye, without exception, there are nearly 5900 stars marked as of sixth magnitude and upwards. (The catalogue contains, however, 8377 stars in all). This catalogue may be regarded as the most complete yet made, so far as the visible stars are concerned. It is on this account that I have selected it as the basis of my large Star-Atlas, which includes all the 5900 stars above referred to.—R. A. P.]

† This drawing is the reproduction, on a small scale, of one of the maps of the beautiful Ecliptic Atlas published by M. Chacornac.

of those visible is consequently much more limited. We may add, in conclusion, that the more decided the scintillation, the more easy is it to distinguish very faint stars.

A word now on the number of stars that can be seen with the help of the telescope. Here we shall find the numbers which our imagination had erroneously led us to believe are visible to the naked eye.

According to the illustrious Director of the Observatory of Bonn—Argelander—the seventh magnitude comprises nearly 13,000 stars; the eighth, 40,000; and lastly, the ninth, 142,000. The calculations of Struve give the total number of stars visible in the entire heavens, by the aid of Sir William Herschel's 20-feet reflector, as more than 20,000,000. But, without doubt, these approximate numbers are much below the real ones. It will be seen, besides, that the richness of the different parts of the heavens in stars is very unequal. The bright zone known under the name of the Milky Way alone contains, according to Herschel, 18,000,000.*

Nothing is more curious than to examine, both with the naked eye and by the aid of a telescope, the same part of the sky. There, when the eye scarcely distinguishes a few scattered stars, the telescope reveals thousands. The two figures (127 and 128) will enable those of our readers who do not possess a telescope to judge of the surprise experienced by those who make this observation.

Fig. 128.—The same part of the constellation of the Twins (Gemini) seen with the naked eye.

These drawings represent the same part of the constellation of the Twins. The naked eye is able to see six stars. Now the same celestial region, seen by the aid of a refractor of six inches aperture, contains 3205 stars, varying from the third to the thirteenth magnitudes. It appears as a perfect mass of luminous points; and were we to apply to the same region instruments still more powerful, the eye would then discover at depths, so to speak infinite, stars of all the smaller magnitudes.

* M. Chacornac considers this estimate as even less than the number of stars comprised between the first and thirteenth magnitudes. 'For my part,' he remarks 'according to Sir William Herschel's guages, and those of the Ecliptic Charts, I estimate at 77,000,000 the number of stars comprised in the first thirteen magnitudes, if we take the mean indicated in the preface to the Catalogue of Bessel's Zones, reduced by Weiss.' What would the number become if we added to these already prodigious estimates, all the stars of which the various star-clusters now known are composed?

II.

THE CONSTELLATIONS.

General Survey of the Starry Heavens — Constellations visible on the Horizon of London — Northern Circumpolar Zone.

Before studying one by one the phenomena which the starry heavens present to us — before penetrating, so to speak, to the heart of the visible universe, to grasp its marvellous structure, and to embrace in thought its tremendous extent, it is well to familiarise ourselves with the groups of stars such as they are presented to the eye of an inhabitant of the Earth. The movements with which the so-called fixed stars are endowed, are effected, as we have before said, with extreme slowness: it follows, therefore, that the artificial groups or constellations preserve for a long period the same configurations. This constancy of form, joined to the difference of brightness of the principal stars, will enable us to extricate ourselves from the apparent chaos produced by so many luminous points scattered on all sides on the celestial vault. When we shall possess, in a manner, a mental map of the sky, we shall be able to follow with more interest the particular features which distinguish its various regions, which are as varied in reality as they are at first uniform in appearance.

In order to make this survey of the heavens we must choose a station. Let it be London. As our globe, by virtue of its diurnal movement, completes an entire rotation on its axis in about twenty-four hours, it follows that the portions of the celestial vault, visible at our station, will completely defile before us during that time. Twenty-four hours, then, would suffice us to make our survey, if the illumination of the atmosphere did not efface the stars during the day. The succession of day and night, in fact, allows us only to see a portion of the visible stars in a given place at the same time of the year.

Fortunately, however, owing to the movement of the Earth in its orbit, this difficulty disappears. In consequence of this movement, each night shows us fresh stars, whilst those first visible disappear. In the course of a year, then, the Earth presents a dark hemisphere to every part of the sky — to all those parts, at least, which are visible on the horizon of our station.

Lastly, it must not be lost sight of, that even then one entire part of the celestial vault will ever remain invisible to us Londoners. Let us recall what is the effect of the diurnal movement of rotation on the aspect of the heavens in any given place like London, the station we have chosen. A point situated at a certain height above its horizon, and towards the north and on the meridian, remains immovable. It is one of the poles. Starting from this point in our survey, the stars seem to describe, from rising to setting, larger and larger circles, in proportion as they are situated further from the pole. As long as the lower arcs of these circles do not touch the horizon, the stars situated on them do not rise or set, and therefore remain constantly visible: these are the northern *circumpolar stars.*

Beyond these, however, the circles described plunge partly below the horizon; they increase as far as the equator, on the other (the south) side of which the stars describe shorter and shorter arcs. The last ones in our survey scarcely rise above our horizon, and when they do, shortly set and disappear.

It follows, then, that there is a zone of stars which never rises above the horizon of London, and which remains for ever invisible to all places of the Earth having the same latitude. These stars are those which surround the southern pole of the heavens, and which an observer would become acquainted with by degrees, in approaching the equatorial regions of the Earth.*

The whole of the heavens, then, in our middle latitudes, may be considered as forming three zones; the first always visible at night when the sky is clear, whatever may be the time of year, the second visible in part only on any given night, the third always invisible.

Let us successively pass these three zones under review. Let us occupy ourselves first with that which is always in sight when the sky is clear, on all points of the Earth which have the same northern latitude as London. From the mouths of the Thames and Rhine, as far as the southern extremity of Kamtschatka, passing by Antwerp, Cassel, Central Poland, Orenbourg, Southern Asiatic Russia, and Northern China, in the Old World, and the Aleutian Islands, Queen Charlotte's Island, and the southern parts of British North America in the New, all the inhabitants of the parallel of which we speak view the same spectacle during the whole year; the hour only, at which the various constellations are on the meridian of the different places, differs.

Suppose it midnight, at the end of autumn, near the 20th of December; it is the night of the winter solstice. Let us look towards the north. Let

* By virtue of the two movements of the Earth, and of its spherical form, the portion of the celestial sphere visible in any part of the globe varies with the latitude of the place.

At the Equator the whole sky, both northern and southern, passes before our view at night, during the entire year. The two poles lie on the horizon, of which they mark the north and south points; the celestial equator crosses the sky from east to west, passing through the zenith.

In proportion as we travel from the Equator towards one or other pole, the portion of the visible sky diminishes even down to the half, for at the poles themselves only one-half of the heavens, north or south, according to the pole, is seen. The celestial equator then forms the horizon, and the celestial pole is in the zenith.

[A little thought will show us that, as seen from the poles, the stars never set, they perpetually describe circles parallel to the horizon. At the Equator, all rise and set every day; the movements of the equatorial stars being vertical. In mid latitudes, the paths of the equatorial stars are intermediate between these two main directions.]

us imagine a circle which, touching the horizon at the north point, extends somewhat beyond the zenith.* The centre of this ideal circle will be found a little above a point nearly equidistant between the zenith and the horizon : it is the Northern Pole of the Heavens. Near this point is seen a rather brilliant star of the second magnitude ; it is named the Pole Star. As it is important to know how to recognise this star, the position of which remains nearly invariable during the whole course of the year, we will show how this may be done.

If we examine fig. 129, we shall find a group of seven stars, six of the second magnitude, one of the fourth. It composes a constellation of the northern heavens known for ages under the name of the GREAT BEAR. Let us scan well this part of the sky, whence we shall soon make many alignments

Fig. 129.—The sky of the horizon of London. Northern Circumpolar constellations.

to help us in our survey of the starry heavens. The seven stars of which it is composed may be divided into two groups, the first of which, towards the upper part, forms a quadrilateral, which is called the *body* of the Bear, whilst the three lower stars form the *tail*. The two extreme stars of the body are called the *pointers*.† Six of the seven principal stars of this constellation are of nearly equal brilliancy, and of the second magnitude. But it is easy to perceive, with the naked eye, that the star in the body of the Bear nearest to the tail is inferior in brilliancy to the others : it is now, indeed, only a fourth-magnitude star, although in the seventeenth century it was as bright as its neighbours.

* The zenith is the point of the heavens situated vertically above the head of the observer.

† The Great Bear has also been called 'Charles' Wain.'

The star in the middle of the tail (or shaft, if we think of Charles' Wain) is accompanied, on the left, by a very small star called Alcor, easily enough distinguished by an ordinary eye.* The naked eye perceives 138 stars in the Great Bear, amongst which, besides the principal seven, are eight stars of the third magnitude, and six of the fourth; the others belong to the two last orders of brightness perceptible to the unassisted vision. From the Great Bear let us return to the Pole Star.

To do this, let us prolong the straight line which joins the pointers (so called because they point to it), carrying our eye along this line towards the centre of the portion of the sky in our sight when looking north. At a distance of about five times the space which separates these two stars we shall find the Pole Star. The Pole Star plays an important part in the northern heavens, since, being very near the pole, it is, so to speak, one of the pivots of the ideal axis round which the Earth executes its real diurnal rotation, and the Heavens their apparent one in the opposite direction. It follows, therefore, that it appears immovable, and always preserves the same elevation above the horizon, while the other stars describe round it circles of unequal size. Thus the Great Bear, situated to the east of the pole at the time we have chosen for the commencement of our inspection, mounts towards the zenith as the night advances. Towards six o'clock in the morning it will be above, or to the south, of the Pole Star; whilst at six in the evening it will occupy a position diametrically opposite, below the pole and near the horizon.

As all the stars participate in the movement, it is clear that, as their relative positions do not change, the figures of the groups remain always the same. This must be well borne in mind. To the west of the Pole Star, at the same height above the horizon as the Great Bear, and at nearly the same distance from the pole, is seen another group of six stars, of which two are of the second magnitude, three of the third, and one of the fourth. This is the constellation Cassiopea,† which contains sixty-seven stars visible to the naked eye. The six which we have mentioned form a kind of reversed chair, or a bad W, the figure of which, once thoroughly caught, renders this constellation easy to recognise.

Between the Great Bear and Cassiopea is the Little Bear, of which the Pole Star is the most brilliant star. Of the twenty-seven stars visible to the naked eye which compose it, there are seven which form a figure having a great resemblance to the seven stars of the Great Bear, but arranged in an inverse order: the four intermediate stars are seen with difficulty.

Below the Little Bear a series of stars forms a sinuous line prolonged nearly to the pointers, and terminated at one extremity by a group of four stars arranged in the form of a trapezium. This is the Dragon,

* Humboldt affirmed that Alcor could be but rarely seen with the naked eye in Europe. Let our readers judge of its present brightness for themselves.

† By drawing a line from the middle star of the Great Bear (the least brilliant of the seven), to the Pole Star, and prolonging it to a nearly equal distance, the star Beta (β) Cassiopeæ is reached.

which, among 130 stars visible to the naked eye, contains only one of the second magnitude and nine of the third.

Cepheus, the Giraffe, and the Lynx, are three other constellations near the pole: the first between the Little Bear and Cassiopea; the second opposite the Dragon; the third on the same side as the second. Neither one nor the other offers anything very remarkable, especially the Giraffe and the Lynx, all the stars in which constellations are at most of the fourth magnitude.

Among all the stars which, on the horizon of London, never set, the brightest is a star of the first magnitude, known under the name of Capella, in the constellation of Auriga.

About the 20th of December, at midnight, Capella is near the zenith. This remarkable star can be found by prolonging the line which joins the two stars of the quadrilateral of the Great Bear, nearest the pole. Auriga, which contains sixty-nine stars visible to the naked eye, comprises, besides Capella, one star of the second magnitude, and three others between the third and fourth.

In the number of the constellations visible, at least partly, during the whole year, the stars of which, as they surround the pole, have, as we have seen, received the name of Circumpolar stars, must be ranked Perseus, situated near Auriga. It occupies, at the time we have chosen, a western position, relatively to this latter constellation, above Cassiopea. Of eighty-one stars visible to the naked eye, one is of the second magnitude, six are of brightness superior to the fourth. Among these latter is Algol, noted for its variable light, alternately passing from the second to the fourth magnitudes. We shall speak, further on, at some length on this singular star.

Before continuing our description of the celestial vault, and of the groups into which the stars have been formed, we will say one word on the aspect of the Northern Circumpolar Zone.

We have supposed, to describe it, that the time of observation was midnight, on the 20th of December. But it is easy to find the actual appearance and the positions of the various constellations for any hour of the night or any night of the year. We know that the entire rotation of the diurnal movement is effected in twenty-four sidereal hours. In six hours, therefore, a quarter of the total movement is accomplished, and it therefore follows that a constellation — such as Cassiopea, for example — which at midnight is to the left of the pole, was above it at six o'clock in the evening, and will be found below it, near the horizon, at six in the morning.

III.

THE CONSTELLATIONS (Continued).

Our Survey (continued), Equatorial and Southern Constellations visible on the Horizon of London.

Let us return to the stars visible at midnight on the 20th of December.

This immense zone very nearly embraces half the horizon from east to west, passing by the south, and extending in altitude to the zenith. It comprises the most beautiful constellations and the most brilliant stars in the heavens. It is divided obliquely by the Milky Way.

Orion occupies nearly the middle view. This magnificent constellation forms a quadrilateral, higher than it is broad, in the centre of which three stars of the second magnitude are arranged in a straight line.

Two of the stars of the quadrilateral, named Betelgeuse and Rigel, are of the first magnitude. Betelgeuse is remarkable for the reddish tint of its light. Among the 115 stars visible to the naked eye, besides the two most brilliant, are included four of the second magnitude, and five between the second and the fourth.

In prolonging towards the north-west the line formed by the three stars in the belt of Orion—the name given to them—the eye perceives a red star of the first magnitude: this is Aldebaran, the most beautiful star of the constellation of the Bull. Aldebaran is in the midst of a group of small stars named the *Hyades*. A little farther, in the same direction, will be found the *Pleiades*, so easy to recognise in the heavens by reason of the six stars visible to the naked eye, which compose this interesting group. The Bull contains 121 stars visible to the naked eye below the second magnitude.

If now we prolong towards the south-east of Orion the line which has found for us Aldebaran on the north-west, we perceive, near the edge of the Milky Way, the constellation of the Great Dog, which includes Sirius, the most brilliant star in the two hemispheres, remarkable on account of its scintillation and by its dazzling whiteness.

Towards the west, and nearly at the same height as Betelgeuse, shines *Procyon*, on the other side of the Milky Way. This is a star of the first magnitude, and the most brilliant one in the constellation of the Little Dog. Betelgeuse, Sirius, and Procyon, form a triangle, the three sides of which are nearly of the same apparent length (fig. 130). This circumstance enables us easily to recognise these stars.

Above Procyon, and towards the zenith, *Castor* and *Pollux* point out the Twins, which include, besides these two stars of the first and second magnitudes, fifty-one stars visible to the naked eye. Towards the west, and by the side of the Pleiades, lies the constellation of the Ram, and, a little below, those of the Whale and Eridanus, neither of which, in those parts visible to us in London, contain any stars of the first magnitude.

But while we are enumerating and contemplating this brilliant portion of the heavens, the stars defile across it, set, and disappear in the west, whilst others rise in the east, revealing new constellations.

Before passing these under review, we may mention that the southern horizon presents the same aspect at the epochs and hours mentioned below:—

Midnight	20th of December.
Six o'clock in the evening .	22nd of March.
Noon	20th of June.
Six o'clock in the morning .	22nd of September.

From the 20th of December, the time of the winter solstice, to the 22nd of March—the vernal equinox—by reason of the Earth's jour-

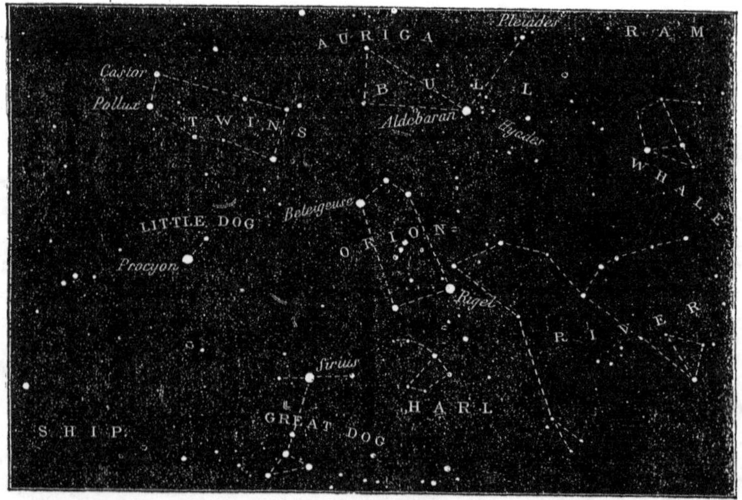

Fig. 130.—The Heavens on the horizon of London. Equatorial zone. Orion.

neying along its orbit, the part of the heavens opposed to the Sun, and therefore visible at night, changes progressively. By this movement from west to east, we gradually see new eastern constellations at the same hours of the night.

Thus, by the 22nd of March, at midnight, the aspect of the southern starry vault has almost entirely changed, and in place of Orion, which is then setting, the Lion occupies the centre. The Milky Way is inclined to the west, and cuts the horizon towards the north.

The principal stars of the Lion form a kind of trapezium, the western side forming a half-circle like a sickle. It is at the lower extremity of the handle of this instrument that Regulus, a star of the first magnitude, which is also named the Lion's Heart (*Cor Leonis*), shines. *Denebola* is the star situated at the other extremity of the trapezium. Of the seventy-five stars visible to the naked eye in this constellation, without counting Regulus, there are three of the second magnitude and five of the third. Three stars of the first order shine with Regulus in the heavens visible to us, at the time we have chosen. In the south-west, Procyon is not yet set. Then, at the same altitude as this star, but to the east of the Lion, is SPICA in the VIRGIN, which will soon ascend the meridian; and, lastly, ARCTURUS, the most brilliant star in the constellation Boötes. *Spica*, *Arcturus*, and *Denebola* form the summits of a triangle, the sides of which are nearly equal, and of which the line which joins the two latter stars forms the base, nearly parallel to the horizon (fig. 131).

The Virgin and Boötes are, with the Lion, the most important constellations in view. The first contains a hundred, and the second eighty-

Fig. 131.—The Heavens on the horizon of London. Equatorial zone. The Lion.

five stars visible to the naked eye, amongst which sixteen exceed in brilliancy stars of the fourth magnitude. Between the Lion and Boötes, a cluster of stars lying very near together is perceived: this is BERENICE'S HAIR. To the east of Arcturus, six stars, arranged in a half circle, the most brilliant of which is named *Alpheta*, form the NORTHERN CROWN, below which are found the Head of the SERPENT and OPHIUCHUS. Lying round Spica, and a little below, towards the horizon, are distinguished the BALANCE, the CROW, and the CUP. The two first constellations only contain a few stars of the second magnitude. Lastly, in the mist on the horizon appear a few stars of the SCORPION and the CENTAUR, constellations which we shall again meet in our survey of the celestial zone which surrounds the Southern Pole.

To conclude our examination of the constellations visible on the 22nd of March, at midnight, we must notice the HUNTING DOGS, above Berenice's Hair; the LITTLE LION, above the Lion; the CRAB, to the west of Regulus; and, lastly, close to the horizon and the Milky Way, the WATER SNAKE, where brilliantly shines *Cor Hydræ*, a variable star of the second magnitude, and the UNICORN, below Procyon.

The zone which we have just described occupies, on the horizon of London, the same position at the following epochs and hours:—

March 22nd	Midnight.
June 20th	Six o'clock in the evening.*
September 22nd	Noon.
December 20th	Six o'clock in the morning.

On the 20th of June, at midnight, another part of the equatorial zone passes before our eyes.

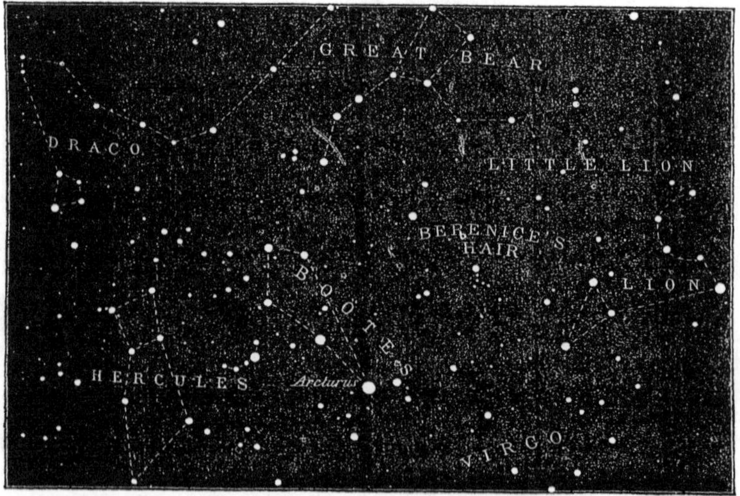

Fig. 132.—The Heavens of the horizon of London. Equatorial zone.

The constellations of the Northern Crown and Boötes, the Serpent, the Balance, and the Virgin, which, on the 22nd of March, occupied the eastern part of the starry vault, are now at the west. Arcturus is situated vertically above Spica. The Milky Way, now divided into two large branches, rises obliquely from the southern horizon towards the north-east.

Three stars of the first magnitude shine at unequal heights in three different constellations. These are, going from west to east, *Antares*, or the Heart of the Scorpion, which scarcely rises above the horizon near the

* We must here make, with reference to the 20th of June, the same remark for six o'clock in the evening in summer as we have already done for midday: the brightness of the atmosphere renders the stars invisible.

Milky Way. Afterwards comes *Vega*, in the LYRE, which is nearly in the zenith, and, lastly, at a mid height, *Atair*, in the EAGLE.

A few words on the constellations now in view.

We have first, to the west of the Northern Crown, nearly in the zenith, HERCULES, which, in a total number of 155 stars visible to the naked eye, includes only two approaching the second magnitude, and ten between the third and fourth. It is towards a point in this constellation, as we shall see anon, that our Sun is actually travelling, carrying with him all his system of planets, satellites, and comets.

To the east of Hercules is the Lyre, where we have already noticed the brilliant and white Vega, easily recognised by the four stars which form below it a little parallelogram.

Still going towards the west, to the left of the Lyre, the constellation of the SWAN is noticed: this traverses the Milky Way, and its most

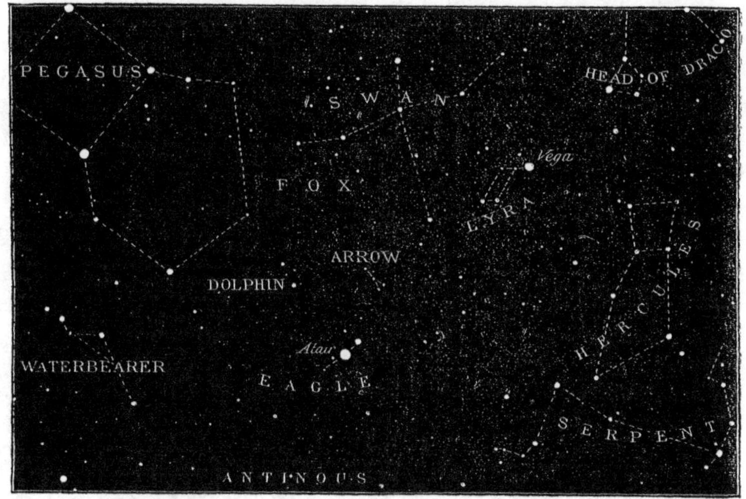

Fig. 133.—The Heavens of the horizon of London. The Lyre, Swan, and Eagle.

brilliant star, *Alpha Cygni*, is between the first and second magnitudes. This star forms, with four others of the third magnitude, a large cross, which at this hour is inclined to the horizon, and serves to distinguish the constellation to which it belongs.

Alpha Cygni forms also, with Atair and Vega, a large isosceles triangle, that is, a triangle two sides of which are nearly equal. In the Swan is found a small star which, though scarcely visible to the naked eye, is celebrated in astronomical annals as being the first the distance of which has been measured. The Swan contains 145 stars perceptible to the unaided sight.

The FOX, the ARROW, the DOLPHIN, between the Lyre, the Swan, and the Eagle, contain no remarkable star.

Near the horizon towards the east are perceived the constellations of the WATERBEARER and of the Goat; then, partly in the Milky Way, the ARCHER. Here we again meet the stars of the Scorpion, amongst which is Antares, which will soon disappear under the horizon, with the four stars with which it forms a sort of fan.

Above the Scorpion, OPHIUCHUS and the SERPENT are entirely visible. Four stars of the second magnitude, and seventeen between the second and the fourth, are met with in these constellations.

And here we finish our survey of the equatorial zone of stars visible at midnight at the summer solstice. This zone presents the same appearance at the four following epochs:—

June 20th	Midnight.
September 22nd	Six o'clock in the evening.
December 20th	Noon.
March 22nd	Six o'clock in the morning.

It remains for us, in order to finish our description of the stars

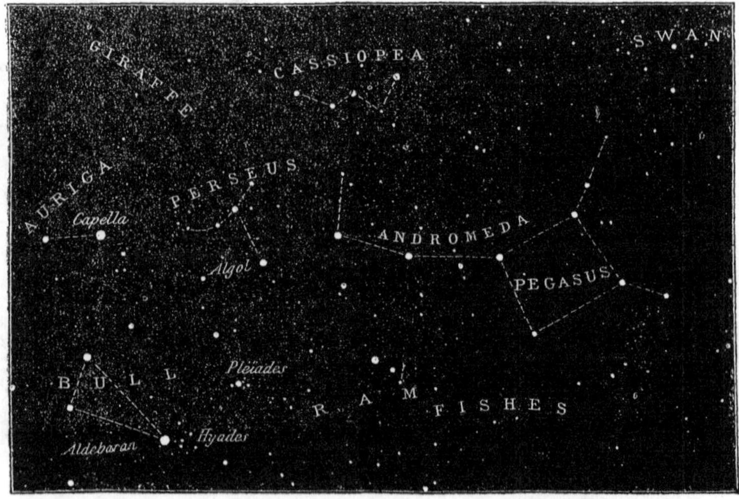

Fig. 134.—The Heavens of the horizon of London. Equatorial zone.

visible above the horizon of London, to pass in review the constellations of the equatorial zone, as they appear at midnight at the autumnal equinox.

If at that time—the 22nd of September, at midnight,—we turn our eyes towards the south, we embrace in our view all the region of the sky which extends from the west to the east as far as the zenith.

In the west appears Atair, in the Eagle, and higher up the Swan; at the east, the Pleiades, and the BULL, in which constellation shines Aldebaran. Orion, already partly visible, will soon mount above the horizon. We have surveyed, between December and September, three quarters of the sky, which have defiled before our eyes, or rather the whole starry vault, if we include the stars now visible.

Towards the middle of the heavens, a little nearer the zenith than the horizon, lies a large square of four stars, three of which are of the second and one of the third magnitudes. Close to this, and on the eastern side, are three other stars of the second magnitude, about the same distances apart; these make of the square which we have mentioned a much more extended figure, having a great resemblance to the group of the seven principal stars of the Great Bear. Of these seven stars, three belong to the constellation of PEGASUS, three to ANDROMEDA, and, lastly, the most eastern one is no other than Algol, the variable star in Perseus.

Andromeda and Pegasus contain between them 191 stars visible to the naked eye, amongst which twelve only exceed the fourth magnitude.

Between the *square of Pegasus* and the Bull we meet with two constellations, the FISHES and the RAM: this latter contains only two rather brilliant stars, situated at nearly equal distances from the Pleiades and the two eastern stars of the square of Pegasus. Below the Fishes and the Ram is the WHALE, some of the stars of which are below the horizon.

Among ninety-eight stars visible to the naked eye in this constellation, six are between the second and fourth magnitudes, and two of the second.

Among the first, one is very remarkable on account of the periodical variations of its brightness, which sometimes cause it to appear as a star of the fourth magnitude, and sometimes efface it sufficiently to render it invisible; this is *Mira* (the marvellous), or ω Ceti.

To the west of this constellation, we again find the Waterbearer and the Goat, then, quite to the south, and touching the horizon, the stars of the SOUTHERN FISH, amongst which we may distinguish, if the atmosphere be pure, and terrestrial objects do not intervene, *Fomalhaut*, a beautiful star of the first magnitude.

The zone, which we have passed under review, offers the same aspect at the following epochs and hours:

September 22nd	Midnight.
December 20th	Six o'clock in the evening.
March 22nd	Noon.
June 20th	Six o'clock in the morning.

Let us add, in terminating this rapid review of the southern part of the sky visible in London, that the figures which have helped us to recognise the different constellations may also be used at other epochs of the year, and at other hours of the night. Only, the stars still preserving the same relative positions, will be diversely inclined to the horizon. The more the hour is advanced beyond midnight, then the more will the western stars have disappeared, while more new stars at the east will be seen. This constant change, which results from the diurnal movement of the Earth, will be produced in the same manner, if we pass from one day to the other, or from one month to the following one, so that at the same hour of the night the stars successively visible in the same part of the sky are situate in constellations more and more eastern.

We have already said that this second apparent movement of the starry vault is due to the translation of the Earth in its orbit. This is effected with great slowness. Thus, for example, the displacement, which requires six hours of diurnal rotation, demands three whole months of annual revolution.

IV.

THE CONSTELLATIONS (Continued).

Our Survey of the Starry Heavens (continued)—Southern Circumpolar Zone—Stars invisible at London.

From the northern hemisphere of the Earth, where we have been placed until now to observe the starry vault, let us transport ourselves to the southern one. Let us choose a place, the distance of which from the Equator is precisely the same as that of our first post, that is to say, one situated on the parallel which passes through the antipodes of London. Let us suppose ourselves, for example, placed on a part of the coast of Patagonia, near to the south point of South America. There, all the stars forming the Northern circumpolar zone, which on the parallel of Paris never set, would be constantly invisible. Looking away from the Equator, that is to say, towards the North, we shall see pass before us, from one end of the year to the other, all the constellations of the equatorial zone which we have just described.

But the stars will here be found arranged in an entirely inverse order, at least relatively to the horizon; so that the two stars of the great quadrilateral of Orion, which in London formed the base, appear as the upper side; Sirius, which appears in the northern hemisphere to the left and below Orion, will be here found to the right, and higher on the horizon. This change of aspect is easily explained by the complete change of the observer's position. But if we look southwards, we shall be able to observe a number of stars unknown to the terrestrial zone which extends from the parallel of London as far as the northern pole. These are the constellations which surround the southern pole of the heavens, and which never set on our new horizon. If, then, we pass in review this zone, we shall have terminated our description of the whole celestial vault.

Let us choose the 20th of December, the period of the winter solstice,—the commencement of the warm season in the southern hemisphere. It is midnight, and the perfectly pure atmosphere permits us to contemplate the sky in all its splendour. The Milky Way, ramified into diverse branches, rises slightly inclined on the horizon, on the left, that is, the eastern side.

But what at first most strikes us in the celestial picture spread out before us is the multitude of brilliant stars which follow the course of the Milky Way as far as the zenith, and, passing over our heads, go behind us, to rejoin Sirius, Procyon, Aldebaran, nearly on the northern horizon.

Let us begin by the constellations which compose this glorious girdle.

Nearly at the height of the pole, four stars, one of which is of the first, and two of the second magnitude, form an elongated figure lying parallel to the horizon. These are the principal stars of the SOUTHERN CROSS—the Pole-star of the South.

Below the most brilliant star of the Cross, and between two branches of the Milky Way, two stars of the first magnitude point out the great constellation of the CENTAUR, in which the eye perceives five stars of the second magnitude. The Centaur extends to the east and north of the Cross, which it nearly entirely surrounds. We shall, in a future chapter,

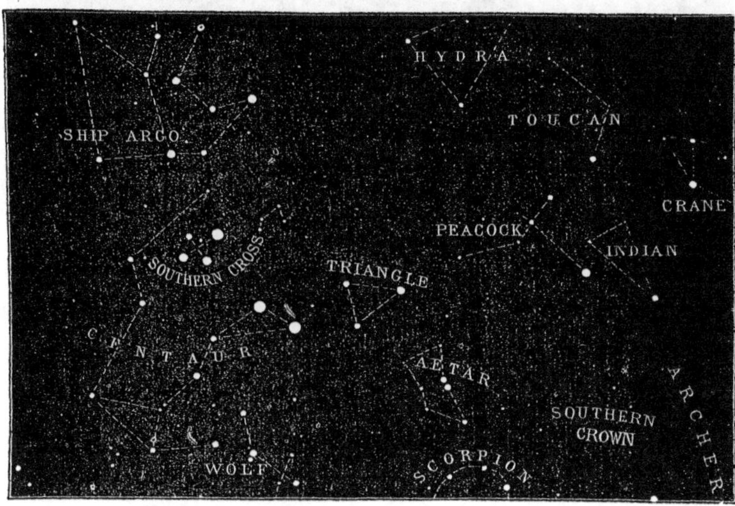

Fig. 185.—Stars invisible at London. Southern Circumpolar zone. The Southern Cross.

have occasion to speak of the brightest star of this constellation, which is not only remarkable for its light; we shall see that it forms a system of two suns, revolving one round the other; and also that it is the nearest to us among the stars the distances of which have been measured.

Below the Centaur, and near the horizon, appear a great number of stars of the third and fourth magnitudes, which form the constellation of the WOLF. One detached branch of the Milky Way traverses the WOLF, and is lost in the Scorpion, of which only a few stars have risen at this hour above the horizon.

The ALTAR and the SOUTHERN TRIANGLE, which lie along the Milky Way in looking towards the pole, and in which there is nothing remarkable to notice, bring us back, above the Cross, to the magnificent constellation of the SHIP, or ARGO. Here a multitude of bright stars, arranged round the pole, give to this region of the sky an incomparable splendour. *Canopus,* looked upon in old times as the most brilliant star in the celestial vault after Sirius, is at this hour close to the zenith and nearly in the meridian; whilst above *Alpha Crucis, Eta Argûs* astonishes us by its unusual magnificence. This singular star, which, varying in brilliancy at different times for some two hundred years, has at length reached and surpassed the brilliancy of Canopus, and has banished it to the third rank in the scale of the stars of the first magnitude.

From the Ship we pass, without meeting any remarkable constellation, by the FLYING FISH, DORADUS, and the RETICULE, and we arrive at

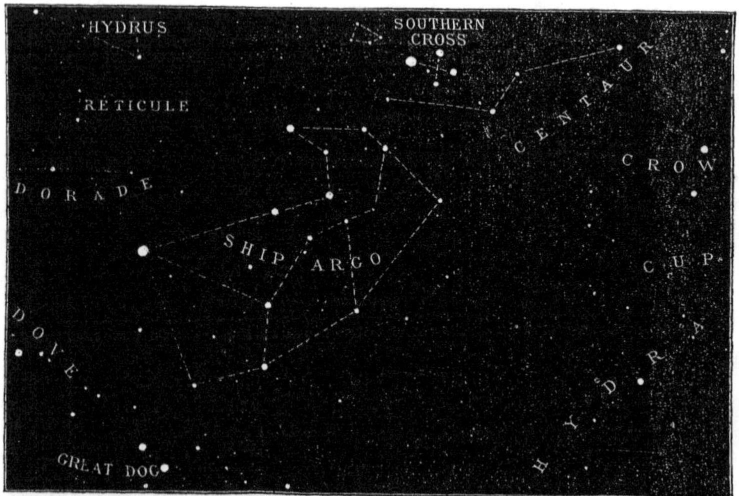

Fig. 136.—Stars invisible at London. Southern Circumpolar zone. Argo.

ERIDANUS, of which we have already noticed the part visible at London. It is at the extremity of this constellation, nearest to the pole, that *Achernar*, a beautiful star of the first magnitude, shines. To the right of Achernar, three stars, one of the second, the two others of the third order, form the PHŒNIX, below which, returning to the horizon and to the meridian, are found TOUCAN, the CRANE, the INDIAN, and the PEACOCK. Two stars of the second magnitude, and some of the third, distinguish these constellations, the positions of which can be exactly recognised in figs. 135 and 137.

In this enumeration of the circumpolar constellations of the South, we have said nothing of the stars situated at the Pole itself. The reason is simple; there are none deserving mention, and, with the exception of the star β *Hydræ*, none approach the third magnitude.

There is not, then, in the southern sky, any star analogous to *Polaris* in the northern heavens. But we have already seen that this poverty of the polar regions is singularly compensated by the number and brightness of the stars which entirely surround the zone which we have just described.

Let us add, that outside the Milky Way, and in the vicinity of the least brilliant parts of the zone, appear two objects which give to the starry vault a very singular aspect; they are two whitish clouds of unequal size,

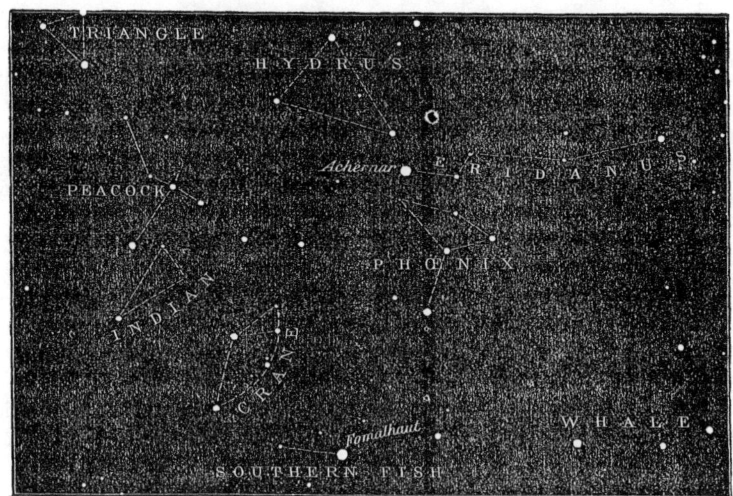

Fig. 137.—Stars invisible at London. Southern Circumpolar zone.

which seem, at first sight, detached portions of the Milky Way itself; these are the GREAT AND LITTLE CLOUDS which astronomers still designate under the popular name of Magellanic Clouds. We shall subsequently describe in detail these curious appearances.

Now, that the appearance of the sky is known to us, we will examine into it a little more closely, and study in detail these thousands of fires, these suns and groups of suns, which the telescope multiplies with such an astonishing profusion.

V.

DISTANCES OF THE STARS.

Distances of some Stars from the Earth—Time required by Light to reach the nearest Stars—A rough sketch of the Dimensions of the Visible Universe.

THE stars are suns.

Each of those luminous points, which the unassisted sight reveals to us by thousands on the vault of heaven, which the telescope shows by millions in the depths of space, shines with its own light. Each star is a focus from which, doubtless, bodies analogous to the planets of our own system, and forming with their central sun a system similar to ours, receive light and heat. The stupendous conception, which affirms the whole visible universe to consist of an almost infinite multitude of suns, is no longer a gratuitous hypothesis, or a simple conjecture; it is one of the most firmly established truths of astronomy.

The data which science now possesses relating to the immense distances of the stars, of those even nearest to the Sun, place the fundamental fact, that each star is a light-source, and does not shine with radiance borrowed from the Sun, beyond all doubt.

We will in this place go over the evidence on which this assertion depends. We shall by-and-by endeavour to give an idea of the methods which have furnished it.

As long as we were dealing with our own system, we found it possible to express the various distances by taking the diameter of our own globe as a standard measure—as a unit. Thus we found the mean distance from the Earth to the Sun to be about 12,000 Earth diameters, or 95,000,000 miles; and the vast distances which separate the Sun from the planets, situated on the confines of the Solar system, were expressed in the same manner. But when, breaking the bounds of our Solar system, astronomers wished to measure and to express the distances of the stars, even of the nearest among them, they soon found that the former unit, or sounding-line, vanished into a point compared with the immensity to which they had to apply it.

Nay, even the radius of the terrestrial orbit itself, a measuring-rod of some 95,000,000 miles in length—a distance which a cannon-ball would require twelve years to traverse—was soon found insufficient, and still remains so for a great many stellar distances; but the improvements continually effected in the methods of observation, and in the measuring instruments themselves, have at length enabled some of our most celebrated astronomers to measure approximately the distances of some few stars, and to tell us how many radii of the Earth's orbit they are removed from us.

The first result obtained was in the case of a star, nearly invisible to the naked eye, situated in the constellation of the Swan, and marked 61 in the star-maps and catalogues.* The distance of this star, the first in the order of discovery, the second in the scale of magnitude, is nearly three times as great as that of one of the brightest stars of the heavens, Alpha (α) Centauri, which according to our present knowledge is the nearest to us of all the stars.

Alpha Centauri is distant from us more than 200,000 times the mean distance of the Sun from the Earth—more than 19,000,000,000,000 miles. The most powerful imagination in vain tries to picture this fearful distance; in vain the mind would heap line upon line, number upon number, to bridge the immensity of this abyss. Let us see if, by some other means, by images, or comparisons, we can—though certainly not with the precision which attaches to numbers—appeal to our senses to comprehend this fact.

Every one knows with what wonderful rapidity light travels; the light-waves are propagated at the rate of 192,000 miles a second. Now, a very simple calculation will show that a light-ray, leaving α Centauri, will not reach our eye till the end of three years and seven months. When, on the surface of our Earth, on this grain of sand belonging to the system governed by our Sun, we endeavour to picture to ourselves a long distance—a hundred or a thousand miles, for instance—it is with difficulty we can form an idea of it. We can only represent it well to ourselves by associating with the sense of sight the perception of time: we ask ourselves, for example, how many hours or days are necessary to accomplish the distanee. What is, then, this distance of 192,000 miles † which light traverses in a second? This distance is an abyss to our imagination.

But, lastly, supposing we could grasp, as in a bird's-eye view, this distance, already so considerable, let us associate it with the short duration of a second; and then let us imagine that a single day of twenty-four hours contains 86,400 such intervals: and let us stay to contemplate the enormous distance to which the luminous ray would arrive after a day's journey—it will have plunged into space to a depth seven times greater than the distance of Neptune. Still, according to what we have just stated, it would not have accomplished the thousandth part of its route; it

* The fame of this first and important determination is due to the illustrious astronomer Bessel. Peters, the two Struves, Henderson, Maclear, Schlüter, and Wichmann, have also distinguished themselves in these researches.

† The velocity of light here given, as we have said before, will possibly require modification. Some remarkable experiments, based on a method both exact and ingenious [the application of Wheatstone's rotating-mirror], have led M. Leon Foucault to a much reduced value. The velocity of the light is, according to him, about 184,000 miles a second; and his modification entails a corresponding reduction in the number which expresses the distance from the Earth to the Sun.

Until a complete discussion of this question shall have established the correctness of these new values, and until they shall be generally accepted, we have preferred to retain the old ones, though there is little doubt that the new ones are nearer the truth. The inconvenience, if there be any, is reduced by the fact that the *relative* distances between the various bodies of the Solar system remain intact, as also those which give the distances of the stars expressed in radii of the terrestrial orbit. The time which the light from these bodies takes to reach us is also, of course, unaltered.

must continue its course for 1300 days with the same tremendous velocity, journeying ever on during three entire years before it attains the nearest star—that brilliant sun of the southern heavens, α Centauri. Such, in every direction, are the dimensions of the space devoid of stars which surrounds our Solar system.

And, nevertheless, the stars nearest to us only are here in question. From α Lyræ, from the sparkling Sirius, light requires more than twenty years to reach us; from the Pole Star, half a century is needed. Lastly, to traverse the space which separates Capella from the world on which we live, or, as it may be stated, 425,980,000,000,000 miles, 72 years, or a man's whole lifetime, would be required.

Shall we endeavour to obtain, from another point of view, an idea of these distances? Suppose a spectator placed at one of the extremities of the line which joins our Sun to α Centauri. At this point, the entire radius of the Earth's orbit would be hidden by a thread of a $\frac{1}{25}$ inch in diameter, held at a distance of 650 feet from the eye; that is, a line 95,000,000 miles in length, looked at broadside on at this distance, would appear but as an imperceptible point.

We give below a table of the principal distances already determined expressed in radii of the Earth's orbit; they can be converted into miles by multiplying them by 95,000,000 miles, the length of that orbit.

We give also the number of years required by light to travel the different distances:

	Radii of Earth's orbit.	Years.
α Centauri	211,330	3·6
61 Cygni	550,920	9·4
Vega	1,330,700	21·0
Sirius	1,375,000	22·0
ι Ursæ Majoris	1,550,800	25·0
Arcturus	1,622,800	26·0
Polaris	3,078,600	50·0
Capella	4,484,000	72·0

Other smaller distances are also known, but with less precision; nearly all are still greater than those here given. None are less than the distance of α Centauri.

Thus, if we imagine a sphere having for its centre the Sun, and for its radius 200,000 times the mean distance of the Sun from the Earth, none of the innumerable stars which we see shining during our nights will be comprised within it. And nevertheless, the volume of this ideal sphere contains 275,000,000,000 times the entire volume of our planetary sphere—the radius of which stretches from the Sun to Neptune. The comets have here full scope to accomplish their most excentric revolutions, and to describe ellipses bordering on the parabola.

If we now imagine our Sun plunged in space, to the distance of the nearest star, and calculate, according to the laws of optics, what will be the reduction of its light, we find that it will but put on the brightness of a star of the second magnitude, that it will shine with the brilliancy of the Pole Star, and the principal stars in the constellation of the Great Bear.

Is it now understood how impossible it is that the stars can shine by reflected light? At the distance at which the nearest of them are from the Sun they receive from the focus of our world a light the intensity of which, as we have just shown, does not exceed that of a star of the second magnitude. If each star were a dark body, the light which it would receive from the Sun would be at most equal to that received by us on our darkest nights, when but a single star pierces through a thick stratum of clouds. And even this feeble glimmer would require to again traverse the immense abyss which separates the star from the Earth, before it reached us twinkling and brilliant as we see it. We might then affirm, on this ground alone, which supplies most incontestable evidence, the astronomical truth, which we announced at the beginning of this chapter. [But there is much more convincing proof to which we shall refer anon.]

The stars, then, are suns. Each of them is a focus of light and heat, and probably the centre of a system which comprises, like ours, planets, satellites, and comets. Each star, in fact, may represent a system.

The distances of some stars being aproximately known, is it possible to deduce from them their real dimensions, as has been done in the case of the planets and the Sun? It is not, and for a simple reason: the apparent diameter of the most brilliant stars is so small that it defies all measurement. The finest spider's web, placed at the focus of an optical instrument, entirely hides the disk of these bodies. When, by the movement of the Moon across the constellations, the limb of our satellite reaches a star, the occultation is instantaneous. The extinction of the light, instead of being gradual, is sudden and complete. This fact is not extraordinary, when we consider that the diameter of the Sun, removed to the distance of the nearest star, would not measure a hundredth of a second of arc,—an angular quantity so small that it is entirely inappreciable.

But if we suppose that the intrinsic intensity of the light be the same, for Sirius, for example, as for the Sun of our system, we shall arrive at pretty clear, if only conjectural, views on the dimensions of this magnificent star. On this hypothesis, the diameter of Sirius would be fifteen times that of our Sun; so that, even in granting to its light an intrinsic brightness triple that of the Sun, the dimensions of Sirius would still be five times greater, and its volume would be 125 times that of the Sun.

Doubtless these numbers are below the reality; doubtless, also, in the multitude of worlds, so distant and so different from ours, the most varied dimensions distinguish the central bodies and the spheres in which their direct action is felt.

So much for our first sketch of the dimensions of the visible universe. We shall return to this interesting subject, when we describe the structure of this vast *ensemble*, such as the most recent investigations in sidereal astronomy present it to us.

We shall also consider not only isolated stars, but systems of suns, and the series of groups forming clusters more and more numerous, and more and more extensive.

VI.

MOVEMENTS OF STARS.

Stars not Immovable in Space—Measure of their proper Motions: Velocities of some of them—Translation of the Solar System through Space.

It was for a long time believed that the stars preserved invariably their relative positions; that they and the Sun also were immovable in space. Hence, the term *fixed stars*, which has so long been assigned to them, in opposition to the wandering ones, or *planets*. Modern astronomical observations, rendered much more precise by the perfection of the instruments now employed, has at length exploded the idea of the immovability of the star.

Movement is the common law of all bodies. In our Solar system, the planets and their satellites are endowed, as we have seen, both with a movement of rotation round their centres, and with a movement of revolution round their common focus. As to the Sun, it is now known that he also turns on his axis in about twenty-five days; and, lastly, comets likewise possess rapid movements, which carry them to great distances beyond the limits of the planetary world.

More than this, the Sun himself moves through space, and draws with him all his numerous train, and yet the distances and relative positions of the different stellar bodies undergo no apparent change. Member of a vaster system, and one still unknown, he describes in thousands—in millions—of centuries, perhaps, his immense orbit.

The same thing holds with all the other suns or stars; the movements of a great number among them have been demonstrated, and already even we possess some knowledge of the direction and velocity of these movements.

Let us endeavour to show, by the aid of a familiar comparison, how it is possible to assure ourselves of these facts.

Let us suppose ourselves immovable in the centre of an extensive plain, crossed by roads and railways in various directions, on which pedestrians, carriages, and trains, are travelling with varying velocities. If these moving bodies are near us, they appear to move with great relative rapidity. But the more distant they are, the more their apparent velocity will diminish, until, when on the horizon, they appear to move with a slowness, which nearly approaches a state of rest; at this moment, if we examine them with a telescope, their apparent velocity will again recover somewhat of the rate it had lost, but only to vanish again in proportion as the distance becomes more considerable.

It is thus with the proper movements of the stars: at first completely imperceptible, they have at length been revealed to astronomers furnished with powerful instruments, and provided, moreover, with measuring apparatus of infinite delicacy. It has thus been shown that many stars are displaced with unequal velocities and in different directions. But we must not be mistaken in the magnitude of these movements, or think we can detect them in a single observation; it requires, indeed, the patient observations of years to establish them.

Let us quote some examples.

The brightest star of Boötes, Arcturus, requires a whole century to traverse only the eighth part of the diameter of the Moon. α Centauri, in the same interval of time, is displaced a quantity measured by the fifth of this diameter. Many others move more slowly still. The most rapid movements are those of the star 61 Cygni, the distance of which has, as we have seen, been measured, and of two stars of the southern heavens, one in the constellation of the Indian, the other in the Ship.

Nevertheless, these three bodies would each require more than 300 years to move across the starry vault a distance equal to the Moon's diameter.

Of course it is only here a question of apparent velocity. To determine the real velocity, the distances of the stars of which the proper motion is measured must be known; now, this element is known—at least for some among them.

It has thus been found that Arcturus moves through space with a velocity not less than 197,000 miles an hour, or 54 miles a second. We give a table of some of the velocities* which have been determined:—

	Miles a second.
Arcturus	54
61 Cygni	40
Capella	30
Sirius	14
α Centauri	13
Vega	13
Polaris	$1\frac{1}{2}$

Thus these stars, which were believed to be fixed, are in perpetual motion; nay, the velocity of some of these distant worlds much exceeds that of the planetary bodies, which varies, as we have seen, between three and thirty miles a second. The Earth, which moves in its orbit with such prodigious rapidity, travels three times more slowly than Arcturus.

How have we arrived at the knowledge of the fact that the Solar system itself in its entirety moves through space? Another familiar comparison will help us to answer this question. Let us place ourselves again in the centre of an extensive plain, bordered at the horizon on every side with rows of trees differently grouped. So long as we ourselves are at rest, these objects keep the same relative positions and distances. But if we move in any one direction, what happens? As we walk, the trees in front of us open out—are gradually separated; while behind us, on the contrary, they will gradually get nearer together, will close up; whilst on either side they will seem to recede in a direction contrary to our movement; these are, it is clear, merely effects of perspective. But between all

* These velocities are possibly still greater, since the paths in space may be inclined, whereas their projections are here in question.

these apparent movements in various directions, and the direction of our walk, there is an intimate connexion, the study of which, if we were not conscious of our movement, would enable us to detect it.

Now the immense expanse of the heavens is our plain, and the trees on the horizon are the stars and the constellations, and the traveller whom we have imagined to walk in a given direction is the Sun and its system.

There are, however, between our supposition and the reality differences which somewhat complicate the problem. The stars, as we have seen, have a real movement of their own, and there are other apparent movements, owing to the movement of revolution of the Earth, and the combination of this movement with the velocity of light. It has, therefore, been necessary to unravel these complicated movements, and to sift out the real from the apparent ones.

If to these difficulties we add those which result from the extreme delicacy of the measurements required, and of the variation of the measuring instruments themselves, an idea will be formed of the sagacity, patience,

Fig. 138.—Point of the heavens towards which the Solar System is travelling in its movement of revolution.

and genius, which have been necessary to arrive at such magnificent conclusions.*

Towards what portion of the sky, then, are we travelling? According to the most recent calculations, the Sun is advancing towards a point situated in the constellation Hercules† with such velocity that in a year it traverses more than once and a half the radius of the terrestrial orbit, or 153,000,000 miles—about 4 miles a second!

The movement of the Sun takes place, possibly, round a centre still unknown to us. The present opinion of astronomers is in favour of the

* The astronomers who have attempted, discussed, and solved this beautiful problem, are, among others, Sir W. Herschel, Argelander, O. Struve, Mädler, and Peters.

† On the straight line which joins the two stars π and μ of this constellation, at a quarter of the separating distance from the first.

Pleiades being the centre of this movement, but precise knowledge on this point is difficult to arrive at.

If the stars move unequally and in different directions,—if the Sun progress towards a certain point in the heavens, how will this eventually show itself in the aspect of the starry vault? By a continual change, which will ultimately give to the constellations groupings vastly differing from those under which they are at present seen. 'The Southern Cross,' says Humboldt, 'will not always keep its characteristic form, for its four stars travel in different directions and with unequal velocities. At the present time it is not known how many myriads of years must elapse until its entire dislocation.' We may, then, rest quiet, and study the sky as it is, without fearing present confusion: let us leave to our descendants of the year 9000 to determine the position which the star of the Hunting Dogs, known as No. 1830 Groombridge, will then occupy. It may possibly be found in Berenice's Hair!

[The Astronomer Royal has recently devised a method by which the whole problem of the Sun's proper motion has been solved *de novo*, and on principles undoubtedly far more exact than any yet applied. It may be thus described. Let us conceive that the Sun has a certain motion in space: that is, let us assign a velocity v and a direction indicated by certain mathematical relations,—the angle, namely, at which the line of the Sun's path is inclined to three fixed lines in space at right angles to each other. Now, when this is done, we can deduce an expression for the apparent motion of each star on the celestial sphere, on the supposition that the assumed solar motion is stopped. In order to do this, however, we must adopt some hypothesis as to the probable distances of the stars of various orders, and also as to the probable errors in the estimated proper motions of the stars. These considerations being attended to, and the sum of all the motions (or rather of their squares) deduced on the above assumption, we have then to find what values for v and for the three angles referred to above, make the sum *least*. These values are the *most probable* elements of the Sun's motion. It will be noticed that the process is free of all hypothetical considerations except those depending on the distance of the fixed stars, and on the probable nature of errors of observation. The results obtained by Airy's method, skilfully worked out under the superintendence of Mr. Dunkin of the Greenwich Observatory, accord most satisfactorily with those obtained by other methods. *But*, although the result which gives the greatest reduction of the stars' apparent motions, accords well with former results, the reduction is not so great as theoretically it might be expected to be. The present writer has shown that from the observed average proper motions of the different orders of stars, the distances of the fainter stars have probably been overrated,—and that the reduction will be materially increased when this consideration is taken into account. By mapping the stellar motions, he has also shown that signs of *star-drift* exist in certain regions of the heavens, which tend to account for the smallness of the corrections deduced by Airy's method.—R. A. P.]

VII.

DOUBLE AND MULTIPLE STARS.

Distinction between Optical and Physical Doubles — Characteristics of the latter — Movements of Revolution of Double Stars — Multiple Systems.

There is, in the vicinity of Vega, the brightest star in the constellation of the Lyre, a small star which appears elongated to some possessed of very keen eyesight, and this appearance suggests that it may really be composed of two luminous points; indeed it is only necessary to examine it with an opera-glass to see that it really consists of two stars separated by an interval equal to about the ninth part of the apparent diameter of the Moon.*

Here, then, we have an example of a coarse and easily divided double star, which a keen eye or an opera-glass of small magnifying power is sufficient to separate into its components. But this is not all; if we employ an instrument of considerable optical power to examine each of the two stars of which the coarse double is composed, we find that each component itself consists of two stars so near together that the intervals separating them are not more than the $\frac{1}{70}$th part of the total distance of the couples themselves,† so that we have here a *double-double* star. A star which appears single to the naked eye becomes quadruple when examined with a powerful telescope.

A century ago, only about twenty double stars were known; now, however, we possess catalogues of more than 6000.‡ Now, is the union of two suns in a small space of the starry vault to be looked upon as purely accidental, or must we rather consider it to indicate a real physical connexion of the two bodies—a real system?

On the first supposition, the proximity of the two stars to each other would be attributed to an effect of perspective; the stars themselves, though widely differing in their distance from us, lying in the same line of sight. In the second case, the two suns are at nearly equal distances, and their apparent connexion proceeds from the relative smallness of the interval which separates them.

Hence a shifting of double stars into optical and physical pairs. As soon as the number of double stars began to increase, it was thought extremely probable that groupings of this kind might not all be owing to the effects of perspective; and the existence of real systems of suns was suggested, before even observation had directly confirmed it; this suggestion has since been abundantly justified.

Out of a total number of 6000 double stars known at the present time,

* 3′ 27″. The star is Epsilon (ε) Lyræ.

† Struve.

‡ Kirch, Bradley, Flamsteed, Tobie and Christian Mayer, Sir W. Herschel, in the last century; the two Struves, Bessel, Argelander, Encke and Gall, Preuss and Mädler, and Sir John Herschel, in the first half of the present one, have assisted in the discovery of these pairs, now so numerous and so interesting.

650 have been demonstrated to be physically connected systems—two suns, turning round a common centre of gravity. There are still more complicated groups—systems of three, or four, or even more suns. In the constellation of Orion, near the centre of the glorious nebula which we shall soon describe, there is a system where the unaided sight only distinguishes a luminous point. With the help of a powerful telescope, however, this point is divided into four stars; these can be seen in a small telescope, in the form of a *trapezium;* but when the telescope of 5 or 6-inches aperture is used, two of the stars in the trapezium are themselves seen to be accompanied by two other very small stars, forming altogether a group of six suns (fig. 139). 'Probably,' says Humboldt, 'the sextuple star, θ Orionis (generally called the "trapezium of Orion"), constitutes a real system, for the five smaller stars have the same proper motion as the principal one.' We may add, that Mr. Lassell has discovered a seventh star in this remarkable system, so that θ Orionis is a septuple star. An attentive study of this group, on which the attention of astronomers is fixed, as it forms such an admirable test-object for their instruments, will eventually show us what truth there is in Humboldt's statement; the various stars will be seen to progress in their orbits, and science will be enriched with a new fact well worthy the attention of geometers:—the reciprocal and simultaneous movement of seven suns.

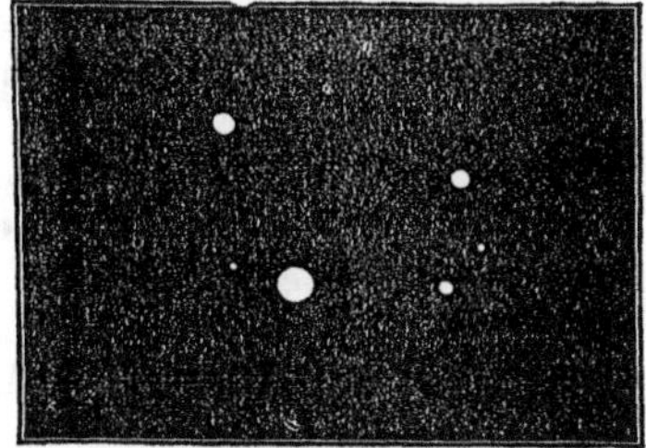
Fig. 139.—The trapezium of Orion. (Sir J. Herschel.)

What magnificence, what variety is there in the constitution of the sidereal universe! Our Solar system places before us the grand spectacle of a central star surrounded with more than a hundred planetary bodies and thousands of comets harmoniously executing their eternal evolutions round the focus of their heat, their light, and life.

In the unfathomable space which surrounds our system, have been revealed to us, at prodigious distances, millions of stars, which are so many suns, surrounded doubtless, for the most part, with a *cortége* of planets like our own. And more than this, among these myriads of systems, we become acquainted with some which present to us the more marvellous association still of suns grouped by twos, and threes, and fours, moving round each other in the same manner as with us the planets move round their common centre.

Not only is the division of double stars into optical and physical couples not arbitrary—founded as it is on precise observations—but it has furnished valuable data for the solution of several most important problems in stellar astronomy. A word on this subject. We can at once recognise that the two components of a double star. or a real or physical system, when the movement of revolution of one round the other is observed.

Thus, the satellite of Castor,* and those of the stars, η Cassiopeæ, *p* Serpentarii, ξ Ursæ Majoris, have completed an entire revolution since the epoch (1780) of the first observations.

The physical couples are again distinguished by another character,—a common proper motion; that is to say, when this is in the same direction and extent, it is extremely probable that we are dealing with a veritable system, although their movement of revolution is so slow that we cannot detect it. As to the optically double stars, they are distinguished by the opposite characteristics; in other words, no movement of revolution can be detected in them, and the proper motion of one is not participated in by the other. Such is the case with the optical couples formed by the companions of Vega, Atair, Pollux, and Aldebaran.

If the double stars of the first kind—the physically connected ones—have increased man's knowledge of the constitution of the Universe, by showing the identity of the laws which govern the stellar worlds with those of the movements of the planets, the optical double stars have furnished, as we shall see in a future chapter, the means of measuring distances, and thus of sounding the depths of the heavens.

We will now proceed to give some details of the principal double stars, the movements of which have been observed and the orbits calculated.

There exists in the constellation of the Great Bear, very near that of the Lion, a star designated in the catalogues by the Greek letter ξ, known as a double star since 1782. The two components of this system are, one of the fourth, the other of the fifth magnitude. The movement of revolution of the second round the first† having been detected, a French astronomer, Savary, determined by calculation the elements of the orbit. The period of revolution is sixty-one years, whence it follows that, since the discovery of the system, the orbit has been entirely traversed, and that one-third of the second period is already completed.

The elliptical or oval form of the orbit of this binary is very decided; its excentricity is comparable to the orbits of our periodical comets, since, even among the telescopic planets, there is no orbit which differs so much from a circle. But among the double stars there are some the orbits of which are still more elongated. Such is that of α Centauri, the period of revolution of which exceeds seventy-eight years.

We may cite the following periods of double stars which have been determined:—

ζ Herculis	36 years
ζ Cancri	59 ,,
μ Coronæ Borealis	66 ,,
p Ophiuchi	92 ,,
γ Virginis	150 ,,
61 Cygni	452 ,,

* Castor is a binary system to which, according to Struve, doubtless belongs a third star, which participates in the proper movement of the two others. Here then are two suns accompanied with a third sun fifteen times more distant from the first than is the second.

† Or, rather, the movement of each star round the common centre of gravity of the system.

There is, as is seen by this table, great variety in the periods, the latter surpassing the first by twelve times. But it is probable that some still more divergent will be found. In Berenice's Hair, and in the Lion, there are two pairs, the first of which has a period of less than fourteen years, whilst the second completes its orbital movement in twelve centuries.*

If we have been able to determine the form of the paths described by these pairs of suns, and the duration of their periodical movements, we are still—to speak generally—far from knowing the absolute dimensions of the orbits: to determine these we must, of course, know the distances of the stars from us. We know this, however, in the case of α Centauri and 61 Cygni.

The mean distance from each other of the two stars which compose the second of these systems is not less than 1,019,000,000 miles. Compared to the distances of the planets from the Sun, this distance is comprised between those of Saturn and Uranus. The orbit of the companion of 61 Cygni has a mean radius of about forty-five times the distance of the Sun from the Earth, or more than 4,275,000,000 miles. Let us bear in mind, that such dimensions are quite lost to the unaided sight; so immense is the distance of these stars that a powerful telescope only can divide them.

That astronomy has arrived at such a point of perfection as to be able to calculate the elements of such distant systems is indeed an admirable result, and a proof of the power of calculation when supported by observations worthy of confidence. But this is not all: it is now demonstrated, that the laws which regulate the stellar systems are identical with those which govern the bodies of our own system; we have thence been able to form an approximate estimate of the masses of these bodies. Thus it has been found that 61 Cygni—that small star scarcely visible to the naked eye—weighs more than a third of our Sun.

Quite recently, the exactitude of these theoretical deductions has received a brilliant confirmation. Every one knows Sirius, the brightest star of the heavens. While studying with minute care the proper movement of this magnificent sun, the illustrious Bessel—one of the greatest astronomers and geometers of the century—suspected the existence of a satellite, the mass of which, acting on the central star, produced variations in its movement. Was this satellite a dark body analogous to our planets, or a secondary sun, the light of which is lost in the dazzling rays of Sirius? On this point nothing was known; other astronomers attempted the same problem, and one of them, M. Peters, calculated for the unknown orbit a period of fifty years. Such was the state of things when an American optician, Mr. Alvan Clark, on the 31st of January, 1862, in turning a new and powerful telescope on Sirius, discovered the satellite, the cause of the observed perturbations. Since that time it has been again seen by

* Both these periods are, however, uncertain.

other astronomers;* and it now remains to verify by observation the orbit and period calculated before its discovery.

When a branch of science, scarcely known two centuries ago, and cultivated steadily less than a hundred years, arrives at such results, what may we not hope for the future progress of sidereal astronomy?

Doubtless, many points will long remain in the domain of conjecture. But, without overstepping probabilities, it will gradually be more and more possible to form a correct idea, both of the unity of the laws which govern the celestial bodies, and of the infinite variety of the phenomena which they offer to man's observation.

We may thus liken the innumerable suns scattered over the heavens to the central body of our own system. Doubtless, round each revolve other bodies, some like our planets, others, perhaps, gaseous, like our comets. The phenomena of day and night, and of the seasons, again occur in those secondary worlds, rendered invisible by their immense distance. By carrying ourselves to the phenomena of our planetary system, we can conceive those eternally going on in the worlds of which we speak.

But how much more varied still must be the phenomena in those systems, composed of two or three, or even more suns, with their varying lights and heats, sometimes combined and sometimes experienced in succession. Let us imagine ourselves, for example, on one of the planets of the triple sun ψ Cassiopeæ; the movements of rotation and revolution of such a planet, combined with the movements of revolution of the three light-giving bodies, would bring on its horizon sometimes one, sometimes the other of the suns of the system, and sometimes, also, two or there at a time. To periods of day and night would succeed periods of continuous day; and the temperature and seasons would vary also by reason of ever new conditions. To these we must add the varieties of colour which characterise the lights of the component stars of the system,—varieties which would produce on the planet sometimes red days, sometimes green or blue ones, or even days illuminated by a light compounded of these three colours, in varying proportions: an idea will thus be formed of the odd effects of light, and singular contrasts which objects must present according to the hour of the day and the time of the year.

That brings us naturally to say a few words on the colour of the stars in the simple or multiple systems.

* The Rev. W. R. Dawes in England, MM. Chacornac and Goldschmidt at Paris, Mr. Lassell at Malta, Father Secchi at Rome.

VIII.

COLOURED STARS.

Variety of Colours presented by the Stars—Colours of Single Stars—Colours of Double and Multiple Stars—Variations observed in Colour; presumed Causes of their Changes.

THE rapid variations of brightness, which a star presents to the naked eye, are ordinarily accompanied with instantaneous changes of colour; and to these two phenomena combined has been given the name of 'scintillation.' It is, however, known that these changes do not take place in the star, but are caused by our atmosphere, through which the luminous waves reach our eye.

But, independently of these apparent and ever-changing tints, the stars possess real and constant colours, arising from real differences in the nature of the light which they emit.

This we can all see for ourselves. If we observe some of the most brilliant stars in the heavens, it will be remarked that the light of Sirius, of Vega, of Regulus, and of Spica, is perfectly white, whilst Betelgeuse, the brightest star in Orion, and Aldebaran, show a decided red tint.

The Greek astronomers, as remarked by Arago, only recognised red and white stars. Now, however, that this branch of observation is carefully cultivated, all colours, all the tints of the rainbow, have been detected in the light of different stars.*

Among the single stars of reddish tint, we may quote Arcturus, Antares, and a star in the Whale, the famous Mira Ceti, which we shall again soon meet with among the variable stars. Procyon, Capella, and Polaris, are yellow. The light of Castor is green, and that of α Lyræ is of a decided blue tint. Nevertheless, white is undoubtedly the colour of the great majority of stars.

These diverse and permanent tints can only be attributed to real differences in the nature of the light emitted by each sun. If the hypothesis of a photosphere, or incandescent gaseous envelope, now admitted by many of our astronomers in the case of the Sun, be extended to the physical constitution of the stars, it suffices to suppose a different chemical composition in the photospheres of these bodies, or different absorbing

* Observations of this nature are very delicate: and although the use of telescopes renders them more certain, as the star is deprived of nearly all its scintillation, they are still subject to errors, proceeding both from the personality of the observer and the peculiarities of his instrument. We are surprised that there has not yet been instituted a precise mode of observation, in employing, for example, a chromatic scale, the degrees of which would serve for terms of comparison with the coloured lights of the stars.[1]

[1] Since the publication of the first edition of this work, we have received from Admiral Smyth a memoir by that celebrated observer, who proposes a chromatic scale precisely of the kind referred to. The title of this memoir, published in London in 1864, is 'Sidereal Chromatics, or the Colours of Multiple Stars.'

processes going on in their atmospheres, to explain the differences of colour. Doubtless, also, the degree of the temperature of the incandescent media will go for something in influencing the phenomena.

It is in the double and multiple stars that the colour of the light is presented with all its brightness and richness. The greatest variety distinguishes the colours of the components of these systems, already so remarkable from so many other points of view.

The illustrious and laborious astronomer of Dorpat and Poulkowa, M. W. Struve, who has consecrated thirteen years of watching to the examination of 120,000 stars, amongst which he has found more than 3000 double stars, thus writes on this subject: —

'The attentive observation of the bright double stars teaches us, that, besides all those which are white, all the colours of the spectrum are to be met with; also, when the principal star is not white, its light borders on the red side of the spectrum, whilst that of its satellite offers the bluish tint of the opposite end. Nevertheless, this law is not without exception; on the contrary, the most general case is that the two bright stars have the same colours. I find, indeed, among 596 bright double stars, —

375 the two components of which have the same colour and the same intensity;
101 of the same colour, with a different intensity;
120 of totally different colours.

'Among the stars of the same colour, the most numerous are the white, and of the 476 stars of this kind I have found

295 in which the two components are white;
118 „ they are yellow or reddish;
63 „ they are bluish.'

It was at first believed that the blue colour was a simple effect of contrast, owing to the feebleness of the light of the smaller star, compared to the yellow and more brilliant light of the principal one. But if this optical illusion be sometimes met with, observation shows that it is accidental, and that blue stars do really exist. Indeed Struve has as often met with a blue satellite to a white star, as to one of a decided yellow. Besides, couples are mentioned of which the components are both blue. Such are the double stars, δ Serpentis and 59 Andromedæ. Lastly, there is in the Southern heavens a group composed of a multitude of stars, which are all blue.

All possible shades, we have before said, are met with in the coloured double stars. White is found mixed with light or dark red, purple, ruby, and vermilion. Here we have a green star with a deep blood-red companion, there an orange primary accompanied by a purple or indigo-blue satellite. The triple star, γ Andromedæ, is formed of an orange-red sun, accompanied with two others, the light of which is of an emerald-green colour. [If, indeed, one be not blue and the other yellow, the green resulting from the close juxtaposition of the two.] Two stars, the distances and period of whose revolutions we have already cited (61 Cygni and α Centauri), have each for their components two orange-yellow suns.

According to Sir John Herschel, a group, situated in the Southern Cross, near the star Kappa, is extremely remarkable. It is composed of 110 stars, of which seven only exceed the tenth magnitude. Among the principal ones, two are red and ruddy, one is of a greenish blue, two are green, and three others are of a pale green. 'The stars which compose it, seen in a telescope of diameter large enough to enable the colours to be distinguished, have the effect,' says Herschel, 'of a casket of variously coloured precious stones.' *

We have already remarked, that it is necessary to distinguish between the real and constant colours of the stars and the instantaneous and oft-renewed variations due to scintillation. Nevertheless, the constancy of the real colour is not absolute.

It seems at length to be an undoubted fact, that certain stars do change colour. Sirius is the first example of this. The ancients represented it as a red star, while at present this sun is distinguished by its brilliant whiteness.

Two double stars, one of the Lion, the other of the Dolphin, noted as white by Herschel, are now composed of primaries of golden yellow, accompanied by a reddish-green star in the first pair, and a bluish-green one in the second.†

But, after all, this variation of colour will seem less astonishing when we see how much the brightness of the light of the stars itself is subjected to variations.

The cause of the colours of the stars, and of the changes of tint they undergo, is still, as we have before remarked, not entirely accounted for. 'It must be left to time and careful observation,' says Arago, 'to teach us if the green or blue stars are not suns in the process of decay, if the different tints of these bodies do not indicate that combustion is operating upon them at different degrees.'

All that can be at present said with certainty is, that the celestial spaces, far from presenting to us immutability and immobility, are the theatre of incessant movement and continuous transformation. The study of variable stars, and of new or temporary stars, which have suddenly appeared to disappear as suddenly, will again furnish us with decisive proof of a truth that has taken us so long to learn.

* 'Astronomical Observations at the Cape of Good Hope,' p. 17.

† This variation does not seem to be explained by the difference of the instruments used, since the mirrors of Herschel's telescope gave rather a reddish tint to all objects; and it was Struve who first established their colour with the large Poulkowa refractor.

IX.

VARIABLE STARS.

Periodical Changes of Brilliancy of Mira Ceti, and Algol in Perseus—Other Variable Stars—Explanation of these Changes—Hypothesis of the Rotation of Stars.

There is in the constellation of the Whale a star marked on the maps by the Greek letter ο (Omicron), which astronomers know also under the Latin name of *Mira* (the marvellous). This star has been long remarked on account of the periodical variations of its brightness. During each interval of eleven months it passes through the following phases:

During fifteen days it attains and preserves its maximum brightness, which is equal to that of a star of the second magnitude. Its light afterwards decreases during three months, until it becomes completely invisible, not to the naked eye only, but even to our telescopes.*

It remains in this state during five whole months; after which it reappears, its light increasing in a continuous manner during three other months. Its cycle of variability is then ended, and it attains again its maximum brightness to pass a second time through the same phases. These singular variations have been known since the end of the sixteenth century; but the exact measure of the period was only effected a century later. At the present time it is known with great precision, and is valued at 331 days, 15 hours, and 7 minutes.

In truth, irregularities have been discovered in the period of Mira; but these irregularities also are subjected to a periodicity which renders the phenomena still more interesting. The greatest brilliancy does not always rank it in the same magnitude. Sometimes it scarcely exceeds the fourth, whilst at certain epochs (in 1799, for example,†) its light was almost as brilliant as that of the first magnitude, and it was scarcely inferior to Aldebaran.

Mira is not the only example of the periodical change of brightness of stellar light; and the duration of the variations is not always so long as in it. Algol, in the head of Medusa, in the constellation of Perseus (fig. 140), is at least as interesting as Mira, but its period is much shorter, and it is never invisible, even to the naked eye. A star of the second magnitude during two days and thirteen and a half hours, it suddenly decreases, and in three hours and a half descends to the fourth magnitude. Then its brightness regains the ascendant, and at the end of a fresh interval of three hours and a half attains its maximum. All these changes are effected in less than three days, or, more exactly, in 2 days, 21 hours, 49 minutes.

* We are surprised that observations of this singular star have not been pursued with the most powerful instruments during the period of invisibility. It is only known that it is then below the eleventh magnitude.

† The 6th November, as cited in Humboldt's 'Cosmos.'

Among the variable stars with long periods, Betelgeuse, one of the four stars of the great trapezium of Orion, may also be mentioned, the period of this star is nearly 200 days. There is a star in the Swan, the variations of which are effected in 406 days. Three of the seven stars of the Great Bear vary in periods imperfectly known, but they certainly embrace several years.

Fig. 140.—Variable star Algol in Perseus.

In the number of variable stars with short periods, δ Cephei is distinguished by the regularity of its changes of brightness, which last 5 days, 8 hours, 40 seconds. This star has been observed since 1784.

Lastly, there is a great number of stars, the variability of which is proved without their periods having yet been determined, either because these periods are irregular, or because the time they occupy is very considerable.

The preceding examples will suffice to give an idea of the interest attached to these singular phenomena, the cause of which, although suspected, is still unknown. The periodicity even of the changes observed indicates that the variations of brightness are possibly produced by a movement of rotation of the variable itself, or by the movement of revolution of a dark or opaque body round the luminous body.

On the hypothesis of the rotation of the variable stars, it has been held that the different sides of the body vary in luminosity, and even, in certain cases, are completely dark.* Spots of large dimensions, analogous to solar spots, and encroaching on a part of the surface of these suns during long intervals of time, have been suggested to account for the phenomena.

On the other hand, if each star be considered the focus of the movements of dark bodies similar to our planets,—an hypothesis which is far from being completely improbable,—it must happen to a certain number of them, that the planes of the orbits of these secondary bodies, if prolonged, would pass through our system. In this case, at each revolution there would be an eclipse to our eyes of the central body, a partial or total eclipse, according to the dimensions and the respective distances of the dark satellite and its sun. Many satellites of unequal periods would then explain the different phases of variability.

* The idea of Maupertuis, that among the suns there are, doubtless, some of which the forms differ from a sphere, and which are presented to us, by reason of a movement of rotation, sometimes in section, sometimes in plan, scarcely seems in accordance with the principles of mechanics, which account for the figures of celestial bodies.

Another explanation of the variability of certain stars has been suggested by the fact, that, during the minimum of brightness, some of these bodies have appeared surrounded with a kind of mist. This is, that the variability is owing to the interposition of nebulous masses travelling through space, and which, not being self-luminous, would veil, or even quite extinguish, the stars in question.

[The question of variable stars, one of the most puzzling in the whole domain of astronomy, has recently engaged the attention of Mr. Balfour Stewart, who has done so much good work on the Sun,—which by the way, is doubtless a variable star. He remarks, 'We are entitled to conclude, that, in our own system, the approach of a planet to the Sun is favourable to luminosity, and especially in that portion of the Sun which is next the planet. Let us take variable stars. The hypothesis which, without being physically probable, gives yet the best formal explanation of the phenomenon there represented, is that which assumes rotation on an axis, while it is supposed that the body of the star is not equally luminous on every part of its surface. Now, if instead of this, we suppose such a star to have a large planet revolving round it at a small distance, then, according to our hypothesis, that portion of the star which is near the planet, will be more luminous than that which is more remote; and this state of things will revolve round as the planet itself revolves, presenting to a distant spectator an appearance of variation, with a period equal to that of the planet. Let us now suppose the planet to have a very elliptical orbit; then for a long period of time it will be at a distance from its primary, while, for a comparatively short period, it will be very near. We should, therefore, expect a long period of darkness, and a comparatively short one of intense light, precisely what we have in temporary stars.']

Among the variable stars, [as if in proof of Mr. Stewart's hypothesis,] binary couples are noticed. Such is γ Virginis, of which we have had occasion to cite the movement of revolution. The two stars which compose it have changed in brightness, and the most brilliant has become inferior to the other at the end of some years. The variable star, α Cassiopeæ, is also a double star; according to Struve there are many others. 'That which is especially of great importance,' remarks that eminent astronomer, is, that it can be demonstrated from this variability of double stars, that they move round an axis of rotation, and that, in consequence, we have found a fresh analogy between these systems of many suns and our planetary system.' On the hypothesis of dark satellites, it will be seen that, if the analogy seized upon is different, it is not less curious.

According to Mr. Hind, the colour of a great number of variable stars is red; but that is not an essential characteristic; if Mira is of a red colour, the light of Algol is white.*

* [We are enabled, by the kindness of Messrs. Knott and Baxendell, to add here a woodcut (fig. 140*a*), which will give the reader an idea of the method adopted by our observers in this class of observations.

By successively contracting the aperture of the telescope, stars of all magnitudes

As we advance in the study of the stellar world, the apparent uniformity of the heavens, in which the indifferent spectator at first only sees a multitude of luminous points always the same, always immovable, gives place to a most rich and varied picture. The number of phenomena of which we are the witnesses is only equalled by the moulds of time and space in which they are cast.

We have seen, in the Solar system, the most wonderful order governing the combination of the movements of the bodies which compose it, and the simplicity of the means by which the most astonishing differences are everywhere produced. In the sidereal world, the same harmony governs the suns even, the changes of which, as we have seen, are subjected to laws and regulated periods.

It must not be thought, however, that it is necessarily thus with all celestial phenomena, and that regularity is the characteristic sign of the movements or transformations of stars. We are about to describe some phenomena which bear, for the most part the appearance of sudden catastrophes, or which, when they occurred gradually, were rapid enough for observers to register all their phases. These sudden changes will doubtless strike the imagination; but our reason will none the more look upon them as prodigies, habituated as it is to see everything subjected to laws: *Omnia reguntur numero, pondere et mensurâ !*

can be made to disappear. Finding by experiment with what aperture stars of known magnitude became just extinguished, the aperture at which a star so disappears becomes an index of its magnitude. Preparatory, therefore, to commencing operations on a variable star, the observer furnishes himself with a chart of the surrounding stars, with a selected list of conveniently situated comparison stars, whose magnitude is carefully measured in the manner we have indicated. The 'comparison stars' are lettered for convenience of reference. The observer then compares the variable with those stars on the list which differ least from it in brightness, and carefully estimates the difference in tenths of a magnitude. He thus obtains several independent values for the magnitude of the variable at the date of observation. The mean of these is adopted for the night. The successive observations are laid down on cross-ruled paper, the dates of observation forming the abscissæ, and the mean magnitudes the co-ordinates. Through the points thus obtained a curve is laid down; this is the *light-curve*, and from it the dates of maximum and minimum brightness are determined.]

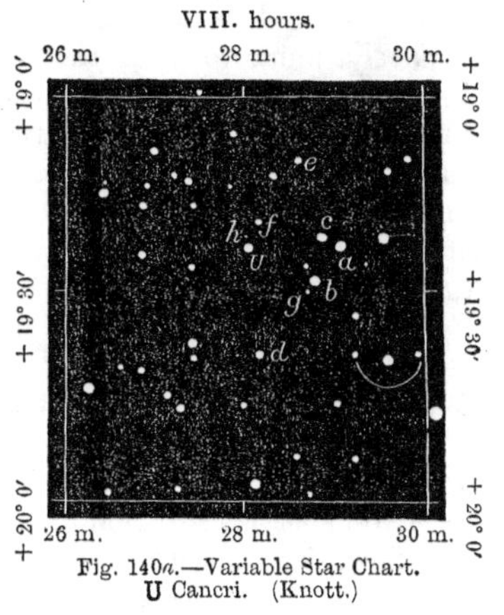

Fig. 140*a*.—Variable Star Chart. U Cancri. (Knott.)

X.

TEMPORARY STARS.

New Stars—Temporary Star of 1572—Lost Stars—Explanation of these Sudden Appearances and Disappearances.

'One night,' writes Tycho Brahé, 'as I was examining as usual the celestial vault, the aspect of which is so familiar to me, I saw with unspeakable astonishment, near the zenith, in Cassiopea, a star of extraordinary brightness. Struck with surprise, I could scarcely believe my eyes. To convince myself that there was no illusion, and to obtain the testimony of other persons, I called the workmen occupied in my laboratory, and I asked them, as well as all the passers-by, if they saw, as I did, the star which had so suddenly made its appearance. I learnt later, that in Germany the coach-drivers and others of the people had acquainted the astronomers of a strange appearance in the sky, and thereby furnished occasion for a renewal of the accustomed railing against scientific men.'

It was in the course of November, 1572, that this strange apparition took place.

The new star observed by Tycho had none of the appearances of a comet; no nebulous head, no tail accompanied it; it, moreover, remained completely immovable in the same point of the heavens during the seventeen months that it was visible. It twinkled in an extraordinary manner, and at first its brightness exceeded that of Vega, Sirius, and even Jupiter at its smallest distance from the Earth. 'It could only be compared,' says Tycho, 'to that of Venus in quadrature.' It also remained visible in the day, at noon, when the sky was clear. But, by degrees, its light diminished in intensity.

In January, 1573, it was already less brilliant than Jupiter; from the month of April it passed from the first to the second magnitude; after this it rapidly decreased, and disappeared at last in March, 1574.

Not only was this extraordinary star variable in its brightness, but even its colour was subjected to rapid changes; first, white during the first two months, the period of its greatest brilliancy; afterwards it passed to yellow, then to red. Tycho then compared it to Mars, to Betelgeuse, and especially to Aldebaran. Lastly, in the spring of 1573, the red colour reappeared, and remained until the end of its visibility.

Several similar appearances have been noticed in more remote times in various regions of the sky; two of them are especially interesting. They were observed in 945 and in 1264, between Cepheus and Cassiopea, nearly in the same position as that taken up by the *Pilgrim*, the name given to the star of 1572. If this identity were actually established, temporary stars would then be shown to be no other than periodical variable stars, a conclusion at which we have before hinted; and the only difference between them would arise from the inequality of the cycle of variability, and of the intensity of the variations.

[From a careful reduction of the places recorded by Tycho Brahé, Argelander has arrived at the following figures, as giving its position for 1865 :—

R.A.		Decl.
h m s		
4 19 57·7	. . . . .	$+63^{\circ}\ 23'\ 55''{\cdot}4$

taking up the theory that this temporary star is really a long-period variable, he has been inquiring whether any suspicious star exists in or near the above place. He finds that D'Arrest has observed a star of the $10\frac{1}{2}$ magnitude, in the following position :—

R A.		Decl.
h m s		
4 19 30	. . . . .	$+60^{\circ}\ 22'{\cdot}9$

Many years ago, observers sought in vain for a star in this position, and, it may be, that D'Arrest's star may be the great temporary star of 1572 slowly recovering its light. Nor are the intervals between the dates we have mentioned widely different; the mean of them gives 1885 as the epoch of its maximum.]

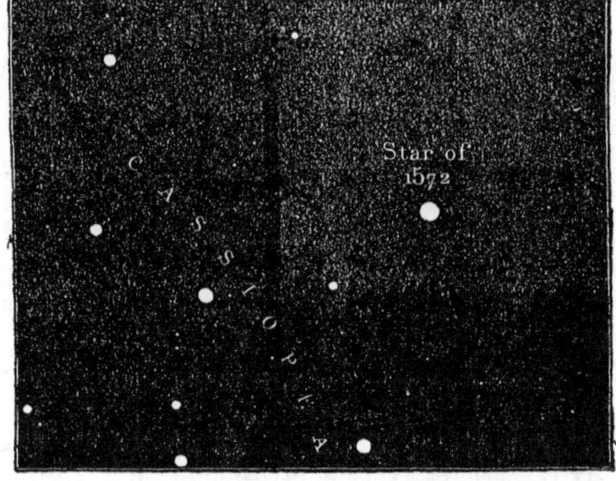

Fig. 141.—New and temporary star of 1572, in Cassiopea.

Since the observation of Tycho Brahé, many temporary stars have been seen in the constellations of Serpentarius and Cygnus.*

But the most brilliant of all these—that of 1604, which was, however, inferior to that of 1572—was especially remarkable by its vivid scintillation; it disappeared like the first, leaving no trace behind.

Among these stars some have been recorded which, after having varied in brightness, have remained visible, preserving permanently their last phase of brightness.

Lastly, some stars, the first appearance of which was not observed, have disappeared. Hence the names *temporary stars*, *new stars*, and *lost stars*, given to these three kinds of stars respectively.

* Most of the new or temporary stars have made their appearance either in or near the Milky Way. Tycho hence concluded that these bodies were formed of the matter of which this great nebula was then thought to consist; but this opinion, at present, is inadmissible, since it is now known that the Milky Way is entirely composed of distinct stars.

To what causes must these truly extraordinary phenomena be ascribed? If we suppose these stars to be variable, it is still difficult to explain these quick changes of brightness, these nearly sudden appearances of bodies, which at once attain their greatest brightness.

It has been attempted to account for them by supposing them to be endowed with very rapid movements; but, of all the hypotheses, this is evidently the most improbable. Arago, examining this question,* shows, that to pass from the first to the second magnitude by a simple change of distance, a star would require six years, in the case of a star travelling with the velocity of light, or 192,000 miles a second. Now, the star of 1572 underwent this change in a month, and we must suppose for it a velocity 72 times greater, that is to say, a velocity 200,000 times greater than that of any known star.

On the other hand, if these phenomena are explained by some stupendous process of combustion—some sudden conflagrations taking place on the surfaces of bodies until then obscure, by progressive extinction inducing first a decrease of brightness, and afterwards disappearance—such catastrophes are well adapted to strike our imagination, and to destroy the ancient idea of the immutability of the heavens.

Perhaps electric and magnetic powers play some part in the production of these gigantic *coups de théâtre*. Humboldt seems inclined towards this idea. He protests against the hypothesis of destruction, of the actual combustion of the stars which have disappeared. 'That which we see no more,' he says, 'has not necessarily ceased to exist. . . . The eternal play of apparent creation and apparent destruction does not prove an annihilation of matter; it is a pure transition towards new forms, determined by the action of new forces. Some stars which have become obscure, may again suddenly become luminous, by the renewal of the same conditions which, in the first instance, developed their light.'

It is, perhaps, yet more difficult to imagine these variations due to movements of rotation. The various faces must, indeed, be supposed to be of a prodigiously unequal brightness; and, even in that case, the sudden appearances could scarcely be accounted for, attaining, as they do, at once, the maximum intensity. The changes of colour would be likewise inexplicable on this hypothesis.

Lastly, some astronomers attribute these appearances and disappearances to the movement of nebulous masses, not self-luminous; a kind of cosmical cloud, interposed between the star and our system, might produce an eclipse, and this eclipse might cease when the 'clouds' had entirely passed. Thus, lost stars, as well as new and temporary stars, would be at once explained.

It is difficult to say which is the most probable of these hypotheses. The truth is that, although the phenomena which have suggested them are facts,—authentic facts,—we are yet quite at a loss to assign a cause for them.

* 'Annuaire du Bureau des Longitudes, 1842,' p. 327.

We will bring this chapter to a close with a description of the most astonishing of all the phenomena of this kind,—namely, the variations of the star η Argûs; a singular star, which can be classed neither among the temporary nor among the variable stars.

Fig. 142.—Variable star, Eta Argûs.

Towards the end of the seventeenth century this star was only of the fourth magnitude; less than a century after, in 1751, it attained the second. Sixty years later, it again descended to its first brightness, increasing anew until the year 1826. From that epoch, it has passed through the most astonishing phases, oscillating between the first and second magnitudes, sometimes equal to α Crucis, then to α Centauri; surpassing Canopus, and approaching lastly to Sirius. The rapidity of these changes, their unequal periods, the long duration of this state of variability, the impossibility of finding a law more or less regular, all contribute to make this beautiful star one of the most curious objects of the sky.

Let us think for a moment on the actual phenomena, which give rise to such metamorphoses. Let us reflect on the vicissitudes necessarily undergone by the planets which move round such a strange sun, arising from the variations in the intensity of its light and heat, and on the stupendous changes which are the necessary consequence. Perhaps our Sun has been, or will be one day, the scene of like variations, which are only, after all, the manifestations of the eternally active forces which govern all systems.*

XI.

STAR-GROUPS.

Natural Groupings of Stars—Groups Visible to the Naked Eye—The Pleiades—The Hyades—Præsepe.

Are the stars that are visible to the naked eye spread orderless on the celestial vault? or is there not between those, apparently most closely connected, some real or physical connexion which requires us to rank them in natural groups?

* A contemporary astronomer, Mr. F. Abbott, who has followed the variations of η Argûs until now, informs us that after having, in 1843, attained the brilliancy of Sirius, it diminished progressively, passing through all the orders of intermediate magnitudes between the first and sixth. In 1863 it was no longer visible to the naked eye.

These questions have been already partly solved, by what is known of the double and multiple star-systems. Soon, exploring the regions of the sky visible by means of the telescope, we shall have to pass in review a multitude of stellar associations, in which suns are found so compact and so numerous, and the form of the groups so regular, that it is impossible to deny their reciprocal dependence.

But long before the discovery of these islands, these archipelagos of worlds, scattered with such astonishing profusion over the infinite, the naked eye had already distinguished a certain number of groups, the stars composing which were so near together that it was impossible to doubt their physical connexion.

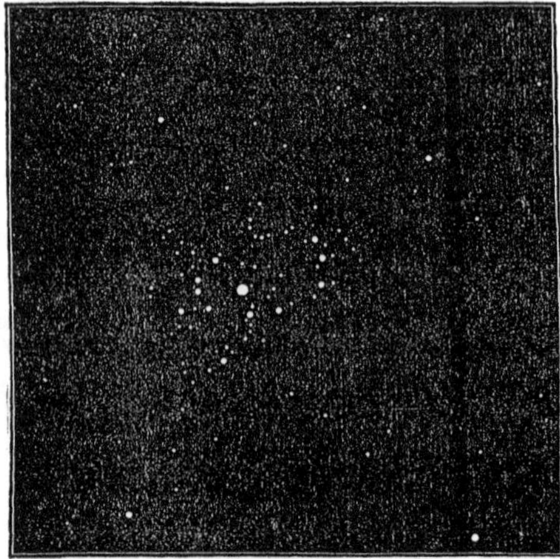

Fig. 143.—The Pleiades. (Harding.)

Such, for example, is the group of the Pleiades. Such, again, are the groups known under the names of the Hyades, of Præsepe, and of Berenice's Hair. All are visible to the naked eye, and good eyes distinguish without difficulty the principal stars of the first-named groups. The Pleiades (fig. 143) are situated in the constellation of the Bull, which we can distinguish so easily, to the north-west of Orion and Aldebaran.

Of about eighty stars, which form the group of the Pleiades, six are visible without the help of telescopes. Formerly, the Latin poet tells us, seven were counted, which may be held to prove that one of them is variable, and has diminished in brightness, or else has disappeared.

[But the power of different eyes in distinguishing stars in a group of this kind, varies extremely, and Ovid's remark,—

'Quæ septem dici, sex tamen esse solent,'

although it still ordinarily applies, must not be insisted on too strongly. One member of the family of the Astronomer Royal habitually sees seven stars, and on rarer occasions twelve—those shown in the accompanying diagram (fig. 144).]

The most brilliant, Alcyone, is of the third magnitude; Electra and Atlas are of the fourth; Merope, Maïa, and Taygete, of the fifth. Three others again have received particular names, although they are below the limit of ordinary vision; these are Pleione, Celeno, and Asterope, from the sixth to the eighth magnitude. All the others are only visible by the aid of a telescope; but with an ordinary glass it is possible to distinguish a large number. The Pleiades * are known under the name of the *Hencoop*, doubtless because Alcyone appears in the group as a hen surrounded with her chickens.

Fig. 144.—The Pleiades as seen with the naked eye.

The *Hyades*, which are near the Pleiades, form a less numerous and more scattered group. The bright light of Aldebaran, which is, as is known, of the first magnitude, renders them more difficult to distinguish with the naked eye.

They appear in the rainy season. Hence their name of Hyades, from the Greek word which signifies 'to rain.'

The connexion of the stars which compose this group is not so striking as in the case of the Pleiades. Nevertheless, it seems difficult to admit that they are quite independent of each other's attraction. In examining the position of these two groups in the vicinity of the Milky Way, and observing that both are situated in the prolongation of a branch of the great zone, we are almost entitled to consider them as two clusters of stars belonging to the immense stellar stratum which surrounds us, and in the midst of which it will be seen that the Sun himself is placed.

In Berenice's Hair, most of the stars are visible to the naked eye, and are perfectly distinguished in the sky, a little to the east of the Lion. No very brilliant star in the vicinity inconveniences the eye by effacing their light.

The next group is situated in the Crab, and is known under the name of *Præsepe*; it is visible to the unassisted sight; but it is impossible to distinguish the separate stars without the help of a telescope. Nevertheless, an instrument of moderate power easily separates them, and they then take the aspect represented in fig. 146.

The groups which we have just described form a transition between the stars scattered over the celestial vault and the more condensed clusters, the

* The ancient poets also called them Hesperides or Atlantides. The name of Pleiades is stated to have been derived from πλεῖν, which signifies 'to navigate:' because, according to Lalande, in the spring and near the epoch when they rise with the Sun, the season for navigating the Mediterranean commences. Others say that these stars were dreaded by mariners, on account of the rains and storms which seemed to rise with them, which they attributed to their influence.

undefined aspect of which caused them formerly to be designated under the general name of *Nebulæ.* [This designation, however, is now much more limited, as we shall see by-and-by.]

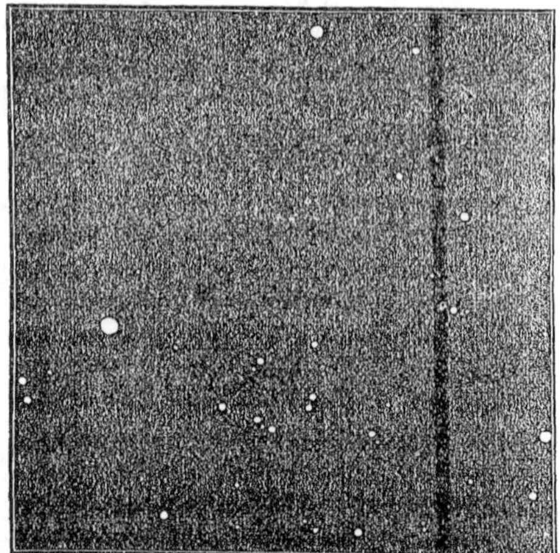

Fig. 145.—The Hyades. (Harding.)

Doubtless, if we could place ourselves in space, and contemplate from a sufficiently distant stand-point, the whole of the stars which appear to us isolated, we should see them condensed into one or several distinct groups, analogous to those of the Pleiades; whilst, were we to penetrate into the midst of one of these compact clusters, we should see the stars of which it is formed separated, and scattered over the celestial vault in such a way as to give it the aspect of our own heavens.

[It is certain, however, that even among the stars visible in our own heavens, laws of aggregation and segregation can be noticed. Instead of that generally uniform distribution over the heavens which has so long been assumed to prevail, there are regions where lucid stars are gathered together in much greater numbers than elsewhere, and others where such stars are remarkably infrequent. The present writer has indicated the regions of greatest richness and poverty. In the northern heavens the rich regions cover the north polar constellations, and extend to Lacerta, Cygnus, Lyra, and Hercules. In the southern they surround almost centrally the greater Magellanic Cloud, and cover nearly half of the southern heavens. But the Milky Way is also a region of great richness, as respects lucid stars (that is, stars visible to the naked eye), not only where it crosses the before-named rich regions

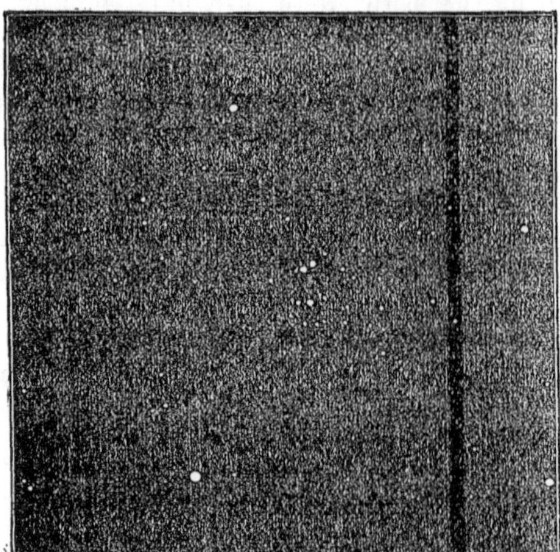

Fig. 146.—Præsepe in Cancer.

but throughout its whole extent. In the southern heavens stars are nearly three times as richly spread over the Milky Way as over the heavens generally; in the northern the proportion is not quite so great, but is still large. When we note that the Milky Way compared with the rest of the heavens as regards extent, is as 1 to 10, while, as regards the number of stars the ratio is as 1 to about 4¼, we see at once that there is a well-marked aggregation of stars along the Milky Way. Yet the gaps and *lacunæ* in the Milky Way, and the regions of the sky bordering upon it, are singularly bare of stars. The conclusion is obvious, and may be regarded as demonstrated, that the lucid stars seen on the Milky Way are really immersed among these stars (which must needs therefore be much smaller), whose combined light produces the milky light of the galaxy.—R. A. P.]

XII.

STAR-CLUSTERS.

Clusters of Stars of Globular and Spherical Form — Enormous number of Stars in certain Clusters—Clusters in Perseus, Centaurus, Toucan, Aquarius, &c.—Curious Forms of some Clusters.

Among star-clusters, a very small number, as we have before remarked, are bright enough or considerable enough to be visible to the naked eye. In all of these, the stars are so close together, that it is impossible not to recognise in them real stellar groups,—real companionship,—real systems of Suns.

[Of this class, the cluster in Perseus is at once a striking example, and one of the most glorious objects in the heavens. Let the reader search for its faint glimmer in the Milky Way, between the bright stars in Cassiopea and Perseus, and turn even a small hand-telescope upon it, the sight will well repay him; but if a six-inch or a larger aperture can be used, he will never forget the glorious picture unfolded before him.]

Their generally rounded form gives them a cometary aspect, and observers, not completely familiar with the divers regions of the sky, may easily be, and indeed sometimes are, mistaken in their nature; although the permanence of their form, and especially of their position, is a characteristic which should suffice to distinguish them from comets.

There are also some clusters, although these are not numerous, the contours of which are very irregular; in these, the number of the stars is generally much smaller than in the clusters of globular form, and their distribution is also very different. If we look at the figures 1, 2, 3 (see Frontispiece), we shall be struck with the remarkable condensation of the luminous points at the centre. This condensation is easily explained, if we suppose that the real form of the cluster is nearly that of a spherical globe. Then, even on the hypothesis that the stars are equally distributed, it will be understood, that, as the visual ray traverses its centre throughout all the extent of its diameter, and as in approaching the borders, it traverses smaller and smaller portions, the laws of perspective will account for the apparent collection of the luminous points at the centre.

But the increase of brightness from the border to the centre is often more rapid than the hypothesis of an equal distribution of the stars in the interior will sanction. It has been held, therefore, that, besides the apparent or purely optical condensation, there exists a real condensation, which is produced, doubtless, by the influence of the central forces, resulting from the separate attractions of each of the suns which compose these systems.

'How can these isolated systems,' says Humboldt,* 'be maintained? How can the suns, which crowd at the interior of these systems, accomplish their revolutions freely and without clashing?'

These questions, which apply to all clusters, are the most difficult of all the problems of celestial mechanics. But it must not be forgotten that these stellar aggregations are situated at great distances, and that their particles, so to speak, which seem to us so near one another, have between them intervals perhaps as considerable as the distance of our Sun from the nearest star. Their movements are, therefore, doubtless effected with all freedom, through spaces as vast as the general equilibrium necessitates, and with a relative slowness proportionate to the dimensions of their orbits. The number of stars contained in clusters of a globular form is often prodigious.

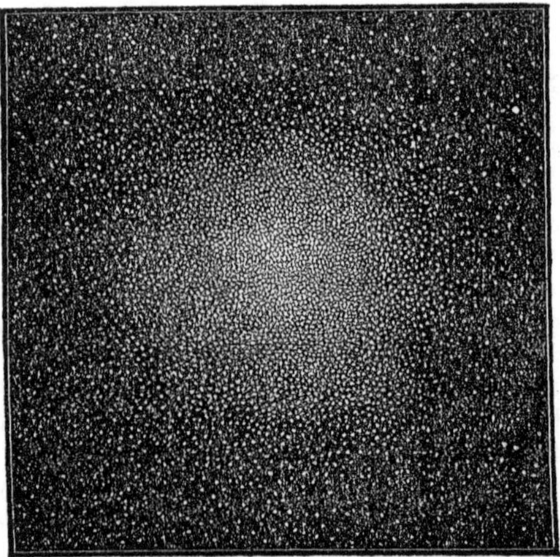

Fig. 147.—Star-cluster near ω Centauri. (Sir J. Herschel.)

We have seen that the cluster of the Southern Cross, so curious on account of the varied colours of its components, only contains 110 stars, but Herschel has calculated that many clusters contain 5000 collected in a space, the apparent dimensions of which are scarcely the tenth part of the surface of the lunar disk.

Such is the cluster situated between the two stars η and ζ Herculis (Frontispiece, No. 2), one of the most magnificent in our northern heavens on fine nights; this cluster is visible to the naked eye as a lumi-

* 'Cosmos,' vol. iii. p. 153.

nous spot of rounded form ; in the telescope, it is resolved into a multitude of stars, and preserves its globular appearance, but is fringed on the borders with several threads of outlying stars.

The cluster near ω Centauri (fig. 147) is also visible to the naked eye, and shines as a star of the fourth or fifth magnitude; it is resolved, by very powerful instruments, into a multitude of stars greatly condensed towards the centre, the light of which varies between the thirteenth and fifteenth magnitudes.

The beautiful cluster in Aquarius, which Sir J. Herschel's drawing exhibits as fine luminous dust (Frontispiece, No. 4), when examined through the Earl of Rosse's powerful reflector appeared (fig. 148) like a magnificent globular cluster, entirely separated into stars.

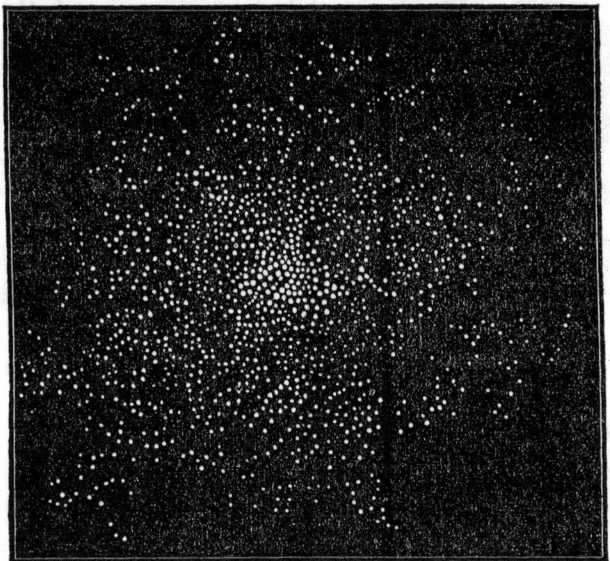

Fig. 148.—Cluster in Aquarius. (Lord Rosse.)

But the most beautiful specimen of this kind is, without doubt, the splendid cluster in Toucan, quite visible to the naked eye in the vicinity of the smaller Magellanic Cloud, in a region of the southern sky entirely void of stars. The condensation at the centre of this cluster is extremely decided; there are three perfectly distinct gradations, and the orange red colour of the central agglomeration contrasts wonderfully with the white light of the concentric envelopes.

The clusters of spherical form are ordinarily the richest, and the telescope has the least difficulty in analyzing them into stars.

Nevertheless, among the others there are some, the resolution of which, until lately impossible, has been accomplished by the use of telescopes of

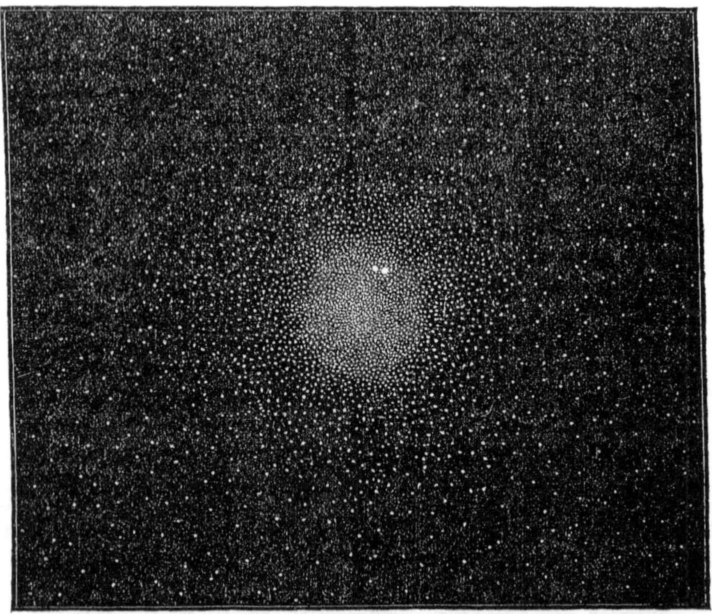

Fig. 149.—Cluster in Toucan. (Sir J. Herschel.)

the greatest optical power. Such is the oval nebula in Andromeda, of which more anon.

Here are some curiously formed clusters (fig. 150), in which every indi-

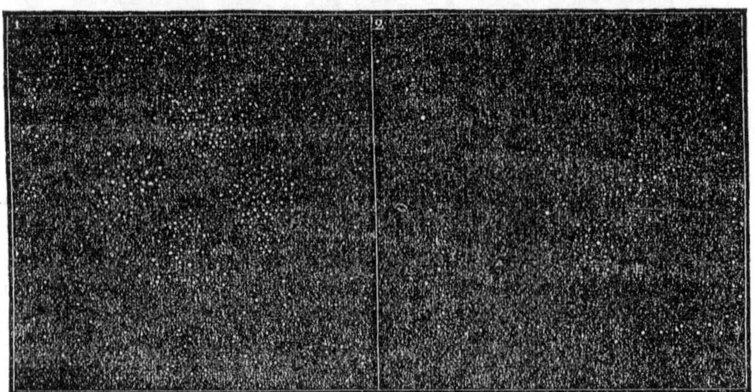

Fig. 150.—Clusters of singular forms. (Sir. J. Herschel.)
1. Cluster in Scorpio. 2. Cluster in the Altar.

cation of concentration has disappeared. The drawing which represents the cluster in the Twins (Frontispiece, No. 6) shows it to be intermediate between the irregular groups, and the clusters of decidedly spherical form which we have passed under review. At the summit of a kind of pyramid —the form of this singular cluster—the luminous points seem to press towards a preponderant mass. In the clusters in figure 150, nothing similar is seen.

The clusters are not equally distributed over the heavens; they are most numerous in the Milky Way, and in the two Magellanic Clouds. The region richest in globular clusters is situated in the southern hemisphere, and forms an important portion of the Milky Way, comprised between the constellations of the Wolf, Altar, Scorpion, Southern Cross, and Sagittarius.

In describing the most beautiful of the star-clusters, that of Toucan, we remarked that the central part is rose-colour, surrounded with a white concentric border. The cluster being entirely resolved into stars, this coloration evidently belongs to each of the components; a fact which will not surprise us, after that which has been seen of the simple and double coloured stars.

The cluster in the Southern Cross, which, as we have seen, is formed of a great number of white stars, interspersed with some red, green, and blue stars, appears as a white cluster. On the other hand, we have quoted a cluster of the southern sky entirely composed of blue stars.

The colour of these star-clusters is then easily explained by the predominant colour of the stars of which they are composed.

XIII.

THE MILKY WAY.

General Aspect of the Milky Way—Its Course through the Northern and Southern Constellations—Resolvability into Stars and Star-Clusters—Impenetrability of certain regions of the Milky Way.

WITH the exception of the Magellanic Clouds, of which more anon, and a few star-clusters, all the star-groupings which we have yet reviewed are invisible to the naked eye. Their extremely small apparent dimensions contribute to this result, bearing in mind the prodigious distances at which they lie from the solar world,—distances which so considerably weaken the brightness of the component stars.

It is not thus with the Milky Way. The light of this immense zone is, one might almost say, bright; its extent, which embraces the entire circumference of the starry vault, and its breadth, are so considerable, that it is readily distinguished at the first *coup d'œil*, whenever the apparent movement of the heavens brings it above the horizon.

This last circumstance occurs, it is true, every night of the year and in all latitudes; but the Milky Way is much better visible when it rises to a great height; and to see it best we must, therefore, choose certain epochs of the year or certain hours of the night.

The general appearance of the Milky Way is that of a long nebulous train, which follows very nearly the circumference of a grand circle of the celestial vault. First of all, it may be remarked, that it is divided into two principal branches throughout nearly half its entire length. Its breadth is very variable; sometimes it contracts so as to occupy no more than six to eight times the lunar diameter, at others it spreads out to an extent four times as great.

Before stating what is known of the composition and structure of this immense congregation of stars, let us describe it as a whole, noting the principal constellations which it traverses in both hemispheres. We will avail ourselves for this purpose of the two Plates XIX and XX, which show it as it is seen in a small telescope, with the variations in form and brilliancy which its different ramifications present.

The northern half of the Milky Way extends from the constellations of the Eagle and the Serpent to the Unicorn, at the altitude of, and near, the belt of Orion. Divided into two branches from the Equator as far as the Swan, it passes by Atair, and traverses the Arrow and the Fox, besides the constellations before named. Near the Swan a dark opening is observed in it, a kind of gap through which the sight plunges into the distant regions of the sky beyond the regions occupied by this zone. One branch is directed towards the Little Bear and Cepheus, and it is in this part that it approaches nearest to the northern pole of the heavens. It afterwards bears away under the form of a single and narrow branch, which traverses Cassiopea, passes by the Waggoner very near Capella, borders the eastern portion of the Twins, and of the Little Dog, and the southern portion of Orion. Before arriving at this point, a branch leaves the main portion in Perseus, and stretches as far as the Pleiades, where it is lost.

The northern portion of the Milky Way presents the greatest intensity in the Eagle and in the Swan: in Perseus and near the Unicorn, it is the least luminous.

Let us now follow its course through the southern hemisphere. After having crossed the Equator and passed Sirius, it enters the Ship, gradually increasing in brightness; it is then divided into several branches which extend fan-like over a large area, and disappear all at once, reappearing further on in the same constellation.

These branches are again united in the Centaur and Southern Cross, at a point where the breadth of the Milky Way is at its minimum. Here is the famous *Coal-Sack*, a dark gap in the form of a pear; surrounded on every side by the nebulous zone, the eye can only perceive in it one or two stars.

Very near α Centauri, the Galaxy is divided anew into two principal

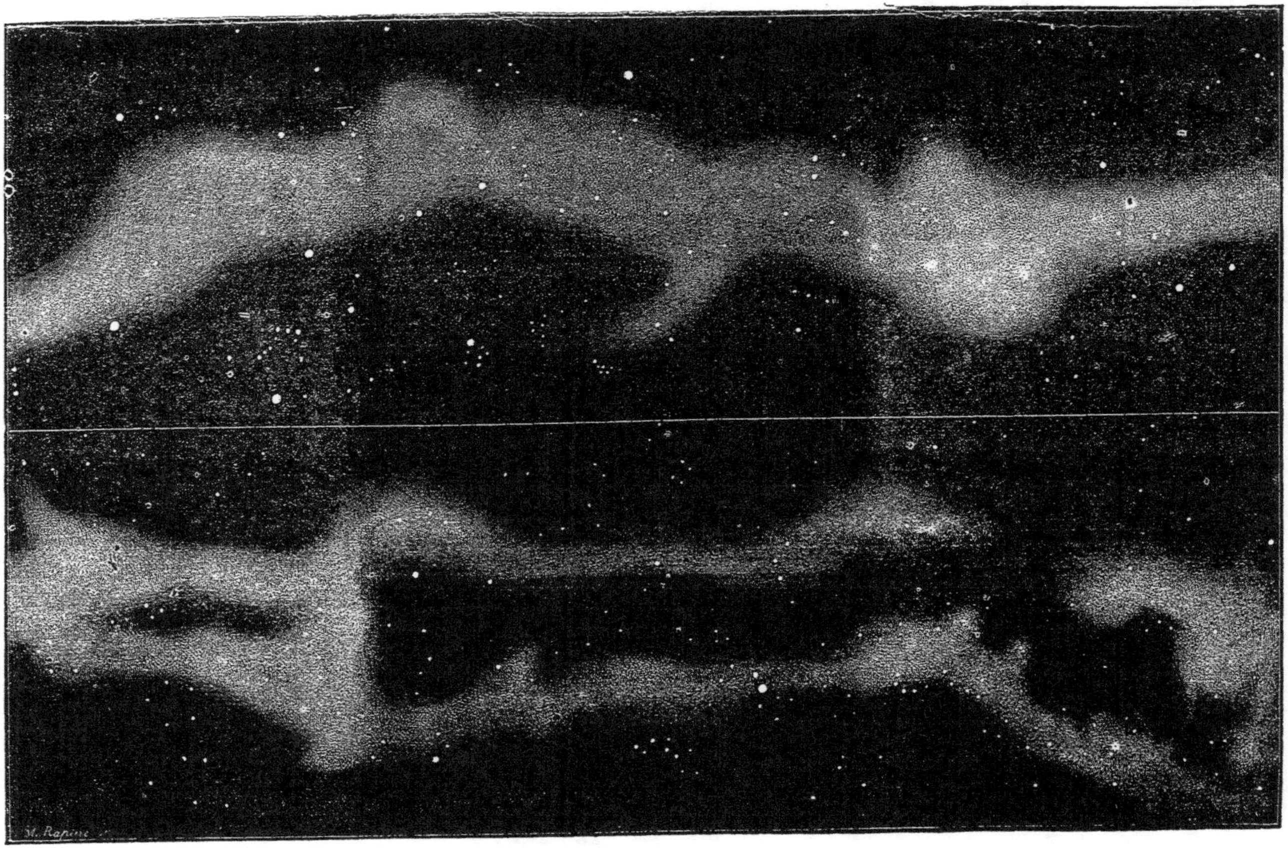

NORTHERN MILKY WAY

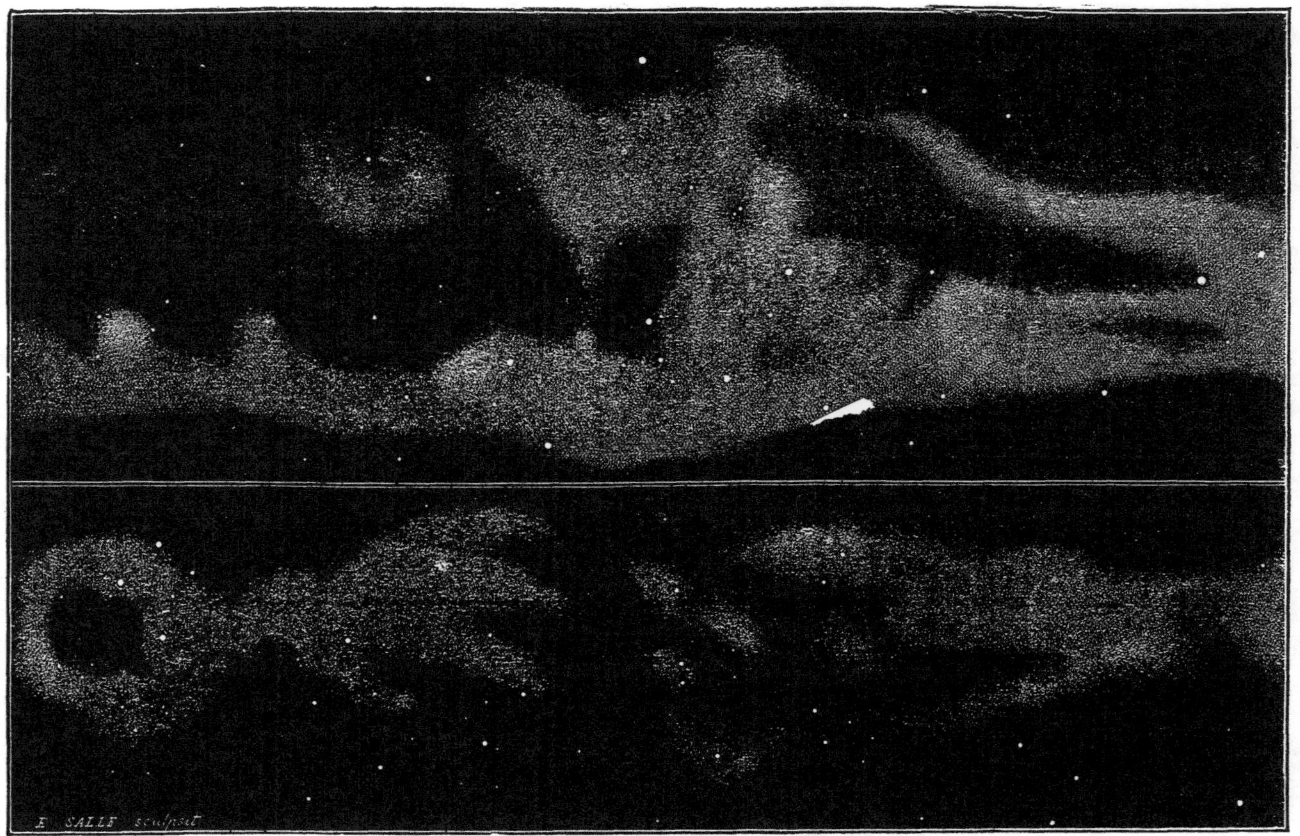

SOUTHERN MILKY WAY.

branches, with numerous ramifications, and the bifurcation continues through the Wolf, the Altar, the Scorpion, and Sagittarius, as far as the Serpent. Then the two branches again cross the Equator and rejoin the northern part of the Milky Way, at the point where our description began.

In this immense course, which embraces, as we have said, a complete great circle of the celestial vault, the glimmer of the star-cloud is extremely variable. We have seen that the brightest part of the northern Milky Way is that which traverses the Eagle and the Swan. In the southern hemisphere, the part comprised between the Ship and the Altar is still more remarkable. But, as Humboldt has observed, there is a circumstance which still more increases the magnificence of the Milky Way in the southern hemisphere; this is the vicinity of a long zone of very brilliant stars, which we have already remarked in reviewing the constellations,—a zone which begins at Sirius in Canis Major, traverses the Ship and the beautiful stars of the Cross, the Centaur and the Scorpion. According to an English observer, Captain Jacob, the rising of this portion of the heavens is heralded by a general illumination of the sky, so decided that he compares it to the light of the new moon.

When the Milky Way is examined by the help of telescopes, it is resolved into a multitude of stars very near together, but very irregularly arranged. Star-clusters of irregular form are especially very numerous; but globular clusters are only found in the brightest portion of the southern zone. 'If some regions,' says Humboldt, 'present large spaces where the light is uniformly spread, there are others where spaces, shining with very bright lights alternating with others poor in stars, cover the sky with an irregularly luminous network. We find, also, even in the interior of the Milky Way, dark portions where it is impossible to discover a single star even of the eighteenth or twentieth magnitudes. At the sight of these absolutely void regions, it is impossible not to believe, that the visual ray has really penetrated into space, traversing the entire thickness of the stellar stratum which surrounds us.'*

In many parts, this nebulous zone has been so completely resolved that the stars appear projected on a black ground, absolutely deprived of all nebulosity. But in other regions, a whitish glimmer is still perceived behind the stars, which shows that in these directions the Milky Way is really impenetrable.

We shall by-and-by examine, what is, in all probability, the real form of the Milky Way, and what inferences may be drawn from it as to the general structure of the visible Universe.

* Humboldt, 'Cosmos,' vol. iii. p. 159.

XIV.

PHYSICAL AND CHEMICAL CONSTITUTION OF THE STARS.

STARS are Suns. This is the last verdict of Science on the constitution of these so prodigiously distant bodies. For a long time the fact has been dawning on us, and already men of science and genius have based on this idea brilliant researches on the general structure of the Universe.

But how could we hope to be able to pass beyond the domain of conjecture in this matter? Were we to imagine that optical instruments, refractors, and reflectors, the construction of which is already so perfect, would acquire by new progress a power superior to that they now possess, and penetrate to depths of space a thousand times more considerable than those they already reach, what would result?

That many of the suns nearest to us might then be scrutinized, at 200, 600, or 1000 times the distance of our Sun: this would be a step certainly not to be despised, but at most we should only be able to estimate their real dimensions by the measure of their apparent diameters, which might then possibly become sensible.

Fortunately for us, this unexpected, if indeed not impossible, perfection of optical instruments, is not requisite. Thanks to an admirable method of analysis, which enables us to affirm by observation of a luminous spectrum the presence or absence of certain substances in the light-source, —in a word, thanks to *spectrum analysis*, we are now able to say, that such and such a metal, as iron, copper, or mercury, exists in a certain star; that another contains sodium or manganese. Already have we discovered, in Sirius, Aldebaran, α Orionis, Vega, and others, the presence of many substances known in our world, and of others with which we are not acquainted: and this new branch of astronomy promises the most interesting and abundant harvest.

In presence of such astonishing conquests of Science, we do not know truly which to admire the most, the magnificent chain of natural phenomena which enables us to conclude from one fact, actual or present, another fact past or future, of which the theatre is, as it were, at an infinite distance; or the power of penetration of the human mind which patiently seizes each link in the chain of facts, and connects the most distant and the most invisible with those which are at our very doors.

[Let us endeavour to give an idea of this branch of research, and of the progress already made. We have already referred, in our Chapter on the Sun, to the solar spectrum, which was familiar to man's gaze in the rainbow, that child of showers and rain-drops, long before Philosophy claimed it or utilised its teachings. What nature does by means of a rain-drop, physicists accomplish by means of a prism; and the first teaching of the prism was, that a beam of light is not a single thing, but a bundle of things, called rays, each with its own special mission, as if each had a master of its own, and had a different tale to tell or note to sing. And so it has. Let all the rays in a sunbeam sing in chorus, and the chord which falls on our eye, as sound would fall on our ear, is *white*. Now, let the beam be sent through the prism, and let the latter work its spell; the chord has vanished. In place of it we find each ray with a coloured note, and may liken the glorious coloured band, which we call the solar spectrum, to the key-board of an organ; each ray a note, each variation in colour a variation in pitch; and as there are sounds in nature which we cannot hear, so there are rays in the sunbeam too subtle for our eyes.

But observe the spectrum of the sunbeam more closely; there are gaps which we may liken to silent notes. How is this? Let us try an experiment; let us light a match, or anything which burns white, and observe its spectrum. It is *continuous*, that is, from reddest red, through the whole gamut of colour, to the visible limit of the violet, each ray accomplishes its special mission, tells its tale and sings its song. There are no silent notes, no dark lines breaking up the band.

Let us try another experiment. Let us burn something which does not burn white, some of the metals will answer our purpose. We see at once by the brilliant colours which fall upon our eye from the vivid flame, that a different chord is struck; but let the prism work again its spell, and tell us the notes.

This time we shall find, not only that the spectrum is not continuous, but that the chord consists perchance of only two, three, four, or more *single notes*, as if on an organ, instead of striking down all the keys, we but sounded one or two notes in the base, tenor, or treble.

Again, let us try still another experiment. Let us so arrange our prism, that while a sunbeam is decomposed by its upper portion, a beam proceeding from such a light-source as sodium, iron, nickel, copper, or zinc, may be decomposed by the lower one. We shall find in each case, that when the *bright lines* of which the spectrum of the metals consists flash before our eyes, they will occupy absolutely the same positions in the lower spectrum as some of the *dark bands*, the silent notes, do, in the upper solar one.

Here, then, is the germ of Kirchhoff's discovery, on which his hypothesis of the physical constitution of the Sun is based; here is the secret of the recent additions to our knowledge of the stars, for stars are suns, and Nature's laws are the same for all.

Vapours of metals and gases absorb those rays which the same metals and gases themselves emit.

We are now in a position to inquire, what has become of those rays, which the dark lines in the solar spectrum tell us are wanting—those rays which were arrested in their path, and prevented from bearing their message to us. Before they left the regions of our incandescent Sun, *they were arrested by those particular metallic vapours in his atmosphere, with which they beat in unison;* and our assertion, that this and that metal exists in a state of vapour in the Sun's atmosphere, is based upon their non-arrival; for so marked, various, and constant are the positions of the bright bands in the spectra we can observe here, and so entirely do they correspond with certain dark bands of the spectrum of the Sun, that it can be affirmed, that the chances against the hypothesis being right are something like 300,000,000 to 1.

So much for the Sun. Fraünhofer was the first to apply this method to the stars; and we have lately reaped a rich harvest of facts, in the actual mapping down of the spectra of several of the brightest stars, and the examination more or less cursory of a very large number. In all, the plan of structure has been found to be the same; in all we find an atmosphere sifting out the rays, which beat in unison with the metallic and gaseous vapours which it contains, and sending to us the residuum, a broken spectrum abounding in dark spaces. But how eloquent is silence sometimes! Who would think, that in those gaps would lie the secret of the physical constitution of distant worlds, and detailed information as to the constituent materials?

Let us see what Dr. Miller and Mr. Huggins, two of the latest labourers in the field, can tell us.

Take the spectrum of Aldebaran, for instance; the coincidence of the bright bands of light given out by sodium, magnesium, hydrogen, calcium, iron, bismuth, tellurium, antimony, and mercury, with dark lines in the solar spectrum, has been proved, seven other elements being tried and rejected. In Betelgeuse, the coincidence of sodium, magnesium, calcium, iron, and bismuth, has been proved.

The seventy or eighty lines already measured and mapped in each of these stars, represent some of the stronger only of the numerous lines which are seen in their spectra. Already we are beginning to think that in the spectra of the stars the chemist is introduced to many new elements.

It has been mentioned as a very suggestive fact, that the lines of hydrogen corresponding with C and F of the solar spectrum are wanting in the spectra of α Orionis and β Pegasi, and these two stars only, out of more than fifty stars examined.

β Pegasi	contains	sodium, magnesium, perhaps barium.
Sirius	,,	sodium, magnesium, iron, hydrogen.
Vega	,,	sodium, magnesium, iron.
Pollux	,,	sodium, magnesium, iron.

How forcibly are we here reminded of that gigantic query of the immortal Newton, 'Are not the Sun and stars great earths vehemently hot?' for surely α Orionis, with its atmosphere containing five of our elements, and Aldebaran, with nine, cannot be vastly different in constitution from our Sun, the atmosphere of which contains ten—possibly fourteen—according to our present knowledge.*

We have also, as has been pointed out by the observers we have named, pretty certain proof of the idea which has long been floating in many minds as to the cause of the colours of the stars, though their variability in colour, which has lately been so strongly insisted upon, is still to be explained. They remark:—'As spectrum-analysis shows that certain of the laws of terrestrial physics obtain in the Sun and stars, there can be little doubt that the immediate source of solar and stellar light must be solid or liquid matter maintained in an intensely incandescent state, as the result of an exceedingly high temperature. For it is from such a source alone that we can produce light, even in a feeble degree comparable with that of the Sun. As the continuous spectrum of the light from incandescent solid and liquid bodies appears to be connected with the state of solidity or liquidity, and not with the chemical nature of the body, it is highly probable that the light, when first emitted from the photospheres of the Sun and stars, should be in all cases identical, *the differences of colour* depending upon the *differences of constitution of the investing atmosphere*, and these again intimately connected with the chemical constitution of the stars. The light of the stars will vary in consequence of the loss of different rays. For, in proportion as the dark lines occur more largely, or are more intense in particular parts of the spectrum, so will those colours be weaker, and the colours of the other refrangibilities will equally predominate.'

This, however, is but one of the sides of the inquiry. We are now furnished with many others. Thus for instance, we must for the future look upon α Orionis and β Pegasi as worlds without hydrogen! while, probably, the atmosphere of Sirius is more charged with vapours than is that of our Sun.

These observations, as a whole, show that the stars differ from each other and from our Sun, only by the lower order of differences of special modification, and not by the more important differences of distinct plans of structure. There is, therefore, a probability that they fulfil an analogous purpose; and are, like our Sun, surrounded with planets, which by their attraction they uphold, and by their radiation illuminate and energize. It is remarkable that the elements most widely diffused through the host of stars are some of those most closely connected with the constitution of the living organisms of our globe, including hydrogen, sodium, magnesium, and iron.]

* ELEMENTS IN THE SUN.

Sodium.	Copper.	Cobalt, *doubtful.*
Iron.	Zinc.	Strontium ,,
Hydrogen.	Calcium.	Cadmium ,,
Magnesium.	Chromium.	Potassium, *probably not.*
Barium.	Nickel.	

The above according to Kirchhoff, except Hydrogen.

BOOK THE SECOND.

THE NEBULÆ.

[ONE of the most important discoveries of modern times has been that which has furnished evidence of a fact, long ago conjectured by the master minds among us, namely, that *Nebulæ* are something different from masses of stars, and that their cloud-like appearance is to be ascribed to something besides their possible distances, and the still comparatively small optical means one can bring to bear upon them. The discovery is still so recent, that there has not yet been time to sort out the real from the apparent nebulæ. But we are, at all events, justified for the purpose of our present sketch, in accepting as *nebulæ* everything hitherto classed as such, although it is nearly certain that the powerful means of differentiation which spectrum-analysis has now placed at our command will place many of them in the category of distant star-clusters, if, indeed, it does not in time indicate a transitional state.]

If we examine the space in Andromeda, which separates the square of Pegasus from Cassiopea, we shall readily perceive, a little below the line which joins these two constellations, a luminous mass—a little whitish cloud of elongated form, in which the eye cannot distinguish any stars.

If we employ a telescope even of great power, the form becomes more defined, and the oval seems more decided, but the soft and pale glimmer of this little celestial cloud retains its nebulous appearance, and there is still no trace of a star.

This is a nebula well known under the name of the Great Nebula in Andromeda.*

The celestial spaces are strewn with a multitude of similar objects, varied in dimension, brightness, and form. All have received, on account of the cloudy appearance which they offer at first sight, the name of *Nebulæ*. A very limited number are visible to the naked eye, a circumstance explained by the smallness of their apparent dimensions, the feebleness of their light, and in some cases the vicinity of relatively bright stars. In the telescope they appear by thousands; more than 5000 are now known; and this number increases in proportion as the different regions of the sky are explored with more powerful instruments.

The question, What are the nebulæ? has long been asked. Were

* Simon Marius, or Mayer, observed and described this nebula in 1612. It was the first which attracted the serious attention of astronomers. Forty-four years later, Huyghens discovered the great nebula which surrounds the sextuple star θ Orionis; since that period, and especially since the end of the eighteenth century, the catalogues of nebulæ have been enriched with numerous observations, and a complete branch of astronomy has been developed.

they agglomerations of diffused matter? celestial luminous clouds? or were they groups of condensed stars, which extreme distance rendered separately invisible?

When studying the natural groups of stars, such as the Pleiades, we remarked that some eyes only distinguish a confused glimmer. To such, the Pleiades put on the appearance of a nebula—a circumstance reproduced in the case of a great many clusters, which, where the best eyes only distinguish an ill-defined luminous mass, are transformed, as we have seen, by telescopes into a multitude of distinct stars.

Hence, in the old classification, the first class of nebulæ comprised the star-clusters. Astronomers gave this name to all nebulosities, which telescopes entirely separated into stars.

A second class comprised those partially separated into stellar points, but in which some portion resisted resolution.

Lastly come the nebulæ, properly so called, in which the most powerful telescopes distinguished no stars.

But this classification was held to be quite relative, and depending entirely on the optical power of the instrument, the sight of the observer, and purity of the sky at the time of observation.

[This was true in the main, and still remains so; but as we shall see by-and-by, we now recognise in the nebulæ proper a distinct physical constitution.]

Before commencing our detailed description of the nebulæ, let us say a word on their distribution over the starry vault. This is very unequal in the northern hemisphere, and in those parts of the southern one visible in the northern temperate zone.

The greatest number is found in a zone which scarcely embraces the eighth part of the heavens. The constellations of the Lion, the Great Bear, the Giraffe, and the Dragon, those of Boötes, Berenice's Hair, and the Hunting Dogs, but principally the Virgin, from this zone, which extends as far as the middle of the Centaur; it is known under the name of the *nebulous region of Virgo.*

Nearly at the opposite pole of the sky, another agglomeration of nebulæ embraces Andromeda, Pegasus, and the Fishes, and extends lower than the first-named constellation, into the southern heavens.

It is noteworthy that the regions nearest the Milky Way are the poorest in nebulæ, whilst the two richest regions lie at the two poles of that great belt in which the stars are so numerous and condensed. The nebulæ are more uniformly spread over the zone which surrounds the South Pole; they are at the same time much less numerous. On the other hand, there are two magnificent regions there, which alone contain nearly 400 nebulæ and star-clusters.

I.

NEBULÆ OF REGULAR FORM.

Circular, Elliptical, Annular, and Spiral Nebulæ—Annular Nebula in Lyra—Spiral Nebulæ in Canes Venatici, Virgo, and Leo.

The forms, apparent dimensions, and intensity of the light of nebulæ, are extremely varied. The very different distances, doubtless, by which they are removed from us, have something to do with these appearances; but

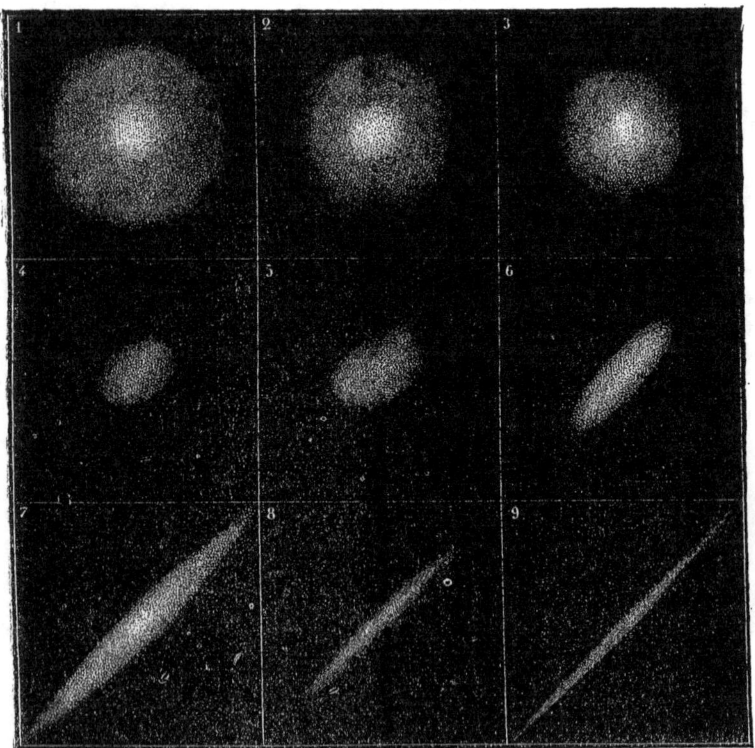

Fig. 151.—Nebulæ of circular and oval forms. (Sir J. Herschel.)

it is probable also that their real structure and dimensions, and the state and temperature of the matter of which they are formed, also influence their apparent characters. In the present transitional state of our knowledge all classification is purely arbitrary, and it will be understood that its only object is to infuse a little order into our inventory. We shall then be guided in our description by the apparent forms assumed by the nebulæ; and we will begin with the nebulæ of regular shape.

The round, globular, or spherical form is very frequent. It may possibly be found that, in many cases, the nebulæ which affect these appearances are nothing else than star-clusters; their immense distances, or the extreme smallness of the stars which compose them, may prevent our distinguishing separately the luminous points, which, even in the most powerful telescopes, only present a confused phosphorescent glimmer. Great probability is lent to this hypothesis, as we have before hinted, by the fact, that each new triumph of optical skill results in a resolution of some nebulæ, before irreducible, and helps us at the same time to discover new nebulæ, at greater depths of space.

Fig. 151 gives some examples of circular and oval nebulæ, chosen

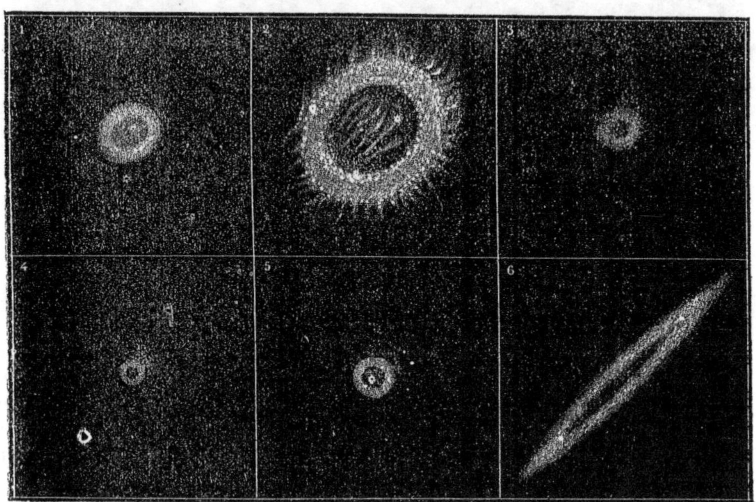

Fig. 152.—Annular Nebulæ.
1. In Lyra (Sir J. Herschel). 2. The same (Lord Rosse). 3. Annular nebula in Cygnus. 4. In Ophiuchus. 5. In Scorpio. 6. Nebula near γ Andromedæ.

from a numerous collection of similar objects. The perfectly rounded form of some is seen to pass, by imperceptible gradations, to the most elongated ellipses, at last approximating to a straight line. Near the centre of some of these nebulæ a marked condensation of light is also noticed, which indicates an analogy with the spherical star-clusters. In some globular nebulæ the brightness does not increase in a continuous manner from the circumference to the centre; the gradation is replaced by concentrical strata, analogous to those which we noticed in the cluster in Toucan. This circumstance affords another point of resemblance between the resolved globular clusters and the nebulæ of the same form.

The oval form probably belongs to very flattened condensations presented to us edgewise, the degree of flattening being attributed either to their real form, or to an inclination more or less decided towards the region of the sky which our system occupies. Among the nebulæ of round or oval form, there are only a few which present another very peculiar and curious structure: we refer to the annular or perforated nebulæ.

One very interesting example is situated in the constellation of the Lyre, not far from Vega, between the two stars β and γ of that constellation. A nebulous ring of oval form surrounds a darker space, the pale uniformly spread glimmer of which resembles a 'light gauze' stretched across the ring. Such is the appearance which this singular object at first presented (fig. 153, 1).

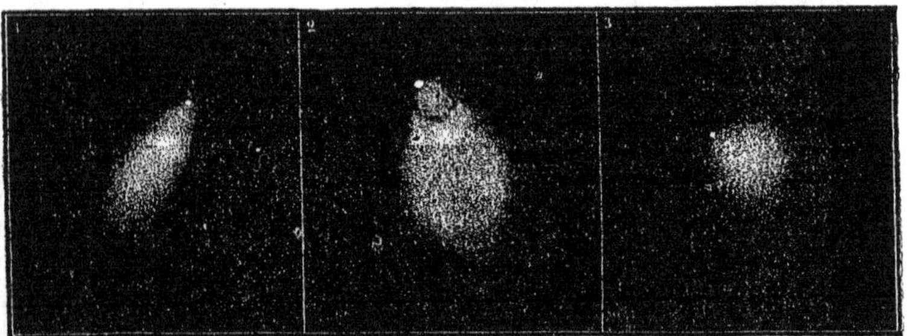

Fig. 153.—Conical or cometary nebulæ.—1. In Eridanus (Sir J. Herschel). 2. In the Unicorn (Lord Rosse). 3. In the Great Bear (Sir J. Herschel).

Lord Rosse's telescope has since partially resolved the ring into luminous points, and has shown parallel lines in the opening; the exterior borders are also stellated with fringes (fig. 152, 2).

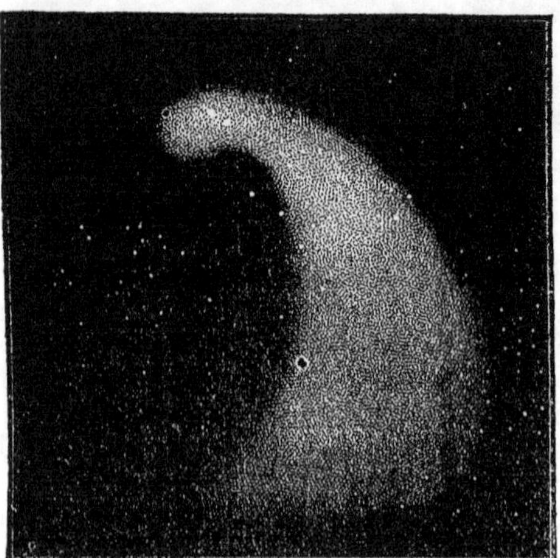

Fig. 154.—Nebula in Argo. (Sir J. Herschel.)

We reproduce here, from the drawings of Sir J. Herschel, two other annular nebulæ, one oval, the other round. The first (fig. 152, 3), which is very similar to the nebula in Lyra, is situated between the constellations of the Swan and the Fox; the second (fig. 152, 4) in Ophiuchus.

The oval form of the ring is already decided in the nebula numbered 5, which presents, moreover, a singularity which we shall again soon meet with: two stars are situated on the ring, at the extremities of its smallest diameter. But in an annular nebula (fig. 152, 6), near the beautiful triple star γ Andromedæ, the ring is excessively elongated; and two stars are there also symmetrically placed, only this time it is at the extremity of the major axis of the ellipse.

This regularity in the forms of a great number of nebulæ is doubtless apparent only. It partly disappears when they are examined with very powerful instruments; that is to say, when brought nearer to us they reveal the details of their structure. Then the large masses of light not being preponderant, the form loses its symmetry, as may be seen in the two drawings which represent the annular nebula in Lyra (fig. 152, 1, 2).

Again, always bearing in mind that the classification which we have adopted is an arbitrary one, we may rank among the regular nebulæ those which affect the conical or parabolic form, similar to that of some comets. We give here (fig. 153) three examples of these nebulæ, the form of which

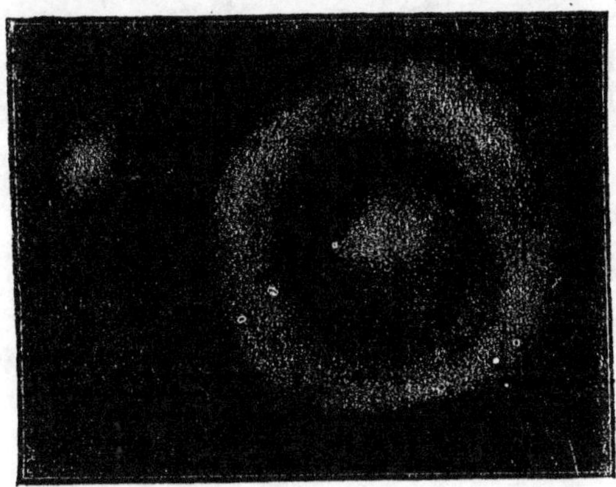

Fig. 155.—Nebula in Canes Venatici. (Sir J. Herschel.)

is analogous to some star-clusters; for example, the cluster numbered 6 in the frontispiece, which shows the same luminous concentration at the apex.

Here, again, is a nebula (fig. 154), which by its widening form approaches the cometary nebula, but which seems to suggest at the same time, by its singular outline, the first approach to a spiral nebula.

In all the nebulæ which we have examined, the regularity of form is manifested by a symmetry, such that each object is divided in two equal parts by its axis. But it is important to insist on the fact that this regularity often disappears when optical instruments of greater illuminating power show the different portions with more clearness. It is often surprising to see a nebula thus transformed to the eye in a most complete manner. In no example is change of form so decided as in the nebula in Canes Venatici.

Let us look at the preceding figure.

We see, at the centre of a ring, double throughout half its contour, a bright, globular nebula, accompanied by a smaller nebulosity of round form, situated outside the ring and at some distance away. It was under this form that it was first seen and drawn by Sir J. Herschel.

Observed later by Lord Rosse, with the help of his magnificent tele-

Fig. 156.—Spiral form of the nebula in Canes Venatici. (Lord Rosse.)

scope, the same nebula was presented under a form of wonderful strangeness (fig. 156). Brilliant spirals, unequally luminous, and overstrewn with a multitude of stars, diverge from the centre, and become separated one from the other more and more as they recede from it, at last being lost in a direction common to all. The exterior filaments of this prodigious spiral of stars join the smaller exterior globular nebulæ which at first appeared isolated from the ring.

Lastly, according to the most recent observations of M. Chacornac, this latter nebula itself affects the spiral form, its contours being connected with the spirals of the principal nebula.

The imagination remains confused in presence of such a grand spectacle. It loses itself in endeavouring to calculate the total dimensions of this immense system, by assuming a probable distance for the atoms of

Fig. 157.—Spiral nebula in Virgo. (Lord Rosse.)

this star-cluster. We are startled at the depth of the abysses into which the human gaze plunges. What strange forces have produced this hurricane of matter—perhaps of suns? Is the spiral the original form of those gaseous matters, the condensation of which may give, or has given, birth to each individual of this gigantic association?

These are questions which the mind puts to itself, the complete solution of which will doubtless demand many centuries. Shall we ever be able to recognise in these groups variations of form, distinct from those due to the varying power of the various instruments and the difference of sight of observers? In a word, shall we ever be able to prove the movements of the constituent parts of the nebulæ?

The spiraloid form is not confined to the nebula we have described. It is quite as clearly defined in the nebula in Virgo represented in fig. 157. The luminous branches of this spiral, four in number, are clearly separated by dark intervals, and divided besides by darker spirals, which indicate strings of matter less condensed. All diverge from a central nucleus where a much more decided light indicates a powerful concentration.

The number of nebulæ in which the spiraloid form is observed was at first rather small. But in proportion as the sky is explored by more powerful instruments the number has increased. In the important memoir published by Lord Rosse in 1861,* we have noted forty spiral nebulæ, and thirty more in which this form is suspected.

Fig. 158.—Spiral nebulæ. (Lord Rosse.) 1. Of the Lion. 2. Of Pegasus.

In a nebula of the northern heavens, situated on the confines of the Great Bear and of Boötes, the centre is like a large globular nebula with a very marked condensation, whence radiate branches arranged in the form of spirals. In several points of these branches other centres of condensation are noticed. Sir J. Herschel had classed this among the nebulæ of rounded globular form, doubtless because the central nebulosity was the only one revealed by his telescope. Some few stars are scattered here and there on the ground which it occupies. In the two nebulæ in fig. 158, which are situated, the first in the Lion, the second in Pegasus, the spiraloid form is less decided. The spirals approach nearer to an elliptical form and are enveloped one in the other.

* 'On the Construction of Specula of six-feet Aperture; and a Selection from the Observations of Nebulæ made with them.'—*Phil. Trans.* 1862.

II.

NEBULÆ OF IRREGULAR FORM.

Large Nebulous Masses affecting no Symmetrical Form—Diversity of Aspect with Instruments employed—Nebulæ in the Constellations of Andromeda, the Lion, Fox, Sobieski's Shield and the Bull—Great Irregular Nebulæ of Orion and Argo.

All the nebulæ we have just described are distinguished by a regularity and a symmetry of form which, joined to a condensation of the light either in one central point, or along converging curves, indicate some bond linking together all the constituent portions of each. It is impossible not to recognise in them so many systems, although as yet we are ignorant of their precise nature. And it is possible that a number amongst them are not

Fig. 159.—Nebula in Andromeda.

yet decomposed into stars, owing to the immensity of their distance, or, what comes to the same thing, the insufficient power of our telescopes.

Besides these regular aggregations, there are other large nebulous masses which affect the most various forms, completely removed from all symmetrical appearance. But such is the variety, such the richness of these systems, that we can pass from the nebulæ of spherical form to others, the most *bizarre* and irregular, by every imaginable gradation.

Let us examine the glimmer of lengthened oval form represented in fig. 159.

The condensation of light noticed at its centre makes it resemble, according to the expression of the first observer—Simon Marius, 'the flame of a candle seen through a leaf of transparent horn.' It is the nebula of Andromeda, which we have already mentioned. Its symmetrical form, which caused it to be once classed among the regular nebulæ, has disappeared in the powerful refractor of Cambridge, U.S. (fig. 160). The nebulous masses which compose it have been found to be separated by two long canals, and it has been partly resolved into stars. Bond has counted more than 1500. The general primitive form is still recognised at the centre of the nebula, but it is singularly altered, and instead of one central point of luminous condensation, several excentrically situated may be noticed.

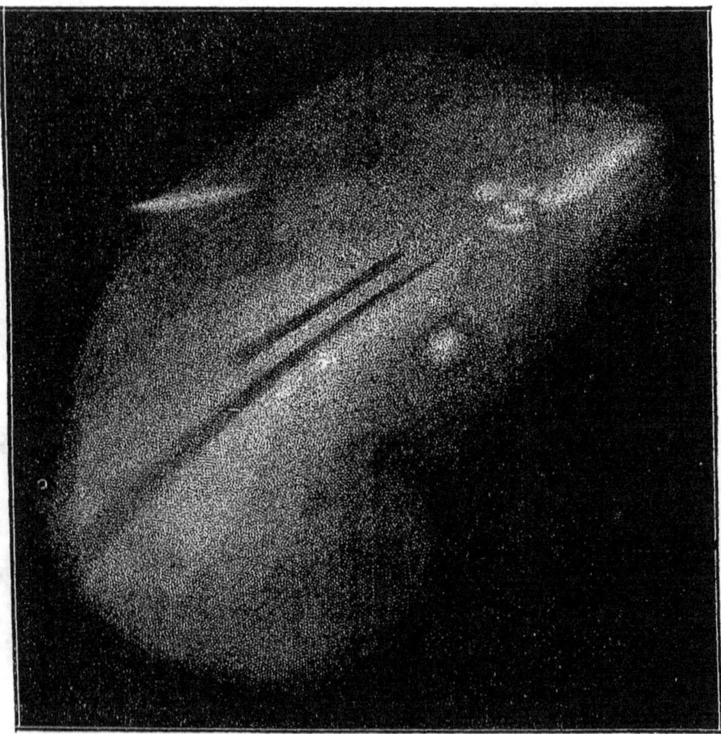

Fig. 160.—Nebula in Andromeda. (G. P. Bond.)

Another nebula of elliptical form situated in the constellation Leo, and represented in the drawing (fig. 151, 7), as seen by Sir J. Herschel, has been observed in a different form (fig. 161) in Lord Rosse's telescope: the central nucleus is composed of envelopes which take an annular spiral form, and the extremities of the oval are marked by luminous *striæ* placed on each side of the axis, like the vertebral column of a fish.

Lastly, another remarkable example of these optical transformations, purely apparent, as they only depend on the power of the instruments, is furnished by a nebula situated in the constellation Vulpecula. Sir J.

Fig. 161.—Elliptical annular nebula of the Lion. (Sir J. Herschel.)

Herschel, to whom we owe the first drawing of this nebula (fig. 162) gave it the name of the 'Dumb-bell.'

Two luminous masses, symmetrically placed and bound together by a rather short neck, the whole surrounded with a light nebulous envelope of oval form, gave it a very marked appearance of regularity. This aspect was, however, modified by Lord Rosse's telescope of three-feet aperture, and the nebulous masses showed a decided tendency to resolvability. Later still, with the six-feet telescope, numerous stars were observed standing out, however, on a nebulous ground. The general aspect retains its primitive shape, less regular, but striking nevertheless (fig. 163).

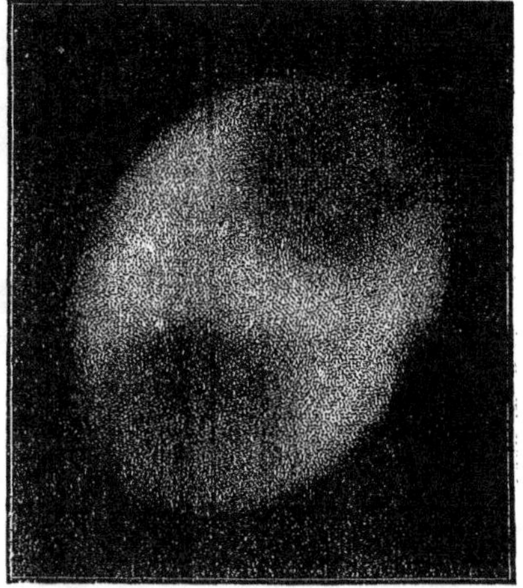

Fig. 162.—Dumb-bell nebula. (Sir J. Herschel.)

The irregular nebulæ are sometimes presented under the most fantastic forms. Sometimes they affect long vaporous trains, which here and there send out their branches; sometimes these shapes are *bizarre* in the extreme. Such is the nebula in Sobieski's Shield. An elliptical portion is terminated by two appendages, one of which is nearly rectilinear, and gives it the form of the Greek capital letter Omega (Ω). In the middle of one of the angles (fig. 164), two luminous condensations are remarked similar to the spherical, or globular clusters.

A form, still more singular, is that of the nebula in Taurus, which,

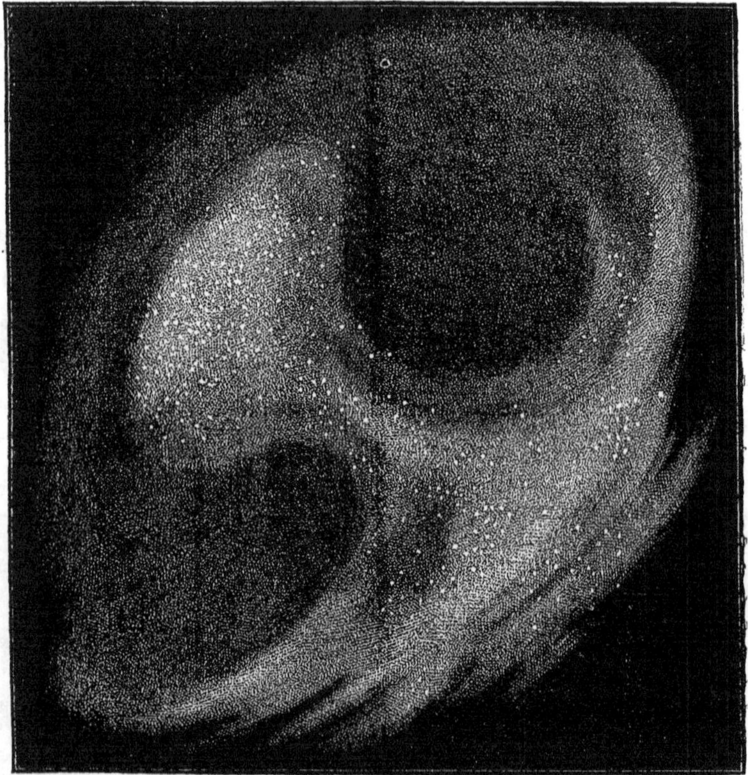

Fig. 163.—Dumb-bell nebula. (Lord Rosse.)

viewed in instruments of slight illuminating power, appears like a regular oval. As seen in Lord Rosse's large telescope, it resembles (fig. 165) a gigantic lobster, the antennæ and claws of which are figured by long strings of stars.

In the centre of one of the two Magellanic Clouds which we have already referred to as among the most beautiful objects of the southern sky (we shall describe them further on in some detail), is a nebula the complex form of which serves as a transitional point for us to pass to the large

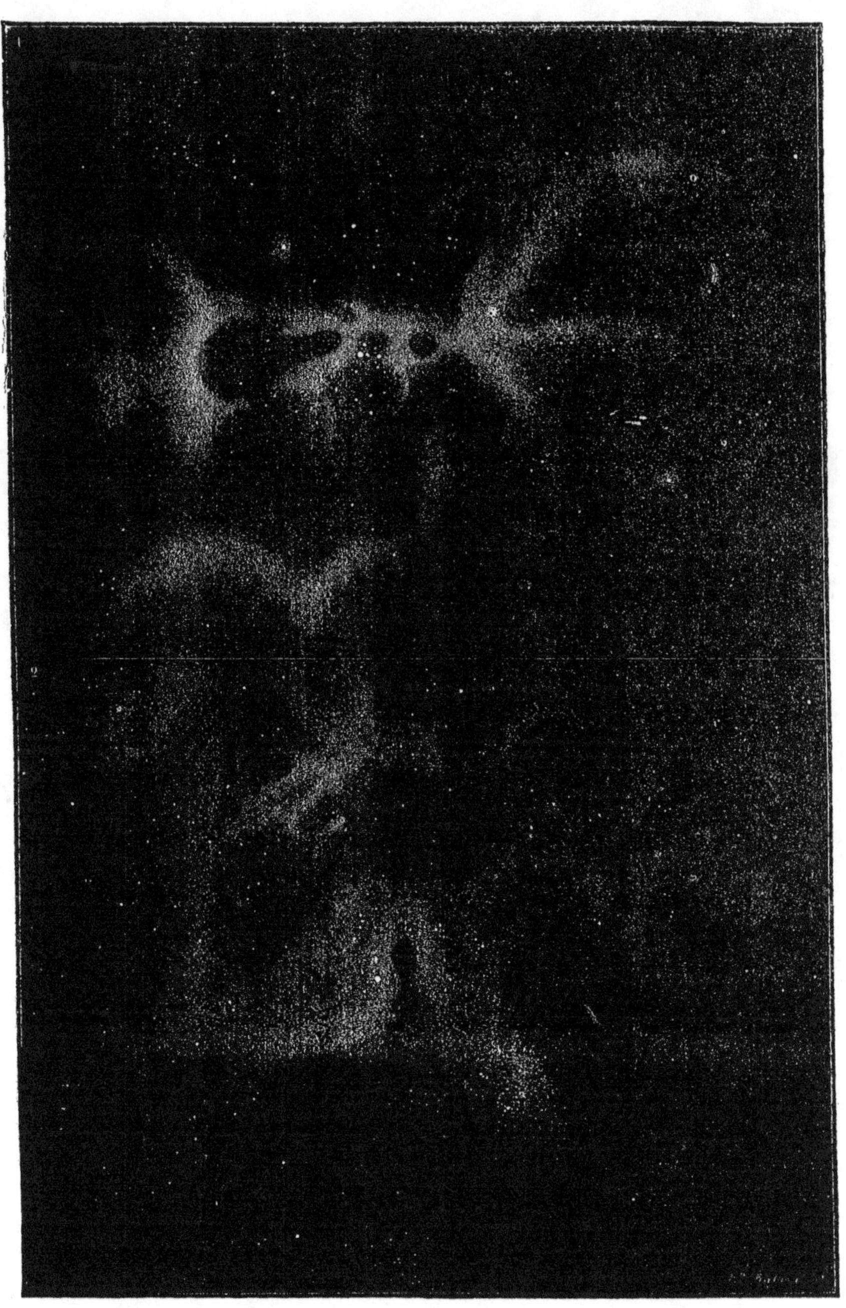

NEBULÆ IN DORADUS AND SURROUNDING ETA ARGÛS.
(Sir J. Herschel.)

irregular nebulæ. It is the nebula of Doradus (Plate XXI). The central part is composed of three bright annular masses; the two smallest are circular; the largest, of the form of a pear, is surrounded with much paler appendages, studded with a great number of small stars.

Imperceptibly we arrive at the large nebulæ, the shapeless forms of which resemble clouds disturbed and torn by the tempest. But, here again, we find in the glimmers of these distant agglomerations, indications of resolution into stars, [or into something, of which more anon.]

Human language has no expression capable of rendering the sentiments of admiration, of profound stupefaction, into which the thought is plunged, when, thanks to the marvellous power of our telescopes, our sight penetrates the distant strata of the sky, in which these unearthly objects shine.

The largest nebulæ of irregular form are found in the vicinity of the Milky Way, among the most brilliant constellations of the starry sky.

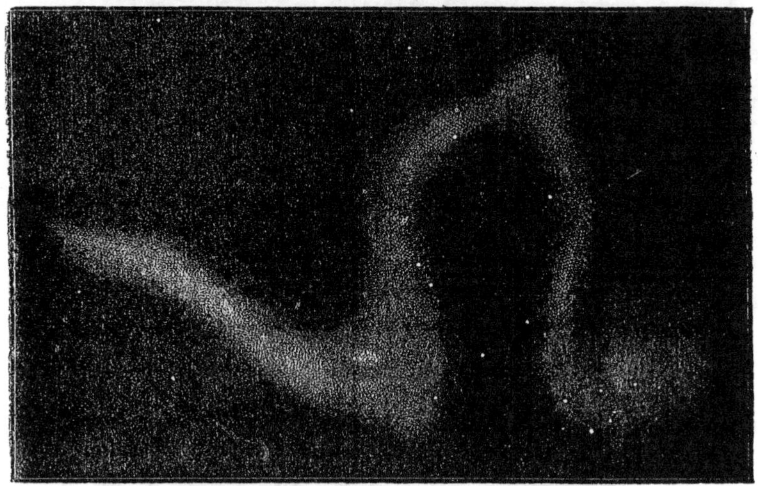

Fig. 164.—Nebula in Sobieski's Shield. (Sir J. Herschel.)

Let us give some details of the two most interesting.

One, situated in Orion, surrounds the magnificent sextuple star θ, which we have described when speaking of the systems of multiple Suns. The other surrounds a star equally noteworthy, η Argûs, so remarkable on account of its quick and capricious variations of brightness. The drawings, which we here give of these two great nebulæ (Plates XXI and XXII), according to two illustrious observers, Sir J. Herschel and G. P. Bond, relieve us of a description which would necessarily be vague and incomplete.*

* It is almost impossible to reconcile the two drawings of Bond and Herschel, without admitting the supposition of a considerable change to which the most

Since Huygens discovered the nebula of Orion in 1656, this magnificent object has been observed with a constantly increasing care, and the different regions, more or less luminous, which compose it have been described in every detail. By degrees, the stars which overspread the expanse have been recognised as more numerous; and astronomers have arrived at the conviction that it is resolvable.

Sir J. Herschel compares the brightest portion to the head of a monstrous animal, the mouth of which is open, and the nose of which is in

Fig. 165.—Nebula in Taurus (Crab nebula). (Lord Rosse.)

the form of a trunk. Hence, its name, the 'Fish-mouth Nebula.' It is at the edge of the opening, in a space free from nebulæ, that the four brightest of the components of θ are to be found; around, but principally above, the trapezium formed by these four stars is a luminous region with a *mottled* appearance, which Lord Rosse and Bond have partly resolved.

luminous region has been subjected during the interval elapsed between the epochs of the two observers.'—*Liapounov*, '*Observations of the Great Nebula of Orion, made at Cazan.*

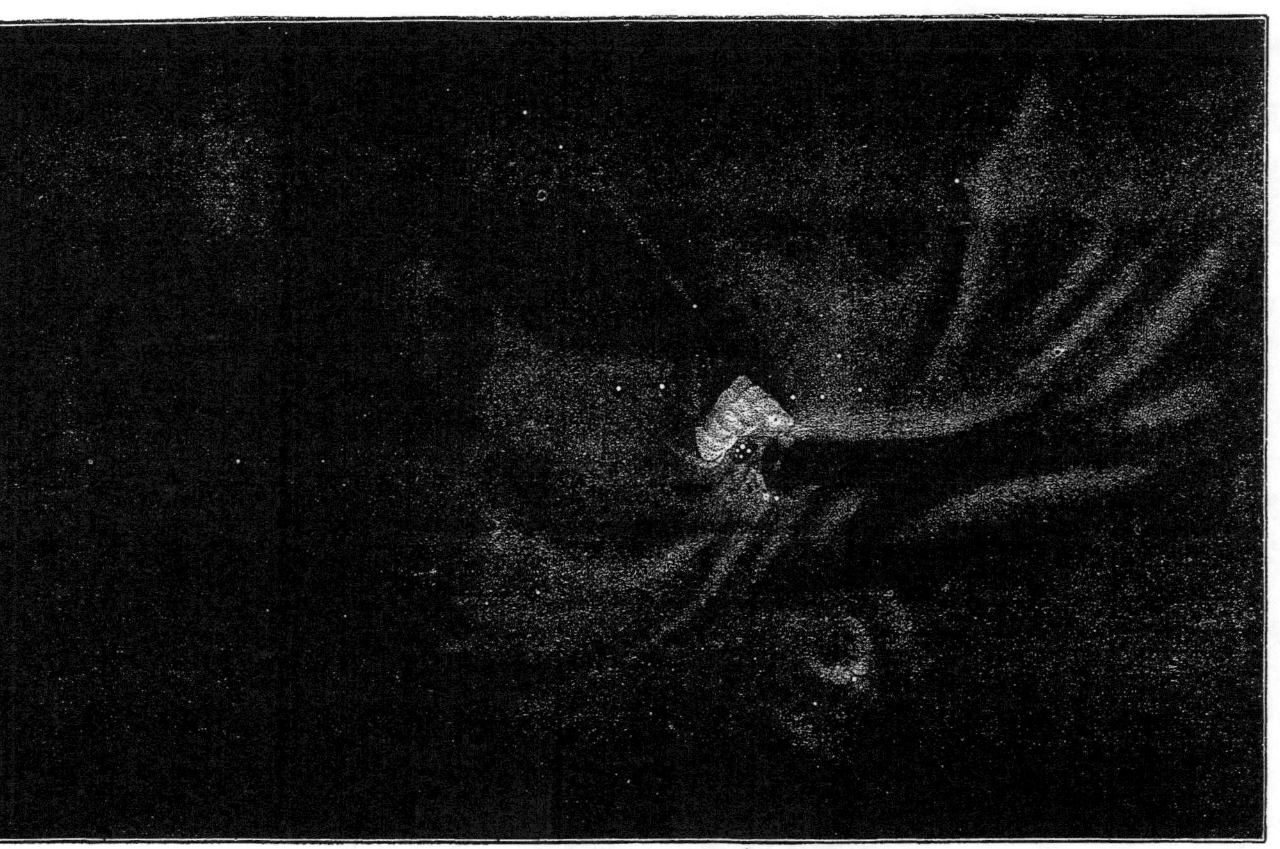

NEBULA OF ORION.
G. P. Bond.)

This region is remarkable on account not only of the brilliancy of its light, but also of the numerous centres where this light is condensed, and each of which appears to form a stellar cluster. The rectangular form of the whole is also worthy of attention. The nebulous masses surrounding it, the light of which is much fainter than that of the central region, are lost gradually; according to Bond, they assume a spiral form, as indicated in the drawing executed by that astronomer.

[It has now been placed beyond all doubt that the changes of form have taken place in the course of our most modern observations.]*

According to Sir J. Herschel, the great nebula of Orion occupies a space on the sky the apparent dimensions of which have the same extent as the lunar disk. He seems to believe that it is attached to the Milky Way—that it is perhaps the prolongation of the branch which leaves the main trunk in Perseus, and extends itself towards the Pleiades and Aldebaran.

[This, however, is now no longer probable.]

The nebulosity which surrounds η Argûs (Plate XXI), like that of Orion, does not present any symmetry in its form or in its outlines. It is situated in the Milky Way, in the midst of a region so rich in stars, that more than 1200 have been counted in the area occupied by the nebula. The stars, however, do not seem to form part of the nebulosity, but rather appear to be simply projected on it.

Towards the centre of the nebula, and close to the star η, an opening of a lengthened and rounded form is noticed, which leaves in view the dark ground of the sky. [This has been named by Mr. Abbott, a careful observer, 'the Crooked Billet.'

The evidences of change in this nebula are even more decided than in that of Orion. This object indeed may supply a link of the greatest importance, for we read that the objects of which it is composed (not stars) 'are now of a larger character, and more refulgent than nebulous matter in general.']†

* 'The observations as to the distribution and brightness of the nebulous matter do not imply any change of form, but many fluctuations in the brightness of the different parts. The general impression which I have received from these observations is, that the central part of the nebula is found in a state of continual agitation, like the surface of the sea.'—*O. Struve, Observations at Poulkowa,* '*Memoirs of the Academy of Sciences of St. Petersburg,* 1862.'

[Since this was written, M. Otto Struve, Father Secchi, and many observers in this country, have completely established the fact that a change of form has taken place.]

† [Mr. Abbott, in 'Monthly Notices of the Royal Astronomical Society,' April 1853, p. 193.]

III.

PLANETARY NEBULÆ AND NEBULOUS STARS.

Planetary Nebulæ—Variation of Aspect—Nebulous Stars.

THE name of *Planetary Nebulæ* has been given to those the form of which is that of a disk uniformly luminous, an appearance which causes them to resemble a spherical body slightly illuminated by borrowed light,—in a word, a planet. In fig. 166 are represented a few of these nebulæ of circular form.

That which distinguishes these nebulæ from those we have previously described is the equality of their light and the absence of all luminous condensation at the centre.

It is only on the very borders of the nebulous disk, that a slight diminution in the intensity of the light can be perceived. It cannot be held that they are extremely distant clusters of stars of spherical or ellipsoidal form, since, as we have seen, even on the supposition of an equal distribution in space of the components of the group, perspective alone

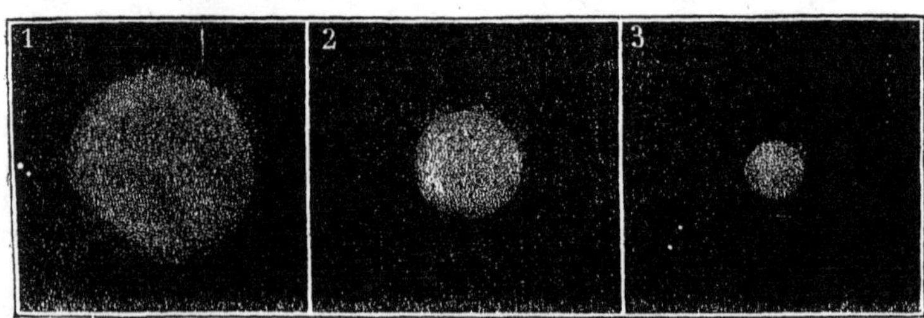

Fig. 166.—Planetary nebulæ. (Sir J. Herschel.)
1. In Ursa Major. 2. In Pisces. 3. In Andromeda.

would give an apparent condensation towards the centre. Again, are any of them by any possibility veritable clusters of flattened form presented to us with their circular surfaces perpendicular to our line of sight? Or, as remarked by Sir J. Herschel, are the stars of these nebulæ in the form of a hollow spherical shell?

[These questions, so long asked, are, as we shall see, now partially answered.]

The planetary nebula in Ursa Major, the light of which is uniformly distributed in Sir J. Herschel's drawing (fig. 166), has been seen under quite another aspect through the large telescope of Lord Rosse. The disk is changed into a double luminous crown, surrounded with a fringed border, two points appearing at the centre of the nebulosity which have every aspect of stars (fig. 167).

Another example of these changes is furnished us by the planetary

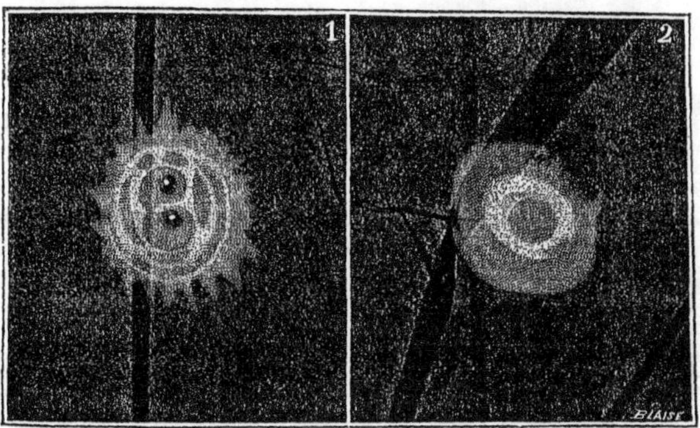

Fig. 167.—Planetary Nebulæ. (Lord Rosse.)—1. In Ursa Major. 2. In Andromeda.

nebula near κ Andromedæ, which, perfectly round in the drawing of Herschel (fig. 166, 2), appears under the form of a luminous ring in that of Lord Rosse (fig. 163).

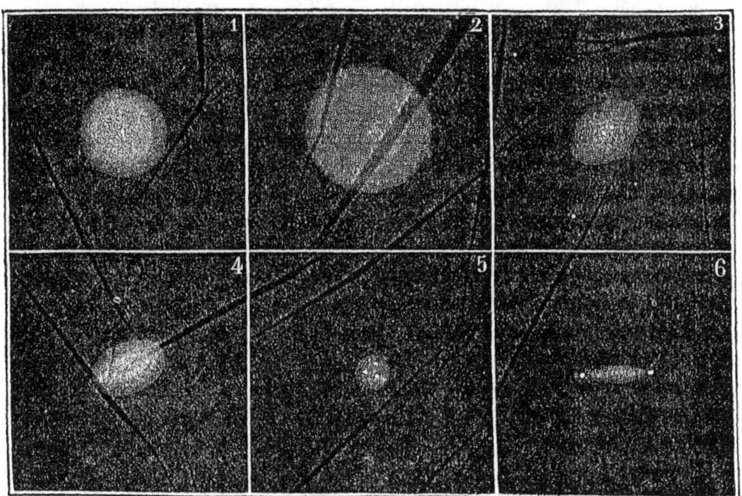

Fig. 168.—Nebulous stars. (Sir J. Herschel.)
1. In Cygnus. 2. In Perseus. 3. In the Centaur. 4. In Sagittarius. 5. In Auriga. 6. In Andromeda.

Let us finish our list, so marvellously rich in various forms of nebulæ, by mentioning those which have received the name of 'nebulous stars.'

These are no other than nebulæ, sometimes circular, sometimes oval, sometimes annular, but always regular; in the interior of which appear one or several stars standing out distinctly from the nebulosity, and being moreover symmetrically placed.

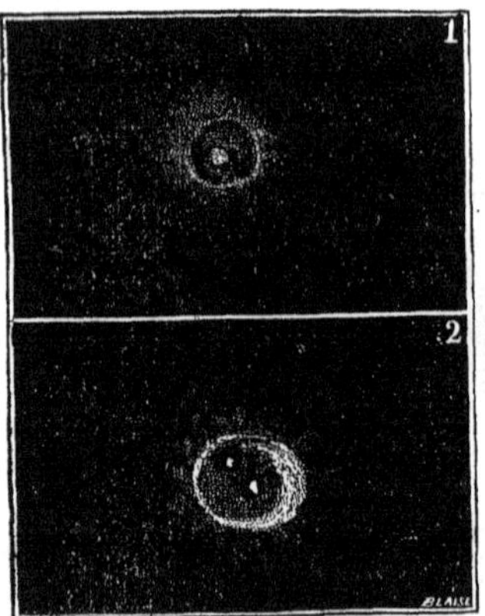

Fig. 169.—Nebulous stars. (Lord Rosse.) 1. In Gemini. 2. In Argo.

If the nebula be circular, the star occupies the centre; in the case of an elliptical form, two stars are seen placed as if they were the two foci of the curve. One is figured in fig. 168, 5, where three stars are regularly disposed at the angles of an equilateral triangle, whilst another very elongated nebula has two stars, placed outside the extremities of the greatest diameter. Here, as in the planetary nebulæ, very powerful telescopes enable us to see, instead of a disk feebly but equally illuminated, forms which are much more irregular, and in which the light is distributed in a much more unequal manner.

Such are the nebulæ represented in fig. 169, taken from the original drawings of Lord Rosse. It has also been asked if we may not see, in these nebulous stars, suns enveloped with an atmosphere of considerable dimensions, rendered visible at these enormous distances by the light of the stellar foci. This opinion is certainly not deprived of probability, although again we may consider nebulous stars as clusters of a multitude of very small ones, having at their centre a sun, single, double, or even multiple, of which the great brilliancy suffices to explain its particular visibility.

Sir J. Herschel describes a planetary nebula, the light of which is about equal to that of a star of the sixth or seventh magnitude, its diameter about 12″, its disk slightly elliptical, with a sharp, clear, and well-defined outline, 'having exactly the appearance of a planet, with the exception only of its colour, which is a fine and full blue verging somewhat on the green.'* The same astronomer describes three other nebulæ, the colour of which is a clear sky-blue.

As these latter nebulæ are all planetary nebulæ, if the hypothesis of a diffused matter be admitted, it must be supposed that its light possesses a particular colour.

* 'Outlines of Astronomy,' 8th Edition, p. 645.

IV.

DOUBLE AND MULTIPLE NEBULÆ.

Groups of Nebulæ—Probability of a Physical Connexion between the Components—Multiple Nebulæ in the larger Magellanic Cloud.

We have noticed nebulæ accompanied by systems of double or multiple stars, placed in a manner so symmetrical in the midst of the nebulosity that it is impossible to doubt the existence of a real connexion between the stars and the nebulæ. Evidently these are physical groups of a special constitution.

There exist also groups of nebulæ analogous to groups of stars, that is to say, the components are physically, and not merely optically, connected. We again find in these interesting associations the same varieties of aspect and form as in the simple nebulæ.

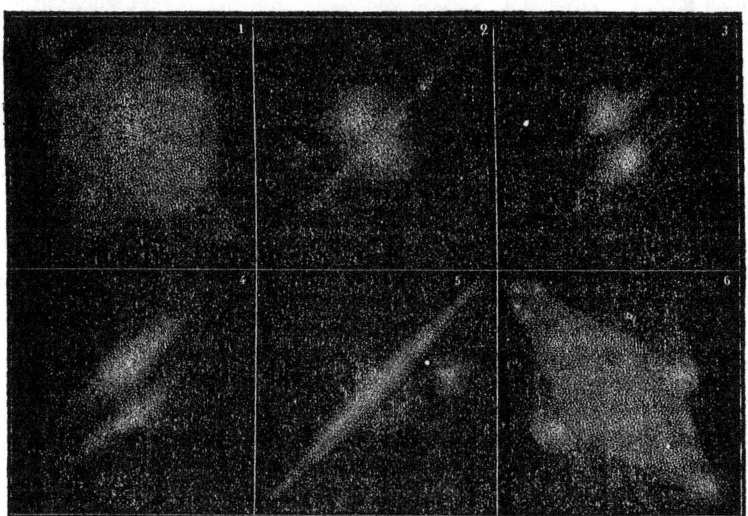

Fig. 170.—Double and multiple nebulæ. (Sir J. Herschel.)—1 and 4. In Virgo. 2 and 5. In Coma Berenices. 3. In Aquarius. 6. In the Nubecula Major (Great Cloud of Magellan).

Some appear formed of two globular clusters, in which the central condensation indicates not only a spherical figure, but probably also the existence of real centres of attraction; examples of this are seen in fig. 170. Sometimes the components appear entirely separate and distinct, sometimes they encroach one on the other; but whether these appearances are optical only, or whether there be a real physical connexion, we know not.

Sometimes, again, one of the components is round or globular, whilst the other takes an elongated elliptical form. The nebula represented in fig. 171 is composed of two rounded masses, terminated by brilliant appendages, enveloped by a nebulosity common to both, the whole surrounded by light luminous arcs similar to fragments of a nebulous ring.

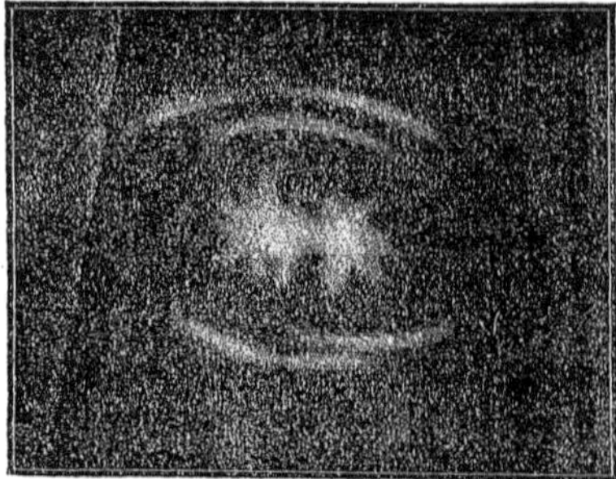

Fig. 171.—Double nebula. (Lord Rosse.)

The number of the nebulous centres is often very considerable. Sometimes it is as high as seven, as in the multiple nebulæ observed by Sir J. Herschel, of which we reproduce a curious specimen (fig. 170, 6). The group in question is one of the numerous clusters which form the largest of the two Clouds of Magellan. We may gather from this circumstance that the connexion of these seven nebulæ is purely optical, if the general nebulosity which envelopes them all does not indicate a physical union.

For the rest, the connexion of the components in the multiple nebulæ will not, doubtless, be demonstrated in the same manner as we have seen that of the systems of the double stars. In these latter systems, the movements of revolution of one of the suns round the other can be studied, because their distance, however stupendous, renders this movement observable in a limited number of years.

On the other hand, the multiple nebulæ are supposed to be banished to such infinite depths in the abysses of the heavens, that any movement would remain imperceptible. Thousands of years—thousands of centuries, perhaps—would be necessary for us to become sure of any change in the position of the whole. Our telescopes will in vain increase their power, and the sight become more penetrating. We cannot anticipate time. Compared to the life of the worlds, our life is but a second, as our entire system is but a point in the expanse of the infinite.

V.

MAGELLANIC CLOUDS.

Position of the Two Magellanic Clouds in the Southern Sky—Structure of the Little and of the Great Cloud—Star-Clusters; Isolated Stars and Nebulæ which they contain.

When we look on the region of the celestial vault which surrounds the South Pole, we cannot help being struck with the contrast presented by the small quantity of stars which it contains, with the brilliant zone which borders on the Milky Way, from Orion and Argo, to the Centaur, passing by the Southern Cross. One solitary star of the first magnitude, Achernar, more distant from the Pole than are the beautiful stars of the Centaur and of the cross, shines in this part of the sky.

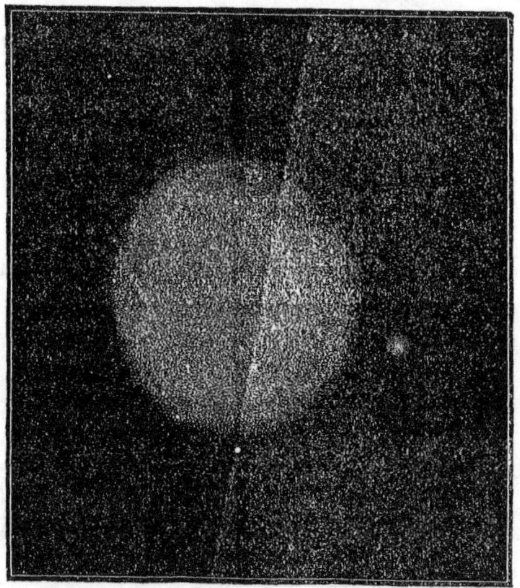

Fig. 172.—Magellanic Clouds. The Small Cloud.

But even this circumstance renders the singular aspect of the two nebulous spots, which seem two detached pieces of the great Galactic Zone, still more striking. These half-stellar, half-nebulous systems, unequal in magnitude and brightness, but easily seen with the naked eye in a clear moonless night, are situated, one, the larger and more brilliant, between the Pole and Canopus, in the constellation of Doradus; the other, the smaller and less brilliant, ordinarily invisible during the full moon, in Hydrus, between Achernar and the Pole.

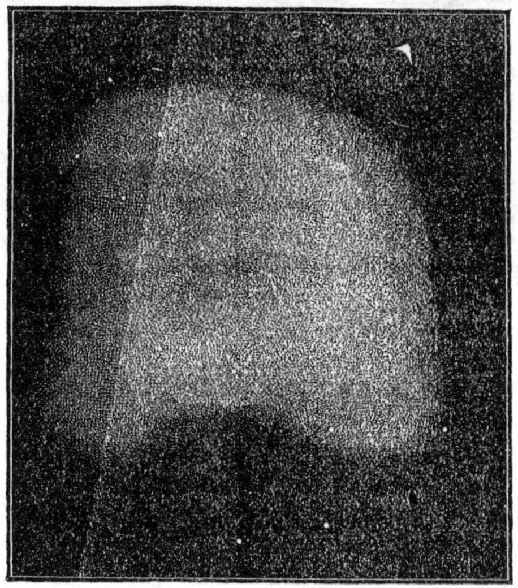

Fig. 173.—Magellanic Clouds. The Great Cloud.

Both are known by astronomers and navigators under the name of 'Cape Clouds,' or, again, 'Magellanic Clouds.' And, to distinguish them, we have again the Great Cloud (*Nubecula Major*) and the Small Cloud (*Nubecula Minor*). In figs. 172 and 173 the general form of these two nebulæ is represented.

The Clouds of Magellan are distinguished from all other nebulæ which we have as yet described by their great apparent dimensions, and by their physical structure; this last character distinguishes them from most of the branches and offshoots of the Milky Way, with which, we may also add, they do not appear connected in any way.

The Great Cloud extends over a space which embraces not less than forty-two square degrees—about two hundred times the apparent surface of the lunar disk. The Small Cloud occupies an extent four times less than the other; according to Humboldt, it is surrounded 'with a kind of desert,' where, it is true, shines the magnificent stellar cluster of Toucan, of which mention has been before made. If the exterior aspect of these two remarkable nebulæ and their situation in a celestial region poor in stars give to the southern sky a peculiar appearance, their real structure makes them one of the wonders of the heavens. Examined by the

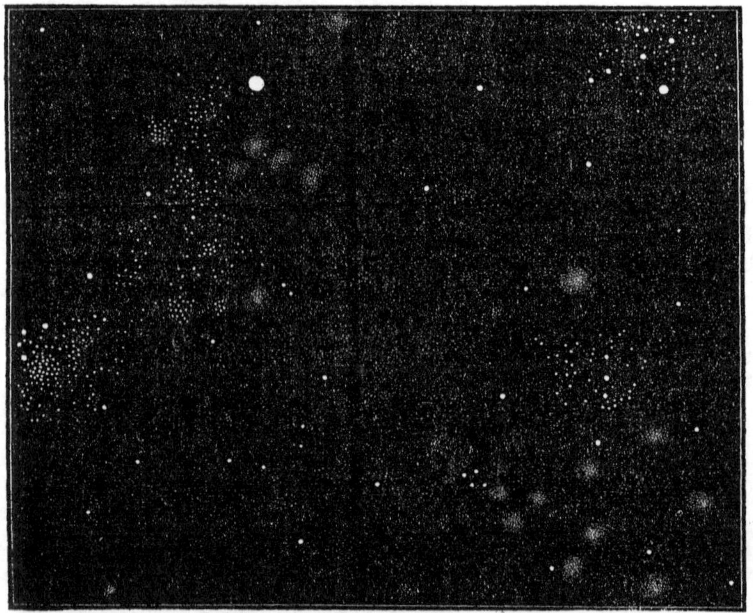

Fig. 174.—Clouds of Magellan. A portion of the Great Cloud. (Sir J. Herschel.)

aid of a powerful telescope by Sir J. Herschel, during his stay at the Cape of Good Hope, they were both decomposed in a manner of which fig. 174, which represents a portion of the Great Cloud, gives an idea.

We have first a great number of single stars, the brightness of which varies betweeen the fifth and eleventh magnitudes; then star-clusters, some of irregular form, others—and the largest number—taking a globular, spherical, or oval shape; lastly, nebulæ, some separate, others grouped in two, three, &c., most of them rounded and regular. Some of them, known under the name of Nebulæ of Doradus, already described and represented in Plate XXI, are situated in the Great Cloud. 'This nebula,' says

Humboldt, 'scarcely occupies the $\frac{1}{300}$th part of the area of the Cloud; and Sir J. Herschel has already measured in this space the position of 105 stars, of the fourteenth, fifteenth, and sixteenth magnitudes, standing out on a nebulous background of unbroken and uniform brilliancy, which has resisted the most powerful telescopes.'

The double and multiple Nebulæ are also much more numerous here than in the other zones of the heavens, richest in objects of this nature.

Thus, we repeat, the constitution of these irregular Nebulæ appears quite different from that of the Milky Way, from which we may also add they are some distance removed. They are distinguished also from other known Nebulæ, and seem like miniatures of the entire heavens.

A word now on the structure of each of the two Clouds. In the Great Cloud, Herschel has counted 582 single stars, amongst which one only is of the fifth magnitude; six others are of the order immediately inferior, and would doubtless be visible to the naked eye if their light were not effaced by the general glare. Then come 291 Nebulæ and 46 star-clusters, forming so many distinct groups.

In the Small Cloud, the single stars are proportionally more numerous, since 200 have been counted, amongst which three are of the sixth magnitude, whilst it only includes thirty-seven Nebulæ and seven star-clusters. These immense aggregations, the elements of which are themselves swarms of suns, remind us of the largest, in appearance at least, of all the clusters which the eye contemplates in the depths of the sky—the Milky Way.

VI.

PHYSICAL CONSTITUTION OF NEBULÆ.

All the Nebulæ, scattered throughout the depths of the sky, were but lately considered to be so many agglomerations of stars, differing only from star-clusters by their general form, and the grouping of the components. But it has often been thought that, among these celestial clouds, there were some, at all events, composed of diffused vaporous matter, or at least formed by the accumulation of bright corpuscules, of great relative tenuity, and as such, possessing no analogy with the other celestial bodies—with suns.

The hypothesis of a nebulous matter endowed with its own light and scattered in immense masses over the expanse of the infinite, was proposed originally by astronomers whose instruments were unable to resolve these cosmical clouds. The large Nebulæ especially, like that which surrounds the star θ Orionis, of irregular form, lent great probability to this hypothesis. But the resolution of the globular Nebulæ, one by one, at length resulted in the idea of a real nebulosity being confined to the irregular Nebulæ.

But later still, modern observations, made with instruments of great power, by degrees showed an apparent identity of composition with the stellar clusters in a great number of these last Nebulæ. Thousands of little stars appeared, where before a phosphorescent milky glimmer, according to the expression of astronomers, of an indefinable and characteristic aspect, was noticed. The Nebulæ in Andromeda and Orion, in which observers had remarked no suspicion of stars or stellar sparkling, indicative of probable resolution, have recently been stated to be resolved, at least in part; and as a consequence, the hypothesis of a diffused, nebulous matter lost ground in proportion as our means of observation were increased. But still it was asked, Must it be quite abandoned? The existence of matter of this kind is not incompatible with what is known of the physical constitution of the celestial bodies. Comets, with their vaporous nuclei, which show various degrees of condensation, their envelopes, and tails, so diffused that stars are perceived through them, and their small masses, show that this existence is possible and real. The agglomeration, of whatever nature it be, which produces the zodiacal light, also supports the hypothesis of nebulous matter.

Not long ago, however, in addition to the analogies in colour, distribution, and, above all, in physical connexion, which the Nebulæ present with stars, both single and united in couples, a new analogy was discovered. We refer to the variability of their light, which, paradoxical as it may seem, seemed to render any analogy between them, as far as their physical constitution was concerned, impossible. Of two Nebulæ, both situated in the constellation Taurus, the first, near a star of the tenth magnitude of variable brightness, presented variations which appeared to correspond with those of the stars,* and has since finally disappeared. The second Nebula, situated near ζ, after having gradually increased in brightness during more than three months,† also disappeared.

Some analogous phenomena had been already recorded by Sir W. Herschel. Two stars, surrounded with circular Nebulæ in 1774, presented no traces of these envelopes in 1811. Arago has described another fact, bearing on the same kind of transformation; 'Lacaille,' he remarks, in a note to his Biography of Sir W. Herschel, 'during his stay at the Cape, saw in Argo five small stars in the middle of a Nebula, of which Mr. Dunlop, with much better instruments, could not see the slightest trace in 1825.'

Lastly, as we have before seen, it is impossible to reconcile the observations and the drawings of the Nebula of Orion, made by many contemporary astronomers without being obliged to admit that it has undergone real changes in brightness and in the outlines of its different regions.

* D'Arrest, Hind, Chacornac.

† Observed by M. Chacornac. The disappearance was not decidedly proved for more than six years after the maximum of brilliancy. It would be interesting to know whether a gradual decrease succeeded the phases of increase, or whether the disappearance was sudden.

The variability, the disappearance even, of a star, is explained by the aid of more or less satisfactory hypotheses. This, however, is not the case with a Nebula, if we admit that it is composed of distinct stars.

[Was then the hypothesis of a nebulous matter correct after all, seeing that variations of brightness, progressive or even sudden extinction of light, might be comprehensible in masses of this kind ?

This question, thanks again to spectrum-analysis, we can now answer in a decided affirmative.

On August 29, 1864, Mr. Huggins, whose observations* on stellar spectra we have before referred to, directed his telescope, armed with the spectrum apparatus, to the planetary Nebula in Draco. At first he suspected that some derangement of the instrument had taken place, for no spectrum was seen, but only a short line of light perpendicular to the direction of dispersion. He found that the light of this Nebula, unlike any other ex-terrestrial light which had yet been subjected to prismatic analysis, was not composed of light of different refrangibilities, as we saw that of the Sun and stars to be, and it therefore could not form a spectrum. A great part of the light from this Nebula is monochromatic and was seen in the spectroscope as a bright line. A more careful examination showed another line narrower and much fainter, a little more refrangible than the brightest line and separated from it by a dark interval. Beyond this again, at about three times the distance of the second line, a third exceedingly faint line was seen.

The strongest line coincides in position with the brightest of the air lines. This line is due to nitrogen, and occurs in the solar spectrum about midway between *b* and F. The faintest of the lines of the Nebula coincides with the line of hydrogen corresponding to the line F in the solar spectrum. The other bright line was a little less refrangible than the strong line of barium.

Here, then, we have three little lines for ever disposing of the notion that Nebulæ may be clusters of stars. How trumpet-tongued does such a fact speak of the resources of modern science!

An object-glass collects a beam of light which for ever without such aid would have bathed the Earth invisibly to mortal eye; the beam is passed through a prism, and in a moment we know that we have no longer to do with glowing Suns enveloped in atmospheres enforcing tribute from the rays which pass through them, but with something deprived of an atmosphere, and that something a glowing mass of gas.

Mr. Huggins has not been idle since his discovery, and has observed a large number of nebulæ with the most interesting results.

Not only must we discard the notion—a very pardonable one when we consider how it came to be held—that the glorious cluster in Perseus, or that somewhat more typical one in Hercules, may be taken as an exemplar of all our nebulæ, could we bring sufficient optical power to bear upon them: but the conclusion is obvious, that the detection in a nebula of

* [*Philosophical Transactions*, 1864. Part II. p. 437.]

minute closely associated points of light, which have hitherto been considered as a certain indication of a stellar constitution, can no longer be accepted as a proof that the object consists of *true stars.* These luminous points, in some nebulæ at least, must be regarded as themselves gaseous bodies, denser portions, probably, of the great nebulous mass, since they exhibit a constitution identical with the fainter and outlying parts which have not been resolved. The nebulæ are thus shown by the prism to be enormous gaseous systems, and it appears probable that their apparent permanence of general form is maintained by the continual motions of the denser portions which the telescope reveals as lucid points.

More than this, the proper motion of nebulæ has not yet been inquired into, because everybody, looking upon them as irresolvable star-clusters, thought them infinitely remote. Now, however, that we know that they are *not* clusters of stars, properly so called, it is possible that they may be much nearer to us than we imagine.

The conclusions to which Mr. Huggins has been led, by his observations, are, curiously enough, the very opposite to those which speculation would have predicted. Speculation would have looked upon nebulæ as sun-germs—as composed of the very matter of which Faye has so recently stated the interior of our own Sun to be still composed. The faint glimmer of one of those eloquent lines here, three there, four elsewhere, a faint, continuous spectrum with bright lines in one place, and a well-defined continuous spectrum in another, would, taking the relatively insignificant optical means employed into consideration, have been held to bridge over the gap between star and nebula as successfully as we have now bridged over that which once separated sun and star.]

BOOK THE THIRD.

STRUCTURE OF THE HEAVENS.

I.

OUR OWN UNIVERSE—THE MILKY WAY.

Real Form of the Stellar Stratum which composes the Milky Way—Position of the Sun in the interior of this Stratum—General idea of its Dimensions.

As we have before stated, the Milky Way extends across the heavens, following nearly the circumference of a great circle of the starry sphere, the irregularities of its form, and the inequalities of its breadth in different portions, not being taken into account. It divides the celestial vault into two portions, not quite of the same extent, the smaller of the two being that which contains the constellations of Pisces, Cetus, in short, those near the vernal equinoxial point. It follows, therefore, that the Milky Way includes the region occupied by our Sun. But what is the true form of this prodigious assemblage of stars, which, according to Sir W. Herschel's estimate, deduced from a considerable number of 'guages' of the heavens, contains certainly not less than 18,000,000 stars? The small breadth of the zone, compared with its other dimensions, shows that it is formed of a stratum of suns, distributed irregularly and comprised between two nearly parallel planes, which give the whole the figure of a flattened millstone, the rim of which is split into two portions throughout one half of its circumference.*

It is nearly at the centre of this gigantic collection of stars, about half way between its two surfaces, and near the region where the separation of the zone into two strata occurs, that, lost in this vortex of worlds, our little Solar System lies. The dimensions of the centre of this system—the Sun, which appeared to us at first so great, but which a second look at the stellar universe showed to be those of a star of the second or third order—are now found to represent but an atom of the luminous sand of the Milky Way.

* [Let it be noted, however, before this conclusion is admitted, that it depends on the assumption that there is a general uniformity in the distribution of stars (and also, to a certain extent, in their magnitude) throughout the sidereal system. If the possibility be once admitted, that multitudes of the stars forming the Galaxy are minute compared with our Sun, or Arcturus, or Sirius, then no such conclusion as the above can be accepted until it has been demonstrated. The whole is a question of evidence.—R. A. P.]

The position of the Sun in this zone explains the general aspect of the whole firmament, and shows, besides, that all the stars so universally and singularly distributed, and apparently so distant from those portions of the Milky Way itself which give rise to the appearance, probably form a part of it.

Indeed, when from the point where we are situated, we look in the direction of the length of the stellar stratum, we meet with, so to speak, indefinite 'files' of stars and clusters of stars, which give to the Milky Way its maximum density, and brightness. If, on the contrary, the sight be allowed to travel in directions more and more inclined, the visual ray traverses strata continually decreasing in thickness, and the density should decrease with great rapidity. Lastly, in the direction perpendicular to the thickness of the stratum, the stars should appear dispersed, as they really do in those parts of the heavens apparently most distant from the great nebulous zone. 'Just as we see,' says Sir J. Herschel, in his

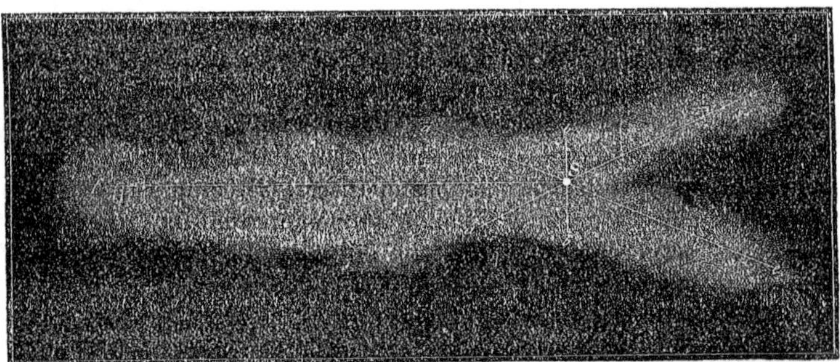

Fig. 175.—Section of the Milky Way ; position of the Sun in it.

'Outlines of Astronomy,' 'a slight haze in the atmosphere thickening into a decided fog-bank near the horizon, by the rapid increase of the mere length of the visual ray.'

Figure 175, which represents, according to Herschel's hypothesis, the Milky Way, in a section perpendicular to its thickness, and along its greatest diameter, which passes through the Sun, renders the explanation we have given easy.

With the help of this conception, we may again refer to the rapid decrease in the number of stars in those regions which, on both sides of the Milky Way, extend as far as the two poles of the great circle which the Galaxy traces on the face of the heavens.

The poles of the Milky Way are situated, the north pole near Coma Berenices, the south pole in the constellation of Cetus. When, from one or other of these points, we advance progressively towards the Milky Way, the mean number of the stars increases, at first very slowly, then, in the vicinity of the galactic plane, with very great rapidity, so that it is about thirty times greater in this plane than in the galactic polar regions.

Until now we have but obtained a general idea of the form of the Milky Way, and of the position which the Sun occupies in the midst of it. To complete our account of what is known of its structure, we must here attempt to give some idea of its real dimensions.

Comparing the photometric brightness of the stars of the different orders of magnitude with the order of probable distances, Sir W. Herschel arrived at the most astonishing conclusions on the dimensions of the Milky Way.

The stars visible to the eye comprise, it is known, the first six orders of magnitude. The illustrious astronomer of Slough established that, in the mean [making certain assumptions as to the average dimensions of the fixed stars], those of the sixth order, that is to say, the smallest stars visible to the naked eye, are twelve times more distant than the stars of the first magnitude. Starting thence, and calculating the space-penetrating power of his telescopes, he arrived at this inference, that he could observe in the depths of the heavens stars situated at a distance 2300 times greater than the mean distance of the stars of the first magnitude. And Herschel recognised, moreover, that the visible extent of the Milky Way, in some regions, increased with the power of the instrument brought to bear upon it, and that even his large 40-feet telescope could not reach the limits of this star-zone, which he therefore declared unfathomable.

Now, when we recall the stupendous distance between the nearest star to our world—such a distance, that light takes years to traverse it—we shall recognise this wonderful fact, namely, that the Milky Way in the direction of the most distant regions accessible to our view, can only be completely traversed by a light-ray in a period of time upwards of ten thousand years. Thus, when applying the eye to the eye-piece of the largest astronomical instruments, we observe, on the not quite dark background of the sky, feeble luminous points, we receive on our retina the impression of an undulatory movement, which was set in motion ten thousand years ago, by the incandescent mass of suns like ours, which form, as he does, part of the same sidereal group.

Calculating the thickness of the Milky Way from its apparent breadth, Herschel arrives at the result, that its thickness is about eighty times greater than the distance of the stars of the first magnitude. Thus, the stellar stratum greatly surpasses in this direction even the space-penetrating power of the human eye. Whence it follows, that, as we have before stated, 'Not only our Sun, but all the stars, that we can see with the naked eye, are deeply plunged in the Milky Way, and form an integral portion of it.'*

[Herschel admitted, however, towards the close of his career as an observer, that the greater richness of certain guages may be due to a greater real richness of stellar aggregation, instead, as he had assumed so far, of a great extension of the Galaxy. There is no direct evidence in favour of the fundamental hypothesis (admittedly an hypothesis) on which Herschel

* Struve, 'Etudes d'Astronomie Stellaire.'

pursued his plan of star-guaging. On the other hand, the present writer has shown that there are very numerous and very weighty arguments against it. These arguments depend chiefly on numerical statistics, not known to Sir W. Herschel, nor until long after his star-guaging had been completed.—R. A. P.]

II.

OTHER UNIVERSES.

'It is extremely probable,' remarked Sir W. Herschel, in a memoir in 1818, 'that some of the nebulæ of cometary form, many of the stellar nebulæ, and a considerable number of nebulous stars, are merely clusters of stars, banished in space to such depths that the penetrating power of the telescope has not yet been able to resolve them.'

This opinion, as we have seen, has now become a certainty, thanks to the power of our modern instruments.*

The stellar clusters and nebulæ are, then, the most distant of celestial objects, which the eye can reach; the accumulation, in a small space, of a multitude of luminous points, allows them only to be distinguished as a whole. The astronomer whose words we have quoted estimated the distance of the 75th cluster of Messier's catalogue at more than 700 times that of the stars of the first magnitude. It is not visible to the naked eye, but it would become so if its distance were reduced to a quarter. If we suppose it removed to five times its actual distance, that is to say, to 3500 times the distance of Sirius, the large Herschelian telescope of 40-feet focus would still show it, but only an irresolvable nebula. It is, then, extremely probable that, among the many nebulæ, indecomposable into stars, beyond the Milky Way, in the depths of the heavens, many are as distant as that of which we speak. Doubtless, many are still more so. Now, to reach us, light-rays must have left stars, situated at such a distance, more than 700,000 years ago. When we reflect on the immensity of such a time, which embraces thousands of centuries, and on the extraordinary velocity of the luminous movement in the bosom of the ether, thought is utterly confounded in the contemplation of such abysses, the extent of which measures, not indeed the dimensions of the Heavens—they are in-

* [Many nebulæ, formerly considered as irresolvable, have been shown to consist of discrete points of light. But it remains yet to be demonstrated that even a single nebula is an external universe. The arrangement of the irresolvable nebulæ over the celestial vault is related in so remarkable a manner to the arrangement of fixed stars, as to suggest the probability, if not the certainty, that the nebulæ lie within the limits of the sidereal system. That *some* do, is beyond all question.—R. A. P.]

expressible—but those portions of them which surround us, and of which Astronomy has studied the structure.

We can now represent the Heavens, even in their majestic whole. In the depths of limitless space, exist numerous assemblages of stars, like so many archipelagoes in an infinite ocean. Each of these Universes is itself formed of a multitude of clusters, in which the suns are grouped like so many systems, the condensation of which is more decided than in the structure generally.

Suns are the individuals of these associations of worlds. But here again is found the tendency to form groups; and double and multiple stars present to us simple systems of two or three suns gravitating one round the other.

Here, then, would end what we could know of the structure of the Universes, if we did not ourselves form part of one of the most simple of these solar systems; if the study of the planetary system, and of its varied organization, did not teach us what part each of these millions of celestial bodies may play in journeying through space, continually radiating afar their rays of heat and light.

Each of these elementary groups may itself be subdivided into smaller groups—into systems of bodies which gravitate round a central body, presenting the wonderful spectacle of a system in miniature. Who knows besides what the study of each of the suns which people the expanse might reveal, if it were given to us to penetrate into the sphere of their action, and to observe the phenomena of which this sphere is the scene? But, if imagination has a right to form conjectures on this subject, it is not so with science; the severe methods of which reject, without condemning them, hypotheses not based on facts and observation, and inferences drawn from facts by rigorous reasoning.

Here ends the purely descriptive part of our task, the object of which has been to give a picture of the phenomena of the Heavens according to actual astronomical knowledge. We may be mistaken, but we hope that more than one reader will wish to penetrate deeper still, and will not be sorry to comprehend, as much as it is possible without previous scientific preparation, the laws which regulate celestial movements, and explain the most complex phenomena. These laws are at once simple and sublime, and are an eternal honour to their discoverers, and a monument of the power of the human mind.

PART THE THIRD.

THE LAWS OF ASTRONOMY.

METHODS AND INSTRUMENTS EMPLOYED BY ASTRONOMERS.

BOOK THE FIRST.

THE LAWS OF ASTRONOMY.

THE marvellous panorama presented by the visible Universe has now passed before our eyes; the Solar System, each component of which we have explored, has shown us in detail what kind of bodies are those suns with which infinite space is strewn; and what may be the conditions of those others bodies, not self-luminous, which circulate round them, what their motions, dimensions, and physical constitution. The sidereal world has in turn revealed to us its magnificence, in its groupings and gigantic assemblages of suns, and we have been enabled to form an idea of the structure and unutterable dimensions of the Universe, or rather of that part of it rendered accessible by the telescope.

Were we to stop here, therefore, the object we had in view in this description of the physical constitution of the Heavens would have been accomplished as far as the limits of this volume would permit. The results of modern investigations have been passed under review, and we have dwelt upon them sufficiently to indicate the interest and importance which attach to them.

And yet, hitherto, we have left in the background, or trenched on but lightly, that part of the subject which makes Astronomy, regarded from an intellectual point of view the most exact, the most admirable, the most sublime of all the natural sciences. We refer to the laws of the motions of the celestial bodies, and to the formulæ, so simple in appearance to us, which have demanded so much mental labour, time, and genius for their

LORD ROSSE'S GREAT TELESCOPE.
At Parsonstown, Ireland.

discovery,—precious conquests of the mind, which have enabled man to penetrate even into the very heart of celestial phenomena; to discover their causes and relationships, and permit us now-a-days to predict the return of the phenomena and to calculate the variations with incomparable precision.

Thanks to these laws, the motions of the celestial bodies, their distances, dimensions, and even weights, have been traced, calculated, and valued. The relative positions of the bodies of the Solar System—planets and satellites, and even comets—positions so extremely variable, influenced by so many causes, can be assigned long beforehand, and thus furnish to the other sciences, and even to practical men,—our sailors, to wit,—most important data.

It is not in a popular treatise on the physical phenomena of the Heavens, such as the present, that an account of these laws, rigorous in its treatment, will be expected; to give this, it would be necessary to call to our aid the mathematical sciences, the language of which, though so clear to those who have made it their special study, is, nevertheless, purely enigmatical to the uninitiated.

But it must not be imagined from this remark, that it is impossible for our readers to gain an idea of these laws, or that they are confined in a sanctuary where the vulgar can enter not. To those whom a rigorous mathematical demonstration would avail nothing, a clear and well-defined exposition, and apt, if even familiar, comparisons, are often sufficient to enable the mind to see the law and the drift of the method. And for such who love to render reason, and to take nothing upon trust, this present Third Part is written.

The laws of planetary motion, as announced by Kepler, and of gravity discovered by Galileo, and extended by Newton to the heavens; the secondary phenomena which result from these fundamental laws, such as planetary perturbations and the tides; the magnificent hypothesis, by means of which Laplace has explained the origin and formation of our system, will occupy the First Book. These will be followed by an account of the methods which have been employed by our philosophers to measure the distances of the Moon, Sun, and Stars; and we hope our account will enable those who still suspect the possibility of such measures, to be convinced of the solidity of the methods employed. Lastly, we shall bring the volume to a close by a description of the principal instruments employed by astronomers, and of one of those edifices, held by some to be shrouded in mystery, where, in the silent night, so many men, devoted to science, have explored and still explore the depths of heaven.

I.

KEPLER'S LAWS.

The Planets describe Ellipses round the Sun — Law of Areas — Connexion between the time of Revolution and the Mean Distances of the Planets from the Sun.

Copernicus, by his discovery of the movement of the Earth and Planets round the Sun, laid the foundations of modern astronomy. Galileo strengthened the building by basing the system upon new proofs. But the real form of the Earth's orbit, and that of the other planets, and the velocity with which they moved in the various portions of those orbits, and their relative distances from the central body, remained still unknown for some time, although the determination of these problems was indispensable for the future progress of the science. For this, however, we had not long to wait. Thanks to the genius and the perseverance of Kepler, in less than a century these different problems were completely solved. Taking, as the basis of his researches, the observations of his master, Tycho Brahé, this great man, after seventeen years of unflagging toil, discovered three laws to which posterity has attached his name. We will now endeavour to give an idea of these laws, which will complete what we have written on the Solar System.

We know that a planet in moving round the Sun describes a continuous curving line, each point of which lies on an ideal plane, which passes through the centre of the Sun. Such an orbit is named in geometry 'a plane curve.' Now, what is the form of this curve, and what is the exact position occupied by the Sun in this plane? Kepler's first law answers these two questions.

The orbit of each planet is an oval curve — an *ellipse*. How, then, can we regularly define an ellipse?

Take a thread, the extremities of which are attached to two nails or pins; press these nails, or pins, into a sheet of paper, or a board, or any plain surface on which the curve in question may be traced; but take care that the thread is longer than the distance between the two fixed points. This done, by the aid of a pencil stretch the thread till it is tight, in such a manner that the point of the pencil can travel over the surface destined to receive its trace. Then let the pencil move along the thread, the latter being always tightly stretched, and the point will trace part of a curve, which can be easily completed by afterwards placing the thread and the pencil on the other side of the line which joins the fixed points. Fig. 176 shows how this may be done, and gives also the form of the curve obtained.

Such is the line which in geometry is termed an *ellipse*.

The two points, at which the extremities of the thread are fixed, have received the name of *foci*, and the two portions of thread, which connect these foci with each point of the ellipse, are called the *radii vectores* of this point.*

It is easy to see that this curve is elongated in the direction of the line which joins the foci. The line A A is called the *major axis* of the ellipse, the middle point of the major axis is the centre of the curve.

If, still retaining the same foci, we describe other ellipses with shorter threads, we shall obtain figures more elongated. The contrary will happen if we use threads of greater length. In the latter case, the ellipses will gradually approach the form of the circle; they will never, however, absolutely reach the circular form.

Lastly, if with a thread of the same length we increase or decrease the distance between the foci, the same differences of form will be obtained. In this case, the length of the major axis will remain the same, but the

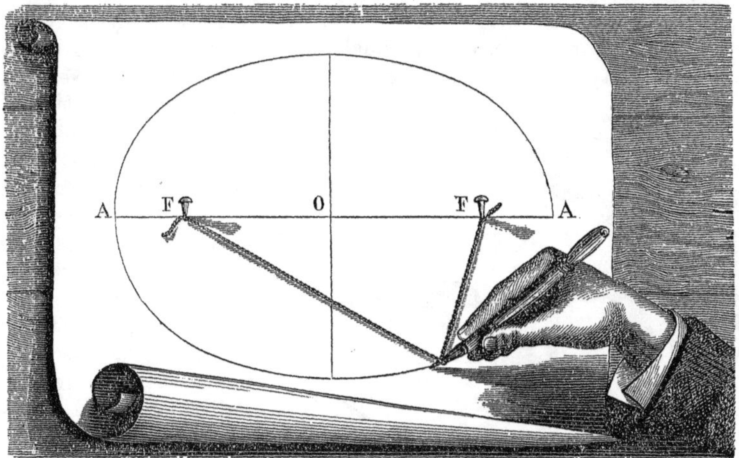

Fig. 176.

more the foci are separated the more oval will become the curve; contrariwise, the nearer they are together the nearer the figure will resemble a circle, finally becoming one when the *foci* are situated in a single point.

We shall now be able to understand Kepler's first law.

Each planet describes round the Sun an orbit of elliptic form, and the centre of the Sun always occupies one of the foci.

We have already seen, that the dimensions of the orbits described by the planets differ among themselves, and that the ellipticity of these orbits is far from being the same for all. Some orbits are nearly circular, as, for instance, those of the Earth, of Neptune, and especially Venus. Others are more elongated in shape; those of Mercury and of the Asteroids which

* As the length of the thread remains constant, the sum of the *radii vectores* is the same for all points of the ellipse. This property serves to define this curve.

lie between Jupiter and Mars. Lastly, the comets of our system have the most elongated orbits, and among them that of Halley's is the most decided.

It evidently follows, from Kepler's first law, that the distance of a planet from the Sun varies continually during its revolution, and takes all possible values between the extreme limits, which correspond to the two positions occupied by the planet at the two extremities of the major axis of the orbit.

Is, then, the velocity of a planet's motion always the same in the different parts of its orbit? No. The movement is by so much the more rapid, as the planet is nearer the Sun. Kepler's second law shows us how this velocity varies.

Let us take a planet in different positions in its orbit, and let us mark off on the orbit arcs described by a planet in the same time, P, P_1, P_2, P_3, P_4, P_5.

We have said that the velocity varies; this evidently is the same as saying that the paths described in equal times are of unequal length: so that the difficulty consists in finding some connexion between these constant variations in length. Let us insert the planet's *radii vectores* in each of the positions chosen; we shall by these means form as many triangles as there are arcs under consideration. Now, the surfaces or arcs of these triangles of which the bases are formed by the arcs described in equal times, are always equal; and therefore, if the length of time be doubled, tripled, &c., the areas of the triangles will be doubled, tripled, &c.

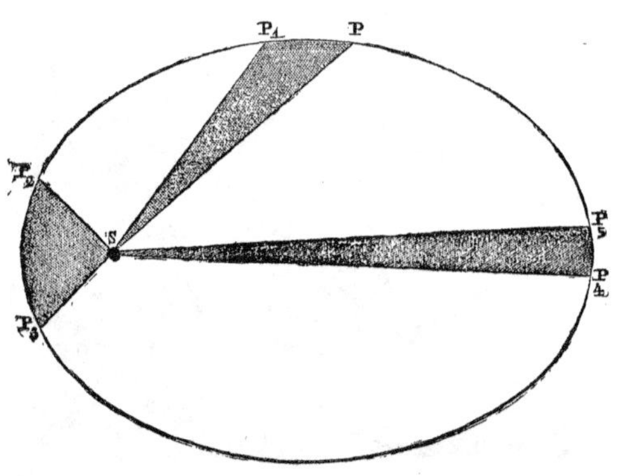

Fig. 177.

Kepler, therefore, thus announced his second law:—

*The areas, described or passed over by the radii vectores of a planet round the solar focus, are proportionate to the time taken in describing them.**

Now, it clearly follows from this second law, that the arcs described in equal times are smaller as the planet recedes from the Sun, and become greater as the Sun is approached. The triangles gain in breadth what they lose in length, and their areas remain constant. In other words, the planet moves faster the nearer it is to the Sun.

Kepler's first two laws apply not only to the orbits of the planets, but

* In planetary orbits one *focus* only is considered—that in which the Sun is placed. In each position of the planet, therefore, there is but a single *radius vector*.

to those of their satellites. Thus, the curves described by the Moon round the Earth considered fixed, is an ellipse, and our globe occupies one of the foci. More than this, the velocity of our satellite is such, that, if we divide its orbit into lengths passed over in equal times, all the triangles formed by the *radii vectores* of the Moon in its different positions will have a surface of similar extent.

We now come to Kepler's third law, that which cost him much more labour. More abstract than the first two, though equally simple in its enunciation, it is of the last importance for a proper comprehension of the subject, and merits in every way our attention.

The first two laws deal with each planet considered by itself, and would hold good if the system were only composed of two bodies, the Sun and a planet. The third law establishes a relationship between every planet in the system.

We must here again call attention to the fundamental fact, that the mean distances of the different planets from the Sun continually increase from Mercury to Neptune, and the same thing holds good for their revolutions round the Sun. But what relationship exists between the length of these periods and the distances, or, in other words, between the periods of revolution and the major axes of the orbits? Such is the problem resolved by the third discovery of Tycho Brahé's disciple.

We will write, in two separate columns, the periods of the revolutions of the principal planets, mean days, and double their mean distances from the Sun in thousandths of double the mean distance of the Earth, as follows:—

	Periods of Revolution Days.	Double mean Distances from the Sun, or Major Axes.
Mercury	87·97	387·1
Venus	224·70	723·3
The Earth	365·26	1000·0
Mars	686·98	1523·7
Jupiter	4332·58	5202·8
Saturn	10759·22	9538·8
Uranus	30686·82	19182·7
Neptune	60126·72	30040·0

Let now the periods of revolution be multiplied by themselves. To multiply a number by itself is to form what is called its square. This first very simple operation will then give the square of the period of the revolutions of the planets; this will form another new column. Let us pass to the second: multiply each number which represents the major axis of the orbits by itself, this will give the squares of these axes. Now multiply each of these squares, not by itself, but by the figures in the column which represent the major axis; this will give the cubes of the major axis, and we shall have a second new column. This done, let us compare two squares in the first column, and two corresponding cubes in the second one. Divide one square by the other, this will give us their ratio; divide in like manner the two cubes, and let us compare the quotients.*

* Let us take Venus and Jupiter for examples. The squares of the times are for Venus 50490·0900, and for Jupiter 18771249·4564. The cubes of the major axis

We shall find them equal. And this will happen whichever two planets we take. Kepler's third law, therefore, is enunciated as follows: —

The squares of the times of revolution of the planets round the Sun are proportional to the cubes of the major axes.

Thus, we need only know the time of revolution of the planets to deduce their major axes, and, as a consequence, their mean distances from the Sun. And as we know the *absolute* value of one of these, we know the absolute value of all. Thus, the knowledge of the *relative* distances of the different bodies of the system depends upon the knowledge of one only — that of the Earth, for example. Further on we shall endeavour to give an idea of the method which enables us to investigate how many radii of the Earth, or how many miles, bridge over the distance which separates us from the centre of our system. We may also add, that Kepler's third law applies to the satellites of any given planet; that is, it has been found to hold in the cases of the satellites of Jupiter, Saturn, and Neptune.

II.

UNIVERSAL GRAVITATION.

Gravity on the Surface of the Earth — Law of the Diminution of the Force of Gravity with increased Distance — The Fall of the Moon towards the Earth — Gravitation is universal — How the Sun and Planets are weighed.

Everything visible and tangible, or, more strictly, everything existing in a solid, liquid, or gaseous state, with which we are acquainted on our planet is subjected to the law of gravity, or, in other words, has weight. What, then, do such expressions as 'weighty,' or 'heavy bodies,' and 'weight' mean? This, namely, that every portion of matter left to itself, either in the atmosphere or *in vacuo*, falls in the direction of the vertical of the place on which it falls. That if the body be sustained and remains in equilibrium, or in repose on a surface, it still exercises a force — a pressure on whatever hinders it from falling lower, a force, of which it is easy to convince ourselves by noting the effort made by the hand, when it forms the supporting surface.*

Experience proves that the direction of this force, known under the name of 'gravity,' lies always in a vertical line; that is to say, in a line perpendicular to the horizon, or to the surface of water at rest. But as

are, for Venus 378,391.648, for Jupiter 140,835,258,325. Divide one square by the other, the quotient is 372. Divide one cube by the other, the quotient is still 372. These quotients would change if we took other planets for examples, but they would still be equal to each other, and it is this equality which forms the subject of Kepler's third law.

* If the body in question be sustained by a spring, the constant tenison of this spring also affords evident proof of the constancy of the force of gravity.

the Earth is sensibly spherical, the verticals of the various places all tend towards the interior of the sphere, very nearly to the actual centre itself.

We owe to Galileo the study of the laws of gravity; those which come into play in the fall of bodies on the surface of our globe. Since the time of this great man, it has been discovered that gravity is a force inherent to the matter even of which the terrestrial globe is composed; it is known, that the energy with which it is exercised depends on the distance of the body which is influenced, so that the energy increases when the distance diminishes, and decreases, on the contrary, when the distance augments.

For example, the flattening of the two poles of the terrestrial globe, or, what amounts to the same thing, the swelling of the spheroid towards the equatorial regions, causes the distance from the surface to the centre of the globe to increase continually as the equator is approached. It should therefore follow, that the attraction of the Earth on heavy bodies is exercised with much greater intensity at the poles than at the equator. This fact is abundantly proved by observation.

The law which regulates this diminution of the force of gravity, when the distance of the heavy body from the centre of the Earth increases, is as follows:—

To understand the law well in its simplicity, let us imagine a heavy body placed on the surface of the Earth, and consequently distant from the centre of the length of the Earth's radius, or in round numbers 4000 miles. Let us place it twice, three times, four times . . . ten times further away. The action of gravity on this body will be four times less at 8000 miles—that is to say, at the second position; nine times less at the following position, sixteen times, . . . a hundred times less at the consecutive distances; in such a manner, that when the distances increase, following the numbers 1, 2, 3, 4, 5, . . . 10, &c., the force of gravity diminishes in the proportion of the squares of these same numbers, or becomes 1, 4, 9, 16, 25 . . . 100 times less, and so on.

The force of gravity is measured by the space fallen through during the first second of the body's fall. So that, if experiment shows that a body requires a second to fall from a height of sixteen feet to the surface of the Earth, when it is removed to a distance double that of the terrestrial radius, it will not travel more than four feet during the first second of its fall; at a distance sixty times as great as the radius of the Earth, it would not fall more than the $\frac{1}{20}$th part of an inch.

This number gives precisely the measure of the diminution of the energy of terrestrial gravity on a heavy body situate in space at the mean distance of the Moon.

If, then, the Earth exercises its action on bodies situated at whatever distances in space, it ought to act on the Moon, and its action should be precisely equal to that which we have just calculated. Such is the question which the genius of Newton put to him, and which he solved, when he showed that the Moon, in moving in its circular orbit, falls towards our Earth that very quantity in a second. It is this incessant fall, combined with the centrifugal movement, which, if left to itself, would impel the Moon into space, which produces the elliptical movement of our satellite in her orbit.

Such is the bold generalisation which served as a point of departure to the great geometer whom we have just named.

He went further; he penetrated more profoundly into the secrets of the sublime mechanics which rule the celestial bodies. He extended to all the bodies of our solar system this law, which is sometimes called 'the law of attraction,' but more correctly, 'the law of gravitation.'

Newton showed, that if the planets move round the Sun, describing elliptical curves, according to the laws the discovery of which is due to Kepler, it is because that they are submitted to a constant force, located, as it were, in the Sun,—a force the direction of which is that of a radius vector, or a right line which joins the planet and the common focus. He showed, also, that all the circumstances of the movements of the planets are well explained by supposing that the force of gravitation is gravity itself, exercised by the Sun on the planets in the inverse ratio of the squares of their distances.

Thus, the same force, which precipitates on to the surface of the Earth bodies abandoned to themselves, is that which maintains the Moon in its orbit. It is a force of similar nature, exercised by the preponderant body of the system—the Sun—which also maintains the planets and the comets in their elliptical orbits, and prevents them from losing themselves in space, following the impulse with which they are animated, and thus breaking up our system.

By what series of reasoning, ideas, calculation, and verifications, Newton arrived at this great discovery, we cannot in this place narrate. Nevertheless, it is as well to know, that Kepler's second law relative to the equality of the areas formed the start-point for his demonstration of the tendency of the unknown force to act towards the Sun; as he found that it necessarily acted in the direction of a radius vector.

The third law of Kepler, combined with the second, led Newton to another inference, namely, that the force varies in the inverse ratio of the distances. Lastly, he showed that the elliptical form of the planetary orbits follows from the very law of the variation of the force in question. The nature of the substances, of which the various planets are composed, is quite independent of the mode of action of gravity, so that the mass of the Sun would act with an equal energy on an unit of the mass of all the planets, if they were all placed at the same distance from the common centre.

But as, by virtue of an universal principle of mechanics, every action of one material body on another necessarily supposes a reaction, that is to say, an action equal and in a contrary direction, it follows, that if the Earth and the other bodies of the solar system gravitate towards the Sun, the Sun also gravitates towards each of them. The same laws rule in each secondary world, composed of a central planet and its satellite.

Modern investigations in the field of sidereal astronomy have extended these laws to the systems composed of two or many suns, and the force thus shown to be diffused everywhere in space, has taken the legitimate name of *universal gravitation;* 'all the molecules of matter gravitate towards each other in the ratio of their masses, and reciprocally as the squares of their mutual distances.'

We will here terminate these considerations—which will be considered abstract ones perhaps, but which it is impossible to pass by in silence in an astronomical work—with a word on one of the truths of that science which is so daring, not to say venturesome, in its attacks upon nature. We refer to the statistics given in astronomical treatises on the mass or weight of the different celestial bodies. Is it possible to know the weight of a star—of the Sun, for instance?

We must first well understand what that means. This is not a question of minute quantities; and if we have expressed in billions of tons the weight of the Sun, it has been for the purpose of placing in relief the immensity of the Sun's mass, or that of the other members of the system.

Astronomers take an unit of mass or of weight in connexion with the quantities which they would measure. They take for the purpose of comparison, either the mass of the Sun or the mass of our globe. So that the question is in some measure transformed into another:—

How many times is the mass of the Sun greater than the mass of the Earth?

If it were possible to place our globe and the Sun successively in presence of the same body, and then to measure the force with which each of the two bodies would act on the third at the same distance, the problem would be solved. For example, we should determine the space travelled by the body in a second of time towards the Earth, then the space travelled in the same time by the body towards the Sun. These two distances, expressed in numbers by means of the same unit, would evidently give the ratio of the masses of the Sun and of the Earth respectively.

Well, at the surface of our globe, experiment tells us that a heavy body traverses during the first second of its fall sixteen feet;* and as, according to Newton's theory, the attraction of a sphere acts on external bodies as if the entire mass of the sphere were concentrated at its centre, we can and must consider the heavy body falling on the surface of the terrestrial globe, as situated at a distance from the centre of attraction equal to the radius of the Earth. Let us bear this in mind.

The mass of the Earth, then, acting on a body situated at a distance of 4000 miles, causes it to fall 16 feet in one second. On the other hand, the Earth itself gravitates towards the Sun; the orbit which it thus describes in a year shows how much it falls towards the Sun during the first second

* [This, of course, varies at different distances from the equator, for a reason we have already stated. The distance is more correctly as follows:—

16 feet 0½ inches at the equator.
16 „ 1 „ at London.
16 „ 1½ „ at Spitzbergen.]

of fall. The distance is found to be ·0099 feet. But we must bring this measure of the attractive energy of the Sun to what it would be at a distance from its centre equal to 4000 miles, or to the terrestrial radius, a distance 23,984 times smaller than the Sun's actual distance.

The law by which Newton found that the intensity of gravitation varies, indicates that the preceding number must be multiplied by the square of 23,984. Effecting this operation, the second result is arrived at:

The mass of the Sun, acting on a body situated at a distance of 4000 miles from its centre, causes it to travel, in the first second, 5,708,763 feet, or 1075 miles.

We can now compare the mass of the Sun with that of the Earth, since we know the actions of these two masses, on a body situated at the same distance from their centres; and it is clear, that the mass of the Sun is by so much greater than that of the Earth, as the number 5,708,763 is greater than 16. Dividing, we find in round numbers 355,000.

We must have, then, 355,000 globes of the same weight as ours to balance the Sun.

To solve this problem, it has been necessary to know the velocity of fall of a heavy body on to the planet. This element is directly observable on the surface of the Earth. In planets which have satellites, this velocity is deduced from the movements of these secondary bodies in their orbits. In the case of the planets without satellites, it is not possible to calculate in this manner the force of gravity on them. But by studying the influence of their masses on the other planets, and the perturbations which they cause in their movements, we have arrived at data equally precise in the case of all the masses of the bodies of the solar world, compared either to the mass of the Sun, or to that of our globe.

III.

Precession of the Equinoxes—Nutation—Planetary Perturbation.

THE rotation of the Earth on its axis produces day; its translation round the Sun gives the year. But, in the same manner as we have distinguished two kinds of day, the one sidereal, the invariable duration of which is due to the movement of rotation, the other solar, which varies in length in the course of a terrestrial revolution, in the same manner also astronomers distinguish two years—the tropical and the sidereal.

If we consider the time which elapses between two successive passages of the centre of the Earth to the same equinox, the spring equinox, for example, we have what is called the tropical year, the length of which, expressed in mean days, is 365·242264 days. If, instead of thus defining the year, we take the time which the Earth requires to return to the point of its orbit, in which the Sun appears to coincide with the same point of the heavens—with the same star— we have the sidereal year, the duration of which, expressed in mean days is 365·2563835 days. The sidereal year exceeds, then, the tropical year by about 20 minutes 20 seconds.

Whence comes this difference, and how can we explain it by the movement of the Earth in its orbit? Let us remember that the equinox occurs when the plane of the terrestrial equator passes precisely through the centre of the Sun. If this plane remained invariably parallel to itself, its line of intersection with the plane of the ecliptic would keep likewise the same parallelism; and it would be always at the same point of the orbit of the Earth that the successive equinoxes would take place. There would not be, then, any differences between the length of the tropical and sidereal year. The length of the latter being the greater, shows that the equinoxial point has fallen back, so that the Earth arrives earlier at this point than it would have done if it had remained immovable. Hence the name the *precession of the equinoxes* given to this phenomenon.

What follows from this fact? That when the Earth occupies the same positions in its orbit year by year, the Sun corresponds with stars more and more to the east, so that, little by little, and progressively, the aspect of the constellations seen at the same seasons is changed.

Let us analyse still more the phenomenon in question. To say that the equinox falls back or retrogrades is the same as saying, that the plane of the equator has varied in position; and as the axis of the Earth is always perpendicular to this plane, it follows that this axis has not remained rigorously parallel to itself. We know, indeed, that it varies in direction, still, however, preserving the same angle with the ecliptic, in such a way as to describe an entire cone in an interval of about 25,870 years; so that at the end of this period, the equinox, having accomplished an entire revolution on the terrestrial orbit, returns to occupy its initial position.

The terrestrial axis, in executing this slow movement on the surface of the starry vault, describes a complete circle. The celestial poles, therefore, are incessantly variable, so that the fixity which we ascribed to them in our description of the heavens is quite relative. In fact, the northern pole, now quite near the Pole Star, is still approaching it. This diminution of angular distance will continue until the year 2120, when they will not be more than half a degree apart. This epoch passed, the pole will recede from Polaris, will pass from the Little Bear to Cepheus, then over the borders of the Swan. In 12,000 years, the bright star nearest to the north pole will be Vega in Lyra, which will then play the part of Pole Star; Canopus, in the southern sky, will be equally found in the vicinity of the other pole.

The phenomenon of the precession of the equinoxes, discovered two thousand years ago by Hipparchus, has during the last century been ascribed to its true cause, of which we will speak a word further on.

Let us now mention another movement of the axis of the Earth, executed simultaneously with that which we have just described. Its period is much shorter, since it is only 18⅔ years.

The conical movement of the axis of the Earth, which produces the precession of the equinoxes, and which is effected in about 26,000 years, changes progressively the direction of this axis, without, however, modifying its inclination to the plane of the ecliptic. In truth, however, this movement does vary by reason of another movement, which causes the axis to oscillate during each period of 18⅔ years around the mean position it would occupy, were it influenced only by the movement of precession. The name of *nutation* has been given to this oscillation—this 'nodding' of the axis of our globe, which gives rises to slight changes, sometimes greater, sometimes less, in the obliquity of the ecliptic.*

All these movements, both those of rotation and translation round the Sun, and those of nutation and precession, are effected simultaneously by the Earth. The motion of our globe has often been compared, and with justice, to that of a top which, while turning on itself with great rapidity, and tracing on the surface which supports it a line which may be likened to its orbit, undergoes also a balancing of its axis of figure or rotation, analogous to the oscillation of the Earth. There is this difference, that the various movements of the Earth are accomplished with mathematical regularity, in periods relatively very long, and according to laws which allow us each instant to assign its true position in space.

Having described the phenomena, let us indicate briefly how they are connected with the great law of the Solar System—with universal gravitation. If the Earth were rigorously spherical, the direction of its axis of rotation would remain always the same, and would preserve indefinitely the parallelism of which we have before spoken. The action of gravity of the other celestial bodies would not change this direction, if we suppose, as observation shows, that the terrestrial poles occupy an invariable position on the globe. But it is known that the Earth is not a sphere, it is swollen at the Equator; it is like a perfect sphere, covered with padding, the thickness of which decreases from the equator to the poles, giving rise to a section resembling an ellipse. At the poles the thickness of the pad is *nil*.

Now, it has been proved that the action of the mass of the Sun on this "padding" is the cause of the continuous retrograde movement of the equinoxial points, which produces a corresponding advance of the successive equinoxes. In the same manner, the action of the mass of the Moon on the same padding produces an analogous, but much more rapid action; that of the nutation of the Earth.†

This is still another kind of influence which affects the movement of

* The maximum of these changes does not reach 10″ of arc.

† We have already seen, that an astronomer of Alexandria, Hipparchus, first discovered the precession of the equinoxes. It is to Bradley (1647), that the discovery of nutation is due. Lastly, the glory of binding firmly these two phenomena to the Newtonian theory of gravitation was reserved for D'Alembert. Laplace has since perfected this beautiful hypothesis.

the Earth, and which is also a consequence of the law of gravitation. This proceeds from the combined actions of the masses of the other planets on the mass of our globe. As the actions of which we speak are reciprocal, what we say of the Earth in this matter is applicable to any other planet; but to dwell on such abstract and complex considerations as these would be to go beyond the purpose of this work. We will, therefore, confine ourselves to pointing out its extreme importance.

Kepler's laws, which we have announced and explained, and from which Newton deduced the law of gravitation, are only rigorously true when we consider a single planet and the Sun. But as the masses of the other planets also act on this planet, each following the general law, there follows a series of modifications which periodically alter its movement. The inclination, the direction of the major axis, the eccentricity of the orbit, are elements which especially vary, in a manner changing at once the position and form of the orbit of the planet. These alterations which, very far from contradicting the law of gravitation, most brilliantly confirm it, are known in astronomy under the name of "planetary perturbations." We have referred to their great importance, not only because they enable us to calculate with precision the future position of the celestial bodies of our system, but, again, because they will serve—and the discovery of Neptune is a proof of our remark—to complete the knowledge which we possess of the Solar System.

In our next chapter we shall discuss the action of the combined forces of the Sun and Moon on the liquid part of the surface of the terrestrial globe, and we shall see manifested, in a manner visible to all, and in extremely short periods, the forces, the perturbations, to which we have referred.

VI.

THE TIDES.

Phenomena of the Ebb and Flow, High and Low-water—Epochs of Spring-tides—Coincidence of the Phenomena with the Positions of the Moon and Sun—Theory of the Tides deduced from the Law of Gravitation—Combined Actions of the Sun and Moon.

If we were to compare the sea to an immense being which lives, moves, and breathes, it is in the tempest we should see its anger, and in calms its sleeping hours, whilst the periodical movements of the tides would typify its regular and constant respiration. But these are poetical fancies on which we do not care to insist. These great phenomena of nature offer an interest so real that they require no more embellishment. The true explanation of the tides, moreover, the connection of the causes which produce them with the great theory of universal gravitation, are quite recent conquests of science. It is scarcely a century since they were first submitted to calculation. They still offer, therefore, to many the attraction of novelty.

Every one knows that twice a-day, at an interval of about 12 hours and 25 minutes, the shores of the ocean present us with the spectacle of the flow of the tide: the tide by degrees rises, gaining on the beach, which it covers to a greater and greater height, and after six hours swelling attains its maximum. It is a beautiful sight to see the agitated waves, which come with increasing fury, to beat the pebbles and the foot of the rocky shore, throwing their salt spray high into the air.

Scarcely is the instant of *high-water* or *flood-tide* attained, than the *flow* or rise of the water ceases; the descent commences, and the *ebb* succeeds to the *flow*. The sea then leaves the beach which it covered, and by degrees re-descends to its point of departure; we have then, *low-water* or *ebb-tide*. Then begins another rising tide, followed by an ebb, and so on.

It must be understood, that the instant of low water is not at the mid-interval which separates two consecutive flood-tides, the flow being of much shorter length than the ebb, or, in other words, the sea takes longer to go down than to rise. This difference varies according to the ports; thus, it is 16 minutes only at Brest, and at Havre, 2 hours and 16 minutes. Such, in the main, is the phenomenon of the tides.

If we were confined to the observations of this periodicity of the movements of the sea, science would not have penetrated very profoundly into the mystery of their causes; it could not predict, as it now does correctly, the height of the tides at the different ports, and the precise times of high water, and thus afford valuable information to navigators.

Before commencing our explanation of the causes, we will conform ourselves to the natural course of science, and look more closely into the facts.

Between two consecutive flood-tides we have, as we have stated, 12 hours and 25 minutes. It follows, therefore, that from one day to another, high-water is 50 minutes behind. Thus the daily period of the phenomenon is exactly equal to the lunar day, the length of which is also 24 hours and 50 minutes, on the average. In other words, the successive retardations of high-water are presented by the successive transits of the Moon over the meridian. If, then, we note the hour of high water in a port, it will be easy to predict the hour for another day. Sailors, profiting by this fact, make their arrangements accordingly, as they require to enter or leave the port on that day.

Let us also notice this: 50 minutes of retardation in one day produce in about 14 days and three-quarters a total retardation of 12 hours; and a retardation of 24 hours, or one day, in 29 days and a half; that is to say, in the period of a lunation. The hours of the tides are, therefore, the same every 15 days, with this difference, that the morning tide becomes the evening one, and reciprocally. At the end of a lunar month the hour becomes identically the same.

The facts which we have already stated deal only with the times of high-water and their variations. Let us now occupy ourselves with the height of the tide.

This height is itself very variable for the same sea and the same port; but here again is presented a remarkable periodicity, which shows that the phenomenon is connected with the relative positions of the Sun, Moon, and Earth.

Near the new and the full moon the flood-tide attains its maximum, whilst the corresponding low-water descends to its lowest point. These are the *spring-tides*, or the '*tides of the syzygies*.' Their height, then, decreases more and more, to the time of the first and last quarter of the Moon. We have, then, the *neap-tides*, or *tides of the quadratures*. Then starting from these two periods, the height of the tide again increases till the next syzygies, that is, until the Moon is again in conjunction or opposition.

But the highest, like the lowest tide, does not really fall on the same day as the lunar phase; in every part of the ocean, there is a difference of 36 hours, or a day and a half. It is, then, the third tide which follows the full and the new moon, which is the highest; the lowest tide, which follows the quadratures, is also the third.

These remarkable coincidences between the times, the periods of high-water, and the positions of the Moon and Sun with respect to the Earth, have given rise for some time to the supposition that the cause of the phenomenon resides in these two bodies. '*Causa*,' says Pliny, '*in Sole Lunâque*.' But of what nature is their influence? This is a problem which it has been given to modern science to solve. Descartes first dared to draw the veil and sound the mystery; and if this great philosopher did not succeed in his attempt, it was on account of his preconceived ideas on the system of the world. The honour still remains to him of having dared. But let us pursue the study of facts.

The height of the tides again varies with the declinations of the Moon and Sun, it is by so much greater as the two bodies are nearer the equator. Twice a-year, towards the 21st of March and the 22nd of September, the Sun is actually in the equator. If, at the same time, the Moon is near the same plane, the tides which occur then are the highest of all. These are the *equinoxial spring-tides*, because the Earth is then at the spring, or autumnal equinox.

On the other hand, the smallest tides take place towards the solstices; if the Moon attains its smallest or its greatest meridional height at the same time as the Sun.

Lastly, the distances of the Moon and Sun from the Earth have also their influence on the height of the tides. Other things being equal, the height of the tide is by so much greater as the two bodies are nearer the Earth. Thus, the tides of the winter solstice are higher than those of the summer one.

Such are the general circumstances which characterise the periodical movements of the sea. But it must not be forgotten, that they are not the only ones; the force and direction of the winds, the configuration and direction of the coasts, the depth and extent of the seas,—circumstances which depend upon position and time—are so many multiplied influences which singularly complicate the tides. Thus, every one is aware that isolated seas, like the Caspian, or those of small extent, and communicating with the ocean by narrow straits, like the Black and Mediterranean Seas, have but imperceptible tides.* The opposite coasts of the Atlantic, which face each other, west and east, have very unequal tides. It is the same with the eastern coasts of Asia, which have strong tides, whilst at the other side of the Pacific, and in the Oceanic Archipelago, the flow, which is very regular, attains but little height.

But speaking only of the European ports, the intensity of the phenomena is extremely variable, even in neighbouring places. Let us take an example; according to the calculations of the tides for the year 1864,† the highest tide was that which followed a day and a half after the full moon of the 15th of September, a little before the autumnal equinox; it occurred on the 17th.

The calculated height of this tide was at Brest, 12 feet; at Granville, 23¼; 10½ feet at Cherbourg; 14 feet at Havre. These numbers, very different for the neighbouring ports, show only the height above the mean level of the sea, that is, the level the water would take if there were no tides. They must be doubled, if we wish to have the height of the flood-tide, above the level of low-water, for the same day. Thus, at the ports of Granville and St. Malo the waters rose on the date mentioned to a total height of about 46 feet. If the wind favours such a tide as this, and increases its violence and its height, great disasters may be feared.

There is a vast difference between the tides of the western coast of Europe and those of the isles of the Southern Sea, which scarcely rise to a height of 20 inches. But there are some still more terrible; and amongst them we will content ourselves with quoting those of the Bay of Fundy in New Caledonia, which rise, it is said, to a height of nearly 100 feet.

The cause of these differences in height is greatly owing to local circumstances. Thus, the ports of the Channel are subject to strong tides, because the moment of the waters meets with an obstacle in the narrowing of the coasts, and the further the gulf is penetrated, the higher is the tide.

The tide is felt in great rivers, to a distance depending upon their size and depth. At the moment of high-water, the waters of the river flow back, re-ascending their course, but the transmission of this river-tide is progressively retarded.

Hence follow the curious phenomena, known in France under the names of *mascaret* and *barre* [such as the 'bore' in the river Severn.]

We will now speak of the causes of the tide.

* According to the observations of the able and regretted G. Aimé, who studied the undulation of the tides at Algiers during two years, the height of the luni-solar tide in that port is nearly 3½ inches on the day of syzygies.

† By MM. Laugier and Mathieu, *Annuaire du Bureau des Longitudes.*

It is the combined actions of the Moon and Sun on the liquid mass with which our globe is three-quarters surrounded, which produce the alternate movements of the ebb and flow.

We have seen, that if two bodies, such as the Earth and the Moon, are present, the molecules of both have a mutual tendency, known under the name of 'gravitation,' the intensity of which varies directly as the masses, and inversely as the square of the distance. Let us now see how this action is exercised by the Moon on the liquid molecules of a sea.

The Earth having the form of a spheroid, the liquid stratum which covers it would have a form exactly similar, and continually the same—except accidental variations due to meteorological causes—if the Moon and Sun did not exist.

Let us consider the Moon at a given moment. Let us connect its centre with the centre of the Earth by an ideal line; this line will meet the

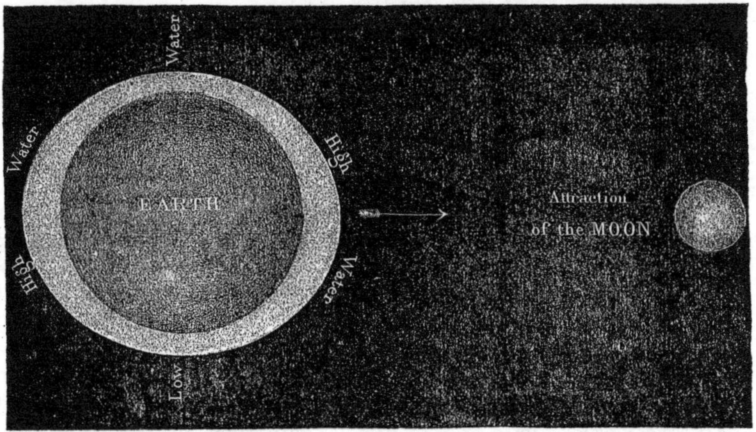

Fig. 178.—Attraction of the Moon on the waters of the sea. Simple lunar tide.

surface of the globe in two points diametrically opposite. The one nearest the Moon will be the place on the Earth at which the Moon is in the zenith. The opposite point will have the Moon at the nadir, every place of the Earth which has the same latitude as the first, will see the Moon on the meridian at that instant.

The attraction of the Moon on the nearest liquid molecules partly counterbalances the attraction of the Earth; it lessens their gravity in the vertical direction. The molecules, which their fluidity and independence separate from the surface to the solid part of the Earth, rise by virtue of that attraction. The same thing happens, but in a less degree, with the neighbouring molecules in the hemisphere turned towards the Moon, the attraction being slighter as these molecules are situated further from the point which lies at the summit of the hemisphere turned towards the Moon.

Hence it follows, that the liquid sheet, with which this hemisphere is covered, is swelled up towards the Moon, and, instead of keeping its spherical form, takes—though not of course in exact proportion—the form of an egg. There is high water at the top, low water at every place which has the Moon on the horizon. If the Earth had no movement of rotation, this tide would be permanent, and the waters would thus remain in equilibrium, or at least would follow the movement of revolution of the Moon; the tides would have no other periods than the lunation. But the Earth in its rotation presents all its surface to the Moon, so that the wave follows the parallel which corresponds to the position of our satellite.

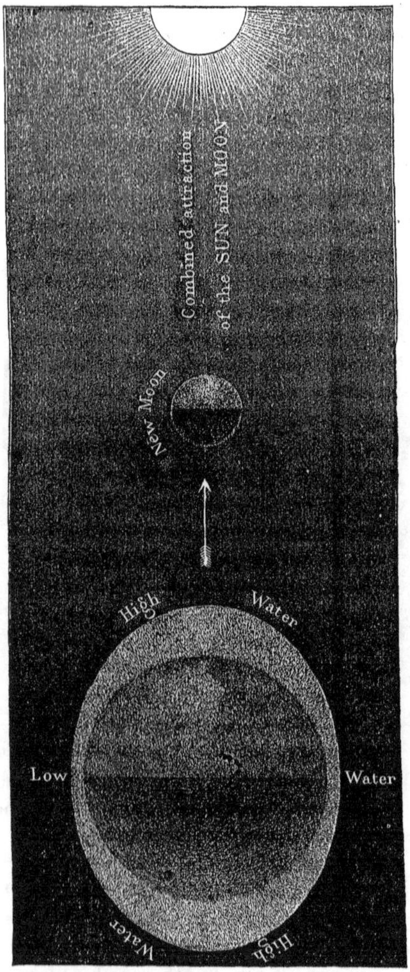

So far we have explained the high and low tide for the hemisphere turned towards the Moon; but how is it that the waters are also swelled up at the same instant on the opposite hemisphere?

This is easily accounted for. The lunar attraction makes itself felt on all the molecules which compose the earth and sea; but its energy is much more slight, as these molecules are more distant. If this action were exercised on every point with equal intensity, there would follow a total displacement towards the Moon, but no change of form. The inequality of attraction causes the most distant molecules to remain behind; their gravity towards the Earth is diminished, and all the liquid strata on the hemisphere opposite the Moon take precisely the same form as those that are in froint. [In a word, on one side, the water is pulled from the Earth, on the other the Earth is pulled from the water.]

Fig. 179—Combined action of the Moon and the Sun on the waters of the sea. Luni-solar tide of the syzygies.

This problem, when submitted to mathematical analysis, indicates for the general form of the surface of the ocean, that of an ellipsoid, swollen in the direction of the diameter of the Earth, which when prolonged passes through the Moon at every instant.

There is then high-water whenever the Moon transits either the upper or lower meridian, that is to say, every 12 hours and 25 minutes, and low-water every time that it is at the horizon of a place; that is to say, at periods of equal duration.

But it is not the Moon alone which acts, there is also a tide produced by the attraction of the Sun. The enormous bulk of that body would produce immense movements of the waters, if its distance, four hundred times greater than that of the Moon, did not counterbalance the attractive

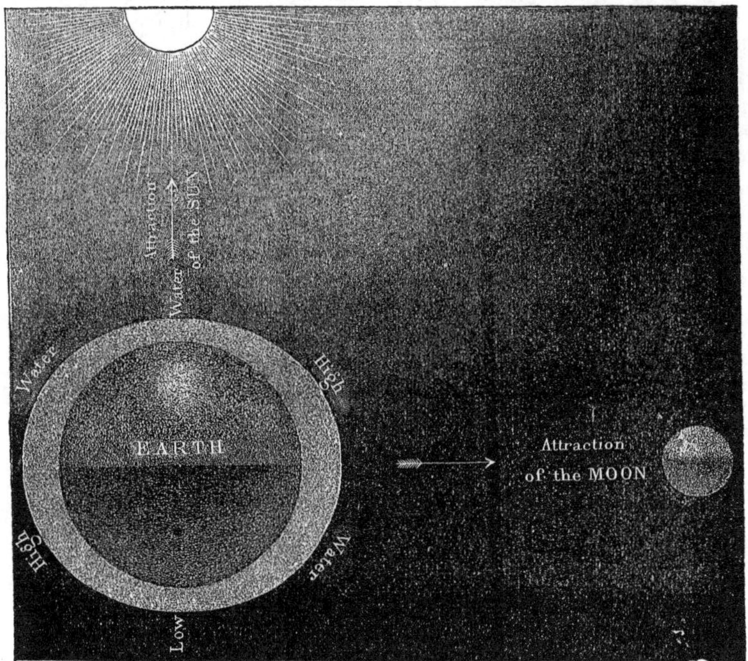

Fig. 180.—Neutralizing action of the Moon and Sun on the waters of the sea. Luni-solar tides of the quadratures.

force due to its mass. The solar tides, although much smaller than the lunar ones, sometimes increase them, at others neutralise them.

They increase them when the two bodies are on the same line with the Earth, which occurs at the syzygies—at new and full moon (fig. 179). The actions of the two bodies neutralise each other, when the Moon is at a right angle to the Sun, and in that case the resulting tide is a minimum (fig. 180).

Calculation shows that the luni-solar action is much more intense when the bodies are nearer the equator: hence, the great equinoxial tides. Lastly, the action varies in the inverse ratio of the cubes of their distance, it is, therefore, clear that the tides are higher when the Moon and Sun are nearer the Earth.

Such in the main is the principle of the theory of the tides. These daily and irresistible movements are subjected to immutable laws; they are, by reason of the density of the water of the sea,—a density inferior to that of the solid nucleus which that water covers—confined within narrow limits. Natural laws suffice to 'put a curb on the fury of the waves.'

[It must be noted, however, that, although the statical equilibrium of a tidal wave is thus accounted for, the dynamical conditions of the problem cannot thus be explained. On the contrary, if we consider only the dynamical relations we shall find that the place of low water should be under the Moon and at the opposite part of the Earth, the place of high water, between these regions. Newton, Laplace, Airy, and others, agree in this view. The theory of the tides remains yet to be established satisfactorily. Much that has been presented in popular treatises as a part of that theory, is in reality but an account of the results of observation.—R. A. P.]

V.

ORIGIN AND FORMATION OF THE SOLAR SYSTEM.

Laplace's Hypothesis of the Origin and Formation of the Solar System—Primitive Nebula—Luminous Nucleus—Formation of Planets and Satellites—Direction of the Movements of Rotation and Revolution.

THE human mind seems so organised that it attaches itself with more obstinacy and perseverance to the pursuit of those questions which it is impossible to solve than to those which are more accessible. At the risk of a kind of intellectual *vertigo,* it loves to lean over the cliffs of those abysses of thought, at the bottom of which lie in confusion the solutions of so many grave problems, the origin and the end of all things, the essence of the first cause, and many other questions which are rather in the domain of metaphysics than of science.

This tendency towards the abstract is, so to speak, irresistible. It is not sufficient for us to fathom, with the telescope, the depths of infinite space, where the eye sees succeeding each other without end suns and clusters of suns; we still wish to know if this progression has an end, a limit. We cannot believe in nothing, and our mind is lost in the contemplation of an indefinite chain of being.

By a like curiosity, we attempt to remount the course of time, and to picture to ourselves the first origin of things. We almost know what is the actual state of the Universe. The discovery of the most general laws authorises us to predict the future state of the celestial bodies, at least in our system. We, therefore, try to know what it is which has given them birth, and, lacking the positive knowledge, which it is so difficult to acquire in such matters, we attach ourselves to the traditions which have been in vogue from the first ages of humanity.

Will there ever be any certain notions on this subject? We know not. But we shall not be sorry to know what are actually the most probable conjectures deduced from those sciences which deserve in the highest degree to be called *positive*.

Geology teaches us that the Earth, at its origin, existed in a fluid state. Formed from an immense agglomeration of gaseous matter, endowed with an excessive temperature, condensed at its centre, it has slowly cooled, then formed a liquid shell enveloped with a high and thick atmosphere. Then, in consequence of the gradual loss of heat, the superficial strata by degrees solidified, until a certain state of general equilibrium has given it the dimensions and form which it now possesses.

Among the many witnesses, which testify to this ancient history of the Earth, there are two which still remain, and which we can now question. These are, on the one hand, the increasing temperature of the strata as we descend, which compels us to consider the interior nucleus of the Earth as being still in an incandescent state; volcanic eruptions are an additional proof in support of this hypothesis. On the other hand, in the form of the terrestrial globe, in its flattening in the direction of its axis of rotation, and the swelling out of the equatorial portion, lies the mechanical proof of the fluid primitive state.

Such are the most certain data which we possess on the ancient history of the Earth, the different evolutions of which can be followed. It is not easy, however, to assign certain epochs to the various phases of this development, but, in such a case, probabilities suffice, and all agree in giving to our planet an age, the antiquity of which is counted by some hundreds of thousands of years.

Is the Earth, then, the only planet of the Solar System to which we must assign such an origin? Here precise data fail us, and it is to analogy that we must appeal for an answer. We have said that facts are wanting. We mistake; there is one which is of great weight; it is the fact of a common flattening, which is certain in Mars, Jupiter, and Saturn, and which the difficulty of measurement only has prevented us from proving in the other planets of the Solar System. It is then extremely probable that at the origin the whole Solar System was formed from an agglomeration of matter in a gaseous state, which by degrees was transformed into distinct bodies, under the influence of a cooling going on during thousands of centuries. We thus arrive at the hypothesis formulated by one of the greatest sons of modern science, Laplace, who has thus attempted to account for most of the phenomena of planetary astronomy.

We shall try to describe in a few words this theory of the origin of the bodies which compose our system.

If we go back in thought to an epoch distant from our own by a considerable series of centuries, the whole Solar System, or, more exactly, all the matter which now forms the different groups, existed in a purely gaseous state, or, as it may be put, under the form of an immense Nebula, extraordinarily diffused, presenting no indication of condensation. In such a condition, the molecules of the nebulosity were so distant one from the other, that the repulsive force with which they are endowed entirely annulled the attractive force by virtue of which, gravitating one round the other, they would tend to form groups. But centuries elapsed; the nebulosity by degrees cooled by incessant radiation into space: the action of the repulsive force diminished, and that of attraction was exercised more and more; it condensed and formed one or many centres in various parts of the nebulosity.

The solar Nebula ought then to have presented at last the aspect of a luminous nucleus enveloped to a great distance by a kind of gaseous atmosphere, in form nearly spherical. Such appear to us in space the nebulous stars; we have seen, indeed, that astronomers consider these last systems as irreducible into stars, or as simple, double, or multiple suns, surrounded with a real nebulosity, either self-luminous or illuminated by the central body. At this period of its formation, the Sun existed alone, the planets and their satellites remained undeveloped in the atmosphere.

But the entire mass was endowed with a movement of rotation, which forced in the same direction either the molecules of the nucleus, or those of the nebulosity. At a given moment, the limits of this latter depended upon the distance at which the centrifugal force due to rotation was in equilibrium with the central force of gravitation. These limits changed, and approached the centre, under the influence of a continual cooling, which induced in consequence a diminution of volume in the Nebula. Hence the abandonment of a zone of condensed vapour, at the distance of the first limits.

By degrees, the celestial atmosphere abandoned a series of zones of vapour nearer and nearer the centre, all being nearly in the plane of the general equator, that is to say, that in which, in consequence of the velocity of the rotatory movement, the centrifugal force was naturally preponderant.

These are the zones which have given birth to the planets, or to the groups of planets and asteroids.

For it to have been otherwise, for the zones detached from the general nebulosity to have kept the form of rings concentric with the Sun, there must have been a perfect equilibrium continuing to exist between the different molecules composing these rings. But, according to Laplace's expression, the chances were greatly against this. The rings divided, and the most considerable *débris*, attaching and incorporating the rest, again formed centres or nebulous nuclei. It is important to remark, that each of them must have been animated with two simultaneous movements, one of rotation round its own centre, the other of translation round the common centre. Moreover, as these two movements were but the continuation of the general anterior movement, their direction remained the same as that of the rotation of all the system, or of the solar nucleus. The planets once formed, we can understand perfectly how these smaller Nebulæ, similar to the larger one, produced the birth of new bodies gravitating and revolving round each of them; such is the origin of the satellites.

Laplace next explained why the satellites formed no more new satellites, and why these secondary bodies present the same side to the planet round which they gravitate; it is that their small distances giving to the attraction of their primary a preponderating influence, the satellites themselves, when still in a fluid state, were swollen up tide-like, towards the planet; and from their rotatory movement followed a time of rotation nearly identical with that of their movement of revolution. After a certain number of revolutions, these periods become rigorously equal.

Such is, in a few words, the magnificent theory which Laplace has presented to the scientific world, with a reserve which testifies to the profound respect which this great genius accorded to the truths demonstrated with all the rigour of science. It must be acknowledged that it is in perfect accord with the laws of general mechanics, and with the facts of both astronomical and physical observation. Without extending the subject further, it is impossible not to be struck with the agreement which the system of Saturn presents with the conception of the illustrious geometer; Laplace insists with reason on this point.

'The regular distribution of the mass of Saturn's rings around its centre, and in the plane of its equator, follows naturally from this hypothesis, and without it it must rest without explanation; these rings* appear

* Some very curious physical experiments, imagined by M. Plateau, account in the most satisfactory way for the phenomena which we have just described; they appear to us well adapted to dissipate the obscurity, which a description of such an abstract conception would naturally leave in the minds of some of our readers.

These experiments consist essentially in freeing a fluid mass from the action of gravity, in such a manner that all its parts may be merely acted upon by their mutual attraction; and in imparting afterwards to this mass a movement of rotation more and more rapid. To do this, M. Plateau places a quantity of oil in a glass vessel, filled with a mixture of water and alcohol, the lower strata of which are less dense than the oil, whilst the upper strata are lighter. The mass of oil descends in the mixture as far as the stratum of the same density, where it remains, taking the form of a sphere.

In this state, the mass of oil is freed from the action of gravity, and the form which it takes is due simply to the mutual attraction of its molecules.

Next, by the help of a metallic disk introduced with care into the sphere of oil, and a stem which passes through its centre and communicates with a handle, M. Plateau imparts to the system a progressive movement of rotation.

When this movement is slow, the sphere is transformed into a spheroid, swelled at the equator, flattened at the poles, under the action of the centrifugal force, which to me to be ever present proofs of the primitive extension of the atmosphere of Saturn, and of its successive contractions.'

[The theory, however, gives no account of the observed relations of planetary magnitude, inclination, axial rotation, &c.; nor of the meteor systems, which are now found to traverse the Solar System in all directions, and with all degrees of excentricity, inclination, and so on. The present writer has shown that these peculiarities, as well as all those accounted for by Laplace, can be explained by the theory that the Solar System resulted from meteoric aggregation rather than (directly) from the condensation of a gaseous mass. See his 'Other Worlds than Ours,' c. ix. —R. A. P.]

developes the movement. The phenomenon accounts then perfectly for the form of the planets.

If the movement becomes more rapid, the flattening becomes more considerable; the spheroid at last becomes indented at its poles, spreading out more and more in the horizontal direction, until the oil, entirely leaving the disk, is formed into a circular ring. At this moment, the phenomenon at once explains both the zones detached at the origin of the solar mass, and the rings of Saturn.

Lastly, if the rotatory movement, rendered more rapid, is continued with a disk of a diameter sufficiently large, the centrifugal force, in driving the particles of the surrounding medium towards the ring, soon separates it into several isolated masses, which form themselves into individual spheres; each of which preserves for a certain time a movement of rotation of its own in the same direction as the ring.

This last phase of the phenomenon offers a striking analogy with that of the formation of the centres of condensation which, on Laplace's hypothesis, are the origin of the planets of our system.

BOOK THE SECOND.

METHODS AND INSTRUMENTS EMPLOYED BY ASTRONOMERS.

I.

CELESTIAL MEASUREMENTS.

General Idea of the Problem by which the Distance of Inaccessible Objects is determined—Solution of this problem on the Earth's surface—Distance of the Earth from the Moon—Solar Parallax, Distance of the Sun from the Earth—Stellar Parallax, Distance of the Stars.

We are now about to discuss one of those problems, the solution of which leaves so many doubts, and gives rise to so much incredulity in the minds of those unacquainted with mathematical science and methods; we refer to the determination of the distances which separate us from the various celestial bodies.

In enunciating the problem generally, we shall put in evidence the essential difficulty, the cause of the incredulity to which we have referred, and which we must attempt to remove. The problem is as follows:—

To measure by means of a conveniently chosen unit the distance of a visible but INACCESSIBLE *point.*

The difficulty lies in the circumstance that the object in question is *inaccessible.* If we speak of measuring a line on the surface of the Earth, the possibility of the operation is at once recognised. Without being in the secret of the methods employed,—methods often very long, very laborious, and very delicate,—it is assimilated vaguely to direct measurement of a small distance by means of a chain or cord; and no one makes a difficulty in admitting, errors excepted, the results of surveys of the surface of our globe.

But how can we ever know the length of the straight line which joins the eye and an object situated in space, out of our reach—the Sun or Moon, for instance? This is the question raised by most persons, when they hear astronomers affirm that the Moon is 240,000 miles from the Earth.

We shall, therefore, show that this problem is one of no real difficulty: the necessary operations are, theoretically, very simple, and it is in the practical carrying out of them that the real difficulty—the impossibility, where the thing is impossible—lies.

We will proceed from the known to the unknown, from the simple to the complex, and we will commence with the problem of the distance of an inaccessible point, situated on the Earth's surface. We shall see that in the main the solution of this case is the same as that of the most difficult ones, and applies equally to the determination of the distances of the heavenly bodies.

We will suppose ourselves in a level field or meadow. We see on the horizon the top of a tower, from which we are separated by some obstacle,

Fig. 191.—Measure of the distance of an inaccessible object.

such as a river. We want to know the distance of this tower from our stand-point without actually measuring or stepping the distance; without, in fact, crossing the water. We shall proceed as follows:—

At C, our standing-point, we plant a stick; at B, in the meadow, we plant another, at a distance which must not be too small compared with the distance of the tower. We now measure accurately by means of a Gunter's chain, or tape, the straight line which joins B and C. Let it be, for example, 468·7 yards.

This is the *Base Line* of our operations.

Now, by means of a theodolite placed successively at C and B, we observe the tower at each station, and the instrument will give us the angle formed by the visual ray with our base-line; that is to say, the angles at the base of the triangle A B C. What do we now know? First, the exact length of the line B C, measured on the ground itself, directly; and secondly, two angles: A C B, which we will suppose to be equal to 80° 29′, and A B C equal to 75°. We shall find these data quite sufficient to lay down a similar triangle on paper, on any scale that we may choose, in such a manner that, by means of a properly divided measure, we may read off the number of yards in the side C A of the triangle. We shall find it 1085 yards, nearly.

The distance sought, therefore, has been found, and the problem is solved.

The precision of the result will depend upon two things: first, the degree of exactness of the measurement of the base; secondly, that of the two angles. This double precision itself depends upon the perfection of the measuring instruments and the skill of the observer. Nor must we forget another important consideration. The choice of the base, both as to its position and length, has a great influence on the result. If it be too small relatively to the distance measured, the form of the triangle is very elongated, and a small error in the measure of either angle may cause a large error in the result. In terrestrial measurements we can, of course, always choose our base; in celestial ones, on the contrary, this is not the case, and a difficulty often practically occurs in this way with which theory has nothing to do.

We now arrive at the application of what we have said, and will begin with the most simple case, that of the distance of the Moon.

Two astronomers arrange to observe in two different parts of the globe. One chooses Dantzig, the other the Cape of Good Hope. We will suppose the two stations, for greater simplicity, situated on the same meridian, so that the time is the same at both stations at the same absolute instant.

They agree to observe the Moon simultaneously, that is, on the same day (or night) at the same hour. These stations A and B (fig. 182) being known, the difference of the latitudes is known; this is the angle A T B formed at the centre of the Earth by the verticals of the two stations.

These are the data of the problem. What we have to find is the length of the distance L T, or the straight line which joins the centre of the Moon with the centre of the Earth, at the time the observation is made.

The first observer, by the aid of a special instrument, measures the angle Z A L, the zenith distance of the Moon's centre. The second observer, at the Cape, does the same for the angle Z′ B L. This is all that need be done. We can now construct on paper a figure similar to the four-sided figure, L A T B. The angle T is known; the lines Z A and Z B are two nearly equal radii of the terrestrial sphere; and the direction of the lines A L and B L is given by the observations. When once this four-sided figure is laid down, we only have to connect the points T and

L, and to find its length, taking the Earth's radius as the unit of measurement.*

We have thus found that the mean distance of the Moon is about 60 radii of the Earth.

We now pass on to the distance of the Sun, and of the divers planets of the Solar System; and we will commence by two remarks, which will simplify our subsequent explanation.

If we refer to the first general problem, of the distance of an inaccessible object, we shall understand, if we look at fig. 181, that the accurate measure of the two angles at the base tells us at once the angle at the apex; or the angle formed by the two straight lines which join the tower and the extremities of the base, [As the sum of the three angles in any triangle is a constant quantity = 2 right angles.]

This angle is called the *parallax* of the tower, and the object of all the problems, dealing with celestial distances, is to determine the amount

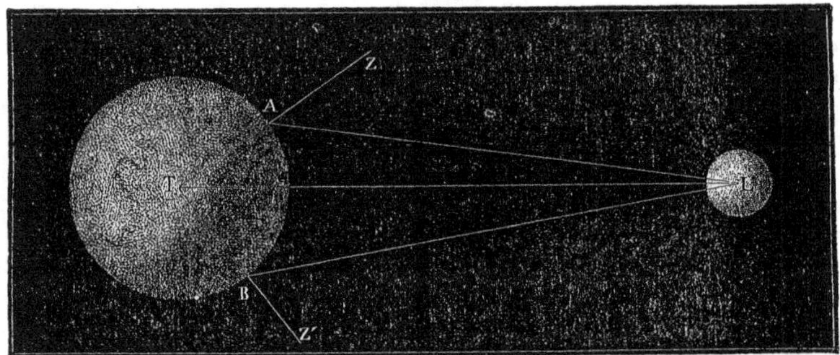

Fig 182.—Measure of the distance of the Moon.

of this parallax. Thus, for the distance of the Moon, what we seek to know is the angle which the base A B (fig. 182) would subtend at the centre of the Moon, or, more generally, the angle subtended by the diameter or radius of the Earth at the Moon.

In the case of the Sun, the problem may thus be stated. Under what angle would the diameter of the Earth appear at the centre of the Sun? or, in astronomical language, What is the Sun's parallax?

The second remark is as follows:—Kepler, by the discovery of his laws, enabled us to determine not the *absolute*, but the *relative* distances of the planets from the Sun. In such a manner that although he was unable to express the *absolute* distance by means of a common unit, in miles for example, the relative dimensions of the orbits were so known, that

* In this example, as in the other, the graphic construction on paper—an exceeding rough method—is not the one actually employed. The real solution is accomplished by a more or less complicated, but sure, mathematical calculation. This calculation admits of a precision which is only limited by the accuracy of the preliminary observations.

he could say, for instance, that the mean distance of Jupiter from the Sun was $5\frac{2}{10}$ that of the Earth, the distance of Venus from the Sun was $\frac{723}{1000}$ that of the Earth, and so on.

So that, when once the distance of any one planet from the Sun is determined, by Kepler's laws we can deduce those of all the rest.

The planet whose distance we have therefore endeavoured to determine is naturally the Earth. How then have we attempted it?

[Here we at once approach a new step in measures, and touch upon one of the noblest problems of Astronomy. We have seen how it is possible to measure distances on the Earth; and how two observers, using their distance on the Earth as a base-line, can determine the distance of the Moon. But the measure of the Moon's distance in no way helps us to get at that of the Sun. The latter is entirely a different operation, and on the correctness with which we can accomplish it depends 'every measure in astronomy beyond the Moon, the distance and dimensions of the Sun,

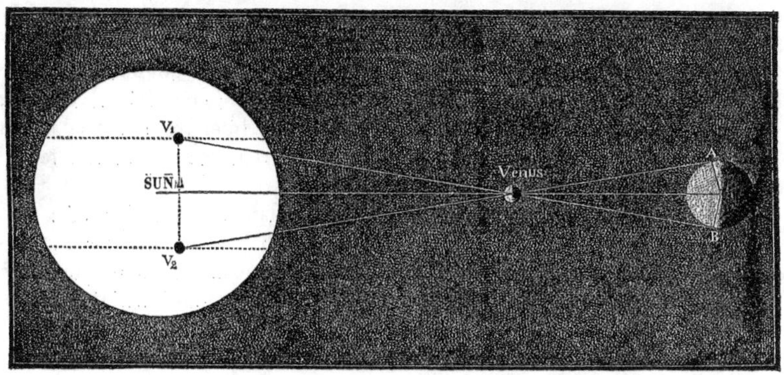

Fig. 183.—Measure of the Sun's distance by the transit of Venus.*

and every planet and satellite, and the distance of those stars whose parallaxes are approximately known.'†

The value of the Sun's distance at present received has been deduced from the transits of Venus in 1761 and 1769, and as these transits afford the most satisfactory means (although, as we have seen, note page 15, there are others) of determining it, we will endeavour to give an idea of the method employed.

We have seen that when Venus crosses the Sun's disk, during its transit, it appears as a round black spot. Let us suppose two observers placed at two different stations on the Earth, properly chosen for observations of the phenomenon, one at a station A in the Northern hemisphere,

* [It will be understood that the distance $V_1 V_2$ in the figure, is enormously exaggerated. The real distance would not exceed the diameter of either of the discs shown in the figure at V_1 and V_2.—R. A. P.

† [The Astronomer Royal in 'Monthly Notices,' vol. xvii. p. 209.]

another at a station B in the Southern one. When Venus is exactly between the Sun and the Earth, the observer at A will see her projected on the Sun at a certain point which we will call V_2, the Southern observer at B will, from his lower station, see the planet—which we will call V—projected higher on the disk at a point which we will call V_1. Now, the angle which we require to know, in order to determine the Sun's distance, is A V_1 B, and the proportion of the measured angle V_2 A V_1 to the desired angle A V_1 B is as V_1 V to A V, or as 72 : 28, very nearly. So that, clearly, all depends upon finding the value of the angle V_2 A V_1. Now, how can this be done?

If the distance between the two stations is sufficiently great, the planet will not appear to enter on the Sun's disk at the same absolute moment at the two stations, and therefore the paths, or the 'chords.' traversed will be different. Speaking generally, the chords will be of unequal length, so that the time of transit at one station will be different from the time of transit at the other. This difference will enable us to determine the difference in the length of the chords described by the planet, and consequently their respective positions on the solar disk, and the amount of their separation. Now, this separation is the angle V_1 A V_2 required. Having this, we can compute the value of A V_1 B, and infer from it the Sun's distance, in fact, if A B were situated at the extremities of a diameter of the Earth, we should know the angle which it would subtend at the Sun; in other words, we should know the Sun's parallax.

But this is on the supposition, that the Earth has no motion of rotation; let us introduce this consideration, and see not only how it modifies the result, but also with what anxious foresight astronomers prepare for such phenomena, and why it was requisite in 1769, and will be again necessary in 1874 and 1882, to go so far from home to observe them.

Let us take the transit of 1882;* we already know the instant and place (true perhaps to a second of time and arc) at which the planet will enter and leave the solar disk—in other words, we know exactly how the Earth will be hanging in space as seen from the Sun—how much the south pole will be tipped up—how the axis will exactly lie—and how the Earth will be situated at the moments of ingress and egress. Now if we draw two planes cutting the centre of the Earth, tangential to those parts of the Sun's limb at which the planet will enter and leave the solar disk, we shall recognise in a moment that some parts of the Earth will see the planet enter the disk sooner than others. Some parts, on the other hand, will see it leave the disk later—in other words, according to the position of a place

* [It happens, unfortunately, that the transit of 1874 has been neglected so far as the application of the method here considered is concerned. It had appeared to the Astronomer Royal, on a general view of the subject, that the transit of 1882 would be preferable. But a very careful analysis of the conditions of the two transits by the present writer (see 'Monthly Notices of the Astronomical Society,' vol. xxix.) has shown that in reality the transit of 1874 will afford far more favourable opportunities for the application of Halley's method than the later transit, during which, indeed, that method can hardly be applied at all.—R. A. P.]

with reference to the plane of which we have spoken, both ingress and egress will be accelerated or retarded as the case may be.

Now, if we can find a place where both the ingress will be accelerated and the egress retarded, and another where the ingress is retarded and the egress is accelerated, we shall get what we want, the greatest difference in the duration of the transit,—the greatest difference in the length of the cord, of which we have before spoken.

'Selecting, then (we quote from a paper by Mr. Airy in the 'Monthly Notices,' vol. xxiv.), the parts of the Earth at which the duration of transit would be shortest, it is seen at once that in the seaboard of the United States of America, the ingress is retarded by a quantity represented by 0·95, and the egress is accelerated by a quantity which, in the mean, is 0·83 nearly; so that the whole shortening is represented by 1·78 (the geometrical possible maximum being 2·00). That locality, therefore, is very favourable.

'Selecting, secondly, the parts of the Earth at which the duration of transit would be longest, it will be found that the choice is more limited, and the practical difficulties rather greater. For the acceleration of ingress at 2^h Greenwich mean time, the observing-station ought to be on the right side of the diagram; and for the retardation of egress at 8^h Greenwich mean time, it ought to be on the left side of the diagram. It is impossible to satisfy these conditions, except by a station on the Antarctic Continent. From this and other considerations, it has been found that the place must be in 7^h East longitude nearly. Such a position can be found between Sabrina Land and Repulse Bay. Here the whole lengthening of transit would be represented by 1·61; a very large amount (the geometrical possible maximum being 2·00). Combining this with the observations at Bermuda, the whole difference of durations would be represented by 3·41 (the geometrical maximum being 4·00). This point near Sabrina Land is, in fact, the only one which is suitable for the observation.'

This method, we see, is sometimes more complicated than that by which the Moon's distance, or that of the inaccessible object, was determined; but they all depend upon the same principle.

We have given, however, but the spirit of the method, omitting all the difficulties met with in practice, and all the consequent complications in the calculations.*

We must next endeavour to show by what methods we have been able

* The reader may perhaps ask why the Sun's parallax is not determined direct by a simple triangulation, as in the other problems we have noticed. The reason is, that the base of the triangle, at its maximum, cannot exceed the dimensions of the Earth's diameter. Now the distance of the Sun is so great that, compared to this base, errors of observation would assume a considerable importance, compared to the extremely small angle to be measured. [For instance, an error, which in the case of the Moon would throw us out only 100 miles, would in the case of the Sun amount to 16,000,000.] This difficulty, therefore, has to be got over by utilising the transits of Venus—a method due to the illustrious Halley, and the most efficacious of those at present adopted.

to determine the distances of the stars, situated beyond our system, or at least of some of them.

The method of triangulation is still the one adopted. But the base is no longer either the radius or diameter of the Earth. Already we know that the angle under which our Earth would be seen at the Sun is extremely small; and it has required all the precision of our modern astronomical data on the planetary movements to obtain a positive result. But the distance of the stars is so considerable, that it is useless to attempt to use a base on the surface of the Earth.

It is, therefore, necessary to choose a base elsewhere, and also some other unit of measurement. Astronomers at once thought of the distance which separates the Earth from the Sun, even before this distance was determined; so that the problem was to determine how many times the Sun's distance was contained in the distance of any given star.

Fig. 185.—Apparent variation in the height of a tower at different distances.

Let us see in what manner we have been able to use this immense base-line, which, as we know, contains some 24,000 terrestrial radii. Let us again take a familiar comparison for an example, and imagine on abserver placed in the centre of an extensive plain. Before him, on the horizon, is a tower, the top of which appears to be of a certain height above the general level of the plain. Now, it is evident that this apparent height depends upon the distance of the observer from it, and that the height will increase as he approaches the object, and decrease as he recedes from it. Let us glance at fig. 185. When the observer is at B, the visual ray, B S, has caused the summit of the tower to stand out on the background of clouds at *b*. If he move from B to A, approaching the tower, the new visual ray, A S, will form a greater angle with the surface of the plain than the first,

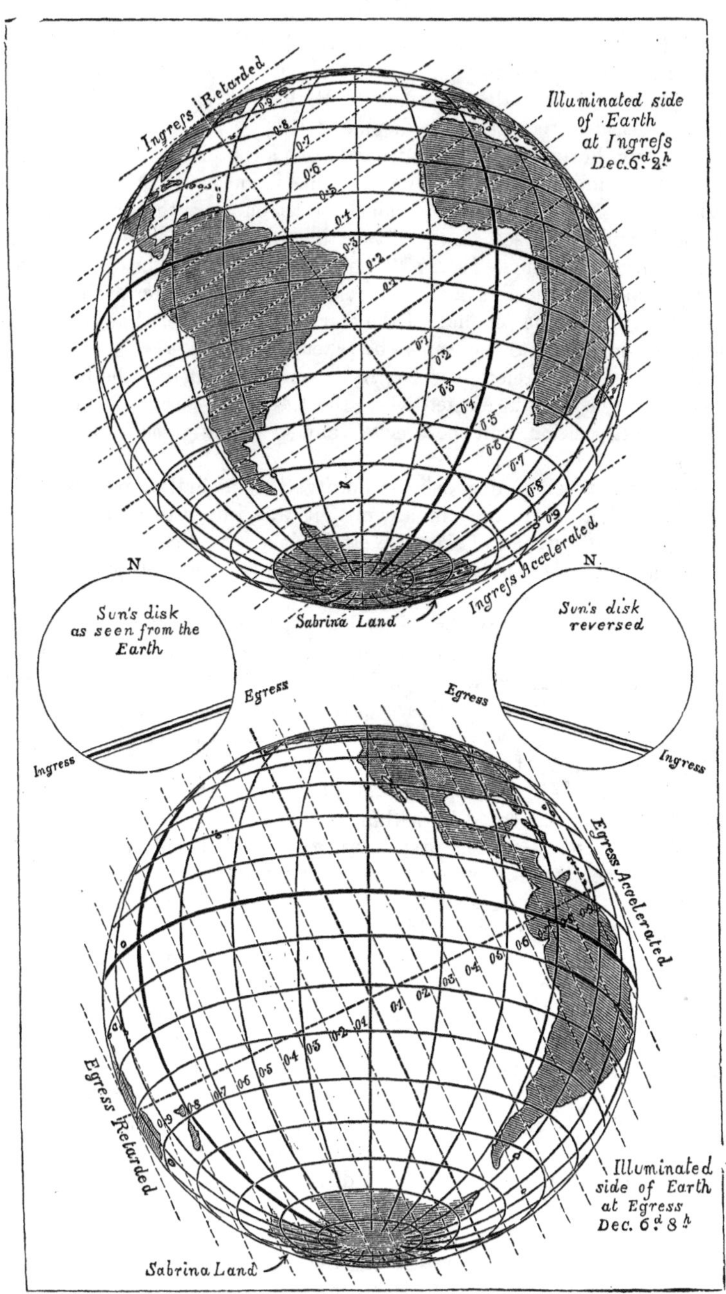

Fig. 184.—Transit of Venus, 1882.

and the top of the structure will have gradually elevated itself from *b* to *a*. By how much? By an angular quantity exactly equal to that under which an eye placed at S would see the base A B, that is to say, the line of length of which measures the observer's displacement.

Well, the horizontal plain represents to us the plane of the terrestrial orbit; the summit of the tower is a star, the distance of which we seek; its height above the plane is what is called by astronomers the star's latitude; and the distance traversed, A B, will be that which the Earth accomplishes in six months, a distance of some 190 millions of miles. The displacement, *b a*, is, in fact, the parallax of the star referred to the diameter of the Earth's orbit; it is double the parallax of the star if the radius of that orbit—the distance of the Earth to the Sun—be taken as an unit.

The question, therefore, consists in determining whether the latitude of the star has sensibly augmented when the Earth has passed from the first to the second position, and the precise value of this augmentation, if there be any.

A large number of most delicate observations at first showed no appreciable variation in latitude; in a word, it was impossible to detect any change, even of a second of arc, in a star's place. So that the visual angle under which form one of these stars a distance of some 190,000,000 miles is seen,—is almost *nil*.

Now, in order that any given length, a yard for instance, viewed in front, may be reduced so that it will subtend an angle of one second only, it must be removed from our eye to 206,000 times its own distance.

It results, therefore, from this, that the stars are removed from us *at least* 206,000 times the distance of the Sun from the Earth—206,000 times 190,000,000 miles. Let us imagine in space a sphere—having the Earth for centre, and this tremendous distance for radius; it is perfectly certain that not a single star could lie within it.

However interesting this first datum may be, it is only a negative one. But astronomers were not discouraged. They increased the perfection of their methods, and suggested a second still more delicate than the first. We will endeavour to give an idea of it.

Let us return to our observer. We will suppose that he has not been able to detect any appreciable increase in the apparent height of the tower, in consequence of the extreme smallness of the displacement compared with the distance of the object observed. Nevertheless, this increase, however small it may be, is a reality. How then can he detect it? In this manner.

Instead of only looking at the top of the tower, he will compare its position with a neighbouring point—neighbouring at least in appearance—and will then commence his approach. One of two things must happen, either the two points are at the same distance from the eye, or one is further off than the other.

In the first case, the variation in the height will be the same for both, and the method will not succeed. In the second case, the top of the tower rising higher than the point with which it is compared, which we will suppose the more distant, their reciprocal distances will vary. Now, on the one hand, it is much more easy to measure the variation where it is confined within small limits, than where it becomes relatively a considerable quantity. On the other hand, the small apparent movements due to different causes, and the inevitable errors of observation and instrument, as they affect in a like manner both points observed, may all be neglected. Such is, shortly, the second method employed by astronomers, the success of which has enabled us to determine, with a great exactitude, our distance from some of the stars.

Comparing with the greatest care, and for several years in succession, the apparent position of several couples of neighbouring stars, [one of which, by virtue of its proper motion, we know to be nearer to us than the other,] we have been enabled to determine the visual angle, which the diameter of the Earth's orbit subtends at the nearest. We have already dealt with the results of this method of observation.

Such are, in their most elementary form, the methods employed by astronomers in measuring celestial distances. If, by means of the foregoing explanations we have been enabled to convince our readers of the certainty of the results, and to dispel the doubts which some among them may have entertained on the possibility of the solution of this problem, our end is gained. But it must be fairly stated that, if the spirit or principle of the methods be easy to comprehend, the practical working out of them is extremely difficult; all the resources of the mathematical sciences, all the most precise astronomical knowledge, so patiently accumulated during so many centuries, all the precision of our measuring instruments, have been indispensable for arriving at their exact solution. We have said nothing of the talent of observation, the sagacity, and sometimes the genius, of the philosophers who have employed them.

II.

ASTRONOMICAL INSTRUMENTS.

VISIT TO AN OBSERVATORY.

Instruments for obtaining Magnified Images of Celestial Objects—The Astronomical Telescope—Newtonian, Herschelian, Gregorian, and Silvered-Glass Reflectors—Instruments used in Observatories: Transit Circle, Equatorial.

The surprise and admiration excited by a description of the marvels which astronomers have discovered in the depths of the heavens are always accompanied by a strong desire to see for oneself. Hence arises a very pardonable curiosity to know more of the instruments by means of which the circle of our knowledge of these magnificent phenomena is being continually widened. Telescopes, both refractors and reflectors, are eagerly sought after; but those most frequently met with are ordinarily so small, that when we compare them with the large instruments now used in observatories the sentiment of curiosity is rather over-excited than satisfied.

We have mentioned Observatories—Temples of the most sublime of the sciences which in the eyes of the profane, that is, of a large majority of the public, are looked upon as mysterious sanctuaries where, in the silent night and away from the busy hum of men, philosophers are in intimate communication with the innumerable worlds which people the Universe. How many there are among us,—we speak of those interested in science,—anxious to inspect one of them if even cursorily. In order, therefore, to do what we can to satisfy this wish, we give in this last chapter a short description of the principal instruments to be found in them.

We may divide astronomical instruments into three distinct classes:—

Those which serve to increase the power of the human eye, or, in other words, to lessen distances. Such are telescopes, divided into refracting and reflecting telescopes, or, as they are called, *Refractors* and *Reflectors*;

Those which have for their object the measurement of angles, and by means of which we determine the positions of the stars; *Divided Circles* and *Micrometers* are the principal instruments in this class, and they are always used in conjunction with telescopes;

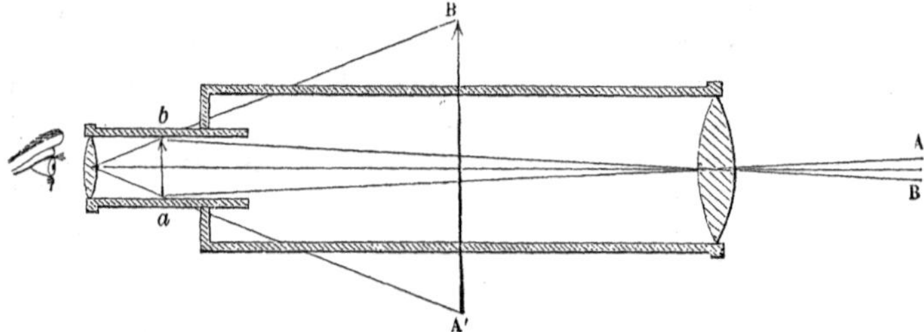

Fig. 186.—Theoretical Section of the Astronomical Telescope.

Lastly, those which enable us to estimate time with all the precision requisite in astronomical calculations [that is, to the tenth part of a second]; such are *Astronomical Clocks* and *Chronometers*.

We must limit ourselves here to the first class, those which, by giving us a magnified image of the object, bring it apparently nearer to us, and thus assist our sight. By reason of its etymology (τῆλε, far, and σκοπεῖν, to see), the term *Telescope* is applied to all those instruments which fulfil this condition, whatever be their construction.

In Refractors, the light is made to pass through a combination of lenses, called the *Object-glass*, and is *refracted*, or bent, to the focus. In Reflectors, the rays are received on a mirror, or *Speculum*, and are *reflected* to the focus. This is the fundamental distinction between the two classes: in both the aërial image formed at the focus is examined in the same manner.

The following description will enable us to understand the specific character, which we have thus defined in such a general manner.

The *Astronomical Telescope* is a refractor formed, as we have seen, of two systems of lenses, one held in position by a cylindrical tube; the one turned towards the object is termed the *Object-glass*, and on it falls the beam of rays emitted by the object viewed; this is grasped by the object-glass, and made to converge, at a certain distance behind it, to a spot called the *focus*, where it forms an image of the object observed. This image *a b* in the figure, is examined by the aid of a magnifier, in precisely the same manner as a naturalist examines an insect or a plant. The eye, in looking at the image of the object by means of this lens — which again may be and generally is a combination of lenses — observes it magnified, and can examine its details. Hence it is called an *eye-piece.*

Such is in principle the construction of an Astronomical Telescope. It must be observed that it is not the object itself which is observed by means of the eye-piece but its image, and it is the image alone which is magnified.

[A word now as to the *power* of the telescope, and, first, as to its *illuminating power.* The aperture of the object-glass, that is to say, its diameter, being larger than that of the pupil of our eye, its surface can collect more rays than our pupil; if this surface be a thousand times greater than that of our pupil, it collects a thousand times more light, and consequently the image which it forms at its focus is a thousand times brighter than the image thrown by the lens of our eye on to our retina.

Having this image at the focus, the *magnifying power* of the telescope comes into play. This, in the general opinion, is the most important element of power. It varies with the eye-piece employed, the ratio of the focal length of the object-glass to that of the eye-piece giving its exact amount. Bearing in mind that what an astronomer wants is a good clear image of the object observed, we shall at once recognise that magnifying power depends upon the perfection of the image thrown by the object-glass and upon the illuminating power. If the object-glass does not perform its part properly, a slight magnification blurs the image, and the telescope is useless. Hence, many large telescopes are inferior to much smaller ones in the matter of magnifying power, although their illuminating power is so much greater. Hence, again, the immeasurable superiority of refractors over reflectors in this particular; for, although by virtue of their illuminating power they are admirably adapted for observations of nebulæ, where the best definition of the image is required, they are found sadly wanting.

There is another matter to be mentioned. In the case of stars, — which, by reason of their immense distance, appear as points, — no increase in the size of the disk, except the one mentioned further on, follows the application of higher magnifiers; with planets this is different; each increase of power increases the size of the image, and therefore decreases its brilliancy, as the light is spread over a larger area. Hence the magnifying power of a good telescope is always much higher for stars than for planets, although at the best, it is always limited by the state of the air at the time of observation.]

If the material of which the object-glasses are composed is equally pure, and their definition equally fine, those with the largest apertures possess the greatest magnifying power.

To return to the object-glass. It is composed generally of two lenses, in juxtaposition, or nearly so, one bi-convex, *the crown*, the other bi-concave, *the flint*. This combination is required to destroy the *chromatic aberration*, which, without it, would surround the image with a halo of coloured light, and destroy the purity of the image. The eye-piece also is composed generally of two or more separate lenses, the object of which is to reduce the distortion of the image as seen through a single lens, and to increase the *field of view*.

In fig. 186 is given a section or interior view of an astronomical telescope, similar to the one figured in fig. 187.

[Among the most remarkable and powerful refractors of the present day, we may mention that at Chicago, of 18½ inches aperture, the work of the celebrated American optician, Alvan Clark, and those of Pulkowa and Cambridge, U.S., each of 15 inches aperture, from the *atelier* of Merz, the successor of the celebrated Fraunhofer. While we write, our English opticians, Messrs. Cooke and Sons, are mounting an object-glass which they have just completed, of the enormous aperture of 25 inches, which at one bound surpasses almost our most sanguine hopes, and restores England to the place it held in the optical art in the time of Dollond.]

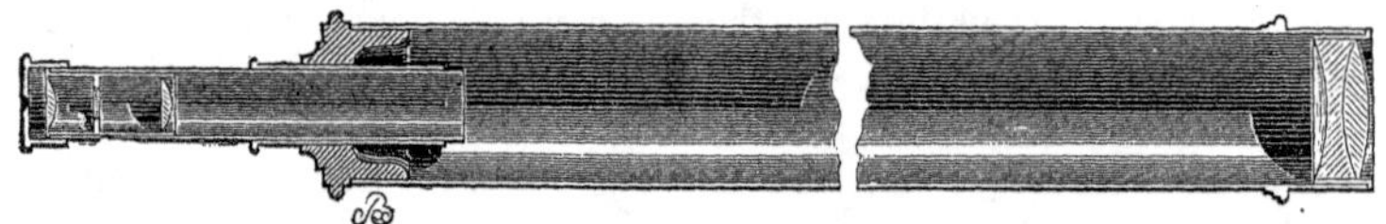

Fig. 187.—Section of the Astronomical Telescope.

We now come to the Reflector, which, as we have seen, differs from the refractor in having a concave mirror to reflect light, instead of an object-glass to refract it. The mirror requires to be ground and polished with the most consummate care and skill as its surface is not spherical, as are those of object-glasses, but parabolic.

The arrangement of the mirror and the eye-piece is of course different from that adopted in the refractor, as the mirror is opaque, and its concavity must be turned towards the sky. We give three sections of reflectors of different constructions as designed by their inventors, Newton, Gregory, and Herschel.

In the first of these instruments (fig. 188) the luminous rays, after reflexion from the principal speculum M, are again reflected from a smaller one *m*, inclined at an angle of 45°, in such a manner as to throw the beam to the side of the tube, to which is fixed the eye-piece, which performs, as we have said, the functions of a magnifier. Thus, in Newton's construction, the observer is placed sideways, at a right angle to the direction of the rays which enter the telescope.

In the Gregorian form (fig. 189) the great speculum is pierced at its centre, and the aperture holds a tube containing the eye-piece: the small mirror is placed in front of the large one, its reflecting surface opposite to it and perfectly parallel. There is, therefore, a double reflexion, as in the Newtonian form, but the eye of the observer is directed to the object viewed. This double reflexion naturally much enfeebles the light.

The 'front-view' reflector,—Herschel's form (fig. 190),—has not this disadvantage; there is but one mirror M, inclined at the bottom of the tube in such a manner as to throw the image to the lower edge of the

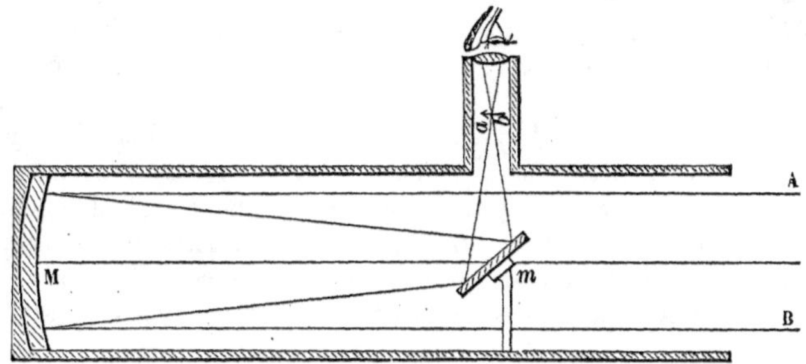

Fig. 188.—Newtonian Reflector.

end of the tube turned towards the object. This arrangement is only good in the case of large specula, because the observer, who is compelled to turn his back to the object observed, cuts off part of the beam of light by his head.

In reflectors, the loss of light by reflexion is much greater than that caused by absorption in refractors; so that with equal apertures the illuminating power, and therefore the magnifying power, of reflectors are very much less.

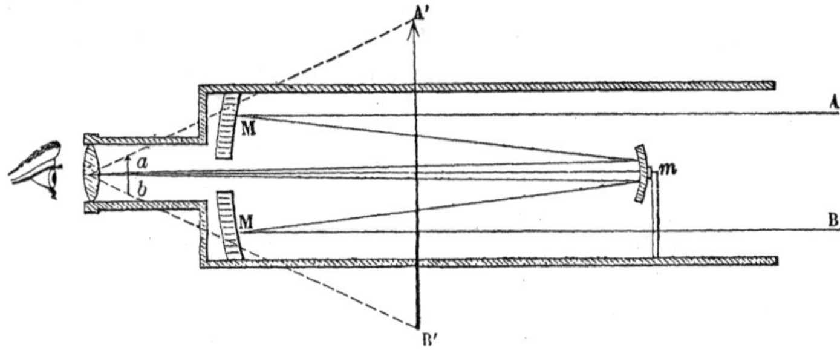

Fig. 189.—Gregorian Reflector.

Some years ago a skilful physicist, M. Léon Foucault, who is so well known from his delicate experiments on the velocity of light and his invention of the gyroscope, suggested the construction of glass mirrors, coated with an exceeding thin film of silver, chemically deposited, an arrangement which would much reduce the price of telescopes and would render their polishing extremely easy. We reproduce here (Plate XXIV) the magnificent instrument he has constructed for the Observatory of Paris (it has subsequently been removed to Marseilles). This reflector is constructed on the Newtonian principle.

Among the remarkable reflectors at present in use, we must mention that constructed by the Earl of Rosse, and erected at Parsonstown, in Ireland. This colossal instrument is of 60 feet focal length, and the mirror is 6 feet in aperture. We have seen what good use the illustrious constructor of this instrumental marvel has made of it in discovering new nebulæ, which had resisted all feebler efforts. The instrument cost 12,000*l.* Plate XXIII gives, according to the 'Speculum Hartwellianum,' views both of the telescope and of the structure which supports it and permits its proper handling.

Nowadays, when the heavens are explored in all parts by tried observers, provided with the most perfect instruments, it becomes more and more difficult to add to our knowledge of the physical constitution of our system and of the other sidereal systems. While the telescope was young, very small instruments were sufficient to secure the most glorious discoveries. Galileo saw the satellites of Jupiter by means of a telescope

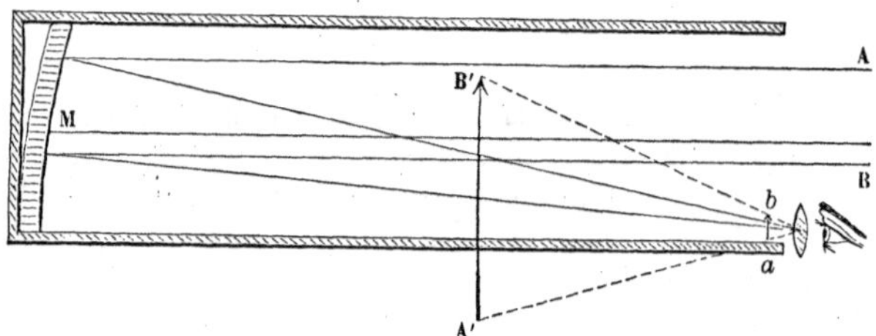

Fig. 190.—'Front View' Reflector.

which magnified seven times; and never used one which magnified more than thirty-two times. Let us add, lest amateurs should be discouraged, that a small telescope of less than three inches aperture, and with magnifying powers varying from 60 to 300 times, is sufficient to enable one to pursue useful investigations. M. Goldschmidt discovered fourteen minor planets with a telescope such as we have described; and he has seen the satellite of Sirius with it also.

[We are glad to know that in England the number of medium-sized refractors, by which so much good work has been done, is rapidly increasing. The illustrious Secchi, we think, has too hastily condemned small telescopes; and—bearing in mind the double-star work done by the Rev. W. R. Dawes with a small telescope, and the maps of the Moon and Mars we owe to the observations of Beer and Mädler, who used a smaller instrument still—the increase in the use of even small telescopes is a subject for much congratulation.

In this climate of ours, which by the way is not so bad, astronomically speaking, as some Anglophobes would make it, a 6-inch glass is doubtless the size which will be found the most constantly useful; larger aperture being frequently not only useless, but hurtful. Still, 4 or $3\frac{1}{4}$ inches are

GREAT SILVER-ON-GLASS REFLECTOR.

Constructed by M. Foucault.

apertures by all means to be encouraged; and by object-glasses of these sizes, made of course by the *best* makers, views of the Sun, Moon, planets, and double stars, may be obtained, sufficiently striking to set many seriously to work, as amateur observers, and with a prospect of doing good, useful work.

Thus in the matter of double stars, a telescope of 2 inches aperture, with powers varying from 60 to 100, will show the following stars double:

Polaris.	γ Arietis.	α Geminorum
α Piscium.	ρ Herculis.	γ Leonis.
μ Draconis.	ζ Ursæ Majoris.	ξ Cassiopeæ.

A 4-inch aperture, powers 80-120, reveals the duplicity of

β Orionis.	α Lyræ.	δ Geminorum.
ε Hydræ.	ξ Ursæ Majoris.	σ Cassiopeæ.
ε Boötis.	γ Ceti.	ε Draconis.
ι Leonis.		

And a 6-inch, powers 240-300,

ε Arietis.	λ Ophiuchi.	ι Equulei.
δ Cygni.	20 Draconis.	ζ Herculis.
32 Orionis.	κ Geminorum.	

The testing of a good glass refers to two different qualities which it should possess. Its quality, as to material and the fineness of its polish, should be such that the maximum of light shall be transmitted. Its quality, as to the curves, should be such that the rays passing through every part of its area shall converge absolutely to the same point, with a chromatic aberration not absolutely *nil*, but sufficient to surround objects with a faint dark blue light.

The convenient altitude at which Orion culminates in these latitudes renders it particularly eligible for observation; and during the first months of the year, our readers who would test their telescopes will do well not to lose the opportunity of trying the progressively difficult tests, both of illuminating and separating power, afforded by its various double and multiple systems, which are collected together in such a circumscribed region of the heavens, that no extensive movement of their instruments—an important point in extreme cases—will be necessary.

Beginning with δ, the upper of the three stars which form the belt, the two components will be visible in almost any instrument which may be used for seeing them, being of the second and seventh magnitudes, and well separated. The companion to β, though of the same magnitude as that to δ, is much more difficult to observe, in consequence of its proximity to its bright primary, a first-magnitude star. Quaint old Kitchener, in his work on telescopes, mentions that the companion to Rigel has been seen with an object-glass of $2\frac{3}{4}$-inch aperture; it should be seen, at all events, with a 3-inch. ζ, the bottom star in the belt, is a capital test both of the dividing and space-penetrating powers, as the two bright stars of the second and sixth magnitudes, of which the close double is composed, are but just over $2\frac{1}{2}''$ apart, according to Secchi's last measurements.

The small star below, which the late Admiral Smyth, in his charming book, 'The Celestial Cycle,' mentions as a test for his object-glass of 5·9 inches in diameter, is now plainly to be seen in a 3¾. The colours of this pair have been variously stated, Struve dubbing the sixth magnitude—which, by the way, was missed altogether by Sir John Herschel—olivaceasubrubicunda.'

That either our modern opticians contrive to admit more light by means of a superior polish imparted to the surfaces of the object-glass, or that the stars themselves are becoming brighter, is again evidenced by the point of light, preceding one of the brightest stars in the system, composing σ. This little twinkler is now always to be seen in a 3¾-inch, while the same authority we have before quoted—Admiral Smyth—speaks of it as being of very difficult vision in his instrument of much larger dimensions. In this very beautiful compound system there are no less than seven principal stars; and there are several other faint ones in the field. The upper very faint companion of λ is a delicate test for a 3¾-inch, which aperture, however, will readily divide the closer double of the principal stars, which are about 5″ apart.

These objects, with the exception of ζ, have been given more to test the space-penetrating than the dividing power; the telescope's action on 52 Orionis will at once decide this latter quality. This star, just visible to the naked eye on a fine night, to the right of a line joining α and δ. is a very close double. The components, of the sixth magnitude, are separated by less than two seconds of arc, and the glass which shows a *good white black division* between them, free from all stray light, the spurious disk being perfectly round, *and not too large*, is by no means to be despised.

The 'spurious disk,' which a fixed star presents, as seen in the telescope, is an effect which results from the passage of the light through the object-glass; and it is this appearance which necessitates the use of the largest apertures in the observation of close double stars, as the size of the star's disk varies, roughly speaking, in the inverse ratio of the aperture of the object-glass.

Then, again, we have a capital test-object in the great 'Fishmouth Nebula, by far the most glorious of its class in the Northern hemisphere, and surpassed only by that surrounding the variable star η Argûs in the Southern. And although, of course, the beauty and vastness of this stupendous and remote nebula increase with the increased power of the instrument brought to bear upon it, a large aperture is not needed to render it a most impressive and awe-inspiring object to the beholder. In an ordinary 5-foot achromatic, many of its details are to be seen under favourable atmospheric conditions. Those who are desirous of studying its appearance, as seen in the most powerful telescopes, are referred to the plate in Sir John Herschel's 'Results of Astronomical Observations at the Cape of Good Hope,' in which all its features are admirably delineated, and the positions of 150 stars which surround θ in the area occupied in the Nebula, laid down.

This star, to which we wish to call especial attention, is situate (see

TRANSIT INSTRUMENTS AND MURAL CIRCLES OF THE PARIS OBSERVATORY.

fig. 139) opposite the bottom of the 'fauces,' the name given to the indentation which gives rise to the appearance of the 'fish's mouth.' This object, which, as we have seen, has been designated the 'trapezium,' from the figure formed by its principal components, consists, in fact, of six stars, the fifth and sixth (γ' and α') being excessively faint. Our previous remark, relative to the increased brightness of the stars, applies here with great force; for the fifth escaped the gaze of the elder Herschel, armed with his powerful instruments, and was not discovered till 1826, by Struve, who, in his turn, missed the sixth star, which, as well as the fifth, has been seen in modern achromatics of such small size as to make all comparison with the giant telescopes used by these astronomers ridiculous.

Sir John Herschel has rated γ' and α' of the twelfth and fourteenth magnitudes—the latter requires a high power to observe it, by reason of its proximity to α. Both these stars have been seen in an ordinary 5-foot achromatic, by Cooke, of $3\frac{3}{4}$-inches aperture, a fact speaking volumes for the perfection of surface and polish attained by our modern opticians.

Observations should always be commenced with the lowest power, gradually increasing it until the limit of the aperture, or of the atmospheric condition at the time, is reached: the former being taken as equal to the number of hundredths of inches which the diameter of the object-glass contains. Thus, a $3\frac{3}{4}$-inch object-glass, if really good, should bear a power of 375 on double stars where light is no object; the planets, the Moon, &c., will be best observed with a much lower power.

It is always more or less dangerous to look at the Sun directly with a telescope of any aperture above two inches, as the dark glasses, without which the observer would be at once blinded, are apt to melt and crack from the concentrated heat. We must, however, except the cases in which a Dawes' solar eye-piece is employed, its smaller field of view, and consequently reduced beam admitted to the eye, obviate the objections attaching to direct vision.

A diagonal reflector, however, which reflects an extremely small percentage of light to the eye, and by reason of its prismatic form refracts the rest away from the telescope, affords a very handy method of solar observation. When this is used, it is possible even to light a cigar at the focus, while the Sun is observed in the most satisfactory manner by the rays intercepted by the reflector.

Care should be taken that the object-glass is properly adjusted. This may be done by observing the image of a large star out of focus. If the light be not equally distributed over the image, or the diffraction rings are not circular, the screws of the cell should be carefully loosened, and that part of the cell towards which the rings are thrown very gently tapped with wood, until perfectly equal illumination is arrived at. This, however, should only be done in extreme cases; it is here especially desirable that we should let *well* alone.]

We will now describe some of the most important work carried on in observatories. One of the first rooms we enter,—we suppose ourselves in the Paris Observatory,—is that in which the meridian instruments are placed. Here at once our attention is riveted by telescopes, divided circles, and clocks, that is to say, by instruments which amplify our vision, measure angles and positions, and measure and divide time.

Three telescopes, of which one is fixed in the centre of a large circle, attached to a wall at the end of the room, and of which the nearest is the most modern and the most powerful, have all the same allotted task, that of showing us with precision the moment at which the stars pass through the plane of the meridian, and of measuring their angular distances from the zenith, whence their position with regard to the celestial equator can be deduced.

The first instrument is styled a *mural circle*, the others are *transit instruments.*

In all these instruments the telescopes are arranged to turn freely on their axes, placed horizontally in a direction east and west, or perpendicularly to the plane of the meridian. The axis of each telescope, therefore, never leaves this plane; and as the daily movement of the Earth brings by turns all the stars on the meridian, it is always possible to observe the exact instant of the transit, or passage, of one of them through this plane. To render this observation easy, the transit instruments are provided with a series of fine spider webs placed at the focus; these are shown in fig. 191. The higher the power employed, the more rapidly does the star move across the field of view, and the more necessary does it become to notice the exact instant at which the star passes behind the different 'wires,' as they are called, the error of observation being diminished by taking the mean of the times of the transits across all of them.

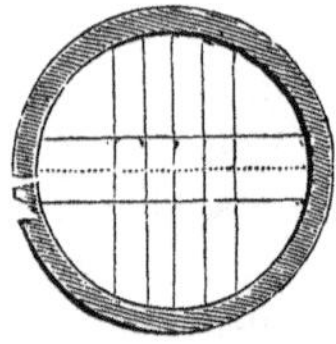
Fig. 191.

We see in Plate XXV, by the side of the meridian instruments, two astronomical clocks regulated to sidereal time and beating sidereal seconds. The noise of the beat is sufficient to enable the observer to follow the time; this he estimates to within a tenth of a second, in such a manner as to know most exactly the instant of transit when it takes place between two successive beats.

Visitors will scarcely care to regulate their watches by the time kept by these clocks, which, as we have before said, is sidereal, or star time, reckoning throughout twenty-four hours, the transit of the first point of Aries being the star-point.

The mural circle consists of a metallic circle divided into degrees and fractions of a degree, and placed in the meridian. A movable telescope attached to its centre allows us to observe a star at the moment of transit; the direction of the telescope shows the angular distance between the actual position of the star and the zenith; hence we can conclude its declination, the angular distance of the star from the celestial equator.

The mural circle, therefore, serves also as a transit circle; reciprocally we now attach divided circles to transit instruments by means of which the

GREAT EQUATORIAL OF THE PARIS OBSERVATORY.

zenith distance is measured. The magnificent transits, both on the one model, with which both Greenwich and Paris are now endowed, perform both these important functions.

From the transit-room we must now pass to the dome, under which is placed the large equatorial of 15 inches aperture.

As the meridian instruments enable us to observe the stars only for a few moments as they are passing the meridian, it becomes necessary to have large telescopes to follow them through those regions of the heavens through which they are carried by the diurnal movement.

This desideratum is accomplished by means of the *equatorial.*

As we see on Plate XXVI, the telescope is fixed on an axis, on which it can move up and down as it were, keeping the same right ascension; this axis is attached to another, parallel to the axis of the Earth: and when this last axis is in motion, the telescope can change its right ascension. It is, therefore, also free to move in every direction by a combination of these two movements. The other most important parts of this instrument are as follows; firstly, the telescope: then a divided circle, at right angles to the declination axis, this measures the declination or the angle distance of a star from the celestial pole a second circle at right angles to the polar axis, and therefore in the plane of the equator, which measures right ascension.

There is also a clock-work movement, which carries the instrument in one direction as fast as the diurnal movement of the Earth is carrying it in the other. From this results that, if the telescope be directed towards a celestial object, such object can be kept in the field of view for hours. This affords a great facility for observations of the planetary disks, sun-spots, the heads of comets, &c.

The equatorial may also be used for determining celestial positions, the divided circles, which enable us to find stars and other objects in the day time, being used for this purpose.

We would gladly have entered into some particulars of the way in which the measurement of angles is accomplished, and of the instruments used, of the precision at which astronomers have arrived, thanks to the ingenious methods and the progress of mechanical and optical art. We should then have referred to micrometers, divided circles, heliometers and other instruments employed in observations. But our description of the instruments used by astronomers is already long. We must, therefore, refer to special treatises those who are desirous of entering more into detail in these matters. Our object will have been sufficiently gained if in exciting curiosity we have succeeded in giving the desire to study a science so capable of elevating the mind, and of affording it the purest and noblest enjoyments.

INDEX.

London: Strangeways and Walden, Printers, Castle St. Leicester Sq.

www.ingramcontent.com/pod-product-compliance
Lightning Source LLC
LaVergne TN
LVHW021131110826
845150LV00005B/1000

* 9 7 8 1 4 2 5 5 4 9 8 4 8 *